THIRD EDITION

OPEN QUESTIONS
An Introduction to Philosophy

EMMETT BARCALOW

Western New England College

New York   Oxford
OXFORD UNIVERSITY PRESS

Oxford University Press

Oxford   New York
Auckland   Bangkok   Buenos Aires   Cape Town
Chennai   Dar es Salaam   Delhi   Hong Kong   Istanbul   Karachi
Kolkata   Kuala Lumpur   Madrid   Melbourne   Mexico City   Mumbai   Nairobi
São Paulo   Shanghai   Singapore   Taipei   Tokyo   Toronto

and an associated company in Berlin

Published by Oxford University Press, Inc.
198 Madison Avenue, New York, New York 10016
http://www.oup-usa.org

Oxford is a registered trademark of Oxford University Press

ISBN 978-0-19-515500-6

Printing number: 9 8 7 6 5 4

Printed in the United States of America
on acid-free paper

CONTENTS

3 BODY AND MIND   56

4 PERSONAL IMMORTALITY AND PERSONAL IDENTITY 110

5 FREEDOM AND DETERMINISM 135

6 KNOWLEDGE, TRUTH, AND JUSTIFICATION 177

7 KNOWLEDGE AND SKEPTICISM 236

8 MORALITY   271

9 MORAL JUSTIFICATION   302

10 TWO THEORIES OF RIGHT AND WRONG   337

11 JUSTICE AND RIGHTS   378

12 LIBERTY AND DEMOCRACY   436

A READING PHILOSOPHY   465

B WRITING A PHILOSOPHY PAPER   466

GLOSSARY/INDEX   469

READINGS CONTENTS

* means new to this edition

PREFACE

This third edition of *Open Questions* has the same goals as the first edition. Given that many of today's college students have modest reading skills, asking beginning students in philosophy to read primary texts is an exercise in frustration for both student and teacher. Students find what they read incomprehensible (when they bother to read what has been assigned). Teachers spend so much time lecturing in order to enable the students to understand what they have (supposedly) read that discussion, the lifeblood of philosophy, evaporates. The students I encounter need a textbook that has been written specifically for them rather than works that have been written for professional philosophers or for a cultivated audience that is already interested in and knowledgeable about philosophy.

My approach is unapologetically analytical. It begins with fairly basic or fundamental philosophical problems and questions: Does God exist? Are human beings composed of a combination of physical and nonphysical substances? Are human choices and decisions ever free? How much do we know about the universe? What are the standards of reasonable belief? Are any moral claims true? Are some moral beliefs more reasonable than others? How can we determine what we should do or how we should live? What moral rights do people have? What makes social institutions just or unjust? How much liberty should people have? What is the best form of government? Analytical philosophy, as I understand it, employs a fairly commonsense approach to philosophical questions that begins with a clear explanation of the alternative answers to the question or solutions to the problem (often, competing philosophical theories). Once the alternative answers or theories have been set out, the next question is, Which alternative answer is most plausible or reasonable? The alternative answer or solution that has the weight of reasons in its favor is the most reasonable one, the one that is most likely to be true. Trying to ascertain which of competing alternative answers to a question or solutions to a problem is most reasonable requires constructing and evaluating arguments. Analytical approaches to philosophy, then, focus on arguments. Words or concepts that are crucial to an argument or theory must be explained and defined. Analytical approaches to philosophy stress the *analysis* (definition or characterization) of fundamental concepts such as *cause, free, know,* and *right* as important for evaluating arguments and arriving at truth and understanding.

Open Question, then, focuses on constructing and evaluating arguments in order to ascertain which of competing answers or solutions to philosophical questions and problems are most reasonable. It also analyzes fundamental concepts where appropriate. In the book I try to provide clearly written, well-organized, and lively explanations of the different philosophical theories that have been accepted as solutions to basic philosophical problems. Although the book is organized thematically in terms of problems rather than historically in terms of philosophers, I try to introduce students to the answers that well-known philosophers have given to our questions. (The book focuses primarily on the Western philosophical tradition because that reflects my own interests and expertise.) I also try to provide the arguments both for and against the various theories in as neutral a way as possible so that students may use what they learn to help them form their own opinions on the issues. My goal is to provide them with the tools that will enable them to think for themselves.

Major Features of This Text

Each chapter begins with a detailed list of chapter objectives so that students may know what they are expected to get from the chapter. Chapter headings have been organized to provide a roadmap of the logical structure of the chapter to aid student comprehension. Many brain teasers have been scattered throughout each chapter—questions for class discussion or for student reflection on the material. Each chapter ends with questions designed to motivate class discussions and a set of suggested readings. Important information, such as definitions, is placed in the margins for easy reference. There are two appendices, one on reading philosophy and the other on writing a philosophy paper. There is a glossary of important terms and a detailed index for easy reference. The text also has an instructor's manual available online.

What is New in This Edition?

I have made changes in all chapters, although Chapters 1, 4, and 6 were rewritten completely. These changes include:

- Chapter objectives have been added to each chapter.

- Chapter 1 has been compressed. I have added information about the major subfields of philosophy, revised the presentation of best explanation arguments to make it more understandable, and deleted coverage of the concepts of a statement's being necessarily true, true, and possibly true.

- Chapter 3 has been expanded to include more coverage of physicalism; explanations of behaviorism, functionalism, identity theories, and supervenience were added. Material on how brain research supports physicalism has been expanded and reorganized to make it more coherent.

- A section on self-knowledge has been added.

- In Chapter 4 more attention has been paid to how personal identity is linked to bodily identity. More emphasis has been placed on the relevance of personal identity to the possibility of personal immortality.

- Chapter 6 covers the importance of belief, realism and antirealism, deciding to believe, the right to believe, justification of noncontingent statements, self-knowledge and introspection, barriers to self-knowledge, justification and perception, alternatives to perception for knowledge of the physical world, distorters (such as interest, passion, and the mass media), and the ethics of belief.

- Chapter 8 has been reorganized and now begins rather than ends with the divine command theory. Other moral theories, such as subjectivism and relativism, are presented as responses to problems with the divine command theory. The distinction between moral objectivism (realism) and moral nonobjectivism has been emphasized and made clearer.

- Chapter 9 now features expanded coverage of social justifications of morality. Material on reflective equilibrium and responses to the question "Why be moral?" have been added.

- Chapter 11 now provides a discussion of equal opportunity.

- Chapter 12 now includes a discussion of Feinberg's analysis of four liberty limiting principles: the harm principle, the offense principle, hard and soft paternalism, and legal moralism.

Readings have been changed and the space devoted to them compressed. A short selection from Benjamin Franklin's autobiography has replaced the longer selection from Locke in Chapter 2. The selection from

Churchland has been deleted from Chapter 3. The selections from Locke and Sri Aurobindo in Chapter 4 have been replaced by a short selection from Walpola Rahula. The selection from Sarvepalli Radhakrishnan in Chapter 5 has been replaced with a selection from Jean Paul Sartre. The selections from Price and from Bradley and Swartz has been replaced by a selection from Bertrand Russell. The selection from Popper in Chapter 7 has been deleted. The selection from Ayer in Chapter 8 has been replaced by brief selections from Saint Augustine, Moses Maimonides, and two Buddhist scriptures. The selection from Warnock has been moved to Chapter 9. The selections from Foot and the Mo Tzu in Chapter 9 have been replaced by the selection from Warnock and a selection from Plato. The selections from Mill and Waldron in Chapter 12 have been replaced by selections from Rousseau and Constant.

Sharing Pedogogical Ideas

Getting students to read assigned material is an ever more serious and aggravating problem. When students come to class unprepared, discussions languish and are rarely fruitful. However good *Open Questions* may be, it will not help you much if students don't read it. I would like to share with you some strategies that seem to be working for me. These ideas are not my own. Most were suggested to me by colleagues from other departments at Western New England College who have wrestled with the same problems. Some of these solutions I resisted for years.

I have finally had to admit that many students will not read assigned material unless there is a carrot and a stick. Therefore, after much resistance, I now give regular quizzes, one for each chapter. When we begin a new chapter, there is a three- to six-question quiz on it that takes five to six minutes; 20 percent of a student's final grade is determined by performance on the quizzes. This is designed almost exclusively to coerce students into reading the chapter or face immediate consequences. After some experimenting, I now permit students to use any notes they may have taken on the chapter in taking the quiz. (Quizzes are open notes but not open book.) When they take notes on what they are reading, they read more carefully, better understand what they have read, and remember more. When they take a quiz, they are in effect reviewing their notes. I have found that with this system most students read and take notes on the assigned material, a refreshing change from the days when I did not give regular quizzes. Most students are better prepared for class now.

My examinations now consist exclusively of essay questions. In order to provide students with a learning experience as well as a test situation, I pass out the essay questions the class period before they are scheduled to take the examination. (It is not a sample, it is the very examination they will take.) I encourage students to form study groups to work on the essay questions so that they can learn from one another. The collaborative learning stops at the door, though. When taking the examination they must not use any notes or books. Everything has to be stored in their heads. In this way I hope to get their best thoughts rather than their most hurried or anxiety-ridden thought. (My essay questions are very general. For example: Which is most reasonable, Hard Determinism, Soft Determinism, or Libertarianism? Defend your answer. In doing so, be sure to explain each theory carefully and to define or explain concepts crucial to the theories.)

I have also learned about the importance of revision from my colleagues in the English department. Following their advice, I now employ peer editing for papers. When a paper is assigned, students bring two copies of a preliminary draft to class and exchange papers, forming groups of three in which each reads the papers of the other two. I provide them with peer editing guidelines, an outline of what makes a good as opposed to a bad paper. They have until the next class period to critically evaluate their peers' papers and make concrete recommendations for revision. During the next class period I give them about twenty minutes to form groups of three to discuss each other's papers. After receiving feedback from two readers, students have a week to revise their own papers and submit a final draft to me. In this way I try to ensure that students do not hand me what should be merely a first draft of their papers written the night before. I also hope to force them to revise their work even if I have not read a draft of it.

I hope that these ideas will be useful to you. They have been helpful to me.

Acknowledgments

My thanks to the reviewers who made suggestions for revision of the third edition of *Open Questions:* Jim Druley, Irvine Valley College; Theodore Guleserian, Arizona State University; John Modschiedler, College of DuPage; and Wayne D. Riggs, University of Oklahoma. Any defects or mistakes remaining in the text are my own responsibility.

I'd also like to thank some of my teachers for their inspiration. Had it not been for Nelvin Vos of Muhlenberg College, my freshman composition teacher more than thirty years ago, I might not have decided to devote my life to college teaching. His enthusiasm and intelligence made the world of ideas so exciting, exhilarating, and challenging that I decided then and there to do what he did so well—teach in college. I have never regretted the decision. I learned about high intellectual standards (painfully), standards that I have never quite been able to meet to my own satisfaction, from Isaac Levi and James Higginbotham at Columbia University more than twenty years ago.

Finally, I would like to thank my mother, father, and sister. My sister, Carol, somehow helped instill in me a love of reading when I was six or seven years old. We used to have reading races in the morning to see who could read more pages in an hour. Since she was older, she usually won. Occasionally she let me win. Through her example she got me to view reading as a pleasure, a priceless gift for which I am in her debt. I also want to thank my mother and (now deceased) father for trying to make me a good person. They encouraged me to care more for what's right and decent than for money, power, or fame. Whatever little bit of good may be in my character I owe to them.

PHILOSOPHY

Objectives

Students are expected to:

- know the basic subfields of philosophy and some of the basic questions addressed in philosophy.
- understand the difference between a philosophical and a nonphilosophical question.
- understand what an argument is.
- know how to construct and critically evaluate an argument.
- understand and apply the concept of validity.
- understand and apply the concept of soundness.
- understand and apply the concept of inductive strength.
- understand and apply the concept of cogency.
- understand and apply arguments to the best explanation.

Introduction

Have you ever wondered whether God exists, whether we really have souls, or whether human life has meaning? Have you ever wondered how to distinguish what's true from what's false, or wondered whether we know as much as we claim to know? Have you ever wondered whether there's a real difference between right and wrong? If so, then you've asked philosophical questions.

The word *philosophy* comes from the Greek language and means love of wisdom. However, that's not very helpful in enabling us to understand what philosophy is. For one thing, it leaves us with the question, "What is wisdom?" Some people have said that philosophy begins with a sense of wonder. In the previous paragraph I asked whether you had "wondered" about certain things, so philosophy may very well begin in wonder. But to wonder is to ask questions, so perhaps philosophy is the attempt to answer philosophical questions. But that leaves us with the problem of what makes a question philosophical rather than nonphilosophical.

Some questions are philosophical, some aren't. Here are examples of what virtually everyone would agree are nonphilosophical questions.

What caused the Civil War?

Why was Julius Caesar assassinated?

How long do lions generally live?

Is there a cure for AIDS?

What caused inflation in the United States in the 1980s?

Does intelligent life exist beyond our solar system?

Why can ants crawl on the ceiling?

On the other hand, almost everyone would agree that the following questions are philosophical.

Does God exist?

Do we have nonphysical souls or minds?

Is everything that happens predetermined?

What makes a belief reasonable?

Is it morally wrong to have sex or get pregnant if you're not married?

Should people be free to use heroin and cocaine?

What's the difference between philosophical and nonphilosophical questions? It's not that there's universal agreement on the answers to non-philosophical questions while there isn't on philosophical questions. There are many nonphilosophical questions that provoke intense debate. And it's certainly not that nonphilosophical questions are important while philosophical questions aren't. Many people think that the answers to some philosophical questions are more important than the answers to most nonphilosophical questions. For example, for many people, the answer to the question of whether God exists is a lot more important than, say, the answer to the question, "What's the atomic weight of gold?"

Perhaps, though, it's that nonphilosophical questions have correct answers while philosophical questions don't. Thus, we might say that there is only one correct answer to the question, "How long do lions generally live?", but no one correct answer to the question, "Does God exist?" However, it's not clear why we should think that philosophical questions do not have correct answers. When we are faced with a statement and its negation, for example, "You are 21" and "You are not 21," one of them must be true and the other false, even if we don't know which is true and which false. Either you're 21 or you're not, and there's a correct answer to the question, "Are you 21?" Similarly, we face "God exists" and "God doesn't exist." One of them must be true and the other false, even if we don't know which is true. Either God exists or doesn't exist. The answer to the question, "Does God exist?" is either yes or no. It can't be both and it can't be neither. So there is only one correct answer to the question, "Does God exist?"[1]

Many people say that the difference between philosophical and non-philosophical questions is that we can answer nonphilosophical questions fairly decisively by examining the evidence of the senses. For example, sensory evidence will tell us with a high degree of certainty how long lions generally live. Even in cases where there's controversy, for example, over whether there's intelligent life beyond our solar system or why Julius Caesar was assassinated, in principle the question could be answered with a high degree of certainty if we accumulated enough observational (empirical) evidence. On the other hand, with philosophical questions, although observational evidence is by no means irrelevant, observation can never provide enough evidence to show with certainty which answer is correct. There's probably enough truth in this to make it an acceptable starting point for distinguishing philosophical from nonphilosophical questions, but we should be wary of hard and fast distinctions. As we progress in our studies, we may discover that questions occur on a continuum, and there's no clear dividing line between philosophical and nonphilosophical questions. Some questions are more easily answered by appeal to observational evidence than others. But for now, let's say that philosophical questions are less easily answered decisively by appeal to observational evidence and that philosophy is the attempt to answer these philosophical questions.

Subfields of Philosophy

Philosophy is a complex discipline with a lot of subfields. Here we'll just list some of the major subfields and identify them by the kinds of questions they ask.

Logic

Logic is the study of arguments. An argument is a formal structure of statements used to defend a claim, for example, (1) We should not vote for a dishonest candidate, (2) Jones is a dishonest candidate; therefore, (3) we should not vote for Jones. Logicians describe and evaluate arguments, attempting to provide criteria of good arguments. Logicians also analyze such concepts as truth and necessity.

---

[1]We may disagree on what "God" means or what characteristics something must have to correctly be named "God," but if we agree on what "God" means, then either that thing exists or it doesn't.

Metaphysics

Metaphysics is the study of what is. It tries to determine what kinds of things exist in the world. Metaphysicians wonder whether—in addition to ordinary physical objects that range in size from subatomic particles to galaxies—certain nonphysical things exist such as numbers, properties, God, angels, minds or souls, and mental states and events. Metaphysicians also wonder about the ultimate structure of the universe. Is everything tied together by tight causal relationships? If so, is there room for human freedom?

Epistemology

Epistemology is the study of knowledge and belief. Epistemologists try to understand what knowledge and belief are and the nature of truth. They try to identify the differences between justified and unjustified or reasonable and unreasonable beliefs.

Ethics or Moral Philosophy

Ethics is the study of morality, including such concepts as right and wrong, good and evil, virtue and vice. Ethicists or moral philosophers try to determine whether there's a real difference between moral right and wrong, as well as to provide ways of distinguishing between right and wrong, good and bad, and virtue and vice. They provide models of moral justification and argument. They try to answer such questions as, "How should people behave? What kind of lives should people live?" Less abstractly, they may also try to answer such moral questions as, "Is abortion or capital punishment immoral?"

Political Philosophy

Political philosophy focuses on politics, broadly conceived. One philosophical question is, "What is politics?" If we think of politics broadly as the struggle for power, then political issues arise almost everywhere we look, not only with human creations called governments. Political philosophers explore such questions as, "What is the best form of government? What makes a social system, government, or law just? What are rights and what rights should people have? How much liberty should people have? What duties do people have toward their societies? What duties do societies have toward their individual members?"

Philosophy of Science

Philosophy of science explores questions that arise in science. For example, "What is science? How does science differ from other human activities? What are scientific explanations? What are scientific theories? How do scientists confirm theories? How reliable is science?"

Aesthetics

Aesthetics is the study of art and beauty. Aestheticians ask such questions as, "What is art? What makes a particular artistic creation beautiful or valuable? Are some works of art better than others? What standards are applicable to different arts, such as painting, sculpture, photography, film, music, and dance? What role does art play in human life?"

History of Philosophy

History of philosophy is the study of the contribution of individual philosophers to the discipline of philosophy, such as Plato, Aristotle, Augustine, Aquinas, Hume, and Russell.

Open and Closed Questions

There's no universal agreement about the correct answers to the questions that philosophers try to answer. That's why they're called open questions. If there's substantial disagreement about the correct answer to a question, it's an open question. If there's almost universal agreement about the correct answer to a question, it's a closed question. Examples of closed questions include "How tall is Mount Everest?" and "Who was the first president of the United States?" People don't argue about what's the correct answer to these questions. To answer a closed question, we need only consult a reliable source of information, such as a science textbook or encyclopedia.

Open questions haven't been answered to everyone's satisfaction, and reasonable people disagree about which of the proposed answers is true. For example, many people think that the question "Did a single individual kill John Kennedy?" is an open question. Other examples of open questions are "Who was Jack the Ripper?" "Was there really a King Arthur?" "Is there intelligent life elsewhere in our galaxy?" "Do ghosts exist?"

We must be careful not to assume that open questions don't have correct answers. Just because people don't agree about what's the correct answer doesn't mean that there isn't a correct answer. For example, there can only be one correct answer to the question of how many people were involved in the assassination of John F. Kennedy. Either Oswald acted alone or he didn't.

Whereas people can consult an expert to answer closed questions, they must, in a sense, become their own experts to answer open questions. An open question is an invitation to think for ourselves. The philosophical questions we'll address in this book are all open questions. They don't have answers that everyone agrees with. That means we have to think for ourselves and decide what answers we think are true or most reasonable.

What It's Most Reasonable to Believe

Philosophy is both a creative and a critical enterprise. Creativity comes in when philosophers create theories to answer philosophical questions. The critical part comes in when we try to decide which claims and theories are true. To do that, we must look at the reasons for and against competing claims. We do that sort of thing all the time outside philosophy. Suppose you were in a discussion about who was the best basketball player, actor, or rock-and-roll band. The creative part is coming up with the names. The critical part is deciding which answer is most reasonable. To decide which basketball player, actor, or band is best, you would feel obliged to provide a *reason* when you suggested or rejected someone. To answer a question, you sift through the reasons for and against the answers each person suggested. To provide a reason is to provide an *argument* for your view.

We might think of the process of deciding what it's most reasonable to believe as a bit like weighing two objects. We place the reasons or arguments for a belief in one arm of the scale, the reasons or arguments against the belief in the other arm of the scale, and determine which side is "heavier" or better. The side that has the weight of reasons in its favor is probably true.

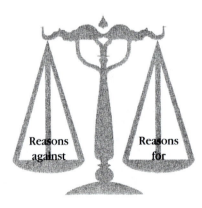

One might be tempted to claim that whatever a person believes is reasonable, at least for that person. Nevertheless, most philosophers are committed to the view that while some beliefs are reasonable, others are unreasonable. For example, some right-wing extremist groups believe that

> the United Nations plans to conquer the United States, using a secret strike force made up of the National Guard and foreign troops, assisted by Los Angeles street gangs. . . . Some think that United States currency is imprinted with secret bar codes so that Government officials in vans equipped with microwave scanners can count how much money people have.[2]

If some people believe these claims, must we say that it is reasonable for them to believe the claims?

On reflection, most people probably would concede that some beliefs are more reasonable than others. Surely it is more reasonable to believe that U.S. astronauts once landed on the moon than it is to believe that the government of the United States faked the moon landings by showing films made in a studio on Earth. But if there is a difference between what it is reasonable to believe and what it is not reasonable to believe, what's the difference?

Reasonable and unreasonable beliefs are linked to arguments. As a first approximation, we might say that a belief is reasonable if the arguments for it are stronger than the arguments against it, while it's unreasonable if the arguments against it are much stronger than the arguments for it. What are arguments, and how do we distinguish between good and bad arguments?

Evaluating Arguments

An argument is a set of statements consisting of one or more premises and a conclusion. The premises are reasons for thinking that the conclusion is true. Here's an example.

All whales are mammals.
All mammals have lungs.

_____

Therefore, all whales have lungs.

The first two statements, above the line, are the premises; the last statement, below the line, is the conclusion.

---

[2]*New York Times,* 23 April 1995, 32.

Validity

We use arguments to prove things. The premises constitute the proof of the conclusion. But we need to be careful about the concept of "proof." There are different standards of proof. The argument above, whose conclusion is that whales have lungs, proves that whales have lungs in that if the premises are true, the conclusion must be true. Arguments like this are called **valid.** In a valid argument, the conclusion could not possibly be false if all the premises are true.

Valid: A valid argument must have a true conclusion if all its premises are true

Consider the following claims:

John is either a math major or an English major.

John is not an English major.

What follows from them? If they're both true, then John must be a math major. Thus, the following argument is valid.

John is either a math major or an English major.
John is not an English major.

Therefore, John is a math major.

Consider another set of claims.

All dogs have fleas.

Lassie is a dog.

What follows from this? If they're both true, then Lassie must have fleas. Again, the following, then, is a valid argument:

All dogs have fleas.
Lassie is a dog.

Therefore, Lassie has fleas.

Validity is a concept applied when evaluating arguments according to **deductive** standards. Deductive arguments intend to be valid. With valid deductive arguments, the premises **entail** the conclusion. A set of statements {x} entails a statement p if, given {x}, p must be true. The premises of a valid deductive argument can also be called **conclusive reasons** for its conclusion. They guarantee truth.

Deductive: A deductive argument is intended to meet the criteria of validity

Not all arguments are valid. Suppose we know that all cats are mammals and all dogs are mammals. Even if that's true, it doesn't follow that all dogs must be cats. So the following argument isn't valid because it's not the case that the conclusion must be true if all the premises are true:

Entail: p entails q means that if p is true, q must be true

Conclusive reasons: Reasons that guarantee truth

All dogs are mammals.
All cats are mammals.

Therefore, all dogs are cats.

BRAIN TEASERS

Is the following argument valid?

All English majors love to read.
John loves to read.

Therefore, John is an English major.

Can an argument still be valid if not all of its premises are true? Yes. Consider this argument.

All turtles are mammals.
All mammals have hearts.

Therefore, all turtles have hearts.

Suppose I point out that the first premise is false: turtles are not mammals. Is the argument then invalid? No. If all its premises had been true, then its conclusion would have had to be true. That's all it takes for an argument to be valid. A valid argument doesn't have to have true premises. Rather, a valid argument must be one such that if its premises were true, then its conclusion would have to be true.

But suppose that an argument has a false conclusion. Could it still be valid? Yes. Again, consider an example.

All angels have wings.
Your philosophy teacher is an angel.

Therefore, your philosophy teacher has wings.

The conclusion is false. (So is the second premise.) But the argument is nevertheless valid because if all the premises were true, then the conclusion would have to be true. Contrast that with the following invalid argument.

All angels have wings.
My pet parakeet has wings.

Therefore, my pet parakeet is an angel.

Here, it's not the case that if all the premises are true, then the conclusion has to be true.

BRAIN TEASERS

If an argument has a true conclusion, does it follow that it must be valid?

We may wonder why validity is important. The answer is that if we argue or reason validly, then if we begin with truth, we're guaranteed to end with truth. We won't move from true beliefs or claims to false beliefs or claims.

Soundness

If an argument is valid, it doesn't guarantee that its conclusion is true. In a valid argument, the conclusion must be true if all its premises are true. An argument is sound, however, if it's valid and all its premises are true. In evaluating an argument, then, we must ask not only whether it's valid, but also whether all its premises are true.

Inductive Strength

Not all arguments aspire to be valid. Consider the following:

Almost all Engineering majors are good at math.
John is an Engineering major.

Therefore, John is good at math.

Inductively strong argument: The conclusion of an inductively strong argument is probably true if all its premises are true

The premises of this argument don't guarantee that its conclusion is true; the conclusion could be false even if all its premises are true. But this argument may be a good argument anyway. If its premises are true, the conclusion is probably true. In that case, it would be inductively strong. With an **inductively strong argument,** if its premises are true, its conclusion is probably true. With a valid argument, if its premises are true, its conclusion must be true. Here we are applying inductive rather than deductive standards.

All valid arguments are equally valid; we can't say that one argument is more valid than another. But not all inductively strong arguments are equally strong. Consider the following two arguments.

99 percent of college students are under age 50.
Jean is a college student.

Therefore, Jean is (probably) under age 50.

90 percent of children in U.S. cities attend segregated schools.
Brad lives in a U.S. city.

Therefore, Brad (probably) attends a segregated school.

The first is stronger than the second in that its premises make its conclusion more probable. The probability that the conclusion of the first argument is true, given its premises, is .99; the probability that the conclusion of the second argument is true is .90.

Consider some other examples of inductively strong arguments.

No known human being has lived to be 150 years old.
I am a human being.

Therefore, I will not live to be 150 years old.

This argument is not deductively valid, but it is inductively strong. It's not valid because the fact that no known human being has lived to be 150 years old doesn't guarantee that I won't. I could be an exception. Or new medical advances might make a life span of 150 years quite reachable. Nonetheless, it's highly probable that if no known human being has lived to be 150, I won't either. The premises make the conclusion highly probable, so the argument is inductively strong.

Inductive strength can also be increased with additional information or premises. Suppose that a detective investigating the theft of diamonds from a jewelry store reasons as follows:

Johnson's fingerprints were found in the jewelry store.
Johnson has a history of thefts similar to this one.
Johnson was seen loitering about the jewelry store the day before the theft.

Therefore, Johnson (probably) is the thief.

The evidence provides some reason for thinking that Johnson is the thief, but it is not likely to be enough to convince a jury.

However, as the detective continues to investigate, additional evidence may make the conclusion more and more probable. Suppose that the detective questions Johnson about his whereabouts the night of the theft and Johnson provides an alibi that is later shown to be a lie. That increases the probability that Johnson is the thief, making the case or argument stronger. Suppose further that an eyewitness claims to have seen Johnson near the jewelry store the night of the theft. With the addition of these two premises, the argument is stronger.

Johnson lied about his whereabouts the night of the theft and cannot provide a satisfactory alibi.

Someone claims to have seen Johnson near the jewelry store the night of the robbery.

Finally, suppose that the detective finds the stolen jewels in Johnson's car. Surely we now have a very strong case against Johnson, perhaps a conclusive case.

Johnson's fingerprints were found in the jewelry store.
Johnson has a history of thefts similar to this one.
Johnson was seen loitering about the jewelry store the day before the theft.

Johnson lied about his whereabouts the night of the theft and cannot provide a satisfactory alibi.
Someone claims to have seen Johnson near the jewelry store the night of the robbery.
The stolen jewels were found in Johnson's car.

Therefore, Johnson (probably) is the thief.

The second argument is much stronger than the first because of the added evidence or premises.

BRAIN TEASERS

Is the argument now valid?

Could the accumulation of even more evidence make the argument inductively weaker?

But there's more to inductive strength than just the relation between premises and conclusion. Consider the following argument.

All the swans we have observed have been white.

Therefore, (probably) all swans are white.

Is it inductively strong? If yes, how strong is it? It's difficult to tell, because we need to answer a number of questions. First, how many swans have been observed? If we've observed only a few swans, say ten or twenty, then the argument is pretty weak. If we've observed hundreds or thousands of swans, the argument may be strong. However, we also must ask where we saw the swans. Suppose that we've observed several hundred swans and they've all been white, but the only place we've seen them has been in Massachusetts. Then the argument is pretty weak because there may be other kinds of swans in other places. The argument would be a lot stronger if we've seen swans from lots of different places across the globe and they've all been white. (In the nineteenth century, black swans were found in remote areas of Australia. Before that, everyone thought that all swans are white.) But we also need to be sure that we've seen swans of different sexes and at different stages of their lives. Suppose we've seen hundreds of swans, but they've all been females or none have been very young or very old. The point is that inductive strength isn't only a matter of numbers; we need to be sure that we've observed a fair representative sample of swans.

This is important in some philosophical contexts. For example, many people say that the universe looks as though it was designed rather than evolved as a product of the chance operation of natural forces. They argue as follows:

What I see in the universe appears to be the product of conscious, intelligent design.

Therefore, the universe is (probably) the product of conscious, intelligent design.

But all too often, people confine their attention to Earth. If we look beyond Earth at the other planets in our solar system, at other solar systems in our galaxy, and at other galaxies, does the universe still appear to be the product of conscious design? We must remember that Earth is one minuscule fraction of the universe. Then, too, people often look at only a limited range of phenomena on Earth and see what appears to be design. They ignore the insect world, or the plant world, or the animal world. If the argument is to be inductively strong, we must ensure that we've observed a fair representative sample of what exists in the universe.

In evaluating an argument, then, the first thing we should ask is whether it's valid or inductively strong. If it's neither valid nor inductively strong, it's not a good argument. If it's inductively strong, the stronger it is, the better. And of course, we have to ask whether the premises are true.

Cogency

The best arguments are **cogent.** An argument is cogent if and only if it meets three conditions. First, it's either valid or inductively strong. Second, the evidence we have makes it at least highly probable that all its premises are true. (It would be even better if it were certain that all its premises are true, but certainty is often unobtainable.) Third, all the available, relevant information has been taken into account in its premises. No information that's relevant and (perhaps easily?) obtainable has been omitted or overlooked. We are fully justified in believing the conclusion of a cogent argument.

Cogent: An argument is cogent if: it is valid or inductively strong, the evidence makes it highly probable that all its premises are true, and all available relevant information has been taken into account

BRAIN TEASERS

Are any of the following arguments either valid or inductively strong?

All fish have gills.
Whales don't have gills.

Therefore, whales aren't fish.

All fish have gills.
This creature has gills.

Therefore, this creature is a fish.

Some people who use cocaine began by smoking marijuana.

Therefore, someone who smokes marijuana will probably use cocaine.

Best Explanation Arguments

There is one form of inductive argument that deserves special treatment, in part because it is especially important in science and philosophy. We can call them Best Explanation arguments. If some hypothesis (H) is the best explanation for some fact or phenomenon (P) that we know to be true, then that gives us some reason for thinking that H is true. Best Explanation arguments have the following general structure:

P is true.
H is the best explanation of why P is true.

Therefore, H is (probably) true.

What do explanations look like? One influential view claims that explanations have the structure of arguments. Suppose that I put water in my birdbath yesterday but when I came out this morning, I discovered that there's a block of solid ice where I put the liquid water. How can I explain the transformation? I could explain it by saying that the water froze because its internal temperature dropped below 32 degrees Fahrenheit. Formally, the explanation would look like this.

Water freezes when its internal temperature drops below 32 degrees Fahrenheit.
The internal temperature of the water I put in the birdbath yesterday dropped below 32 degrees Fahrenheit.

Therefore, the water froze.

The first premise expresses what has been called a law of nature. Natural laws are generalizations about how nature works. The second premise describes the changes or conditions that, linked to the natural laws, explain why the event described in the conclusion occurred. It makes the event described in the conclusion understandable, something we could have expected.

Can we use this same pattern to explain why the internal temperature of the water dropped below 32 degrees? Yes we can. It is a law of nature that heat, which is the mean kinetic energy of a collection of molecules, migrates from areas of higher temperature to areas of lower temperature. Like water, air is a collection of molecules. The water in my birdbath was in contact with the surrounding air. Thus, the air temperature must have dropped below 32 degrees, causing heat (energy) in the water to migrate from the water to the air, lowering the temperature of the water. Formally, the explanation would look like this.

> Heat migrates from areas of high temperature to areas of low temperature.
> The temperature of the air surrounding the water dropped below 32 degrees Fahrenheit.
>
> ───────────────────────────────
>
> Therefore, the temperature of water dropped below 32 degrees Fahrenheit.

The first premise of the explanatory argument is the statement of a natural law, while the second is a description of a change (event) that played a causal role in the water changing from a liquid to a solid.

The explanation also relies on a theory, the atomic theory of matter. According to this theory, physical matter is composed of atoms, which combine to form molecules. Matter can exist in one of three states: solid, liquid, and gas, depending on its temperature (the energy level or activity of the ever moving atoms and molecules). Both air and water are composed of collections of molecules. We can think of theories as collections of statements, many of which express laws of nature.

Here we can gain further insight into the best explanation arguments. Suppose that when I put the water in the birdbath yesterday the thermometer read 50 degrees Fahrenheit. When I go outside the next morning, I see that the water in my birdbath turned to ice, but I also see that the thermometer says that the outside temperature is now 40 degrees. Can I infer that some time during the night the air temperature dipped below 32 degrees, even though I didn't actually see it happen? Yes I can. The temperature's dropping below 32 degrees is the best explanation of the fact that the water turned to ice overnight. Thus:

> P occurred (the water turned to ice)
> H (the air temperature dipped below 32 degrees) is the best explanation of P's occurring.
>
> ───────────────────────────────
>
> Therefore, H is (probably) true.

In scientific explanations, the laws and theories appealed to can often be confirmed by appeal to experiment and observation. Suppose I left an iron bar outside for a week. After a week, I discover that there's an orange powder on it. It's rust. Is rust something deposited from the air onto the iron bar? I can devise an experiment to find out. (Before continuing, try to think up an experiment that would enable you to answer this question.) What can I do? I can take an iron bar and weigh it, then leave it outside for a week. Suppose after a week it has rust on it. I can then weigh it again. If it weighs less with the rust on it than it did without the rust, it doesn't seem likely that rust is something deposited on the iron bar from the air. Suppose it weighs more with the rust on it than it weighs without rust. Then maybe rust is something deposited on the iron bar from the air and it's nothing to worry about.

But we're not finished. What we should do next is scrape off the rust and weigh the bar a third time. If we find that the bar weighs the same the third time that it did the first time, it would show that rust is probably something deposited from the air. But suppose we find that the bar weighs less on the third weighing than it did on the first weighing?

In fact, if we performed this experiment carefully, we'd find that the weight of the bar is different at all three instances. It weighs more with the rust than without. It weighs less than it did the first weighing after the rust is scraped off. So the rust must be a combination of the iron and something else from the air. Appealing to the atomic theory of matter and other experiments, we now know that iron rusts when atoms of iron bond with atoms of oxygen. So we could explain rusting in this way:

> When atoms of oxygen come in contact with atoms of iron, they bind together.
> When iron and oxygen bind, they form an orange molecule called rust.
> This iron bar came in contact with oxygen.
> _____
>
> Therefore, this iron bar rusted.

The law of nature appealed to in the first premise can be confirmed or disconfirmed by performing experiments. That's an important feature of most scientific explanations. But many people say that it's not individual laws that are confirmed and disconfirmed by experiment, but rather whole theories. For example, the first premise of the above explanatory argument makes sense only within the context of the atomic theory of matter, a complicated edifice or structure of claims. Some parts of scientific theories are further back from what can be easily confirmed or disconfirmed by experiment than others.

But scientific explanations don't always directly appeal to laws of nature. Consider the most widely accepted explanation for the extinction of the dinosaurs. That explanation seems almost like a story that provides us with understanding. According to this explanation, a large piece of a comet or asteroid struck Earth, launching an enormous amount of debris into the atmosphere. This debris—particles of dust, dirt, and smoke—blocked most of the sun's rays for months or years. Because of this, an enormous amount of plant life died. Large dinosaurs that ate the plants then starved to death. Next, dinosaurs that ate those dinosaurs starved to death. Perhaps smaller plant eating dinosaurs that didn't need to eat as much food might have survived, but because they were reptiles and cold blooded, the drop in temperature caused by the blockage of the sun's rays might have made them too sluggish to be able to forage for food or caused them to freeze to death. Small mammals that are warm blooded would have had a much better chance to survive in these altered conditions. This story would explain why the dinosaurs died out so quickly and so completely. Since it's the best explanation, we're justified in believing that a piece of a comet or asteroid struck earth and caused the sudden extinction of the dinosaurs.

But scientists won't immediately begin to believe a good explanation unless there's some supporting evidence that comes from observation and experiment. Therefore, they looked for evidence to confirm the theory. They found what appeared to be a huge depression in the Gulf of Mexico that would be consistent with a crater caused by the impact of a meteor. Soil samples around the depression at soil depths of the time the dinosaurs became extinct showed traces of elements most likely to come from a meteor. Soil samples at other places in the world from the same time showed traces of the same elements. Because there is evidence that the hypothesis of a giant meteor hitting Earth is true, it's more widely accepted.

However, philosophical explanations aren't scientific explanations, even if philosophers sometimes appeal to scientific explanations and theories in defending their philosophical theories. Philosophical theories are further back from what's confirmable and disconfirmable by observation and experiment than are scientific theories.

Let's look at an example of a philosophical explanation. I am quite certain that I have mental states: beliefs, desires, sensations (such as pains and itches), emotions and feelings (such as love and hate), and attitudes. I also believe that other people besides me have mental states. What best explains how or why people such as me can have mental states? One possible explanation is that we have nonphysical minds that enable us to have mental states. So I might explain it as follows:

A being can have mental states only if it has a nonphysical mind that enables it to have mental states.
Human beings have mental states.

Therefore, human beings have nonphysical minds.

This is a philosophical rather than a scientific explanation because the law appealed to in the first premise isn't confirmable or disconfirmable by any experiment. But it's still an explanation.

A best explanation argument proceeds as follows:

Humans have mental states.
Having a nonphysical mind best explains how humans can have mental states.

Therefore, humans (probably) have nonphysical minds.

Best explanation arguments aren't limited to science and philosophy. Suppose that you're in a hotel room and you awake smelling smoke. You touch the wall next to the bed and it's hot. What should you conclude? Clearly, you're justified in concluding that there's a fire nearby. A fire would explain what you've observed.

Smoke is usually caused by fire.
Fire causes nearby things to get hot.
There's a fire nearby.

Therefore, I smell smoke and feel that the wall is hot.

A fire explains why I smell smoke and feel heat when I touch the wall. So I could reason:

I smell smoke and feel heat when I touch the wall.
The best explanation of the smoke and heat is that there's a fire.

Therefore, there's (probably) a fire.

Therefore, I'm justified in believing that there's a fire even though I don't see one because it's the best explanation of what I do observe.

Why Are Things This Way Rather Than Some Other Way?

When we seek explanations, we want to know why things are as they are rather than some other way. I ask why the water turned to solid rather than remaining a liquid or why the airplane exploded rather than didn't explode. A good explanation of a phenomenon must show why that phenomenon occurred rather than some other phenomenon. It must at least make the phenomenon that occurred highly probable and the alternative phenomena that didn't occur improbable.

The water froze because its temperature dropped below 32 degrees. In the context of the explanation, which appeals to the law that water freezes when its temperature drops below 32 degrees, the water had to freeze. It couldn't have remained a liquid or turned to a solid. The explanation makes those two possible phenomena very improbable, perhaps impossible. If the water had remained a liquid or turned to a gas instead, then we would have had to come up with a completely different explanation for those phenomena. We couldn't explain them by saying that the water's temperature dropped below 32 degrees.

A plane crashes. I ask why it crashed. Someone says that it's because God wanted it to crash. I ask, What if it hadn't crashed? Why would it have not crashed? The same person replies, Because God didn't want it to crash. All passengers died. I ask why. The answer I get is that God wanted it that way. I say, suppose only half died. How would we explain that? The answer I get is that God wanted it that way. Thus, no matter what happens, I get the same answer. What explains everything explains nothing. If I will get the same explanation regardless of what happens, I don't get an explanation of why this happened rather than something else.

Consistency with Background Information

If a possible explanation is in conflict with (is inconsistent with) information or beliefs that are widely accepted as obviously true, then it is not as good an explanation as one that is not in conflict with such information or beliefs.

Suppose that you time yourself in running from point A to point B and back again to point A. According to your stopwatch it took you 42 minutes: 20 minutes to run from A to B and then 22 minutes to run back from B to A. You wonder why it took you longer to run from point B back to point A than it took you to run from A to B. There are several possible explanations. One is that the distance from B back to A was greater than the distance from A to B. Another is that your stopwatch ran more quickly when you ran from B back to A than it did when you ran from A to B. Another is that you ran more slowly from B to A than you did when you ran from A to B (probably because you were tired). Which of these possible explanations is the best explanation?

I hope you will agree that the first explanation is the worst (least plausible) explanation because it is in conflict with something that all adults normally know and are certain of: the distance between any two points A and B is the same as the distance between B and A. (We assume that you took the same path from B to A as you took from A to B.) If the first explanation were the true explanation, then something that all adults normally know and are certain of would be false. But there is no good reason to think that this fundamental assumption is false if there are other possible explanations that are not in conflict with this fundamental assumption.

That leaves the second and third potential explanations. How likely is it, given what you know, that your stopwatch speeded up after you ran from A to B? Stopwatches can malfunction, but suppose it's generally been reliable. Compare that with the probability, given what you know, that you ran faster during the first half of your run than during the second half. You know that people get tired. Given what you know, the third explanation does the least violence to what you know, that is, it requires the least revision in your background beliefs.

Simplicity

All other things being equal, a simpler explanation is better than a more complicated or complex explanation if each will satisfactorily explain a phenomenon. For example, human beings can go through a variety of moods that affect their behavior. They can be happy one day and sad the next, hopeful then hopeless, calm then angry, pacific then violent, elated then depressed. Many people believe that a human being's mental life is a function of his or her soul; that is, they believe that it is one's soul that is or makes one happy or sad, calm or angry, pacific or violent. If we accept this theory (called Dualism, which we critically examine in Chapter 3), we can explain changes of mood either by claiming that changes within an individual's soul cause them or by claiming that whenever an individual's mood changes, he or she has a new soul. In the first explanation, each individual has one and only one soul and changes in it may cause the individual to change from being happy to sad. In the second explanation, each individual has many souls; when an individual changes from being happy to sad it is because a happy soul has been replaced by a sad soul. The first explanation is simpler than the second because it requires the existence of only one soul per person rather than many souls per person. Thus, one explanation is simpler than another if it postulates the existence of fewer things.

Suppose that one day you and a friend are having a discussion. He tells you that it is at least possible that when you go to sleep, the entire universe is annihilated, ceasing to exist, and then is recreated upon your awakening. There are thus two possible explanations for why the universe is there when you wake up each morning. One is that it was there the whole time you were sleeping. The other is your friend's explanation, that it was annihilated but then recreated. I think that almost all of us would consider the first explanation more plausible than the second because it is simpler. In the second we have to postulate the existence of some mechanism or thing that annihilates the universe when you go to sleep and a mechanism or thing that recreates it upon your awakening. We also have to explain how or why that happens. We face no such problems with the first explanation. The first explanation requires fewer processes, events, and things than the second explanation and therefore is simpler. Since both can adequately explain the phenomenon to be explained (the fact that the universe is there each time you awaken from sleep), the second, simpler explanation is more plausible.

Facts and Theories

People often say things such as, "That's not a fact, it's only a theory." The implication is that theories are second or third rate in comparison to facts.

A theory is a statement or set of statements intended to explain something. Darwin's theory of evolution is intended to explain why or how there are so many different species of living organisms. The heart of the theory is the statement that species that exist today evolved from other species, many of which are now extinct. The theory also provides an explanation of how this occurs. When an organism reproduces, its offspring is not an exact copy. Over long periods of time, changes (mutations) can accumulate so that some members of the thousandth or millionth generation can be so very different from the original organism that they constitute a separate species. The mechanism of evolution is thus random variations in offspring and natural selection.

What is a fact? Examples might be: Earth is smaller than the sun, water freezes at 32 degrees Fahrenheit, plants need water to live, and cats kill mice. What do all of these have in common? For one thing, they're all true statements, so perhaps a fact is nothing but a true statement.

BRAIN TEASERS

What else could a fact be?

Thus, if it's true that a meteor hitting Earth caused the extinction of the dinosaurs, then it's a fact that a meteor hitting Earth caused the extinction of the dinosaurs. If currently existing species evolved from earlier forms of life, then it's a fact that currently existing species evolved from earlier forms of life.

But many people would probably say that not all true statements are facts. After all, no one saw the meteor hit Earth and no one has found a big chunk of it. So isn't it still just a theory? How can a theory also be a fact? Perhaps a fact is a true statement that has been proved to be true by direct observation. Thus, it's a fact that quarters are round because it's true and we can just see that it's true. A theory can't also be a fact because we can't just see that a theory is true the way we can just see that quarters are round.

It may be that our ordinary usage of the term "fact" is fuzzy. We often use it in ways that suggest that it just means a true statement. For example, if someone says, "Michael Jordan was the greatest basketball player," and you agree, you might say, "That's a fact." If someone says that the United States never started a war and you're not sure of that, you might ask, "Is that a fact?" But many of us also tend to make a sharp distinction between theories and facts. That suggests that facts are more than true statements. But it may be that we're better off just defining a fact as a true statement. That way, we can talk of currently unknown facts that someone may discover. And we can distinguish between facts for which we have a lot of evidence and facts for which we have little evidence. Then, we can also say that some theories are also facts—the true ones. Similarly, we can talk of theories that have been highly confirmed or "proved," theories that have been disconfirmed or disproved, and theories for which there are varying amounts of evidence.

Two Principal Philosophical Questions

There are two very general philosophical questions that naturally arise for almost every philosophical issue:

1. What do you mean?
2. What reasons are there for believing that this claim is true?

Suppose that someone claims that God exists. Philosophers might first ask, "What do you mean by 'God'?" Until one knows what "God" means (or refers to), one cannot know whether the claim is true or false.

The second question that philosophers ask is "What reasons are there for believing that this claim is true?" That might be rephrased as "What evidence do you have?" Philosophers demand justification. They are hesitant to accept various claims, especially controversial claims, without reasons and arguments. Philosophers look for and then critically examine the justifying reasons that support a claim—reasons for believing that the claim is true rather than false. That is because philosophers assume that there's a connection between reasons and truth. A claim for which there are good justifying reasons is more likely to be true than a claim for which there aren't good justifying reasons.

Questions for Discussion and Review

1. If an argument is neither deductively valid nor inductively strong, does that prove conclusively that its conclusion is false? Explain and defend your answer.

2. If an argument is valid, does that prove conclusively that its conclusion is true? Explain and defend your answer.

3. If the conclusion of an argument is true, does that show that the argument is good—either deductively valid or inductively strong? Explain and defend your answer.

4. Which of the following arguments are deductively valid? Which are inductively strong? Of the inductively strong arguments, which are stronger? Explain and defend your answers.

   a. All college students love to read.
      Jones is a college student.
      _____
      Therefore, Jones loves to read.

b. All college students love to read.
Jones loves to read.

Therefore, Jones is a college student.

c. Thunderstorms sometimes occur under conditions C.
We now have conditions C.

Therefore, we're (probably) going to have a thunderstorm.

d. I have driven drunk many times without getting into an accident.

Therefore, if I drive drunk now, I probably won't get into an accident.

5. John promised to meet you at 5:30 at the corner of Main and Broadway on Monday in order to go to dinner and see a movie. John is very reliable and as far as you know has never broken a promise. It is now 5:40 and John has not appeared. Which of the following potential explanations is the best explanation? Why?

a. John has gotten stuck in rush hour traffic and is being delayed.
b. John has been in an accident and is either seriously injured or dead.
c. John has been kidnapped.

6. You arrive home one night to find your apartment a shambles inside. Furniture is overturned, books and clothing are strewn all over the floor, windows are broken. Which of the following are potential explanations? Explain and defend your answers.

a. There has been an earthquake.
b. Your upstairs neighbor coughed.
c. Robbers ransacked your apartment.
d. There was a lunar eclipse.

7. You notice that whenever you plunge a thermometer into boiling water, initially the mercury in the column drops, and then rises. How might you explain the initial drop in the column of mercury in the thermometer?

8. Mammals such as cows, squirrels, rabbits, wolves, dogs, cats, monkeys, and human beings are variations on the same general model. Roughly, they all have four limbs, a torso, and a head; a mouth, a nose, two ears, and two eyes in their heads; a heart, a liver, lungs, and a brain inside their bodies; a skeleton with similar bones such as ribs and vertebrae. They are also composed of the same kinds of cells on the cellular level. What would explain these systematic similarities?

Suggestions for Further Reading

Francis Watanabe Dauer. *Critical Thinking*. New York: Oxford University Press, 1989. A rigorous, careful introduction to reasoning, appropriate mainly for advanced students. See especially Chapters 2 and 5.

Howard Kahane. *Logic and Philosophy*, 6th ed. Belmont, CA: Wadsworth, 1990. A clear, readable introduction to formal and informal logic. See especially Chapters 1, 16, 17, and 18.

Willard Quine and Joseph Ullian. *The Web of Belief*, 2d ed. New York: Random House, 1978. A lively, stimulating look at many of the issues of this chapter. See especially Chapters 6, 8, and 9.

2 GOD AND PHILOSOPHY

Objectives

Students are expected to:

- understand the terms theist, atheist, and agnostic.
- understand the concept of God.
- understand the First Cause argument for God's existence.
- understand the Design argument for God's existence.
- understand the argument from evil against God's existence.
- understand the concept of faith.
- critically evaluate arguments for and against God's existence.

Introduction

When thunder crashed and lightning sprang across the sky, the ancient Greeks thought that Zeus, king of the gods, was at work. An earthquake, on the other hand, signaled the activity of Poseidon, the earthshaker. The Greeks, like the ancient Romans, believed in many gods—Zeus, Poseidon, Athena (goddess of wisdom), Hera (queen of the gods), Ares (god of war), Apollo (god of the sun and artistic creation)—living a divine life in their home on Mount Olympus. The ancient Egyptians worshipped a variety of gods, principal of whom was Re, the sun god. Similarly, the ancient Norse people, better known as the Vikings, believed in a host of gods, including Odin and Thor. It seems that through all of human history, a vast number of people have believed that behind or above the ordinary world of physical objects and events lies another order of existence, a divine and sacred world populated with humanlike individuals, the gods of what we now call mythology.

The belief that there are many individual gods is called *polytheism*. The Greeks, Romans, Egyptians, and Vikings were all polytheists. In modern Western culture, however, polytheism has largely given way to *monotheism*, the belief that only one God exists. Today, most Westerners scoff at the idea of many gods and dismiss as mere superstition the belief in the existence of such gods as Zeus and Thor. Modern theists believe that transcending the world we see, the world of ordinary physical objects from galaxies to atoms, is God, maker of heaven and earth. I will take theism and monotheism as synonymous. A theist believes that one and only one God exists.

One can be a theist and believe that God exists and yet reject all organized religions. For example, you could consistently reject all forms of Christianity, Judaism, Islam, Hinduism, or Buddhism as human devised systems of thought and practice that have many falsehoods included among their beliefs, and yet still be a theist who believes that God exists. Similarly, you could deny that the Bible (or the Koran) is the word of God, instead maintaining that what was written in these books was written by human beings, and yet still be a theist who believes that God exists. Of course, a Christian, Jew, or Muslim is a theist, but the opposite does not hold; you can be a theist without belonging to or accepting any of the world's organized religions.

A great many people today in the West are theists, but ours is an age of disbelief and unbelief as well as belief. There are those who deny or doubt that God exists, who look upon theism as a remnant of irrational superstition, as mere mythology like the polytheism of ancient peoples. They look upon God as nothing but a figment of human imagination. There are also those who simply cannot make up their minds. They find that they can't prove to their own satisfaction that God exists, and they can't prove to their own satisfaction that God doesn't exist. So they suspend judgment. They remain uncommitted. There are three positions one could take, then, toward the claim that God exists:

A theist believes that God exists.

An atheist believes that God doesn't exist.

An agnostic suspends judgment, neither believing nor disbelieving in God.

Theism: Belief that God exists

Atheism: Belief that God does not exist

Agnosticism: Suspension of judgment about God's existence

Which view is most reasonable, **theism, atheism,** or **agnosticism?** Obviously, one doesn't come to such questions wholly neutral and uncommitted. Many of us come to the question of whether God exists with pretty firm convictions about what the right answer is. So how do we approach the question philosophically?

Suppose we ask whether King Arthur and Queen Guinevere really existed or were merely legends, or whether Robin Hood and Maid Marian really existed. If we are rational, we will try to answer such questions by carefully examining the evidence and arguments, both those that try to prove that they did exist and those that try to prove that they didn't. We will try to determine which view is supported by the best reasons. Similarly, to determine whether theism, atheism, or agnosticism is most reasonable, we ought to investigate critically the arguments for and against God's existence.

The Concept of God

Suppose someone asked whether Xtlpzl really exists. Undoubtedly you would wonder who or what "Xtlpzl" refers to. Until you know that, you can't answer the question about whether Xtlpzl really exists. The same things apply when we ask about God's existence. It would help to know who or what "God" refers to.

In the Western religious tradition (Christianity, Judaism, and Islam), God (or Allah) is supposed to be the most perfect and powerful entity conceivable. According to this conception, God is the name of the creator of the universe from nothing, an entity outside space and time that is eternal, all-powerful, all-knowing, and perfectly good. In addition, God is said to be like a person in that God can feel love, anger, and compassion. Therefore, when we ask whether God exists, we are asking whether the term God really names anything, that is, whether the thing that the word God refers to really exists.

Not all names refer to something that really exists. Consider George Washington and Sherlock Holmes. There really was a George Washington, but there never was a Sherlock Holmes. Sherlock Holmes is a fictional character. Is God a fictional being like Sherlock Holmes or a real being like George Washington?

Arguments for God's Existence

Philosophers often claim that whether it is reasonable for you to believe something depends on whether you have evidence for it or arguments supporting it. What evidence or arguments are there for supporting the claim that God exists?

I Believe That God Exists
Because That Is What I Was Taught

When asked why they believe that God exists, students often say, "I believe that God exists because that is what I was taught." That might give one kind of explanation, but does it provide a *justification*? Is "That's what I was taught" a justifying reason? It would be if we thought of it as part of an argument. Here is one version:

I was taught that God exists.
Everything that I was taught is true.

Therefore, God exists.

This is a valid argument. If its premises are true, its conclusion must be true. But is it a good argument? That depends on whether we think that the second premise of the argument is true (or beyond reasonable doubt). However, it is awfully doubtful that everything you have been taught is true. For one thing, almost all of us at various times have been taught things that are inconsistent with one another. At one time in your life you may have been taught that Santa Claus and the Easter Bunny exist and then at a later time in your life taught that they don't exist. Then at least one of the things that you were taught was false. And most of us find from our own experience that not everything we were taught is true.

We could weaken the argument as follows to make it more plausible:

I was taught that God exists.
Most of what I was taught is true.

Therefore, (probably) God exists.

Although this argument is not deductively valid, it is inductively strong. The premises, if true, make the conclusion probable. A good case could be made that the second premise is true; most of what you were taught is true. So as it stands, this argument is inductively strong. But how strong is it? Recall that it is important with inductive arguments to take account of as much relevant information as we can before reaching a conclusion. Also it is important to examine the arguments on the other side. So perhaps it is premature to put much weight on this argument. What do you think?

The First Cause Argument

Another argument for the existence of God is the First Cause argument. Its best-known champion was Thomas Aquinas (1225–1274), one of the most influential of Roman Catholic theologians and philosophers. Aquinas insists that the existence of God can be proved, and he provides five inter-related arguments, his famous "five ways" of proving that God exists. His second argument deals with the chain of causality:

> The Second Way is taken from the idea of the Efficient Cause.[1] (1) For we find that there is among material things a regular order of efficient causes. (2) But we do not find, nor indeed is it possible, that anything is the efficient cause of itself, for in that case it would be prior to itself, which is impossible. (3) Now it is not possible to proceed to infinity in efficient causes. (4) For if we arrange in order all efficient causes, the first is the cause of the intermediate, and the intermediate is the cause of the last, whether the intermediate be many or one. (5) But if we

---

[1]Aquinas took over from Aristotle a complicated notion of four kinds of "cause," one of which is the "efficient" cause. For our purposes, the term *efficient* can be ignored.

remove a cause the effect is removed; therefore, if there be no first among efficient causes, neither will there be a last or intermediate. (6) But if we proceed to infinity among efficient causes there will be no first efficient cause, and thus there will be no ultimate effect, nor any intermediate efficient causes, which is clearly false. Therefore it is necessary to suppose the existence of some first efficient cause, and this men call God.[2]

Most of us are inclined to think that things that exist have a cause of their coming into existence. As Aquinas puts it, "We find that there is among material things a regular order of efficient causes." Where did you come from? Obviously from your parents. Aquinas says that nothing can be the cause of itself, so you didn't cause yourself to come into existence. Where did your parents come from? They came from their parents. Where did their parents come from? From their parents. How far backward in time do we go? We can go back a thousand years, perhaps a million years. However far back in time we go, we'll encounter something that is the cause of things coming after it, ancestors of you and of your parents and of your parents' parents and so on. Or take an oak tree. It came into existence, and there was a cause. That cause was an earlier oak tree. What caused that earlier oak tree to come into existence? A still earlier oak tree. It seems that each thing with which we are familiar came into existence at some time, and its coming into existence was caused by something. Scientists tell us that even Earth had a beginning in time. They even say that the entire physical universe itself came into existence 12–15 billion years ago in the "Big Bang."

Aquinas maintains that "it is not possible to proceed to infinity in efficient causes." That is, according to him, an infinite chain of causes going backward eternally into the past is simply impossible. You don't have an infinite number of ancestors going backward into the eternal past; the oak tree doesn't have an infinite number of ancestors. It seems that Aquinas is claiming that there can't be a causal chain in which A_1 is brought into existence by the activity of A_2, which is brought into existence by the activity of A_3, which is brought into existence by the activity of A_4, . . . which is brought into existence by the activity of A_{999}, and on and on through an infinity of causes stretching backward into the infinite past. But then there must have been a first link in this causal chain, if Aquinas is right; a first link caused the second link to come into existence, which caused the third link to come into existence, and so on. A last link requires a first link. According to Aquinas, the First Cause couldn't be a cause of itself, nor could it have come into existence without a cause, so it must have always existed. It must be eternal. There exists, then, an eternal, uncaused First Cause, and this First Cause is God, Aquinas claims.

---

[2]Thomas Aquinas, "The Five Ways," from *Summa Theologica*. Quoted in *Philosophy of Religion: An Anthology*, ed. Louis Pojman (Belmont, CA: Wadsworth, 1987), 4.

We have to be careful, though, about the claim that there can't be an infinite causal chain, or causal series. Aquinas recognizes that there can be an infinite series and perhaps even an infinite temporal series extending backward in time to the infinite past. But he claims that there cannot be an infinite causal series. That claim, as interpreted by most commentators today, isn't as straightforward as it might at first appear.[3]

Suppose we have an A (for example, an oak tree) that is a member of a causal series of A's or a link in a causal chain of A's. Its coming into existence was caused by a prior A. Aquinas admits that this causal series of A's can be infinite, with an infinite number of A's, each caused by a preceding A, stretching backward into the infinite past forever:

$$\ldots -A_6 -A_5 -A_4 -A_3 -A_2 -A_1$$

Past $\longleftarrow$——————— Present

A_1 was caused by A_2, which was caused by A_3, and so on. But now a new question arises for Aquinas. Each individual A has a cause, but what is the cause of the series, or chain, of A's? How did the universe come to include A's at all? Must there not be a cause of the series of A's, whether it's infinite or finite?

Assuming that everything that exists has a cause, the series of A's requires a cause, just as each individual A requires a cause. Let's say that B is the cause of the series of A's. We then get the following:

$$\underbrace{-A_6 -A_5 -A_4 -A_3 -A_2 -A_1 \ldots}_{B}$$

But now what about B? B either has a cause or doesn't. If it doesn't have a cause, it's the First Cause, God, and that ends the matter. If it does have a cause, it isn't the First Cause. Let's assume that B isn't the First Cause. Therefore, it had a cause—a prior B—which in turn had a cause. It's just one member of a causal series or link in a causal chain of B's, each B caused by a prior B:

$$\underbrace{A_6 -A_5 -A_4 -A_3 -A_2 -A_1 - \ldots}$$
$$B_1$$
$$|$$
$$B_2$$
$$|$$
$$B_3$$
$$|$$
$$B_4$$
$$\vdots$$

---

[3]See, for example, William J. Wainwright, *Philosophy of Religion* (Belmont, CA: Wadsworth, 1988).

Whether the causal chain or series of B's is infinite or finite, the same question arises with relation to that series as arose with relation to the series of A's. How did the universe come to include the series of B's? What is the cause of the series of B's? Perhaps it's a C. If the C has no cause, it's the First Cause and thus God. If it has a cause, it's not the First Cause. As before, let's assume that the C that caused the series of B's is itself a member of a causal series. We then generate a more complicated pattern than before:

$$A_6 - A_5 - A_4 - A_3 - A_2 - A_1 - \ldots$$

$$\left. \begin{array}{c} B_1 \\ | \\ B_2 \\ | \\ B_3 \\ | \\ B_4 \\ | \\ B_5 \\ \vdots \end{array} \right\} C_1 - C_2 - C_3 - C_4 - \ldots$$

The series of A's is caused by B1, one of a series of B's. The series of B's is caused by C1, one of a series of C's. It doesn't take long to see that such an infinite series of causal chains becomes absurd. Must we not introduce D as the cause of a series of C's? If that's not the First Cause and it's one of a series of D's, we must introduce E as cause of the series of D's, and so on.

$$A_6 - A_5 - A_4 - A_3 - A_2 - A_1 - \ldots$$

$$\left. \begin{array}{c} B_1 \\ | \\ B_2 \\ | \\ B_3 \\ | \\ B_4 \\ | \\ B_5 \\ \vdots \end{array} \right\} C_1 - C_2 - C_3 - C_4 - \ldots$$

$$\left. \begin{array}{c} D_1 \\ | \\ D_2 \\ | \\ D_3 \\ | \\ D_4 \\ \vdots \end{array} \right\} E \ldots$$

Aquinas thinks it absurd that there could be such an infinite series of causal chains. He thinks, then, that there must be a First Cause that provides an end to the absurd population explosion of causal chains. And the First Cause is God. Let me set out the structure of the argument as I've attributed it to Aquinas, and then we can evaluate it to see whether Aquinas has succeeded in proving that God exists:

THE FIRST CAUSE ARGUMENT

1. Everything that exists had a cause of its coming into existence.
2. Nothing can be the cause of itself.
3. There cannot be an infinite series of causal chains.
4. Therefore, there had to be a First Cause.
5. The First Cause must be God.

6. Therefore, God exists.

One thing to notice is that the argument is valid. If all its premises are true, its conclusion must be true. The question is whether all its premises are true. Supporters of the First Cause argument believe that all its premises are true. (Some supporters might say that while some premises of the argument are undoubtedly true, other premises are, more weakly, just probably true. Other supporters might say that it is beyond reasonable doubt that each premise is true.) Critics of the First Cause argument do not think that all of its premises are beyond reasonable doubt. Most critics focus on the first, third, and fifth premises. Because they think that these premises are doubtful, they do not think that the argument "proves" that God exists.

Must Everything That Exists Have a Cause?   Almost all of us, on reflection, accept the thesis of *Determinism,* the thesis that every event has a cause. (Some people might maintain that the thesis of Determinism is not merely true, but necessarily true, meaning either logical necessity or physical necessity.) For our purposes, an event is simply a change. If a leaf changes color from green to red or water changes from a liquid to a solid, that's an event. If a painting comes into existence, that's an event. Any change in the properties of an object or the relations between objects is an event, as is an object's coming to or ceasing to exist. And almost all of us assume that events have causes.

If the temperature of the room begins to rise, we assume that there is a cause of its rising. If there has been a tree in front of your house but one day it is gone, you would surely assume that there was a cause of its ceasing to be there. Similarly, if something comes into existence, almost all of us assume that there must have been a cause of its coming into existence.

Consider yourself. You came into existence as a result of the activity of your parents. They in turn came into existence as a result of the activity of their parents. They came into existence as a result of the activity of their parents, and so on. We can go back hundreds, perhaps thousands of generations in time to the first human beings, then beyond to precursors of modern humans. But always one thing's coming into existence is caused by the activity of a prior thing or things.

Must everything that exists have a cause? If the answer is yes, there is a problem, because then it must be the case that if God exists, God had a cause. And then the cause of God would have had a cause and that cause would have had a cause and . . . We would face the kind of infinite population explosion that Aquinas rejected. How can we resolve this?

A supporter of the First Cause argument might point out that according to the thesis of Determinism, every event has a cause rather than every "thing." When we say that you had a cause, we mean that the event of your coming into existence had a cause. When we say that a "thing" has a cause, we mean that the event of that thing's coming into existence had a cause. According to the thesis of Determinism, anything that came into existence must have had a cause of its coming into existence. But suppose that a thing has always existed. Suppose it never came into existence because it has always existed; it is eternal. In that case there would have been no event of its coming into existence. And if there was no event of its coming into existence, it would not have a cause, because it is events rather than things that have causes. But even though it would not have a cause, that would not be inconsistent with the thesis of Determinism because it would not entail the existence of an uncaused event.

We can restate the first premise of the First Cause argument, then, as follows:

> Everything that has come into existence had a cause of its coming into existence.

If something came into existence, it must have had a cause (of its coming into existence). However, this makes no such claim about something if it never came into existence but rather has always existed. If something never came into existence because it never was nonexistent, then it does not have to have had a cause. Therefore, if God is eternal and has always existed, God doesn't have to have a cause. Only things that have not always existed must have causes. So God could be the first cause although Him/Herself uncaused.

The First Cause argument relies on the assumption that the physical universe that extends in time backward into the past and forward into the future must have had a cause, although God does not have to have had a cause. But what if the physical universe extends backward into the past eternally? What if the physical universe has always existed, just as God is supposed to have always existed? In that case, the thesis of Determinism would not entail that the physical universe must have had a cause any more than it entails that God must have had a cause. If the universe has always existed, then there was no event of the universe's coming into existence any more than there was an event of God's coming into existence. If the universe has always existed, it is not at all obvious that it must have had a cause.

Has our universe always existed? Scientists claim that our universe was "created" by a colossal explosion called the Big Bang 12–15 billion years ago. (The evidence for this event is the fact, discovered by astronomers in the twentieth century, that the universe is expanding like a balloon, with galaxies hurtling away from each other at tremendous speed just like debris from an explosion. The speed at which galaxies fly apart is used to estimate the age of our universe or the time at which the Big Bang occurred.) Some maintain that the Big Bang represents the creation of the physical universe from nothing, that prior to the Big Bang there was nothing and after the Big Bang the physical universe came into existence. If the thesis of Determinism is true, there must have been a cause of the Big Bang. In turn, that would mean that there must have been a cause of the physical universe's coming into existence. But was there literally nothing in existence before the Big Bang? If something was in existence before the Big Bang, then events associated with it might be the cause of the Big Bang.

Many people in the West assume that the physical universe has not always existed, that it came into existence at the time of or as a result of the Big Bang. However, many people in the East deny that. According to Buddhism, the universe has always existed. "Buddhism sees no need for a creator of the world, as it postulates no ultimate beginning to the world, and regards it as sustained by natural laws."[4] How could that be? How could the Big Bang not be the event of the universe's coming into existence out of nothing?

One possibility is that the Big Bang was an explosion of (or in) something that already existed, perhaps a kind of "stuff" even more basic than energy or the smallest subatomic particles, quarks, of which physical objects in our universe are supposedly composed. This basic material, whatever it might be, or perhaps some basic building blocks of the very structure of space-time, has always existed. Perhaps the Big Bang transformed but did not create it. In fact, if there is enough matter in the universe to slow and then reverse the expansion of the universe, there may be another Big Bang in the future as the universe collapses. One might speculate (it is merely speculation) that the Big Bang that created the universe as we know it was merely the most recent in an infinite series of Big Bangs, a series made up of an eternal process of Big Bang followed by expansion, contraction, and collapse leading to another Big Bang.

Which model is more plausible, the one above or the one below?

[4]Peter Harvey, *An Introduction to Buddhism* (Cambridge: Cambridge University Press, 1990), 36.

In the first model, there is no need to postulate a creator of the universe, because it has always existed in some form, although not necessarily in its present form. And each Big Bang has a cause, but not necessarily God. Each Big Bang is caused by the collapse of the universe during its contraction phase, creating gigantic internal forces that eventually cause another colossal explosion. The time between Big Bangs could be a hundred billion years or a thousand billion years. (This assumes that there is enough matter in the universe so that the combined forces of gravity will reverse the expansion.) In the second model, the Big Bang was the first, the event at which the universe was created from nothing. And the most likely cause of the Big Bang was God.

However, critics of the First Cause argument might maintain that so far as we know now, the first model is no less plausible than the second model. In that case, the universe doesn't have to have a cause and the Big Bang could have had a cause other than God.

Is There a Problem About an Infinite Series of Causal Chains?
According to the third premise of the First Cause argument, there cannot be an infinite series of causal chains. This does not mean that there cannot be an infinite series of events going back into the past. The point here may be subtle. Perhaps we can think of it in the following way: Aquinas may ask why the physical universe exists, whether it is eternal or not. That is, Aquinas may seek a causal explanation for why there is something rather than nothing. Even though it is obvious that there is a physical universe, the physical universe might not have existed. Why is it that the physical universe exists rather than doesn't exist? Why is there something (the physical universe) rather than nothing?

Aquinas might maintain that there must be a cause of (or causal explanation for) why the universe exists rather than doesn't exist. Then there must be a cause of (or causal explanation for) why the cause of the universe exists rather than doesn't exist. Then there must be a cause. . . . Here we go again. There is a threat of an infinite causal chain and an infinite population explosion again, which Aquinas thinks is absurd. He thinks that the cause of why the universe exists rather than doesn't exist is God. There is something rather than nothing because God made there be something. But Aquinas thinks that we don't need an explanation for why there is a God rather than no God.

It would be nice if we could explain why the universe exists rather than doesn't exist, why there is something rather than nothing. But critics of Aquinas maintain that we can't. They think that appealing to God as the explanation of why there is rather than isn't a physical universe is mere speculation and that it would be more honest to say simply, "We don't know." They think that explanations must stop somewhere; but should explanations stop with God or with admissions that sometimes we just don't know, that we cannot answer every "Why?" question? We can stop the threat of an infinite series of causal chains with God (we don't need to or cannot explain why God exists rather than doesn't exist) or with the universe itself (we don't need to or cannot explain why the universe exists rather than doesn't exist).

Must a First Cause Be God?   Even if there is a First Cause, critics of the First Cause argument ask, "Why think it's God?" Recall that our idea of God is rather complex; it includes the ideas of being an all-powerful, all-knowing, and perfectly good humanlike being. Critics ask: Is there any reason to think that the First Cause has all of the characteristics attributed to God? For example, why think that the First Cause is anything at all like a human being, having consciousness and personal characteristics such as being capable of love, forgiveness, compassion, and so on? Why couldn't the First Cause be an impersonal force or field of energy? And why think that the First Cause is perfectly good? Or all-knowing? Similarly, why think the First Cause is eternal? Perhaps the First Cause existed when it caused the Big Bang, but does that guarantee that it still exists today? The claim that the First Cause is God, a being having all the characteristics we attribute to God, is nothing but an arbitrary assumption, according to critics of the First Cause argument.

BRAIN TEASERS

1. Do you think that the First Cause argument proves that God exists? Why or why not?
2. Do you think it is more likely that the universe has always existed or that it had a beginning in time? Explain and defend your answer.

The Design Argument

Look around you. Everywhere you look, there is evidence of order. The planets revolve about the sun in their regular orbits millennium after millennium; the seasons come and go with astonishing regularity. Most astonishing of all is the order of living things. Earth is just close enough to the sun to sustain this incredible variety of life. A bit closer and it would have been too hot for life, a bit farther away and it would have been too cold for life. Earth seems set in just the right place. Consider the delicately balanced ecosystems that gave birth to and sustain life. One species feeds on another species and in turn becomes the food of a third species. Think of the incredible complexity and organization of the simplest one-celled creature. Or think of the marvel of engineering an ant represents! We surely at least feel tempted to ask who painted the wings of the monarch butterfly. Or consider the humblest bird. Who designed its wings and body so that it could fly? Who designed the sonar by which bats fly? Who designed the gills of fish that enable them to live in water? When we consider the fact that Earth is hospitable to life and that life in incredible profusion and variety exists on Earth, it's difficult not to conclude that it's all the result of intelligent design and purpose. It all looks as though it were designed.

Finally, consider yourself. Isn't it tempting to conclude that human beings are the product of intelligent design? Doesn't it seem that it required an engineer of incredible talent to design the human eye? Think of all the cells and organs cooperating to sustain the life and functioning of a human being: heart, lungs, digestive system, blood, liver, and kidneys. Then think of the astonishing capabilities of the human brain. It has composed symphonies, created powerful supercomputers, built sprawling cities of cement and steel that cover the globe and pierce the clouds, and sent vessels out to explore the cold, dark depths of space. Human beings have created scientific theories of unimaginable complexity and profundity. They are capable of feeling love and hate, joy and sorrow, compassion, and a thousand other emotions. Is there anything more incredible than a human being? Isn't it tempting to think that human beings were designed and created by a higher power?

Could all this order, structure, and organization simply be the product of chance, or must this order be the product of an intelligent designer? The Design argument tries to use the obvious fact of order and structure to prove that God exists. According to many thinkers, the order in the universe and the existence of life itself appear to be products of intelligent design. The best explanation for their appearing to be the product of intelligent design, according to these thinkers, is that they are the product of intelligent design. The designer, of course, is God:

THE DESIGN ARGUMENT

1. The universe has an orderly structure, or organization.
2. The best explanation of this structure is that it was produced by the conscious activity of an intelligent designer rather than by the chance operation of natural forces.
3. The designer is God.

---

4. Therefore, God exists.

The argument is an argument to the best explanation. It starts with a fact to be explained—the order of the universe—and asks what best explains the fact that there is this order, this appearance of design. According to this argument, the intelligent, purposive activity of a designer is a better explanation than is the chance operation of nonconscious natural forces. Therefore, it's reasonable to believe that there is a designer and that the designer could only be God.

Probably the best-known advocate of the Design argument was William Paley (1743–1805), a British clergyman. Paley likens the universe to a humble watch. He points out that if we came across a watch on a desert island, we would have as much evidence as we could desire that there had been a maker of the watch. It wouldn't matter that we hadn't seen it made or that there were no other signs of intelligent life on the island. We would not be tempted to suppose that the watch had somehow been formed by the chance operation of natural forces on the island. We would know that an intelligent watchmaker had made it.

Paley says that the universe shows more signs of design than a watch. Just as we conclude that there must have been a watchmaker, we should conclude when we see the order and design of the universe that there was a designer. Paley argues that the designer of the universe could only be God.

Must Species Have Been Created by God?   As plausible as this reasoning seems, it has been severely challenged by critics of the Design argument. For one thing, critics point to the theory of evolution in biology. According to scientists, more complex organisms have evolved from less complex organisms over vast periods of time. All the life we see around us evolved from very humble origins over billions of years, they maintain. According to this theory, life started with single-celled organisms and gradually evolved into all the forms we see around us, including ourselves. Living organisms, according to biologists, were not designed by a conscious intelligence.

Take a monarch butterfly or an ant. Don't they seem to be either exquisite works of art or extraordinary machines? Take a bird with its wings that enable it to fly or a bat with its sonar that enables it to navigate at high speed in the dark without bumping into things and knocking its brains out. Take a human being with eyes, ears, and a brain. Despite the fact that all these appear to be the product of intelligent design, many scientists insist that appearances are deceptive. They claim that these creatures were all produced not by design but by the operation of purely natural forces, by chance.

How could that be? Charles Darwin (1809–1882), the father of modern biology, had an explanation: descent with modification and natural selection. Each generation that reproduces brings forth offspring that are not exactly identical to their parents. This is what Darwin calls descent with modification. You are not identical to either of your parents. Similarly, not every dog, cat, or horse is a carbon copy of either of its parents.

Some of the offspring who differ from their parents are less well-adapted to their environment than are their parents, others are just about as well adapted, but some few are better adapted. That is, some offspring are, in a sense, "improved models." Whether an individual offspring is better adapted or less well adapted to its environment than its parents is a matter of chance. An organism that is an improved version, that is better adapted to its environment than are others of its kind, has a higher probability of surviving and reproducing. It may be able to pass on to its offspring any traits that gave it an edge in its struggle for survival. This is natural selection.

Given descent with modification and natural selection, through hundreds of millions of years, small changes handed down to subsequent generations accumulate until they make big changes. It's like building a pile of one-inch blocks, one stack at a time. In the first stack you put one block, in the second stack you put two blocks, in the third stack three blocks, and so on. Each stack of blocks would be only an inch taller than the preceding one and an inch shorter than the next one. The changes would be small. But let them accumulate. How tall would the millionth stack be? Almost sixteen miles tall! Yet we began with something an inch tall. Evolution is like that, according to Darwin's theory. Imagine the changes that could occur over hundreds of millions of generations. So according to evolutionary theory, no one designed the life forms we see around us. They gradually evolved through chance variation and natural selection.

Most scientists claim that a great deal of evidence confirms the theory that the creatures that exist today are descended from, and hence modifications of, creatures that existed millions of years ago. And they claim that all of the available evidence goes against the theory that the creatures we see around us today, including human beings, were specially designed and created by an intelligent being. A critic of the Design argument, then, says that it's simply *not necessary* to introduce a designer to explain the wealth of living creatures that Earth contains. Thus, there's no reason to believe that there was a designer.

It's not that evolutionary biology is inconsistent with God's existence. It's entirely possible that God exists and that evolutionary biology is true. God could have ordained that species and organisms would come into existence through evolutionary processes. For example, the contemporary philosopher and theologian Arthur Peacocke has written:

> We now see in a new way the role in evolution of the interplay between random chance micro-events and the necessity which arises from the stuff of this world having its particular "given" properties. These potentialities a theist must regard as written into creation by the creator himself in order that they may be unveiled by chance exploring their gamut. God as creator we now see as somewhat like a composer who, beginning with an arrangement of notes in an apparently simple tune, elaborates and expands it into a fugue by a variety of devices. In this way the creator may be imagined to unfold the potentialities of the universe that he himself has given it, selecting and shaping by his providential action those that are to come to fruition.[5]

---

[5]Arthur Peacocke, "Biological Evolution and Christian Theology," in *Philosophy of Biology,* ed. Michael Ruse (New York: Macmillan, 1989), 340.

Must the Environment Have Been Created by God?   Even if the critics of the Design argument are right and the living creatures we see around us were not designed, can't one argue that an environment hospitable to living organisms must be the product of design? Doesn't it seem almost miraculous that the environment is hospitable to life at all? A supporter of the Design argument could concede that evolution might explain the marvelous diversity of living organisms and the origin of today's species without introducing the activity of an intelligent designer. But what of the environment that supports life and the evolutionary process? Surely the environment seems *designed* to support life.

Critics of the Design argument are not impressed with this appeal and think that the appearance of having been designed to support life is deceptive. It may appear as though the environment was created to be suitable for the organisms in it, but critics think it more likely that the life forms conformed themselves to the environment available. They point out that only life forms that can live in the earthly environment could have arisen here. The environment came first, the organisms later. The environment determined what could come into existence here and what couldn't. According to critics of the Design argument, then, the environment wasn't especially designed for the organisms we see around us.

But even if that were true, couldn't a theist argue that only the intelligent activity of a designer could explain the fact that an environment capable of supporting life and the evolutionary process exists? Even if the environment wasn't designed especially for the forms of life in it, wasn't it designed to support life of some kind? Why does Earth support life whereas the other planets in our solar system don't (as far as we know)? Surely someone designed Earth so that it's capable of supporting life.

Critics of the Design argument might appeal to probability to show that a world hospitable to life could be the product of mere chance rather than conscious intelligence and purpose. For example, given that there are twenty or thirty large bodies in our solar system (planets and their moons), couldn't chance account for one of them being hospitable to life? Think of a game of cards. In one hand of poker it's fairly unlikely that in a fair deal in which the cards have been randomly shuffled you'll be dealt four aces. But if you play thirty hands, the odds are much better that in one of them you will be dealt four aces purely by chance. Similarly, if there are thirty planets and moons rather than one, there's a greater chance that at least one of them will have conditions suitable for life.

But the critic can point to greater odds than merely 30 to 1. There are about 100 million stars in our galaxy alone. Scientists now believe that many of them have planets circling them. Among 100 million stars with perhaps tens of millions or hundreds of millions of planets and large moons, isn't it likely that at least some of them would be suitable for life (of some kind)? In 100 million hands of poker, isn't it likely that many, many hands of four aces will be dealt? Further, our galaxy is only one of tens of millions of galaxies. Scientists say that there are 10^{20} stars visible to optical and radio telescopes; that's 100,000,000,000,000,000,000 visible stars. Scientists are certain that there are many others we have not yet been able to detect. Isn't it overwhelmingly likely, critics of the Design argument say, that however rare may be the conditions suitable for life, many places in the universe will be suitable, quite by chance, because of the astounding number of places available? (Of course, life need not be as we find it on Earth.) Surely with that many stars and that many planets, the critics maintain, some will be suitable for life of some kind. Therefore, they argue, we can explain the existence of worlds hospitable to life without introducing God. Given the vast number of combinations that nature has to experiment with, it's highly probable that some of them would be favorable to life.

Must Life Have Been Created by God?   Even if you think that the critics of the Design argument are right, another question arises. How could living things come into existence at all? Even if there is a hospitable environment available, how could life itself come into existence to take advantage of the hospitable environment? Could nonliving things produce living things by the chance operation of natural forces? Isn't God's causal activity the best explanation of the origin of life itself? Even if it is a matter of chance that some planets are hospitable to life, and even if the theory of evolution is true, where did the first living organisms come from, however simple and primitive they may have been? Surely only God can explain the origin of life itself.

In opposition to this argument, many scientists believe that a purely natural rather than a supernatural explanation of life's origin will be found. They believe they've gotten closer and closer to such a purely physical explanation, as the physicist Paul Davies points out in his book *God and the New Physics:*

> The favoured scenario for the origin of life is the "primeval soup." The primitive Earth, with its abundant supply of water, enriched by simple organic compounds formed from chemical reactions in the atmosphere, would have possessed innumerable ponds and lakes in which a vast range of chemical processes would have taken place. Over millions of years, molecules of greater and greater complexity would form until, with the threshold crossed, life itself would have arisen purely from the random self-organization of complex organic molecules.
>
> Support for this scenario came with the celebrated Miller–Urey experiment in 1953. Stanley Miller and Harold Urey, of the University of Chicago, attempted to simulate the conditions believed to have prevailed on the primeval Earth. . . . After a few days, the experimenters found their "pool" of water had turned a red colour and contained many of the chemical compounds that are important in life today, such as amino acids.[6]

---

[6]Paul Davies, *God and the New Physics* (New York: Simon & Schuster, 1983), 68–69.

Davies points out that the steps from prebiotic soup to life remain mysterious. But, as he puts it, "a lack of understanding does not imply a miracle."[7]

None of this, of course, rules out a creative God, but it does suggest that divine action may be no more necessary for biology than it is for, say, producing the rings of Saturn or the surface features of Jupiter.[8]

Davies's point is that science may be able to find a purely natural explanation for the origin of life. Therefore, critics of the Design argument may insist that we don't even need a designer to explain the origin of life. Supporters of the argument, however, may reply that scientists have not yet come up with such a natural explanation. Until scientists come up with plausible and well-confirmed theories about the origin of life that are complete and detailed, a theist may say that divine action is still the best explanation for the origin of life.

Must the Designer Be God?   A final problem with the Design argument should be mentioned. Even if there had to be a designer of the universe, what reason is there to think that it had to be God? David Hume (1711–1776) points out that any orderly design we see could have been produced not only by the intelligent activity of one supremely perfect and powerful God but also by the cooperative effort of many lesser gods. He notes that most complex human projects are not individual efforts but joint efforts. Take a house or a ship. These are usually built by several people working together. The bigger the job, the more workers seem required. Is it not at least as plausible, Hume asks, that the organization of the universe is the product of the cooperative effort of many gods rather than the product of one supremely perfect and powerful God?

> A great number of men join in building a house or ship, in rearing a city, in framing a commonwealth: why may not several deities combine in contriving and framing a world? This is only so much greater similarity to human affairs. By sharing the work among several, we may so much further limit the attributes of each, and get rid of that extensive power and knowledge, which must be supposed in one deity.[9]

Even if the Design argument could prove that only one designer was responsible for the order and design we see around us, could it prove that the one designer is the God of Judaism and Christianity, who is eternal, all-perfect, and the creator of the universe from nothing? If the order in the world is the product of intelligent activity, is there any reason to think that the designer has existed from eternity, still exists, and will exist eternally into the future? Is there any reason to believe that the designer is or was perfectly good? Is there any reason to believe that the designer not only shaped the

---

[7] Ibid., 70.

[8] Ibid., *God and the New Physics,* 70.

[9] David Hume, "Dialogues Concerning Natural Religion," in *David Hume on Religion,* ed. Richard Wollheim (New York: Meridian, 1963), 140–141.

structure of the universe but also created it from nothing? A designer may work with raw materials already at hand and not create the material to which order is given. To be God, the designer must have all the characteristics definitive of God, but critics of the Design argument maintain that there is simply no reason to believe that a designer must have all of those characteristics—eternal, all-powerful, and so on—and thus be God.

An Argument Against God's Existence: The Argument from Evil

So far, we've examined and evaluated two important arguments that try to prove that God exists. One influential argument, however, attempts to prove that God doesn't exist: the argument from Evil. This argument is in a sense the mirror image of the Design argument. Whereas the Design argument uses the facts of ordinary existence—order and structure—to try to prove that God exists, the argument from Evil uses a different selection of the facts of ordinary existence—pain and suffering—to try to prove that God doesn't exist.

It's undeniable that there are pain and suffering in the world; the world is not entirely benign. Animals are eaten alive by other animals for food; whole species have become extinct; among human beings there is poverty, loneliness, ignorance, disease, starvation, and violent death. Surely if God exists and both created and designed this world, a nontheist says, God would have done a much better job of it. In this view, God would have created a world with far less evil (not necessarily no evil). A world with so much unnecessary pain and suffering doesn't seem to be a world God would create, so God probably didn't create it. God probably is a figment of people's imaginations and doesn't exist, this argument concludes.

ARGUMENT FROM EVIL

1. Some of the evil (pain and suffering) in the world is unnecessary.
2. If God existed, there would be no unnecessary evil in the world.

---

3. Therefore, God does not exist.

Is There Any Unnecessary Evil?

It seems difficult to deny that evil exists, if by evil we mean pain and suffering. The existence of pain and suffering is hard to deny. We all know that death can sometimes be long, slow, and painful. All living things die, and often their deaths are horrible to contemplate. Illness can sap a living creature's vitality and kill it inch by slow inch. There are deaths from starvation and dehydration in drought-stricken areas, infant malnutrition, birth defects, and natural disasters such as earthquakes, floods, and tornadoes. There are war and political turmoil, the gas chambers and killing fields of totalitarian regimes. Then there are those illnesses that don't kill but disable or disfigure. There is also the mental anguish that people are prone to because of the loss of a loved one, unrequited love, loneliness, or mental incapacity. Not only humans suffer but also other living things. Think of the animal caught in a trap to die a slow death.

Although it seems hard to deny that evil exists, it's not so obvious that some of the pain and suffering is unnecessary. What would make pain and suffering necessary, and what would make them unnecessary? Pain and suffering are necessary if there's an important good that cannot come into existence without them—if they are means to an important end. For example, a doctor gives you a painful injection of an antibiotic to cure an infection. The pain of the injection was necessary for the important good of receiving medication to combat the infection. Or take an athlete who trains vigorously. Vigorous training can produce pain, but it contributes to the greater good of physical strength and endurance necessary for competing and winning. As coaches are fond of saying, "No pain, no gain."

Pain and suffering are unnecessary when they are pointless, when they don't contribute to any greater good. If a dentist could cure a cavity without drilling and without any pain but drilled anyway, the pain of the drilling would be unnecessary. Let's say, then, that an evil is necessary when it meets three conditions:

1. The evil produces good.
2. The good could not have come into existence other than through the evil.
3. The good outweighs (is more valuable than) the evil.

The first premise of the argument from Evil states that some evil (pain and suffering) is unnecessary. But is it beyond reasonable doubt that some of the evil in the world is unnecessary? Can critics of theism show that some evil is unnecessary? Can they demonstrate pain and suffering that are absolutely pointless, that either produce no good, produce a good that could have come into existence without the evil, or produce a good that was not sufficiently valuable to outweigh the evil?

Take a baby born with a severe birth defect that will drastically limit her life span and quality of life. A supporter of the argument from Evil might point to this birth as an example of unnecessary evil. What good can come from it that outweighs the evil? There are a blighted life, the mental anguish of the parents and other relatives, and the enormous financial burden of medical costs. A nontheist might say, "Surely here is unnecessary evil."

How might a theist respond? A theist might try to show that significant good comes from the evil. For example, the theist might maintain that people familiar with the situation become more compassionate, more generous. The suffering ennobles those who observe the suffering or those who suffer. Suffering can build character and bring people together. Thus, theists might try to show that, contrary to first impressions, the evil in question is necessary for the production of some important and valuable goods that justify the pain and suffering.

But what of teenagers killed in a car accident? The millions of innocent men, women, and children murdered in Hitler's concentration camps? The child with muscular dystrophy? The patient slowly dying in pain from terminal cancer? The aged and infirm person with Alzheimer's disease wasting away in loneliness in an old-age home? Supporters of the argument from Evil who think that evil proves that God doesn't exist will ask what good comes from these evils and whether the good can be said to outweigh the horrible pain and suffering. They will ask whether theists can prove that good comes from them, that the good could have come about in no other way, and that the good outweighs the evil.

Supporters of the argument from Evil are also likely to bring up the question of who benefits from the pain and suffering. Can the infant with severe birth defects be said to benefit from her defects? Sometimes it's not those who suffer who are said to benefit but rather those who observe and respond to the suffering. Perhaps they grow in compassion, benevolence, sympathy, wisdom, or kindness as a result of experiencing the suffering of others. Nontheists may well ask whether God would be either compassionate or just to impose suffering on some or permit some to suffer in order to benefit others. My knowledge of a child who dies of malnutrition may expand my sympathies and benefit me, but the child doesn't benefit because he dies. Should God permit this child to suffer and die from malnutrition in order to benefit me, even if it makes me a better person?

Evil and Human Freedom

Many theists have claimed that God must permit or tolerate even unnecessary evil in order to protect and respect human freedom. Much of the pain and suffering we see are caused by human action. Rape, murder, genocide, and some illnesses are the direct result of human decisions. The same is true of many instances of mental anguish. Theists who dispute the argument from Evil claim that God could prevent much of the evil in the world only by riding roughshod over human freedom, preventing murderers from murdering and rapists from raping. Human freedom is very valuable, so it's better for God to tolerate pain and suffering and preserve human freedom than to interfere with human freedom, they say.

Two varieties of evil are traditionally distinguished: natural and human. Natural evils are events or states of affairs such as earthquakes, droughts, tornadoes, some birth defects, and the painfulness of certain diseases. Human evils are exemplified by war, murder, torture, and assault. The free-will defense, if successful, can be successful only with human evil. Earthquakes and droughts are not caused by human choices, so human freedom is irrelevant here. Nontheists can point out that a god could have created Earth without the potential for, say, earthquakes, droughts, tornadoes, and volcanoes without at all interfering with human freedom. Similarly, God could have created human beings less susceptible to intense pain and physical injury and illness. Nontheists could ask how human freedom would be compromised or interfered with if we lived in a world that never had earthquakes, droughts, and other natural disasters, a world in which human beings and other animals were subject only to mild discomfort rather than intense pain.

Then, too, nontheists might argue that with minimal interference, God could prevent some of the more horrible effects of the misuse of human freedom. Everyone dies. What if God had caused Hitler to die of a heart attack or stroke in 1935, thus preventing World War II and all of the horrors of the Nazi Holocaust? Would that have been an interference with human freedom? If it had interfered somehow with human freedom, wouldn't the prevention of World War II and the Holocaust have been worth it? God is by definition all-knowing and so knew at the beginning of time that Hitler would cause the deaths of tens of millions of innocent people if not stopped. Even if causing Hitler to have a fatal stroke or heart attack in 1935 would have interfered with his freedom, was preserving his freedom really more important and valuable than preventing the deaths of tens of millions of innocent people?

Nontheists think that an appeal to human freedom can't show that all the suffering in the world is necessary, as we have seen, because they believe that freedom is irrelevant to natural evil and that God could prevent much human evil without significantly undermining human freedom. But some nontheists also dismiss the free-will defense because they doubt that human beings have free will. Some people claim that human freedom is an illusion. According to them, human beings think that their actions and behavior are free, but they're mistaken. I will not address the question of human freedom in this chapter because Chapter 5 is devoted to an analysis of that issue.

Faith

Many theists say that a person's religious beliefs are "just a matter of faith." Rarely are people argued into theism by the First Cause or Design arguments, and rarely are people argued out of theism by the argument from Evil or by coming to believe that critics are right in thinking that the First Cause and Design arguments are defective. Religious belief often seems independent of evidence or rational argument. When people say that religious beliefs are a matter of **faith,** one thing they may mean is that religious beliefs are held independent of evidence and argument.

Many people approve of faith, but some critics of faith think it's wrong to believe something without adequate evidence. Suppose I believe that it will rain on this date five years from now. I have no evidence that it will rain then and no evidence that it won't rain then. My belief is a matter of faith; I have no evidence for the belief, and I have no evidence against the belief.

W. K. Clifford (1845–1879) was a persistent critic of faith. He claims that belief "is desecrated when given to unproved and unquestioned statements, for the solace and private pleasure of the believer . . . or even to drown the common sorrows of our kind by a self-deception." He concludes, "To sum up: it is wrong always, everywhere, and for anyone, to believe anything upon insufficient evidence."[10] In Clifford's view, if there isn't sufficient evidence to prove that God exists, one should be an agnostic, suspending judgment on the question of God's existence. If the weight of evidence is against God's existence, one should be an atheist. To believe that God exists when one doesn't have adequate evidence is wrong, according to Clifford. It's as unreasonable to believe that God exists when you don't have adequate evidence for that belief as it would be to believe that it will rain five years from today.

Faith: Belief held independent of evidence and argument

The contemporary philosopher Robert M. Adams, a theist, concedes, "If belief is to be praised at all, we are accustomed to think that its praiseworthiness depends on its rationality, but the virtuousness of faith for Christians seems to be based on its correctness and independent of the strength of the evidence for it."[11] But Adams points out that the reasonability of a belief is in many contexts less important than its truth. It's often more important that one's beliefs be true than that they be reasonable. Adams thinks that applies to religious beliefs. Theists are quite confident that theism is true, so they may be less concerned that their belief in God be reasonable. Adams asks:

> What is the good of faith or trust? The answer that Christian thinkers have most often given to the question is that as it is our highest good to be related in love to God, and as we have to believe that he exists and loves us in order to be related to him in that way, we need faith in God in order to attain our highest good.[12]

---

[10]W. K. Clifford, "The Ethics of Belief," in *Philosophy of Religion: An Anthology,* ed. Louis Pojman (Belmont, CA: Wadsworth, 1987), 386–387.

[11]Robert M. Adams, "The Virtue of Faith," in *The Virtue of Faith and Other Essays in Philosophical Theology* (New York: Oxford University Press, 1987), 9.

[12]Ibid., 20.

Some people insist that standards of reasonableness are simply not applicable to religious belief. They say that questions of reasonableness and unreasonableness shouldn't be asked about religious belief, that religious belief isn't either rational or irrational but nonrational. Perhaps religious belief is and ought to be more a matter of feeling and emotion than a matter of reason and evidence.

What reason can there be for claiming that reason is irrelevant to religious belief, that standards of reasonableness don't and shouldn't apply to religious belief? One reason is that religious belief must be a matter of free decision and commitment. If religious belief were reasonable, in this view, it would in a sense be demanded by reason and hence coerced. Only if religious belief is contrary to evidence can it be wholly a free decision. The contemporary philosopher William Rowe writes:

> Indeed, it is sometimes argued that the very nature of religion requires that its beliefs rest on faith, not on reason. For, so the argument goes, religious belief requires unconditional *acceptance* on the part of the believer, an acceptance, moreover, that results from a *free decision* to become a believer. But if religious belief were based on reason, reason would either establish the belief beyond question or it would merely render the belief probable. In the first case, where reason proves the belief, the informed intellect would compel belief and leave no room for the exercise of a free decision. And in the second case, where reason merely shows the belief to be probable, if religious belief rested entirely on reason then the unconditional acceptance of religious belief would be unwarranted and absurd. Perhaps, then, religious belief does rest on faith, rather than reason.[13]

Do you agree that religious belief is "just a matter of faith," of belief independent of evidence and argument? Why or why not? Do you think that faith is a good thing or a bad thing? Why?

Experiencing God's Presence

For some people, belief in God's existence is due neither to rational argumentation, such as the First Cause argument, nor to "mere" faith. Rather, their belief is grounded in personal experience. Surely personal experience is the best evidence. But what sort of experience are we talking about? Sometimes it is experience of what one might call the "miraculous." If you know someone who escaped a horrendous accident unscathed or who, against all odds, recovered from a serious illness, you

---

[13]William L. Rowe, *Philosophy of Religion: An Introduction* (Belmont, CA: Wadsworth, 1978), 170–171.

might consider that a "miracle." What is a "miracle"? Let's define a miracle as an event that is directly caused by God's activity.

One problem, of course, is how to decide whether an event really is a miracle. An event is a miracle if and only if it has a supernatural rather than a natural cause. If I see bloody tears seeping from the eyes of a statue, am I seeing a miracle? If I see someone escape a horrible accident unscathed, have I witnessed a miracle? I may believe that I have seen a miracle, but I could be mistaken. The bloody tears of the statue may be a hoax. The person's surviving the accident could be the result of a lucky coincidence of purely natural causes.

However, there is another kind of personal experience that could be evidence for God's existence. That is what we might call the experience of "sensing" God's presence. One might "feel" God's presence at certain times—for example, during prayer or meditation. The experience of "feeling" or "sensing" God's presence is not the same as literally seeing God with one's eyes or hearing God with one's ears (sense perception). Unfortunately, it is difficult to describe the experience in any detail to one who has not had it.

If I have had a personal experience that I would call "sensing God's presence," I might believe that the best explanation of this experience is that I really was sensing God's presence. In that case, the personal experience I have had (and later the memory of that experience) would for me be very strong evidence that God exists. Just as my seeming to see an oak tree in my yard would be very good evidence for me that there is an oak tree in my yard, so, too, my seeming to sense God's presence would be very good evidence for me that God exists.

However, would my sensing God's presence be good evidence of God's existence *for you*? My experience cannot have the same authority for you as it might have for me. After all, you would be relying on my claim that I had this experience. Can you know that I am telling the truth, that I really had the experience I claim to have had? Even if I am sincere and I had an experience that I think was a sensing of God's presence, can you know that I am correct about the nature of this experience? Could it have been something else, such as a hallucination or a general feeling of contentment and tranquility? Could I be mistaken in thinking that an experience I have had was one of really sensing God's presence? Second- and third-person claims about personal experiences of God do not provide nearly as strong evidence of God's existence as one's own first-person experiences may.

◣◗ CHARLES DARWIN (1809–1882)

RELIGIOUS BELIEF

Whilst on board the *Beagle* I was quite orthodox, and I remember being heartily laughed at by several of the officers (though themselves orthodox) for quoting the Bible as an unanswerable authority on some point of morality. I suppose it was the novelty of the argument that amused them. But I had gradually come, by this time, to see that the Old Testament from its manifestly false history of the world, with the Tower of Babel, the rainbow as a sign, etc., etc., and from its attributing to God the feelings of a revengeful tyrant, was no more to be trusted than the sacred books of the Hindoos, or the beliefs of any barbarian. The question then continually rose before my mind that would not be banished,—is it credible that if God were now to make a revelation to the Hindoos, would he permit it to be connected with the belief in Vishnu, Siva, &c., as Christianity is connected with the Old Testament. This appeared to me utterly incredible.

By further reflecting that the clearest evidence would be requisite to make any sane man believe in the miracles by which Christianity is supported,—that the more we know of the fixed laws of nature the more incredible do miracles become,—that the men at that time were ignorant and credulous to a degree almost incomprehensible by us,—that the Gospels cannot be proved to have been written simultaneously with the events,—that they differ in many important details, far too important as it seemed to me to be admitted as the usual inaccuracies of eyewitnesses;—by such reflections as these, which I give not as having the least novelty or value, but as they influenced me, I gradually came to disbelieve in Christianity as a divine revelation. The fact that many false religions have spread over large portions of the earth like wild-fire had some weight with me.

Beautiful as is the morality of the New Testament, it can hardly be denied that its perfection depends in part on the interpretation which we now put on metaphors and allegories.

But I was very unwilling to give up my belief;—I feel sure of this for I can well remember often and often inventing daydreams of old letters between distinguished Romans and manuscripts being discovered at Pompeii or elsewhere which confirmed in the most striking manner all that was written in the Gospels. But I found it more and more difficult, with free scope given to my imagination, to invent evidence which would suffice to convince me. Thus disbelief crept over me at a very slow rate, but was at last complete. The rate was so slow that I felt no distress, and have never since doubted even for a single second that my conclusion was correct. I can indeed hardly see how anyone ought to wish Christianity to be true; for if so the plain language of the text seems to show that the men who do not believe, and this would include my Father, Brother and almost all my best friends, will be everlastingly punished.

And this is a damnable doctrine.

Although I did not think much about the existence of a personal God until a considerably later period of my life, I will here give the vague conclusions to which I have been driven. The old argument of design in nature, as given by Paley, which formerly seemed to me so conclusive, fails, now that the law of natural selection has been discovered. We can no longer argue that, for instance, the beautiful hinge of a bivalve shell must have been made by an intelligent being, like the hinge of a door by man. There seems to be no more design in the variability of organic beings and in the action of natural selection, than in the

---

course which the wind blows. Everything in nature is the result of fixed laws. But I have discussed this subject at the end of my book on the *Variation of Domestic Animals and Plants,* and the argument there given has never, as far as I can see, been answered.

But passing over the endless beautiful adaptations which we everywhere meet with, it may be asked how can the generally beneficent arrangement of the world be accounted for? Some writers indeed are so much impressed with the amount of suffering in the world, that they doubt if we look to all sentient beings, whether there is more of misery or of happiness;—whether the world as a whole is a good or a bad one. According to my judgment happiness decidedly prevails, though this would be very difficult to prove. If the truth of this conclusion be granted, it harmonises well with the effects which we might expect from natural selection. If all the individuals of any species were habitually to suffer to an extreme degree they would neglect to propagate their kind; but we have no reason to believe that this has ever or at least often occurred. Some other considerations, moreover, lead to the belief that all sentient beings have been formed so as to enjoy, as a general rule, happiness.

Every one who believes, as I do, that all the corporeal and mental organs (excepting those which are neither advantageous or disadvantageous to the possessor) of all beings have been developed through natural selection, or the survival of the fittest, together with use or habit, will admit that these organs have been formed so that their possessors may compete successfully with other beings, and thus increase in number. . . .

That there is much suffering in the world no one disputes. Some have attempted to explain this in reference to man by imagining that it serves for his moral improvement. But the number of men in the world is as nothing compared with that of all other sentient beings, and these often suffer greatly without any moral improvement. A being so powerful and so full of knowledge as a God who could create the universe, is to our finite minds omnipotent and omniscient, and it revolts our understanding to suppose that his benevo-

lence is not unbounded, for what advantage can there be in the sufferings of millions of the lower animals throughout almost endless time? This very old argument from the existence of suffering against the existence of an intelligent first cause seems to me a strong one. . . .

At the present day the most usual argument for the existence of an intelligent God is drawn from the deep inward conviction and feelings which are experienced by most persons. But it cannot be doubted that Hindoos, Mahomadans and others might argue in the same manner and with equal force in favour of the existence of one God, or of many Gods, or as with the Buddists of no God. There are also many barbarian tribes who cannot be said with any truth to believe in what we call God: they believe indeed in spirits or ghosts. . . .

Formerly I was led by feelings such as those just referred to, (although I do not think that the religious sentiment was ever strongly developed in me), to the firm conviction of the existence of God, and of the immortality of the soul. In my Journal I wrote that whilst standing in the midst of the grandeur of a Brazilian forest, "it is not possible to give an adequate idea of the higher feelings of wonder, admiration, and devotion which fill and elevate the mind." I well remember my conviction that there is more in man than the mere breath of his body. But now the grandest scenes would not cause any such convictions and feelings to rise in my mind. It may be truly said that I am like a man who has become colour-blind, and the universal belief by men of the existence of redness makes my present loss of perception of not the least value as evidence. This argument would be a valid one if all men of all races had the same inward conviction of the existence of one God; but we know that this is very far from being the case. Therefore I cannot see that such inward convictions and feelings are of any weight as evidence of what really exists. The state of mind which grand scenes formerly excited in me, and which was intimately connected with a belief in God, did not essentially differ from that which is often called the sense of sublimity; and however difficult it may be to explain the genesis of this sense, it can hardly be advanced as an argument for the existence of God, any more than the powerful though vague and similar feelings excited by music.

With respect to immortality, nothing shows me how strong and almost instinctive a belief it is, as the consideration of the view now held by most physicists, namely that the sun with all the planets will in time grow too cold for life, unless indeed some great body dashes into the sun and thus gives it fresh life.— Believing as I do that man in the distant future will be a far more perfect creature than he now is, it is an intolerable thought that he and all other sentient beings are doomed to complete annihilation after such long-continued slow progress. To those who fully admit the immortality of the human soul, the destruction of our world will not appear so dreadful.

Another source of conviction in the existence of God, connected with the reason and not with the feelings, impresses me as having much more weight. This follows from the extreme difficulty or rather impossibility of conceiving this immense and wonderful universe, including man with his capacity of looking far backwards and far into futurity, as the result of blind chance or necessity. When thus reflecting I feel compelled to look to a First Cause having an intelligent mind in some degree analogous to that of man; and I deserve to be called a Theist.

This conclusion was strong in my mind about the time, as far as I can remember, when I wrote the *Origin of Species;* and it is since that time that it has very gradually with many fluctuations become weaker. But then arises the doubt—can the mind of man, which has, as I fully believe, been developed from a mind as low as that possessed by the lowest animal, be trusted when it draws such grand conclusions? May not these be the result of the connection between cause and effect which strikes us as a necessary one, but probably depends merely on inherited experience? Nor must we overlook the probability of the constant inculcation in a belief in God on the minds of children producing so strong and perhaps an inherited effect on their brains not yet fully developed, that it would be as difficult for them to throw off their belief in God, as for a monkey to throw off its instinctive fear and hatred of a snake.

I cannot pretend to throw the least light on such abstruse problems. The mystery of the beginning of all things is insoluble by us; and I for one must be content to remain an Agnostic.

 BENJAMIN FRANKLIN (1706–1790)

FRANKLIN'S RELIGIOUS PRINCIPLES FROM HIS AUTOBIOGRAPHY

I had been religiously educated as a Presbyterian; and tho' some of the Dogmas of that Persuasion . . . appear'd to me unintelligible, others doubtful . . . , I never was without some religious Principles; I never doubted, for instance, the Existence of the Deity, that he made the World, & governed it by his Providence; that the most acceptable Service of God was doing Good to Man; that our Souls are Immortal; and that all Crime will be punished and Virtue rewarded either here or hereafter; these I esteemed the Essentials of every Religion, and being to be found in all the Religions we had in our Country I respected them all, tho' with different degrees of Respect as I found them more or less mix'd with other Articles which without any Tendency to inspire, promote or confirm Morality, serv'd principally to divide us & make us unfriendly to one another.

From *The Autobiography*, in *Writings*, ed. J. A. Leo Lemay (New York: The Library of America, 1987).

◢ MOHANDAS K. GANDHI (1869–1948)

GANDHI'S POLITICAL PRINCIPLES

I came to the conclusion long ago, after prayerful search and study and discussion with as many people as I could meet, that all religions were true, and also that all had some error in them, and whilst I hold my own, I should hold others as dear as Hinduism. . . . So we can only pray if we are Hindus, not that a Christian should become a Hindu, or if we are Moslems not that a Hindu or a Christian should become a Moslem, nor should we even secretly pray that anyone should be converted, but our inmost prayer should be that a Hindu should be a better Hindu, a Moslem a better Moslem and a Christian a better Christian. . . . I broaden my Hinduism by loving other religions as my own. . . .

I disbelieve in the conversion of one person by another. My effort should never be to undermine another's faith but to make him a better follower of his own faith. This implies the belief in the truth of all religions and respect for them. . . .

Let no one even for a moment entertain the fear that a reverent study of other religions is likely to weaken or shake one's faith in one's own. The Hindu system of philosophy regards all religions as containing the elements of truth in them and enjoins an attitude of respect and reverence towards them all. . . . Study and appreciation of other religions need not cause a weakening of [regard for one's own religion], it should mean extension of that regard to other religions.

. . . Hinduism leaves the individual absolutely free to do what he or she likes for the sake of self-realization for which and which alone he or she is born.

. . . I do not believe in the exclusive divinity of the Vedas [Hindu scriptures]. I believe the Bible [and the] Koran to be as much divinely inspired as the Vedas. . . .

Religions are different roads converging to the same point. What does it matter that we take different roads so long as we reach the same goal? In reality there are as many religions as there are individuals.

From *The Essential Gandhi*, ed. Louis Fischer (New York: Vintage, 1962).

Questions for Discussion and Review

1. Construct an argument to try to persuade an atheist or agnostic that God exists.

2. Construct an argument to try to show a theist that God doesn't exist.

3. Do you think most people would believe that God exists if they had not been taught at an early age that God exists? Why or why not? If belief in God is learned, what, if anything, does that tell us about belief in God?

4. If you believe in God, explain why in your own words. If you don't believe in God, explain why. What, if anything, would make you change your beliefs about God's existence or nonexistence?

5. Jews believe that the Old Testament portion of the Bible is the word of God; Christians believe that both the Old and New Testaments are the word of God;

Muslims believe that the Koran is the word of God dictated to the prophet Muhammad; Mormons believe that the Book of Mormon was dictated by God to the prophet Joseph Smith. How would you defend a claim that a certain book was the word of God? How might a believer convince or persuade a nonbeliever that such a book was the word of God? What if each believer maintains that his or her belief is a matter of faith?

6. Tom says he knows that God exists because he miraculously escaped serious injury in a horrible automobile accident. Does his experience prove that God exists? Why or why not?

7. Sara says she knows that God exists because she has experienced, or "seen," God; she has felt God's presence. Does her experience prove that God exists? Why or why not?

8. God supposedly cares about and loves human beings. Does God also care about and love other living creatures? Defend your answer.

9. What reason is there for thinking that there is only one God?

10. Does it matter whether we can prove or disprove God's existence? Why or why not?

11. Some people claim that the universe looks as if it was designed by a good and benevolent designer only if one ignores much of reality. For example, consider this description of a horrific event from Elspeth Huxley's autobiographical account of growing up in Africa early in the twentieth century:

> [Baby chicks] had hatched the day before; in the night a column of *siafu*, those black, purposeful, implacable, and horribly sinister warrior ants, had marched through the nest. In the morning the yellow chicks were limp, bedraggled, soiled little corpses with their insides eaten out, lying in the nest. The hen was alive, and that was the worst part of it, for the ants had swarmed over her and eaten half her flesh away and her eyes, and she lay there twitching now and then, as if to demonstrate that unreasoning persistence of life that is the very core of cruelty.[14]

Such events are commonplace in nature. How would you reconcile such events with the view that the universe was created by a wise, good, and benevolent creator?

Suggestions for Further Reading

Robert M. Adams. *The Virtue of Faith and Other Essays in Philosophical Theology*. New York: Oxford University Press, 1987. A collection of

---

[14]Elspeth Huxley, *The Flame Trees of Thika* (New York: Penguin Books, 1959), 40.

essays on many of the topics of this chapter by one of the most eminent philosophers of religion, writing from a theistic perspective.

Peter Angeles, ed. *Critiques of God*. Buffalo: Prometheus Books, 1976. A collection of essays devoted to the case against belief in God.

Paul Davies. *God and the New Physics*. New York: Simon & Schuster, 1983. A contemporary physicist's skeptical analysis of religious belief in view of the findings of modern science.

John H. Hick. *Philosophy of Religion,* 3d ed. Englewood Cliffs, NJ: Prentice-Hall, 1983. A classic, highly readable textbook that examines a host of philosophical issues raised by theism and religious belief, written from a theistic perspective.

Louis Pojman, ed. *Philosophy of Religion: An Anthology*. Belmont, CA: Wadsworth, 1987. A good anthology of primary sources, historical and modern, on many aspects of theism and religious belief representing a variety of perspectives.

William L. Rowe. *Philosophy of Religion: An Introduction*. Belmont, CA: Wadsworth, 1978. A rigorous treatment of many of the issues in this chapter.

William L. Rowe and William J. Wainwright, eds. *Philosophy of Religion: Selected Readings*. New York: Harcourt Brace Jovanovich, 1989. A good anthology of primary sources, historical and modern, on many aspects of theism and religious belief from a variety of perspectives.

William J. Wainwright. *Philosophy of Religion*. Belmont, CA: Wadsworth, 1988. A rigorous treatment of many of the issues in this chapter suitable mainly for advanced students.

3 BODY AND MIND

Objectives

Students are expected to:

- understand the differences between living and non-living things.
- understand theories that explain life by appeal to non-physical souls.
- understand Aristotle's three grades of soul: nutritive, sensitive, and rational.
- understand natural or scientific explanations of life processes.
- understand consciousness as the capability for having a variety of mental states.
- understand Cartesian Dualism as an explanation of consciousness.
- understand the main objections to Cartesian Dualism.
- understand varieties of Robust Physicalism: Philosophical Behaviorism, Functionalism, and Type and Token Identity theories.
- understand Minimal Physicalism (or supervenience).
- understand some of the scientific research that leads some people to accept Physicalism.
- understand the concept of self-knowledge and its problems.

Life

You're a human being and you're alive. Some people consider those two facts to be rather mysterious. After all, as a human being, you're a physical object. Rocks, clocks, cars, cameras, and computers are physical objects, too, but they're not alive. Of course, you're not the only physical object that's alive, nor are human beings the only living organisms. Moss, mice, and moose; ticks, tarantulas, and tigers; frogs, fish, and ferrets are also alive. A fundamental way of cutting up reality is to divide things into those that can be alive and those that cannot be alive. But how can we explain why some physical objects are alive while others aren't?

Living things die. Some people consider that fact rather mysterious, too. For example, consider a familiar sight on our highways. A squirrel, hit by a car, lies dead in the road. How can something that once was alive cease to be alive? Perhaps living things have something in their bodies that makes them alive and that, when it leaves their bodies, causes them to die. Some people once thought that there is a special vital fluid or vital energy that when present causes life and when absent causes death. However, although scientists searched for it, they couldn't find it. But if it was a special physical stuff and it existed, they certainly should have been able to find it. That they looked for it but couldn't find it led them to conclude that it doesn't exist. That certainly would explain why they couldn't find it.

But if there is no special physical vital fluid or energy that is responsible for life, perhaps it is something nonphysical. Nonphysical things can't be observed and found the way physical things can be. So perhaps that's why they couldn't find it. The nonphysical thing responsible for life was called the soul by ancient peoples.

BRAIN TEASERS

1. If purely nonphysical beings exist, such as angels and demons, are they alive?

2. If the android Data from the television series *Star Trek: The Next Generation* or the robot C3PO from the *Star Wars* movies really existed, would they be alive?

3. If we say that a computer or a battery is dead, do we mean that it is literally dead, in the same way that a dead cat is dead?

Soul as the Explanation of Life

In ancient times, people believed that something special had to be added to a purely physical object in order to make it come alive. This same thing, when it departed from the living body, made it dead. They believed that a purely physical object is inherently lifeless as a stone. They called that something special a soul. Thus, to return to the poor squirrel lying in the road, when it was alive and climbing trees, eating nuts, and running into the road, it was alive; it was alive because it had a soul that made it alive. When the car hit it, its soul departed from its body and thereupon it died.

It's natural to ask, What is a soul? Let's step back for a moment and look at how we might define other sorts of things. What is a clock? It's something that tells the time of day. It can be round or square, big or little, with or without hands. What is a cup? It's an object capable of holding liquids for drinking. It can be made of china, glass, plastic, or paper. It can be round, square, or any shape in between. It can be big or little, tall or short, wide or narrow, with or without a handle. We have given functional definitions of clocks and cups, defining them in terms of what they can do or what can be done with them, not in terms of what they look like or what they're made of.

BRAIN TEASERS

1. Define the following things: a reading lamp, a flashlight, an engine, a chair, a bed, a saw.

2. Define the following: a steak knife, a butter knife, a hunting knife, a bread knife.

Probably it is best to define souls functionally, too, in terms of what they do. If we think of souls as necessary for life, we can define them as things that enable physical objects to be alive. We may not know much else about souls, but as long as we know what they do, we have a grasp of what they are. But maybe we do know something else about souls. One of the greatest and most influential philosophers of the ancient world, Plato (427–347 B.C.E.), insisted that souls are immaterial or nonphysical. On reflection it seems plausible. If something needs to be added to a physical object to make it alive, how could that something be just another physical object? But what makes something nonphysical rather than physical?

Physical objects such as a bullet shot from a gun have a variety of physical properties: it's composed of molecules which in turn are composed of atoms; it has mass, weight, shape, color, temperature, location in space-time, and velocity. If something is nonphysical, then it has none of these physical properties. It isn't composed of atoms and molecules. It has no mass, weight, shape, color, temperature, or location in space-time.

Contemporary science teaches us that there are a variety of odd things in the universe that aren't quite like bullets and other ordinary physical objects, for example, energy and electro-magnetic fields. But there are overlaps in the properties they have. A bit of energy doesn't have a color, shape, or temperature. But Einstein taught us that matter and energy are interchangeable, in some way different manifestations of the same underlying reality. That's why $E = MC^2$ and why nuclear bombs are so powerful. They transform a little bit of matter (or mass) into a whole lot of energy. The amount of energy in a unit of mass is equal to that unit of mass multiplied by the speed of light (C) squared, which is an awfully big number. Therefore, energy has a location in space-time. So do electromagnetic fields.

It's not easy to define what makes something physical rather than nonphysical because the things that science counts as physical differ so dramatically. Therefore, it is probably best to define the physical as whatever is referred to by the terms or concepts of the natural sciences (physics, chemistry, biology, astronomy, geology, and all their subfields). This is important for two reasons. First, the existence of an object referred to by the terms of a scientific theory is entailed by the truth of that theory. (If a theory that employs the concept of an electron is true, then electrons exist.) Second, if a term occurs in a scientific theory, then at least in principle it is possible to use perception and observation (directly or indirectly) to detect the existence or presence of things referred to by those terms. (If the terms "electron" and "bacterium" occur in scientific theories, then in principle it is possible to employ perception [directly or indirectly] to detect their existence or presence; for example, a cloud chamber for detecting electrons and a microscope for detecting a bacterium.)

Something is nonphysical, then, if it is not referred to by any terms or concepts employed in the theories of the natural sciences. The term "soul" is not used in any scientific theories. Nor are souls detectable by perception and observation, whether directly or indirectly. Thus, souls are nonphysical and have none of the properties we attribute to things that are physical.

Kinds of Soul: Aristotle's Theory

There are profound differences as well as similarities among living things. For example, dogs don't behave the way trees do. Unlike trees, dogs move around in their environment, sniffing, eating, barking, licking people's faces, chasing cats, jumping up and down, and digging holes. It's pretty clear from their behavior that dogs can see, hear, smell, taste, and feel. There's no reason to believe that trees can. Most people also think that dogs can feel such sensations as pains and itches. The best explanation of why a dog scratches itself is that it has an itchy sensation. The best explanation of why a dog yelps or howls when kicked hard is that it feels a painful sensation. Some people even think from observing their behavior that dogs can have feelings, such as fear, and emotions, such as love. There are no reasons to believe that trees can have feelings or emotions.

BRAIN TEASERS

1. Can dogs love their owners? What reasons are there for thinking that they can? What reasons are there for thinking that they can't?

2. What do we mean when we say that one person loves another? Do we mean the same thing if we say that a dog loves its owner? What about if we say that an owner loves her dog?

There are differences between trees and dogs, but also differences between dogs and human beings. Dogs can't read a philosophy book, understand calculus, play chess, write a poem, tell or appreciate a joke, design and build a house, or understand how a radio works. Human beings can do all of those things. How are we to explain these evident differences, as well as similarities, among living things?

Plato's pupil Aristotle (384–322 B.C.E.) had a theory. Like Plato, Aristotle thought that soul is required to explain life, but he does not see all souls as alike. He postulates three kinds of soul, which he characterized in terms of their different capabilities, or functions. The most primitive kind of soul is the *nutritive soul,* which is responsible for the basic life processes of growth, nutrition, and reproduction. The sensitive soul is a more sophisticated form of soul that provides the capacity for undergoing the basic life processes that the nutritive soul does, but adds to that the capacity to perceive, move around, and have sensations and emotions. Finally, the *rational soul* provides all the capacities provided by the nutritive and sensitive souls plus the capacity to reason. Thus, trees have only a nutritive soul, and it is because they have a nutritive soul that they are alive and behave as living things do. It is because trombones don't have any soul that they are not alive. Dogs have a sensitive soul, which allows them to do more than trees can do, such as perceive and feel. Finally, human beings have a rational soul, which allows them to reason. The rational soul enables humans to write and read books, do mathematics, understand scientific theories, participate in religious belief and practice, and compose music. Because they don't have rational souls but only sensitive souls, dogs can't do any of these things.

NUTRITIVE SOUL	SENSITIVE SOUL	RATIONAL SOUL
growth	growth	growth
nutrition	nutrition	nutrition
reproduction	reproduction	reproduction
	perception/sensation	perception/sensation
	movement	movement
		reasoning

Souls also can explain death. An organism dies when (and because) its soul departs from its body. It's a little like when your car runs out of gasoline. When all the gasoline has been used up, your car's engine won't work any more. Similarly, when a cat's soul departs from its body, its body won't work any more. Of course, the difference is that gasoline is a physical substance while the cat's soul isn't.

If, as ancient peoples thought, something can be alive only if it has a soul, then there is evidence of the existence of souls, namely, living things. We could construct an argument for the existence of souls as follows.

Something is alive only if it has a soul.
Living things exist.

Therefore, souls exist.

But are we justified in believing that something is alive only if it has a soul?

Problems for Souls

Few people in Western culture today believe that all living things have souls and that the existence of soul best explains life. Most scientists explain life and the complex behavior of living things without introducing the idea of soul. To be alive, for them, is not to be animated by a soul but to behave and function in certain ways: to grow, to utilize energy for nutrition, to reproduce. It would probably strike most people as ridiculous to talk about the soul of a gnat, a tree, a rosebush, or a mosquito. Almost all of us are certain that such things are purely physical objects.

Even more puzzling, microscopic organisms called cells are alive (as we'll see below). And every living thing is composed of millions and millions of cells. For example, every one of a cat's organs (as well as your organs), such as its (and your) heart, blood, lungs, liver, muscles, and brain, is composed of cells organized into tissues and sheets of tissues. Therefore, if a soul is necessary for life, then each cell in the body of a living organism has its own soul. In that case, wouldn't it be difficult to speak of the soul of a cat or human being, since each has millions and millions of souls, one for each of its cells? If we still want to say that a carrot, cat, or human being has one soul, we would have to explain how millions of individual cell-souls combine to form one carrot, cat, or human soul.

But things are even worse than that for souls as an explanation of life. There's an embarrassing question that it's difficult not to ask. How exactly do souls explain life? For example, how do they enable living things to do what only living things can do? For example, how does a soul give a cell the ability to reproduce itself, to convert food into energy, to grow? Just saying that a soul does it without explaining how it does it seems fishy. It's even more mysterious when we consider that if souls explain life, then something nonphysical is supposed to cause physical things to happen in a physical organism. But how could nonphysical things cause physical things to happen? Does appeal to a nonphysical soul really contribute anything to our understanding of life?

But good scientific and philosophical practice recommends that we don't abandon a theory, even if it's inadequate, unless we have a better theory with which to replace it. The appeal to nonphysical souls to explain life is a theory. An important question, then, is whether we have a purely physical theory that can do a better job of explaining life than the theory of souls can. People who are naturalistically inclined claim that we can explain scientifically how and why an organism, such as a cell, behaves in ways definitive of living things. They claim that there is no need to bring in nonphysical souls to explain life. And if we can provide satisfactory explanations for the behavior of cells and other living things without bringing in nonphysical souls, then Occam's Razor applies. We shouldn't postulate the existence of more things than are necessary to adequately explain the phenomena we observe. So we shouldn't postulate the existence of souls to explain life.

BRAIN TEASERS

If all living things have souls, then every cell in your body has its own soul. In that case, do you have one soul or millions of souls? If somehow we can truly say that you have one soul, what is the relation between your soul and the millions of souls of your cells?

Physical Explanations of Life

People who tend toward naturalism try to give purely physical or scientific explanations of life. A good place to start is with the structure of physical things, for example, you. You have parts, such as skin, hair, bones, muscles, blood, heart, lungs, liver, kidneys, and brain. These parts (organs) in turn are composed of sheets of tissues. Sheets of tissues are composed of tissues. Tissues are composed of cells. Cells have parts that are composed of molecules. Molecules are composed of atoms. Atoms are composed of subatomic particles, such as electrons, protons, and neutrons. So far, so good. But atoms and molecules are not alive. You are. How can something that's alive be built from components that are not alive? And where in this organizational structure does life emerge?

According to scientists, the transition occurs at the level of the cell, which is the basic building block of all life on Earth. Subatomic particles, atoms, and molecules are not alive. Cells are alive, as are the organisms composed of cells. Somehow, joining together the right number of the right nonliving molecules under the right conditions creates a living cell. How can that be?

First, though, why do we say that a cell, a microscopic organism that cannot even be seen with the naked eye, is alive? There's no doubt that you're alive, but are your cells really alive? Let's first remind ourselves of what distinguishes the living from the nonliving. It's a matter of what living things can do that nonliving things can't do. Why do we consider an oak tree to be alive but not a stone? Unlike a stone, an oak tree can grow and reproduce. It takes in nourishment from the environment (light from the sun, carbon dioxide from the air, and water and nutrients from the soil) and transforms them into physical energy to perform work. It excretes waste (oxygen). An individual cell, unlike the molecules of which it is composed, engages in exactly the same basic life processes. A cell reproduces, grows, and transforms what it takes in (food) into energy for work and waste to be excreted. That is the criterion distinguishing the living from the nonliving. Then how can we explain the fact that a cell is alive but is composed of nonliving parts? That's the point where the mystery of life really begins.

Cells are composed of molecules that are composed of atoms that are composed of subatomic particles. There are at least ninety-two different kinds of naturally occurring atoms in the universe called elements. Of all the elements, carbon is the key to life on Earth. All the billions of forms of Earthly life are based on carbon.

> The source of the vast molecular diversity in living things is the bonding capacity of . . . carbon. Carbon's power lies in its versatile structure: four unpaired electrons in its outer [electron] shell, which allow it to form covalent bonds with up to four other atoms, make possible enough different molecular connections to generate an almost endless variety of carbon-based . . . molecules.[1]

There are four major types of complex organic compounds: carbohydrates (composed of atoms of carbon, hydrogen, and oxygen, such as $C_6H_{12}O_6$ [the molecular formula for sugars], lipids (also composed of carbon, hydrogen, and oxygen, but with a much smaller proportion of oxygen and frequently the addition of other elements), proteins (composed of carbon, hydrogen, oxygen, and nitrogen, and usually sulfur, binding together to form very complex molecules called amino acids, which in turn combine to form proteins), and nucleic acids (composed of nucleotides that are composed of "a five-carbon sugar, a phosphate group, and an organic nitrogen-containing base).[2] These large, complex carbon-based molecules are the building blocks of cells and their parts.

These carbon-based molecules, created by natural processes under the right conditions, built up more and more complex levels of organization as a result of random collidings and chemical interactions. Eventually, the components of cells were created, leading to the existence of cells.

But how do cells work? That is, how does science explain how cells do the things that are definitive of life? The boundary of the cell is its cell membrane. The membrane of a particular kind of cell permits some molecules to enter the interior of the cell and some to exit from it. It is selective about this, because it serves as a barrier to either entry or exit for

---

[1]William T. Keeton and James L. Gould, *Biological Science*, 4th ed. (New York: W. W. Norton, 1986), 47. (All information about life in this section comes from this text.)
[2]Ibid., 68–69.

most molecules. The selective permeability permitting ingress to some molecules and exit for others is explained in terms of complex chemical reactions at the membrane. Inside a cell are other structures called organelles that are encompassed by their own membranes that selectively permit entry or exit to some molecules. The work of the membrane requires physical energy. The energy stored in the covalent bonds of glucose, one of the sugars, "is usually, directly or indirectly, the source of the energy that powers cells."[3] Nothing nonphysical is needed to explain the functioning of the cell membrane. In fact, appeal to anything nonphysical would retard rather than enhance understanding.

The most important of the organelles of a cell is the nucleus (only bacteria lack a nucleus). According to Keeton and Gould,

> The nucleus plays the central role in cellular reproduction, the process by which a single cell divides and forms two new cells. It also plays a crucial part, in conjunction with the environment, in determining what sort of differentiation a cell will undergo and what form it will exhibit at maturity. And the nucleus directs the metabolic activities of the living cell. In short, it is from the nucleus that the "instructions" emanate that guide the life processes of the cell as long as it lives.[4]

The nucleus in turn has two major structures within it: the chromosomes and the nucleoli. Chromosomes are composed of DNA, which forms the genes, and protein. The genes "are the very hub of life; they encode all the information necessary for the synthesis of the enzymes regulating the myriad independent chemical reactions that determine the characteristics of cells and organisms."[5]

The capacity to reproduce is one of the most fundamental life processes. How does a cell reproduce? Does a nonphysical soul enable it to reproduce? No. By a process called mitosis, a nucleus divides to form two identical copies of itself. It does this by first separating the chromosomes into two complete sets which move to opposite ends of the nucleus, after which a new cell wall or membrane emerges to separate the two halves of the nucleus, after which they divide, creating two nuclei where before there was one. The two nuclei move to opposite ends of the cell and the same process of division occurs, so there are two identical copies of the same cell. All of these processes occur as the result of complex chemical reactions that require physical energy.

Living cells are composed of nonliving molecules. Are cells still being created out of molecules? Could we play Doctor Frankenstein on the cellular level and create new forms of living cells from nonliving molecules? In 1858 a German physician, Rudolf Virchnow, theorized that "all living

---

[3]Ibid., 52.
[4]Ibid.,111–112.
[5]Ibid., 113.

cells arise from previously existing cells . . ., and that there is therefore no spontaneous creation of cells from nonliving matter."[6]

In 1862, Louis Pasteur confirmed this hypothesis in a series of experiments; scientists today accept the theory as at least beyond reasonable doubt. It means that the transition from large, complex nonliving carbon-based molecules to living cells is not a process that continues in the present. New living cells are not continually created from nonliving molecules. Instead, the transition from the nonliving to the living occurred long ago in the past. In fact, scientists have found evidence that living cells first came into existence on Earth billions of years ago, a few hundred million years after Earth was formed.

At least three explanations of the emergence of life on Earth have been proposed: (1) The right atoms met and joined together to make the right molecules that in turn met and joined together to make cells as a result of divine activity and intervention. (2) This process was the result of chance. Given that there were probably hundreds of billions of interactions among atoms, by chance the right combinations would occur under the right conditions, such as two atoms of hydrogen meeting an atom of oxygen and binding to create a molecule of water (H_2O). In turn, these molecules would bump into and bind with other molecules to create more complex levels of organization until the threshold was passed and the cell was formed. (3) Cellular life emerged elsewhere in the universe and came to Earth in some unknown way, such as on a comet or asteroid that collided with Earth. Of course, this explanation still relies on either (2) or (3) to explain how life emerged somewhere else in the galaxy or universe.

Scientists today say that the conditions that were conducive to the formation of living cells from nonliving molecules no longer exist. They occurred only in the first several hundred million years of Earth's existence. But if scientists can discover what those conditions were like and can duplicate them, then perhaps they could create new forms of cellular life from the right combinations of nonliving molecules. Perhaps Doctor Frankenstein's dream is not impossible.

According to people who tend toward naturalism, all the life processes of cells and all the life processes of higher level structures composed of cells, including organs (liver, heart, lungs, blood, brains) and organisms (hay, heather, haddock, hamsters, and humans), can be explained scientifically. Appeal to nonphysical souls to explain life processes explains nothing. Therefore, naturalists reject the argument:

1. Living organisms exist.
2. Something is alive only if it has a nonphysical soul.

---

3. Therefore, nonphysical souls exist.

---

[6]Ibid., 84.

The defect in the argument is with the second premise. It is unreasonable to accept it because there is no evidence at all for it.

Mind as the Explanation of Consciousness

Today, few people try to explain life by appeal to something nonphysical. Most people probably accept the view that life can be explained purely physically or scientifically, even if the details about how living cells first formed are currently unknown. However, many people try to explain another feature of the universe—consciousness—by appeal to something nonphysical.

What we might call common sense says that stones are neither alive nor conscious, that trees are alive but not conscious, but that dogs (and humans) are both alive and conscious. Common sense is less certain about other forms of life, such as insects.

BRAIN TEASERS

Which of the following do you think are conscious?

Computers, individual living cells, mosquitoes, bees, spiders, cobras, crocodiles, lobsters, swordfish, sparrows, mice, cats, elephants, whales, monkeys, gorillas.

But what is consciousness? One of the most basic aspects or components of consciousness seems to be the capacity to perceive the world. If we believe that trees cannot perceive, that counts against considering them conscious; if we believe that dogs can perceive, that counts in favor of considering them conscious. Beings on Earth that can perceive do so with one or more of the familiar five senses: sight, hearing, smell, taste, and touch. Mammals such as dogs and humans see with their eyes, hear with their ears, taste with their tongues, smell with their noses, and feel/touch with their skin, or rather, with the sensory nerves in their skin. A traditional way of speaking about human perception is to claim that our senses give us perceptual sensations. Our eyes give us visual sensations; our ears give us auditory sensations; and so on. Thus, I see a red car only if I have a visual sensation of a red car. I hear a police siren only if I have an auditory sensation of a police siren.

How are we to understand what perception is? For example, can a being perceive only if it has one or more of the five senses that we have? Can there be other senses or other sensory organs?

BRAIN TEASERS

> If purely spiritual beings, such as angels or ghosts exist, and if they can perceive the world, do they perceive by means of sensory organs, such as eyes and ears?

Perhaps we should ask exactly what our senses do. One way of looking at it is to view perception as a means of acquiring information about the world. Our sensory organs, then, are receptors sensitive to certain kinds of stimuli from the world, stimuli that carry information about the world. Our receptors receive and in a sense decode the information. Thus, light carries information that our eyes can receive and decode; sound carries information that our ears can receive and decode.

BRAIN TEASERS

> Humans are sensitive to light and sound waves in a fairly narrow band of the spectrum of such waves. Our noses and tongues are sensitive to only some molecules. Our skin receptors are sensitive to only certain stimuli (textures, temperature, pressure). Are we sensitive to all of the possible sources of information about the universe? Might other forms of life have ways of acquiring information about the world that differ radically from the ways that we acquire information about the world?

Perceptual sensations are a kind of mental state. Thus, to see something is to be in a certain kind of mental state. This suggests that consciousness is tied to the capacity to have mental states.

Some sensations, especially those associated with the sense of touch, have certain important properties of their own. If you feel pain from a cut, we could say that you are having a painful sensation. If you feel itchy from a mosquito bite, you are having an itchy sensation. If you feel a chill and shiver or feel dizzy and fall, you are having a sensation of chilliness and a sensation of dizziness. These sensations are also said to be mental states.

There is a great variety of mental states. There are *beliefs*. You may believe that the square root of 25 is 5, that George Washington was the first president, and that God exists. There are *desires*. You may desire to get an A in your philosophy course or desire to have pizza for lunch. There are *feelings* and *emotions*. You may be depressed or bored, love your parents, fear bees, or feel hopeful. Mental states abound. You may *understand* the theory of evolution, *imagine* that people are out to get you, *wish* that you will get a good job, etc.

There is another rather complex and special kind of mental state that we could call self-consciousness or self-awareness. As the name suggests, it is a consciousness or awareness of oneself as a separate being. You're aware of yourself as a separate being: you're aware of not merely being part of an undifferentiated whole. You're different from the ground you stand on, the chair you sit in, the book you read, the teacher you listen to. You also know what you are. You have a rich set of concepts that you apply to yourself and the world. Perhaps you know you're Jaimie Rodriguez rather than Ben Teller. You undoubtedly know that you're a human being, not a cat, dog, or horse. Perhaps you know also that you're someone's child and someone else's grandchild, that you're a student with a certain major, perhaps a parent, a member of a certain religion, a worker. You know a lot about yourself. You know what your desires, feelings, emotions, plans, and preferences are. Self-consciousness or awareness, at least human self-consciousness or awareness, presupposes possession of a very rich set of concepts that one can apply to oneself and to the rest of the world to identify who or what one is and who or what one is not.

Self-consciousness or consciousness of oneself, again at least at the human level, presuppose both a concept of time (past, present, and future) and of oneself as a being having an existence spread through time. You're aware of yourself as existing now, but you also know that you existed in the past and you may remember many of your own past experiences. You're also almost certainly imagining that you'll continue to exist in the future. You may feel absolutely certain that you'll still exist tomorrow. You may be fairly certain that you'll still exist ten years from now. You may hope and believe, though not feel certain, that you'll still exist fifty or sixty years from now.

There are also mental processes. Among the most general processes are thinking and reasoning. They can involve reaching a conclusion from data or solving a problem. If you're trying to discover whether Marilyn Monroe was murdered, ascertain the causes of World War I, solve a problem in physics, or dream up a marketing campaign for pet rocks, you're thinking and reasoning.

If consciousness is the capacity to have mental states and to engage in mental processes, and if there is a variety of such states and processes, then consciousness could be a matter of degree. Perhaps it would sound odd to speak of one thing's being more conscious than another, but it may sound less odd to speak of one thing's having a more sophisticated level of consciousness than another. The level of sophistication of a being's consciousness might be thought of as a function of how many kinds of mental states it can have. For example, a being that has a more complex self-consciousness than another might be said to have a higher level of consciousness. A being that has fewer (or no) beliefs, desires, feelings, or emotions could be said to have a less sophisticated level of consciousness than a being that has more.

BRAIN TEASERS

1. Of the beings on the following list, which would you say are conscious and which are not? Why? Of those that you think are conscious, do you think that some have a higher level of consciousness than others? Why? Living cells, flowers, ants, butterflies, birds, cows, foxes, dogs, chimpanzees, dolphins, elephants, humans.

2. What role does the capacity to communicate play?

3. Can a dog have beliefs, desires, hopes, and fears? Can it love? Can it feel depressed and lonely? Which mental states require concepts that dogs probably don't have?

4. If the android Data from *Star Trek: The Next Generation* or the robot C3PO from *Star Wars* existed, would they be conscious? Why or why not? Where would they fit in the table of levels of consciousness? Why?

Minds

How can we explain consciousness, the fact that some living beings can have a variety of mental states? One answer is that they have minds. Because, and only because, you have a mind, you can believe that global warming is a serious threat to the world, desire that governments do something about it, hope that action will not come too late, love your parents and siblings, and feel depressed about people's indifference to the threat. Because, and only because you have a mind, you know who and what you are and what you want to be. What, then, is a mind? Let's define a mind functionally, as we did with the concept of life. Let's say that a mind is that which causes and contains mental states. If we don't like the idea that minds "contain" mental states, we can instead say that mental states are "realized" in a mind.[7] So minds are things in which mental states are realized. Thus, a being can have mental states only if it has a mind; if it has no mind, it cannot see, have an itch, feel depressed, love its parents,

---

[7]Perhaps an analogy will help with the term "realize." Consider the sentence "Jack and Jill ran up the hill" (abbreviated as J). We could say that J is realized on the page of this book and on every copy of this book because it's printed there. If I wrote J on the blackboard, we could say that it is also realized on the blackboard because it's written there in chalk. If I engraved it on marble it would be realized on the slab of marble.

understand how the world works, desire to eat, fear flying, or believe it will rain.

BRAIN TEASERS

Can a mental state exist yet not be "contained" or "realized" in anything?

A major question, then, is whether minds are physical or nonphysical. Dualists maintain that purely physical organisms—organisms composed only of matter and energy and capable only of chemical reactions—cannot have mental states. In their view, then, minds must be nonphysical. Physicalists, on the other hand, as we will see, think that minds are purely physical. In fact, they say that the minds of creatures on Earth are nothing but their brains.

Descartes' Argument For Dualism

The French philosopher René Descartes (1596–1650) maintained that mental states or properties, such as the state of desiring to be an astronaut, are radically different from physical properties, such as the property of weighing 200 pounds and of being six feet tall. He thought that because there are two radically different kinds of *property* or state in the universe—physical and mental—there must be two radically different kinds of stuff or *substance* in the universe that has these two different kinds of property. If one kind of stuff—matter—is physical, then the other kind of stuff—minds—must be nonphysical. Thus, Descartes accepted two forms of Dualism: Substance Dualism (the claim that nonphysical substance exists or that nonphysical entities exist) and Property Dualism (the claim that there are mental properties that are different from and not reducible to physical properties). Let's consider the difference between substance and properties.

Traditionally, philosophers distinguished between independently existing things or entities and their properties. (From now on I'll just use the term "entity.") For example, a lump of sugar is an entity. I could describe it by saying that it's a cube, white, and sweet, and that it dissolves in hot liquids (is soluble). When I describe it, I'm listing some of its properties. Thus, the lump of sugar has the properties of being white, being a cube, being sweet, and being soluble. Since it's sugar, it also has the property of being sugar. On the other hand, since it's not green and spherical and isn't salt, it doesn't have the properties of being green, being spherical, or being salt.

Most philosophers assume that properties cannot exist all by themselves. Properties must belong to (or be had by) something and must be attached to other properties. Take the property of being white. Snow, chalk, salt, and sugar can all have that property (they're all white). But can the property of being white just exist alone in the universe, not attached to anything, such as a piece of chalk or a snowflake, or to other properties? Surely nothing can have only the property of being white. If something is white, it must have a surface, so it must have the property of having a surface. It must have a certain molecular structure that enables it to reflect light of certain wavelengths, so it must have the property of having a certain molecular structure. It must be composed of something, so it must have the property of being snow, or of being paint, or of being salt.

Let's try a thought experiment. Imagine that we could detach from a lump of sugar every property that it has. We detach the property of being white, of being a cube, of being solid, of being soluble in hot liquids. We even strip from it the property of being sugar (as well as the properties that make it sugar rather than salt, flour, talcum powder, or chalk dust). What would we have left? If we say that nothing would be left, then only properties exist and somehow they can hook together to form things such as lumps of sugar. The British philosopher David Hume (1711–1776) sometimes seemed to embrace that idea.

On the other hand, many philosophers rejected that idea because then there would be nothing that "has" the properties. Many philosophers have claimed that there would be something left if we were to detach all the properties from a lump of sugar. What would be left is what the properties attach to: substance. According to this view, a physical object is composed of a bit of substance with various properties attached to it. A lump of sugar is composed of substance plus the properties of being white, being a cube, being sweet, being soluble in warm liquids, and being sugar.

Substance is mysterious stuff. According to the traditional view, substance has no properties of its own; it's like a kind of flypaper to which properties adhere, but flypaper that has no properties of its own, not even the property of being sticky. But many philosophers have found it attractive to postulate the existence of substance to act as the stuff that has properties and holds them together to form an object. Otherwise there are only properties with nothing to which they can adhere.

Descartes accepted the distinction between properties and substance. He thought that substance exists but that there are two very different kinds of substance: physical and mental. Physical substance (matter) is what physical properties collect in or adhere to; mental substance is what mental properties collect in or adhere to.[8]

---

[8]If we don't think that the concept of substance is useful, we can just use the concept of an entity and its properties. We could then say that Descartes believed that there are purely physical entities that can only have physical properties and nonphysical mental entities that can only have mental properties.

Substance Dualism and Human Nature

Of course, we're most interested in ourselves. According to Descartes, we can truly say of ourselves that we're a certain height and weight, a certain shape, and that we have certain beliefs, desires, feelings. That is, we can truly say of ourselves that we have a variety of physical and mental properties. Therefore, according to Descartes, we're composed of two kinds of substance: physical (our bodies) and nonphysical (our minds). Our bodies have our physical properties while our minds have our mental properties. It's your nonphysical mind, not your body or part of your body, such as your brain, that thinks, believes, feels, remembers, dreams, decides, sees, loves, and hopes. It's your body, not your mind, that has a certain mass, weight, shape, color, and temperature.

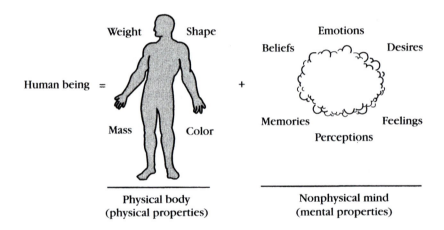

Weight	Shape	Emotions
		Beliefs · Desires
Human being =	+	
Mass	Color	Memories · Feelings
		Perceptions
Physical body		**Nonphysical mind**
(physical properties)		**(mental properties)**

The Relation Between the Physical and Mental

According to Descartes, our minds and bodies causally interact with each other. That means that events and states in your mind can cause physical events in your body and vice versa. (Of course, mental states and events can cause other mental states and events, and physical states and events can cause other physical states and events.) For example, a tack puncturing your foot (a physical event) causes you to feel pain (a mental event) and causes you to say "ouch," (a physical event); fear (a mental state) may cause you to sweat or run (physical events) and to hope your friend will come soon (a mental event); deciding to exercise (a mental event) may cause you to move your legs as you run (a series of physical events). This relation between the physical and mental is called Interactionism.[9] Common sense seems to be on the side of Descartes. It seems somehow "natural" to believe that people are a combination of physical bodies and nonphysical minds and that minds and bodies causally interact in both directions—events in the mind causing things to happen in the body and events in the body causing things to happen in the mind. But common sense is often wrong, and what it seems "natural" to believe is often false.

Problems for Descartes

We'll focus here on four problems facing Descartes: the mystery of causal interaction, the unobservability of minds, the problem of evolutionary development, and the problem of fetal development.

The Mystery of Causal Interaction

According to Descartes, mental states, events, and processes in a nonphysical mind cause physical events, states, and processes in a physical body, and vice versa. However, causal interaction between entirely different kinds of things—between physical things and nonphysical things—seems rather mysterious to many people. Causal interaction appears to be a physical phenomenon. Some people wonder how such radically different realms of reality as the physical and nonphysical could affect each other causally.

Let's look at ordinary cases of causal interaction. I pick up my coffee mug and raise it to my lips. What caused the coffee mug to rise? My hand gripping the mug exerted an upward force on it that was greater than the force of gravity that kept it sitting on my desk. Forces are purely physical things, although they are obviously different from physical objects composed of matter, such as the mug itself. We consider forces to be part of the physical universe because the concept of a force is an integral part of scientific theories. So forces belong on the physical side of the physical/nonphysical divide. In turn, the exertion of the force by my hand required the expenditure of energy, and like force, energy belongs on the physical side of the physical/nonphysical divide.

What caused my hand to rise? The forearm to which it is attached rose, and that rose because (here "because" is a causal concept)

---

[9]Not all Substance Dualists accept Interactionism. Some believe that mental events can only cause other mental events and that physical events can only cause other physical events. Others believe that physical events can cause mental events as well as other physical events, but that mental events cannot cause either physical events or other mental events.

muscles in my arm contracted. The contracting muscles exerted forces that raised my forearm. (This, too, required the expenditure of energy.) The muscles in my arm contracted because electrical impulses travelling from my brain triggered reactions in the muscle cells, causing them to contract. (The chemical and electrical reactions at the cellular level are pretty complicated.)

Many people find it inconceivable that a purely nonphysical thing can cause events to occur in a physical thing. The causal explanation of my raising my mug to my lips involved discrete physical objects literally touching each other. (My hand, attached to my forearm, gripped the mug; the arm muscles touch the bones of my forearm; the nerves touch the muscles of my forearm at one end and my brain at the other end; the electrical impulses originate in my brain and physically travel down the nerves until contact is made with my arm muscles.) It also involved appeal to forces and energy. The problem is that something nonphysical has no spatial location (that's a physical property), no mass, and no surfaces capable of touching or being in contact with a physical object. It also seems that something purely nonphysical cannot create forces or energy, either. The force of gravity on Earth, for example, is created by Earth's mass, just as the sun's force of gravity is caused by its mass. The so-called strong force that holds the nucleus of an atom together, the weak force that binds the electrons to the nucleus, and electromagnetic forces that attract and repel are purely physical forces caused by the interactions of purely physical objects. (Subatomic particles are on the physical side of the physical/nonphysical divide, but they're fundamentally different from macroscopic objects composed of atoms, such as snowflakes, grains of sand, and mountains.) Energy, according to Einstein's theory of Relativity, which has been strongly confirmed countless times, is in a sense another manifestation of mass. Mass can be converted to energy and energy can be converted into mass. ($E = MC^2$ means that the energy in a given bit of matter is equal to its mass [M] multiplied by the speed of light [C] squared.) Thus, something that has no mass cannot possibly have or create any energy and thus is incapable of exerting any forces on things. On this view, something nonphysical cannot possibly cause my brain cells to send electrical impulses down my arm to cause my arm muscles to contract so that I would lift my coffee mug to my lips.

But is it a fatal problem? Couldn't a supporter of the claim that the nonphysical and physical can causally interact simply say that science has not identified and detected all of the forms of energy in the universe, that there is a nonphysical form of energy that can create forces that in turn can cause physical things to happen, such as the firing of brain cells in my brain? Of course, one can say anything. The problem is that there appears to be no evidence for the existence of nonphysical forms of energy. If we require evidence for existence claims, we are unlikely to accept this claim.

BRAIN TEASERS

In the movie *Ghost,* Patrick Swayze, a new ghost, learns from an older ghost in a subway station how to move objects by touching them; for example, how to move a can by kicking it. The key, says the older ghost, is concentration. Swayze learns how to move coins, shut doors, and even push people. But if, as a ghost, Swayze has no physical properties such as mass, is it possible for him to do the things he does? If the answer is yes, how might we explain such an ability of ghosts, other than by appealing to "concentration"?

The Unobservability of Minds

For many people, seeing (or feeling) is believing. Most of us believe that something exists only if we can perceive it. Some people reject nonphysical minds simply because they can't observe them or detect their presence or existence by physical means. What can't be observed or detected, they say, probably doesn't exist. After all, if someone tells me there's an elf in my garden but I can't perceive it, I'm not going to believe it's there. That's why Demi Moore in the movie *Ghost* at first refuses to believe that Patrick Swayze's ghost has returned. She can't see, hear, smell, taste, or touch him.

But what about our belief in subatomic particles, energy, and magnetic fields? We can't perceive them. To make the human senses the measure of what is real, of what really exists, would be folly. However, we believe in subatomic particles, energy, and magnetic fields because we can detect them by physical means. We can detect a magnetic field by observing the behavior of a nail or iron filings. We can detect an electron in a cloud chamber by observing the condensed droplets of water in the path the electron took. We can detect energy by the work it does. (Also, these things are crucial parts of explanatory theories that have been highly confirmed by experience. As some thinkers, such as the American philosopher W. V. Quine, have emphasized, it is whole theories that are confirmed by appeal to observation, not necessarily parts of theories and individual claims, such as that energy exists. But there isn't even any indirect way of detecting the presence of a nonphysical mind (or ghost). If it can't be detected, then surely it doesn't exist.

A Dualist might respond, first, that we can detect nonphysical things by their effects. Demi Moore comes to believe in the reality of Patrick Swayze's ghost because he makes a penny climb up a door. Perhaps we have evidence of nonphysical things by their effects. Second, a Dualist might say that when it comes to nonphysical minds, wherever there is evidence of consciousness, there is evidence of the presence and existence of mind. When a human being uses language, for example, we have evidence of consciousness and thus evidence of the presence of a mind. Whenever we see a living organism engaging in what appears to be complex, purposive behavior, we have evidence of the existence of a mind. That is, minds are indirectly detectable even if they're not publicly perceivable.

Introspection: Awareness of One's Own Mental States

Finally, a Dualist might respond that he or she has in some sense observed a mind—namely, his or her own. You see, hear, touch, smell, and taste things. But you're also aware of an "inner" world, the world of your own thoughts, feelings, hopes, desires, and memories. This awareness of your own mental states isn't the result of perception. Philosophers have coined the term **introspection** for awareness of one's own mental states. A Dualist could say that she is aware of her own mind's existence through introspection of the contents of her mind.

Introspection: Source of knowledge of our own mental states

The Problem of Evolutionary Development

Critics of Dualism also point to the problems raised for Dualism by evolutionary biology. According to science, as we have seen, all living organisms evolved gradually from more primitive origins. Life started with one-celled, self-replicating molecules. At what point in evolutionary history did nonphysical mind enter the picture? What was the first species in evolutionary history to have a nonphysical mind? For example, did dinosaurs that first appeared about two hundred million years ago and that became extinct about sixty million years ago have nonphysical minds? Did the species from which, according to biologists, modern humans evolved have them? Or is it, as Descartes thought, that minds entered the evolutionary stream only with human beings?

And how are we to explain how or why nonphysical minds somehow "melded" with purely physical beings to give them consciousness, however rudimentary that consciousness might be? Where did they come from? Did they already exist in some nonphysical plane of existence? Did they come into existence only when human beings appeared? It's difficult to see how exactly nonphysical minds help explain consciousness.

A theist, of course, might claim that God created nonphysical minds and at some point in evolutionary history embodied them so that they could interact with a body through the brain. And a theist could insist that God created minds of various degrees of sophistication and complexity, the sophistication of the mind of an organism being a function of the development of the organism's brain.

The Problem of Fetal Development

A human being begins its existence as a single fertilized egg. It then undergoes a slow process of development in the womb that takes nine months. Where in fetal development does a nonphysical mind join with the physical body? Does the fertilized egg at the moment of conception already have a mind? Many people don't think so. Does it have a mind after one month of development? Three months? At birth?

Where does the individual's nonphysical mind come from? Does it exist disembodied in some nonphysical plane of existence before it melds with the developing human organism? Does it come into existence only when it melds with the developing human? How does it meld to provide consciousness?

Physicalism

The problems for Descartes have led many people to try to find an alternative theory about the nature of human beings. The central concern is the claim that there are two radically different kinds of substance in the world and that human beings are a combination of these two substances somehow joined together to form one organism. Critics of Descartes deny that human beings are composed of a combination of two kinds of substance. Instead, they maintain that we are composed of only one substance: physical matter. According to them, we are made up of atoms that combine to form molecules that combine to form larger and more complex structures, such as skin, blood, bone, and organs such as lungs, liver, and brain. That is all we are composed of; we have no nonphysical parts.

The claim that human beings are composed only of physical matter is called *Physicalism* (some philosophers call it *materialism*). Jaegwon Kim defines what he calls *minimal physicalism* in terms of three principles:

> *Mind-Body Supervenience:* The mental supervenes on the physical in that any two things (objects, events, organisms, persons, etc.) exactly alike in all physical properties cannot differ in respect of mental properties.[10]
>
> *Anti-Cartesian Principle:* There can be no purely mental beings. . . .
>
> *Mind-Body Dependence:* What mental properties a given thing has depends on, and is determined by, what physical properties it has.[11]

---

[10]One property X supervenes on another property Y just in case X varies as Y varies. Thus if the property of your fearing snakes supervenes on a certain state of your brain, then if the brain state changes, you will no longer fear snakes. However, if the brain state does not change, you will continue to fear snakes.

[11]Jaegwon Kim, *Philosophy of Mind* (Boulder CO: Westview Press, 1996), 10–12.

Minimal physicalism claims essentially that Substance Dualism is false (there are no mental substances), but it leaves open the possibility that Property Dualism is true (there are mental properties that are not identical or reducible to physical properties). But if Property Dualism is true, then according to Minimal Physicalism, your mental properties are dependent on the physical properties of your body or parts of your body. Thus, if you believe that snow is cold, your believing it is not a property of your non-physical mind but rather, a property that is dependent on the physical properties of your body (especially on the properties of your brain).

On the other hand, a more robust form of Physicalism rejects Property Dualism as well as Substance Dualism and denies that there are special mental properties that are substantially different from physical properties. One version of this more robust Physicalism rejects mental properties entirely. Other versions claim that mental properties are either identical to or somehow reducible to physical properties of your brain.

All Physicalists deny that humans are composed of two kinds of substance—physical matter and nonphysical mind or soul. But Minimal Physicalists concede that humans have two kinds of properties—physical and mental, thus claiming that one kind of substance—matter—can have two different kinds of properties. More robust Physicalists either deny that mental properties exist or maintain that they are in some way identical or reducible to physical properties, such as physical properties of a brain.

We might diagram the Physicalist's view, in contrast to the Cartesian Dualist's view, as follows:

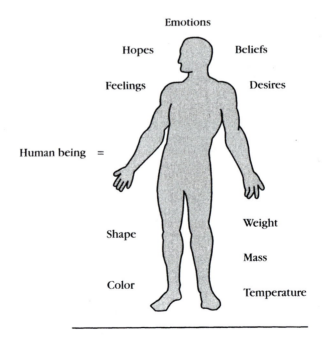

Physical matter

According to Minimal Physicalists, it is one's brain that enables a human being to see, think, feel, remember, love, desire, and so on. According to Physicalists, what Cartesian Dualists think of as one's nonphysical mind or soul is nothing but a person's brain and central nervous system.

Mind (in Humans) = Brain

Almost all philosophers and psychologists today are at least Minimal Physicalists in that they reject Substance Dualism. They differ, though, on how to deal with mental properties. Rejecting Substance Dualism in favor of some form of Physicalism has several advantages. First, it is simpler. Instead of two radically different kinds of entity, there is only one. Second, it explains how, where, and why consciousness emerged in the evolutionary process: consciousness emerged whenever a species developed a sophisticated enough brain. (Rosebushes aren't conscious, because they don't have brains. Flies aren't, because whatever brains they have are not nearly sophisticated enough. Dogs, elephants, and humans are conscious because they have sufficiently sophisticated brains.) Third, it resolves the problem of where in fetal development a mind appears in a human: it appears when the brain is sufficiently developed and functioning at a high enough level. The only problem remaining is that of causal interaction between the mental and the physical. If physical properties cause mental properties and vice versa, how can that be explained?

Minimal and Robust Physicalism

Robust Physicalists try to resolve the problem of causal interaction by either denying that there really are mental properties, or by claiming that mental properties are either identical to or reducible to physical properties. That is, they reject Property Dualism. Minimal Physicalists may accept property Dualism.

Robust Physicalism: Philosophical Behaviorism

Philosophical or logical behaviorists (sometimes called radical behaviorists) either deny that mental states exist or maintain that mental states play no role in human behavior and so can be ignored. If there are no mental substances or mental states, events, and processes, then there is no divide between the physical and mental; everything is physical. They define psychology as a science of human behavior and maintain that as a science, psychology must confine itself to what can be publicly observed. Science tries to develop laws and theories that explain certain phenomena in a certain domain of inquiry, theories and laws that are testable or confirmable by appeal to what can be publicly observed. Physics and chemistry try to explain the behavior and properties of subatomic particles, atoms, and molecules. Biology tries to explain the basis and properties of living things. What is the domain of inquiry of psychology? If it's human psychology that we're interested in is explaining human behavior.

What is Behavior?

What is behavior? The quick answer is that it's what we do that is publicly observable, that is, movements of our bodies and parts of our bodies. But consider the following list of movements of your body and parts of your body: you raise your arm to ask a question, you move your arm in response to your hand's coming in contact with a very hot object, you cough, you utter sounds to answer a question, you utter sounds in response to bumping your shin into a chair, your heart beats, muscles in your intestines push food along during the process of digestion, your head moves because a ball hit it, you hit a ball with your head while playing soccer, you read a book, you hold a book in your hands. Are they all the same? Common sense says no.

Surely there's a difference between the movement your head makes when it's unexpectedly hit by a ball and the movement it makes when you hit a ball with your head while playing soccer. Similarly, there seems to be a difference between your uttering sounds when you cough and your uttering sounds when you're answering a question, as well as between having your arm move when your hand touches a very hot object and your raising your arm to answer a question. In each case, the second item of the pair is something you do *intentionally* according to common sense. Each item of the pairs requires a different kind of explanation.

Why did you cough? Let's assume you have chest congestion because of a cold. The coughing is a reflex action and we certainly can explain why you coughed without bringing in any mental states as part of the explanation. But can the same be said of your uttering sounds to answer a question? First, notice that it will be difficult even to describe this behavior without using concepts that belong on the mental side of the physical/mental divide. The sounds you utter asking a question are not the same as those you utter when you cough. How should we describe the sounds? We must say that they're words, for example, "Are purely behavioral explanations really adequate and complete?" So what is it exactly that you're doing? We can't just say, "You're uttering sounds," because you do that when you cough, sneeze, scream, hiccup, snore, issue an order, describe an object, explain something, pray, and ask a question.

So suppose we say that what you're doing is asking a question. That's simple enough. But consider what must be the case for it to be true that what you're doing is asking a question rather than coughing, sneezing, screaming, praying, or issuing a command. You must be using a language, such as

English. In order to use a language, you must understand it and understand the particular sentence you're uttering. To understand is on the mental side of the mental/physical divide. To ask a question, you also must want the individual you're asking to understand the question and answer it. To want is a mental concept. Similarly, you must believe that the individual to whom your question is addressed can hear you and she understands the language you're using. Both believing and hearing are mental concepts. So merely describing your behavior seems to require the use of mental concepts.

The kinds of behavior that psychologists try to explain include such things as carrying an umbrella, drinking coffee, shooting a gun, kicking a ball, and writing a sentence on a piece of paper. These are actions, a form of behavior that is called intentional behavior. Common sense says that intentional behavior can be described and adequately explained only by appeal to mental concepts.

BRAIN TEASERS

Can we describe your kicking a ball in order to try to score a goal (as opposed to your kicking a ball by accident) without using any mental concepts?

Behaviorist Explanations of Actions

Common sense says that we can explain intentional behavior or actions only if we include descriptions of a subject's mental states. For example, we might explain why someone pulled the trigger of a gun by saying that he wanted to wound or frighten someone and he believed that he could accomplish this by aiming a gun at him and pulling the trigger. If we ask why someone carried an umbrella to work, we might say that he believed it was likely to rain, believed that if it rained and he had no protection he would get wet, that he wanted to stay dry, and that he believed that a raised and open umbrella would keep him relatively dry.

Philosophical Behaviorists maintain that we can describe and explain actions without having to describe any of the subject's mental states. We can adequately and completely explain such behavior in terms of stimuli and responses, and negative and positive reinforcement. Let's look at an example of nonhuman behavior to clarify this. A white rat will get food if and only if it presses a bar. It engages in random movements in its cage and eventually, quite by accident, it presses the bar. Food is released, which gives it positive reinforcement. Initially, it might not connect pressing the bar with getting food, so it may continue to engage in random behavior. Eventually, after accidentally pressing the bar a number of times and getting food, and having no other form of behavior produce food, it begins to press the bar again and again.

Why does the rat press the bar? Common sense is tempted to say that the rat now knows or believes that pressing the bar produces food and that it wants food because it's hungry. It's following an elementary psychological law according to which (all other things being equal) if a subject wants something X and believes that doing Y will produce X, then it will do Y.

But this common sense explanation appeals to a rat's mental states. We can observe its behavior but not its mental states. So why should we think that appeal to its mental states is the true explanation of its behavior? Why think it has mental states at all? Well, it depends on whether we can produce another explanation of its behavior that is adequate and that does not appeal to the rat's mental states. What would such an explanation look like?

Behaviorists say that the rat presses the bar because it was conditioned to press the bar. The behavior of pressing the bar, originally random, was positively reinforced. An elementary psychological law is that positively reinforced behavior (all other things being equal) will persist as long as it continues to be positively reinforced. That adequately explains the rat's behavior without appealing to, or attributing to the rat, any mental states. As for defining positive and negative reinforcement, something is a positive reinforcer of behavior X if it increases the probability of X occurring; it is a negative reinforcer of behavior X if it reduces the probability of X occurring.

Suppose we want to condition a rat to not pass through a certain opening in its cage. To do this, we give it a shock each time it passes through the opening. Soon, the rat avoids the opening. The shock is a negative reinforcer that extinguishes behavior. Now common sense psychology says that the rat feels pain when shocked and for that reason avoids the opening. To common sense, the fact that the shock causes pain explains why it is a negative reinforcer. However, behaviorists say that there is no need to claim that the shock causes pain to the rat. Pain is a mental state and there are no good reasons to attribute mental states to rats. Instead, we should say that the shock just is a negative reinforcer because it reduces the probability of the behavior in question. Can we explain why it is a negative reinforcer rather than either a positive reinforcer or no reinforcer of any kind? No.

What about human behavior? Suppose that we're trying to explain why you either proposed marriage to someone or accepted a proposal of marriage. (Consider what is entailed by describing the behavior as making or accepting a marriage proposal.) Common sense would explain it by attributing certain mental states to you. One obvious explanation is that you acted as you did because you love (or believe that you love) the person, you believe you'll be happy if you marry someone you love, perhaps you believe you won't be happy unless you marry this person, and you want to do what will make you happy. Of course, that might not be the true explanation. It could be that you believe you'll be happy if you marry someone who is rich, you want to make yourself happy, and you believe that the person is rich. Or it could be that you want to hurt your parents and you believe that you will do so if you marry this person. Common sense explanations of your behavior appeal to your mental states, especially your beliefs and desires.

Behaviorists maintain that we can satisfactorily explain your behavior without appealing to any of your mental states, just as we did in the case of the rat pressing the bar. You were conditioned to ask or say yes. Perhaps you were conditioned to have the tendency to enter into marriage by both positive reinforcers for marrying (social approval) and negative reinforcers for remaining single (social disapproval). Critics of Behaviorism deny that we can satisfactorily explain your action if we do not appeal to any of your mental states.

Of course, in many cases conditioning explains why we have the mental states we do. Why does Carmen wish to marry for money rather than for love? It may be that she was conditioned to believe that love is a fiction and that money always brings happiness. Why does Cassandra want to have ten children? Perhaps she was conditioned to want to have a large family. Why does Carol love Billy? Perhaps she was conditioned to love someone with his characteristics. But these behavioral explanations do not replace explanations that appeal to mental states; rather, they explain why we have the mental states we do. And it is not obvious that all mental states can be explained by appeal to conditioning. Why do you believe that new-fallen snow is white? Why do you believe that if all humans are mortal, and you are a human, then you are mortal? The explanations of your believing these things don't seem to involve conditioning.

BRAIN TEASERS

Try to provide a behaviorist explanation of your decision to marry a specific individual. Remember that it must not mention any of your mental states. Do you think that the explanation is wholly adequate? Why or why not?

Try to provide a behaviorist explanation of a behaviorist's uttering the sentence "Behaviorism is true" that does not mention any of the behaviorist's mental states.

Behavioral Translations of Mental Terms

Philosophical behaviorists claim that we can adequately translate any sentence containing mental concepts into a sentence that does not contain any mental concepts. If that is the case, we can dispense with all talk of mental states. Sentence P adequately translates sentence Q if and only if P and Q have the same meaning. Thus, consider "The average American family has 2 children." Is there such a thing as the average American family? Where shall we look for it? We can eliminate reference to "the average American family" by translating the original sentence into, "The number of children in American families divided by the number of American families is two." Or we could say, "On average, American families have two children." Now we no longer have to say that there is some entity called the average American family. The two sentences have the same meaning as the first sentence and we can see that we were mistaken in thinking that the first sentence says there is an entity called "the average American family." If we can do the same thing with sentences containing mental concepts, we can say that mental states are no more real than is the average American family.

Let's first look at explanations of rat behavior. Suppose that a rat is shocked and it then jumps, writhes, and emits a shrill shriek. Common sense is tempted to say that the behavior provides evidence that the rat feels pain because that is behavior that we normally associate with pain. But do rats feel pain? We can't observe or feel the rat's pain; all we can observe is its behavior. But what can we mean when we say, "The rat's in pain?" Behaviorists try to provide a purely behavioral meaning. For example, they might say that "X is in pain" means that under certain input conditions (stimuli), such as receiving a shock or sustaining an injury or damage, x will have certain behavioral outputs, for example, it will utter certain noises (cries, whimpers, squeals, screams) and make certain bodily movements (such as wincing, cringing, jumping, shuddering, writhing, or limping). Thus, they say that we can translate a sentence such as "The rat is in pain" into a different sentence with the same meaning, such as "The rat has the tendency to emit high pitched shrieks and to jump and writhe." Because the second sentence does not contain any mental concepts, we can treat pain as we did the average American family. And then we do not have to attribute pains to the rat.

But do any sentences that contain no mental terms truly mean the same as "The rat is in pain"? If not, then the behaviorist strategy fails, because the sentences used to translate "The rat is in pain" must mean the same thing. That is just what it means to say that one sentence is an adequate translation of another. The answer seems to be no: no sentence that contains no mental concepts means the same as "The rat is in pain." We can't say the same thing (the rat's in pain) without using the concept of pain. And common sense seems to be still on safe ground in explaining the rat's behavior by attributing the mental state of pain to it.

Let's turn to humans. Can we explain human actions without appealing to the subject's mental states? First, can we say all we mean without using mental concepts? Suppose we say that you love someone. Can we say the same thing without using the concept of loving? Perhaps we could say that x loves y means that if x sees y, x will smile, especially if there has been a long separation; that if x is close to y, x will hold y's hand, kiss y, or hug y. Perhaps on appropriate occasions x will say to y, "I love you." And so on. But do these things mean the same as "x loves y"?

There are problems with this. First, there are no necessary behavioral responses for many mental states. Take loving. What forms of behavior will x necessarily engage in if x loves y? It's hard to think of any. There are many actions that could be produced by love (marrying, giving presents, putting the loved one's interests before one's own, saying "I love you," sending a birthday card, engaging in sex), but each form of behavior could occur even where there is no love and love could occur where none of these forms of behavior are engaged in. So no sentence that only refers to these forms of behavior could possibly mean the same as "x loves y." Therefore, a sentence that only describes a subject x's observable behavior cannot be an adequate translation of "x loves y."

A deeper problem is that behaviorists think that we can define mental states individually without mentioning other mental states. Take the claim that "x loves y" entails that if x is close to y, x will hold y's hand, kiss y, or hug y. (This is a weaker claim than the claim that it means the same thing.) X will do these things only if certain other things are true. X must see and recognize Y. X must have no desire to avoid public displays of love. X must understand that holding hands, hugging, and kissing are conventional signs of love and must want to behave in a way that signals her love to y. X must want y to understand her (x's) behavior as a sign of love. All these conditions require us to attribute mental states to x. (We might be tempted to say that surely having an itch necessarily produces scratching. But suppose that you don't want to scratch even though you're itchy. Perhaps you bet someone that you have so much self-control that you won't scratch even when very itchy. Perhaps you don't want to give away the fact that you have an irritation that's causing you to itch.)

If we cannot even describe people's actions without using mental concepts that attribute mental states to them, why should we think that we can adequately explain their actions without having to appeal to their mental states? How can we explain why Phyllis married John (or said "I do" at a wedding ceremony) without appealing to any of Phyllis's mental states?

There is another problem for behaviorists. Common sense says that mental states are the causes of behavior, not merely identical to tendencies to behave in certain ways. Suppose we ask what caused x to kiss y. Common sense says that the love x feels for y caused the behavior.

Few philosophers or psychologists today accept Philosophical Behaviorism. Most of them think we cannot adequately describe or explain human behavior without attributing mental states to them. The majority that embraces Physicalism seeks a different theory about mental states.

Robust Physicalism: Functionalism

If sentences containing mental terms cannot be translated into sentences that replace the mental terms with terms referring only to observable behavior, perhaps other kinds of translation can be accomplished building on the common sense idea that mental states play a causal role in human behavior.

Let's look at the mental state of pain first. Suppose we say that x is in pain. X could be a human, a hippopotamus, a cat, or an alien, such as E.T. If we can attribute pain to a variety of beings, we must know what pain is. O.K., what is it? It's a mental state. But there are lots of mental states: pains, itches, burning sensations, sensations of cold, hearing a siren, seeing a tree, wanting to go to Disney World, fearing pain, anticipating pain, believing that there's no gain if there's no pain. What makes a state one of being in pain or feeling a pain rather than some other mental state, such as remembering a painful experience, having an itch, or fearing pain?

In addition to asking "What is a pain? What is a belief? What is a desire?" and so on, we can ask simpler questions. "What is a chair? What is a clock? What is a knife?" We all know what chairs are and we can easily recognize them almost all the time. But what do all chairs have in common? They don't all have four legs, although many of them do. A chair could have three or five legs. They're not all made of wood. Some are made of metal. They don't all have arms.

Is a beanbag chair really a chair? It doesn't have legs, let alone arms. It doesn't have an identifiable seat. It doesn't even keep its shape; it's a blob. But surely we're right in calling it a chair because it's something we can sit in, and that's what a chair is. A chair is defined in terms of its function.

What about a clock? A clock is something that tells time. What about a knife? That's harder because there are different kinds of knives. There are steak knives, butter knives, paring knives, bread knives, and so on. But each kind of knife is defined functionally. A butter knife is a knife suitable for cutting and spreading butter. A steak knife is a knife suitable for cutting steak without too much effort.

Functionalists in psychology try to provide functionalist definitions of mental states. Mental states are defined in terms of (1) the physical stimuli and physical states and events that typically cause them, (2) typical kinds of behavior that they cause, and (3) typical mental states that accompany or are caused by them. For example, a functionalist might say that pain is a mental state that (1) is typically caused by various kinds of physical damage (a cut, abrasion, burn, broken bone), (2) typically causes, in suitable circumstances (including the presence of certain other mental states), characteristic kinds of behavior (winces, moans, gritting of teeth, cries, bodily writhings, reaching for a pain killer), and (3) typically causes, in suitable circumstances (including the presence of certain other mental states) certain kinds of mental states (fear, anger, frustration, the desire to reduce the pain).

The Functionalist analysis of pain does not try to eliminate reference to mental states nor does it try to define a mental state in isolation from other mental states. Further, it suggests that mental states are real because it presents them as causes of behavior and other mental states and processes. A Functionalist who is also a Robust Physicalist may say that the mental state of an organism's being in pain, while a real state of the organism, is related in some way to physical states of the organism. One possibility is that mental states are identical to physical states of the being's brain or whatever plays the role of the brain in its life. Another is that mental states are reducible to physical states. A third is that mental states supervene on physical states.

Identity Theories

There are at least two kinds of identity theory. One claims that every type of specific mental state, such as being in pain, wanting to have two children, and believing that fire is hot, is identical with exactly the same physical state, no matter who or what has the mental state. The other claims that every individual's mental states are identical to some physical state of that individual, but that other beings having the same mental states may be in very different physical states, with their mental states identical to those (different) physical states they're in. The first is a *Type Identity Theory* while the second is a *Token Identity Theory*.

What's the difference between a type and a token? We can begin to understand the distinction by considering how many sentences appear below:

Crows are black.

Crows are black.

Crows are black.

In one sense there are three, but in another sense there is only one. There are three instances of the same one sentence. We can express this using the type/token terminology by saying that there is only one sentence type but three tokens of that sentence type.

How does this apply to mental states? Suppose that three different individuals, a, b, and c, all believe that crows are black. How many beliefs are there? In one sense there is only one but in another sense there are three. There is only one belief type—the belief that crows are black—but there are three different *tokens* of that belief type: A's belief that crows are black, B's belief that crows are black, and C's belief that crows are black. Individuals A, B, and C have the same belief.

A *type* identity theory identifies a particular mental state type, such as believing that crows are black, with a specific physical state. Thus, every instance of believing that crows are black, no matter whose belief it is, is identical to the same exact type of physical state. Let's say that the belief that crows are black is identical in individual A to a certain configuration of certain nerve cells in his brain. Then anyone's or anything's belief that crows are black is identical to the same kind of configuration of the same kind of brain cells.

But that's implausible. People's brains are probably as different as their fingerprints. Thus, while individual A's belief that crows are black may be identical to a certain configuration of nerve cells in his brain and B's belief that crows are black may be identical to a certain configuration of nerve cells in his brain, there is no obvious reason to believe that their brain states must be exactly the same. In fact, probability is on the side of their being different. And what if there are nonhuman beings that believe (or can believe) that crows are black? If there is intelligent life elsewhere, it could easily come to believe that crows are black. But their brains would surely be very different from ours. In that case, their belief that crows are black could not possibly be identical to brain states that are exactly like ours. Thus, a type identity theory seems implausible.

On a *token* identity theory, an individual token of a mental state is identical to a certain physical state of the subject who has the mental state. My believing that crows are black is identical to a certain physical state of my brain while your believing that crows are black is identical to a certain (probably different) physical state of your brain. An alien's belief that crows are black would then be identical to a certain physical state of its brain (or whatever part of it functions as a brain).

Why would anyone want to identify mental states with physical states? It explains mental causation. If mental states of a person are nothing but certain of their physical states, then there's no puzzle about causal relations between the physical and mental. It's all causal relations among purely physical states and events. But there's a problem. If each token of a specific mental event, such as believing that rattlesnakes are poisonous and fearing rattlesnakes, is identical to a different physical state, then it's difficult to see how we can construct scientific laws and theories about them. Consider the "law" that if someone believes that rattlesnakes are poisonous, fears poisonous snakes, and tends to avoid what she fears, then she will fear rattlesnakes and tend to avoid them. If the type identity theory were true, then in each individual the belief that rattlesnakes are poisonous, fearing poisonous snakes, and fearing rattlesnakes would be identical to the same three physical states. The physical states would cause the avoidance behavior. The law would be expressed in terms of one set of physical states always (or generally) causing another kind of physical state. This law would apply to everyone. But on a token identity theory, everyone who falls under this law will have different physical states to which their beliefs and fears are identical. If we express the law in terms of the physical states to which the mental states are identical, there will then be a different law for each individual. Suppose that in individual x the belief that rattlesnakes are poisonous is identical to brain cell configuration a, his fear of poisonous snakes is identical to brain cell configuration b, and fearing rattlesnakes is identical to brain cell configuration c. However, in individual y the belief that rattlesnakes are poisonous is identical to brain cell configuration d, her fear of poisonous snakes is identical to brain cell configuration e, and her fear of rattlesnakes is identical to brain cell configuration f. The law that applies to x is then: if one has brain cell configuration a, b, and c, then he will tend to avoid rattlesnakes. But the law that applies to y is: if one has brain cell configuration d, e, and f, then one will avoid rattlesnakes.

But critics of the identity theory think that it misses something vital. Pain hurts. It has what are called phenomenal properties or qualities. Pains feel different from itches. To define them functionally and to identify them with purely physical states seems to overlook this fact. Perhaps it's less a problem with some of the propositional attitudes, such as believing, but even fearing something feels a certain way to the subject.

If an individual's mental states are not identical to specific physical states of their brains, then perhaps they're reducible to such states. But what does reduction mean here? Let's look at some examples. We can reduce temperature to the mean kinetic energy of a group of molecules. That is, when we are measuring the temperature of a thing, such as a pool of water, whether we know it or not we're measuring the mean kinetic energy of the group of water molecules making up the pool. Temperature is thus reducible to the mean kinetic energy of a collection of molecules. Similarly, lightning is an atmospheric electrical discharge. Thus, lightning is reducible to an electrical discharge. But when we reduce one thing to another, we seem to be saying that we don't have two things—temperature and mean kinetic energy—we have one thing referred to by two different terms. (But the two terms, "temperature" and "mean kinetic energy," are not synonymous.) So reduction seems to imply identity. Thus, if we reduce having a pain to being in a certain brain state, we seem to imply that having a pain is identical to being in that certain brain state.

Minimal Physicalism: Supervenience

Many physicalists fall back on the view that mental states supervene on physical states. Roughly, that means that every mental state of a subject is caused or determined by some physical state of the subject. That means that there cannot be a mental state without there being a physical state that underlies it. But the mental states are not identical or reducible to those physical states.

This is not a robust version of Physicalism because it admits the existence of irreducibly mental properties of a subject, even though they are not properties of a nonphysical substance. Instead, they are irreducibly mental properties caused, at least in humans, by states of our brains. Thus, they may be said to be nonphysical states of our brains that are caused by physical states of our brains. This is a version of Property Dualism rather than Substance Dualism. But this view leaves us with the puzzle of how irreducibly mental states can be both effects and causes of physical states of our brains.

How Research on the Brain Seems to Support Physicalism

Brain research has revealed a whole host of connections between the brain and those states, processes, and events that we consider mental. Certain areas or systems of the brain are responsible for (or play a crucial role in) specific mental functions, such as perception, feelings and emotions, and memory. It's difficult to understand the role of the brain in mental life if Substance Dualism is true. But brain research does not seem to enable us to decide between minimal and robust Physicalism. Mental states could be identical or reducible to physical states of the brain, or instead mental states may be irreducibly mental, although supervening on the brain and its processes and states.

Let's remind ourselves that there are many kinds of mental states. There are sensations. They include pains, itches, and the experience you have feeling sandpaper with your hand. Another kind is the intentional states or propositional attitudes. Unlike sensations, often called "raw feels," intentional states have content that can be expressed by a proposition. Let p represent any proposition. Intentional states include beliefs (believing that p), desires (desiring that p), and fear (being afraid that p). There are also perceptions, emotions, feelings and moods, such as seeing the Washington Monument, loving your parents, feeling sympathy for refugees, and being depressed. What is the role of the brain in these various mental states?

Sensations　Suppose that you stumble into a chair in the dark, hitting your shin. What happens? You feel pain. But how does that happen? Contact between your shin and the chair triggers certain nerve cells in your skin that then emit electrical impulses that travel from your leg to your brain. One kind of neuron or nerve cell in your brain is crucial in this—so-called C-fibers. You feel pain only if your brain's C-fibers fire.

In many cases we can control pain. During surgery, anesthesia eliminates pain. Anesthetizing a patient involves purely physical substances and interactions. Presumably anesthesia prevents the C-fibers from firing, which in turn prevents pain. Ibuprofen and aspirin can reduce pain. Perhaps they do so by reducing the intensity of the electrical impulses emitted by the C-fibers. In any case, pain sensations seem to be caused by brain activity. Similar things may be said about other sensations.

Intentional States   Intentional states have content that can be expressed by a proposition. That means that if our intentional states are caused by and are "in" our brains, then our brains must be able to do what sentences and propositions do—represent information. Take the belief that dogs are mammals. That dogs are mammals is information. Thus, the sentence "Dogs are mammals" contains or represents information. Someone who understands English can convey or receive that information. But can brain states contain or represent information the way that sentences in a language can? At first sight that may seem absurd, but remember that computer hardware can store or represent information. I'm storing the entire contents of this book on the hard drive of my computer and on a computer disc. It's stored solely by means of electrical impulses. Brain cells work by means of electrical impulses. Perhaps the brain stores information in a way that's similar to the way a computer does.

Memory is crucial for the intentional states. You can't believe that dogs are mammals unless somewhere in your memory is the information that dogs are mammals. You can't fear snakes (or fear that a snake will bite you) unless you have stored in your memory the information that snakes bite and some of them are poisonous. You also must have concepts stored in your memory, such as the concept of a dog, a mammal, and a snake. What role does the brain play in memory?

Memory   Memory is the ability to store and retrieve information. Scientists distinguish among several types of memory. For example,

> *Episodic memory* refers to the conscious recollection of the personal past. . . . *Semantic* memory contains the general knowledge of the world. . . . *[P]rocedural* memory means the ability to perform skill-based operations. . . .[12]

Episodic memory enables us to remember what we had for breakfast this morning as well as our first day of college. It enables us to remember our own experiences, such as a vacation taken ten years ago. Semantic memory enables us to remember what we believe to be facts about the world, such as that colds are caused by viruses, World War II occurred from 1939 to 1945, and water freezes at 32 degrees Fahrenheit. Procedural memory enables us to remember how to do things, such as tie our shoelaces, ride a bicycle, or repair a leaky faucet.

Memory is vitally important to our lives. Imagine what it would be like if you couldn't remember what things look like, such as people's faces, so that you were unable to recognize and reidentify people, such as your family members and friends, and you couldn't recognize a door or a lion because you don't remember what they look like and what they

---

[12]Hans J. Markowitsch, "Anatomical Basis of Memory Disorders," in *The Cognitive Neurosciences*, ed. Michael S. Gazzaniga (Cambridge, MA: MIT Press, 1995), 768.

are. Imagine what it would be like if you couldn't remember anything about your past, even your past of five minutes ago. What if you couldn't remember any language, such as English? You wouldn't be able to read, write, or speak. Perhaps you wouldn't even be able to think. Human life without memory is inconceivable.

As we said, memory involves storing information for later retrieval and use. Several questions arise. Where are memories stored? How are they stored? How are they retrieved? Substance dualists say that memories are stored in our nonphysical minds. They probably would say they have no idea how they are stored and retrieved. Nonphysical minds are beyond the reach of scientific inquiry, which limits itself to the physical world.

Physicalists, who claim that our minds are our brains, say that memories are stored in the brain. Given this hypothesis, scientists then try to employ scientific methods to explain how they are stored and retrieved. Part of this attempt to explain involves identifying the sections of the brain that are responsible for memory. Individual memories are probably stored in discrete parts of the brain. However, it's likely that the processes of storage and retrieval involve many systems of the brain working together.

Is there any evidence that memories are stored in our brains rather than in nonphysical minds? One form of evidence is the consequences of brain damage and injury. If damage to a part of the brain leads to the loss of memories, one plausible explanation is that the lost memories were stored in the damaged part of the brain. Another possibility is that the damaged part of the brain plays a role in retrieving the memories. Let's examine some of the studies.

BRAIN TEASERS

If nonphysical minds store and retrieve memories, why would damage to certain parts of the brain lead to memory loss or impairment?

In one memory test, subjects are given three letters and asked to produce as many words that begin with these letters as they can in one minute. Subjects with lesions on a certain section of the frontal lobes of their brains do significantly worse on this test than do subjects who do not have lesions on this area of their brains. "For example, Janowsky et al. (1989) found that patients with bilateral or left unilateral lesions of the frontal lobes produced significantly fewer words on this task (21.5 words produced) than control subjects (37.5 words produced)."[13] In the supermarket fluency test,

---

[13]Arthur P. Shimamura, "Memory and Frontal Lobe Function," in *The Cognitive Neurosciences,* 807–808.

subjects are asked to name as many items as they can think of that could be purchased at a supermarket. Patients with frontal lobe lesions exhibited fewer retrievals than control subjects. . . . Impairment on tests of word retrieval may be related to difficulties in organizing and searching information in semantic memory.[14]

Thus, one plausible explanation of these findings is that the temporal lobes of our brains play a crucial role in the storage and/or retrieval of our semantic memories.

More dramatic memory deficits are possible. Oliver Sacks, a neurologist, tells the tragic story of a patient of his, Jimmie G. In 1975, Jimmie G. was a forty-nine-year-old man. However, Jimmie G. believed at that time that the year was 1945 and that he was still nineteen. He had vivid memories of his first nineteen years, but had absolutely no memories of his life after that date. Every memory from age nineteen to age forty-nine had been permanently obliterated. He could form no new memories. Dr. Sacks informed Jimmie G. that he had forgotten the last thirty years of his life. Jimmie G. was shocked, but he promptly forgot what Dr. Sacks had told him. He still believed that the year was 1945 and that he was nineteen. Each time he saw Dr. Sacks, he forgot about it and thought he was meeting him for the first time. In testing Jimmie G., Dr. Sacks put his watch, tie, and glasses on his desk so that Jimmie could see them, asked him to remember what he had put on his desk, and then covered them. A few minutes later he asked Jimmie what was under the cover. Jimmie didn't remember. He didn't even remember Dr. Sacks asking him to remember.

According to Dr. Sacks, Jimmie G.'s inability to remember anything after 1945 was due to the destruction of a part of the brain crucial for long-term memory, the mammillary bodies. This part of Jimmie G.'s brain was destroyed by acute alcoholism.[15] A plausible explanation of Jimmie G's problem is that the part of his brain that was destroyed either is where his episodic memories are stored or that that part of his brain is crucial for retrieving those memories.

Perception   How is it that we can perceive the world, that we can have experiences such as seeing a cloud, hearing a siren, feeling a tickle or itch, smelling a rose, or tasting peanut butter? Human beings (and other vertebrates) have a variety of specialized sensory receptor cells throughout their bodies that are sensitive to stimuli such as "pressure, heat and cold, concentrations of particular chemical compounds, vibrations, light, electric and magnetic fields, and so on."[16] For example, human skin has

---

[14]Ibid., 808.

[15]Oliver Sacks, "The Lost Mariner," in *The Man Who Mistook His Wife for a Hat* (New York: HarperCollins, 1987).

[16]Keeton and Gould, *Biological Science*, 491–492.

at least five kinds of sensory receptors: those sensitive to pain, cold, heat, pressure, and touch. Your hair and fingernails don't have any pain receptors. That's why you can cut your hair and nails but not your skin without feeling pain. Receptors for taste on the tongue and for smell in the nose are sensitive to the presence of certain kinds of chemicals. The human eye has two kinds of receptors at the back that are sensitive to light: rods and cones.

When exposed to a stimulus to which it is sensitive, the polarization of the membrane of a sensory cell changes in response. A change in polarization causes the receptor cell to fire, sending an electric charge or signal along a pathway of nerves that eventually leads to the section of the brain responsible for processing the signal. In human beings, signals (electrical impulses) from sensory cells travel through a complex network of nerves to the cerebral cortex, the surface layer of the cerebrum, where specialized areas of the brain receive and process the signals. Signals from sensory cells in the eyes sensitive to light are channeled to the visual area of the cerebral cortex, called the visual cortex; signals from cells in the nose are channeled to the olfactory lobes where they are processed; and so on. The electrical and chemical activity of the brain as it processes these signals gives rise to perception. As a result of the activity of the specialized sections of the brain responsible for processing the signals from the appropriate sensory cells, we perceive the world—we see, hear, smell, taste, and feel things.

Damage part of the system and we lose the sense. If the sensory cells in our eyes that are sensitive to light are damaged or destroyed, our vision is impaired or destroyed. We may become blind. Similarly, if there is damage to the nerves that carry the signals to the section of the cerebral cortex responsible for vision or there is damage to that section of the cerebral cortex itself, we may become blind. The physical basis of perception is fairly well understood by scientists. There does not seem to be any need to postulate the existence of some nonphysical substance—a nonphysical mind—to explain perception. Seeing, hearing, and the other senses seem to Physicalists to be purely physical processes and states. To Physicalists, the state of seeing a clock on the wall is a purely physical state of an organism explained in purely physical terms. They do not think that understanding is enhanced by claiming that the brain's physical activity creates a nonphysical state of perceiving something in a nonphysical substance, a mind.

Feelings and Emotions   We commonly talk sweepingly of our having feelings and emotions. However, it's difficult to distinguish between them or define them. Is loving something a feeling or an emotion? What about fearing something or being depressed or angry? I say that I "feel" sympathy or compassion for someone, but does that make them feelings? Why aren't they classified as emotions? What is an emotion? What is a feeling?

For our purposes, these are not questions we need to answer. Whatever feelings and emotions are and however they are to be distinguished, we have a lot of mental states that fit under one or the other of these concepts. Let's look individually at some of them in terms of brain research.

Fear Scientists have discovered some "fear circuits" in the brain. A central player in the fear circuit is the amygdala. Lesions on its central nucleus interfere with fear conditioning. (This makes it more difficult to condition an organism to feel fearful, or at least to have fear responses as measured by increased heart rate.) Studies showed that the amygdala "receives inputs from cortical areas associated with the major sensory modalities. . . ."[17] In turn, it sends signals to other brain areas that lead to various forms of responses associated with fear: blood pressure increases, sudden freezing or motionlessness, startle responses, and the release of stress hormones. Thus, inputs from the senses travel to the amygdala and outputs travel to various parts of the brain to produce responses generally thought to be caused by fear. This has led some scientists to theorize that the subjective mental state of pain is caused by or supervenient on brain activity that crucially involves the activity of the amygdala.

The fact that certain drugs injected directly into the amygdala of nonhuman animals can suppress reactions associated with anxiety and fear while injection of other drugs can produce reactions associated with anxiety and fear lends support to the view that the amygdala is a crucial part of the brain in producing the mental state of fear.[18]

Similarly, according to one researcher, Edmund T. Rolls, removing the amygdala from monkeys makes them tame and reduces their emotional responsiveness. Rats with lesions on their amygdala show less fear of new items placed in their environment.[19]

By stimulating various parts of the hypothalamus with microelectrodes, researchers have been able to identify centers in the hypothalamus that control hunger, thirst, . . . as well as sexual desire, pleasure, pain, hostility, and so on. It is possible to induce behavior appropriate to each of these states by inserting microelectrodes surgically into the control centers of experimental animals and then stimulating the centers electrically. Rats with electrodes in their pleasure centers will spend virtually all their time pressing levers that turn on a tiny current in those centers, ignoring food and water almost to the point of starvation. Animals with electrodes in appropriate parts of the hypothalamus can be made to feel sated one moment and hungry the next, cold and then hot, angry and then calm. Cats wired in this way may be friendly one

---

[17]Joseph E. Ledoux, "In Search of an Emotional System in the Brain: Leaping from Fear to Emotion and Consciousness," in *The Cognitive Neurosciences*, 1051.

[18]Floyd E. Bloom, "Cellular Mechanisms Active in Emotion," in *The Cognitive Neurosciences*.

[19]Edmund T. Rolls, "A Theory of Emotion and Consciousness, and Its Application to Understanding the Neural Basis of Emotion," in *The Cognitive Neurosciences*, 1051.

moment and in a rage the next. They can be made to break off an attack on a mouse and cower in a corner in fear of the very creature they were attacking only a second earlier.[20]

Mental Imagery   Try to imagine a circle. Now imagine a circle where the line marking its circumference is red. Now imagine a circle whose line marking its circumference is black and whose interior is red. Next, try to imagine a square. Now imagine a square whose interior is green. If you have been able to imagine or visualize these things, then one way of describing it is to say that you have had a series of mental images. These mental images are like pictures in your mind.

Where is New York City in relation to Philadelphia? If I'm asked this question, I imagine a map of the central Eastern part of the United States with points representing New York and Philadelphia. On my mental map, the point representing New York City is almost directly above the point representing Philadelphia. Knowing map conventions, I answer that New York City is almost due north of Philadelphia. I rely on mental imagery to answer the question. Suppose I ask you where Denver is in relation to Boston or what is the shape of Italy. How would you come up with the answers?

Suppose I ask you to describe an elephant and a giraffe. You might say that an elephant is large and stocky, that it has a trunk, and that it's gray. On the other hand, a giraffe is very tall and has a very long neck and long thin legs. It also is spotted, with brown and white the predominant colors. Do either of them have fur? You might know and say that elephants don't have fur but that giraffes do. But how do you know what they look like? Of course, you may have seen them in person or have seen pictures of them on television or in magazines, but if you're not now looking at pictures of them or at them in the flesh, how do you remember what they look like? One possibility is that you have mental images of them stored in memory and that you retrieved those images when I asked the question. You then in some sense "looked" at the images to describe an elephant and a giraffe. Mental states have the capacity to represent information and perhaps some of them represent information pictorially.

Behaviorists deny that we have mental images because mental images are not publicly observable. One way to answer that is to say that I know that I have mental images, and knowing that, I know that mental images exist. There is no argument that could persuade me that I don't have mental images. However, I don't know whether you have mental images. Only you can answer that. (Of course, you don't know that I have mental images, either, because I could be lying when I say I do.) However, since many people who appear to be pretty much like me have said that they have mental images and have described them, and since mental imagery

---

[20]Keeton and Gould, *Biological Science,* 521.

seems to be a crucial requirement for certain abilities (for example, the ability to know whether the Mediterranean Sea is at the north or south end of Africa and to describe what a bird looks like), it seems reasonable for me to believe that others also have mental images.

BRAIN TEASERS

Return to imaging an elephant. Is it facing right or left? If you can answer this question, does that show that mental images truly exist?

Are mental images objects in or states of a nonphysical mind, or instead do they at least supervene on the brain? Physicalists say that mentally picturing things to ourselves involves the brain storing images derived from perception (brain states represent the information pictorially) and then retrieving them.

What evidence do we have of the brain's responsibility for mental imagery? Certain kinds of brain damage impair the ability to form mental images. In addition, several ways of detecting brain activity have showed a variety of brain systems or areas becoming more active during mental imagery tasks. Also, as we might expect if we assume that having mental images is like actually seeing things and arises because the brain is able to store visual memories:

> in most but not all cases of selective visual impairments following damage to the cortical visual system, patients manifest qualitatively similar impairments in mental imagery and perception. This provides some evidence for the hypothesis that imagery and perception share at least some modality-specific cortical representations.[21]

That is, if a consequence of brain damage is that a subject cannot see a certain observable feature, she also cannot have those features in her mental images. So seeing an elephant and having a visual image of an elephant probably involve the use of some of the same areas and systems of the brain.

Thinking   Having minds, we're able to think. According to Physicalism, we think with our brains, not with something nonphysical. What is thinking? Is there any evidence that it's our brains that think?

According to Stephen Kosslyn, a Harvard psychologist,

> The term *thinking* is notoriously vague, but we can all agree that it hinges on two kinds of properties. First, information must be represented

---

[21]Martha J. Farah, "The Neural Bases of Mental Imagery," in *The Cognitive Neurosciences*, 968.

internally; and second, that information must be manipulated in order to draw inferences and conclusions. Most of what we mean by "thinking" corresponds to reasoning, to determining what follows from specific circumstances or how to reach a goal given a set of initial conditions.[22]

Suppose I give you two items of information—(1) either A killed B or B killed A and (2) A didn't kill B—and ask you what follows from that information. (What does follow from it?) If you answer that B killed A follows from it, you were thinking. Similarly, suppose I give you the information that twenty percent of college freshmen smoke and that C is a college freshman, and then ask you what follows from that. (What does follow from that?) You might reply that there's a twenty percent probability that C smokes and an eighty percent probability that C doesn't smoke. If I then give you the information that only ten percent of female college freshmen smoke and that C is a female, you will probably revise your answer. Again, you were thinking.

Thinking is a mental process. It doesn't always lead to observable behavior. I assume that you were reading the previous paragraph to yourself and that if you were answering the questions, you did nothing that could count as observable behavior. Some behaviorists say that thinking is simply talking to oneself or self-talk. However, neither talking to oneself nor self-talk can possibly count as observable behavior. (Who is talking to whom if I am talking to myself? If I utter no sounds, and do not open my mouth, move my lips and tongue, or use my vocal cords, what observable behavior have I engaged in?) Thinking occurs internally.

If I can't tell that you're thinking just by observing you, can there be any evidence that the brain is involved in thinking? Psychologists have devised a number of interesting experiments that give information about the brain's activity during thinking.

Subjects were asked to silently start with 100 and continue subtracting seven from it. After performing the task they were asked the results. Then they were asked to subtract three from a series of numbers starting with fifty and to continue even to negative numbers. In another experiment, subjects were asked to say to themselves a well-known jingle, then say it again to themselves deleting every third word. In yet another experiment, subjects were asked to visualize walking out the front door of their houses and alternately turning left then right at each corner. They were asked after a minute or two where they were.

During these processes, the psychologists measured regional cerebral blood flow (rCBF) throughout the brain. (Researchers assume that increased blood flow to an area of the brain indicates that increased brain activity is occurring in that area.) They found an increase in rCBF in a variety of regions of the brain during these thinking tasks; however, the regions activated for one thinking task were not exactly the same as those

---

[22]Stephen M. Kosslyn, *The Cognitive Neurosciences*, 959.

activated for another thinking task.[23] This seems to suggest that thinking is caused by or depends on the brain's activity.

Conclusions

Research on the brain is still in its early stages. But Physicalists maintain that what we have already learned about the brain makes it plausible that what Cartesian Dualists have called the mind is nothing but the brain, a purely physical object. In their view, the results of research strongly suggest that mental states are physical states of or realized in the brain rather than nonphysical states of or in a nonphysical substance.

The dependence of the mental on brain activity seems undeniable. If the area of the brain responsible for a certain form of perception is damaged or destroyed, the relevant sense is impaired or destroyed. For example, one may become blind or suffer hearing impairment. If the area of the brain responsible for speech is damaged, one may no longer be able to speak. Similarly, memories may be erased as a result of brain damage. Electrically stimulating certain areas of a patient's brain can produce certain emotions and feelings, including fear, isolation or loneliness, disgust, sorrow and depression, anxiety, guilt, ecstasy, and sexual excitation.[24] Thought and emotion are also affected by chemical changes in the blood that affect the brain. Drugs can induce hallucinations, reduce anxiety or depression, bring on euphoria, reduce aggressiveness, and so on. Certain drugs or brain injuries can drastically alter a person's whole personality. Surely, Physicalists say, all these things show that the mind is the brain.

What Are We?

Physicalists maintain that we're composed only of physical stuff, even if some of them think that we have mental states that are not identical or reducible to physical states. But many people disagree and claim that we have a nonphysical part. Some say we have two parts, others three. For example, Descartes believed that we have two parts, a physical body and a nonphysical mind. He identified the soul with the mind. Others say that we have a physical body and two nonphysical parts, one the mind, the other the soul or spirit. Thus, we are three rather than two. Perhaps some people think we are composed of four or five parts, only one of them physical.

---

[23]P. E. Roland and L. Friberg, "Localization of cortical areas activated by thinking." In *Frontiers in Cognitive Neuroscience,* ed. Stephen M. Kosslyn and Richard A. Anderson (Cambridge, MA: MIT Press, 1992).

[24]"Brain Development" in *The Oxford Companion to the Mind,* ed. R. L. Gregory (New York: Oxford University Press, 1987), 527–529.

It's difficult to see how we can employ scientific methods to ascertain how many nonphysical parts we have when we can't use scientific methods to ascertain whether we have any nonphysical parts at all. How can we know how many nonphysical parts we have? Is it two or a hundred and two? And what are the differences between mind on the one hand and soul or spirit on the other if we say that they are different entities? Perhaps we could provide functional definitions for them in terms of what they do, defining a mind as what does so-and-so and a soul or spirit as what does such-and-such.

Of course, none of the research on the brain proves that we are not composed of nonphysical as well as physical stuff. But Physicalists say it's a lot simpler to say we're composed only of physical stuff. We avoid a lot of insoluble puzzles and arbitrary speculation that way. And they say that claiming we're composed of one or more nonphysical parts doesn't help us to explain anything in compensation for the increased complexity. So, what are we? Are we composed only of physical stuff or are we a combination of matter combined with nonphysical stuff?

Self-Knowledge

According to Plato, inscribed over the Temple of Apollo at Delphi were the words, "Know thyself." What kind of knowledge did Apollo mean? If I know my name, height, weight, birth date, and occupation, do I know myself? If that's all I know about myself, I don't know much. Apollo surely meant that we should know our own inner selves, our own minds. We are directed by Apollo to know our own mental states—what we believe, want, like, dislike, love, hate, fear, worship, respect, and care about. We are directed to know our own character, personality, values, capabilities, attitudes, and preferences.

At first, we might think that nothing could be simpler. Of course I know myself and you know yourself. After all, common sense says that we each have privileged access to our own minds. That means that I have direct access to and can know the contents of my mind but not yours and you have direct access to and can know the contents of your mind but not mine. I can't know what you're thinking, what you want, believe, and feel, but you can. I can't feel your pains and itches, but you can.

But immediately, a question arises about privileged access. Some people claim that they can read minds, that they can know immediately and directly what someone else is thinking and feeling. They claim it's not based on inferences from the individual's behavior but rather based on a kind of direct access to the individual's mind. So maybe our access to our own minds isn't so privileged after all.

BRAIN TEASERS

Do some people truly have the ability to read other people's minds? If yes, how might we explain such an ability?

The common sense conception of privileged access has two other aspects. One is infallibility, the other is omniscience. If we are infallible regarding our own minds, it means that we can't possibly be mistaken if we believe something about ourselves. Necessarily, if we believe it, it's true. Thus, suppose that I seem to hear a sound. I could be mistaken if I believe that I really do hear a sound, but could I possibly be mistaken in believing that I seem to hear a sound, that I'm having a particular auditory experience? If my knowledge of my own mind is infallible, then the answer is no. Or suppose I believe that I prefer steak to lobster or believe that I'm sad. Could I possibly be mistaken about that? Not if I have infallible knowledge of my own mind. If we are omniscient regarding our own minds, then we are necessarily aware of our own mental states; they cannot be hidden from us. Thus, if you dislike the color blue, then you must be aware of it and know that you dislike the color blue.

If we have infallible and omniscient knowledge of ourselves, then knowing ourselves is easy. It just requires that we turn our attention inward on ourselves rather than outward on the world. But Plato thought that the task of knowing ourselves is one of the most difficult (and important) we face. In fact, he probably thought that few of us really know ourselves well. How can that be?

First, it's doubtful that we have infallible knowledge about ourselves. We often speak of self-deception, for one thing. For example, we might say that people often think they're braver, smarter, kinder, more tolerant, and more generous than they really are. Consider yourself. Suppose you believe that you love (in the sense of romantic love) a certain person. Could you be mistaken? Many people think you could be. So it's doubtful that we have infallible knowledge of our own minds.

BRAIN TEASERS

Even if we don't have infallible knowledge of all of our own mental states, might we have infallible knowledge of some of them? That is, might there be some mental states that, if we believe we have them, we couldn't possibly be mistaken about it? If yes, which ones?

What about omniscience? Is it impossible to have any of our own mental states hidden from us? Could we have desires, fears, attitudes, and beliefs that we're not aware of? Many people think it is possible. For example, they say that you could think that you're free of prejudice when in fact you're not. You could be prejudiced about anything from race, ethnicity, and religion, to accent, sexual orientation, and body shape, and yet not be aware of it. In fact, even if you reflected on it, you still might not be aware of it. You could value money more than anything and be unaware of it. If they're right, then we don't have omniscient knowledge of our own minds, either.

BRAIN TEASERS

Even if we don't have omniscient knowledge of all of our own mental states, might we have omniscient knowledge of some of them? That is, might there be some mental states that could not possibly be hidden from us? If yes, which ones?

If we don't have infallible or omniscient knowledge of our own minds, then the task of knowing ourselves isn't as easy as was first suggested. There are three stumbling blocks. One is that most of the time most of us have our attention directed outward rather than inward. The technical term for directing our attention inward is introspection. Many of us are not very introspective. Perhaps our culture does not encourage us to be introspective and know ourselves. Second, even if we become introspective, we can deceive ourselves about ourselves because we're capable of a lot of self-deception. Finally, even if we become introspective, a lot about ourselves may remain hidden from us unless we dig deeply and work hard at it. Even then, things may remain hidden.

BRAIN TEASERS

Why do you think that Apollo considered it very important for us to know ourselves? Do you agree with him?

Death

We saw early in this chapter that souls have been used to explain death. That is, if souls are necessary for life, then obviously, when a soul detaches itself from a body, that body can no longer live. If Physicalists don't believe in souls, how do they think of and explain death?

Suppose that you stop breathing. Are you dead? Today, doctors say not necessarily. With the proper treatment provided swiftly enough, you could start breathing again and return to normal functioning. That's what happens sometimes when people who are drowning are rescued and artificial respiration revives them. But suppose your heart stops beating.

Surely you're dead then. Again, not necessarily. Heart attack victims have had their hearts restarted when they receive prompt medical attention.

Well then, when are you declared dead? The ultimate test of death that has been widely accepted in this century is brain death. An EEG measures the electrical activity of our brains. As long as there is a certain amount of electrical activity in the various parts of our brains, our brains are still alive and functioning. However, if there is no electrical activity in your brain as measured by two consecutive EEGs separated by at least twenty four hours, you're declared brain dead. Brain dead means dead. Even if you're still breathing and your heart is beating because you're on life-support, you're dead.

Physicalists ask how appeal to a nonphysical part helps us explain death. To them, death is straightforwardly physical. The brain dies; the systems and activities controlled by the brain (consciousness, respiration, digestion, secretion of hormones, muscular movements) permanently cease to function. Cells throughout the body die, no longer nourished by the blood. The body begins to disintegrate. We don't need to explain the death of the cells by saying that their souls left them. We don't need to explain the system shutdowns by appeal to souls that are responsible for their functioning. (Does a soul cause the heart to beat and one's lungs to take in oxygen and transfer it to the blood?) The brain dies because its cells die.

If you have a soul and it's different from your mind, what does it do? What is its function? Why does it leave your body when your brain dies?

 PLATO (427 B.C.–347 B.C.)

PHAEDO

Come, then, [Socrates] said, let me try to make my defence to you more convincing than it was to the jury. For, Simmias and Cebes, I should be wrong not to resent dying if I did not believe that I should go first to other wise and good gods, and then to men who have died and are better than men are here. Be assured that, as it is, I expect to join the company of good men. This last I would not altogether insist on, but if I insist on anything at all in these matters, it is that I shall come to gods who are very good masters. That is why I am not so resentful, because I have good hope that some future awaits men after death, as we have been told for years, a much better future for the good than for the wicked.

Well now, Socrates, said Simmias, do you intend to keep this belief to yourself as you leave us, or would you share it with us? I certainly think it would be a blessing for us too, and at the same time it would be your defence if you convince us of what you say.

I will try, he said. . . .

Do we believe that there is such a thing as death?

Certainly, said Simmias.

Is it anything else than the separation of the soul from the body? Do we believe that death is this, namely, that the body comes to be separated by itself apart from the soul, and the soul comes to be separated by itself apart from the body? Is death anything else than that?

No, that is what it is, he said. . . .

When Socrates finished, Cebes intervened: Socrates, he said, . . . men . . . think that after it [the soul] has left the body it no longer exists anywhere, but that it is destroyed and dissolved on the day the man dies, as soon as it leaves the body; and that, on leaving it, it is dispersed like breath or smoke, has flown away and gone and is no longer anything anywhere. If indeed it gathered itself together and existed by itself and escaped those evils you were recently enumerating, there would then be much good hope, Socrates, that what you say is true; but to believe this requires a good deal of faith and persuasive argument, to believe that the soul still exists after a man has died and that it still possesses some capability and intelligence.

What you say is true, Cebes, Socrates said, but what shall we do? Do you want to discuss whether this is likely to be true or not?

Personally, said Cebes, I should like to hear your opinion on the subject. . . .

. . . Let us examine it in some such a manner as this [said Socrates]: whether the souls of men who have died exist in the underworld or not. We recall an ancient theory that souls arriving there come from here, and then again that they arrive here and are born here from the dead. If that is true, that the living come back from the dead, then surely our souls must exist there, for they could not come back if they did not exist, and this is a sufficient proof that these things are so if it truly appears that the living never come from any other source than from the dead. If this is not the case we should need another argument.

Quite so, said Cebes.

Do not, he said, confine yourself to humanity if you want to understand this more readily, but take all animals and all plants into account, and, in short, for all things which come to be, let us see whether they come to be in this way, that is, from their opposites if

they have such, as the beautiful is the opposite of the ugly and the just of the unjust, and a thousand other things of the kind. Let us examine whether those that have an opposite must necessarily come to be from their opposite and from nowhere else, as for example when something comes to be larger it must necessarily become larger from having been smaller before.

Yes.

Then if something smaller comes to be, it will come from something larger before, which became smaller?

That is so, he said.

And the weaker comes to be from the stronger, and the swifter from the slower?

Certainly.

Further, if something worse comes to be, does it not come from the better, and the juster from the more unjust?

Of course.

So we have sufficiently established that all things come to be in this way, opposites from opposites?

Certainly.

There is a further point, something such as this, about these opposites: between each of those pairs of opposites there are two processes: from the one to the other and then again from the other to the first; between the larger and the smaller there is increase and decrease, and we call the one increasing and the other decreasing?

Yes, he said.

And so too there is separation and combination, cooling and heating, and all such things, even if sometimes we do not have a name for the process, but in fact it must be everywhere that they come to be from one another, and that there is a process of becoming from each into the other?

Assuredly, he said.

Well then, is there an opposite to living, as sleeping is the opposite of being awake?

Quite so, he said.

What is it?

Being dead, he said.

Therefore, if these are opposites, they come to be from one another, and there are two processes of generation between the two?

Of course.

I will tell you, said Socrates, one of the two pairs I was just talking about, the pair itself and the two processes, and you will tell me the other. I mean, to sleep and to be awake, to be awake comes from sleeping, and to sleep comes from being awake. Of the two processes one is going to sleep, the other is waking up. Do you accept that, or not?

Certainly.

You tell me in the same way about life and death. Do you not say that to be dead is the opposite of being alive?

I do.

And they come to be from one another?

Yes.

What comes to be from being alive?

Being dead.

And what comes to be from being dead?

One must agree that it is being alive.

Then, Cebes, living creatures and things come to be from the dead?

So it appears, he said.

Then our souls exist in the underworld.

That seems likely.

Then in this case one of the two processes of becoming is clear, for dying is clear enough, is it not?

It certainly is.

What shall we do then? Shall we not supply the opposite process of becoming? Is nature to be lame in this case? Or must we provide a process of becoming opposite to dying?

We surely must.

And what is that?

Coming to life again.

Therefore, he said, if there is such a thing as coming to life again, it would be a process of coming from the dead to the living?

Quite so.

It is agreed between us then that the living come from the dead in this way no less than the dead from the living and, if that is so, it seems to be a sufficient proof that the souls of the dead must be somewhere whence they can come back again.

I think, Socrates, he said, that this follows from what we have agreed on.

Consider in this way, Cebes, he said, that, as I think, we were not wrong to agree. If the two processes of becoming did not always balance each other as if they were going round in a circle, but generation proceeded from one point to its opposite in a straight line and it did not turn back again to the other opposite or take any turning, do you realize that all things would ultimately have the same form, be affected in the same way, and cease to become?

How do you mean? he said.

. . . My dear Cebes, if everything that partakes of life were to die and remain in that state and not come to life again, would not everything ultimately have to be dead and nothing alive? Even if the living came from some other source, and all that lived died, how could all things avoid being absorbed in death?

It could not be, Socrates, said Cebes, and I think what you say is altogether true.

I think, Cebes, said he, that this is very definitely the case and that we were not deceived when we agreed on this: coming to life again in truth exists, the living come to be from the dead, and the souls of the dead exist. . . .

[Cebes] is sufficiently convinced I think, said Simmias, though he is the most difficult of men to persuade by argument, but I believe him to be fully convinced that our soul existed before we were born. I do not think myself, however, that it has been proved that the soul continues to exist after death; the opinion of the majority which Cebes mentioned still stands, that when a man dies his soul is dispersed and this is the end of its existence. What is to prevent the soul coming to be and being constituted from some other source, existing before it enters a human body and then, having done so and departed from it, itself dying and being destroyed?

You are right, Simmias, said Cebes. Half of what needed proof has been proved, namely, that our soul existed before we were born, but further proof is needed that it exists no less after we have died, if the proof is to be complete.

It has been proved even now, Simmias and Cebes, said Socrates, if you are ready to combine this argument with the one we agreed on before, that every living thing must come from the dead. If the soul exists before, it must, as it comes to life and birth, come from nowhere else than death and being dead, so how could it avoid existing after death since it must be born again? What you speak of has then even now been proved. However, I think you and Simmias would like to discuss the argument more fully. . . .

We must then ask ourselves something like this: what kind of thing is likely to be scattered? On behalf of what kind of thing should one fear this, and for what kind of thing should one not fear it? We should then examine to which class the soul belongs, and as a result either fear for the soul or be of good cheer.

What you say is true.

Is not anything that is composite and a compound by nature liable to be split up into its component parts, and only that which is noncomposite, if anything, is not likely to be split up?

I think that is the case, said Cebes.

Are not the things that always remain the same and in the same state most likely not to be composite, whereas those that vary from one time to another and are never the same are composite?

I think that is so. . . .

And the invisible always remains the same, whereas the visible never does?

Let us assume that too.

Now one part of ourselves is the body, another part is the soul.

Quite so.

To which class of existence do we say the body is more alike and akin?

To the visible, as anyone can see.

What about the soul? Is it visible or invisible?

It is not visible to men, Socrates, he said.

Well, we meant visible and invisible to human eyes; or to any others, do you think?

To human eyes.

Then what do we say about the soul? Is it visible or not visible?

Not visible.

So it is invisible?

Yes.

So the soul is more like the invisible than the body, and the body more like the visible?

Without any doubt, Socrates. . . .

Judging from what we have said before and what we are saying now, to which of these two kinds do you think that the soul is more alike and more akin?

I think, Socrates, he said, that on this line of argument any man, even the dullest, would agree that the soul is altogether more like that which always exists in the same state rather than like that which does not.

What of the body?

That is like the other.

Look at it also this way: when the soul and the body are together, nature orders the one to be subject and to be ruled, and the other to rule and be master. Then again, which do you think is like the divine and which like the mortal? Do you not think that the nature of the divine is to rule and to lead, whereas it is that of the mortal to be ruled and be subject?

I do.

Which does the soul resemble?

Obviously, Socrates, the soul resembles the divine, and the body resembles the mortal.

Consider then, Cebes, whether it follows from all that has been said that the soul is most like the divine, deathless, intelligible, uniform, indissoluble, always the same as itself, whereas the body is most like that which is human, mortal, multiform, unintelligible, soluble and never consistently the same. Have we anything else to say to show, my dear Cebes, that this is not the case?

We have not.

Well then, that being so, is it not natural for the body to dissolve easily, and for the soul to be altogether indissoluble, or nearly so?

Of course.

You realize, he said, that when a man dies, the visible part, the body, which exists in the visible world, and which we call the corpse, whose natural lot it would be to dissolve, fall apart and be blown away, does not immediately suffer any of these things but remains for a fair time, in fact, quite a long time if the man dies with his body in a suitable condition and at a favourable season? If the body is emaciated or embalmed, as in Egypt, it remains almost whole for a remarkable length of time, and even if the body decays, some parts of it, namely bones and sinews and the like, are nevertheless, one might say, deathless. Is that not so?

Yes.

Will the soul, the invisible part which makes its way to a region of the same kind, noble and pure and invisible, to Hades in fact, to the good and wise god whither, god willing, my soul must soon be going—will the soul, being of this kind and nature, be scattered and destroyed on leaving the body, as the majority of men say? Far from it, my dear Cebes and Simmias, but what happens is much more like this: if it is pure when it leaves the body and drags nothing bodily with it, as it had no willing association with the body in life, but avoided it and gathered itself together by itself and always practised this, which is no other than practising philosophy in the right way, in fact, training to die easily. Or is this not training for death?

It surely is.

A soul in this state makes its way to the invisible, which is like itself, the divine and immortal and wise, and arriving there it can be happy, having rid itself of confusion, ignorance, fear, violent desires and the other human ills and, as is said of the initiates, truly spend the rest of time with the gods. Shall we say this, Cebes, or something different?

This, by Zeus, said Cebes.

But I think that if the soul is polluted and impure when it leaves the body, having always been associated with it and served it, bewitched by physical desires and pleasures to the point at which nothing seems to exist for it but the physical, which one can touch and see or eat and drink or make use of for sexual enjoyment, and if that soul is accustomed to hate and fear and avoid that which is dim and invisible to the eyes but intelligible and to be grasped by philosophy—do you think such a soul will escape pure and by itself?

Impossible, he said.

It is no doubt permeated by the physical, which constant intercourse and association with the body, as well as considerable practice, has caused to become ingrained in it?

Quite so.

We must believe, my friend, that this bodily element is heavy, ponderous, earthy and visible. Through it, such a soul has become heavy and is dragged back to the visible region in fear of the unseen and of Hades. It wanders, as we are told, around graves and monuments, where shadowy phantoms, images that such souls produce, have been seen, souls that have not been freed and purified but share in the visible, and are therefore seen.

That is likely, Socrates.

It is indeed, Cebes. Moreover, these are not the souls of good but of inferior men, which are forced to wander there, paying the penalty for their previous bad upbringing. They wander until their longing for that which accompanies them, the physical, again imprisons them in a body, and they are then, as is likely, bound to such characters as they have practised in their life.

What kind of characters do you say these are, Socrates?

Those, for example, who have carelessly practised gluttony, violence and drunkenness are likely to join a company of donkeys or of similar animals. Do you not think so?

Very likely.

Those who have esteemed injustice highly, and tyranny and plunder will join the tribes of wolves and hawks and kites, or where else shall we say that they go?

Certainly to those, said Cebes.

And clearly, the destination of the others will conform to the way in which they have behaved?

Clearly, of course.

The happiest of these, who will also have the best destination, are those who have practised popular and social virtue, which they call moderation and justice and which was developed by habit and practice, without philosophy or understanding?

How are they the happiest?

Because it is likely that they will again join a social and gentle group, either of bees or wasps or ants, and then again the same kind of human group, and so be moderate men.

That is likely. . . .

Questions for Discussion and Review

1. What's the difference between saying that something exists and saying that it's alive?

2. Can appeal to anything nonphysical help us explain either life or death?

3. How might we explain how a nonphysical soul enables a physical organism to reproduce and grow?

4. Consider the robots from the *Star Wars* motion pictures, as well as the android Data from *Star Trek: The Next Generation*. If they really existed, would they be alive? Would they be conscious and have mental states?

5. Do you think it's possible to create machines—robots or androids—capable of having mental states and capable of being conscious? Would it require giving a machine a nonphysical mind or soul? What, if anything, does your answer presuppose about the truth of Dualism?

6. Are you conscious? Do you have mental states? How do you know?

7. Do you think that other human beings are conscious and have mental states? Why or why not?

8. Do only human beings have mental states? If not, what other living beings do you think can have mental states? What kind of mental states do you think they can have? What evidence or arguments do you have to support your views?

9. If other living beings besides humans have mental states, does that mean that they are composed of physical and nonphysical substance joined together?

10. Philosophical behaviorists claim that there are no good reasons to attribute mental states to any beings, even human beings. They say that we can explain both human and animal behavior completely and adequately without having to appeal to the being's mental states. Do you agree? Why or why not?

11. If we humans have mental states, do you think that they are identical to or reducible to physical properties of our brains? Why/Why not?

12. What do you know about yourself? How would you answer the question, "Who are you?" How do you know these things about yourself?

13. Do you have infallible knowledge of any of your own mental states?

14. Can any of your own mental states be hidden from you? Are there any that could not possibly be hidden from you? How might we explain how some of our own mental states can be hidden from us?

Suggestions for Further Reading

Aristotle. *On the Soul*. A classic treatment of the relation between soul and body. (Many editions.)

Brian Beakley and Peter Ludlow, eds. *The Philosophy of Mind: Classical Problems/Contemporary Issues*. Cambridge, MA: MIT Press, 1992. An excellent anthology blending classical and contemporary philosophers.

Quassim Cassam, ed. *Self-Knowledge*. Oxford: Oxford University Press, 1994. A collection of articles by contemporary philosophers in the prestigious Oxford Readings in Philosophy series. Some of the articles are quite advanced, but several are fairly accessible to interested students.

Paul M. Churchland. *Matter and Consciousness*. Cambridge, MA: MIT Press, 1984. The first part provides a brief, readable, lively, and authoritative introduction to many of the issues of this chapter.

René Descartes. *Meditations on First Philosophy*. Descartes's classic work, a must for anyone interested in the issue of the relation between mind and body. See especially Meditation 6.

Owen Flanagan. *Consciousness Reconsidered*. Cambridge, MA: MIT Press, 1992. An attempt to defend Physicalism.

R. L. Gregory, ed. *The Oxford Companion to the Mind*. New York: Oxford University Press, 1987. A wonderful source of information on a huge variety of topics relating to the issues of this chapter. It contains brief, encyclopedia-like entries that are fun just to browse through.

Jaegwon Kim. *Philosophy of Mind*. Boulder, CO: Westview Press, 1996. A rigorous and complete survey of the issues by one of the leading philosophers in the field. Suitable mainly for advanced students.

Wallace Matson. *A New History of Philosophy*, vols. 1 and 2. New York: Harcourt Brace Jovanovich, 1987. A brief, readable, reliable account of the views of the most important philosophers in the Western tradition. Volume 1 contains chapters on Plato and Aristotle. Volume 2 contains a chapter on Descartes.

Plato. *Phaedo*, in *Plato: Complete Works*, John Cooper, ed. Indianapolis: Hackett, 1997. An entertaining and moving discussion of the existence and immortality of the soul.

David Rosenthal, ed. *The Nature of Mind*. New York: Oxford University Press, 1991. An excellent anthology of recent articles by eminent philosophers.

PERSONAL IMMORTALITY AND PERSONAL IDENTITY

Objectives

Students are expected to:

- understand the concept of a person.
- understand the role that our bodies play in personal identity, whether they are necessary or sufficient for it.
- understand the Same Body criterion of personal identity.
- understand the Same Soul criterion of personal identity.
- understand the Same Psychological Essence criterion of personal identity.
- understand the Continuity of Consciousness criterion of personal identity.
- understand what must continue to exist if a person is to continue to exist after the body's death.

Introduction

You have a present life that extends backward into the past and forward into the future. What ties together this past, present, and future into *Yours truly,* past, present, and future? What makes you the same person as the infant born roughly two decades ago and the middle-aged person who'll exist two decades from now? What will happen to you when your body dies? Will you continue to exist? If so, how? For how long? A year? A decade? A century? Forever? In this chapter we'll examine the possibility of existence after death and its relation to the issue of personal identity. We will examine several criteria of personal identity: (1) the Same Body criterion, (2) the Same Soul criterion, (3) the Same Psychological Essence criterion, and (4) the Continuity of Consciousness criterion.

We ended the last chapter with a brief discussion of death. Many people are uncomfortable thinking or talking about death because they fear it so intensely. But not everyone fears it. Our attitude toward death is probably determined in part by our beliefs about what happens to us after death.

Some things about death are obvious. When we die, most parts of our bodies disintegrate pretty quickly. After a few months, about all that's left of us are bones. Our bones could continue to exist for a long time. After all, we have discovered fossilized bones of dinosaurs that are hundreds of millions of years old. Even if our bones aren't fossilized, they will probably continue to exist for centuries after the rest of our bodies have disintegrated.

Suppose that I die in 2048 at the grand old age of 100, and that by 2049, all that's left of me is my bones. What happened to me? Some people say that I have simply ceased to exist. There is no more me. I'm gone forever; I'll never return. Others, however, say that I probably still exist even though my body has been reduced to a pile of bones. But how could I still exist? Part of the puzzlement I feel may be over the question of who or what I am. What is the "me" (Emmett Barcalow) that still exists? Surely I'm not just a pile of bones. But if I'm not just a pile of bones, who or what am I?

Obviously, I'm not just a pile of bones, but perhaps I am nothing but this physical body that has not yet died and disintegrated, whose fingers are now typing the words of this sentence. In that case, my existence began when this body was born (or was conceived) and it will end when this body dies and disintegrates into a pile of bones or dust. When it's gone, I'm gone. But is that plausible? Am I really nothing but my body? Are you really nothing but your body?

Suppose you lost both your arms and legs. You'd have lost a good part of your body. Suppose further that your eyes, heart, lungs, kidneys, and liver were removed and replaced with artificial organs. (We're imagining that medical science has advanced considerably.) You'd have lost even more of your body. Now how much of you would remain? Would that still be you? I think that most of us would say that it would still be you, the same person, even though your body has undergone drastic alterations. But why would most people say that it would still be you, that you're the same person even though your body has changed?

Surely not all of our properties are equally central to who we are. If my physical appearance changed completely because I was burned in a fire, losing all my limbs, transforming my flesh so that my face now bears no resemblance to my face before the fire, my major internal organs being replaced by artificial ones, I still think it would be me, Emmett Barcalow. (Of course, my transformation would probably have a profound impact on me. For example, I would probably feel depressed and angry.) So what's essential to being me?

BRAIN TEASERS

If I underwent all these changes, do you think it would still be me? Why/Why not?

Let's approach the same issue from a slightly different angle. Suppose that someone claims to love you. You ask why. The individual says, "Because you're young, beautiful/handsome, well built, and strong." That might satisfy you, but suppose you ask anyway, "What else about me do you love?" The individual replies, "Nothing. That's it." You press harder. "Surely there are other things about me you like or love." The reply: "Oh, yes. You're rich and famous. I love that about you, too." Nonplussed, you ask, "But what about when I grow old and I'm no longer handsome or beautiful? What if I'm also no longer rich and famous? Will you still love me?" Suppose the individual replied, "Of course not."

We generally call people like that superficial. What do we mean? We mean that they only care about our physical appearance or our bodies, that they ignore or fail to value what we think of as most central to ourselves, to who or what we are. But what things are those? If they're not our purely physical properties, then they must be our mental properties, such things as our knowledge, character, personality, and values. It matters whether we're sensitive or insensitive, kind or cruel, imaginative or unimaginative, warm-hearted or cold-hearted, friendly or unfriendly, introverted or extroverted, tolerant or intolerant, generous or miserly; it matters whether we have a sense of humor and what kind of sense of humor we have; it matters what our beliefs, values, preferences, interests, ideals, hopes, dreams, and plans are. We might say that the "outer you" is far less central to who you are than is the "inner you," that the "inner you" is the "real you."

This line of thinking suggests that our mental properties are what's essential to who we are, that our identities as persons are determined by our mental properties rather than by our physical properties. That would explain why I think it would still be me even if most of my physical properties have changed because my body was badly burned. It would still be me if my mental properties remain largely unchanged.

Death and Other Happenings

The question of what's essential to our identities as people is relevant to the issue of what happens to us after our bodies die. We'll still exist as the person we once were after our bodies die only if what's essential to us as people still exists. So we have to figure out what that is.

Suppose Joan claims that she'll still exist when her body dies. The "real" her, she says, what is most essential to her, the person she is, is not her physical properties but her mental properties. Being a Dualist, she explains that all her mental properties are embedded in her nonphysical mind or soul, so as long as her mind exists and contains her mental properties, she'll exist, and she'll be wherever her mind or soul is. Her body is not necessary for her continued existence as a person. Is she right?

We may also wonder whether we'll still exist even if our bodies haven't died and disintegrated. That is, are our bodies sufficient for our continued existence as people? If our bodies are still in existence and alive (lungs and heart working, etc.), do we still exist? Consider someone suffering from the end stages of Alzheimer's Disease. Let's call her Bonnie. Bonnie may no longer be able to remember or recognize her loved ones. She may not remember where she lives or know where she is at the current moment. She may not remember anything of her past life, even of the recent past, such as what she had for breakfast this morning. Her personality and character may have altered drastically. She may not be able to recognize ordinary objects any more, such as a set of keys. In a very real sense, she may not know who she is. Is she still the same person she was before the onset of Alzheimer's Disease? If not, is she literally a different person? Some would say it's the same person; others would say that Bonnie is gone and that a new person has taken her place.

Or consider someone lying in a hospital bed in a chronic vegetative state because of profound brain damage. Let's call him Bill. Suppose that all of Bill's consciousness has been permanently obliterated. He can no longer perceive, think, or dream. His memories are erased. He is no longer capable of having any mental states. Is it Bill lying in the bed? Is the *person* Bill, who existed prior to the damage to his brain, still in existence? Some would say it's still Bill, but others would say that the individual in the bed used to be Bill but is Bill no longer. Not that it's a new person taking his place. Rather it's not a person at all. The entity in the bed once embodied the person Bill, but it no longer embodies any person.

Again, suppose that Carla claims to be the reincarnation of Cleopatra. That is, she says that she is Cleopatra. Could she really be Cleopatra? What would have to be the case for her to really be the same person as Cleopatra? One thing seems to be certain. However beautiful she may be, her body isn't Cleopatra's because Cleopatra's body died and turned to dust a long time ago.

Then, too, suppose that John says that while his body was anesthetized on the operating table, he went roaming around the hospital peeking into every nook and cranny. He saw and heard a variety of things, then he returned to his body when it began to awaken from the effects of the anesthesia. Could he really have been roaming the hospital while his body was on the operating table? What would have to be the case for that to be true?

Science fiction and horror fantasy sometimes depict body exchanges. For example, a movie may show an evil person exchanging bodies with a good person, leaving the good person confined in the body that's about to be executed for the evil person's crimes. Are such things possible? What would have to be the case in order for it to be possible?

Finally, consider a newborn infant. Is it yet a person, or instead should we say that the infant will become a person as it develops? Some would say it is a person already; others would say that it will become a person in the future, whether it's a year, five years, or twenty years. Our answer depends on what we think is required to be a person in general, as well as what's required to be a specific individual person.

What Role Do Our Bodies Play in Personal Identity?

One way of expressing the issue brought up by the above examples is, "What role do our bodies play in personal identity?" There are several views we could take, depending on the answers we give to the following three questions: (1) Are our bodies necessary for personal identity? (2) Are our bodies sufficient for personal identity? (3) Are our bodies both necessary and sufficient for personal identity? If our bodies are necessary for personal identity, then you don't exist if your body doesn't exist and you exist only where your body exists. On the other hand, if our bodies are sufficient for personal identity, then if your body exists, you exist and you are where it is. Finally, if our bodies are both necessary and sufficient for personal identity, then you exist if and only if your body exists and you exist where and only where your body exists.

Are Our Bodies Necessary for Personal Identity?

Are our bodies necessary for personal identity? If yes, then Joan won't continue to exist as Joan when her body dies, Carla can't possibly be Cleopatra reincarnated, it wasn't John who was roaming the hospital while John's body was anesthetized on the operating table, and body exchanges are logically impossible. Some people say that if these things follow from the claim that our bodies are necessary for our personal identity, then our bodies aren't necessary for our identities as persons.

British philosopher Bernard Williams maintained that our bodies are necessary for personal identity. Why did he think that? He asks us to imagine that an individual, say Julian, claims to be the reincarnation of Julius Caesar.[1] That is, Julian claims that he is, or is identical to, Julius Caesar who once ruled Rome and was assassinated in 44 B.C.E. Of course, you'd be skeptical. (Who wouldn't?) But suppose he proceeds to speak perfect Latin (Caesar's native tongue) and we find out that he never studied or learned Latin. Then he tells us stories about his life and times. Experts in

---

[1]Actually, Williams uses Guy Fawkes as an example, but most of us in the United States know little or nothing about Guy Fawkes.

Roman history confirm their accuracy and say that only specialists could know all the things he knows. But further, he goes on to tell tales of Caesar's life that no one in the world knows about. He explains many of his actions that have puzzled historians for centuries. In fact, he exhibits all the personality and character traits historians have attributed to Caesar. But Julian's body is not identical to Julius Caesar's body. Caesar's body turned to dust ages ago.

Williams admits that if everything seems to fit, we may be sorely tempted to conclude that Julian really is Julius Caesar reincarnated. However, Williams points out that we're not forced to conclude that Julian really is Julius Caesar. We could say, instead, that Julian has a character and personality very like Caesar's and that he has acquired knowledge of Caesar's life and past, including the language he spoke and wrote, in ways we're not familiar with, such as clairvoyance. His memories of Caesar's life are vicarious. He can't remember these experiences the way that Caesar could (from the inside, as it were) because he, Julian, wasn't there. (His body certainly wasn't there.)

But why resist the temptation to conclude that he really is Julius Caesar reincarnated? Why say that because his body is not identical to Caesar's body, he can't really be Caesar? The problem, as Williams sees it, is that this claim might lead to a violation of a basic logical rule of identity: It's necessarily true that if A = C and B = C, then A = B. Williams points out that it's possible that someone else besides Julian, call him Gulian, could be in the very same situation, claiming to be the reincarnation of Julius Caesar and presenting the exact same case for his claim as Julian. If we admit that Julian is Julius Caesar, then we must admit that Gulian is Julius Caesar, too. But then two different individuals in two different bodies at different spatial locations would be identical to each other. They'd be the same person! If Julian = Julius Caesar and Gulian = Julius Caesar, then Julian = Gulian. Williams points out that that would be absurd and logically impossible.[2]

How can we avoid such absurdity? According to Williams, we should deny that either Julian or Gulian is Julius Caesar. On what grounds? Because neither has a body that is identical to Julius Caesar's body. How can we make precise this claim of Williams?

Questions or assertions of identity generally presuppose a context that involves time. For example, police might wonder whether the person they have in custody now is (is identical to) the person who committed a specific murder last month. Or you might wonder whether the person you saw yesterday in the supermarket is (is identical to) the person who taught your first grade class. The general form of an identity question is

---

[2]Bernard Williams, "Personal Identity and Individuation," in *Problems of the Self: Philosophical Papers, 1956–1972* (Cambridge: Cambridge University Press, 1973).

something like this: Is x at time t_1 the same person as y at time t_2? Thus, according to Williams,

> person x at t_1 is identical to (is the same person as) y at t_2 only if x's body at t_1 is identical to (is the same body as) y's body at t_2.

BRAIN TEASERS

What makes x's body at t_1 identical to or the very same body as y's body at t_2?

Aristotle tells about the ship of Theseus. Let's call it the *Argo*. When it was built, it was in perfect condition. But over the years, many parts deteriorated and had to be replaced. Sails went first. Then ropes. Then planks. After many years, every single part of the ship had been replaced. Not one of its original parts remained. Is it still the same ship, the *Argo*?

But is Williams right? If the view that Julian at t is Julius Caesar reincarnated might lead us to say on the same grounds that Gulian, too, at t is Julius Caesar reincarnated, we seem to have a problem. Could two different individuals in two different bodies in two different places really be the same person?

Here's one possible response. Suppose that Julian and Gulian were born the very same instant, t_1, in two different places and that they claim that at birth they were each reincarnations of Julius Caesar, who was born in 100 B.C.E. (The same reasoning will apply whenever they were born and whenever they claim to have become reincarnations of Julius Caesar.) Once they were born, we could say that Julian is reincarnation A and Gulian is reincarnation B of Julius Caesar. Through time, reincarnation A has a whole new set of experiences, a new life history to add to the base of Julius Caesar's history. Similarly, reincarnation B has a new set of experiences, a new life history, that are different from those of A. Incarnation A is then made up of Julius Caesar's life plus Julian's life. Incarnation B is made up of Julius Caesar's life added to Gulian's life. The instant that Julius Caesar was reincarnated into two different bodies, he divided into two separate people. But both A and B are incarnations of Julius Caesar, although after t_1 their life paths diverge. Both have an existence going back to 100 B.C.E. when Julius Caesar was born. Now, at time t_2, A and B are not the same person, although both are reincarnations of Julius Caesar. We might diagram the situation like this.

		$-----$ Julius Caesar A (Julian)
Julius Caesar $-----$		
		$-----$ Julius Caesar B (Gulian)
100 B.C.E.	t_1	t_2

If this makes sense, then Williams's argument does not seem to show that our bodies are necessary for personal identity.

BRAIN TEASERS

Can you think of any other arguments that might show that our bodies are necessary for personal identity?

Are Our Bodies Sufficient for Personal Identity?

Are our bodies sufficient for personal identity? That is, if at t_1 body x is Julian, then if at t_2 that same body still exists and lives, must it still be Julian? If yes, then the individual suffering from the end stages of Alzheimer's Disease is still literally the same person she was before the onset of her disease, the individual in a chronic vegetative state is still the same person he was and that person still exists, and again, body exchanges are impossible.

In the movie *Total Recall*, the character played by Arnold Schwarzenegger discovers one day that he is not the person he thought he was. He discovers that someone wiped out all his real memories and replaced them with false memories. He remembers nothing of his real past life. Instead, he thinks that he's been married for many years to a woman he's only known for a few weeks, and he seems to remember details of their life together, a life he never really had. More than his memories have been changed. He has had a complete personality and character alteration. He was a bad guy, the ruthless right-hand man of a tyrant. After the transformation, he's a good guy. He has a totally new set of values and principles. A variety of virtues have replaced his vices. He learns about the transformation near the end of the movie. As a bad guy, he had agreed to undergo the transformation so that he could infiltrate a group of freedom fighters led by someone who could read minds. Only if Arnold's mind was altered could he hide who he is from the leader. Now Arnold knows who he is. Or is it who he was? His boss wants to transform him back into the bad guy he was. But Arnold doesn't want to be transformed back into a bad guy. He wants to remain the good guy he is.

Suppose that the transformation occurred at time t_2. At an earlier time, t_1, Arnold was a bad guy. At t_3, Arnold was a good guy who didn't want to be transformed back into the bad guy he was. At t_4, alas, his boss has transformed him back into the bad guy he was at t_1 by returning his original (real) memories to him and altering his personality, character, beliefs, desires, preferences, values, principles, and attitudes back to what they were. How should we think about this situation? On the one hand, we could say that it's the same person at all times because it's the same body, although that person has undergone some very dramatic changes in mental characteristics. On the other hand, we could say that we really literally have different people in the same body at different times. Let x be Arnold's body. The two possibilities are:

	ALTERNATIVE 1	ALTERNATIVE 2
t_1	x = person A	x = person A (bad guy)
t_3	x = person A	x = person B (good guy)
t_4	x = person A	x = person A (bad guy)

If we choose alternative 1, we seem to assume that our bodies are sufficient for personal identity, that is, that if body x at t_1 is person A, then body x at t_2 must still be person A. Thus, if body x exists and is alive, then person A must still exist. However, if we choose alternative 2, we seem to assume that our bodies are not sufficient for personal identity.

BRAIN TEASERS

Which alternative do you think makes more sense? Why?

Patients who are in a chronic vegetative state present similar puzzles. Suppose that John is in such a state because of profound brain damage due to a car accident. Let's assume that doctors are correct when they say that all of John's mental states and his capacity to have mental states have been permanently obliterated. He can't see, hear, smell, taste, or feel; he can't think, remember anything, or dream. He isn't aware of the outside world or aware of himself. We might describe his situation by saying that he no longer has a mind. There are two different ways that we could think about this situation. We could say that the body in the bed is still John and that therefore the person named John still exists. On the other hand, we could say that the body in the bed once was the person John but that the person John no longer exists. We would still call the physical object in the bed "John," but that is only because that is how this physical object has been referred to for many years.

It might matter very much how we think about this situation. It might be real and not a movie. We might be asked to take the body off life support, in which case its life processes will cease. If we think that it is no longer the person John who we have loved, that the person John has already ceased to exist, it may make the decision easier. On the other hand, if we think that it's still the person John, that the person John still exists but won't exist any more if we decide to pull the plug on life support, it will probably make the decision much harder.

BRAIN TEASERS

Which way of thinking about John in this situation makes more sense to you? Why?

Suppose there's something that can keep your body alive for at least a thousand years. The only drawback is that after a hundred years, you'll be in the same situation as someone in a chronic vegetative state: all aspects of your consciousness will be permanently obliterated. Would you still exist?

It's up to you to decide whether you think that our bodies are necessary or sufficient for personal identity. From here on, though, we're going to explore the negative answer to this question. If our bodies are neither necessary nor sufficient for personal identity, then what is either necessary or sufficient? To answer that question, we need to look more carefully at the concept of a person.

What is a Person?

A rock isn't a person. Nor is a bicycle, car, or computer. Snails, codfish, blackbirds, and crocodiles aren't people, either, nor are dogs and cats. However, you and I are people. What makes you and I people?

In order to be a person, one must have a fairly rich mental life. This includes perceptions, beliefs, desires, thoughts, feelings, and emotions. One must have self-awareness, as well as awareness of the world one inhabits. One must be able to remember, imagine, reason, and communicate. We're people because we have these characteristics. Snails, crocodiles, and dogs aren't people because they don't have these characteristics.

Given what it takes to be a person, it seems plausible to conjecture that those very same characteristics are crucial to the identities of persons. What's necessary or sufficient for something to be the same chair or the same tree at t_1 and t_2 may be rather different than what's necessary or sufficient for something to be the same person at t_1 and t_2.

That is, perhaps what's crucial for our identities as persons, for our being not just a person but a specific person different from every other person, is a cluster of mental characteristics. In that case, what makes me me, what is essential to being me, is a specific cluster of thoughts, feelings, beliefs, desires, emotions, values, preferences, interests, experiences, and memories. What makes you "you," on the other hand, what is essential to being you and what makes you a different person than me, is another, different cluster of specific mental characteristics—a different set of thoughts, feelings, beliefs, and so on. Let's call the cluster of mental states that makes me "me" my *psychological essence*.

The cluster of mental states that makes you "you" is your psychological essence. Our psychological essences are different; therefore, we're different people.

Psychological Essences as Necessary and Sufficient for Personal Identity

If this is correct, then having the same psychological essence is necessary and sufficient for personal identity. Thus, for example,

> Physical body x at t_1 is the same person as physical body y at t_2 if and only if x and y embody the same psychological essence.

Note that according to this criterion, though, not only is it not necessary or sufficient for personal identity that one be embodied in the same body at t_1 and t_2, but it is not necessary to be embodied in any physical body. If it's logically possible for our psychological essences to exist disembodied, then it's logically possible for us to exist disembodied. (Whether it's physically possible is another matter.) Thus, it also follows that:

> Person A in place p_1 at time t_1 still exists as person A in place p_2 at time t_2 if and only if A's psychological essence in p_1 at t_1 is in p_2 at t_2.

Death and Other Happenings, Again

If we accept the view that a particular psychological essence is necessary and sufficient for personal identity, then we might think in the following way about the cases we discussed earlier.

> Joan will continue to exist as Joan after her body dies and disintegrates, provided that her psychological essence continues to exist.

> An individual suffering from the end stages of Alzheimer's Disease is still the same person, provided that his psychological essence still exists in his body.

> An individual in a chronic vegetative state is still a person and the same person, provided that his psychological essence still exists in his body.

> Carla is a reincarnation of Cleopatra, provided that Cleopatra's psychological essence is in Carla's body.

> John was roaming about the hospital while his body was on the operating table provided that his psychological essence was not in his body at the time but instead was at various places in the hospital at various times.

A and B have exchanged bodies, provided that A's psychological essence is now in the body that once contained B's psychological essence, and vice versa.

Arnold's body has embodied two different people at different times (bad guy A and good guy B) provided that A's psychological essence is not identical to B's psychological essence.

Even if I've lost most of my body and have been disfigured, I'm still the same person in that body, provided that the body contains the same psychological essence as before.

But puzzles arise if we accept psychological essences as necessary and sufficient for personal identity. For one thing, our psychological essences change second by second as we have new thoughts, experiences, beliefs, questions, doubts, fears, likes, and dislikes. I visit a new city and store hundreds of mental images I didn't have before. I change my mind and alter my beliefs, adding new ones and subtracting old ones. I forget things. Last Wednesday I remembered what I had for breakfast that day. Now I don't remember. I now have an itch that I didn't have a moment ago. Yesterday I had a stomach ache that I don't have today. Last week I felt depressed, but I don't feel depressed this week. Ten years ago I loved comic books, but now I'm completely indifferent to them. Ten years ago I loved someone I can't stand now; now I love someone I didn't even know ten years ago. I learned how to do something this year that I didn't know how to do before. So what makes my psychological essence today the same as the psychological essence I considered mine ten or twenty years ago and the psychological essence I'll consider mine ten or twenty years from now?

Same Psychological Essence

We sometimes say of someone that he's not the same person now that he once was. Consider someone who was a cold-blooded killer but who "got religion" and is now meek and mild as a lamb and wouldn't harm a hair on anyone's head. Call him Dillinger. If we say that Dillinger is now a "new man," that he's no longer the same person he once was, do we mean that he's literally no longer Dillinger but is a completely different person? That seems far-fetched. Surely we're speaking figuratively when we say things like that. What we mean is that he's not the same kind of person he once was. He's still Dillinger, just Dillinger transformed.

If we took such talk literally, we'd be in trouble. We'd have to say that the individual who once was Dillinger is Dillinger no longer, he's a different person. Therefore, we'd not be justified in punishing him for Dillinger's crimes, anymore than if we picked a stranger at random and punished him for Dillinger's crimes. The person in the body that once was

Dillinger's body is not Dillinger. Where is Dillinger? Presumably, he would no longer exist unless the transformation was reversed.

Some transformations in our psychological essences do not make us literally different people. Your beliefs can change without it being the case that you're literally no longer the same person. Similarly for your desires, and other mental states. Some parts of our psychological essences, then, are more essential to our identities as persons than others. Some things can change and it's still the same psychological essence, but if others change, it's no longer the same psychological essence. What's most important?

Let's contrast first-person identity judgments with second- and third-person identity judgments. Let's say that there was a person in 1970 who had a job at an insurance company that he detested. Who was that person? I believe it was me. I believe that I in the present am identical to that person who existed in 1970. What makes me think I am that person?

I can't plausibly say that I think it was me because my psychological essence now is the same as the psychological essence of that person in 1970. For one thing, after all these years there are probably profound differences between the psychological essence of 1970 and my psychological essence now. But even more important, how do I know what was included in the psychological essence of 1970? If I do know, it can only be because I remember it. I remember (from the inside) what that person thought, felt, etc. And I might say that I simply remember being this person. Similarly, consider what might lead you to suspect that you are the reincarnation of someone who died before you were born. Surely, only your having memories of that person's experiences. If you have no memories of being Julius Caesar, then you are unlikely to suspect that you might be Julius Caesar reincarnated. From a first person perspective, memory seems to be among the most crucial determinants of personal identity.

But memory is also important from a second and third person perspective. We would be tempted to say that Julian is a reincarnation of Julius Caesar only if his claims to remember being Caesar are compelling. If Julian admits that he doesn't remember anything of Caesar's life and doesn't remember being Caesar, his claim to be a reincarnation of Caesar is absurd. But if he can provide many details of Caesar's life, some known only to experts, some unknown but plausible given what we do know of Caesar's life and times, then we will probably feel tempted to say that he's a reincarnation of Caesar because he remembers being Caesar.

Perhaps, then, memory is central to personal identity, a necessary and sufficient condition of our identities as persons. That was British philosopher John Locke's (1632–1704) view. We could express this suggestion in the following way.

> Person A at time t_1 is identical to Person B at a later time t_2 if and only if B at t_2 remembers at least some of the mental states (especially experiences) of A at t_1.

If someone claims to be the reincarnation of Cleopatra but has no memories of Cleopatra's life, no memories of being Cleopatra, it wouldn't seem reasonable to accept her claim. Similarly, if someone is suffering from the end stages of Alzheimer's disease and has no memories at all of her past life, not recognizing her friends and relatives and not knowing who she is or was, it may be difficult to view her as literally the same person she was before the onset of Alzheimer's. But there are problems with the Memory criterion.

The Gallant Officer Objection to the Memory Criterion

Although the Memory criterion of personal identity has considerable plausibility, several problems arise. One set of problems was pointed out by the philosopher Thomas Reid (1710–1796).[3] Reid imagines the case of the gallant officer, which I'll paraphrase and place in more modern times. Suppose that in 1950 a young boy, let's call him John Jones, is caught stealing apples and is severely punished. At a later time, 1968, Jones, now a young army officer, does something heroic: he rescues two comrades from certain death. Still later, in 2001, Jones is a retired general. In 2001, Jones remembers having rescued his two comrades in 1968 but doesn't remember having stolen the apples in 1950. In 1968, however, as a young army officer, he distinctly remembered having stolen the apples in 1950. The problem is that if memory is both necessary and sufficient for our identities as persons, then (1) Jones in 2001 is identical to the young officer in 1968, (2) the young officer in 1968 is identical to the apple stealer of 1950, but (3) Jones in 2001 is not identical to the young apple stealer in 1950. This is paradoxical because it's necessarily true that if A = B and C = B, then A = C. Reid's example violates this because A is identical to B and C is identical to B, but A is not identical to C.

There is one possible way to resolve this problem. We could distinguish between direct memory and indirect memory. Thus suppose that at noon you remember eating pancakes for breakfast this morning at 8:15. In that case, at noon you are the person (you're identical to the person) who was eating pancakes at 8:15. At noon you're also taking a test. Midnight arrives. Now you remember taking the test at noon but you don't remember eating pancakes for breakfast at 8:15. In fact, you remember almost nothing you did or experienced from the time you got up at 7:30 to the time you went to your first class at 9:00. According to the memory criterion, then, at midnight you're not identical to the person who ate

[3]Thomas Reid, "Mr. Locke's Account of Our Personal Identity." In *Personal Identity*, edited by John Perry. Berkeley: University of California Press, 1975.

pancakes at 8:15 although you are identical to the person who was taking a test at noon.

However, at midnight, you remember taking the test at noon. We could say, then, that you remember being the person who at noon was taking a test. The person at noon taking the test also remembered eating pancakes at 8:15. So at midnight you remember being the person who at noon remembered eating pancakes at 8:15. We might say that at midnight you directly remember taking a test at noon, and at noon you directly remember eating pancakes at 8:15. However, at midnight you do not directly remember eating pancakes at 8:15. But since at midnight you directly remember being the person who at noon directly remembered eating pancakes at 8:15, we could say that you indirectly remember eating pancakes at 8:15 and that therefore you indirectly remember being the person who ate pancakes at 8:15. If this distinction between directly and indirectly remembering makes sense, we might say that person A at t_1 is identical to person B at t_2 if and only if B at t_2 either directly or indirectly remembers being A at t_1.

If this makes sense, then we can say in reply to the gallant officer objection that in 2001 retired General Jones is identical to the boy who stole the apples in 1950 because although he doesn't remember stealing the apples, he does remember being the person who in 1968 remembers stealing the apples. Therefore, he indirectly remembers stealing the apples. And indirect memory is satisfactory as a necessary and sufficient condition of personal identity.

Forgetting

But even if we can expand the memory criterion to include indirect as well as direct remembering, there's still a problem. While it may be plausible to consider direct and indirect memories as sufficient conditions of our identities as persons, it seems less plausible as a necessary condition. In the above example, at midnight you remembered taking a test at noon. At the same time you were taking the test, you remembered eating pancakes at 8:15. That's why I said that at midnight you remembered being the person who at noon remembered eating pancakes at 8:15. But suppose that at 11:30 a.m. you remembered eating pancakes at 8:15, but that at midnight you don't remember anything at all about what you did or experienced at 11:30 a.m. The way we've been talking, you don't directly remember being the person who at 11:30 directly remembered eating pancakes at 8:15, although you directly remember being the person who at noon directly remembered eating pancakes at 8:15. (Whew! Perhaps you'd better read this paragraph again. It's awfully complicated.) Can we say anyway that you're (identical to) this person who existed at 11:30 a.m.?

Yes, at least if at each instant of time, you directly remember what you did and experienced the previous second or minute. Then there's a chain of direct rememberings going back into the past to your first memories. Thus, suppose that at midnight you remember some of what you did and experienced at 11:59 p.m. and at 11:59 you remembered some of what you did and experienced at 11:58 p.m. This chain of direct memories would go back to 11:30 a.m. Provided that there are no breaks in the chain, then at midnight you do indirectly remember being the person who at 11:30 remembered eating pancakes. Then that person at 11:30 would be you.

But suppose there are breaks in the chain of memories. Suppose that as a result of a blow to the head you develop permanent amnesia. Say you were hit on the head January 15. Afterwards, you are never able to remember anything of your life between January 5 and January 25, including being hit on the head. Twenty days of your life are permanently erased from your memory. If memory is necessary for personal identity, then we would have to say that the person who did and experienced a variety of things between January 5 and January 25, including getting hit on the head, was not you. We could diagram the situation like this where x is your physical body and person A is you now at some time after January 25.

X = Person A (you)	X = Person B	X = Person A
	Jan. 5	Jan. 25

Most of us would find this claim absurd.

BRAIN TEASERS

Why would we have to say that person is not you if either direct or indirect memories are necessary for our identities as persons?

Memory is important, but it's not the only element making up one's psychological essence. There are beliefs, desires, feelings and emotions, personality and character traits, values, preferences, abilities, and so on. If all your states of consciousness had been drastically altered during the time period January 5 to January 25 by the blow to the head, it might make sense to say after that that the person wasn't really you. But what if that's not the case? Then it seems implausible to maintain that between January 5 and January 25 a different person was embodied in your body.

This complicates matters. It may be that at this point, all we can say is that our continued existence as the people we have been requires that enough of our psychological essences continue to exist. How much is enough? We may not be able to give a precise rule. Instead, we may have to judge on a case-by-case basis. Thus, we may be forced to express this criterion quite roughly.

Person A at t_1 is identical to person B at t_2 if and only if enough of A's psychological essence is identical to B's psychological essence.

How the Self Depends on the Body

By examining the claim that it's our psychological essence that's both necessary and sufficient for our identities as persons, we may have given the false impression that our physical bodies are ultimately irrelevant. Our bodies are crucial.

The term "psychological essence" is not one we ordinarily encounter. Instead, we generally talk of a "self." For example, we might say such things as, "I talk to myself," "I myself prefer coffee to tea," "I want to know myself," "I can't hear myself think," "I want to think for myself," "I want to look out for myself," "I want to be good to myself," "I can't look at myself in the mirror," "I'm self-conscious," and "I'm too selfish."

If I talk about knowing myself, that presupposes that there is a self to be known. My "self" is me. Your "self" is you. What is a self? One conjecture is that it is a psychological essence. My self would then be my psychological essence and your self would be your psychological essence. In this section, let's focus on the concept of the self and try to get clear on its relation to physical bodies.

Selves are dynamic. They change over time. My self when I was five, twenty-five, and forty-five differ in a variety of ways, many of them profound. I don't think I was born with a self. I think it developed and probably only began to coalesce when I was two or three.

How did my self evolve if I wasn't born with it? What things affected its development through the years, making it the self it now is (making me the person I now am)?

My body had a profound impact on my self, determining a lot of its nature (of my nature as a person). For one thing, I was born male. The male hormones secreted by my body and other physical features peculiar to males probably had an important influence on shaping my self (me). If I had been born female, I probably would have a different self. (Part of this difference, as we'll see below, probably is due to interactions with other people, the way they would have treated me if I had been born female instead of male, but I doubt that all the differences are due to this.)

The anatomy of my brain surely had a profound influence on my self. If I had been born severely brain damaged, I would surely have had a different self. Similarly, if my level of intelligence, creativity, and so on is due at least in part to the capabilities of my brain, then again, my brain had a profound impact on the nature of my self.

Other influences might play a role in the development of one's self. For example, someone who is unusually large and strong may have a different self than he would have had if he had been average or below average in these characteristics. It would probably influence his self-image, as well as how he is perceived and treated by other people. He may be more self-assertive, aggressive, and confident than he would have been if he hadn't been unusually large and strong. On the other hand, someone who is smaller and weaker than average may be less assertive, self-confident, and aggressive than he would have been if he had been average or above average in these ways. (Of course, it could work the other way. He may over compensate and be more assertive and aggressive than average.) He might be picked on by others rather than being admired, respected, even feared by others. That can have a profound effect on the self that develops.

Similarly, someone who is especially attractive may develop a different self than he would have had if he had been average or below average in appearance. The same occurs for someone who is overweight or underweight. These purely physical characteristics can shape our lives and selves. They influence how we see ourselves, and how others see and treat us. Therefore, they influence how we experience the world and our lives in it.

Again, consider someone who is physically challenged or ill: someone who is born deaf or blind, someone confined to a wheelchair, or suffering from a debilitating illness. Surely such things will affect the self that develops, often profoundly.

Our interactions with other people also influence the formation of our selves. Someone who is loved and adequately cared for will probably develop a different self than she would have if she had been unloved and either neglected or abused. The same occurs for someone who is frequently taunted and picked on by others. Our training, education (formal and informal), and conditioning, provided to us by others, also influence the selves that we develop. These all involve interactions among our physical bodies and the bodies of other people.

Consider also the way our racial and ethnic backgrounds can be crucial for our identities, for who we think we are, for the selves we develop. If I had been born African-American or Latino, instead of Caucasian, the self that is me would have been different, perhaps profoundly different. I would probably have experienced forms of prejudice and discrimination, subtle and unsubtle, that I am wholly unaware of. Finally, what if I had been born with a different sexual orientation, which appears to be at least strongly influenced by our genetic and biological makeup? Surely my self would have been very different.

BRAIN TEASERS

How would you be different if you had been born a member of the opposite sex?

How would you be different if you had been born into a different racial or ethnic group?

How would you be different if you had been born into a different economic class?

How would you be different if you had been born with very different physical characteristics, such as height, weight, and attractiveness?

How would you be different if you had been born with a different sexual orientation?

The physical bodies we're born with play a large role in determining our psychological essences, the selves we develop.

Identifying and Reidentifying People

How do you know that the person who taught your philosophy class today is the very same person who taught your philosophy class last week? We'd probably say that the person teaching it today looked, sounded, and acted exactly the same as the person who taught the class last week. In that case, we infer that the physical body at the front of the class today is the same physical body that was in front of the class last week. (We infer that it's not the person's twin or a look-alike.) And we infer that if it's the same physical body, it's the same person.

How do you recognize your family and friends? Suppose you're sitting at the table on Thanksgiving. You occupy one chair. A variety of human beings occupy other chairs. How do you know they're human beings? Obviously, they look like human beings; they don't look like elephants or zebras. You can tell they're human by looking at them. But what you're looking at are physical bodies. Who are these human beings? There's your mother, your father, your maternal grandmother and grandfather, your Uncle Bill and Aunt Mary, your two sisters, and your brother. But how do you know that the humans at the table are these people? They look, sound, and act like them. You infer that they're the same bodies that had been these people in the past and therefore that they are still these people in the present. But then you're identifying and reidentifying people by appealing solely to physical characteristics of physical human bodies. You're not actually perceiving their psychological essences or selves and identifying them on the basis of that. So perhaps ordinarily we identify and reidentify people only by means of perceivable characteristics of their physical bodies.

Can a Criterion of Personal Identity Ignore the Physical Body?

Given the role that our bodies play in the development of our selves—our psychological essences—and the role that bodies play in identifying and reidentifying people, we may wonder whether a criterion of personal identity can ignore the body. If psychological essences are necessary or sufficient for our identities as persons, that seems to leave out our bodies. But can we be the same person—the same self—in any body or in no body?

Disembodied Persons

The only people that most of us are acquainted with are embodied in physical bodies. If there are nonphysical beings that have psychological essences or selves, such as angels or ghosts, most of us have no direct experience of them.

A self or psychological essence has parts, namely, the individual mental characteristics making up a self. As we saw in the previous chapter, almost all philosophers think that the cluster of mental characteristics that make up a self must be realized (contained or embedded) in something. The traditional name for that something is substance. Physicalists think that each human self is (and must be) realized in a specific bit of physical substance, a human body. Dualists think that each human self is realized in a specific bit of nonphysical substance, a soul or mind. According to Dualists, a self can be disembodied—not realized in any physical body.

The idea of a disembodied self presents problems, given how the self is dependent on the body. Would an African-American woman still be the same person or have the same self if disembodied, given that it doesn't obviously make sense to call a disembodied person African-American or female?

BRAIN TEASERS

Could a person still be Cleopatra if reincarnated into a man's body?

Could a person still be Julius Caesar if reincarnated into a woman's body?

Would you still be the same person if you're disembodied and are no longer a man or a woman, no longer experiencing sexual desire (which seems to be governed by the body's hormones), neither homosexual, heterosexual, nor bisexual, neither tall nor short, neither fat nor skinny, neither strong nor weak, neither handsome nor plain? In short, if you no longer have any physical characteristics?

Dualism, Personal Identity, and Existence After Death

If Dualism is true, a person's psychological essence or self is realized in a nonphysical substance. Let's call it your soul. How long do souls exist? A hundred years? A thousand? A million? Forever? Will you continue to exist as long as your soul continues to exist?

There is a problem. If you are your self or psychological essence, then your soul will still be you only so long as your self continues to be realized in your soul. If your psychological essence is ever erased from your soul, the way a movie might be erased from a tape, then that soul would no longer be (or be the realization of) you. Just as if I have a taped copy of the movie *Star Wars* and I erase it, the tape still exists but it is no longer a tape of *Star Wars*. If I record another movie on the same tape—for example, *Alien,*—it is now a tape of *Alien* rather than a tape of *Star Wars*. Similarly, if your soul continues to exist but your self has been erased from it and replaced with a different self, then that soul is no longer a realization of you. If your self is not realized in any other bit of substance, then surely you have ceased to exist even though your soul still exists.

If your soul will continue to exist for a very long time after your body dies, how long will it continue to realize your self? Can selves be erased from souls? Or is it a kind of permanent realization, the way the information embedded in a compact disc can be made permanent?

 WALPOLA RAHULA

THE DOCTRINE OF NO-SOUL: *ANATTA*

What in general is suggested by Soul, Self, Ego, or to use the Sanskrit expression *Ātman,* is that in man there is a permanent, everlasting and absolute entity, which is the unchanging substance behind the changing phenomenal world. According to some religions, each individual has such a separate soul which is created by God, and which, finally after death, lives eternally either in hell or heaven, its destiny depending on the judgment of its creator. According to others, it goes through many lives till it is completely purified and becomes finally united with God or Braham, Universal Soul or *Ātman,* from which it originally emanated. This soul or self in man is the thinker of thoughts, feeler of sensations, and receiver of rewards and punishments for all its actions good and bad. Such a conception is called the idea of self.

Buddhism stands unique in the history of human thought in denying the existence of such a Soul, Self, or *Ātman*. According to the teaching of the Buddha, the idea of self is an imaginary, false belief which has no corresponding reality, and it produces harmful thoughts of 'me' and 'mine', selfish desire, craving, attachment, hatred, ill-will, conceit, pride, egoism, and other defilements, impurities and problems. It is the source of all the troubles in the world from personal conflicts to wars between nations. In short, to this false view can be traced all the evil in the world.

Two ideas are psychologically deep-rooted in man: self-protection and self-preservation. For self-protection man has created God, on

From *What the Buddha Taught* (New York: Grove Press, 1974). Footnotes omitted.

whom he depends for his own protection, safety and security, just as a child depends on its parent. For self-preservation man has conceived the idea of an immortal Soul or *Ātman,* which will live eternally. In his ignorance, weakness, fear, and desire, man needs these two things to console himself. Hence he clings to them deeply and fanatically. . . .

According to Buddhism, our ideas of God and Soul are false and empty. . . . These ideas are so deep-rooted in man, and so near and dear to him, that he does not wish to hear, nor does he want to understand, any teaching against them. . . .

We have seen earlier, in the discussion of the First Noble Truth . . . , that what we call a being or an individual is composed of the Five Aggregates, and that when these are analysed and examined, there is nothing behind them which can be taken as "I," *Ātman,* or Self, or any unchanging abiding substance. That is the analytical method. The same result is arrived at through the doctrine of Conditioned Genesis which is the synthetical method, and according to this nothing in the world is absolute. Everything is conditioned, relative, and interdependent. This is the Buddhist theory of relativity. . . .

The question of Free Will has occupied an important place in Western thought and philosophy. But according to Conditioned Genesis, this question does not and cannot arise in Buddhist philosophy. If the whole of existence is relative, conditioned and interdependent, how can will alone be free? Will, like any other thought, is conditioned. So-called "freedom" itself is conditioned and relative. Such a conditioned and relative "Free Will" is not denied. There can be nothing absolutely free, physical or mental, as everything is interdependent and relative. If Free Will implies a will independent of conditions, independent of cause and effect, such a thing does not exist. How can a will, or anything for that matter, arise without conditions, away from cause and effect, when the whole of existence is conditioned and relative, and is within the law of cause and effect? Here again, the idea of Free Will is

basically connected with the ideas of God, Soul, justice, reward and punishment. Not only is so-called free will not free, but even the very idea of Free Will is not free from conditions.

According to the doctrine of Conditioned Genesis, as well as according to the analysis of being into Five Aggregates, the idea of an abiding, immortal substance in man or outside, whether it is called *Ātman,* "I," Soul, Self, or Ego, is considered only a false belief, a mental projection. This is the Buddhist doctrine of *Anatta,* No-Soul or No-Self.

In order to avoid a confusion it should be mentioned here that there are two kinds of truths: conventional truth and ultimate truth. When we use such expressions in our daily life as "I," "you," "being," "individual," etc., we do not lie because there is no self or being as such, but we speak a truth conforming to the convention of the world. But the ultimate truth is that there is no "I" or "being" in reality. As the *Mahāyāna-sūtrālaṅkāra* says: "A person (*pudgala*) should be mentioned as existing only in designation (*prajñapti*) (i.e., conventionally there is a being), but not in reality (or substance *dravya*)." . . .

[T]he Buddha analyses being into matter, sensation, perception, mental formations, and consciousness, and says that none of these things is self. But . . . according to the Buddha's teaching, a being is composed only of these Five Aggregates, and nothing more. Nowhere has he said that there was anything more than these Five Aggregates in a being. . . .

[T]he Buddha said . . . "O bhikkhus, when neither self nor anything pertaining to self can truly and really be found, this speculative view: "The universe is that *Ātman* (Soul); I shall be that after death, permanent, abiding, ever-lasting, unchanging, and I shall exist as such for eternity"—is it not wholly and completely foolish?"

Here the Buddha explicitly states that an *Ātman,* or Soul, or Self, is nowhere to be found in reality, and it is foolish to believe that there is such a thing.

Questions for Discussion and Review

1. Karen Ann Quinlan suffered irreversible brain damage, which put her into what doctors call a chronic vegetative state. If all of Quinlan's consciousness has been permanently obliterated and her mental life and functioning have permanently ceased, does the person Karen Ann Quinlan still exist?

2. Suppose that Dualism is true and at death your soul, in which your self has been realized during life, detaches from your body and continues to exist. Will your self continue to be realized in your soul? Why or why not? For how long?

3. If souls exist, for how long do they exist?

4. In the Steve Martin/Lily Tomlin movie *All of Me*, Steve Martin's body is partly taken over by Lily Tomlin's soul. If the body that once only contained Steve Martin's soul now also contains Lily Tomlin's, do we have two separate people in one body? Can a body have more than one soul or person in it simultaneously?

5. Are souls reincarnated in other bodies after death?

6. Suppose that Guru Svengali tells me that my soul once was Albert Einstein's soul, that after Einstein's death, his soul was reincarnated in my body. However, I don't remember being Einstein and I have none of Einstein's genius. Assuming you believe Guru Svengali's claim, what would you conclude?

7. Tom, who has been on death row for ten years, having been convicted of murder, has altered profoundly. Once he was violent, filled with hatred and rage, unable to govern his temper, and filled with self-loathing. He had no self-respect or respect for other people. He was a substance abuser who used drugs and abused alcohol. He believed that God does not exist and had no religious convictions. Psychologists attribute his character at least in part to the fact that he was neglected and physically abused as a child. Five years ago he underwent a religious conversion. (Assume that he is not faking it.) It has altered not only his beliefs, but also his desires, character, personality, and actions. He has become a model prisoner who teaches and counsels other prisoners. He is no longer filled with rage or self-loathing. He believes fervently that every human being is precious and should be treated with great respect. He is no longer violent; he is mild and gentle and he has a strong desire to do all in his power to refrain from hurting others. He feels great remorse for what he did in the past. You are the governor. Tom's attorney has submitted to you a request to have Tom's sentence changed to life in prison. His attorney says that Tom is no longer the same person who committed the crimes for which he was convicted. What would you do and why? (You may not refuse solely on the grounds that you don't

believe that Tom has really changed. You do believe it. Nor may you agree to commute his sentence solely on the grounds that you are against the death penalty. You support it.)

8. People routinely use transporters to travel from place to place on the various Star Trek movies and television programs. According to explanations offered in the movies and programs, transporters disassemble a person molecule by molecule and reassemble the person molecule by molecule at a different location. If this mode of transportation were physically possible, would the person at the sending platform at the beginning of the process and the person on the receiving platform at the end of the process be the same person? Why or why not? What, if anything, does this reveal about our concept of personal identity?

9. Would it make sense to say that our selves are realized in our brains? Would it be probable?

10. At time t_1 Abe is realized in body A and Brad is realized in body B. At time t_2, an evil neuroscientist takes Abe's brain from body A and transplants it into body B and takes Brad's brain from body B and transplants it into body A. At t_2 where is Abe? At t_2 where is Brad?

11. Consider fictional characters such as the android Data from *Star Trek: The Next Generation* or R2D2 from the *Star Wars* movies. If robots or androids like these characters are ever created, will they be people? Why or why not?

Suggestions for Further Reading

Daniel Kolak and Raymond Martin, eds. *Self and Identity: Contemporary Philosophical Issues.* New York: Macmillan, 1991. An excellent anthology of articles by contemporary philosophers.

John Locke. *An Essay Concerning Human Understanding,* ed. Peter H. Nidditch. Oxford: Oxford University Press, 1975. Book 2, Section 27 contains Locke's discussion of personal identity and his memory theory.

John Perry. *A Dialogue on Personal Identity and Immortality.* Indianapolis: Hackett, 1978. An interesting, enjoyable dialogue about personal identity and the possibility of surviving bodily death.

John Perry, ed. *Personal Identity.* Berkeley: University of California Press, 1975. A good anthology of classic and recent contributions to the debate over the proper criteria of personal identity.

Amelie Oksenberg Rorty, ed. *The Identities of Persons.* Berkeley: University of California Press, 1976. An anthology of fairly demanding, timely articles on personal identity and related issues.

Sydney Shoemaker and Richard Swinburne. *Personal Identity*. Oxford: Basil Blackwell, 1984. Two opponents square off on the proper criteria of personal identity and the possibility of surviving bodily death.

5 FREEDOM AND DETERMINISM

Objectives

Students are expected to:

- understand the Compatibilist and Incompatibilist concepts of freedom.
- understand the thesis of Determinism.
- understand what causal claims mean.
- understand Hard Determinism.
- understand Indeterminism/Libertarianism.
- understand Soft Determinism.
- understand the concepts of causal responsibility and moral responsibility.
- understand Fatalism.

Introduction

Do human beings have free will? In this chapter we'll examine three views on this question. Hard Determinism is the theory that every event is predetermined by prior events, leaving no room for human freedom. Indeterminism is the theory that not every event is predetermined by prior events; human actions aren't predetermined and thus can be free. Finally, Soft Determinism, or Compatibilism, is the theory that Determinism and freedom can be reconciled—that all events, including human actions, are predetermined by prior events, but that such predetermination doesn't entail that human beings aren't free.

Causality and Personal Identity

When you decide to raise your right arm, the right arm of your body rises rather than the right arm of my body. Similarly, when I decide to raise my right arm, the right arm of my body rises but not the right arm of your body. You are in control of your body; I am in control of my body. When you decide to run or walk, it is your body that runs or walks, not someone else's body.

We often talk of our minds being in control of our bodies. My body is the body that my mind is realized or embodied in and controls; your body is the body that your mind is realized or embodied in and controls. This way of talking suggests that you are your psychological essence rather than a particular physical body. However, it suggests that you (your psychological essence) are connected to one particular physical body and not others. The connection between the cluster of mental states that constitutes you or your psychological essence, on the one hand, and the physical body that is yours, on the other, appears to be causal. (This seems to be an accurate description of the situation whether one is a Dualist or a Physicalist.) Mental events that occur as part of the history of your psychological essence cause physical events to occur in a certain physical body. That physical body is your body. Thus, if you decide to raise your right arm (a mental event), your right arm will rise (unless physically prevented, as by paralysis or some obstruction). Your deciding to raise your right arm will cause your right arm to rise (but not mine).

The causal connection between a person and his or her physical body is generally assumed to be two-way. Mental events of yours cause physical events in your body, and physical events in your body cause mental events in you. For example, consider perception. You see through your eyes, not mine; I see through my eyes, not yours. You hear with your ears, not mine; I hear with my ears, not yours. Physical stimuli affecting your body cause physical events in your perceptual systems that cause you (not me) to perceive things; physical stimuli affecting my body cause physical events in my perceptual systems that cause me (but not you) to perceive things.

If your mental states have no causal connection to events that occur in a certain body, it makes no sense to say that body is your body.

Causality and Determinism

A crucial assumption of the First Cause argument for God's existence introduced in Chapter 2 is that every event has a cause. There was a cause of the event of your coming into existence, a cause of that cause, a cause of that cause, and so on. According to the First Cause argument, there must be a causal chain going backward into the past, each link of which has been caused by a preceding link. Thus, C_1 is caused by C_2, which is caused by C_3, which is caused by C_4, and so on. According to Aquinas, every event had to have a cause. If the physical universe came into existence at the instant of the Big Bang, then that event must have had a cause. According to theists, that cause was God. If events can occur without causes, then the universe could have come into existence without a cause. In that case, there would be no reason to say that God must be the cause of the universe. There must be a First Cause only if every event has a cause.

The concept of causality seems to be crucial both for arguments for God's existence and for our ideas about mind, body, and personal identity. In fact, the concept of causality seems to be one of our most fundamental concepts because much of our thinking about the world involves causal connections among events. The way that most of us think about the connection between our bodies and ourselves is causal. Much of our thought is devoted to finding the causes of things. We seek the cause of a disease such as cancer, the cause of an accident such as the collapse of a building or a plane crash, the cause of a person's death, the cause of leaves' changing color in the fall, and so on. Causal connections among events are pervasive.

Suppose that you discover a new dent in your car. The creation of the new dent was an event. Did it have a cause? If it had a cause, the cause was probably a solid object such as another car hitting your car. But did it have a cause, or could it have been an event that simply had no cause? The problem is to understand how the new dent in your car could have gotten there without a cause. Most people would probably say that that makes no sense. How could you get a dent in your car without something causing the dent?

Similarly, suppose that someone dies under mysterious circumstances. The local coroner conducts an autopsy to discover the cause of death. After weeks of analysis, the coroner releases her report. She couldn't find a cause of death, so she concludes that there was no cause of death. Can we make sense of the claim that someone died but there was no cause of his dying? Or consider an accident investigation. Suppose that after investigating a plane crash the investigators concluded that there was no cause of the crash. Would that be believable? Most people would say no. They think that every event has a cause, even if in many cases we don't know what the cause was.

Thesis of Determinism: Every Event has a Cause

The claim that every event has a cause is called the thesis of Determinism. According to the thesis of Determinism, there are no uncaused events.

BRAIN TEASERS

Is there any event you can think of that probably did not have a cause? How would you defend the claim that it probably or possibly did not have a cause?

The Meaning of Causality

We have used the term cause, but we have not defined it. What is a cause? First off, the causal relation is a relation between events. That means that the causal relation is a relation between one event, an effect, and another event, its cause. Thus, we must understand what a claim that has the schematic structure "Event c caused event e" means. (Such a statement is called a singular causal statement.) For example:

His being shot (c) caused his death (e).

A car's hitting my car (c) caused a new dent in my car (e).

A sudden wind shear (c) caused this plane to crash (e).

Singular causal statements are distinguished from causal generalizations of the form "Events of *kind C* cause events of kind E." Examples of causal generalizations would be "Hitting a car causes dents in it" and "Wind shear causes plane crashes."

Causality is a relation between events. It is events that are caused, and it is events that are causes. But what is an event? An event is a change, such as change in the properties of a thing or in the relations between two or more things. Examples of events are a leaf's changing color, a bit of water's changing from liquid to solid, an object's moving from location x to location y, a plane's crashing, a person's dying, an arm's changing its position, a building's coming into existence, a pond's ceasing to exist, and so on.

What is the nature of the causal relation between events? Almost all of us assume that causes always precede their effects. That is, if c caused e, then c occurred earlier than e. First comes the cause, then comes the effect. Lighting the fuse on the dynamite comes before the explosion. But that is not all we mean when we make a claim that some event c caused another event e. According to an influential tradition in philosophy, we mean that there is a necessary connection between c and e. For example, the European philosopher Baruch or Benedict de Spinoza (1632–1677) said, "From a given determinate cause the effect follows necessarily."[1] British philosopher David Hume (1711–1776), in one of his analyses of the causal relation, maintained that the idea of a "necessary connection" between a cause and its effect is of great importance.[2] Similarly, the German philosopher Immanuel Kant (1724–1804) said, "The very concept of a cause . . . manifestly contains the concept of a necessity of connection with an effect."[3] According to this tradition, "c caused e" means something like this:

Given that c occurred, e had to occur.

Consider the claim that Jones's drinking arsenic caused him to die. That means, on our present analysis,

---

[1]Baruch Spinoza, "Ethics," in *The Collected Works of Spinoza,* vol. 1, ed. and trans. Edwin Curley (Princeton, NJ: Princeton University Press, 1985), Pt. 1, axiom 3.

[2]David Hume, *A Treatise of Human Nature,* 2d ed., ed. L. A. Selby-Bigge, rev. P. H. Nidditch (Oxford: Oxford University Press, 1978), 77.

[3]Immanuel Kant, *Critique of Pure Reason,* trans. Norman Kemp Smith (New York: St. Martin's Press, 1929), B5, 44.

> Given that Jones drank arsenic, he had to die.

Similarly, the statement "Jones's drinking arsenic will cause him to die" would mean "If Jones drinks arsenic, then he has to die."

The first problem is how to understand the "had to." Philosophers claim that if the causal relation involves necessity, it is physical rather than logical necessity. Thus, we could restate our analysis as

> Given that Jones drank arsenic, it was physically necessary that he die.

It is a law of nature that humans die if they ingest arsenic.

A singular causal statement presupposes that there is a law of nature, but not a law of logic, linking events of one kind with events of another kind. Thus, "The temperature's dropping below 32 degrees F caused the water to freeze" presupposes that it is a law of nature that water freezes at 32 degrees F. If the internal temperature of water drops to or below 32 degrees F, it "has to" freeze.

But there is a problem. It is physically necessary that human beings die if they ingest arsenic only under certain conditions. If a human being ingests a minute quantity of arsenic, she might not die because she hasn't ingested enough to kill her. Similarly, if she takes an antidote to arsenic immediately after ingesting it or if she gets prompt medical attention and her stomach is pumped, she may not die. So it is physically necessary that human beings die if they ingest arsenic only under certain conditions. If Jones has ingested arsenic under the right conditions (she has ingested enough to kill her and nothing such as ingestion of an antidote or a stomach pumping follows), she has to die. The same occurs with water freezing. Water will freeze at or below 32 degrees F if it is pure water at a certain atmospheric pressure. If it is not pure water or is not "at sea level," it may not freeze even if its temperature is below 32 degrees F. Therefore, we need to incorporate the notion of appropriate conditions into our analysis of singular causal statements. Thus, "c caused e" means

> Given that c occurred *under the right conditions,* e had to occur (it was physically necessary that e would occur).

Determinism

Determinism and Causal Chains

Most of us assume without even thinking about it that Determinism is true, that every event has a cause. The idea of an event that had no cause at all seems outlandish to most people. However, Determinism seems to have rather unsettling implications. Take a particular event e, a plane crash. If Determinism is true, then it must have had a cause. That cause is a prior event, e_1. If Determinism is true, then e_1 had a cause, e_2. That cause was a still earlier event, e_3. If Determinism is true, then that event had a cause. We wind up with a causal chain like the following going backward into the past, where e is the plane crash and c_1 is the event that caused it:

$$...c_6 \longrightarrow c_5 \longrightarrow c_4 \longrightarrow c_3 \longrightarrow c_2 \longrightarrow c_1 \longrightarrow e$$

As we saw in Chapter 2, this causal chain either goes backward into the infinite past or ends with the First Cause.

If c_1 caused e, then given that c_1 occurred, e had to occur. If c_2 caused c_1, then given that c_2 occurred, c_1 had to occur. That supports the following argument:

> Given that c_1 occurred, e had to occur.
> Given that c_2 occurred, c_1 had to occur.
> Given that c_3 occurred, c_2 had to occur.
> Given that c_4 occurred, c_3 had to occur.

> Therefore, given that c_4 occurred, e had to occur.

Of course, we could go back further in time in the causal chain, perhaps ten or twenty years, and we would reach the same conclusion: given that c_{1546} occurred, e had to occur. In a universe in which Determinism is true and every event has a cause that preceded and physically necessitated it, events occur in a kind of lockstep. If e has a cause, event c_1, then given that c_1 occurred (under the right conditions), e had to occur. No other event was physically possible. If the internal temperature of water drops to 32 degrees F, under the right conditions, it has to turn to a solid; it cannot remain a liquid or turn to a gas.

Determinism Versus Indeterminism

Consider the following two diagrams, in which c_1 is the event of a drop in the internal temperature of a glass of water to 32 degrees F:

Deterministic Universe

$c_1 \longrightarrow$ Water changes from liquid to solid

Indeterministic Universe

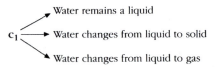

In a Deterministic universe, where every event has a cause, given that c_1 occurred, there is only one physically possible future effect: the water must change to ice. The water (physically) cannot remain a liquid or change to a gas. On the other hand, in an Indeterministic universe, where events can be uncaused, there may be several physically possible futures. After its temperature drops to 32 degrees F, the water may change to ice, it may remain a liquid, or it may change to a gas.

If Determinism is true, then since the beginning of the universe, if it had a beginning, there has been only one physically possible history. The events at one instant cause all of the events of the next instant. What happens, then, happens necessarily. Thus, if Determinism is true, someone with God's knowledge of all of the laws of nature and a complete knowledge of everything there is to know about the universe at a particular time t could predict with absolute certainty everything that will occur after t for as far into the future as she wishes to predict. In an Indeterministic universe, by contrast, there are many physically possible futures.

Deterministic Universe

a ———▶b ———▶c

Indeterministic Universe

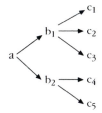

In the Deterministic universe a causes b; therefore, given a, b must occur. Because b causes c, c must occur. So given that a occurred, c must occur. We can explain why c occurred by saying "because b occurred," and we can explain why b occurred by saying "because a occurred."

However, in the Indeterministic universe, alternative states are physically possible. Given that a occurred, either b_1 or b_2 could occur. If b_1 occurs rather than b_2, it was not physically necessitated by a. We cannot explain the occurrence of b_1 by appealing to a's occurrence, because a causal explanation is designed to show why one thing rather than another occurred. The occurrence of a can't explain why b_1 rather than b_2 occurred, because given a, either b_1 or b_2 could have occurred. In the Indeterministic universe, there is no cause to explain why b_1 occurred, rather than b_2. Similarly, there are various physically possible succeeding states for each of b_1 and b_2. Given a, any of states c_1–c_5 could occur. The future is not determined by the past. Even God could not predict the future in an Indeterministic universe.

Determinism and Human Behavior

Suppose that one morning you enter the college snack bar and buy and drink a cup of hot coffee. The action involves various bodily movements: moving your legs to walk into the snack bar, speaking to order coffee or reaching out to pour yourself a cup of coffee, taking money from your pocket to pay the cashier, bringing the cup to your lips, swallowing the coffee, and so on. If Determinism is true, then there was a cause of your bodily movements. Let's focus on the mental causes. Many people claim that we can explain what you are doing only by appealing to some of your mental states. You are buying and drinking a cup of coffee because you decided or chose to. Deciding and choosing are categorized as mental events. Your deciding or choosing to buy and drink a cup of coffee caused you to do the things you did, caused the movements of your body. This is called mental causation. Using a traditional terminology, your decision led to an act of will, a volition, that caused the various physical changes in your body that led to your bodily movements.

You decide to →	You will that your body →	You buy and
buy and drink	perform the actions of	drink coffee
coffee	buying and drinking coffee	
(decision)	(volition or act of willing)	(action)

If your deciding or choosing to buy and drink a cup of coffee was not the cause of the movements of your body, then it is difficult to see what we could mean in saying that what occurred was your action. Movements of your body are your actions if and only if they are caused by your mental states. Movements of your body that are not caused (at least in part) by your mental states are not your actions.

Your choosing to drink a cup of coffee was an event. If Determinism is true, then this had a cause. What would be the cause of an act of choosing? Why did you decide to buy and drink a cup of coffee? Let's suppose you had the following options:

nothing	water	hot coffee
hot tea	iced coffee	iced tea
a soft drink	hot cocoa	fruit juice
milk	chocolate milk	beer

What caused you to choose hot coffee rather than some other alternative? The cause of a decision need not be something simple. A causal explanation of an action as simple as deciding to drink hot coffee may be quite complicated. In general, the cause of a decision is a combination of the agent's beliefs, desires, and preferences. Let's assume that the best explanation of your deciding to drink hot coffee rather than something else looks like this:

1. You are cold.
2. You want to feel warmer.
3. You believe that drinking a hot liquid will make you feel warmer.
4. You believe that drinking a cold liquid will make you feel colder.
5. Therefore, you want to drink a hot liquid.
6. You feel tired.
7. You want to feel less tired.
8. You believe that drinking a liquid that contains caffeine will make you feel less tired.
9. Therefore, you want to drink a liquid that contains caffeine.
10. You believe that coffee and tea contain caffeine.
11. You believe that water, fruit juices, soft drinks, milk, and beer do not contain caffeine.
12. You prefer drinking a beverage that tastes good to you rather than one that does not.
13. You like the taste of coffee.
14. You do not like the taste of tea.
15. You do not like the taste of milk if you are not eating anything.
16. You do not like the taste of beer in the morning.
17. You are on a diet and want to avoid high-calorie beverages.
18. You believe that hot cocoa and chocolate milk are high-calorie beverages.
19. You believe that hot coffee is a low-calorie beverage.

Items 1–19 would explain why you decided to have hot coffee rather than making some other decision. We could call the whole set of states and events {1–19} the "cause" of your decision, or we could identify some of the events associated with {1–19}, such as your coming to desire a hot beverage that contains caffeine, as the "cause" of the decision and the other components as the "conditions" under which the decision occurred. In any event, {1–19} causally explains why you decided at that time to have hot coffee rather than nothing at all or some other beverage.

We are not usually aware of all of the factors immediately influencing a decision we have made, especially when the decision is not the result of a long process of deliberation. Many of our decisions are more or less immediate; we decide without taking time to think about it, to weigh the pros and cons of the alternatives. The fact that your decision to have hot coffee had a cause does not mean that you debated within yourself about whether or not to have hot coffee and consciously went through items 1 through 19 before reaching your decision. But the fact that you did not reason out your decision by consciously thinking about all those items does not mean that they did not cause you to make the decision you did.

BRAIN TEASERS

At the supermarket you reach out and take a can of tomato soup from the shelf and place it in your shopping basket. There were twenty different kinds of canned soup and fifty qualitatively identical cans of tomato soup on the shelf.

1. Was there a cause of your deciding to buy a can of tomato soup? If yes, what might have been the cause? If no, explain how there might be no cause of your decision to buy a can of tomato soup.

2. Was there a cause of your selecting the particular can of tomato soup that you took from the shelf? If yes, what might that cause have been? If no, explain how there might have been no cause of your selecting that can out of fifty qualitatively identical cans of tomato soup.

If we think of {1–19} as the cause of your decision, we are committed to saying that given {1–19}, you had to choose hot coffee rather than nothing at all or any of the other alternatives. For example, if {1–19} was true of you, how could you have chosen iced tea instead of hot coffee? Of course, you could have chosen iced tea if the conditions had been different—for example, if you liked the taste of tea better than the taste of coffee and you felt hot rather than cold. But a Determinist would say that under the exact conditions specified (assuming that no other factors can influence your decision), you couldn't possibly have decided differently. You had to choose hot coffee rather than making some other choice. Assuming for the sake of argument that there are no other factors that could influence this decision, we might think of it as a law of nature that anyone of whom {1–19} is true will decide to have hot coffee rather than any other alternative. If you know that {1–19} is true of Jones, then you can predict with absolute certainty that Jones will decide to buy hot coffee.

In reality, other factors can influence your decision. Suppose further that

20. You believe that coffee contains substances that cause cancer and heart disease.

21. You believe that tea contains no harmful substances.

22. You do not want to ingest substances that cause cancer or heart disease.

23. You care more about your health than about the good taste of beverages.

Under these different conditions {1–23}, you would not decide to have hot coffee. Instead you would decide to have hot tea. Similarly, if you had no money and could not buy anything at the snack bar, then despite {1–19} you could not drink hot coffee. But according to Determinists, if we could exhaustively specify all of the factors that can influence a decision, then given that set of complete factors, only one possible decision can result.

According to Determinists, all of our decisions have causes. The causes consist of a combination of the agent's mental events and states, such as desires, beliefs, and preferences. But if Determinism is true, then each component of the cause in turn has a cause. Your feeling cold has a cause; your feeling tired has a cause; your believing that drinking a warm beverage will make you feel warm has a cause; your believing that drinking a beverage that contains caffeine will make you feel less tired has a cause; your liking the taste of coffee and not liking the taste of tea has a cause; and so on. But if Determinism is true, then each of these has a cause and their causes have causes and those causes have causes and . . . The result is a causal chain of your decision. Let c_1 be {1–19}, the cause of your decision to drink coffee. C_1, in turn, has a cause, c_2. C_2 will be more complicated than c_1, because c_2 includes the causes of each component of c_1. C_2 has a cause, c_3, which may be even more complicated, and so on.

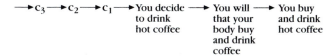

Given c_1, you had to decide to drink hot coffee; given c_2, c_1 had to be the case; given c_3, c_2 had to be the case; and so on. We could continue the causal chain into the past to a time before you were even born. Each link of the chain causally necessitates the next link so that given the prior link in the chain, the next link has to occur. That means that given the first link in the chain, the last link and every link in between are causally necessitated and have to occur. There cannot possibly be any different links than there are. A plausible line of reasoning thus leads to a startling conclusion: given events that occurred before you were even born, you had to decide to drink hot coffee when you did.

If Determinism is true, every decision and choice you have made or will make was (will be) causally necessitated by events that occurred before you were even born. Before you were born it was predetermined, in a sense preprogrammed, that you would decide to go to college, to attend the college you are attending, to major in your particular field, and to register for this course. Of course, the causal chain that necessarily led to these decisions is so complicated and vast that only God could trace it out. Similarly, every decision you will make in the future is already predetermined or preprogrammed, although again only God could have the vast amount of knowledge required to trace out the future course of your life. In a Deterministic universe, there is only one physically possible future.

Determinism and Human Freedom

An Incompatibilist Analysis of Freedom

Incompatibil-ism: An action or decision cannot be both caused and free

If your decisions are predetermined—caused by prior events that have causes that in turn have causes, and so on—are any of your decisions or actions free? The philosophical view known as **Incompatibilism** holds that an action or decision cannot be both free and caused or determined. On this view, if it was already determined before you were born that you would decide to go to college, then it makes no sense to say that your decision or choice was "free." How could your decision to go to college be free if, given events that occurred before you were born, it was physically necessary that you would decide to go to college? If Determinism is true, then given the way the universe was prior to your decision, you had to decide to go to college. You could not have made any other decision under those circumstances; therefore, your decision was not free.

Incompatibilists earn the name because they say that human freedom and Determinism are incompatible. In their view, if Determinism is true, then human freedom is an illusion. People can be free only if Determinism is false. Therefore, we must choose between human freedom and Determinism. Either we (a) accept the truth of Determinism and give up freedom as a mere illusion or (b) accept the reality of human freedom and give up Determinism as false. We can't accept both that Determinism is true and that people's decisions can be free.

In evaluating the Incompatibilist position, as with many philosophical issues, questions of meaning become central. What does it mean to call a decision "free" as opposed to "unfree"? According to Incompatibilists, only decisions that are uncaused can be free; decisions that are caused are not free.

Most Incompatibilists say that a decision is free only if, given the circumstances of the decision, the person could have done something else.

INCOMPATIBILIST ANALYSIS OF FREEDOM

Person S's decision at time t to do x was free only if, at t, S could have done something other than x.

According to the Incompatibilist analysis of freedom, your decision to go to college was free only if, at the time and under the circumstances, you could also have decided not to go to college.

The problem with Determinism is that if it is true, you couldn't have made any other decision at the time. It is like the decision to buy and drink hot coffee that we analyzed earlier. In that case, given {1–19}, you had to decide to buy and drink hot coffee; no other decision was possible. If Determinism is true, then there was a similar complex set of mental states (desires, beliefs, preferences) and conditions at the time of your college decision that caused you to decide as you did. Given that precise set of circumstances, you had to decide for rather than against college. Therefore, Incompatibilists say, your decision was not free.

BRAIN TEASERS

Was there a cause of your deciding to go to college rather than not go to college? If yes, what was the cause (or causal explanation)? If no, defend your answer. If your decision was caused, was it then unfree? Why or why not?

Incompatibilists thus face a choice. They must either give up human freedom as an illusion or give up Determinism as false. Those who give up human freedom are called Hard Determinists. Those who give up Determinism as false are called Indeterminists or Libertarians.

Hard Determinism

Hard Determinists reason as follows:

1. Determinism is true.
2. If Determinism is true, no human decisions or actions are free.

3. Therefore, no human decisions or actions are free.

Hard Determinists believe that it is easier to give up human freedom than to give up Determinism. They think that Determinism is obviously true, that every event has a cause. If Determinism is false, then there are some events that have no cause. Hard Determinists feel certain that there are no such causeless events. Therefore, they believe that it is more reasonable to maintain that no human decisions are free than to maintain that there are some events that have no cause.

Indeterminism/Libertarianism

Indeterminists or Libertarians take the opposite position. They reason as follows:

1. Some decisions that people make are free.
2. If Determinism is true, no human decisions or actions are free.

3. Therefore, Determinism is false.

Both Hard Determinists and Indeterminists/Libertarians are Incompatibilists; that is, they both accept the second premise of the argument.

However, Indeterminists/Libertarians feel certain that some decisions are free. They think that when you decided to go to college, you could just as easily have decided not to go to college under the circumstances. They feel more certain that some decisions are free than that Determinism is true. Therefore, they reject Determinism as false. They claim that some events are not caused—that is, causally necessitated by prior events. (It is vital to note that Indeterminism, the claim that Determinism is false, entails only that some events are uncaused; it does not commit one to the absurd view that no events have causes.) Those causeless events are mental events—decisions that people make.

Compare the Hard Determinist view with the Indeterminist/ Libertarian view of decision making.

Hard Determinist View of Decision Making

$\{$Circumstances of decision$\}$ ⟶ Decide to go to college

Indeterminist/Libertarian View of Decision Making

$\{$Circumstances of decision$\}$ → Decide to go to college
→ Decide not to go to college

The set of circumstances under which you made the decision might have included the following:

1. Your family and friends encouraged you to go to college.

2. You believed that your family and friends would disapprove if you decided not to go to college.

3. You did not want to have your family and friends disapprove of you.

4. You want a good job or career.

5. You believe that earning a college degree will improve the chances of your having a good job or career.

6. You like school and want to learn more.

7. You and your family have enough money to afford college.

8. You have no good reason not to go to college, such as a good job or boyfriend/girlfriend you would have to leave.

Of course, if the circumstances had been different, you might have made a different decision.

According to Hard Determinists, your decision was caused by the prior set of circumstances. Given the circumstances, only deciding to go to college was possible. Under those circumstances, you could not have decided not to go to college. According to Indeterminists/Libertarians, in contrast, given those circumstances, you could have decided either to go to college or not to go to college. Although you decided to go to college, you could have decided not to go; there was no cause of your deciding to go rather than not go. The circumstances under which you made the decision do not causally explain why you decided to go rather than not go; they did not cause the decision. The decision was uncaused, and hence "free."

Soft Determinism/Compatibilism

Many philosophers are reluctant to reject Determinism as false or human freedom as an illusion. On one hand, they think that Determinism is obviously true and that there cannot be uncaused events. On this they agree with Hard Determinists and disagree with Indeterminists/Libertarians. On the other hand, they do not think that all human actions or decisions are equally unfree. They think that there is a significant difference between free and unfree actions. Here they agree with Indeterminists/Libertarians and disagree with Hard Determinists.

Let us first concentrate on human behavior or actions. Soft Determinists, sometimes called Compatibilists, do not believe, as Hard Determinists do, that all human actions are unfree. Consider the items on the following list:

Sneezing because of an allergy

Falling because you slipped on ice

Bumping into someone because you were pushed from behind

Sneezing because you wanted to pretend that you have a cold

Falling because you wanted to fake an accident

Bumping into someone because you wanted to jostle him

Soft Determinists believe that it makes no sense to say that all the items on the list are equally unfree actions. They think that there is a significant difference between the first three and the last three. These differences are ignored if we simply say that all six are unfree actions.

What is the difference? It is not that actions of the first sort are caused while actions of the second sort are not caused. Rather, it is the nature of the cause. Actions of the first sort were not caused by your volitions and decisions, but rather by an external force or influence over which you had no control. When you sneezed because of an allergy, allergens entered your body through your nose, causing histamines to form that caused the reflex action of sneezing. You didn't decide to sneeze and then, in an act of volition, will yourself to sneeze. If you had wanted not to sneeze, you still would have sneezed; you had no control over your sneezing. The same kind of analysis applies to the next two items on the list.

On the other hand, if you sneezed because you wanted to pretend that you have a cold, your sneezing was a result of your decisions and volitions. You decided to sneeze and then, in an act of volition, willed yourself to sneeze. If you had wanted not to sneeze, you would not have sneezed; you had control over your sneezing. The same kind of analysis applies to the remaining two items on the list.

Thus we have two different kinds of causes for actions:

External force $\longrightarrow$ action

Decision $\longrightarrow$ volition $\longrightarrow$ action

In the first, the whole cause is an external force; the agent's decisions and volitions play no immediate causal role in producing the action. (I say "immediate" because the agent's decisions and volitions may have caused him to be in the situation he's in, although not the action that occurs in the situation. The agent may have decided to smell a flower that led to his sneezing or to walk on the icy sidewalk that caused him to fall. His decision to smell the flower or walk on the icy sidewalk was an indirect but not an immediate cause of his sneezing or falling.) In the second, the agent's decisions and volitions play an immediate causal role in the action. Soft Determinists think that actions in which the agent's decisions and volitions play an immediate causal role should be called free rather than unfree. Therefore, Soft Determinists think that at least some human actions are free, even though they are caused. In their view, an action is unfree if the agent's decisions and volitions are not part of the immediate cause of the action. An action is free if the agent's decisions and volitions are part of the immediate cause of the action.

Similarly, Soft Determinists believe that human decisions can be free even if they are caused. Suppose that you decide to fall intentionally in order to fake an accident and in turn fake injuries because you want to get money by suing or threatening to sue. The causal chain would look like this:

| You want to fake a fall to get \$ | $\longrightarrow$ | You decide to fall | $\longrightarrow$ | You will your body to fall | $\longrightarrow$ | You fall |

Your action of falling has a cause—namely, your deciding to fall. Your decision to fall has a cause—namely, your desire to fake a fall in order to get money. (Strictly speaking, your wanting to take a fall in order to get money is part of the cause rather than the whole cause.) According to Incompatibilists, whether Hard Determinists or Indeterminists, your decision to fall was not free because it had a cause. On the other hand, soft Determinists reply that since the cause (or part of the cause) of your decision was your own mental states—your beliefs, desires, and preferences—the decision was free rather than unfree. If you decided to fall because a gunman said that he would shoot you if you did not fall to the ground, then the decision would not be free, it would be coerced. But if you decided to fall because you wanted to fall in order to get money rather than because of some external coercion or compulsion, then the decision was free. Thus, Soft Determinists say that because there are differences in the causes of decisions, it makes no sense to say, as Hard Determinists do, that all decisions are unfree regardless of the nature of their causes.

Soft Determinists are Determinists; they agree with Hard Determinists that every event has a cause. Thus, they think that every human action has a cause; the idea of an action that had no cause makes no sense to them. Often part of an action's cause is the agent's own mental states— most basically, beliefs, desires, and preferences. They believe that these beliefs, desires, and preferences have causes, and those causes have causes, and those causes have causes, and . . . But Soft Determinists agree with Indeterminists/Libertarians, that some human actions and decisions are free. Soft Determinists may be thought to reason as follows:

1. Determinism is true.
2. Some human actions and decisions are free.

---

3. Therefore, Determinism and freedom are compatible.

Soft Determinists are also called Compatibilists because, unlike Incompatibilists, they believe that Determinism and human freedom are *compatible*. That is, we can have both Determinism and freedom. That is, Soft Determinists reject the second, Incompatibilist premise of the arguments of Hard Determinists and Indeterminists/Libertarians alike. That Incompatibilist premise is the assumption that if Determinism is true, then no human actions or decisions are free.

The Compatibilist Analysis of Freedom

The logical question to ask is, "How can freedom and Determinism be compatible?" Haven't Incompatibilists shown that an action cannot be free if it is caused? According to them, person S's doing action X at time t was "free" only if S could have done something other than X at t. But if Determinism is true, then given the circumstances at t, S had to do X at t; S could not have acted or decided differently.

The answer is that Soft Determinists/Compatibilists reject the Incompatibilist analysis of freedom. They don't think that "free" means what Incompatibilists say it means. They deny that S's doing X at t was "free" only if S could have done something other than X at t. If this were true, then your decision to drink hot coffee would have been free only if you could have done something else even though {1–19} was true of you. But Soft Determinists think that makes no sense.

Soft Determinists believe that you could have done something other than get hot coffee *if the circumstances had been different*. But under circumstances {1–19}, you could make no other decision. No matter how often we might roll back time to return to the instant you were making the decision, you would always make the same decision, hot coffee. The decision could change if and only if the circumstances under which you made the decision changed. But if the circumstances changed, your decision could change. If some of your desires or beliefs had been different, your action might have been different.

Soft Determinists claim that your action of buying and drinking hot coffee was free if it was immediately caused by your volition. You could have done something else if you had wanted to do something else. They think that's enough for freedom. You were free because you could have done something else *if* you had wanted to do something else, if you had had different desires, beliefs, or preferences.

COMPATIBILIST ANALYSIS OF FREEDOM

An *action* is free if part of its immediate cause is the agent's own mental states (beliefs, desires, preferences), that is, if you're doing what you want to do.

BRAIN TEASERS

1. Tom intentionally kicked his TV set because he was angry. (a) Was there a cause of his kicking his TV set? (b) Was his being angry part of the cause? (c) Was his action of kicking his TV set free or unfree? Defend your answers.
2. Must there have been a cause of his becoming angry?
3. Did Tom freely choose to become angry?

An Incompatibilist Objection to the Soft Determinist Analysis of Freedom

Incompatibilists object that if Determinism is true, as Soft Determinists maintain, then an action is causally necessitated by a set of desires, beliefs, preferences, and so on, which is causally necessitated by an earlier set of mental states, which is causally necessitated by a still earlier set of mental states, and so on back to events that occurred before the agent was born. Thus, given the events that occurred before the agent was born, he had to have the set of mental states that caused the decision that caused her action. If Determinism is true, an agent does not have control over the internal and external forces and influences that shape her personality and character, or over what mental states she will have at any given time. For instance, in our coffee example, you did not choose to be cold or tired, to like the taste of coffee and dislike the taste of tea, or to have the desire to feel warm rather than cold and alert rather than tired. If the mental states that cause our actions are not under our control but were predetermined before we were even born, and if given these states we have to decide and act as we do, then it makes no sense to call our actions and decisions free.

Soft Determinist Objections to Indeterminism/Libertarianism

Soft Determinists have two problems with Indeterminism/Libertarianism. First, Soft Determinists believe that it is highly unreasonable to reject Determinism. But they also do not see how rejecting Determinism can save human freedom. How can the fact that an action or decision is uncaused make it free? Suppose that your right arm rises in class. If there was no cause of your arm's rising, would that make it a free action of yours? Surely not. It wouldn't even make sense to call it an "action" *of yours*. It would be something that happened to you rather than something that you did. But does it even make sense to say that there might have been no cause of your arm's rising?

Indeterminists might agree that there must have been a cause of your arm's rising and that part of its cause was your desire to raise your arm. But they would maintain that somewhere in the causal chain there must have been an uncaused event if the action was free. But there still remains the question how an action's or mental event's being uncaused can make it free. Therefore, Soft Determinists believe that rejecting Determinism in order to preserve human freedom is fruitless.

BRAIN TEASERS

1. Tom kicked his TV. If there were no cause of his action, would it be a free action? Would it be an action of his? Why or why not?

2. Tom kicked his TV because he was angry. If there was no cause of his becoming angry, would that make his action free? Why or why not?

3. Tom became angry because he strongly disagreed with a political editorial on TV. He kicked his TV because he was angry. If there was no cause of his strongly disagreeing with the political editorial, would that make his action free? Why or why not?

Reasons and Causes

One point of contention in the debate about freedom and Determinism involves the difference between reasons and causes. When we explain human behavior, we often give the reasons why people behaved as they did. This kind of "intentional" explanation appeals to the agent's mental states, such states as belief, fear, desire, love, and so on. We have treated these reasons for behavior, the agent's mental states, as causes. But are reasons causes? Is intentional explanation a variety of causal explanation? Does it make sense to say that a complex set of mental states {1–19} (the reason why you decided to get hot coffee) is the cause of your deciding to get hot coffee?

Probabilistic Causality?

Another point of entry into the controversy about freedom and Determinism involves the analysis of causality. According to our analysis of the relation of causality, causality involves necessity. We claimed that "Event e_1 caused event e_2" means "Given that e_1 occurred, e_2 had to occur." Perhaps causes make events more probable rather than making them physically necessary. Wesley Salmon says that if the probability of event e_2 given that event e_1 occurs is greater than the probability of event e_2 given that event e_1 does not occur [(prob. e_2, given e_1) > (prob. e_2, given not e_1)], it makes sense to say that e_1 could be the cause of e_2.[4] Perhaps "Event e_1 caused event e_2" means (or, more modestly, entails) "Given that e_1 occurred, it was more probable that e_2 would occur." Thus, suppose we have the following situation. Event e_1 occurs. There are three possible (though mutually exclusive) events that could follow: e_2, e_3, and e_4. Their probabilities, given e_1 and given not e_1, are shown in the following diagram:

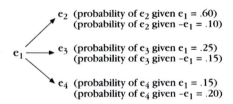

According to the present analysis of probabilistic causality, if e_2 occurs we could say that e_1 was its cause because e_2's occurrence is more probable if e_1 occurs than if it does not occur. Thus, even though e_2's occurrence was not made necessary by e_1's occurrence, and even though given e_1's occurrence there were several alternative possibilities, we would not say that e_2's occurrence was uncaused. It did have a cause, namely, the occurrence of e_1.

---

[4]See the essays by Wesley Salmon in *Causation*, ed. Ernest Sosa and Michael Tooley (Oxford: Oxford University Press, 1993).

However, if e_3 occurs, we could say the same thing. The occurrence of e_1 caused it because e_3's occurrence is more probable if e_1 occurs than if e_1 does not occur. But in both cases, does the occurrence of e_1 really causally explain why that event occurred rather than one of the other possible events? If e_2 occurred, why did it occur rather than e_3 or e_4? Critics of this approach to causality claim that we must introduce other events or conditions in addition to event e_1 in order to give a causal explanation (the cause) of why e_2 occurred rather than e_3 or e_4. But then if e_2 did occur instead of one of the other events, perhaps it occurred not simply because e_1 occurred but because, in addition, those other conditions and events that would have produced e_3 or e_4 did not occur. The idea is that there must be hidden causal factors besides e_1 that necessitate e_2. Event e_1 is part of the cause since it makes e_2 more likely, but it is not the whole cause. Although most philosophers seem to be still committed to the claim that the causal relation between events involves a necessary connection, some deny it.

BRAIN TEASERS

How would you analyze the meaning of a singular causal statement of the form "Event e_1 caused (or was the cause of) event e_2," such as "Kicking the TV caused the glass of the picture tube to crack"?

What Difference Does It Make Whether We Are Free?

Many philosophers are unsatisfied with all three positions on the issue of freedom and Determinism. They are not entirely comfortable with any of the proposed solutions to the problem. However, no fourth position has been developed (or discovered) that has attracted many philosophers. Even some philosophers who accept one of the three positions (Hard Determinism, Indeterminism, or Soft Determinism) do not feel wholly comfortable with their choice. That is why it remains an open question. To fully understand the point of it all, we need to ask ourselves whether we care whether we are "free" and, if so, why.

Human Freedom and Self-Respect

If there is a law against walking on the grass, you are not free to walk on the grass. We might call this political freedom. Political freedom and unfreedom deal with constraints and coercion imposed by human laws that limit what we may do or not do by punishment or the threat of punishment. The more forms of behavior that are forbidden or required by law, the less politically free we are; the fewer forms of behavior that are forbidden or required by law, the more politically free we are. Most people prefer more political freedom to less political freedom because more behavior is then up to them rather than controlled by someone else. Most of us want our actions to be under our own control rather than under someone else's control. But Determinism has nothing to do directly with political freedom and unfreedom.

However, looking at political freedom may reveal why we care about the kind of freedom that some people believe to be threatened by Determinism. We can call that freedom metaphysical. We want to have alternative possible actions open to us from which we may choose. We also want our actions and decisions to be under our own control rather than under someone or something else's control. We want what we do to be "up to us." If we have no possible alternatives available to us, if we must do what we do under the circumstances, then we don't really have choices. If we believe that that is the case, we may begin to view ourselves as being like a puppet controlled by forces over which we have no control or like a leaf carried along by a strong wind. We can't do anything other than what we do, any more than a puppet or windblown leaf can. We want to feel that we are in control of our destiny, that our future is, at least in part, open and up to us. Few of us would feel comfortable thinking that we are "mere" puppets or windblown leaves.

BRAIN TEASERS

If Determinism is true, in what ways would we be like puppets or wind-driven leaves? In what ways would we differ from puppets or wind-driven leaves? Would it matter to you if you were in relevant ways like a puppet or a wind-driven leaf? Why or why not?

Paradoxically, some people derive comfort from the thought that "Whatever happens has to happen." If tragedy strikes, they say with a sigh, "It was meant to be." Additionally, many people happily believe astrology's claim that the stars control our destiny. They enthusiastically believe (or hope) that people can predict the future course of their lives. But how can anyone accurately predict the future course of someone's life unless, in a sense, that individual's entire biography has already been written so that it can be read?

Causal Responsibility

If John shot Jean, killing her, John caused Jean's death. If he hadn't shot her, the death she died would not have occurred. (If he shot her intentionally, then he's morally responsible for her death in the sense that he's blameworthy. If he shot her accidentally, he may not be blameworthy.) But is John's action of shooting Jean the sole or whole cause of Jean's death? Put another way, is John alone causally responsible for Jean's death? Suppose that Tom hired John to kill Jean. Then surely Tom is also partly causally responsible for her death. If Tom hadn't hired John to kill her, Jean would not have been shot. We may say that Tom causally contributed to Jean's death. Sharing causal responsibility for her death, he shares moral responsibility for it. Both John and Tom should be prosecuted for murder, even though it was John, not Tom, who shot Jean.

Now suppose that John bought the gun he used to kill Jean from Brad. Does Brad share causal responsibility for Jean's death with John and Tom? Surely he causally contributed to her death by providing the gun used to kill her. If he hadn't sold the gun to John, Jean would not have been shot with it. But we may feel uncomfortable about this. After all, if Brad hadn't sold Tom this gun, someone else would have sold him another one and he would have shot Jean with it. Jean would still have died. But suppose that Brad knew that John was going to use the gun to kill Jean. Most of us would consider him at least partly morally responsible and blameworthy for her death. We may even think that he should be prosecuted for contributing to her murder. But he can share moral responsibility for her death only if he also shares causal responsibility for it. The question of moral responsibility can arise only if the question of causal responsibility has already been settled. We seem driven to the view that he shares causal responsibility whether or not he knew that John was going to use the gun to kill Jean. If he didn't know it was going to be used in a murder, he may not share moral responsibility for her death, but it doesn't follow that he doesn't share causal responsibility for it. His action of selling the gun to Tom was part of the cause of Jean's death.

Suppose that Alec introduced Tom to John. That is, Tom wouldn't have known John if Alec hadn't introduced them. Is Alec's action of introducing them part of the cause of Jean's death? Does he share causal responsibility with John, Tom, and Brad? We may be tempted to snort that this is really pushing it, but suppose that Alec introduced Tom to John because John asked him to introduce him to a hit man so that he could hire him to kill Jean. In that case we surely would say that he is part of the cause and shares causal responsibility and moral responsibility for her death. But again, the question of moral responsibility or blameworthiness can arise only if the person shares causal responsibility or is part of the cause. Whether or not Alec knew that Tom was going to hire John to kill Jean, his action is part of the cause of Jean's death.

How far can we go like this? One possibility is that the network of causal relations in the world is so dense that we can causally relate almost every past event to a certain effect. Of course, then we would surely need to distinguish between those events that are in some sense causally close to the effect and those that are causally far removed from the effect. For example, Tom and John's parents would be part of the cause of Jean's death. If they hadn't had Tom and John, then the death Jean died would not have occurred. The manufacturer of the gun used to kill Jean would share causal responsibility, too. (So would Tom and John's grandparents and great grandparents.) Of course, the further away from the effect, the less plausible it is to hold someone morally responsible for it. Even if John's parents having conceived John is part of the cause of Jean's death, surely it would be strange to say that they therefore share moral responsibility for her death and are blameworthy.

BRAIN TEASERS

> Try to trace out the network of events that are part of the cause of your meeting the individual you're dating or are married to, that is, events that, if they hadn't occurred, would have led to your not meeting this individual.

The further someone is from an effect, the less plausible it is to hold her morally responsible for it. The closer to an effect, the more plausible it may be to hold her morally responsible.

Human Freedom, Moral Responsibility, and Punishment

If someone is morally responsible for an effect, the person's action is either blameworthy (worthy of blame) or praiseworthy (worthy of praise). But someone can be morally responsible for something only if they're causally responsible, that is, only if their action is part of the cause. But that provides a necessary condition only. Moral responsibility requires more than causal responsibility.

A person's beliefs, desires, and intentions are also relevant. As we saw, if Brad introduced Tom to John knowing that John is a hit man and that Tom wants to hire him to kill Jean, he shares moral responsibility for Jean's death. But if he didn't know that John is a hit man and didn't know about Tom's plans, he doesn't seem to share moral responsibility; he's not blameworthy.

BRAIN TEASERS

> Mark is a senior vice president for marketing at a major tobacco company. Although he maintains publicly that cigarettes are not addictive and do not cause illness, he believes that they are addictive and do cause such illnesses as heart disease, emphysema, and lung cancer. In

part because of cigarette advertisements targeted at teenagers, at age 15 Cindy begins smoking cigarettes manufactured by Mark's company. She will die at age 59 from smoking related illnesses. Is Mark partly causally responsible for Cindy's death? Is he partly morally responsible for it?

Another requirement for moral responsibility may be freedom. Suppose that Albert collides with Brenda, knocking her out the window of a building. Brenda dies from the fall. Albert is causally responsible, but is he morally responsible? If he collided with Brenda because someone pushed him, he's not morally responsible (blameworthy). But suppose no external force caused him to collide with her; he pushed her. Surely then he's morally responsible. But suppose that he was hypnotized or was controlled by someone who had planted electrodes into his brain. Then he didn't do it freely. We might say that someone is morally responsible only if they freely did the action that is part of the cause. And we usually say that someone doesn't deserve punishment for something unless they are both causally and morally responsible for it.

Suppose that Jack the Ripper, a serial killer, has been apprehended and is on trial for his crimes. To everyone's surprise, he admits that he committed the crimes of which he has been accused. However, he claims that he does not deserve to be punished for it. He makes the following statement to the court:

> I killed those women. However, because this is a Deterministic universe, I did not do it freely. It was predetermined before I was even born that I would kill those women. Events and conditions over which I had no control formed my personality and character—a combination of my genes, my biology, and my early experiences. I killed those women because I was enraged. I was enraged at them because I hate and fear women. I hate and fear women because of experiences I underwent in early childhood; I did not choose to hate and fear women. I have a violent nature, a great propensity for violence. I did not choose to have a violent nature. I do not have the strength of will to resist my violent impulses. They overcome me. They are so powerful that I cannot control them. I did not choose to have such strong impulses or an inability to resist them. The causes of my killing these women had causes that in turn had causes that in turn had causes. Given events that occurred before I was even born, events over which I had no control, I had to decide to kill rather than not kill those women. I couldn't possibly have not decided to kill them. That's because Determinism is true.

> People deserve to be punished only for actions that they are morally responsible for. But people are morally responsible only for actions over which they have control, that are free. It makes no sense to punish someone for an act if the person did not do the act freely.

> Therefore, although I am guilty, I do not deserve to be punished for
> my crimes because I couldn't help it.

If Determinism is true, does it follow that we are never morally responsible for our actions and, therefore, that we do not deserve to be punished for them? Many Soft Determinists maintain that the freedom that their Compatibilist analysis attributes to people is sufficient for moral responsibility. Since Jack the Ripper killed the women because he wanted to kill them, he did it freely according to Soft Determinists. Since he did it freely, he is morally responsible for it and deserves punishment, even though he couldn't have done anything else under those precise circumstances. And he could have done something else if circumstances had been different—for example, if he had not hated and feared women.

Critics do not think that the Compatibilist version of freedom is strong enough to preserve moral responsibility. They think that a person can be morally responsible for an action, and thus deserve punishment (or reward) for it, only if the person could have done something else under those very circumstances.

Fatalism

If Determinism is true, why should people bother deliberating about what to do or take the notion of deciding and choosing seriously? If Determinism is true, then whatever is determined to happen by the past history of the universe is going to happen. In a sense, your biography was written before you were born, so there's no sense in making an effort. Whatever will be will be, whatever you do or don't do.

For example, the date of your death is already determined even if you don't know what that date is. So why should you worry about your health or avoid overly risky behavior? You're going to die when you're going to die, whether or not you smoke, drink, take drugs, play Russian roulette, or dodge cars on the freeway. Nothing you do or don't do can change the course of events that was already determined before you and your parents and your grandparents were born. That unchangeable course of events includes every event of your life, including the day of your death.

Fatalism is the view that *nothing a person does can change the course of events.* Whatever will be will be, regardless of what you do or anyone else does. The clear implication is that one should just be passive and allow the course of events to carry one along. Does Determinism entail fatalism?

You hold a cup of poison and reason as follows: Either you're going to die now or not die now. Whether you're going to die now was determined before you were even born. So it doesn't matter what you do; whatever will be will be, whether or not you drink the poison. What you do has no effect on the predetermined course of events. So it doesn't matter if you drink the poison.

Surely it is clear that whether you will die now depends crucially on what you do. If you drink the poison, you'll die now; if you don't, you may not die. Determinism entails a causal order, and you are part of the causal order. As part of the causal order, you are affected by events around you, but you in turn produce effects. Your actions are not simply effects of causes, they are also causes of effects. If you drink poison, it will kill you. What you do affects the course of events.

But your doing something, such as drinking poison, was determined before you were born, if Determinism is true. Your whole life history was "written" before you were born, and it either does or doesn't include your drinking poison now. But is that fatalism, the doctrine that what you do doesn't matter, that you cannot influence the course of events? Your history can include your drinking poison now only if you drink poison now! Your history will end now only if you drink poison now. It's what you do now that determines what comes next, and the fact that what you do now is but one link in a causal chain extending backward in time to before your birth is irrelevant to the fact that what you do now matters and affects the future.

Sophocles' *Oedipus the King* gives us an example that may help us distinguish between Determinism and fatalism. An oracle informs the king and queen of Thebes that their newborn son, Oedipus, will grow up to kill his father and marry his mother. In order to avoid this fate, they give the infant to a servant and order him to expose the child on a hillside so that it will die. The servant, taking pity on the infant, gives it to a herdsman from the neighboring city of Corinth. Eventually, the infant is adopted by the childless king and queen of Corinth and brought up as their own child. When Oedipus is a man, an oracle informs him that he will kill his father and marry his mother. In order to avoid this fate, he leaves Corinth, believing that his adoptive parents are his natural parents. On his travels he gets into a fight with a stranger and kills him. The stranger was his natural father, the king of Thebes. Oedipus's travels bring him to Thebes, where he saves the city from a monster. Because the city is without a king (no one knows that it was Oedipus who killed him), the city's leaders select Oedipus. In order to cement his position, he marries the queen, ignorant of the fact that she is his natural mother. Despite the efforts of both Oedipus and his parents, fate overtook them: Oedipus killed his father and married his mother. Nothing they did changed it or could have changed it.

Fatalism entails Determinism, but Determinism does not entail fatalism. If fatalism is true, nothing anyone could have done would have altered the inevitable course of events. But fatalism is not true. If the people involved in these events had behaved differently, the future probably would have been different. If the servant to whom Oedipus was given had followed orders and had killed the infant, Oedipus would not have grown up to fulfill the predictions. If the king and queen of Corinth had revealed to Oedipus that he was adopted, he might not have left the city when warned that he was fated to kill his father and marry his mother. The point is, if circumstances had been different, the outcome might have been different. That is consistent with Determinism but not with fatalism.

Borderline Cases

A thief emerges from the dark, points a gun at you, and barks, "Your money or your life." As a result of her threat, you hand over your wallet. Was your action of handing over your wallet free? At that point you certainly desired to hand over your wallet to save your life. So your action was the product of your thoughts and feelings. But surely handing over your wallet as the result of a threat is different from ordering a pizza because you want one. This seems to be a borderline case for Compatibilists. We might say that it has aspects of both free action and unfree action. Action that is the result of coercion doesn't seem to be free in the same way that action that isn't the result of coercion is free. Your alternatives have been reduced by the introduction of a new alternative that is quite unpleasant: a bullet in the heart. But you do hand over your wallet because you want to (in order to avoid the bullet in the heart). How shall we deal with this case on the basis of the Compatibilist version of freedom?

Consider the case of a drug addict or an alcoholic. When an addict takes drugs or an alcoholic drinks, are these free actions? In a sense the addict wants to take the drugs, and the alcoholic wants to take the drink. It's the addict's and the alcoholic's desire that leads them to take the fix or drink. But actions that are the result of addiction don't seem free in the same way that eating a pizza because you want to eat it is free. Actions that are the result of addiction—taking drugs, drinking, smoking, or overeating—seem the result of internal compulsions. How might we handle cases of internal compulsion or addiction? Are they free or unfree?

Desires sometimes conflict. Suppose that you're a smoker who's trying to quit. Right now, you're facing temptation. You have a strong desire to smoke. But that's not the only desire you have. You also have the desire not to succumb to the temptation. You have a desire not to succumb to the desire to smoke! You don't want to be addicted to smoking anymore, but the addiction causes you to have desires for that to which you're addicted.

If you smoke now, thus acting on your desire to smoke, is your action free or unfree? You act on one desire, the desire to smoke, but fail to act on another incompatible desire, the desire not to succumb to the desire to smoke. What if you don't smoke? Is that free? Again, you act on one desire you have, the desire not to succumb to the desire to smoke. But you fail to act on another desire, the desire to smoke.

You might say that the stronger desire will win. If the desire to smoke is stronger than the desire not to succumb to the desire to smoke, the desire to smoke will win. You'll smoke. If it's the other way around, you won't smoke. But do you have control over the strength of your conflicting desires? If the strongest desire always wins out and produces the action, and if one has no control over whether one has a desire and which desire is strongest, can it make sense to call actions produced by one's strongest desire free? You eat a pizza because you want to. Your desire to eat pizza is your strongest desire. On the other hand, an addict takes a fix because he wants to. His desire for a fix is his strongest desire. But are the two actions equally free? Why or why not?

 JOHN LOCKE (1632–1704)

An Essay Concerning Human Understanding

§ 5. This at least I think evident, That we find in our selves a *Power* to begin or forbear, continue or end several actions of our minds, and motions of our Bodies, barely by a thought or preference of the mind. . . . This *Power* which the mind has, . . . is that which we call the *Will*. The actual exercise of that power . . . is that which we call *Volition* or *Willing*. The forbearance or performance of that action, consequent to such order or command of the mind is called *Voluntary*. And whatsoever action is performed without such a thought of the mind is called *Involuntary*. . . .

§ 8. All the Actions, . . . reducing themselves . . . , to these two, viz. Thinking and Motion, so far as a Man has a power to think, or not to think; to move, or not to move, according to the preference or direction of his own mind, so far is a Man *Free*. Where-ever any performance or forbearance are not equally in a Man's power; where-ever doing or not doing, will not equally follow upon the preference of his mind directing it, there he is not *Free*, though perhaps the Action may be voluntary. So that the *Idea* of *Liberty*, is the *Idea* of a Power in any Agent to do or forbear any particular Action, according to the determination or thought of the mind, whereby either of them is preferr'd to the other; where either of them is not in the Power of the Agent to be produced by him according to his *Volition*, there he is not at *Liberty*, that Agent is under *Necessity*. So that *Liberty* cannot be, where there is no Thought, no Volition, no Will; but there may be Thought, there may be Will, there may be Volition, where there is no *Liberty*. A little Consideration of an obvious instance or two may make this clear.

§ 9. A Tennis-ball, whether in motion by the stroke of a Racket, or lying still at rest, is not by any one taken to be a *free Agent*. . . . It is, because we conceive not a Tennis-ball to think, and consequently not to have any Volition, or preference of Motion to rest, or vice versa; and therefore has not *Liberty*, is not a free Agent; but all its both Motion and Rest, come under our *Idea* of *Necessary*, and are so call'd. Likewise a Man falling into the Water, (a Bridge breaking under him,) has not herein liberty, is not a free Agent. For though he has

From *An Essay Concerning Human Understanding*, ed. P. H. Nidditch (New York, Oxford University Press, 1975).

Volition, though he prefers his not falling to falling; yet the forbearance of that Motion not being in his Power, the Stop or Cessation of that Motion follows not upon his Volition; and therefore therein he is not *free*. . . .

§ 10. Again, suppose a Man be carried, whilst fast asleep, into a Room, where is a Person he longs to see and speak with; and be there locked fast in, beyond his Power to get out: he awakes, and is glad to find himself in so desirable Company, which he stays willingly in, i.e. preferrs his stay to going away. I ask, Is not this stay voluntary? I think, no Body will doubt it: and yet being locked fast in, 'tis evident he is not at liberty not to stay, he has not freedom to be gone. So that *Liberty is not an* Idea *belonging to Volition,* or preferring; but to the Person having the Power of doing, or forbearing to do, according as the Mind shall chuse or direct. . . .

§ 11. We have instances enough, and often more than enough in our own Bodies. A Man's Heart beats, and the Blood circulates, which 'tis not in his Power by any Thought or Volition to stop; and therefore in respect of these Motions, where rest depends not on his choice, nor would follow the determination of his Mind, if it should prefer it, he is not a *free Agent. . . Voluntary* then *is not opposed to Necessary; but to Involuntary.*

§ 12. As it is in the motions of the Body, so it is in the Thoughts of our Minds; where any one is such, that we have power to take it up, or lay it by, according to the preference of the Mind, there we are *at liberty.* A waking Man . . . , whether he will remove his Contemplation from one *Idea* to another, is many times in his choice; and then he is in respect of his *Ideas,* . . . at liberty. . . . But yet some *Ideas* to the Mind, like some Motions to the Body, are such, as in certain circumstances it cannot avoid, nor obtain their absence by the utmost effort it can use. A Man on the Rack, is not at *liberty* to lay by the *Idea* of pain, and divert himself with other Contemplations. . . . But as soon as the Mind regains the power to stop or continue, begin or forbear any of these Motions of the Body without, or Thoughts within, according as it thinks fit to preferr either to

the other, we then consider the Man as a *free Agent* again.

§ 14. If this be so, (as I imagine it is,) I leave it to be considered, whether it may not help to put an end to that long agitated, and, I think, unreasonable, because unintelligible, Question, viz. *Whether Man's Will be free, or no.* For if I mistake not, it follows, from what I have said, that the Question it self is altogether improper; and it is as insignificant to ask, whether Man's *Will* be free, as to ask, whether his Sleep be Swift, or his Vertue square: *Liberty* being as little applicable to the *Will,* as swiftness of Motion is to Sleep, or squareness to Vertue . . . *Liberty,* which is but a power, belongs only to Agents, and cannot be an attribute or modification of the *Will.* . . .

§ 22. But the inquisitive Mind of Man, willing to shift off from himself, as far as he can, all thoughts of guilt, though it be by putting himself into a worse state, than that of fatal Necessity, is not content with this: Freedom, unless it reaches farther than this, will not serve the turn: And it passes for a good Plea, that a Man is not free at all, if he be not as free to will, as he is to act, what he wills. Concerning a Man's Liberty there yet therefore is raised this farther Question, *Whether a man be free to will;* which, I think, is what is meant, when it is disputed, Whether the *will* be free. And as to that I imagine,

§ 23.2. That *Willing,* or *Volition* being an Action, and Freedom consisting in a power of acting, or not acting, *a Man in respect of willing . . . cannot be free.* The reason whereof is very manifest: For it being unavoidable that the Action depending on his *Will,* should exist, or not exist; and its existence, or not existence, following perfectly the determination, and preference of his Will, he cannot avoid willing the existence, or not existence, of that Action; it is absolutely necessary that he *will* the one, or the other. . . . A Man must necessarily *will* the one, or the other of them, upon which preference, or volition, the action, or its forbearance, certainly follows, and is truly voluntary: But the act of volition, or preferring one of the two, being that which he cannot avoid, a Man in respect of that act of *willing,* is under a necessity, and so cannot be free. . . .

§ 29. . . . To the Question, what is it determines the Will? The true and proper Answer is, The mind. If this Answer satisfies not, 'tis plain the meaning of the Question, *what determines the Will?* is this, What moves the mind . . . ? And to this I answer, The motive . . . ; The motive to change, is always some *uneasiness*. . . . This is the great motive that works on the Mind to put it upon Action.

 ROBERT BLATCHFORD (1851–1943)

THE DELUSION OF FREE WILL

I. Introduction

The free will delusion has been a stumbling block in the way of human thought for thousands of years. Let us try whether common sense and common knowledge cannot remove it. . . .

The free will party[1] claims that man is responsible for his acts, because his will is free to choose between right and wrong. . . .

When a man says his will is free, he means that it is free of all control or interference: that it can overrule heredity and environment.

We reply that the will is ruled by heredity and environment.

The cause of all the confusion on this subject may be shown in a few words.

When the free will party says that man has a free will, they mean that he is free to act as he chooses to act.

There is no need to deny that. *But what causes him to choose?*

That is the pivot upon which the whole discussion turns.

The free will party seems to think of the will as something independent of the man, as something outside him. They seem to think that the will decides without the control of the man's reason.

If that were so, it would not prove the man responsible. "The will" would be responsible, and not the man. It would be as foolish to blame a man for the act of a "free" will as to blame a horse for the action of its rider.

But I am going to prove to my readers, by appeals to their common sense and common knowledge, that *the will is not free; and that it is ruled by heredity and environment.*

II. Reasons Given for Free Will and Criticisms of Them

1. To begin with, the average man will be against me. He [says he] knows that he chooses between two courses every hour, and often every minute, and he thinks his choice is free. But that is a delusion: His choice is not free. He can "choose," and does "choose." But he can only "choose" as his heredity and his environment cause him to choose. He never did choose and never will choose except as his heredity and his environment—his temperament and his training—cause him to choose. And his heredity and his environment have fixed his choice before he makes it.

2. The average man says, "I know that I can act as I wish to act." But [I ask:] what causes him to wish?

The free will party says, "We know that a man can and does choose between two acts." But [I ask:] what settles the choice?

There is a cause for every wish, a cause for every "choice"; and every cause of every

---

[1][The believers in genuine free will.—Eds.]

From *Not Guilty* by Robert Blatchford, p. 129–145, 1927. Vanguard Press: New York.

wish and choice arises from heredity, or from environment.

For a man acts always from *temperament,* which is *heredity,* or from *training,* which is *environment.*

And in cases where a man hesitates in his choice between two acts, the hesitation is due to a conflict between his temperament and his training, or, as some would express it, "between his desire and his conscience."

[*Example.*] A man is practicing at a target with a gun, when a rabbit crosses his line of fire. The man has his eye and his sights on the rabbit, and his finger on the trigger. The man's will is "free." If he presses the trigger the rabbit will be killed.

Now, how does the man decide whether or not he shall fire? He decides by feeling, and by reason.

He would like to fire, just to make sure that he could hit the mark. He would like to fire, because he would like to have the rabbit for supper. He would like to fire, because there is in him the old, old hunting instinct, to kill.

But the rabbit does not belong to him. He is not sure that he will not get into trouble if he kills it. Perhaps—if he is a very uncommon kind of man—he feels that it would be cruel and cowardly to shoot a helpless rabbit.

Well. The man's will is "free." He can fire if he likes; he can let the rabbit go if he likes. How will he decide? On what does his decision depend?

His decision depends upon the relative strength of his desire to kill the rabbit, and of his scruples about cruelty, and the law.[2]

Not only that, but, if we knew the man fairly well, we could guess how his "free" will would act before it acted. The average sporting Briton would kill the rabbit. But we know that there are men who would on no account shoot any harmless wild creature.

Broadly put, we may say that the sportsman would will to fire, and that the humanitarian would not will to fire.

Now, as both their wills are "free," it must be something outside the wills that makes the difference.

Well. The sportsman will kill, because he is a sportsman; the humanitarian will not kill, because he is a humanitarian.

And what makes one man a sportsman and another a humanitarian? Heredity and environment; temperament and training.

One man is merciful, another cruel, by nature; or one is thoughtful and the other thoughtless, by nature. That is a difference of heredity.

One may have been taught all his life that to kill wild things is "sport"; the other may have been taught that it is inhuman and wrong: That is a difference of environment.

Now, the man by nature is cruel or thoughtless, who has been trained to think of killing animals as sport, becomes what we call a sportsman, because heredity and environment have made him a sportsman.

The other man's heredity and environment have made him a humanitarian.

The sportsman kills the rabbit because he is a sportsman, and he is a sportsman because heredity and environment have made him one.

That is to say the "free will" is really controlled by heredity and environment. . . .

3. But, it may be asked, how do you account for a man doing the thing he does not wish to do? No man ever did a thing he did not wish to do. When there are two wishes the stronger rules.

[*Example.*] Let us suppose a case. A young woman gets two letters by the same post; one is an invitation to go with her lover to a concert, the other is a request that she will visit a sick child in the slums. The girl is very fond of music, and is rather afraid of the slums. She wishes to go to the concert, and to be with her lover; she dreads the foul street and the dirty home, and shrinks from the risk of measles or fever. But she goes to the sick child, and she forgoes the concert.

Why?

Because her sense of duty is stronger than her self-love.

---

[2][Because he was hunting on someone else's private property.—Eds.]

Now, her sense of duty is partly due to her nature—that is, to her heredity—but it is chiefly due to environment. Like all of us, this girl was born without any kind of knowledge, and with only the rudiments of a conscience. But she has been well taught, and the teaching is part of her environment.

We may say that the girl is "free" to act as she "chooses," but she *does* act as she has been *taught* that she *ought* to act. This teaching, which is part of her environment, controls her will.

We may say that a man is "free" to act as he chooses. He is free to act as *he* "chooses," but *he* will "choose" as heredity and environment cause *him* to choose. For heredity and environment have made him that which he is.

A man is said to be free to decide between two courses. But really he is only "free" to decide in accordance with his temperament and training. . . .

How, then, can we believe that free will is outside and superior to heredity and environment? . . .

4. "What! Cannot a man be honest if he choose?" Yes, if he "choose." But that is only another way of saying that he can be honest if his nature and his training lead him to choose honesty. "What! Cannot I please myself whether I drink or refrain from drinking?" Yes, But that is only to say you will not drink because it pleases *you* to be sober. But it pleases another man to drink, because his desire for drink is strong, or because his self-respect is weak.

And you decide as you decide, and he decides as he decides, because you are *you* and he is he; and heredity and environment made you both that which you are. . . .

The apostles of free will believe that all men's wills are free. But a man can only will that which he is able to will. And one man is able to will that which another man is unable to will. To deny this is to deny the commonest and most obvious facts of life. . . .

III. Arguments Against Free Will

. . . Let any man that believes that he can "do as he likes" ask himself *why* he *likes,* and he will see the error of the theory of free will, and will understand why the will is the servant and not the master of the man: For the man is the product of heredity and environment, and these control the will. . . .

Those who exalt the power of the will, and belittle the power of environment, belie their words by their deeds.

For they would not send their children among bad companions or allow them to read bad books. They would not say the children have free will and therefore have power to take the good and leave the bad.

They know very well that evil environment has power to pervert the will, and that good environment has power to direct it properly.

They know that children may be made good or bad by good or evil training, and that the will follows the training.

That being so, they must also admit that the children of other people may be good or bad by training.

And if a child gets bad training, how can free will save it? Or how can it be blamed for being bad? It never had a chance to be good. That they know this is proved by their carefulness in providing their own children with better environment.

As I have said before, every church, every school, every moral lesson is a proof that preachers and teachers trust to good environment, and not to free will, to make children good.

In this, as in so many other matters, actions speak louder than words.

That, I hope, disentangles the many knots into which thousands of learned men have tied the simple subject of free will; and disposes of the claim that man is responsible because his will is free.

JEAN PAUL SARTRE (1905–1980)

EXISTENTIALISM

I should like on this occasion to defend existentialism against some charges which have been brought against it.

First, it has been charged with inviting people to remain in a kind of desperate quietism because, since no solutions are possible, we should have to consider action in this world as quite impossible. We should then end up in a philosophy of contemplation; and since contemplation is a luxury, we come in the end to a bourgeois philosophy. The communists in particular have made these charges.

On the other hand, we have been charged with dwelling on human degradation, with pointing up everywhere the sordid, shady, and slimy, and neglecting the gracious and beautiful, the bright side of human nature; for example, according to Mlle. Mercier, a Catholic critic, with forgetting the smile of the child. Both sides charge us with having ignored human solidarity, with considering man as an isolated being. The communists say that the main reason for this is that we take pure subjectivity, the *Cartesian I think,* as our starting point; in other words, the moment in which man becomes fully aware of what it means to him to be an isolated being; as a result, we are unable to return to a state of solidarity with the men who are not ourselves, a state which we can never reach in the *cogito.*

From the Christian standpoint, we are charged with denying the reality and seriousness of human undertakings, since, if we reject God's commandments and the eternal verities, there no longer remains anything but pure caprice, with everyone permitted to do as he pleases and incapable, from his own point of view, of condemning the points of view and acts of others.

I shall try today to answer these different charges. Many people are going to be surprised at what is said here about humanism.

We shall try to see in what sense it is to be understood. In any case, what can be said from the very beginning is that by existentialism we mean a doctrine which makes human life possible and, in addition, declares that every truth and every action implies a human setting and a human subjectivity. . . .

[T]here are two kinds of existentialist; first, those who are Christian, . . . and on the other hand the atheistic existentialists, among whom I class . . . myself. What they have in common is that they think that existence precedes essence, or, if you prefer, that subjectivity must be the starting point.

Just what does that mean? Let us consider some object that is manufactured, for example, a book or a paper-cutter: here is an object which has been made by an artisan whose inspiration came from a concept. He referred to the concept of what a paper-cutter is and likewise to a known method of production, which is part of the concept, something which is, by and large, a routine. Thus, the paper-cutter is at once an object produced in a certain way and, on the other hand, one having a specific use; and one can not postulate a man who produces a paper-cutter but does not know what it is used for. Therefore, let us say that, for the paper-cutter, essence—that is, the ensemble of both the production routines and the properties which enable it to be both produced and defined—precedes existence. Thus, the presence of the paper-cutter or book in front of me is determined. Therefore, we have here a technical view of the world whereby it can be said that production precedes existence.

When we conceive God as the Creator, He is generally thought of as a superior sort of artisan. Whatever doctrine we may be considering, whether one like that of Descartes or that of Leibnitz, we always grant that will more

---

From *Existentialism and Human Emotions* (New York: Philosophical Library, 1957). Reprinted with permission.

or less follows understanding or, at the very least, accompanies it, and that when God creates He knows exactly what He is creating. Thus, the concept of man in the mind of God is comparable to the concept of paper-cutter in the mind of the manufacturer, and, following certain techniques and a conception, God produces man, just as the artisan, following a definition and a technique, makes a paper-cutter. Thus, the individual man is the realization of a certain concept in the divine intelligence.

In the eighteenth century, the atheism of the *philosophes* discarded the idea of God, but not so much for the notion that essence precedes existence. To a certain extent, this idea is found everywhere; . . . Man has a human nature; this human nature, which is the concept of the human, is found in all men, which means that each man is a particular example of a universal concept, man. . . . Thus, here too the essence of man precedes the historical existence that we find in nature.

Atheistic existentialism, which I represent, is more coherent. It states that if God does not exist, there is at least one being in whom existence precedes essence, a being who exists before he can be defined by any concept, and that this being is man. . . . What is meant here by saying that existence precedes essence? It means that, first of all, man exists, turns up, appears on the scene, and, only afterwards, defines himself. If man, as the existentialist conceives him, is indefinable, it is because at first he is nothing. Only afterward will he be something, and he himself will have made what he will be. Thus, there is no human nature, since there is no God to conceive it. Not only is man what he conceives himself to be, but he is also only what he wills himself to be after this thrust toward existence.

Man is nothing else but what he makes of himself. Such is the first principle of existentialism. It is also what is called subjectivity, the name we are labeled with when charges are brought against us. But what do we mean by this, if not that man has a greater dignity than a stone or table? For we mean that man first exists, that is, that man first of all is the being who hurls himself toward a future and who is conscious of imagining himself as

being in the future. Man is at the start a plan which is aware of itself, rather than a patch of moss, a piece of garbage, or a cauliflower; nothing exists prior to this plan; there is nothing in heaven; man will be what he will have planned to be. Not what he will want to be. Because by the word "will" we generally mean a conscious decision, which is subsequent to what we have already made of ourselves. I may want to belong to a political party, write a book, get married; but all that is only a manifestation of an earlier, more spontaneous choice that is called "will." But if existence really does precede essence, man is responsible for what he is. Thus, existentialism's first move is to make every man aware of what he is and to make the full responsibility of his existence rest on him. And when we say that a man is responsible for himself, we do not only mean that he is responsible for his own individuality, but that he is responsible for all men.

. . . Subjectivism means, on the one hand, that an individual chooses and makes himself; and, on the other, that it is impossible for man to transcend human subjectivity. The second of these is the essential meaning of existentialism. When we say that man chooses his own self, we mean that every one of us does likewise; but we also mean by that that in making this choice he also chooses all men. In fact, in creating the man that we want to be, there is not a single one of our acts which does not at the same time create an image of man as we think he ought to be. To choose to be this or that is to affirm at the same time the value of what we choose, because we can never choose evil. We always choose the good, and nothing can be good for us without being good for all.

If, on the other hand, existence precedes essence, and if we grant that we exist and fashion our image at one and the same time, the image is valid for everybody and for our whole age. Thus, our responsibility is much greater than we might have supposed, because it involves all mankind. If I am a workingman and choose to join a Christian trade-union rather than be a communist, and if by being a member I want to show that the best thing for man is resignation, that the kingdom of man is not of this world, I am not only involving my own case—I want to be resigned for everyone. As a result, my action has involved all humanity. To take a more individual matter, if I want to marry, to have children; even if this marriage depends solely on my own circumstances or passion or wish, I am involving all humanity in monogamy and not merely myself. Therefore, I am responsible for myself and for everyone else. I am creating a certain image of man of my own choosing. In choosing myself, I choose man. . . .

[T]he man who involves himself and who realizes that he is not only the person he chooses to be, but also a lawmaker who is, at the same time, choosing all mankind as well as himself, can not help escape the feeling of his total and deep responsibility. . . . Certainly, many people believe that when they do something, they themselves are the only ones involved, and when someone says to them, "What if everyone acted that way?" they shrug their shoulders and answer, "Everyone doesn't act that way." But really, one should always ask himself, "What would happen if everybody looked at things that way?" There is no escaping this disturbing thought except by a kind of double-dealing. A man who lies and makes excuses for himself by saying "not everybody does that," is someone with an uneasy conscience, because the act of lying implies that a universal value is conferred upon the lie. . . .

There was a madwoman who had hallucinations; someone used to speak to her on the telephone and give her orders. Her doctor asked her, "Who is it who talks to you?" She answered, "He says it's God." What proof did she really have that it was God? If an angel comes to me, what proof is there that it's an angel? And if I hear voices, what proof is there that they come from heaven and not from hell, or from the subconscious, or a pathological condition? What proves that they are addressed to me? What proof is there that I have been appointed to impose my choice and my conception of man on humanity? I'll never find any proof or sign to convince me of that. If a voice addresses me, it is always for me to decide that this is the angel's voice; if I consider that such an act is a good one, it is I who will choose to say that it is good rather than bad. . . .

For every man, everything happens as if all mankind had its eyes fixed on him and were guiding itself by what he does. And every man ought to say to himself, "Am I really the kind of man who has the right to act in such a way that humanity might guide itself by my actions?" . . .

For example, when a military officer takes the responsibility for an attack and sends a certain number of men to death, he chooses to do so, and in the main he alone makes the choice. Doubtless, orders come from above, but they are too broad; he interprets them, and on this interpretation depend the lives of ten or fourteen or twenty men. In making a decision he can not help having a certain anguish. All leaders know this anguish. That doesn't keep them from acting; on the contrary, it is the very condition of their action. For it implies that they envisage a number of possibilities, and when they choose one, they realize that it has value only because it is chosen. . . .

The existentialist . . . thinks it very distressing that God does not exist, because all possibility of finding values in a heaven of ideas disappears along with Him; there can no longer be an *a priori* Good, since there is no infinite and perfect consciousness to think it. Nowhere is it written that the Good exists, that we must be honest, that we must not lie; because the fact is we are on a plane where there are only men. Dostoievsky said, "If God didn't exist, everything would be possible." That is the very starting point of existentialism. Indeed, everything is permissible if God does not exist, and as a result man is forlorn, because neither within him nor without does he find anything to cling to. He can't start making excuses for himself.

If existence really does precede essence, there is no explaining things away by reference to a fixed and given human nature. In other words, there is no determinism, man is free, man is freedom. On the other hand, if God does not exist, we find no values or commands to turn to which legitimize our conduct. So, in the bright realm of values, we have no excuse behind us, nor justification before us. We are alone, with no excuses.

That is the idea I shall try to convey when I say that man is condemned to be free. Condemned, because he did not create himself, yet, in other respects is free; because, once thrown into the world, he is responsible for everything he does. The existentialist does not believe in the power of passion. He will never agree that a sweeping passion is a ravaging torrent which fatally leads a man to certain acts and is therefore an excuse. He thinks that man is responsible for his passion. . . .

To give you an example which will enable you to understand forlornness better, I shall cite the case of one of my students who came to see me under the following circumstances: his father was on bad terms with his mother, and, moreover, was inclined to be a collaborationist; his older brother had been killed in the German offensive of 1940, and the young man, with somewhat immature but generous feelings, wanted to avenge him. His mother lived alone with him, very much upset by the half-treason of her husband and the death of her older son; the boy was her only consolation.

The boy was faced with the choice of leaving for England and joining the Free French Forces—that is, leaving his mother behind—or remaining with his mother and helping her to carry on. He was fully aware that the woman lived only for him and that his going-off—and perhaps his death—would plunge her into despair. He was also aware that every act that he did for his mother's sake was a sure thing, in the sense that it was helping her to carry on, whereas every effort he made toward going off and fighting was an uncertain move which might run aground and prove completely useless; for example, on his way to England he might, while passing through Spain, be detained indefinitely in a Spanish camp; he might reach England or Algiers and be stuck in an office at a desk job. As a result, he was faced with two very different kinds of action: one, concrete, immediate, but concerning only one individual; the other concerned an incomparably vaster group, a national collectivity, but for that very reason was dubious, and might be interrupted en route. And, at the same time, he was wavering between two kinds of ethics. On the one hand, an ethics of sympathy, of personal devotion; on the other, a broader ethics, but one whose efficacy was more dubious. He had to choose between the two.

Who could help him choose? Christian doctrine? No. Christian doctrine says, "Be charitable, love your neighbor, take the more rugged path, etc., etc." But which is the more rugged path? Whom should he love as a brother? The fighting man or his mother? Which does the greater good, the vague act of fighting in a group, or the concrete one of helping a particular human being to go on living? Who can decide *a priori*? Nobody. No book of ethics can tell him. The Kantian ethics says, "Never treat any person as a means, but as an end." Very well, if I stay with my mother, I'll treat her as an end and not as a means; but by virtue of this very fact, I'm running the risk of treating the people around me who are fighting, as means; and, conversely, if I go to join those who are fighting, I'll be treating them as an end, and, by doing that, I run the risk of treating my mother as a means.

If values are vague, and if they are always too broad for the concrete and specific case that we are considering, the only thing left for us is to trust our instincts. That's what this young man tried to do; and when I saw him, he said, "In the end, feeling is what counts. I ought to choose whichever pushes me in one direction. If I feel that I love my mother enough to sacrifice everything else for her— my desire for vengeance, for action, for adventure—then I'll stay with her. If, on the contrary, I feel that my love for my mother isn't enough, I'll leave."

But how is the value of a feeling determined? What gives his feeling for his mother value? Precisely the fact that he remained with her. I may say that I like so-and-so well enough to sacrifice a certain amount of money for him, but I may say so only if I've done it. I may say "I love my mother well enough to remain with her" if I have remained with her. The only way to determine the value of this affection is, precisely, to perform an act which confirms and defines it. But, since I require this affection to justify my act, I find myself caught in a vicious circle. . . .

[I]n coming to see me he knew the answer I was going to give him, and I had only one answer to give: "You're free, choose, that is, invent." No general ethics can show you what is to be done; there are no omens in the world. The Catholics will reply, "But there are." Granted—but, in any case, I myself choose the meaning they have.

When I was a prisoner, I knew a rather remarkable young man who was a Jesuit. He had entered the Jesuit order in the following way: he had had a number of very bad breaks; in childhood, his father died, leaving him in poverty, and he was a scholarship student at a religious institution where he was constantly made to feel that he was being kept out of charity; then, he failed to get any of the honors and distinctions that children like; later on, at about eighteen, he bungled a love affair; finally, at twenty-two, he failed in military training, a childish enough matter, but it was the last straw.

This young fellow might well have felt that he had botched everything. It was a sign of something, but of what? He might have taken refuge in bitterness or despair. But he very wisely looked upon all this as a sign that he was not made for secular triumphs, and that only the triumphs of religion, holiness, and faith were open to him. He saw the hand of God in all this, and so he entered the order. Who can help seeing that he alone decided what the sign meant?

Some other interpretation might have been drawn from this series of setbacks; for example, that he might have done better to turn carpenter or revolutionist. Therefore, he is fully responsible for the interpretation. . . .

Actually, things will be as man will have decided they are to be. . . .

According to this, we can understand why our doctrine horrifies certain people. Because often the only way they can bear their wretchedness is to think, "Circumstances have been against me. What I've been and done doesn't show my true worth. To be sure, I've

had no great love, no great friendship, but that's because I haven't met a man or woman who was worthy. The books I've written haven't been very good because I haven't had the proper leisure. I haven't had children to devote myself to because I didn't find a man with whom I could have spent my life. So there remains within me, unused and quite viable, a host of propensities, inclinations, possibilities, that one wouldn't guess from the mere series of things I've done."

Now, for the existentialist there is really no love other than one which manifests itself in a person's being in love. There is no genius other than one which is expressed in works of art; the genius of Proust is the sum of Proust's works; the genius of Racine is his series of tragedies. Outside of that, there is nothing. Why say that Racine could have written another tragedy, when he didn't write it? A man is involved in life, leaves his impress on it, and outside of that there is nothing, To be sure, this may seem a harsh thought to someone whose life hasn't been a success. But, on the other hand, it prompts people to understand that reality alone is what counts, that dreams, expectations, and hopes warrant no more than to define a man as a disappointed dream, as miscarried hopes, as vain expectations. In other words, to define him negatively and not positively. However, when we say, "You are nothing else than your life," that does not imply that the artist will be judged solely on the basis of his works of art; a thousand other things will contribute toward summing him up. What we mean is that a man is nothing else than a series of undertakings, that he is the sum, the organization, the ensemble of the relationships which make up these undertakings.

When all is said and done, what we are accused of, at bottom, is not our pessimism, but an optimistic toughness. If people throw up to us our works of fiction in which we write about people who are soft, weak, cowardly, and sometimes even downright bad, it's not because these people are soft, weak, cowardly, or bad; because if we were to say, as Zola did, that they are that way because of heredity, the workings of environment, society, because of biological or psychological determinism, people would be reassured. They would say, "Well, that's what we're like, no one can do anything about it." But when the existentialist writes about a coward, he says that this coward is responsible for his cowardice. He's not like that because he has a cowardly heart or lung or brain; he's not like that on account of his physiological make-up; but he's like that because he has made himself a coward by his acts. There's no such thing as a cowardly constitution; there are nervous constitutions; there is poor blood, as the common people say, or strong constitutions. But the man whose blood is poor is not a coward on that account, for what makes cowardice is the act of renouncing or yielding. A constitution is not an act; the coward is defined on the basis of the acts he performs. People feel, in a vague sort of way, that this coward we're talking about is guilty of being a coward, and the thought frightens them. What people would like is that a coward or a hero be born that way. . . .

If you're born cowardly, you may set your mind perfectly at rest; there's nothing you can do about it; you'll be cowardly all your life, whatever you may do. If you're born a hero, you may set your mind just as much at rest; you'll be a hero all your life; you'll drink like a hero and eat like a hero. What the existentialist says is that the coward makes himself cowardly, that the hero makes himself heroic. There's always a possibility for the coward not to be cowardly any more and for the hero to stop being heroic. . . .

Questions for Discussion and Review

1. John Jones has died. After exhaustive tests, the coroner cannot find a cause of death. Therefore, the coroner claims that there was no cause of death; it was a causeless event. Would you believe the coroner? Why or why not?

2. Sheila is afraid of wasps. Is it (a) possible or (b) probable that there is no cause of her being afraid of wasps? Why or why not?

3. Pablo loves Delores but does not love Concetta. Is there a cause of his loving Delores and a cause of his not loving Concetta? Defend your answer.

4. Vanessa was in a car accident. Investigators cannot find a cause. Might there have been no cause? Why or why not?

5. You decided or chose to wear the clothes you are wearing today rather than other articles of clothing. Was there a cause of your deciding to wear these clothes rather than some other clothes? Defend your answer.

6. Tom opened the window because he was hot, he wanted to feel cooler, and he believed that opening the window would make the room cooler. Were his reasons also causes of his action of opening the window? Defend your answer.

7. If an event is predetermined—that is, a link in a causal chain each of whose links is caused by a preceding link in the chain—does it follow that the event is preplanned? Why or why not?

8. If God is all-knowing, then God knows what will occur in the future as well as what is occurring now and what has occurred in the past. How would it be possible for God to know everything that will occur in the future?

9. You set your alarm clock for 6:00 A.M. When the clock registered 6:00 A.M., the alarm went off. Just after the alarm went off, the sun rose over the horizon. Did the alarm clock's registering 6:00 A.M. cause its alarm to go off? Did the alarm's going off cause the sun to rise above the horizon? Explain and defend your answers.

10. Brenda is highly intelligent, physically strong and healthy, energetic, hardworking, self-confident, physically attractive, outgoing, kind, and considerate. She has a sense of humor and is not arrogant or conceited. She is popular and gets good grades in school. Did Brenda freely choose to have these traits and characteristics? Are they under her control? Do these characteristics and traits affect her behavior? (That is, if she had different characteristics, would her behavior probably be different?) Explain and defend your answers.

11. Was your decision to attend this college or university a free decision? Defend your answer.

12. Was your decision to attend this college or university uncaused? Defend your answer.

13. Do you agree with the Incompatibilist analysis of the concept of a "free" action/decision or with the Compatibilist analysis? Why?

14. If an action or decision is free only if it is uncaused or is caused by an uncaused event, how would its being uncaused or caused by an uncaused event make it "free"?

15. Jack the Ripper says that he does not deserve to be punished for his crimes because (a) he was not morally responsible for his actions because (b) his actions were not free because (c) they were caused and predetermined. Do you agree with him? Why or why not?

16. You have an examination tomorrow. You want to study for it because you want to pass it, but your roommate suggests that you party instead. He argues that fatalism is true. If you are fated to pass the exam, you will pass whether you party or study. If you are fated to fail the exam, you will fail it whether you party or study. Your actions will have no effect on whether you pass the exam, so you may as well party because it will be more enjoyable. Do you agree with his reasoning? Why or why not?

17. Sam and Dave are arguing about poverty and welfare reform. Sam says that if people are poor, it is their own fault. If they don't want to be poor, they can easily avoid poverty or lift themselves up from

poverty. All they have to do is work hard. Therefore, he says, poor people don't deserve help from society.

Dave, on the other hand, claims that it is not their own fault if people are poor. He says that often the causes of poverty are beyond their control. He points out that someone born into a poor family has a much higher probability of being poor as an adult than someone not born into a poor family. He says that all kinds of causal factors over which individuals have no control can lead to poverty in adulthood: malnutrition in infancy and childhood that affects physical development, including development of the brain; inferior educational opportunities; and continuous exposure to a variety of forms of serious stress, including crime, drugs, and violence. Dave also points out that the experience of growing up poor can have a profound effect on people's self-esteem, self-confidence, and general character and personality. Additionally, the way they are perceived by others will affect the way people perceive themselves. Poor children, especially children of color, are often looked down on by others. Thus, social and economic conditions shape people's character, personality, and the development of their skills and abilities. People also might be poor because of ill health. Dave says, "You are what your genes, your biology, and your environment made you." Therefore, Dave says, because people who are poor are almost always poor through no fault of their own, they deserve help.

With whom do you agree? Why?

18. Which, if any, do you accept, Hard Determinism, Soft Determinism, or Indeterminism? Why?

Suggestions for Further Reading

Bernard Berofsky, ed. *Free Will and Determinism*. New York: Harper & Row, 1966. A collection of excerpts from classic and contemporary works.

David Hume. *An Enquiry Concerning Human Understanding*. Indianapolis: Hackett, 1977. See especially Secs. 7 and 8. A classic formulation of the Compatibilist position.

Sidney Morgenbesser and James Walsh, eds. *Freedom and Determinism*. Englewood Cliffs, NJ: Prentice-Hall, 1962. A collection of excerpts from classic and contemporary works.

Timothy O'Connor, ed. *Agents, Causes, and Events*. Oxford: Oxford University Press, 1995. An excellent collection of recent work in this area of philosophy.

Ernest Sosa and Michael Tooley, eds. *Causation*. Oxford: Oxford University Press, 1993. A collection of challenging essays on the subject of the nature of the causal relation.

Jennifer Trusted. *Free Will and Responsibility*. New York: Oxford University Press, 1984. A readable contemporary introduction to the issues of this chapter.

Gary Watson, ed. *Free Will*. Oxford: Oxford University Press, 1982. A useful collection of influential articles on some of the issues of this chapter.

6 KNOWLEDGE, TRUTH, AND JUSTIFICATION

Objectives

Readers are expected to:

- understand the difference between knowledge and belief, including the three requirements for knowledge.
- understand the difference between Realist and anti-realist views of truth, including Subjectivism and Relativism.
- understand the distinction between conclusive and nonconclusive reasons.
- understand how beliefs expressed by noncontingent statements can be justified.
- understand how beliefs about our own mental states can be justified.
- reach conclusions about the scope and limits of self-knowledge and introspection.
- understand how beliefs about the world can be justified.
- understand the role of perception in forming and justifying beliefs about the world.
- reach conclusions about the scope and limits of perception.
- reach conclusions about the reliability of alternatives to perception for acquiring information about the world.
- reach conclusions about an ethics of belief.
- recognize and understand distorters of belief and perception.
- understand the role of memory in justified belief.
- reach conclusions about the scope and limits of memory.
- understand the role of probability in justification.
- understand the role of, as well as the scope and limits of, testimony of authorities in justification.

Introduction

People sometimes believe the darndest things. The nine hundred people who died with the Reverend Jim Jones in Guyana in 1979, many of them committing suicide by drinking strychnine-laced Kool-Aid, apparently believed that Jim Jones was divine, a son of God. Similarly, the people who died with David Koresh in the fire that ended the FBI siege of the Branch Davidian compound in Waco, Texas believed Koresh's claims to be divine. Several people committed suicide during the most recent visit of the Hale-Bopp comet because they believed that by doing so, they would be transported to a space ship that was hidden in the comet's tail and would enter another dimension that is more perfect than the dimension we ordinarily inhabit. Many people believed that the world would end on January 1, 2000.

It's Only a Belief

When people disagree, for example, one believing that we have souls and another believing that we don't, they sometimes say, "But it's only a belief; people have a right to believe what they want to." It may be true that people have a right to believe what they want to, in that others don't have a right to force them to believe what they don't want to believe. But what does it mean to say it's *only* a belief? If you believe that people have souls or that cows don't eat meat, they're certainly beliefs, but we seem somehow to diminish them if we say that they're "only" beliefs, as though it would be better if they were something other than beliefs. But what else could they be but beliefs?

One possibility is that we're contrasting beliefs with knowledge. "It's only a belief" may mean that you only believe it, you don't know it. We'll look at the contrast between knowledge and belief shortly, so we'll postpone consideration of this claim. On the other hand, "It's only a belief" may mean that somehow, beliefs are trivial or unimportant. "It's only a belief" may be a little like, "It's only a scratch, it's not serious."

Beliefs are serious if, as most people think, they guide our actions. If people in the middle ages hadn't believed in witches, they wouldn't have slaughtered tens of thousands of innocent people for witchcraft. Similarly, if it weren't for the Nazi's racial beliefs, they wouldn't have murdered millions of men, women, and children in the Holocaust. Black slavery, too, flourished because of racial beliefs. Mother Teresa dedicated her life to the poor and Martin Luther King, Jr. dedicated his life to racial justice because of their beliefs. If "it's only a belief" implies that beliefs are unimportant, it's misguided; what we believe matters.

BRAIN TEASERS

How would your actions be different if you believed that you only have six months to live?

How would your life be different if your religious beliefs were the opposite of what they are now?

Belief and Truth

Beliefs are mental states. Each of us has thousands of different individual beliefs. The content of each individual belief—what you believe—is expressed by a statement. For example, you believe that the sun is 93 million miles from Earth.

Statements are either true or false. For example, the statement "Abraham Lincoln was over six feet tall" is either true or false. If he was over six feet tall, it's true. If he wasn't, it's false. Similarly, "Earth is spherical" is true while "Earth is a cube" is false. Because the statements that are the content of individual beliefs are true or false, it follows that beliefs are true or false. If Abraham Lincoln was not over six feet tall but you believe that he was, then you have a false belief. If he was over six feet tall and you believe that he was, then you have a true belief. Thus, if you believe a statement to be true and it is true, you have a true belief. If you believe a statement to be true but it is false, you have a false belief.

Most of us care about truth. We want our beliefs to be true rather than false. In part it's because we steer through life using our beliefs as a guide. If many of our beliefs are false, we probably will have many of our desires frustrated. It may even shorten our or other people's lives. Suppose you believe that the ice will bear your weight if you skate on it and you act on that belief. If your belief is false, it could be catastrophic for you.

Consider the horrors that have occurred because of false beliefs. Because of their racial beliefs, the Nazis sought to exterminate all of Europe's Jews. Because of their beliefs about racial inferiority and superiority, people in Europe and America enslaved people of African descent. Because they believed that Native Americans were merely brutes, Europeans and their American descendants stole their land, confined them to reservations that often were little better than concentration camps, and sometimes massacred them. Because of beliefs about female inferiority and male superiority, in many parts of the world women were, and often still are, denied the same legal rights given to men.

Beliefs are vitally important. Having true beliefs rather than false ones matters. But when we talk about statements and beliefs being true or false, what do we mean?

If it's true that lions eat meat and false that they eat grass, then lions eat meat and don't eat grass. We could say that it means that lions have the property of being meat-eaters and don't have the property of being grass-eaters. Similarly, if it's true that snow is white and false that it's red, then snow is white and not red—snow has the property of being white but doesn't have the property of being red.

All that may seem obvious and trivial, so what's the point of saying it? Common sense makes a fundamental distinction between what really is the case and what only appears to be the case, between what's real and what's not real. Suppose I report seeing pink elephants in polka dot tights and tutus dancing about my room. Most people would say that although the elephants may appear to me to be there, they're really not. They're imaginary. My room doesn't really contain pink elephants, with or without tights or tutus.

We talk about the real world and reality. We contrast that with the worlds of imagination, fantasy, illusion, and hallucination. The real world or reality is the way things really are. Reality contains Bill Clinton, it doesn't contain Obi Wan Kenobi; it contains dogs and cats, it doesn't contain human vampires and werewolves; it contains New York City, it doesn't contain the City of Oz. In the real world, in reality, New York City is larger than Boston and helium is lighter than air. When we call a statement or belief true, we mean that reality is as the statement claims it to be. If I say it's true that Earth has one moon, I mean that reality contains Earth and Earth has only one moon. If reality is like that, then the claim is true; if reality isn't like that, it's false.

However, some people have said things about truth that may sound strange to common sense. (Remember that common sense can be wrong!) For example, some people say that a statement is true provided that it "coheres" with other statements one believes.[1]

According to this view, truth is not a relationship between a belief and reality or the world. Rather, it is a relationship between one belief and a system of other beliefs. Critics of this view have pointed out that as a consequence, two contradictory statements or beliefs can both be true. A statement may cohere with one individual's or group's system of beliefs but not with another's. Then the statement is true and false—or true within one system of beliefs and false within another. We can't answer, and perhaps can't even ask, the question, But is it really true? Some critics of this view have said that coherence with other beliefs is a good test of truth or justification, but not a good definition of truth. That is, they say that if a statement coheres with other things you believe, then you're justified in believing that it's true. But coherence doesn't guarantee truth. It could cohere with other things you believe and still

---

[1]See, for example, Nicholas Rescher, *The Coherence Theory of Truth* (Oxford: Oxford University Press, 1973).

be false. Therefore, cohering with other things we believe can't be what truth means.

William James said essentially that truth is what works. Sometimes it seems he meant that if our experiences of the world are consistent with what a statement implies they will be, then the statement is true. Thus, if I believe that there's a door in front of me, then it follows that if I reach out, I'll feel the door and doorknob with my hand. Suppose I reach out and, as expected, I feel the door and doorknob. Then my belief that there's a door in front of me is true. The belief "works" in the sense that acting on it leads to the experiences I anticipated. Thus, I consider the belief to be true.

Now "working" in the sense of leading to experiences I expect may well be a sign of truth. But James seems to be saying that truth means nothing but leading to experiences I expected. That doesn't seem to accord with common sense, because according to common sense, truth is a relationship between a belief or statement on the one hand and reality on the other hand. According to common sense, to say that it's true that there's a door in front of me is to say that reality, the real world, includes a real door in a certain place in front of where I'm standing.

American philosopher Charles Sanders Peirce (1839–1914) said that truth is what all inquirers would ultimately agree on. If all inquirers agree that Earth has only one moon, then it's true that earth has only one moon. If this is a definition of truth, it leaves out the idea that truth is a relationship between a belief or statement and the real world. We may be justified in believing something if all inquirers (or experts) agree on it, but is that what we ordinarily mean when we say that a belief or statement is true?

Realism and Antirealism

Realism about truth (also called objectivism) insists that when we say that a belief or statement is true, we mean that there is a certain relationship between the belief or statement and the real world. First, Realism is committed to the view that there is a real world. Different Realists have different views about this. Some say the real world is the world of physical things we perceive with our senses, that is, the physical universe with its physical objects, forces, fields, and energy. Others say the real world is purely mental, not physical, a world consisting only of thoughts and thinkers. According to this view (Idealism), the physical universe isn't real, only "ideas" are real. Common sense generally opposes Idealism and is committed to the view that the physical universe exists and is real.

So-called Quasi Realists say that while truth is a relationship between a statement and reality, reality is in some sense mind-dependent. What exists depends on what someone (humans? God?) believes exists. Realists without qualification are committed to the view that reality is what it is independent of any minds. In their view, even if no minds exist in the universe, there still would be a physical universe. And either planets are part of it or they're not. If they exist, then the statement "Planets exist" is true, whether or not there's anyone around to know or believe it. No mind makes it be the case that there are planets.

Realism and Correspondence

According to many Realists, a statement is true if and only if it "corresponds" or agrees with reality, which is what it is independent of what anyone thinks. Explaining this relationship of "correspondence" or agreement isn't easy, but let's try.

First, let's say that there are states of affairs.[2] For example, there is the state of affairs of Bill Clinton's winning the presidential election of 1996 and there is the state of affairs of Bill Clinton's losing the presidential election of 1996. Similarly, there is the state of affairs of water always freezing at 32 degrees F and the state of affairs of water always freezing at 50 degrees F. States of affairs are odd entities, to say the least, raising a number of puzzles. What exactly are they? Of what are they composed? Let's sidestep these puzzles. I hope we've said enough that you have an idea of what a state of affairs is supposed to be.

What are we to say of the states of affairs of:

A. Bill Clinton's winning the 1996 presidential election, and
B. Bill Clinton's losing the 1996 presidential election?

Philosophers say that both states of affairs "exist." Why? Because we can conceive of them and talk about them. So we need a concept that we can use to distinguish between the relationship between states of affairs (A) and (B) on the one hand and reality on the other. Philosophers say that state of affairs (A) "obtains" while state of affairs (B) does not "obtain."

States of affairs that obtain are called facts. Since the state of affairs of Bill Clinton's winning the 1996 presidential election obtains, it is a fact that Bill Clinton won the 1996 presidential election. Since the state of affairs of Bill Clinton's losing the 1996 presidential election does not obtain, it is not a fact that Bill Clinton lost the 1996 presidential election.

We can now say that a statement or belief is true provided that it agrees with or corresponds to the facts. The statement that Bill Clinton won the 1996 presidential election is true because it's a fact that he won the election. It's a fact that he won the election because the state of affairs of his winning the election obtains. The statement that Bill Clinton lost the 1996 presidential election is false because it doesn't agree with the facts;

---

[2]Not all philosophers will agree with my description of "correspondence" and some object to the use of the terms I'll be introducing.

it isn't a fact that Bill Clinton lost the 1996 presidential election. According to Realism, then, truth is a relationship between statements and facts. Since what the facts are is determined by the way the world really is, truth is a relationship between statements and the world.

Subjectivism About Truth

According to Realism, mind-independent reality determines whether a statement (and therefore a belief) is true or false. Realism is committed to what has been called the law of excluded middle: every statement is either true or false; it can't be both true and false, nor can it be neither true nor false. Realism is also committed to the view that if statements contradict each other, only one can be true. Thus, "The moon is a cube" is either true or false; it can't be both true and false, nor can it be neither true nor false. Since "The moon is a cube" and "the moon is not a cube" contradict, only one of them can be true. Which one is true depends only on the real shape of the moon (and the moon does have a real shape, independent of what anyone thinks).

However, according to Subjectivism about truth, whatever a person believes to be true is true for that person, and there is no other kind of truth. Truth is not a relationship between statements and a real world independent of people's minds, it's only a relationship between statements and individual minds.

Thus, if Tina believes that the world is round and Fred believes that the world is flat, then "The world is round" is true for Tina but not for Fred. Common sense asks, But who's really right? Who has the really true belief? Common sense assumes that they can't both be right, that their beliefs can't both be true because they contradict. However, Subjectivists say that they both have true beliefs, although not objectively true beliefs because no beliefs (or statements) are objectively true or false. This view entails that no one can ever have a false belief.

Realists think that Subjectivism about truth is logically incoherent and based on confusion. Consider the claims that define Subjectivism about truth.

SUBJECTIVISM ABOUT TRUTH (ST)

No statement is objectively true or objectively false. Whatever a person believes to be true is true *for that person,* and there is no other kind of truth.

Surely we must ask whether ST itself is true! If it is not true, then we should not accept it; but if it is true, then it contradicts itself (and a contradiction is necessarily false). But according to Subjectivism, ST is neither true nor false. It may be true for you and not true for me, but it is neither true (period) nor false (period). But how does that help us? If ST is true for you and not true for me, we surely are tempted to ask which of us is correct to ask whether ST is really true. If there is no correct as opposed to incorrect answer to the question "Is ST really true?" then what are we to make of ST?

Furthermore, Realists believe that Subjectivism about truth makes the concept of belief unintelligible. Suppose I believe that there is snow at the north pole and I am a Subjectivist about truth. That commits me to the following:

> I believe that there is snow at the north pole but I believe that "There is snow at the north pole" is neither objectively true nor objectively false.

Similarly, if I believe that there is snow at the north pole and you do not, if I am a Subjectivist about truth I am committed to the following:

> I believe that there is snow at the north pole, but my belief that there is snow at the north pole is no more true or correct than your belief that there isn't snow at the north pole.

If as a Subjectivist I do not believe that p is objectively true, then what can "I believe that p is true" possibly mean? Critics think that Subjectivism about truth makes the concept of belief incoherent.

Realists think that Subjectivism is based on confusion. Suppose a Subjectivist says that "There's snow at the north pole" is true for Joe but not true for Tim. What can that possibly mean? It's difficult to imagine that it could mean anything except that Joe believes that there's snow at the north pole and Tim doesn't. Talking about a statement being true for someone is just a careless and confusing way of saying that the person believes that the statement is true.

Someone might argue that everyone has a right to believe what they want to believe. But it's not clear what follows from this claim, even if it's true. It certainly doesn't follow that whatever a person believes to be true is really true. When people say that everyone has a right to believe what they want to believe, they seem to mean that no one has a right to force others to change their beliefs or to punish them solely for their beliefs. For example, you may believe that human actions are causing global warming and I may not. If we each have a right to believe what we want to believe, then we shouldn't try to force each other to change beliefs or kill each other over our disagreement. But it doesn't follow that we each have a true belief. How can it be true that human actions are and aren't causing global warming?

Furthermore, Subjectivists can't say that the claim that everyone has a right to believe what they want to believe is really true. What if someone doesn't believe that everyone has a right to believe what they want to believe? Then to use the language of Subjectivists, it's not true for them. And so it's not really true. So we can't use the claim that everyone has a right to believe what they want to believe in order to prove Subjectivism, since according to Subjectivism, it's not true.

Another common argument for Subjectivism starts with some statement, such as "God exists," about which people disagree. Subjectivists point out, often correctly, that no one knows whether the statement is true or false. They then claim that if no one knows whether the statement is true or false, then it isn't really true and isn't really false. This argument for Subjectivism is limited to statements that are not known by anyone to be true or false. If many people know that there's snow at the north pole, then Subjectivism doesn't apply to it. It's really (objectively) true that there's snow at the north pole and if someone believes there isn't snow there, that person is mistaken. So a Subjectivism that appeals to this argument isn't a doctrine about all statements or beliefs.

But why should we think that if no one knows the answer to a question, then there's no distinction between true and false answers to it? No human today knows whether there is life on other planets. But why would that lead us to think that the statement "Life exists on other planets" is neither true nor false? What sense can be made of the claim that the question "Is there life on other planets?" has no true or false answer? Subjectivism would then make the process of inquiry incomprehensible. Suppose that Chan is a scientist who wonders whether a combination of substances X, Y, and Z can cure AIDS. At this point, no one knows. As an inquirer, surely he is seeking to discover the truth about whether X, Y, and Z in combination can cure AIDS. Subjectivists tell him that whatever he believes and why ever he believes it, it will be true for him and there is no other kind of truth. According to them, he cannot meaningfully ask, "But can they really cure AIDS?" If Subjectivism is true, then there is no point to scientific research designed to discover truth, because there is no truth to be discovered. If Tom believes that eating rutabagas will cure AIDS, then his belief is as true as any other belief. Nor would the fact that many cancer patients ate lots of rutabagas and didn't have their cancers cured give Tom any reason to revise his beliefs. There are no facts to which our beliefs must conform in order to be true.

Relativism About Truth

According to Relativism about truth (as we will use the term), truth is relative not to individuals but to groups. According to Relativists, whatever a group believes to be true is true for members of that group. The group could be a whole society or it could be some smaller or larger group, such as the group of scientists or Christians. The beliefs of the individual members of the group are evaluated for truth relative to the group of which they are members. A belief is true if it is the same as the group's beliefs but false if it is inconsistent with the group's beliefs. Thus, suppose that Smith is a member of a society X that believes that witches exist. If Smith believes that witches exist, she has a true belief; if she believes that witches don't exist, she has a false belief.

Suppose that there is another society Y that believes that witches don't exist. We probably would be inclined to ask, "Which society is correct? Which has a true belief and which has a false belief? Do witches really exist?" Relativists claim that both societies are correct, that both have true beliefs and neither has a false belief. We can't ask, "Is 'witches exist' really true?" because there is no such thing as a statement's being "really" true. Nor is there a true as opposed to false answer to the question, "Do witches really exist?" Like Subjectivists, Relativists deny that any statement is objectively true or objectively false. But where the Subjectivist claims that whatever an individual believes is true for that individual (and there is no other kind of nonrelative truth), the Relativist claims that whatever a group believes is true for that group (and there is no other kind of nonrelative truth).

RELATIVISM ABOUT TRUTH

No statements are objectively true or objectively false. An individual's beliefs are true if and only if they conform to the beliefs of the group to which that individual belongs. Whatever a group believes to be true is true for that group.

Realists reject Relativism for the same reasons that they reject Subjectivism. We don't need to repeat those reasons here. However, there are two other additional problems facing Relativism. First, when we speak of the beliefs of a group, we can only mean the beliefs of a majority of the members of the group. So if Kim believes that God exists but he belongs to a group where 51% of its members believe that God doesn't exist, then according to Relativism he has a false belief. All that counts in evaluating the truth or falsity of a statement or belief is what a majority of members of the group believe.

Second, people belong to many different subgroups. Where do we locate the standard of truth that applies to them, then? Suppose that Tim is a member of a society X, most of whose members believe in witches, but he is also a scientist, most of whom believe that witches do not exist. Tim believes that witches do not exist. Does he have a true belief or a false belief? If his beliefs are to be assessed relative to society X, then his belief is false. On the other hand, if his beliefs are to be assessed relative to the group of scientists to which he belongs, then his belief is true. But which group's beliefs serve as the criterion of truth for Tim? Relativists do not say.

Realism Revisited

Realists claim that Subjectivism and Relativism about truth fail to distinguish between what is believed to be true or real and what is in fact true and real—between reality, on the one hand, and error, illusion, hallucination, and fantasy, on the other. Subjectivists and Relativists, in denying that truth depends on facts that are what they are independent of our minds, are committed to claims that are almost impossible to defend rationally.

Suppose that because of a reaction to medication, you become temporarily psychotic and believe that if you jump from the tenth floor of the hospital you will soar safely away over the clouds. Subjectivists say that your belief isn't really false. But of course it is. If you jump, you'll fall and almost certainly be killed.

Similarly, suppose that a whole society believes that there are malevolent gods who will destroy them unless they sacrifice young children every week. Relativists say that this society's belief is not false. But of course it is.

The last refuge of anti-realists is to point out that when I say, or everyone in my society says, that there are no gods that require human sacrifice, one individual's or society's belief is being pitted against another individual's or society's belief. Anti-realists might then say that there are no good reasons for claiming that I'm right and someone else is wrong; it's mere dogmatism or arrogance on my part. Sincere belief versus sincere belief always results in a draw.

But wait. Is it really mere dogmatism and arrogance on my part to say that I'm right that you'll fall to the ground if you leap from the tenth floor of the hospital in your psychotic state and you're wrong in thinking that you'll soar off into the clouds? It would be if I had no more reasons for my belief than you have reasons for your belief, or if I, too, were in a temporary psychotic state. But I have ample reasons—an entire lifetime's experience with gravity. You have no reasons other than the delusions caused by your psychotic state.

What about the other society's belief in gods that require human sacrifice? Our society doesn't believe in them, their society does. Isn't it dogmatism and arrogance to say that we're right and they're wrong? But if our society has carefully examined the evidence in favor of the belief that there are gods that require human sacrifice, including any evidence that the other society has, and has found none, and if the other society has no good evidence for its belief, then it's not mere dogmatism and arrogance on our part.

Of course when there's disagreement, it's my belief against yours or our society's belief against the belief of another society. But if I have, or my society has, carefully examined the issue and discovered many good reasons for the belief and few or no good reasons against it, then claiming that my or our belief is the true one is not mere dogmatism or arrogance. On the contrary, it would be almost preposterous to maintain that my or our belief is not the true one.

Sometimes we claim that we don't merely believe something, we know it. For example, I might claim that I know that if you jump from the tenth floor of the hospital in your psychotic state, you'll fall to the ground rather than soar off into the clouds. I also might say that I know that there are no gods that require human sacrifice. Do or can I really know these things? It's difficult to answer that question until we have a clearer idea of what knowledge is.

Three Requirements for Knowledge

Most philosophers think that you can't possibly know that something is true if you don't believe it's true. If you don't believe that bats perceive using sonar, then you don't know it. Believing is a requirement for knowing. In fact, most philosophers think that knowing is a subset of believing. That is, some of our beliefs constitute knowledge, others don't. Knowing isn't something entirely different from believing. Rather, knowing is believing that meets certain other requirements. The set of things we know is a subset of the things we believe.

Which of our beliefs are also knowledge? If you believe that Hitler was the leader of Germany during World War I, do you also know it? Of course not. Hitler wasn't the leader of Germany during World War I, so your belief is false. If you believe something to be true but the belief is false, you can't possibly know it to be true. Only our true beliefs can be knowledge.

Are all our true beliefs knowledge? Suppose that your friend believes that Judy has a crush on him. However, he has absolutely no evidence of this. He admits that she's never spoken a word to him, she's never written a line to him, and he's never seen her looking at him in the special way you look at someone you have a crush on. No one close to her has revealed her secret to him. Nothing at all has occurred that would justify him in his belief. In fact, you suspect that it's a case of wishful thinking, that he believes she has a crush on him only because he has a crush on her.

Suppose, though, that Judy really does have a crush on your friend. Does your friend know that she has a crush on him? Most philosophers say that even though your friend has a true belief, it's not knowledge because something is missing. In order to know that something is true, you must have good reasons or adequate evidence for believing it. If you have good reasons, then your belief is said to be justified. Thus, only our true beliefs that are justified count as knowledge.

BRAIN TEASERS

Does my friend know that Judy has a crush on him if she tells him that she does?

But justification is a matter of degree, unlike truth. All true beliefs are equally true. It wouldn't make sense to say that one true belief is more or less true than another true belief. But it would make perfectly good sense to say that one belief is more justified than another.

Probability is generally considered justification. If the probability of statement p, given the evidence e [pr(p/e)] is greater than .50, then we're justified in believing p. But if the probability of p is only a little bit greater than .50, the justification is pretty weak. Clearly, if pr(p/e) = .75, we're more justified in believing p than if pr(p/e) = .51. And if pr(p/e) = .95, we're even more justified in believing p.

How justified must our true beliefs be to constitute knowledge? Let's use a lottery to explore this. Suppose that there's a fair lottery with 100 tickets, one of which is guaranteed to win. I buy a ticket, so I have a .01 probability of winning and a .99 probability of losing. Being a realist, I believe I'll lose even though I hope I'll win. The winning ticket is drawn and my ticket is a loser. Therefore, I had a justified true belief that my ticket would lose. But did I know that my ticket would lose? Most people, on reflection, would say I didn't know it would lose. Since I could have been mistaken in believing that my ticket would lose, even though the probability of my being mistaken was only .01, I didn't know it would lose. The probability of my being right was not high enough and the probability of my being wrong was not low enough for me to have knowledge.

Then what if I have one lottery ticket out of a million tickets. I believe I will lose because the probability of my losing is .999999 and the probability of my winning is .000001. I turn out to have been right; I lose. I had a justified true belief that I would lose. Did I know I was going to lose? If you say that I didn't know, then you're committed to the view that knowledge requires a very high degree of justification. Some philosophers call that complete justification.

For now, let's say that we're completely justified in believing statement p if and only if the probability of our being mistaken, given our evidence, is zero. That is, we're completely justified in believing p if and only if pr(p/e) = 1 and pr(–p/e) = 0. Thus, there are at least three requirements for knowledge:

KNOWLEDGE

Person S knows that p is true only if:

1. S believes that p is true.

2. p is true.

3. S is completely justified in believing that p is true.

Justification

Whatever justification consists in and whatever degree of justification is required for knowledge, why should we care whether our beliefs are justified? Most philosophers maintain that justification is a guide to truth.

Justified beliefs are much more likely to be true than unjustified beliefs. Therefore, if we consider truth to be valuable, if we prefer true beliefs to false beliefs, then we should try to ensure that we believe only what we're justified in believing. Expressed this way, the concept of justification seems to have an evaluative dimension. It suggests a logical connection between justification and what we should believe, at least if truth is our goal in believing.

There are no degrees of truth. Every true statement or belief is equally true. It doesn't make sense to say that this statement is truer than other statements. (We might say that one statement is closer to the truth than another, but that's a different thing.) However, there are degrees of justification. For example, you would be more justified in believing that you'll be alive a year from now than you would be in believing that you'll be alive fifty years from now. That's an instance of a more general principle: the more probable a claim, the more justified we are in believing it.

If you're justified in believing something, it doesn't follow that you do believe it. You might be justified in believing something that you've never thought of or considered. You may have considered it but rejected it because you didn't recognize that you're justified in believing it.

BRAIN TEASERS

1. Could you be justified in believing something, recognize that you're justified in believing it, and yet not believe it?

2. Could you not be justified in believing something, recognize that you're not justified in believing it, and yet believe it anyway?

3. What, if anything, do your answers suggest about human rationality?

Realists about truth claim that truth isn't relative to what anyone believes or thinks. However, justification is relative. You are probably justified in believing many things that I'm not justified in believing, and vice versa. A member of a jury listening to all the evidence in a case is almost surely more justified in his beliefs about the guilt or innocence of the defendant than someone who has not followed the case very closely. Justification is relative to what people believe and think. It's relative to the evidence that they have. But is it only relative to evidence?

There are at least two different contexts in which the question of justification arises. One is when we are about to add a belief to our stock of beliefs. The question is whether we would be justified in coming to believe it, justified in adding it to our beliefs. For example, a juror has to decide whether to believe that the defendant is guilty or innocent. She also has to decide whether to believe that the evidence proves beyond reasonable doubt that he's guilty. Similarly, someone who doesn't yet have any beliefs about God may face the decision about whether to believe God exists or believe God doesn't exist.

Another context is when someone already believes something. The question is whether she's justified in continuing to believe it, justified in retaining it among her stock of beliefs. That question may depend on whether she was justified in adding it when she first came to believe it. But then again, it may not depend on that. The conditions under which someone is justified in retaining a belief she already has may be different from the conditions under which she's justified in adding a belief in the first place. The flip side of this is that if someone is not justified in continuing to believe something she already believes, then she's justified in ceasing to believe it, in ejecting it from her stock of beliefs. Thus, someone may believe that God exists, wonder whether she's justified in continuing to believe it, and face the decision about whether to stop believing.

Deciding to Believe

Are our beliefs a matter of decision? Do we have control over them so that if we decide to believe something or to stop believing it, by an act of will we can do so? Do we choose our own beliefs? For example, was there a time when you didn't believe in God, then you decided to believe, and by an act of will you began to believe? Could you simply stop believing in God now if you do believe, or begin believing in God if you don't now believe?

BRAIN TEASERS

> Try an experiment. If you do believe in God, try to exercise your will to stop believing it, even if only temporarily. Similarly, if you don't believe, try to exercise your will to begin believing.

I find that there are many things that in a sense I can't help believing. I believe I'm now typing these words into my computer. Therefore, I also believe that I'm in my office and that there's a desk before me with a computer on it. I don't think I decided to believe these things. I just find myself believing them. And I'm not sure that under the circumstances, I could change that and stop believing at this moment that I'm typing these words into my computer. (Perhaps later I could convince myself that I wasn't really doing this, that it was a dream. But right now I can't seem to help believing that I'm really typing these words into my computer.)

We might distinguish between beliefs added almost automatically to our stock of beliefs, and beliefs added only after conscious deliberation and thought. I hear a bird's song as I type. I didn't stop to ask myself, am I really hearing a bird? I automatically came to believe that there's a bird outside my window without thinking at all about it. On the other hand, I came to believe that World War I profoundly changed the world and that its effects are still being felt only after reading and thinking about it. It wasn't automatic.

Suppose that I came to believe that God exists only after much thought and deliberation. Was there an act of will involved? Did I decide, "I will believe now?" Or instead did the evidence and arguments in some sense cause me to come to believe in God so that after reviewing the evidence and thinking about it, I simply found myself believing? Similarly, if after reviewing the evidence I'm unpersuaded and I remain agnostic on the question, did I decide not to believe? Or instead, did I simply find myself not believing after reviewing the evidence?

In order to answer these questions, you probably have to search your own mind and memory to review how you came to believe many of the things you believe. I don't seem to have that much control over what I believe. How much control do you have over what you believe?

The Right to Believe

If you're justified in believing something, should you believe it? Would it be somehow wrong not to believe it? On the other hand, if you're not justified in believing something, either not justified in adding it to your beliefs or in retaining it among your beliefs, should you not believe it? Would it be wrong to begin believing it or to continue believing it? Some philosophers, for example, W. K. Clifford, emphasize that there is an ethics of belief. Clifford claimed that it's wrong to believe something if you don't have adequate evidence for it.

Some people value psychological comfort more than truth, at least in certain areas of inquiry. They say that if believing something satisfies some of our psychological needs, then we're justified in believing it even if we have no evidence for it. Thus, some people say that they're justified in believing that God exists, that they have immortal souls, and that they will continue to exist after their bodies die, even if they have no evidence for these things and no good arguments or reasons for believing them. (Of course, many people who believe these things say that they do have evidence and good reasons.)

William James (1842–1910) wrote an influential paper entitled "The Will to Believe." He later wished he had entitled it "The Right to Believe." In it he tries to defend "the lawfulness of voluntarily adopted faith."[3] By

---

[3]William James, "The Will to Believe," in *The American Intellectual Tradition,* vol. II, 3d ed., ed. David A. Hollinger and Charles Capper (Oxford: Oxford University Press, 1997), 75.

saying that faith is "lawful," James means that it's not contrary to any ethical rules, including any ethical rules governing belief, if there are any, to believe when there's no evidence. But James does not argue that wishful thinking is as lawful as science in the matter of belief. It's only in certain circumstances that faith is lawful.

James begins, "Let us give the name of hypothesis to anything that may be proposed to our belief."[4] For example, neither believing that God exists nor that God doesn't exist, I consider whether to believe in God. The claim that God exists is a hypothesis for me. The context of justification, then, is when we're considering adding something to our stock of beliefs.

A hypothesis is either live or dead for us. If, given my stock of beliefs, the hypothesis is not impossible or so improbable that it's not worth considering, then it's live for me. If it is impossible or extremely improbable, then it's dead for me. For example, given what I believe, the hypothesis that the Pope ordered President Kennedy's assassination is dead for me because it's so wildly improbable. However, given what I believe, the hypothesis that Lee Harvey Oswald did not act alone is live for me because its probability for me is not negligible.

If I face a choice between two hypotheses, that is an option. In the case of God, it's an option because I face two alternative hypotheses: God exists, and God doesn't exist. A live option involves a choice between alternative hypotheses, all of which are live. If the hypothesis that God exists is live for me and the hypothesis that God doesn't exist is live for me, then it's a live option I face. If the hypotheses are inconsistent with each other, that is, if one is true, the other must be false, then that is a forced option. I must believe only one of the alternatives. Since "God exists" and "God doesn't exist" contradict each other, my option is a forced one. Finally, James says that hypotheses that are really important to my life are momentous. Which hypothesis I come to believe will profoundly affect my life. James believed that whether he believed in God would profoundly affect his life, so the hypothesis that God exists and the hypothesis that God doesn't exist are momentous for him.

In many cases, when faced with a live, forced, momentous option, which hypothesis is true can be determined by appeal to scientific evidence and tests. But in some cases they can't, or at least can't in some reasonable length of time. According to James, when we face such an option (but only such an option?), and when we can't get enough scientific evidence in a reasonable length of time to determine which one is true, then we have a right to believe either hypothesis based on our psychological needs. This right to believe is fairly restricted. For example, if we have evidence that a hypothesis is false, the principle does not give us a right to

---

[4]Ibid.

ignore it and believe anyway. Similarly, it would not license us to believe a hypothesis if there's evidence available that it's false, but we refused to look at it so that we don't *have* evidence that it's false.

BRAIN TEASERS

What's the difference between there being evidence for a hypothesis and one's having evidence for it?

James doesn't simply assert this principle; he argues for it. He points out that as inquirers, we have two goals that aren't necessarily compatible. We have a desire to believe what's true and to not believe what's false. That is, we have a desire to acquire true information while avoiding error. If we have no beliefs, we have no true information at all. So we want to acquire a stock of beliefs, and a fairly large stock. We want to do what we can to ensure that if a statement is true, then we believe it.

BRAIN TEASERS

Could someone have absolutely no beliefs? What would it be like if someone had only a few hundred beliefs?

After all, our stock of beliefs is our map or picture of the world. We don't want that to be blank or to have a lot of blank spaces. Now we can minimize the probability that we'll fail to believe a true statement by believing every statement we consider. That way, not many true beliefs will escape us. But of course, if we believe every statement that we consider, we'll add a lot of false beliefs to our stock as well as true beliefs. And we also want to avoid error. We want to minimize the probability of having lots of false beliefs. To do that, we could believe nothing. That way we'll guarantee that we won't have any false beliefs.

James's point is that we have to balance these two equally important but competing objectives—gaining true beliefs (accurate information) and avoiding error. That means taking risks. If we don't believe something, we risk losing a true belief. If we do believe something, we risk adding a false belief. We have to decide which risks are worth taking.

James thinks that if (and probably only if) we would lose something very valuable by not believing because of a fear of error, then we're justified in believing in order to secure that valuable thing. What do we risk losing if we don't believe that God exists? James says that if God does exist, we'll lose the opportunity to have a personal relationship with God. There may be no guarantee that God will have a personal relationship with us if She exists and we believe She exists, but James assumes that we cannot possibly have a personal relationship with God if we don't believe that She exists. Having a personal relationship with Her, if She exists, is of immeasurable value that can only bring us good things.

But do we know that God would be willing to have a personal relationship with someone who believes in Her existence without having adequate evidence for it? How do we know that God values faith? James may have overlooked the possibility that believing in God without adequate evidence, even if the belief is true, could prevent our having a personal relationship with God. If God exists, She gave us our capacity for reason. She may want us to exercise it to the fullest extent and may consider faith the easy way out.

Although James doesn't stress this, he seems to imply that there's great good in believing that God exists if She does, but no bad consequences in believing that God exists if She doesn't. But that's questionable. First, it may depend on what other beliefs one has about God besides Her bare existence. If one believes that God doesn't want people to enjoy themselves in this life too much, and that they'll be punished after death if they do, that might lead to an ascetic lifestyle and the denial of many harmless pleasures. Also, given the way that religious belief has sometimes led to horrible atrocities or been used to justify them, one may wonder whether belief in God is always at worst harmless. Religious divisions have led to inquisitions and wars. Catholic and Protestant Christians slaughtered each other because of their different religious beliefs during the Reformation and Counterreformation. Catholics and Protestants have been at each other's throats in Ireland for centuries. Christians and Muslims fought several Crusades against each other in the Middle Ages, motivated at least in part by religious beliefs. Religion has been used to justify slavery and the subordination of whole classes of people, such as women in Christianity and so-called Untouchables in Hinduism.

What about the other hypothesis, the hypothesis that God doesn't exist? What if you believe that God doesn't exist and you're right? Even if you've avoided error, have you nevertheless lost something valuable that might outweigh avoiding error? James doesn't say, but perhaps it's the psychological comfort that comes with religious belief, even if it's false. If you believe that you have a personal relationship with God, that may fulfill a variety of psychological needs even if it's false.

We might summarize James's reasoning as follows.

BELIEVE GOD EXISTS

If it's true, only good consequences

If it's false, only good consequences

BELIEVE GOD DOESN'T EXIST

If it's false, only bad consequences

If it's true, mainly bad consequences

Then it's reasonable to believe God exists because the consequences will be better for you than if you believe God doesn't exist, regardless of the truth.

BRAIN TEASERS

Do you think we have a right to believe under the conditions that James set out? Do James's views about our having a right to believe under certain circumstances, even if we don't have adequate evidence, presuppose that we have control over what we believe and can decide to believe?

Conditions of Justification

Under what conditions are we justified in believing something? Justification is tied to reasonability. We could rephrase our question as, "Under what conditions is it reasonable to believe something?" One possibility is that you're justified in believing anything you believe, whether you have reasons for it or not. That is,

Necessarily, if you believe that p, then you're justified in believing that p.

Thus, if you believe that the Pope is a space alien in disguise or that the entire universe will cease to exist five minutes from now, you're justified in believing these things. But most people probably would consider that quite implausible. How can you be justified in believing that the Pope is a space alien, how can it be reasonable for you to believe this, if you don't have any good reasons for believing it? This suggests a different principle of justification.

Necessarily, you're justified in believing that p if and only if you have good reasons for believing that p.

Most people probably would consider this an improvement, but there's still a problem. Suppose I have good reasons for believing p, but I also have good reasons for believing not p. We frequently find ourselves having to weigh reasons or evidence both for and against a statement p in order to reach a judgment about whether it would be reasonable to believe it rather than believe the contrary (not p) or suspend judgment. Juries in trials almost always find themselves in this predicament. So perhaps we can improve this principle further.

Necessarily, you're justified in believing that p if and only if (1) you have good reasons for believing that p and (2) you do not have equally (or nearly equally) good reasons for believing that not p.

We could continue to refine this principle to improve on it, but what we have suits our purposes.

BRAIN TEASERS

Is this principle plausible for both contexts—coming to believe something and continuing to believe something?

Reasons

We need to distinguish between different kinds of reasons. First, there are explanatory and justifying reasons. Explanatory reasons explain why something is the case; justifying reasons provide reasons for thinking that a claim is true. The question, "Why do you believe that the Pope is a space alien?" could be a request either for explanatory or justifying reasons. "Because I was brainwashed to believe it" or "because that's what I was taught at an early age" are explanatory reasons. "Because I read it in a supermarket tabloid" or "Because I saw him out of his human disguise" are justifying reasons.

Second, there are conclusive reasons and nonconclusive justifying reasons. Conclusive reasons logically entail what they are justifying reasons for, nonconclusive reasons don't. That the animal I'm looking at is a whale, that all whales are mammals, and that all mammals have lungs are conclusive reasons for believing that the animal I'm looking at has lungs. Conclusive reasons can be recast into deductively valid arguments.

1. The animal I'm looking at is a whale.
2. All whales are mammals.
3. All mammals have lungs.

---

4. Therefore, the animal I'm looking at has lungs.

Statements (1) through (3) are conclusive reasons for believing (4). But they will be conclusive reasons for me only if I believe they're true. Something can be a reason for me only if I believe it; something can be a reason for you only if you believe it.

Nonconclusive justifying reasons only make that for which they are reasons more or less probable. That anyone reading this book is almost certainly a college student or teacher, that almost all college students and teachers are below age seventy, and that you're reading this book are good reasons for believing that you're below age seventy. Nonconclusive good reasons can be recast into inductively strong arguments.

1'. Anyone reading this book is almost certainly a college student or teacher.

2'. Almost all college students and teachers are below age seventy.

3'. You're reading this book.

4'. Therefore, you're (probably) below age seventy.

Statements (1') through (3') are good nonconclusive reasons for believing (4'). They're good but not conclusive because even if (1')–(3') are true, the conclusion could possibly be false. You could be one of the very rare college students or teachers who is seventy or above, and you could be one of the very rare readers who is neither a college student nor a teacher. Nevertheless, I'm justified in believing you're under age seventy, given the reasons I have.

Different kinds of statements or beliefs seem to call for different kinds of reasons. Consider the following list of things I might believe.

Either it will rain today or it won't.

$3^3 = 27$.

I'm holding a book in my hands.

I had pancakes for breakfast this morning.

I have a headache.

I love my wife.

$E = MC^2$.

John Wilkes Booth assassinated Lincoln.

They call for different kinds of evidence or reasons. I would not justify each in the same way.

Justifying Noncontingent Statements

There are two kinds of noncontingent statement, those that are necessarily true and those that are necessarily false. "Either it will rain today or it won't" is necessarily true; "It will simultaneously rain here and not rain here" is necessarily false. Let's look at two lists.

NECESSARILY TRUE STATEMENTS

Either you're over age seventy or you're not over age seventy.

If water is a liquid at room temperature and liquids are wet, then water is wet at room temperature.

If either Sam or Dave is guilty and Sam isn't, then Dave is guilty.

All bachelors are unmarried.

NECESSARILY FALSE STATEMENTS

All lions eat meat but some don't eat meat.

You're simultaneously below age seventy and not below age seventy.

The ball is red all over and blue all over.

Some raisins are dried apricots.

If you believe that a necessarily true statement is true, are you justified in believing it? If yes, what justifies you? What are your reasons? It's tempting to say that you're justified in believing it simply because it's necessarily true, but suppose you don't recognize that it's necessarily true? Some necessarily true statements may be very complicated and difficult to understand. So perhaps we should say that you're justified in believing it if you recognize that it's necessarily true. If you're asked, "What reasons do you have for believing that 'either you're below age seventy or you're not' is true?", about the only reply available seems to be, "Because I recognize that it's necessarily true."

But a persistent questioner will then ask, "And what justifies you in believing that it's necessarily true?" What other answer can we give than, "Because I just recognize that it's necessarily true after I've reflected on it. It can't possibly be false. I realize that there are only two possibilities: you're below age seventy and you're not below age seventy. If you're below age seventy, it's true. But if you're not below age seventy, it's also true. So no matter what your age, it's true. So it's necessarily true, true in all possible circumstances." What enables us to recognize that a statement is necessarily true or necessarily false is our capacity for reason. So for noncontingent statements and beliefs, the reasons that justify us in believing are just our recognitions of necessary truths and necessary falsehoods. Because reason alone enables me to recognize necessary truths and falsehoods (of course, knowledge of the meanings of words is required, too), they are said to be knowable a priori. That means that I can know whether they're true or false prior to (or independent of) any experience of the world. The truth of "Either it will rain today or it won't" is knowable a priori because no one has to rely on experience, such as perceptual experience, in order to know that it's true.

Justification Principles for Noncontingent Statements

We might advance the following justification principle for noncontingent statements based on our ability to reason.

Necessarily, if you recognize that p is necessarily true, then you're justified in believing that p.

Necessarily, if you recognize that p is necessarily false, then you're justified in believing that not p.

Whether contingent statements are true or false, however, can only be known after experience. I don't know whether it's raining here now unless I have experiential evidence. I may listen to hear whether it's raining, look outside to see whether it's raining, look at people who have been outside to see whether they're wet, or listen to a weather report. Contingent statements, then, are said to be knowable only a posteriori, which means that we can know whether they're true or false only after (posterior to) experience.

BRAIN TEASERS

Is it necessarily true and knowable a priori that all fathers are male and all mothers are female?

Self-Knowledge: Beliefs About Our Own Mental States

I claim that I know a lot of things about myself. I know my height, weight, hair color, and eye color. I know who my parents are, where I was born, where I went to school, and what my current job is. I know who my sister is, who my wife is, and where I live. Yes, I know a lot about myself. But that's not the kind of knowledge that the Greek god Apollo had in mind when he admonished people, "Know yourself." He had in mind knowledge of our own mental states: our beliefs, desires, preferences, values, personality and character traits, personal strengths and weaknesses. How do we acquire knowledge of our own mental states? What justifies our beliefs about our own mental states?

"I have a headache," even if true, is not necessarily true.

BRAIN TEASERS

Why is it that "I have a headache" isn't necessarily true even if it's true?

If I assert (to myself or to others) the statement, "I have a headache," ordinarily that signals that I believe I have a headache. If someone speaks or writes a statement, she is generally taken by others to be asserting what she believes. The same thing applies if one asserts something to oneself silently. There's a difference, then, between having a headache and believing that one has a headache.

If asked, we probably would say that we know we have a headache when we have one. Given our analysis of knowledge, that means we believe it, it's true, and we're justified in believing it. What justifies you in believing you have a headache when you have one?

It's difficult to imagine any other response than "What justifies me in believing I have a headache is the fact that I have a headache and I feel the pain." We may be tempted to say that the mental state of having a headache is special in that we can't possibly believe we have one if we don't, and if we have one, then we believe we have it. The first part says that you can't possibly be mistaken if you believe you have a headache. The second part says that your headaches can't hide from you; if you have one, you're aware of it and believe you have it. We'll call the first principle the principle of infallibility and the second principle the self-presentation principle.[5] Thus, the claim is that first-person beliefs about having a headache are infallible and the mental state of having a headache is self-presenting. Let's make these two principles explicit, applying them specifically to headaches.

THE PRINCIPLE OF INFALLIBILITY

Necessarily, if you believe you have a headache, then you do have a headache, and

if you believe you don't have a headache, then you don't have a headache.

THE PRINCIPLE OF SELF-PRESENTATION

Necessarily, if you have a headache, then you believe that you have a headache.

If these two principles are correct, then beliefs about our having a headache seem to be self-justifying in the following sense.

THE SELF-JUSTIFICATION PRINCIPLE

Necessarily, if you believe that you have a headache, then you're justified in believing that you have a headache, and

if you believe you don't have a headache, then you're justified in believing that you don't have a headache.

We're going to examine more fully the mental state of having a headache. But first, a major question is whether all mental states are like having a headache in that first-person beliefs about being in a mental

---

[5]The term "self-presenting" comes from Roderick Chisholm.

state, any mental state, are infallible and the states themselves are self-presenting. If they are, then we can generalize our principles in the following way.

THE PRINCIPLE OF INFALLIBILITY

Necessarily, for all mental states m, if you believe that you're in m, then you are in m, and if you believe that you're not in m, then you're not.

THE PRINCIPLE OF SELF-PRESENTATION

Necessarily, for all mental states m, if you're in m, then you believe that you're in m.

THE SELF-JUSTIFICATION PRINCIPLE

Necessarily, for all mental states m, if you believe that you're in m, then you're justified in believing that you're in m, and

if you believe that you're not in m, then you're justified in believing that you're not in m.

But are even headaches both infallible and self-presenting?

Are first-person beliefs about headaches infallible? Could I believe I have a headache when I don't? Could I believe I don't have a headache when I do? Let's assume that we don't suspect that there's confusion over what "headache" means. For example, I don't rub my jaw the way I would if I had a toothache or my stomach the way I would if I had a stomachache and say, "I have a headache," which would probably indicate that I don't mean by "headache" what others mean. It's difficult to imagine that we could be mistaken in believing we have a headache, other than verbal mistakes. But if we can make verbal mistakes, then perhaps beliefs about having a headache aren't infallible after all.

Suppose I have what in English is called a headache and, although I'm a native speaker of English, I think that headaches are called "toothaches." If asked, I'd say, "I have a toothache." What do I believe? Do I believe that I have a headache or do I believe that I have a toothache? We might be tempted to say that I believe I have a toothache, but suppose you ask me to point to where I feel the pain. If I point to my head rather than to my tooth or jaw, it seems plausible to say that I believe I have a headache, but I'm just misexpressing my belief.

We said earlier that in order to have a specific belief, we have to have the concepts that express the contents of the belief. I can't believe that elephants are large if I don't have the concept of an elephant. What is it to have the concept of an elephant? Do I have to understand the English word "elephant"? No. Do I have to understand some word in some language that means the same as the English word "elephant"? Not necessarily. Imagine that space aliens land on Earth and encounter elephants for the first time. No language they know has a word for elephants. They study these creatures and invent a new word for them in their language.

It seems that they acquired the concept of an elephant before they invented a word for it. So perhaps concepts are not words but instead are things that are designated by words.

To have the concept of an elephant, we must be able to distinguish things that are elephants from the things that aren't elephants. Having the concept of something is a matter of degree. Since elephants are very complicated creatures with lots of properties, the concept of an elephant is itself complicated. It might include every property that all elephants share (or generally share). The concept of an elephant might include, then, being a mammal with certain readily perceivable characteristics, such as having a trunk and big ears, and being, when full grown, as large as a tank. It may include being an animal with a certain diet, a certain way of procreating, a certain way of behaving. It may include being an animal with a certain genetic structure. The concept of an elephant that an expert on elephants has is much richer than the concept of an elephant that I have. We might say that I have a part of the concept of an elephant. As long as it's enough of a part to enable me to accurately distinguish elephants from nonelephants, it's adequate.

What about the concept of a headache? I could have the concept even if I don't have a word for it and even if I apply the wrong word to it. I may think that the English word "toothache" designates the concept of a headache. Nevertheless, couldn't we say that if I've ever had a headache, then I have acquired the concept of a headache, regardless of issues of language? It's just as we might say that the space aliens have acquired the concept of an elephant when they encountered one, even if they had no word for it. In that case, we might wish to say that if I believe I have a headache, then I do have one, even if I misexpress my belief in language. This supports the first clause of the infallibility principle: Necessarily, if you believe you have a headache, then you do. In turn, that justifies the first clause of the self-justification principle: Necessarily, if you believe you have a headache, then you're justified in believing you do.

What about the converse, though? Could you believe you don't have a headache when you do have one? That depends on whether headaches are self-presenting.

Some psychologists cast doubt on this. They point out that other stimuli can in a sense drown out pain. If I'm attending to other things, I may cease attending to my headache and I may not be aware of it any longer. Thus, I could feel my headache between 10:00 and 11:00, get deeply involved in something from 11:00 to 12:00, and then become aware of my headache again. These psychologists theorize that I still had the headache from 11:00 to 12:00 but I wasn't aware of it. If that's the case, headaches aren't self-presenting.

But is that an accurate description? We could say instead that my headache actually went away from 11:00 to 12:00 and then returned when my attention changed. Which is it? It's difficult to know. To what can we appeal to decide the issue?

At this point in our discussion, it seems (to me at least) that we have enough grounds for saying that first-person beliefs about headaches are infallible. However, whether headaches are self-presenting is less clear. But that is enough to justify us in accepting the first clause of the self-justification principle: necessarily, if you believe that you have a headache, then you're justified in believing that you have a headache. But it's less clear that we're justified in accepting the second clause of the self-justification principle: necessarily, for all people x, if x believes she doesn't have a headache, then she's justified in believing she doesn't have a headache. That may be an open question. However, for what it's worth, I'm inclined to accept the second clause.

But do these principles apply to all mental states or just to pain states such as having a headache, a toothache, a stomachache, or an earache? For example, is (romantic) love either infallible or self-presenting? Are our beliefs about loving someone self-justifying? Suppose I believe that I love Linda. Could I be mistaken and not love her although I believe I do? If yes, then beliefs about the mental state of loving are not infallible.

Experience has shown that we can (all too easily) fool ourselves about love. We can easily mistake other emotions or feelings for love, for example, lust or friendship. Love is much more complex than having a headache. Headaches aren't difficult to recognize as headaches, but loving someone entails the existence of a lot of other mental states, as well as patterns of behavior.

If love were like having a headache, a simple sensation, then introspection alone would readily reveal it to us if we, in a sense, search our minds for it. And we wouldn't mistake some other mental content for it, just as, unless we make a verbal mistake, we don't (normally?) mistake itches for pains. If we employ introspection, we must look for the mental states that are part of or signs of love in order to find out whether we love. I have to inspect my mind for the mental states that necessarily accompany love and also for the mental states that necessarily would be absent if I love someone.

BRAIN TEASERS

What mental states necessarily accompany (romantic) love? What mental states are necessarily absent if we love someone?

Another thing I have to look at is my behavior. Romantic love is supposed to make a difference in our behavior. I'll act one way if I love someone and some other way if I don't. I have to observe my own actions to see whether I'm behaving in the ways indicative of love in order to figure out whether I love someone.

BRAIN TEASERS

What are the ways of acting indicative of love?

Are some actions incompatible with love?

If love were as easily recognized and known as having a headache, we would never be faced with the question that can be so knotty and painful—do I really love this person? It would be as plain as whether you have a headache. But it isn't.

First-person beliefs about loving don't seem to be infallible. I can believe I love when I don't. (Evidence of my other mental states and my behavior can enable me to correct my errors, but that just points out that errors are possible.) Is love self-presenting? If I love someone, will I necessarily believe I do? Experience says no. We can love someone and not be aware of it and therefore not believe we love that person. In the movie *When Harry Met Sally,* Harry discovers that he has loved Sally for quite some time but he wasn't aware of it. He didn't believe he loved her. The theme of discovering love that we have but haven't been aware of is common in books, movies, and television. And it's not far-fetched. Many of us have had the experience of discovering we've loved someone for a while when we weren't aware of loving. So it seems clear that love isn't self-presenting, either. And if our beliefs about it are not infallible and the state of loving is not self-presenting, then it's difficult to see how beliefs about loving and not loving can be self-justifying.

If we're right about the mental state of love, then the principles of infallibility, self-presentation, and self-justification, if they apply to some mental states, do not apply to all mental states.

BRAIN TEASERS

Are first person beliefs about depression infallible?

Is depression self-presenting?

Are first-person beliefs about depression self-justifying?

We may not know ourselves, our own minds, as well as we think we do. Apollo's command to know ourselves may be more difficult than we realize. However, it may be that ordinarily, as long as there's no contrary evidence, we're justified in believing whatever we believe about our own mental states, regardless of what mental state it is, and the fact that we believe it is what justifies us. They may be self-justifying in a more restricted sense than the sense we introduced above. There may be conditions on self-justification. One is that we've actually reflected on our belief and tried to answer the question, "Is it true?" Another is that we have no contrary evidence. We might modify the self-justification principle, then, in the following way.

THE MODIFIED SELF-JUSTIFICATION PRINCIPLE

Necessarily, for all mental states m, if you believe that you're in m, you have reflected carefully on the question of whether you're in m, and you have no good reasons for believing that you're not in m, then you're justified in believing that you're in m, and

if you believe that you're not in m, you have reflected carefully on the question of whether you're in m, and you have no good reasons for believing that you're in m, then you're justified in believing that you're not in m.

The principles we have proposed and examined employ the concept of necessity. Should we employ the concept of logical necessity or physical necessity here? Are there some mental states, perhaps having a headache is one, to which the self-presentation and infallibility principles apply in every logically possible world? Put another way, would it be a logical contradiction to say that you believe you have a headache but you don't or that you have a headache but you don't believe you have one? Or instead would it simply be contrary to the laws of nature that govern the actual universe we inhabit, laws that govern all mental states? If it's the latter case, we should employ the concept of physical necessity rather than logical necessity in all the principles we have proposed.

Finally, is the justification in the modified justification principle strong enough for knowledge? Does it provide complete justification? Does it give us self-knowledge?

BRAIN TEASERS

I believe the following things about myself. Which, if any, are infallible? Which, if any, do I know to be true?

I'm hungry.

I want pizza for lunch.

I have no racist beliefs or attitudes.

I believe that men and women are equal intellectually.

I'm kind, not cruel.

I'm shy.

I'm listening to music now.

I have self-respect.

I feel respect for all other people.

I'm not proud or arrogant.

Knowledge of the World Outside Our Minds: Perception

According to a doctrine called Empiricism, all of our beliefs about the world outside our minds—from the very fabric of space-time to the contents of space-time, such as galaxies, stars, planets, continents, oceans, living beings, atoms, subatomic particles, energy, and forces—come from perceptual experience. In addition, the concepts that enable us to have beliefs about the world outside our minds also come from perceptual experience. For example, we can have such concepts as that of a galaxy, star, planet, elephant, dog, and cup only because we have seen them or pictures of them, or have heard or read descriptions of them. The descriptions will employ concepts that in turn have come from perceptual experience; for example, the shape and color concepts that might be used to describe a planet, a cloud, or an elephant.

BRAIN TEASERS

How might perceptual experience have given us the concepts of space and time?

According to Empiricism, if we didn't have any of the five senses, then we wouldn't have any concepts or any beliefs about a world outside us. The universe we inhabit would be forever closed to us. We wouldn't even know that we have physical bodies. We wouldn't be able to think because we would have no concepts to think with. Our senses provide us with a kind of window on the world, the only window we have. Without them, it's not clear what our consciousness would be like or even whether consciousness would be possible for us.

John Locke and David Hume were two early empiricists. Their opponents, called rationalists, claimed that some concepts[6] are innate. For example, Descartes claimed that the concept of God is innate, implanted

---

[6]Early modern philosophers called concepts "ideas," although "ideas" as they used the term included more than concepts.

in us by God. Immanuel Kant, who tried to bridge the divide between rationalists and empiricists, claimed that a number of fundamental concepts are supplied by the mind prior to experience and structure the way we experience the world, such as the concepts of space and time.

Not all people today are empiricists, though it seems that most are to some extent. That is, most people probably believe that all or almost all of our information about the world can only come from our five senses. However, some people claim that there are alternative sources of information about the world besides perception, sources that are as reliable, perhaps even more reliable. For example, one might say that meditation or something akin to a sixth sense can give us knowledge of things perception can't—a spiritual realm of reality inaccessible to our senses. Others say that introspection of our own minds, looking inward rather than outward, can provide us with valuable information about the world. Psychics claim to have ways of knowing that transcend the senses. We'll look at these claims about alternatives to perception below.

In this book we won't delve into the controversies that divided early modern philosophers, although we will look at alternative ways of knowing the world. Instead we will focus on Empiricism because most contemporary philosophers and nonphilosophers, at least in the English speaking world, are empiricists of one kind or another. We'll examine some of the puzzles that Empiricism poses.

Empiricism is not merely a theory about the genesis of our concepts and beliefs about the world. It also provides a theory of justification for our beliefs about the world. According to empiricists, the only evidence or justification we can have for a belief about the world outside our minds is so-called empirical evidence, the evidence provided by our senses. And almost all empiricists claim that a belief about the world isn't reasonable or justified unless the believer has empirical evidence for it.

Suppose that someone believes that most recipients of welfare are just lazy bums who don't want to work. Empiricists say the belief isn't reasonable if the believer doesn't have empirical evidence for it. One question is what counts as empirical evidence. Another is how much empirical evidence is needed.

The best kind of empirical evidence is a series of well-constructed studies where researchers look at and observe welfare recipients. Of course, we can't expect them to look at and observe all recipients. Instead, researchers will look at a fair representative sample of recipients and see whether all, most, many, some, a few, or none fit the description of lazy bums who don't want to work. We'll return in the next chapter to the logic of research studies. For now, let's imagine that such studies have been done. If you're not a researcher yourself who has participated in these studies, how can you acquire reasonable or justified beliefs about the issue?

You could read the studies. You could read summaries of the studies written by experts and published in reputable social science books and journals or in newspapers. That is, you can appeal to legitimate authorities on the subject. If authorities who write about the studies disagree, you can go directly to the studies. If the studies themselves don't all reach the same conclusions, you can suspend judgment and await the results of further studies. But empiricists are united in saying that if you haven't at least read about the results of studies in authoritative sources, then whatever you believe about welfare recipients is unjustified because you don't have any empirical evidence for your beliefs.

BRAIN TEASERS

Can the claims you heard made by politicians count as empirical evidence for your beliefs about the character of welfare recipients?

The researchers who performed the studies had to rely on their own senses. If you read or heard about them, you relied on your senses of seeing or hearing. Let's look at a simple case of perception as a source of knowledge about the world.

I believe that there's a cup of coffee on my desk as I type the words of this chapter into my computer. I'm confident that I'm justified in believing this, but what justifies me in believing it? I see it. Seeing is about the best evidence one can have. Common sense tells me that if I see something x, then I'm justified in believing that x exists. If I see that x has the property of being F, then I'm justified in believing that x has the property of being F. For example, if I see the Pope, then I'm justified in believing that the Pope exists. If I see that the Pope is an old man, then I'm justified in believing that he's an old man. In this case, I see the cup of coffee on my desk so I'm justified in believing that there's a cup of coffee on my desk.

Perceiving X and Perceiving that X is F

Let's examine the concept of perception a bit more carefully. When I see, what do I see? Put most abstractly, I see something. But reality doesn't normally present itself to our minds and senses just as a something. We see objects as things of a certain sort. I don't see an undifferentiated blob of something (or nothing), I see a horse, a piano, a house, a computer, and so on. To see something as a horse, piano, or house requires that I have a fairly rich conceptual scheme, and I perceive things, as it were, through this conceptual scheme.

Imagine that someone who has never seen or heard of a computer is standing in front of one with his eyes open and ample light. In one sense, of course, he sees the computer. But he doesn't see it as a computer since he has no idea of what he's seeing. He doesn't come to believe that he's seeing a computer. Thus, in order to make sense of our perceptual experiences, in order to know what we perceive, we need a system of concepts.

Sometimes it takes practice to actually see things in the sense of differentiating them from their backgrounds or from other things in their environment. It's notorious that students first learning to use a microscope have to learn how to recognize, and thus see, the parts of a cell. Similarly, a radiologist has to learn how to read an X ray in the sense of learning what to look for and how to see what's there in the developed X-ray film.

A lot of our perception is more complicated than just seeing a thing of a certain sort and recognizing what sort of thing it is. Here we can talk of seeing that. I see that painters are painting the house in front of me. I see that my windshield is cracked. I see that my teacher is in the room. (The same applies to hearing, but does it also apply to tasting, smelling, and feeling?) Perceiving is not divorced from other mental activities. The signals carrying information from outside us get filtered and processed through our minds and our system of concepts, they don't come pure.

One important question, then, is how accurate human perception is in giving us information about a world outside our minds if our minds necessarily filter and process the messages.

Perceiving and Justification

I see a cup of coffee on my desk. But in order to see it as a cup of coffee, in order to acquire the belief that there's a cup of coffee on my desk, I have to have the concepts of coffee, a cup, a desk, and possession ("my"). And even if I see it as a cup of coffee, I could be mistaken. For example, it could be a cup of tea. It could be a piece of artwork fabricated to look exactly like a cup of coffee.

But, I say to myself, I know it's coffee and not tea because I remember putting the cup there myself and I remember pouring coffee into it, not tea. (But now I'm not just relying on perception, I'm relying on memory. We'll look at memory as a source of justified beliefs below.) Suppose I'm not content to rely on memory. I'll settle the issue now once and for all. I look carefully at it. It looks like coffee. I sniff. It smells like coffee. I pick it up and drink. It's not a piece of artwork. It's a real cup with real liquid in it that tastes like coffee. Therefore, I conclude that it is coffee. I've confirmed by perception that I see a cup of coffee on my desk; therefore, I've also confirmed that there is a cup of coffee on my desk. (Seeing is a success verb. "I see a clown" is true only if there really is a clown in front of me and I'm seeing her.)

But now another puzzle arises. I didn't realize it before, but my belief that there's a cup of coffee on my desk is actually justified by my belief that

I *see* a cup of coffee on my desk. And that belief is justified, at least in part, by my belief that what's in the cup looks, smells, and tastes like coffee to me. That's not all. It also depends on my belief that if something looks, smells, and tastes like coffee to me, then it must be coffee. My beliefs about what's there in front of me and what I'm perceiving are based on inference. I inferred them from other things. To infer is to reach a conclusion. My inferring took the following form.

1.   What's in the cup looks, smells, and tastes like coffee to me.
2.   If something looks, smells, and tastes like coffee to me, then it must be coffee.
3.   Therefore, it's coffee.

That is, I infer what is the case (what's real) partly from the way things appear to me. Of course, I don't consciously do this. That would be absurd. But on reflection, that seems to be how I came to believe that what's in the cup is coffee.

One inference looks like this.

1.   "There's a cup of coffee on my desk" is inferred from
2.   "I see a cup of coffee on my desk," which is inferred from
3.   "It appears to me that there's a cup of coffee on my desk."

Each of these expresses a belief. So I'm justified in believing there's a cup of coffee on my desk if I'm justified in believing I *see* a cup of coffee on my desk, and I'm justified in believing I see a cup of coffee on my desk if I'm justified in believing that it *appears to me* that there's a cup of coffee on my desk. But am I justified in believing that it appears to me that there's a cup of coffee on my desk?

Some philosophers reply that I am justified in believing this and that what justifies me is that it does appear to me that there is a cup of coffee on my desk. They claim that its-appearing-to-me-that-there-is-a-cup-of-coffee-on-my-desk is a particular mental state. There are various ways that we could describe or designate this mental state.

We could use the language of it "seems to me" that or "looks to me" like. Let's call such mental states perceptual states. Perceptual states are mental states of seeming to perceive something, such as seeming to perceive (see) a cup, seeming to perceive (smell) coffee, and seeming to perceive (hear) a bell.

We've now been driven back to introspection once more. If first-person beliefs about our own perceptual states are infallible, then we can't possibly be mistaken if we believe we're in one, and thus we have the strongest possible justification for our beliefs. Are they infallible? Could I possibly be mistaken if I believe that it appears to me that I see a cup of coffee on my desk? I leave that for you to answer. But even if such beliefs are not infallible, the first clause of the modified justification principle may apply to our beliefs about our mental states:

Necessarily, for all perceptual states s (it appears to me that I'm perceiving that p), if you believe that you're in s, you have reflected carefully on the question of whether you're in s, and you have no good reasons for believing that you're not in s, then you're justified in believing that you're in s.

Then on this view, the justification of our beliefs about perceptual experiences is transmitted to our beliefs about what we're really perceiving, and in turn is transmitted from them to our beliefs about what's really there.

Let's try to come up with justification principles for perception that will specify conditions under which we're justified in believing something on the basis of perception.

JUSTIFICATION BY PERCEPTION

1. Necessarily, for all objects x and observable properties F, if you believe that you're perceiving that x is F, then you're justified in believing that you really perceive that x is F.
2. Necessarily, for all objects x and all perceivable properties F, if you perceive that x is F, then you're justified in believing that x is F.

But we need to modify the first principle because of the various possibilities of error. So let's propose:

1'. Necessarily, for all objects x and observable properties F, if you believe that you're perceiving that x is F, you have reflected carefully on the question of whether you're really perceiving that x is F, and you have no good reasons for believing that you're not perceiving that x is F, then you're justified in believing that you're really perceiving that x is F.

According to this principle, we're justified in believing most of the things we think we're justified in believing, and for the reasons we think we're justified. Thus, I'm justified in believing there's a cup of coffee on my desk and I'm justified in believing I see a cup of coffee on my desk. That accords pretty well with common sense. Whether the degree of justification is sufficient for knowledge will occupy us in the next chapter.

Alternatives to Perception

If God exists, God knows everything. All of God's beliefs are true and completely justified. God can't make mistakes in believing. But God doesn't have any of the five senses, since God isn't physical. So God didn't acquire Her beliefs or concepts via perception, nor did She confirm or justify Her beliefs by means of perception. How does God know what She knows? However God knows, are human beings capable of knowing in the same way? That seems unlikely.

If there are other immaterial beings, such as angels, presumably they know and believe things, too. Whether they're infallible, as God is supposed to be, is probably an open question. How do they know what they know? How do they acquire and confirm or justify their beliefs? It can't be by perception, because they're not physical and our senses are dependent on physical sense organs, such as eyes and ears. However they come to know and believe, can humans come to know and believe, and test their beliefs, in the same way? Again, it seems unlikely.

If there are other forms of intelligent life in the universe that have physical bodies as we do, how do they come to acquire their beliefs about the universe? Do they have something like sensory organs that provide them with information about the world? If they do, how might theirs differ from our sensory organs? For example, we have eyes that are sensitive to a certain range of electromagnetic waves in the spectrum, a range we call visible light. Might they have a sensory organ different from the human eye that is also sensitive to visible light? Might their sensory organs also be sensitive to electromagnetic waves that have a frequency greater than light waves? Less than light waves? (Eagles have eyes that are more acute than human eyes.) Our ears are sensitive to sound waves of a certain frequency, waves of compressed air. Might they have some kind of sensory organs sensitive to the same thing, although built on a different model than human ears? Might their sensory organs be sensitive to a much greater range of waves of compressed air than our ears are? (Dogs have ears more acute than human ears.) Perhaps they have sensory organs sensitive to things in the environment that we are not at all sensitive to. But no matter what their sensory organs are like, we have to make do with the organs we have. We have five senses that are capable of decoding certain information from the environment and not other forms of information. We can't know the world the way an alien being may be able to know the world.

Some humans claim to be psychic. They claim that they can read other people's minds or find out about distant states and events without using any of the five human senses. Can they? Under what circumstances would we be justified in believing that someone really has such abilities? Suppose I told you that I have these abilities, that I'm psychic. Would you instantly believe me? I doubt it. You'd probably ask for empirical evidence. For example, you might ask me to read your mind, foretell the future, or give you information about some event occurring in China now. Of course, I might say I'm reading your mind and you're thinking that I'm a fraud. Or I might predict that someone will die in the next twenty-four hours. Or I might say that a baby is being born in China right now and I can "see" it being born with my "mind's eye." But those probably wouldn't persuade you. The probability of my being right with each one is so high that there's no reason to think I'd have to have special abilities to "see" these things. Of course one of your thoughts is almost certain to be that I'm a fraud. Surely somewhere someone will die in the next twenty-four hours. And in a nation of about a billion and a half people, it's highly probable that someone is now giving birth. And you're probably in no position to confirm whether someone in China really is giving birth at this exact moment, anyway.

My point is that the claim that someone has psychic powers isn't justified unless there's empirical evidence for it. And in fact, empirical evidence is hard to come by. Take predictions of the future by such people as Nostradamus. One might point to all the predictions that came true and say that the only explanation is that Nostradamus had the powers he claimed to have. But if we look closer, we're liable to discover a few things. We may discover that lots of predictions he made haven't in fact panned out. Of course, someone may say that they will if we just give them time. Nostradamus wasn't predicting what was going to happen ten years in the future, but rather hundreds of years in the future. But if we give a prediction that can apply either to the near or very distant future, the probability of the prediction coming true is pretty high. Suppose I say that the United States will some day collapse. In the course of a thousand years, that's almost a certainty. I don't need to be psychic to predict that.

But note that the prediction is ambiguous or vague. I predicted that the United States would "collapse." Is the collapse supposed to be temporary or permanent? What does "collapse" mean? Does a deep economic depression count as a collapse? What about a loss in a major war, a widespread crime wave, a revolt, a plague or famine that kills 10% of the population, or a major political or territorial reorganization? Predictions are often so vague that almost any event could be interpreted as fulfilling the prophecy. Sometimes the predictions are so obscure that we have to guess what they mean, and it's hard to know how we can tell whether our guess is right. Suppose I predict that one day the eagle and the bear will mate. Do I mean that Russia and the United States will some day join together to form one nation? How do you know I mean that? How do you know what I mean?

It's an open question whether any humans have psychic abilities that enable them to know the world without having to use sensory perception. I'll leave it to you to decide how plausible or well defended such claims are.

Empiricists are skeptical about claims that we humans have ways of knowing the world that don't depend on perception. Further, they say that such claims, in order to be worthy of belief or justified, would have to be tested by appeal to perception. If we are told that we can learn a lot about a person's character, history, and future life by learning exactly when the person was born and applying astrological knowledge to it, empiricists claim that we should test it out. We should use perception to find out what a person's history and character are, then see how close the astrologer comes to it. (Beware of vague pronouncements or fairly obvious claims.) Most empiricists think that the empirical evidence available to support the claims of astrology is skimpy at best and that there's a lot of empirical evidence of astrology's failures. For example, if the claims of astrology are true, then every individual born at exactly the same time should have the exact same personality, character, and fate. Do they? Again, I leave you with the open question of whether to accept the claims of astrology to have ways of knowing independent of perception.

Empiricists are convinced that we humans are limited to sensory perception in building our picture of the world. And they claim that we should subject every claim about the world to tests that rely on observation and perception. That leads us back to the question of whether there's an ethics of belief.

An Ethics of Belief?

During the conflict in Kosovo, when NATO forces bombed targets in the former Yugoslavia, reports emerged of massive atrocities committed by the forces of Serb leader Slobodan Milosevic against the Kosovars who were ethnic Albanians. The stories of atrocities came from refugees. Western news organizations reported them, but carefully referred to them as "alleged" atrocities because they did not believe that they had enough empirical evidence to confirm or strongly justify the claims. Only when NATO forces and Western journalists entered the province after Milosevic's capitulation and found ample empirical evidence of massive atrocities, such as mass graves, did Western news media report the claims as fact. There is an ethics of belief and reporting for journalism that requires that claims not be reported as fact unless there's enough empirical evidence to support the claims. It is probably only because (or when) newspapers, magazines, or television and radio news programs rigorously abide by the ethics of belief for reporting that their stories and claims are worthy of belief.

At the same time, the state run television news programs in the former Yugoslavia ruled by Milosevic were giving their audience a completely different picture. They denied that there had been any atrocities. They did not show film footage of corpses and mass graves. When they showed long lines of refugees fleeing the province and destroyed buildings, they blamed it on NATO bombs, not on Serb terror tactics. At the time, studies showed that most Serbs in Yugoslavia, having access only to state run television, believed that their government had done nothing to provoke NATO's air attacks. The news programs hid the truth and fed people an inaccurate picture of reality. Most Serbs fell for it. The Serbian experience shows the dangers of relying on only one or two sources of information. Not all sources are equally reliable. If we have access to multiple sources of information, we're in a better position to correct falsehoods, distortions, and omissions.

Reflecting on journalistic practice, we see that responsible journalists insist on confirming claims by empirical evidence before reporting them as fact. If we don't have empirical evidence for our beliefs, is it unreasonable to believe? Should we not believe?

For example, if I don't have empirical evidence for the existence of angels (because I've never seen, heard, or touched one), would I be justified in believing in them anyway or would it be unreasonable? What if I read of angels in the Bible? Would that constitute empirical evidence? What if someone close to me reports having seen or heard angels?

Here the distinction between coming to believe and continuing to believe may be relevant. Suppose at an early age I read of angels in the Bible and at the time I believed that the Bible is God's word and contains no errors. I then came to believe that angels exist. It would be at best questionable to say that I wasn't justified in coming to believe that angels exist. So, I added to my stock of beliefs the claim that angels exist. At a later date either I have doubts about it or others express to me their doubts about it. Now I wonder whether I should continue believing it or instead should delete it from my stock of beliefs. Suppose I concede that I don't have (personal) empirical evidence that angels exist because I've never perceived one. However, I also don't have empirical evidence that angels don't exist. Would it be reasonable for me to keep the belief in angels among my stock of beliefs, to continue believing in angels, or instead would it be unreasonable? I think that many philosophers would say that you would be reasonable or justified if you stopped believing it (threw the belief out, as it were), but that you also would be (equally) reasonable or justified if you retained the belief and kept on believing in angels. Without empirical evidence that angels don't exist, reason doesn't require you to cease believing in angels.

What about the context of coming to believe? Many philosophers would say that if you start out neither believing that angels exist nor believing that angels don't exist, then you should add a belief in angels only if you have empirical evidence that they do exist. (But is believing under our control? That question arises again.) Obviously one form of empirical evidence would be your own perceptions. If you perceive one, then you're justified in adding a belief in angels to your stock of beliefs. (But you'd have to be careful. Did you only think you perceived one or did you really perceive one?) If someone you fully trust claims to have perceived one, then that would be empirical evidence. (But again, you must be careful. Could he be lying or mistaken?) But angels, being immaterial, aren't really supposed to be perceivable with any of our five senses. So perhaps you'd have to believe in ways of knowing that are alternatives to sensory perception.

There is one other way of being justified. As we've seen, justification can be tied to explanation. No one has ever perceived a subatomic particle, but since they're the best explanation of states and events that we can perceive, we think we're justified in believing in them. The fact that something is the best (or a very good) explanation of things we can perceive counts as a kind of empirical evidence. So perhaps angels are the best explanation of states and events that we do perceive. If you believe or know that, then you'd be justified in adding a belief in angels to your stock of beliefs. But are angels the best or a good explanation of perceivable things? (We'll return to justification and explanation below.)

Distorters

When the Hubble space telescope was first launched into space, scientists discovered that it had flaws. It gave distorted pictures. Fortunately, once they discovered this, scientists were able to correct for the distortions so that they could get clear and accurate pictures. Do we have things built into us that distort our pictures of reality? Are there things in our environment that distort our pictures?

One possibility, of course, is that, given the distinctions among seeing, seeing as, and seeing that, all of our perceivings are systematically distorted by our minds, which filter and process perception. Our minds could be like the Hubble Space Telescope. Of course, we assume that our perception of reality is clear, unclouded, and undistorted, but do we know that?

Some things are well known as distorters. One is personal interest. If I would gain by something's being true, it may help influence me into believing it is true. Similarly, if I would lose by something's being true, it may help influence me into believing it's false. For example, I may see someone I trust and admire cheating, but in a sense, I may not believe my eyes. I may not see him as cheating, but instead may see his actions as more innocent than they are. On the other hand, if I don't like someone, I may see innocent actions as cheating. Similarly, during the NATO action against Serbia over the region of Kosovo, Serbs saw television images of ethnic Albanian refugees streaming out of Kosovo leaving behind burned out villages and towns. They saw it as refugees fleeing NATO bombing rather than as refugees fleeing Serb forces that were practicing "ethnic cleansing" against them, a euphemism for systematic murder, rape, and destruction. They saw bodies of ethnic Albanians on television as the bodies of terrorists killed in action rather than as innocent civilians slaughtered by Serb forces. Their interest in maintaining their self-respect as Serbs and their love for and respect for their country affected the way they perceived the world.

Another distorter is public opinion. Many of us tend to conform and are reluctant to stand out from the crowd, whether the crowd is our neighborhood, family, or circle of friends. It doesn't apply only to our behavior, but also to our beliefs. Many of us are reluctant to have beliefs that are very different from the beliefs of the majority. There's a pressure to believe what most people believe, at least about important matters. If someone knows that 95% of people in his community believe in God, that may influence his beliefs. (Of course, it may have the opposite effect on someone who is rebellious.) If the majority of people in our society believe that members of a certain minority group are inferior, many people will see them as inferior.

Suppose that 10% of the people in a certain society are green, and the dominant ideology says that green people are inferior. Many nongreen people will see green people as inferior. For example, if a nongreen teacher reads a report from a green student, the teacher may see the report as worse than those submitted by nongreen students. The teacher may be completely unaware of how the dominant view is affecting her perception of the student. Or nongreen people may see green people as having vicious or stupid facial expressions. The ways that such biases can affect how we perceive things are almost endless.

A variety of mental illnesses can distort perception. In some cases, someone may seem to hear or see things that aren't there. Some criminals have reported hearing voices egging them on to commit crimes. Some people have a variety of visual hallucinations. In other cases, someone might hear laughter and hear it as people laughing at him behind his back. He might see the most innocent action as hostile and aggressive. Everyone may look untrustworthy to him.

Even independent of mental illness, this problem is especially acute in the realm of politics. During the height of the Cold War between the United States and the former Soviet Union, many United States policy makers perceived almost every action of the Soviet Union as motivated by aggressive desires to expand Soviet territory rather than as defensive actions to hold on to the territory they had. It's clear now that expanding Soviet territory was not always on the minds of Soviet policy makers.

It's become a cliché that the media, especially television, distorts our picture of the world. Studies show that most people get most of their news from television news programs rather than from newspapers. Studies also show that Americans average 30–40 hours per week of television viewing. Is that a problem? Yes. It's notorious that most Americans believe that the world is more dangerous than it really is. That's because so much time of local television news programs is devoted to crime, accidents, fires, and natural disasters. The rule is, "If it bleeds, it leads." Seeing reports of local crime night after night, people begin to believe that you take your life in your hands every time you walk down the street. But crime isn't nearly as common as television news's insatiable appetite for crime stories may lead us to believe. Suppose that you live in a city of a million people and there are 200 murders committed there each year. That's enough murders to allow the local television news programs to cover murders every day. Anyone viewing the local news and seeing stories of murders every day is likely to conclude that the probability of his being murdered is very high and may feel intense fear about it. Given that fear, many people may want the government to do drastic things to lower the violent crime rate.

But if you live in that city, what's the probability of your being murdered? Given only the information that there are 200 murders committed each year, the probability of your being murdered is .0002. That is, you have two chances in ten thousand of being murdered. Suppose, as is almost always the case, most of the murders, say 80%, occur in only a few neighborhoods. Let's say it's five neighborhoods out of 50. And suppose that they're neighborhoods that you're never in. Now what's the probability of your being murdered? It's .000004, four chances in a hundred thousand. Yet, watching television news that covers a new murder almost every day, you're likely to think that the probability of your being murdered is a lot higher.

Television news has been criticized not just because of what it covers, but also because of what it doesn't cover. Critics complain that it provides almost no in-depth analysis of events so that people can understand them. Its coverage is superficial. It might devote only a minute or two of time every so often to a highly complex issue, such as reform of social security and Medicare, not nearly enough time to explain the problems and explore the alternatives, with their strengths and weaknesses. It reports speeches of politicians but doesn't provide much critical analysis of them. Often misstatements and downright lies go uncorrected. In addition, the range of views that is presented is very narrow. From the perspective of people on the left (very liberal to socialist and Marxist), the views that are represented on television tend to be heavily weighted toward the moderate and conservative end of the spectrum. In turn, those who are most conservative maintain that television news has a liberal bias.

Of course, news programs are only a small fraction of the programs on television. While there are scores of television stations that are accessible through cable and satellite, many of which are devoted primarily to education, most of them that have the largest audience are devoted primarily to entertainment. And most people who watch many hours of television almost every day watch it to be entertained, not informed. Its images are far more powerful than the written or spoken word. For many of us, television entertainment programs profoundly shape our view of the world and ourselves. That's now a cliché, because it's so obvious and undisputed. Watching television, many of us think we're looking at the real world.

Many television programs filter out a large part of reality. Ordinary people with ordinary jobs and ordinary looks are rare on television. Most television families are upper middle class; almost none are poor. Most are extremely attractive; men are generally well built and women are thin. When characters are overweight, their weight is often treated as a joke. The same can be said for homosexuals. Elderly characters are often undignified and played for laughs. Few characters on television are deeply religious and almost none have physical challenges or handicaps.

Television programs also provide examples of behavior that viewers may come to see as normal or acceptable. Obviously, there's a lot of violence and sex. But there's also a lot of crude behavior, especially among teenaged characters. Treating people with a certain amount of disrespect almost always gets laughs on comedy soundtracks. Of course, there are notable exceptions to these generalizations, but these generalizations apply to the majority of television entertainment programs. The point is that by watching a lot of television, which the average American does, we may acquire a lot of unjustified beliefs about the world.

BRAIN TEASERS

How much television did you watch each week, on average, from age 8 to 18? How do you think it affected your view of yourself and the world? Do you think it gave you an accurate picture of the way the world is?

Memory

We can remember what we have experienced, as well as remember information we've acquired. The first is experiential memory, the second is propositional memory. Memory is involved in almost every aspect of justification. With our perceptual beliefs, I have to remember what coffee looks, smells, and tastes like in order to be justified in believing that I see a cup of coffee on my desk. I have to remember the concepts I employ in organizing and thinking about my experiences. I can also remember my past experiences. Propositional memory includes the entire body of information I've stored.

Memory involves several discrete processes, the most important of which for our purposes are storage and retrieval. Relying on memory presents risks because we can make errors in both storage and retrieval. This means that memory is not infallible; we can make mistakes. But you already knew that. Like me, you've undoubtedly made many mistakes in remembering. You've stored misinformation and made mistakes in retrieval. Sometimes I've had a distinct memory of parking my car in a certain place, only to discover that I parked it somewhere else. I've forgotten a lot of things, too, such as that I promised to cook dinner on a certain night.

Can memory provide justification? Suppose I believe that I left my car keys on my desk. I'm confident that I'm justified in believing this, but what justifies me? I'd have to say that what justifies me is that I remember leaving them there. But like perceiving, remembering is what could be called a success verb. I remember doing something only if I really did it. Thus, if I remember leaving my car keys on my desk, then I really did leave my car keys on my desk.

On reflection, I have to say that I *believe* I remember leaving the keys on my desk. So what justifies me in believing I left the keys on my desk is that I believe I *remember* leaving the keys on my desk. What justifies me in believing I remember leaving the keys on my desk? Many philosophers claim that we have to appeal to a certain kind of experience we have had. It's not a perceptual experience, one that we might refer to as seeming to perceive x or seeming to perceive that x is F. Instead it's a memory experience that we might refer to as the experience of seeming to remember something, for example, seeming to remember leaving the keys on my desk.

Is this experience either self-presenting or infallible? It's difficult to imagine how I could seem to remember something and yet not be aware of seeming to remember it, so seeming to remember may be self-presenting. As to infallibility, while I might misdescribe my experience, it's difficult to imagine any other way that I could be mistaken about what I believe that I *seem* to remember. We might say that necessarily, if I believe that I seem to remember leaving my keys on my desk, then I do *seem* to remember leaving my keys on my desk.

Similarly, suppose I believe that Thomas Jefferson wrote the first draft of the Declaration of Independence. What justifies me in believing that? I may not be able to point to any source of the information. Instead, it may be that I just remember that he did, although I don't know how or where I first acquired the information or belief. But again, what justifies me in believing I remember this bit of information? It's that I *seem* to remember that Jefferson wrote the first draft.

Common sense says that memory is a source of justified beliefs. Generally, if I seem to remember an experience, I'm justified in believing that I'm accurately remembering it. Similarly, if I seem to remember a bit of information, then I'm generally justified in believing that the information is accurate. But since our memory can play tricks on us, since we can both forget and misremember, we have to be cautious in our principle of justification. The following principle of justification regarding memory seems to accord with the spirit of common sense:

JUSTIFICATION THROUGH MEMORY

Necessarily, if you seem to remember that you had experience E at a time t, and if you have no reason for thinking that you are mistaken, then you are justified in believing that (a) you do remember having experience E at time t and (b) you had experience E at time t.

Necessarily, if you seem to remember that p, and you have no reasons for believing that p is false, then you're justified in believing that p.

If I seem to remember leaving my keys on my desk, and if I have no reason for thinking that my memory is playing tricks on me, then I'm justified in believing that I do remember leaving them there and justified in believing that I did leave them there. Similarly, if I seem to remember that China has over a billion people, then I'm justified in believing that China has over a billion people.

If I'm justified in believing that I remember leaving my keys on my desk, am I completely justified so that I *know* that I left my keys on my desk? We'll tackle that question in the next chapter.

Basic Justifiers

Let's call reason, introspection, perception, and memory basic sources of justification or basic justifiers. Most other forms of justification will ultimately rely on one or more of these basic sources of justification.

Justification and Probability

Probability relations between beliefs also provide justification. Suppose I hear a weather forecast that says there's a 90% chance of rain tomorrow. Surely I'm justified in believing it will rain tomorrow. But as we saw, justification due to probability relations comes in degrees. I'm more justified in believing it will rain if the probability is 90% than I would be if the probability were 70%. I'm less justified than I would be if the probability were 98%.

Probability is relative to evidence. When a weather forecaster says that the probability of its raining tomorrow is 90% (or .90), she means it's 90% given the evidence she has when she made the forecast. The general form of a probability statement is $pr(p/e) = x$, for example, the probability that it will rain tomorrow (p), given the evidence (e), equals 90% (x). Probability ranges from 0 to 1.0. If $pr(p/e) = 0$, then given the evidence, p is impossible. If $pr(p/e) = 1.0$, then its certain that p; it's impossible that not p. Generally, the higher the probability of a hypothesis or claim, given our evidence, the more justified we are in believing it. The less probable it is, the less justified we are in believing it.

Some probability relations are derived from relative frequencies. When a weather forecaster says that the probability that it will rain tomorrow is 90%, she means that in the past, when the weather conditions have been like they are now, it has rained 90% of the time. But not all probability judgments are of that kind. Consider a prosecutor in a murder trial. He lays out the evidence for the jury. The defendant's fingerprints were found on the murder weapon, which was found in a garbage can only a block from where the defendant lives; he had a motive; he had opportunity; he doesn't have a good alibi; the victim's credit cards were found in his home. Therefore, the probability that he did it is so high that it makes it beyond reasonable doubt that he is the murderer. First, it's difficult to precisely quantify the degree of probability of the hypothesis that he's guilty, given this evidence. It's not 1.0. (Why not?) Is it .99? .98? .90? And it's not that when in the past this much evidence has been amassed against someone, he really did it in, say, 98% of the cases. Perhaps it's what's called a subjective probability judgment or measure. I might estimate the probability based on the evidence as .92, you might estimate it as .99. Attempts have also been made to have logical measures of probability, but they're so complex that we won't cover them in this book.

However we're to understand probability judgments, we have to keep in mind that they're relative to evidence. That means they can change. Return to our prosecutor. If the defense attorney, Perry Mason, uncovers additional evidence, it may point to someone other than the defendant. He may discover that the fingerprints and credit cards were planted. He may have an eyewitness to the crime who points to someone else as the murderer. Finally, Mason may get a confession on the witness stand from the real murderer, who breaks down under Mason's relentless cross examination. Given this new evidence, the probability that the defendant did it may drop from the range of .90–.99 down to near zero.

Common sense seems to adopt a principle of justification such as the following.

PROBABILISTIC JUSTIFICATION

If your evidence e makes statement p probable, then you're justified in believing that p is true. The degree of justification is proportional to the degree of probability; the higher the probability, given your evidence, the greater the justification.

But suppose someone deliberately turns his back on evidence that is unfavorable to what he prefers to believe or who does not make any effort to ensure that his evidence is complete. For example, suppose a detective finds Casey's fingerprints on the murder weapon, finds the victim's credit cards in Casey's car, and discovers that Casey doesn't have an alibi. Should he halt his investigation of the crime and go on to other things or should he continue investigating? The detective might believe that the probability of Casey's guilt is so high, given his evidence, that it doesn't make sense for him to spend more time on the case. So he turns the case over to the prosecutor with the evidence he has, which certainly makes Casey's guilt highly probable. Is he justified in believing that Casey is guilty? How probable is it that if he investigated further, he would uncover evidence that someone else did it?

Suppose that the detective, A, has this evidence against Casey, but Casey tells him that he's been framed by a police officer, officer B.

Suppose A refuses to even consider this possibility and does nothing to confirm or disconfirm Casey's allegations. A's evidence against Casey is limited to what he's already accumulated, which certainly makes Casey's guilt highly probable. How justified is he in believing that Casey is guilty?

This is complicated because we humans don't have infinite amounts of time and we have lots of other inquiries to make. A detective may have five open cases with more on the way. He may realize that he can't spend all his time for a month on this investigation; he has to set limits. He has to spend a reasonable amount of time investigating it, but he has to judge when he has sufficient evidence to make him confident that he's solved the case. Such judgments are fraught with risk, but they're risks we must take.

There's no easy answer to the question of how much time we should spend trying to find evidence for and against a hypothesis, whether it's a hypothesis about who committed a crime or whether God exists. Every inquiry must end in a finite amount of time and must end in time to allow the inquirer to go on to other equally or more important inquiries. So we might say that as long as the inquirer has made a good faith effort to be fair and thorough in gathering and assessing evidence for and against a hypothesis, and the evidence she's gathered makes the hypothesis probable, then she's justified in believing the hypothesis. Let's revise the probabilistic justification principle.

PROBABILISTIC JUSTIFICATION

If your evidence e makes statement p probable, and you have made a good faith effort to discover the available evidence both for and against p, then you're justified in believing that p is true.

The degree of justification is proportional to the degree of probability; the higher the probability, given your evidence, the greater the justification.

Justification and Explanation

What justifies scientists in believing that subatomic particles exist? No one can see them, even with sense enhancing instruments such as microscopes and telescopes. Scientists talk of detecting the presence of certain subatomic particles, such as electrons, but given that what they really see are things like blips on dials, how do they know it's electrons they're detecting? And other subatomic particles can't be detected at all. According to current physical theory, the smallest subatomic particle is the quark. Quarks have properties that have been given strange names, such as charm, flavor, and left-handedness. Is talk of quarks just a joke? Are scientists really justified in claiming that quarks exist and have the properties they say they have, however bizarre the names given to the properties?

Scientists believe in quarks, even though they can't perceive them, because quarks are the best explanation of what they do perceive. Explanation provides justification.

I see a tall column of dark smoke on the horizon. I conclude that there's a fire in that location. Am I justified in believing that there's a fire there even though I can't see it? Yes. A fire is the best explanation of the smoke I see. (Of course, it's the best explanation because I've seen smoke caused by fires before and perhaps I've never seen smoke where there hasn't been a fire. I may also know the old adage, "Where there's smoke, there's fire." So perception and memory are tied to justification by explanation.) We might also say that a fire is the most probable explanation of the smoke I see.

Sometimes it's not easy to know what's the best explanation. Suppose that journalists come across the bodies of twenty ethnic Albanian men in a ravine in Kosovo, all having been shot. The government of Slobodan Milosevic claims that they were Kosovo Liberation Army (KLA) soldiers killed in battle by Serb soldiers. Nearby residents claim that they were innocent civilians rounded up by Serb forces and massacred. Who should the journalists believe? Suppose the journalists examine the situation carefully. They note that all the men are clustered together in a relatively small area and they seem to have been shot at close range. They do not see any weapons around. They note that the ages of the men seem to range from the early teens to the late sixties or early seventies. They think that Milosevic's government has many reasons for lying and they have caught it in many lies in the past. They also know that Serb forces loyal to Milosevic's government have been accused of atrocities many times. What's the better explanation? Is it that the residents are lying and the men were KLA guerrillas killed in battle or that they were innocent civilians who were massacred? If the better explanation is that the men were innocent civilians who were massacred, then the journalists would be justified in believing this.

We covered justification by explanation in the first chapter, so we won't spend more time on it here.

Testimony of Authorities

Probably our most important source of justification is the testimony of experts and authorities. Why do I believe that George Washington was the first president of the United States? Because I have read it in many history books. Am I justified in believing it on the basis of having read it in many history books? Yes, because history books written by reputable historians (experts) are generally reliable (within limits). My justification is stronger if all or almost all historians agree that George Washington was the first president of the United States. Similarly, if I read in a physics textbook that $E = MC^2$ and I come to believe it, then

I am justified in believing it because it comes from what we take to be a reliable source.

Suppose I read a book that says that John F. Kennedy was killed by a team of CIA assassins and as a result of reading this, I come to believe it. Am I justified in believing this on the basis of having read it in this one book? If I am justified, the justification is surely not very strong. Partly it depends on what evidence the author presents. Bare assertion is not argument. It also depends on what evidence the author leaves out. But most important, the fact that the views expressed in the book are intensely controversial means that the claims and arguments of one author alone do not provide very strong justification when there are many other authors with equal or greater expertise who deny that what this author says is true. The appeal to an authority to justify a belief does not provide much justification if the acknowledged authorities disagree and the appeal is to only one authority among many.

Similarly, suppose I read a book that claims that the Holocaust did not occur. Would I be justified in believing it? First, I should ask myself whether it is published by a well-known publisher with a good reputation among knowledgeable people. If not, that reduces my justification. Second, I should ask myself whether the author is an acknowledged expert in the field. If not, my justification is reduced. Third, I should ask myself where acknowledged experts in the field stand. Do they all agree with what this book has to say? Do most of them agree with it? Are they divided, many agreeing but many disagreeing? Or is it that most or almost all or all acknowledged experts disagree with what this book has to say? The fewer experts who agree with what this book claims, the less justified I am in believing its claims. Then I have to ask myself, given what I know or believe, how plausible are the claims? Has the author ignored evidence that others have presented? Is the evidence or are the arguments that the author presents good?

Let's try to provide a principle of justification based on the testimony of experts.

JUSTIFICATION FROM THE AUTHORITY OF EXPERTS

We're justified in believing what we hear or read provided that (a) the source is widely accepted as reliable, (b) those with expertise are in substantial agreement on the issue, and (c) what we have read or heard is consistent with what we know.

◣ BERTRAND RUSSELL (1872–1970)

ON THE VALUE OF SCEPTICISM

I wish to propose for the reader's favorable consideration a doctrine which may, I fear, appear wildly paradoxical and subversive. The doctrine in question is this: that it is undesirable to believe a proposition when there is no ground whatever for supposing it true. I must, of course, admit that if such an opinion became common it would completely transform our social life and our political system; since both are at present faultless, this must weigh against it. I am also aware (what is more serious) that it would tend to diminish the incomes of clairvoyants, bookmakers, bishops and others who live on the irrational hopes of those who have done nothing to deserve good fortune here or hereafter. In spite of these grave arguments, I maintain that a case can be made out for my paradox, and I shall try to set it forth.

First of all, I wish to guard myself against being thought to take up an extreme position. I am a British Whig, with a British love of compromise and moderation. . . . I am prepared to admit the ordinary beliefs of common sense, in practice if not in theory. I am prepared to admit any well-established result of science, not as certainly true, but as sufficiently probable to afford a basis for rational action. If it is announced that there is to be an eclipse of the moon on such-and-such a date, I think it worth while to look and see whether it is taking place. . . .

There are matters about which those who have investigated them are agreed; the dates of eclipses may serve as an illustration. There are other matters about which experts are not agreed. Even when the experts all agree, they may well be mistaken. Einstein's view as to the magnitude of the deflection of light by gravitation would have been rejected by all experts twenty years ago, yet it proved to be right. Nevertheless, the opinion of experts when it is unanimous, must be accepted by non-experts as more likely to be right than the opposite opinion. The scepticism that I advocate amounts only to this: (1) that when the experts are agreed, the opposite opinion cannot be held to be certain; (2) that when they are not agreed, no opinion can be regarded as certain by a non-expert; and (3) that when they all hold that no sufficient grounds for a positive opinion exist, the ordinary man would do well to suspend his judgment.

These propositions may seem mild, yet, if accepted, they would absolutely revolutionize human life.

The opinions for which people are willing to fight and persecute all belong to one of the three classes which this scepticism condemns. When there are rational grounds for an opinion, people are content to set them forth and wait for them to operate. In such cases, people do not hold their opinions with passion; they hold them calmly, and set forth their reasons quietly. The opinions that are held with passion are always those for which no good ground exists; indeed the passion is the measure of the holder's lack of rational conviction. . . .

Let us take [an] . . . illustration. It is often said that socialism is contrary to human nature, and this assertion is denied by socialists with the same heat with which it is made by their opponents. The late Dr. Rivers, whose death cannot be sufficiently deplored, discussed this question in a lecture at University College, published in his posthumous book on *Psychology and Politics*. This is the only discussion of this topic known to me that can lay claim to be scientific. It sets forth certain anthropological data which show that socialism is not contrary to human nature in Melanesia; it then points out that we do not know whether human nature is the same in

---

From *Sceptical Essays* (New York: W. W. Norton, 1928). Reprinted with permission from Allen of Unwin.

Melanesia as in Europe; and it concludes that the only way of finding out whether socialism is contrary to European human nature is to try it. It is interesting that on the basis of this conclusion he was willing to become a Labor candidate. But he would certainly not have added to the heat and passion in which political controversies are usually enveloped.

I will now venture on a topic which people find even more difficult in treating dispassionately, namely, marriage customs. The bulk of the population of every country is persuaded that all marriage customs other than its own are immoral, and that those who combat this view only do so in order to justify their own loose lives. In India the remarriage of widows is traditionally regarded as a thing too horrible to contemplate. In Catholic countries divorce is thought very wicked, but some failure of conjugal fidelity is tolerated, at least in men. In America divorce is easy, but extra-conjugal relations are condemned with the utmost severity. Mohammedans believe in polygamy, which we think degrading. All these differing opinions are held with extreme vehemence, and very cruel persecutions are inflicted upon those who contravene them. Yet no one in any of the various countries makes the slightest attempt to show that the custom of his own country contributes more to human happiness than the custom of others.

When we open any scientific treatise on the subject, such as (for example) Westermarck's *History of Human Marriage,* we find an atmosphere extraordinarily different from that of popular prejudice. We find that every kind of custom has existed, many of them such as we should have supposed repugnant to human nature. . . . [R]eading must soon reduce any candid person to complete scepticism, since there seem to be no data enabling us to say that one marriage custom is better or worse than another. Almost all involve cruelty and intolerance towards offenders against the local code, but otherwise they have nothing in common. It seems that sin is geographical. From this conclusion it is only a small step to the further conclusion that the notion of "sin" is illusory, and that the cruelty habitually practiced in punishing it is unnecessary. It is just

this conclusion which is so unwelcome to many minds, since the infliction of cruelty with a good conscience is a delight to moralists. That is why they invented Hell.

Nationalism is of course an extreme example of fervent belief concerning doubtful matters. . . . [T]here is no country where people tolerate the truth about themselves; at ordinary times the truth is only thought ill-mannered, but in wartime it is thought criminal. Opposing systems of violent belief are built up. . . . But the application of reason to these systems of belief is thought as wicked as the application of reason to religious dogmas was formerly thought. . . .

What would be the effect of a spread of rational scepticism? Human events spring from passions, which generate systems of attendant myths. Psycho-analysts have studied the individual manifestations of this process in lunatics, certified and uncertified. A man who has suffered some humiliation invents a theory that he is King of England. . . . In this case, his delusion is one with which his neighbors do not sympathize, so they lock him up. But if, instead of asserting only his own greatness, he asserts the greatness of his nation or his class or his creed, he wins hosts of adherents, and becomes a political or religious leader, even if, to the impartial outsider, his views seem just as absurd as those found in asylums. In this way a collective insanity grows up, which follows laws very similar to those of individual insanity. . . .

The part played by intellectual factors in human behavior is a matter as to which there is much disagreement among psychologists. . . .

[H]ow far are beliefs in fact based upon evidence? . . . [H]ow far is it possible or desirable that they should be?

(*a*) The extent to which beliefs are based upon evidence is very much less than believers suppose. Take the kind of action which is most nearly rational: the investment of money by a rich City man. You will often find that his view (say) on the question whether the French franc will go up or down depends upon his political sympathies, and yet is so strongly held that he is prepared to risk his money on it. In bankruptcies it often appears that some sentimental factor was the original cause of ruin. Political opinions are hardly ever based upon evidence, except in the case of civil servants, who are forbidden to give utterance to them. . . .

This brings me to the question: How far could or should men's actions be rational? Let us take "should" first. There are very definite limits, to my mind, within which rationality should be confined; some of the most important departments of life are ruined by the invasion of reason. Leibniz in his old age told a correspondent that he had only once asked a lady to marry him, and that was when he was fifty. "Fortunately," he added, "the lady asked time to consider. This gave me also time to consider, and I withdrew the offer." Doubtless his conduct was very rational, but I cannot say that I admire it. . . .

[E]nvy, cruelty, and hate sprawl at large with the blessing of nearly the whole bench of Bishops. Our instinctive apparatus consists of two parts—the one tending to further our own life and that of our descendants, the other tending to thwart the lives of supposed rivals. The first includes the joy of life, and love, and art, which is psychologically an offshoot of love. The second includes competition, patriotism, and war. Conventional morality does everything to suppress the first and encourage the second. True morality would do the exact opposite. Our dealings with those whom we love may be safely left to instinct; it is our dealings with those whom we hate that ought to be brought under the dominion of reason. In the modern world, those whom we effectively hate are distant groups, especially foreign nations. We conceive them abstractly, and deceive ourselves into the belief that acts which are really embodiments of hatred are done from love of justice or some such lofty motive. Only a large measure of scepticism can tear away the veils which hide this truth from us. Having achieved that, we could begin to build a new morality, not based on envy and restriction, but on the wish for a full life and the realization that other human beings are a help and not a hindrance when once the madness of envy has been cured. . . . It could be realized to-morrow if men would learn to pursue their own happiness rather than the misery of others. This is no impossibly austere morality, yet its adoption would turn our earth into a paradise.

Can Men be Rational?

I am in the habit of thinking of myself as a Rationalist; and a Rationalist, I suppose, must be one who wishes men to be rational. But in these days rationality has received many hard knocks, so that it is difficult to know what one means by it, or whether, if that were known, it is something which human beings can achieve. The question of the definition of rationality has two sides, theoretical and practical: what is a rational opinion? and what is rational conduct? Pragmatism emphasizes the irrationality of opinion, and psycho-analysis emphasizes the irrationality of conduct. Both have led many people to the view that there is no such thing as an ideal of rationality to which opinion and conduct might with advantage conform. It would seem to follow that, if you and I hold different opinions, it is useless to appeal to argument, or to seek the arbitrament of an impartial outsider; there is nothing for us to do but to fight it out, by the methods of rhetoric, advertisement, or warfare, according to the degree of our financial and military strength. I believe such an outlook to be very dangerous, and, in the long run, fatal to civilization. I shall, therefore, endeavor to show that the ideal of rationality remains unaffected by the ideas that have been thought fatal to it, and that it retains all the importance it was formerly believed to have as a guide to thought and life.

To begin with rationality in opinion: I should define it merely as the habit of taking account of all relevant evidence in arriving at a belief. Where certainty is unattainable, a rational man will give most weight to the most probable opinion, while retaining others, which have an appreciable probability, in his mind as hypotheses which subsequent evidence may show to be preferable. This, of course, assumes that it is possible in many cases to ascertain facts and probabilities by an objective method—*i.e.*, a method which will lead any two careful people to the same result. This is often questioned. . . .

[T]he pragmatist philosophers . . . maintain that there is no such thing as objective fact to which our opinions must conform if they are to be true. For them opinions are merely weapons in the struggle for existence, and those which help a man to survive are to be called "true." . . .

In spite of the pragmatist's definition of "truth," however, he has always, in ordinary life, a quite different standard for the less refined questions which arise in practical affairs. A pragmatist on a jury in a murder case will weigh the evidence exactly as any other man will, whereas if he adopted his professed criterion he ought to consider whom among the population it would be most profitable to hang. That man would be, by definition, guilty of the murder, since belief in his guilt would be more useful, and therefore more "true," than belief in the guilt of any one else. I am afraid such practical pragmatism does sometimes occur; I have heard of "frame-ups" in America and Russia which answered to this description. But in such cases all possible efforts after concealment are made, and if they fail there is a scandal. This effort after concealment shows that even policemen believe in objective truth in the case of a criminal trial. It is this kind of objective truth—a very mundane and pedestrial affair—that is sought in science. It is this kind also that is sought in religion so long as people hope to find it. It is only when people have given up the hope of proving that religion is true in a straightforward sense that they set to work to prove that it is "true" in some new-fangled sense. It may be laid down broadly that irrationalism, *i.e.,* disbelief in objective fact, arises almost always from the desire to assert something for which there is no evidence, or to deny something for which there is very good evidence. But the belief in objective fact always persists as regards particular practical questions, such as investments or engaging servants. And if fact can be made the test of the truth of our beliefs anywhere, it should be the test everywhere, leading to agnosticism wherever it cannot be applied. . . .

I shall assume that there are facts, that some facts can be known, and that in regard to certain others a degree of probability can be ascertained in relation to facts which can be known. Our beliefs are, however, often contrary to fact; even when we only hold that something is probable on the evidence, it may be that we ought to hold it to be improbable on the same evidence. The theoretical part of rationality, then, will consist in basing our beliefs as regards matters of fact upon evidence rather than upon wishes, prejudices, or traditions. According to the subject-matter, a rational man will be the same as one who is judicial or one who is scientific. . . .

So far we have been considering only the theoretical side of rationality. The practical side, to which we must now turn our attention, is more difficult. Differences of opinion on practical questions spring from two sources: first, differences between the desires of the disputants; secondly, differences in their estimates of the means for realizing their desires. Differences of the second kind are really theoretical, and only derivatively practical. For example, some authorities hold that our first line of defense should consist of battleships, others that it should consist of airplanes. Here there is no difference as regards the end proposed, namely, national defense, but only as to the means. The argument can therefor be conducted in a purely scientific manner, since the disagreement which causes the dispute is only as to facts, present or future, certain or probable. To all such cases the kind of rationality which I called theoretical applies, in spite of the fact that a practical issue is involved.

There is, however, in many cases which appear to come under this head a complication which is very important in practice. A man who desires to act in a certain way will persuade himself that by so acting he will achieve some end which he considers good, even when, if he had no such desire, he would see no reason for such a belief. And he will judge quite differently as to matters of fact and as to probabilities from the way in which a man with contrary desires will judge. Gamblers, as every one knows, are full of irrational beliefs as to systems which *must* lead them to win in the long run. People who take an interest in politics persuade themselves that the leaders of their party would never be guilty of the knavish tricks practiced by opposing politicians. Men who like administration think that it is good for the populace to be treated like a herd of sheep, men who like tobacco say that it soothes the nerves, and men who like alcohol say that it stimulates wit. The bias produced by such causes falsifies men's judgments as to facts in a way which is very hard to avoid. . . . In politics and religion such considerations become very important. Most men think that in framing their political opinions they are actuated by desire for the public good; but nine times out of ten a man's politics can be predicted from the way in which he makes his living. This has led some people to maintain, and many more to believe practically, that in such matters it is impossible to be objective, and that no method is possible except a tug-of-war between classes with opposite bias.

It is just in such matters, however, that psycho-analysis is particularly useful, since it enables men to become aware of a bias which has hitherto been unconscious. It gives a technique for seeing ourselves as others see us, and a reason for supposing that this view of ourselves is less unjust than we are inclined to think. Combined with a training in the scientific outlook, this method could, if it were widely taught, enable people to be infinitely more rational than they are at present as regards all their beliefs about matters of fact, and about the probable effect of any proposed action. And if men did not disagree about such matters, the disagreements which might survive would almost certainly be found capable of amicable adjustment.

There remains, however, a residuum which cannot be treated by purely intellectual methods. The desires of one man do not by any means harmonize completely with those of another. Two competitors on the Stock Exchange might be in complete agreement as to what would be the effect of this or that action, but this would not produce practical harmony, since each wishes to

grow rich at the expense of the other. Yet even here rationality is capable of preventing most of the harm that might otherwise occur. We call a man irrational when he acts in a passion, when he cuts off his nose to spite his face. He is irrational because he forgets that, by indulging the desire which he happens to feel most strongly at the moment, he will thwart other desires which in the long run are more important to him. If men were rational, they would take a more correct view of their own interest than they do at present; and if all men acted from enlightened self-interest the world would be a paradise in comparison with what it is. I do not maintain that there is nothing better than self-interest as a motive to action; but I do maintain that self-interest, like altruism, is better when it is enlightened than when it is unenlightened. In an ordered community it is very rarely to a man's interest to do anything which is very harmful to others. The less rational a man is, the oftener he will fail to perceive how what injures others also injures him, because hatred or envy will blind him. Therefore, although I do not pretend that enlightened self-interest is the highest morality, I do maintain that, if it became common, it would make the world an immeasurably better place than it is.

Rationality in practice may be defined as the habit of remembering all our relevant desires, and not only the one which happens at the moment to be strongest. Like rationality in opinion, it is a matter of degree. Complete rationality is no doubt an unattainable ideal, but so long as we continue to classify some men as lunatics it is clear that we think some men more rational than others. I believe that all solid progress in the world consists of an increase in rationality, both practical and theoretical. . . . [R]ationality helps us to realize our own desires on the whole, whatever they may be. A man is rational in proportion as his intelligence informs and controls his desires. I believe that the control of our acts by our intelligence is ultimately what is of most importance, and what alone will make social life remain possible as science increases the means at our disposal for injuring each other.

Education, the press, politics, religion—in a word, all the great forces in the world—are at present on the side of irrationality; they are in the hands of men who flatter King Demos in order to lead him astray. The remedy does not lie in anything heroically cataclysmic, but in the efforts of individuals towards a more sane and balanced view of our relations to our neighbors and to the world. It is to intelligence, increasingly widespread, that we must look for the solution of the ills from which our world is suffering.

Questions for Discussion and Review

1. Does it matter whether our beliefs are true?

2. Suppose that a young child has asked you what "true" and "false" mean. What would you say?

3. Is it true that everyone has a right to believe what they want to believe? What does this tell us about truth?

4. How much control do we have over what we believe?

5. What do you think about Realism?

6. The prosecution at a murder trial presents evidence that the DNA found at the scene of the crime has a .99999999 probability of being the defendant's DNA. Do we know that it is the defendant's DNA? Why/Why not?

7. Does it matter whether our beliefs are justified?

8. What does it mean to be rational? How rational are humans? How rational should humans be?

9. Is justification relative? Explain your answer.

10. Suppose you already believe that God exists and you discover that you don't have adequate evidence for God's existence. However, you also don't have adequate evidence that God doesn't exist. Would it be irrational to continue believing that God exists?

11. Suppose you don't yet have any beliefs about God. You examine the issue and discover that you don't have adequate evidence that God exists and you don't have adequate evidence that God doesn't exist (or that the evidence for and against is roughly equal). Would it be irrational for you to believe that God exists? Would it be irrational for you to believe that God doesn't exist?

12. How much control do we have over our beliefs? Do or can we decide to believe some things and decide not to believe others?

13. Is there an ethics of belief? If there is, what are its rules? How might we defend the rules?

14. Suppose I have a mosquito bite that itches. However, I believe that what I'm feeling is called a "pain." I tell someone that I'm feeling a pain on my right arm. Do I believe that I'm itchy on my right arm or do I believe that I have a pain in my right arm?

15. Could I have an insect bite that itches and yet not be aware of it and not believe that I'm itchy where the insect bite is?

16. How well do you know yourself?

17. List two mental states that you think are self-presenting and two that you think are not self-presenting. Defend your selections.

18. List two mental states, first-person beliefs about which are infallible, and two mental states, first-person beliefs about which are not infallible. Defend your selection.

19. How easy is it to know whether you love someone? If it isn't easy, why isn't it easy?

20. If you had none of the five senses, what do you think your picture of reality (system of beliefs) would be like? Why?

21. Nancy says that her belief that many people who receive government assistance don't deserve it or qualify for it is reasonable because as a clerk in a store, she's seen many recipients of government assistance buy expensive items, wear expensive clothes, and leave in expensive cars. Is she justified? Why or why not?

22. What do you see when you look out the window? Does it make sense to say that you're seeing things through a conceptual scheme? Explain and defend your answer.

23. Do our minds filter and process information from perception? If yes, what do you think are the implications?

24. I'm walking along a country road. I believe that I see a cow in the field. Could I possibly be mistaken? How?

25. What other sources of reliable information about the world do we humans have in addition to our five senses?

26. Do our five senses give us reliable information about the world?

27. Beverly Daniel Tatum, a Black psychologist, tells the following two stories:

    (A) In a study of race relations, one five-year-old Black boy reportedly asked, "Do I have to be Black?" To the question of why he asked, he responded, "I want to be chief of paramedics." His favorite TV show at the time featured paramedics and firefighters, all of whom were White.[7]

    (B) One Sunday afternoon . . . my oldest son and I drove past a Black teenager running down the street. "Why is that kid running?" my son asked. "I don't know," I said absentmindedly. "Maybe he stole something," my son said. I nearly slammed on the breaks. "Why would you say something like that?" I said.

---

[7]Beverly Daniel Tatum, *Why Are All the Black Kids Sitting Together in the Cafeteria?* (New York: Basic Books, 1997), 43.

"Well, you know, in the city, there's a lot of crime, and people steal things," he said. He did not say Black people, but I knew to what cultural images he was responding. Now the neighborhood was very familiar to us. We had spent many Sundays at choir rehearsal and sat in church next to Black kids who looked a lot like that boy on the street. We had never personally experienced any crime in that location. . . . I . . . asked my son to imagine why he, also a Black boy, might be running down the street—in a hurry to get home, late for a bus, on his way to a job at the McDonald's up the street? Then we talked about stereotyping and the images of urban Black boys we see on television and elsewhere. Too often they are portrayed as muggers, drug dealers, or other criminals. My sons know that such images are not an accurate representation of themselves, and I have to help them see that they are also a distorted image of their urban peers.[8]

What reaction do you have to these stories?

28. In July 1999, the NAACP complained that although the major television networks had scheduled 26 shows for the Fall prime-time line up, not a single one had "an ethnic minority character in a leading role."[9] What reaction do you have to this claim?

29. If a world famous athlete says in a commercial that a certain breakfast cereal is very nutritious and healthy, would you be justified in believing it? Why or why not?

30. If you read in the New York Times that ten million people worldwide are infected with the HIV virus that causes AIDS, would you be justified in believing it? Why or why not?

31. If the vast majority of scientists who specialize in climate sciences agree that it's highly probable that human actions are causing global warming, would you be justified in believing that human actions are causing global warming?

Suggestions for Further Reading

Robert Audi. *Belief, Justification, and Knowledge.* Belmont, CA: Wadsworth, 1988. A rigorous treatment of problems of knowledge and justified belief suitable mainly for advanced students.

Roderick Chisholm. *Theory of Knowledge,* 3d ed. Englewood Cliffs, NJ: Prentice-Hall, 1989. A brief introduction to problems of truth,

---

[8]Ibid., 48–49.

[9]"NAACP Plans to Press for More Diverse TV Shows," *New York Times,* 13 July 1999.

knowledge, and belief by an eminent and influential contemporary philosopher. See especially Chapters 4, 5, and 6. Suitable mainly for advanced students.

Samuel Gorovitz, Merrill Hintikka, Donald Provence, and Ron Williams. *Philosophical Analysis: An Introduction to Its Language and Techniques,* 3d ed. New York: Random House, 1979. A readable introduction to some of the concepts of this chapter. See especially Chapter 4, on truth, and Chapter 6, on the analytic/synthetic, a priori/a posteriori distinctions.

David Hume. *An Enquiry Concerning Human Understanding.* Indianapolis: Hackett, 1977. A delightful, readable excursion into some basic issues of philosophy from an early modern empiricist view. See especially Sections 4 and 5.

Immanuel Kant. *Prolegomena to Any Future Metaphysics.* Indianapolis: Hackett, 1977. A brief overview of Kant's ideas, rather formidable for beginning students.

Paul K. Moser and Arnold Vander Nat. *Human Knowledge: Classical and Contemporary Approaches.* New York: Oxford University Press, 1987. A collection of excerpts from classic texts and contemporary articles.

D. J. O'Connor and Brian Carr. *Introduction to the Theory of Knowledge.* Minneapolis: University of Minnesota Press, 1982. A rigorous treatment of some of the problems of this chapter.

Alvin Plantinga. *Warrant: The Current Debate.* Oxford: Oxford University Press, 1993.

Alvin Plantinga. *Warrant and Proper Function.* Oxford: Oxford University Press, 1993. Plantinga's set of books are challenging and important, but suitable only for advanced students.

Louis Pojman. *What Can We Know? An Introduction to the Theory of Knowledge.* Belmont, CA: Wadsworth, 1995. An excellent introduction to the issues of this chapter.

KNOWLEDGE AND SKEPTICISM

Objectives

Students are expected to:

- understand the arguments for Global Knowledge Skepticism.

- reach an informed conclusion about the truth of Global Knowledge Skepticism.

- understand the concept of complete justification and its role in knowledge.

- understand the concept of skeptical possibilities.

- understand the role that the fallibility of memory and perception play in arguments for Global Knowledge Skepticism.

- understand the distinction between real and apparent memories and perceptions.

- understand the differences between the strong and weak senses of "know."

- understand induction.

- understand how to confirm generalizations, including causal generalizations.

Introduction

What do we human beings know? Most of us assume we know that 2 + 2 = 4, Earth is spherical, humans are mortal, and it's usually colder in January than it is in July in the United States. These are part of public knowledge, things we all know. As for yourself, you probably assume that you know that you have a brain inside your skull and that you're now reading a philosophy book. (What else do you assume you know?) But most of us also assume that there are things we don't know. Almost all scientists say that we don't yet know whether human actions are the primary cause of the global warming that has been observed over the last few decades, that we don't know how much warmer Earth will become over the next 50–100 years, and that we don't know what the effects will be.

Recall the distinction among theism, atheism, and agnosticism. Theists believe God exists; atheists believe God doesn't exist; agnostics believe neither but instead suspend judgment. We could say that agnostics doubt both that God exists and that God doesn't exist; that's why they suspend judgment. When someone cannot make up her mind about the correct answer to a question and so suspends judgment, we can call her agnostic regarding that issue. It is doubt that leads people to agnosticism. For example, if I don't believe that the average global temperature will rise 5 to 7 degrees Fahrenheit over the next 25 years but also don't believe that it won't, then I'm agnostic about whether it will or won't.

When we doubt something, we're said to be skeptical. If you doubt that the Loch Ness monster exists, then you're skeptical about the claim that it exists. Doubting that the Loch Ness monster exists, being skeptical about it, implies that you don't believe it exists but also that you don't believe it doesn't exist. Perhaps you're suspending judgment awaiting further evidence.

We're all skeptical about some things. You may be skeptical about the claims of most politicians. You may be skeptical about the claims that environmental threats are serious. Or you may be skeptical about the claims that environmental threats are not serious and that we will find a technological fix for them. Skepticism about a certain set of claims or areas of inquiry can be called local skepticism. Someone may be skeptical about most religious claims, so that her skepticism is localized to that area of inquiry.

The widest kind of skepticism, what we might call global skepticism, entails doubt about every area of inquiry. Someone who is globally skeptical doubts every claim in every area of inquiry. That would mean suspending judgment about everything and believing nothing. That kind of global skepticism is probably impossible. It's difficult to imagine that there could be someone who has no beliefs. Such a person wouldn't even believe that he himself exists!

So far, we've talked as though the only doubt is doubt about the truth of a claim. But we can doubt other things. We can doubt that we're justified in believing a certain claim. I doubt that people are justified in believing the claims of psychics and astrologers. (You may doubt that people are justified in believing the claims of philosophers.) So there can be doubt about truth and doubt about justification. But we can also have doubts about knowledge, or about knowledge claims.

Suppose that you have a very wealthy friend who says she knows that Bill loves her. You may think that your friend is probably right and you may yourself believe that Bill loves her. However, you might doubt that she really *knows* that Bill loves her. If you tell her that she doesn't really know this, you're not necessarily saying that you don't share her belief. You're not necessarily saying that her belief is mistaken. You might not even be saying that she doesn't have good reasons for believing that he loves her. You might think that she's justified in believing that he does. Nevertheless, you're saying that she doesn't know, perhaps even cannot know, what she claims to know. You have doubts about her knowledge claim.

We're all familiar with doubts about knowledge claims. If someone claims to know that there is life on other planets, most of us would probably reply that he doesn't really know this, he only believes it. Similarly, if someone says she knows that God exists, you might reply that she doesn't really know this, even if you yourself believe that God exists. In fact, you might say that while you believe that God exists, and you think you're justified in believing it, you don't know that God exists.

We're all skeptical about some knowledge claims, maintaining that in some cases, people don't really know what they claim to know. What's the basis of this skepticism? Clearly, we think that at least one of the requirements for knowledge has not been met. Sometimes we think that the truth condition has not been met. If someone claims to know that the Loch Ness monster exists, I would be skeptical of their claim to know because I doubt that it's true that the Loch Ness monster exists. (That is, I say he doesn't really know what he claims to know.) Sometimes it's the justification condition. If someone claims to know that there is life on other planets, I would be skeptical of his claim to know because I don't think he can be completely justified in believing that there's life on other planets; there's no evidence for or against it yet. However, because I think it's probable that there's life somewhere else in the universe, I believe (weakly?) that there's life elsewhere, although I would insist that I don't know that there is and neither does he.

Some philosophers, however, take what common sense would consider an extreme position on knowledge claims. No matter what you claim to know, these philosophers say that you don't really know it. Not only do you not know that ghosts exist or that there's life on other planets, you don't know that dogs and cats exist. You don't know that Earth exists and that you're located somewhere on its surface. This kind of skepticism about knowledge claims is pretty radical because it's so global. Let's call it **Global Knowledge Skepticism** or GKS for short.

Global Knowledge Skepticism (GKS): People know almost nothing about the world

GKS seems pretty outrageous, but let's not distort it and make it more outrageous than it is. Suppose that a global knowledge skeptic says that you don't know that Mount Everest exists. First, he's not saying that you don't believe that Mount Everest exists, and he's not saying that he doesn't believe that Mount Everest exists. He may believe, as you do, that Mount Everest exists. Also, he's not saying that it's not true that Mount Everest exists; he's not saying that Mount Everest is just a figment of your imagination. If he's not saying these things, what is he saying? He's saying that you don't know that Mount Everest exists and he doesn't know that Mount Everest exists.

We may be tempted to dismiss him as a lunatic, but if we approach his claim philosophically, we'll ask what reasons he has for his claim. On reflection, it seems clear that there are only a few arguments he can make.

He has to say that your claim to know that Mount Everest exists fails to satisfy at least one of the requirements for knowledge. These requirements are belief, truth, and complete justification. What requirements does he think that your knowledge claim fails to satisfy?

It can't be the belief condition. Surely you know whether you believe that Mount Everest exists; it would be madly presumptuous of the GK skeptic to tell you that you don't really believe it. And it's not the truth condition, either. A GK skeptic won't say that you're definitely mistaken about the existence of Mount Everest. That would be a kind of dogmatism that GK skeptics say they abhor. So there's only one requirement left, the complete justification requirement. GK skeptics maintain that your belief that Mount Everest exists, even if true, is not and cannot be completely justified.

What's required for complete justification? A GK skeptic might begin in the following way. Suppose there's a lottery with a billion tickets and you have one. You believe you'll lose. You're justified in believing you'll lose because the probability of your losing (and thus having a true belief) is .999999999. As expected, you do lose. But did you know you'd lose? GK skeptics think that the average speaker of English, on reflection, would probably say that you don't know that you'll lose. Why? Because however small the probability (in this case .000000001), it's still possible that you could have won, possible that your belief could have turned out to be false rather than true. According to the normal conception of knowledge and complete justification, skeptics think, you know only if you can't possibly be mistaken. It's not enough that the possibility of your being mistaken is very low. In the lottery case, there's only a one in a billion chance of being mistaken. You know only if it's impossible for you to be mistaken.

Let's say that something is absolutely certain for you if you couldn't possibly be mistaken about it. Thus, it may be absolutely certain for you that you believe that Mount Everest exists. That is, you couldn't possibly be mistaken about what you believe regarding Mount Everest. GK skeptics are then saying that knowledge (complete justification) requires absolute certainty.

But if a GK skeptic says that you don't know that Mount Everest exists because you're not completely justified in believing it—that you could possibly be mistaken—you can surely ask him how you could possibly be mistaken. He may ask in return whether you've ever actually seen Mount Everest. If you're like me, you haven't, but you've seen pictures of it and you've heard a lot about it. You can show him an encyclopedia with an entry about Mount Everest, describing it as the tallest mountain in the world. Perhaps it will have a picture. Surely this would convince him that you do really know that Mount Everest exists.

Unfortunately, it wouldn't. The GK skeptic will still say that you could possibly be mistaken. You're liable at this point to wonder about the skeptic's sanity. Does he think that the encyclopedia is wrong? Does he think that everyone on Earth who believes in Mount Everest is wrong, that everyone has somehow been deluded all these years into believing in the existence of a nonexistent mountain? You surely would wonder how so many people could possibly make such a colossal mistake. It just seems incredible.

But the GK skeptic has some surprising arguments. He says first that he doesn't have to show that anyone is actually mistaken about anything. All he has to show is that people *could possibly be mistaken*. And a mistake doesn't have to be at all probable to be possible. It could be highly improbable. It could be very highly improbable.

Our GK skeptic may remind you of a recent movie starring Jim Carrey entitled *The Truman Show*. Truman has been brought up on a movie set, but he doesn't know it. Everything he encounters is a prop. Every person he encounters is an actor. Our GK skeptic might ask you, "You could possibly be in Truman's predicament, and if you are, you wouldn't know it. In that case, the encyclopedia you referred to would be a prop filled with false information. People who speak of Mount Everest would be actors acting out a script. Perhaps one of the script writers invented Mount Everest and created fake pictures of it, then planted the pictures, descriptions, and stories in the prop books, encyclopedias, and newspapers you've read. Perhaps even the television programs you've watched have sometimes included views of this purely imaginary mountain. So you could be mistaken in thinking that Mount Everest exists. In that case, it's not absolutely certain for you that it exists, and you don't really know that it exists."

What the GK skeptic has done is present you with a *skeptical possibility*. These are possible (of course, they're usually not very probable) situations or states of affairs which, if they obtained, could lead you to have false beliefs. And they're situations or states of affairs that, if they obtained, you might not know that they obtained. The GK skeptic's point is that he doesn't have to say that you are mistaken about anything. All he has to do is show that it's possible that you could be mistaken about things you believe. If it is possible, then what you believe is not absolutely certain and you don't know it to be true.

Because you've never really seen Mount Everest, you might be willing to concede the GK skeptic's point that you don't know that it exists, even though you feel pretty certain that it does.[1] But he also said that you don't know that dogs exist. How could that be? You've seen and petted scores, perhaps hundreds of dogs in your life. Even if you're in Truman's predicament, you'd still know that dogs exist since you see them every day.

---

[1] Saying that you feel certain about something isn't the same as saying that something is certain. If you feel certain about something, you have full confidence that it's true. But if you feel certain that p is true, it doesn't follow that p is true. On the other hand, if something is certain for you, you couldn't possibly be mistaken. If it is certain for you, it follows that it is true.

GK skeptics present skeptical possibilities based on the fallibility of memory to undermine your claim to know that dogs exist.

The Fallibility of Memory

We're familiar with how frequently memory plays tricks on us. It's not just that we tend to forget things, although that's true enough. We sometimes misremember things. We may think we remember having done something, such as taking out the garbage, only to discover that we're wrong. We may think we remember having parked our car in one place only to discover that we parked it in some other place.

We can distinguish between real memories and apparent memories. For you to really remember something, such as having taken out the garbage, that something must really have occurred. Someone can really remember an experience or event only if it did, in fact, occur. What about cases, however, in which we think we remember or seem to remember something? Those are apparent memories. Unlike real memories, apparent memories needn't be true. That is, to have a real memory of (to really remember) some event or experience e, e must really have occurred. But one can have an apparent memory of, or seem to remember, e, even though e did not, in fact, occur. Thus, while you can really remember paying a bill only if you paid it, you can have an apparent memory of (seem to remember) having paid a bill even though you didn't really pay it.

Real memories presuppose apparent memories. One remembers having paid a bill when (1) one seems to remember (has an apparent memory of) having paid it, and (2) the apparent memory is accurate. If you paid a bill but don't have an apparent memory of having paid it, you've forgotten it. Remembering requires having an apparent memory. On the other hand, if you didn't pay the bill but you have an apparent memory of having paid it, you're not really remembering, either, you're misremembering. You really remember paying a bill only if you seem to remember paying it and you did pay it. Real memories are accurate apparent memories.

Let's assume that our GK skeptic concedes that you can know that you seem to remember something; you can't be mistaken in thinking that you seem to remember having paid a bill. If you think you seem to remember it, you do seem to remember it. But our GK skeptic says that though it can be certain that you seem to remember something, it's never certain that you really do remember it. Introspection reveals your apparent memories to you, but it can't reveal to you which of your apparent memories are real memories. The fact that you seem to remember something doesn't guarantee that you really remember it.

Memory does sometimes play tricks on us, but how could it play big tricks on us? For example, how could you seem to remember having seen scores of dogs in your life if you didn't really see them? Our GK skeptic might say that you could be under the influence of a drug or medication that is wreaking havoc with your memory, causing you to seem to remember many things that didn't really occur. Or a hypnotist may have planted false memories in you. Recall the movie *Total Recall*. Brain scientists may have implanted false memories in you just as Arnold Schwarzenegger had false memories implanted in him. If God, Satan, angels, or demons exist, presumably they have the power to implant false memories in us. So although you may seem to remember having seen many dogs, it's not absolutely certain that you did.

But suppose that you're now seeing a dog. You're not relying on memory, you're relying on current perception. If you now see a dog, then you know that dogs exist, don't you?

The Fallibility of Perception

GK skeptics say that our senses can play tricks on us just as our memory can. GK skeptics claim that perceiving starts with what we seem to perceive. When we seem to perceive something, we're having a certain perceptual experience. If you seem to see something, it's a visual experience; if you seem to hear something, it's an auditory experience, and so on. In order to see a dog, you have to have a perceptual experience of seeming to see a dog. The perceptual experience may be that of having a visual mental image of a certain dog against a certain background.

If you're really seeing the dog, then your visual mental image of it is caused in the right way by your interactions with the dog. Light is reflected from it into your eyes, complicated electrical and chemical reactions take place along a pathway from your eyes to certain parts of your brain, and then you have the mental visual image of the dog.

GK skeptics point out that a number of things can go wrong in this process. Your visual mental image may not be an accurate representation of what caused it. For example, you could see something as a dog when it's not. You could be looking into a field at a sheep and mistake it for a dog. You seem to see a dog when in fact you're seeing a sheep. So even if you now seem to see a dog, you could be mistaken—it could be something else—so you don't know that dogs exist.

You're likely to reply that when perceptual conditions are not ideal you can make such mistakes, for example, if what you think you're seeing is too far away to see clearly. But suppose the animal you're looking at is right at your feet. Suppose further that there's plenty of light in the room and that you haven't merely given it a quick glance but you're looking intently at it. Surely you couldn't possibly be mistaken under those circumstances. You couldn't mistake a sheep or anything else for a dog. Thus, you know you're seeing a dog, and consequently you know that dogs exist.

But global knowledge skeptics still aren't satisfied. They say that even though I think I see a dog lying at my feet and I think that perceptual conditions are ideal, I don't know that I see a dog. Therefore, I don't know there's a dog at my feet and I can't appeal to that to show that I know that dogs exist. They sharply distinguish between my seeming to perceive something and my really perceiving it. According to them, the fact that I seem to perceive something doesn't guarantee that I really perceive it. I can know that I *seem* to perceive something, but not that I really perceive it.

To seem to perceive something is to have a certain perceptual experience. If I seem to perceive that there is a dog at my feet, I'm having an experience of a dog's image being in my visual field. My visual field includes an image of part of a floor and an image of a pair of human legs and feet.

Some global knowledge skeptics say that introspection infallibly reveals to us what we seem to perceive. According to them, I can't be mistaken about what images are in my visual field. But they say that I can be mistaken about whether the images accurately represent what's really there. To see this, we have to understand how perception works. According to them, stimuli from the world first impinge on our sensory organs. Our organs and brains process the information contained in the stimuli and somehow, a mental representation or image is created in our minds. But such representations or images can be created in other ways, as well, for example, by imagination.

This is rather abstract so let's use a concrete example. If you see a dagger, you see it only because light from the dagger entered your eyes, causing a variety of complicated chemical and electrical reactions that sent messages to the visual cortex and other parts of your brain. As a result, you have a mental image of a dagger in your mind. If something interfered with this process so that a mental image of a dagger wasn't formed in your mind, you wouldn't see the dagger even if it was right in front of you. (This would happen if you were blind.) As a result, you form a perceptual belief that there's a dagger in front of you.

But people can hallucinate. Macbeth seemed to see a bloody dagger before him, but he wasn't really seeing it because there was no bloody dagger there. His visual experience of seeming to see a dagger was real, but it wasn't caused by a real dagger. He believed he was really seeing a dagger right before his eyes, but he wasn't. Thus, the fact that you seem to perceive something doesn't guarantee that you're really perceiving it.

Skeptics believe that we're never in a position to know that our perceptual experiences are caused by or accurately represent objects in the physical world. It's always possible that a perceptual experience has a purely internal cause, as in dreams or hallucinations. We may have a natural tendency to believe that we're really perceiving what we seem to perceive, but we always could be mistaken.

According to skeptics, neither memory nor perception is a completely reliable source of information, and therefore, we're not completely justified in believing what they reveal to us. We may know what we seem to remember and seem to perceive, but we're never completely justified in believing that we're really remembering what we seem to remember or really perceiving what we seem to perceive. It's always at least possible that we're mistaken. Therefore, we can never know that we're really remembering or perceiving something. Since sense perception and memory are our only sources of information about the physical world, skeptics insist that we don't really know anything about the physical world.

The Possibility of Dreaming

Most GK skeptics have not been familiar with the movie *The Truman Show*. They presented other skeptical possibilities to show that we don't really know what we think we know. For example, Descartes, an anti-skeptic who, in trying to refute skepticism, presented some of the strongest arguments for skepticism, used dreaming as a skeptical possibility. He might have said something like the following to you. "Of course at this moment you believe that you've seen pictures of Mount Everest, have heard people talk about Mount Everest, have read about Mount Everest, and even that you just looked at an encyclopedia entry for Mount Everest. You even think that you're now talking to me about this. But you could be dreaming all this right now. You could be dreaming that you're talking to me and that you just read an encyclopedia. Your memories of having seen pictures and heard talk of Mount Everest could be dream memories. If you are just dreaming all this, you wouldn't know it; you'd think it is real. Mind you, I'm not saying that you really are dreaming. I'm not even saying that it's probable that you're dreaming. I'm saying that it's possible. And that's all I need to show that you don't really know that Mount Everest exists; it's not absolutely certain."

Evaluating the Skeptic's Argument

Should we accept skepticism and concede that we know almost nothing about the physical world, or should we reject skepticism and insist that we do know pretty much what we think we know about the world? To many people, there's something initially plausible about skeptical arguments, but their ultimate consequences also strike many people as absurd. According to the skeptic, we don't know that there are other human beings and that there have been wars that killed millions of people; we don't know there are people who are poor, malnourished, and homeless;

we don't know that human beings feel pain when cut or burned; we don't know that there are mountains, seas, and rivers. Yet surely, many people insist, we do know these things. So skeptics must be wrong. But claiming that skeptics are mistaken is a lot easier than showing how or why they're mistaken. Can we show that skepticism is mistaken, if it is?

We can begin by formalizing the skeptic's argument as follows:

SKEPTIC'S ARGUMENT

1. You know that p is true only if it is *certain* that p is true—that is, only if you could not possibly be mistaken about p's being true.
2. If p is a statement about the world outside your mind, the only basis (immediate or ultimate) for your believing p is memory or perception.
3. Memory and perception are not infallible; what you believe based on them is not certain. With any belief based on memory or perception, you could possibly be mistaken.
4. Therefore (from 3), if you believe that p is true on the basis of memory or perception, p is not certain; you could possibly be mistaken about p's being true.

---

5. Therefore, if you believe that p is true and p is a statement about the world outside your mind, then you do not *know* that p is true.

If we reject the skeptic's conclusion, it must be because something is wrong with this argument. The argument appears to be valid, so the problem must be with one or more of its premises.

The Fallibility of Memory and Perception

The third premise of the skeptic's argument maintains that memory and perception do not provide certainty because they are fallible. However, a nonskeptic might say that beliefs based on memory or perception could not possibly be mistaken (and are certain) if the conditions under which they are formed were ideal. If you believe you see and feel a book in your hands and there's ample light, how could you be mistaken? As for memory, you could possibly be mistaken if the event you seem to remember occurred a long time ago, but what if it occurred ten minutes ago? Thus, if you believe that your uncle was at your birthday party that ended less than an hour ago because you seem to remember seeing and talking to him, how could you be mistaken? How could your memory play tricks on you?

However, our skeptic's skepticism is more global than this response seems to concede. In essence, the skeptic points out that there is no conclusive proof that memory and perception are ever capable of giving us accurate information about the existence and nature of a world outside our own minds. The very idea of "ideal" memory and perceptual conditions presupposes that sometimes memory and perception are accurate, but global knowledge skeptics say that we have no proof that perception and memory are ever reliable or accurate. They say that the claim that our senses reveal reality to us is simply an unproved and unprovable assumption. The entire course of your experience could be just one long dream or hallucination. It could be that God or the devil has systematically deluded you, providing you with fake perceptual experiences your whole life. It could be that super scientists have plugged into your brain or mind and are using a super computer to generate a whole set of illusory experiences, so-called "virtual" reality instead of "real" reality. If everything you seemed to perceive throughout the course of your life were merely illusion, you would have no way of knowing it.

The same thing applies to what you seem to remember. Like Arnold Schwarzenegger in *Total Recall,* you could have had illusory memories implanted in your brain or mind by super scientists. So even under ideal memory conditions (or what you think are ideal memory conditions), none of what you seem to remember may have happened.

Are Memory and Perception Our Only Access to a World Outside Our Minds?

The second premise of the skeptic's argument maintains that perception and memory are our only sources of information about a reality outside our minds and they're fallible. Do we have any other form of access to reality that's infallible? What of divine revelation? Meditation? Intuition? A sixth sense? Many people have claimed that memory and perception are not our only sources of information about the universe. There have been claims made on behalf of supernatural and paranormal ways of knowing that Western science and philosophy know nothing about. Sometimes these ways of knowing are thought to show that ordinary sensory perception is hopelessly inadequate to reveal to us the immense richness of reality. It's not that what our senses reveal to us isn't there. Rather, our senses reveal only a tiny part of what is there. Our senses do not reveal to us God, angels, an individual's "aura," an individual's soul, the world's soul, and so on. In other cases, people maintain that what the senses reveal is somehow a distortion or illusion. Our senses reveal to us not how things really are, but merely how they appear to us.

Skeptics doubt that alternative sources of information about the world are in any better position than memory or sense perception. They would ask how one knows that what alternatives to sense perception seem to reveal is reality rather than illusion. They believe that alternatives to sense perception cannot be validated for reliability and accuracy any more than sense perception and memory can.

BRAIN TEASERS

1. Do our senses reveal to us only a small portion of what exists in the universe? How do you know? Explain and defend your answers.

2. Do our senses reveal to us only illusion, not reality? Defend your answer.

3. Are there reliable alternative sources of information about the universe outside our minds in addition to or instead of sense perception? Explain and defend your answer.

Does Knowledge Require Certainty?

The first premise of the skeptic's argument says that you know that p is true only if p is certain—that is, only if you *cannot possibly* be mistaken about p's truth. Skeptics maintain that the standard for complete justification is very high. You are completely justified in believing that p is true only if the probability of your being mistaken about p's truth is zero. Your evidence must be conclusive, must guarantee p's truth. Some nonskeptics maintain that skeptics set the standard of complete justification and thus of knowledge much too high. Some nonskeptics say that knowledge does not require certainty. They maintain that even if it is not absolutely certain that there is a book in front of you, if you seem to see and feel a book and you have no reason for thinking that your senses are deceiving you, then you know that there is a book in front of you.

A problem for nonskeptics is how to make more precise this concept of knowledge that does not require absolute certainty. If complete justification does not require zero probability of being mistaken, what does it require? But even before this enterprise can get off the ground, skeptics say that it is fruitless. They maintain that the concept of knowledge that they have identified is our ordinary concept of knowledge, not some new concept that they have invented. They point to our ordinary use of language. As we suggested earlier, if you have a lottery ticket with a .000001 probability of winning, you still don't know that it will lose because as low as the probability is, it is not zero. The probability of its winning, of your being wrong, is vanishingly small, but it is still possible that it will win; therefore, you do not know that it will lose. Skeptics think that this sort of example shows that we do not say that you know unless you cannot possibly be mistaken, unless it is certain that you are right.

BRAIN TEASERS

1. Suppose that there is one chance in 10 billion that a particular nuclear reactor will experience a meltdown (that is, the probability of a meltdown is .0000000001). Do you know that the reactor will not experience a meltdown? Why or why not?

2. Do you know that you will still be alive an hour from now? Why or why not?

A Strong and a Weak Sense of *Know*

There are certain things that no one knows. No one knows how many hairs Julius Caesar had on his head when he was assassinated. No one knows how many dolphins are now alive. No one knows what, if anything, will cure cancer. But does it make sense to say that no one knows anything? No one knows how many hairs were on Caesar's head, but does it make sense to say that no one knows how many hands you have? No one knows how many dolphins are now alive, but does it make sense to say that no one knows that dolphins exist or how many former U.S. presidents are alive? That would suggest a universal ignorance that flies in the face of common sense.

Imagine your professors admitting that they had no knowledge at all to impart to you: no knowledge in engineering, physics, chemistry, biology, history, psychology, or economics. Wouldn't you be tempted to drop their courses? If no one knows anything, a college or university has no knowledge to impart to students, so why should anyone spend the time and money attending?

But few of your teachers are likely to say that they know nothing or that no one knows anything. They think that they and their colleagues have a lot of knowledge to impart to you, and they'll insist that you acquire some of this knowledge. When they say that they know lots of things, though, perhaps they're applying a less stringent concept of knowledge than are skeptics. In practical life we have to. We're just not as completely ignorant as the claim that we know nothing implies.

Knowledge has practical importance. It terminates inquiry. If we think we know the answer to a question, we can stop investigating it and go on to other things. For example, if we think we know what caused World War I, more investigation is pointless. However, if we think we don't know what caused it, more inquiry is called for. In daily life, chaos would ensue if, as a matter of course, we used the stringent concept of knowledge; then, no matter what the issue or question, we would not be justified in stopping inquiry and going on to other things. For practical purposes, we have to relax our standards and treat some things as if they really are knowledge, even if they don't meet the stringent standards required for genuine knowledge that skeptics apply. For example, if I think I know that a truck is coming toward me, I won't keep wondering whether I really know that a truck is coming; I'll get or stay out of its way. On the other hand, if I say to myself, "I don't really know that a truck is coming," I'm treating it as an open question that calls for further inquiry. That could be disastrous.

The relaxed standards for knowledge, as we apply the concept in practical life, aren't easy to specify. Several considerations seem to be relevant, including whether anyone has challenged a claim to know something and whether there are good reasons for doubting a claim—that is, good reasons for thinking that a claim is false rather than reasons for thinking a claim could possibly be false—and whether there are good reasons for thinking a claim to be true.

In effect, then, we have two senses of *know*. The strong sense is the one that skeptics use:

THE STRONG SENSE OF *KNOW*

Person S knows$_s$ that statement p is true only if p is certain and S could not possibly be mistaken about p's truth.

Know$_s$: The strong sense of know, requiring absolute certainty

In daily life, however, we use a weaker sense of *know*. The following may be a rough approximation of that weaker or less stringent standard:

A WEAK SENSE OF *KNOW*

Person S **knows$_w$** that statement p is true if (1) S believes that p is true, (2) p is true, (3) S has very good (but not necessarily conclusive) reasons for believing that p is true, (4) S has no reasons for believing that p is false, and (5) S has not ignored relevant evidence

Know$_w$: The weaker, everyday sense of know that does not require absolute certainty

Let's look more closely at conditions 3–5. In condition 3, "very good reasons for believing that p is true" is imprecise. Unfortunately, we may not be able to make the idea of "very good reasons" more precise.

Condition 4 requires that you have no reason for believing that you are mistaken. You believe you see a house because you seem to see one. What would be a good reason for believing that there really isn't a house there? If you believe that it is logically possible that you are hallucinating, then is that a reason for believing that you do not really see a house? No. On the other hand, suppose you know that a movie company has built several facsimiles of houses here among the real ones. Is that a reason for believing you don't see a real house? If it is, then you don't know$_w$ that you see a house.

BRAIN TEASERS

Is your belief that a movie company built some facsimile houses in the neighborhood a reason for believing that you don't really see a house?

Condition 4 is specified in terms of reasons that you have. Those reasons are your own beliefs. But there could be reasons for believing or disbelieving that you are unaware of. They would then not be reasons that you have. For example, suppose that facsimile houses were built in this area but you are unaware of this. That then would not be a reason that *you have* for thinking you're not (or may not be) seeing a real house, even though it *may be* a reason for thinking that you're not. Should we require that there not *be* reasons for thinking you're mistaken as well as that you *not have* reasons for thinking you're mistaken in order to know$_w$?

In the weak sense of know, we probably know much of what we think we know.

Perhaps as long as we apply less stringent standards for knowledge in ordinary practical life, we can live with skepticism. Perhaps we can admit that in the strong sense of *know,* we know nothing about the world. But we can say that we're not ignorant; we have much knowledge in the weak sense of *know.*

It's impossible for anyone to exist without beliefs, and it seems incontrovertible that some propositions are more worthy of belief than others. We must have some procedure for selecting what's worthy of belief and what's not worthy, for selecting what propositions to accept, reject, or suspend judgment on. Skeptics insist that memory and sense perception aren't reliable enough to provide knowledge, but perhaps we can give up the concept of knowledge and make do with the concept of justified belief. After all, our main concern is to have justified beliefs, whether or not we say we *know* things. We can focus on questions of whether our beliefs are justified and if they are, how justified they are.

Perception, Observation, and Induction

According to most people, we really do perceive what we seem to perceive. Perception is our starting point in building our knowledge (if we have knowledge) of the universe. We assume that perception is generally reliable. We assume that through perception we acquire accurate information about what the universe is like at the time that we perceive it, that through memory we acquire accurate information about what the universe was like when we perceived it in the past, and that through testimony we acquire accurate information about what other people have perceived.

Perception as we have described it seems passive. It suggests that we simply sit back and receive information about the universe through our senses. However, acquiring knowledge usually requires that we be active rather than passive. Let us use the term observation to indicate the active role we play in acquiring information. Observation is a systematic, controlled, focused, and active kind of perception. For example, no matter how long I sit and stare at a computer, I'm not going to learn much about it unless I become more active. I need to switch it on, play with the keyboard, give it various commands, and watch what happens as I do these things. (I may also need to read manuals for the hardware and software.) To get a better understanding, I need to open it up and look inside it.

Similarly, scientists don't learn anything from just passively looking at the universe. They have to ask a specific question about the nature of the universe, form a hypothesis (a potential answer to the question), and then test the hypothesis by conducting experiments. A scientist has to start with a question. Suppose I wonder whether water is heavier in its solid (ice) state than in its liquid state. I can't be passive if I want to find the answer to this question. What must I do? I have to think of an experiment that will give me an answer. Here's one idea. I could weigh a glass of (liquid) water, freeze it, and then weigh it again. If it weighs more, then that shows or confirms that water in its ice state weighs more than water in its liquid state. If it weighs the same, then that shows or confirms that the state water is in (liquid or solid) has no effect on its weight. But I have to weigh water in its liquid and in its solid state, which is an activity. (I probably should repeat the experiment several times in order to ensure that I have not made a mistake.) I have to rely on perception to do the weighing; I must see the numbers on the scale, and so on. But I must be active rather than passive.

Often considerable imagination is required in order to devise an experiment to test a hypothesis or answer a question. One of the characters in the movie *Smoke* tells a story about Sir Walter Raleigh and Queen Elizabeth I. (I do not know whether the story is true, but it is good enough to repeat even if it is merely apocryphal.) One day Raleigh wondered aloud in the queen's presence how much smoke weighs. (Because it rises, one might be tempted to think that smoke has no weight, or perhaps negative weight.) Queen Elizabeth said that no one can weigh smoke. Raleigh said he could. What did he do? (Try to devise an experiment of your own before reading further.)

Raleigh took an unlighted cigar and weighed it. Then he smoked it, being careful to place the ashes in a dish. When he had finished smoking the cigar, he put the remaining stub in the dish, and weighed it along with the ashes he had accumulated. The remains of the smoked cigar weighed less than the unsmoked cigar. Raleigh said that the difference in weight between the smoked cigar and the unsmoked cigar was the weight of the smoke.

Suppose that I want to find out whether a combination of substances x, y, and z will slow the effects of the AIDS virus. I'll never know if I simply look at the three substances. I have to perform experiments. I have to give various combinations of the substances (for example, 26% x, 34% y, and 40% z) in various strengths to HIV-positive patients and see how long it takes for full-blown AIDS to develop. I have to compare the results of these experiments with control groups who also are HIV-positive but who do not receive the experimental x, y, z treatment. If there is no difference between the control groups and the groups who receive the experimental x, y, z treatment, then that shows or confirms that x, y, z has no effect on AIDS. On the other hand, if individuals in the treatment group on average develop full-blown AIDS two years later than individuals in the control group, then that shows or confirms that x, y, z slows the development of AIDS. (Scientists always require that such experimental results be repeated before they are willing to accept them as authoritative.) Again, I must be active in performing experiments and doing research. Knowledge is not acquired by being passive.

BRAIN TEASERS

What experiments might you perform in order to answer the following questions?

1. Does caffeine contribute to heart attacks?

2. Does the position of the stars at one's birth determine what one's personality and character will be?

3. Can psychics see into the future?

If we want to know whether a particular human being has a brain, whether a particular whale has lungs, or whether a particular cow eats meat, we can observe the particular individual creature. We can look inside the human being or whale and we can present various meats to a cow to see whether it will eat any of them. But suppose we want to know whether all human beings have a brain, whether all whales have lungs, or whether all cows are herbivorous (vegetarians). We cannot observe every human being, whale, or cow that has ever existed, exists now, and will exist. So can we *know* (even know$_w$) whether any generalization is true based on observation of only some things of the kind in question?

The traditional term for reaching conclusions about all members of a certain class of things based on observation of only some members of the class is induction. I employ induction if I conclude that all whales have lungs because every whale that has been observed has had lungs. Can induction provide knowledge, even knowledge$_w$? Skeptics deny that it can because the evidence from observation cannot conclusively guarantee that the generalization is true. Even if a million whales have been examined and each has had lungs, that does not prove conclusively that all whales have lungs. Observers may have overlooked the lungless whales. Even if observers have been very careful and have observed a fair sample of whales, ensuring that they have observed specimens from every breed (genus) of whales, from both sexes, from a variety of ages, and from many different geographical regions, they might have overlooked the lungless whales. (One question, of course, is whether we would even call an animal a whale if it was exactly like a whale in all respects except that it had gills rather than lungs.) Thus, skeptics say that even if every observed whale has had lungs, we do not know that all whales have lungs.

There is another problem with induction that was pointed out by British philosopher David Hume. Hume pointed out that when we make universal generalizations, they apply to the future as well as to the present and past. If all whales have lungs, then a whale born a hundred years from now will have lungs. Therefore, if I know that all whales have lungs, I know that any whale born a hundred years from now will have lungs. Or suppose I believe that apples are not poisonous to human beings because people have been eating apples for centuries without being poisoned. If I know that apples are not poisonous to human beings, then I know that if ten years from now I eat an apple that has not been tampered with, it will not poison me.

Hume points out that any generalization that has implications for the future depends on a crucial assumption that cannot be proved. It assumes that the future will be like the present and past in relevant respects. A generalization about whales' having lungs assumes that the universe won't change so that a hundred years from now whales no longer have lungs. A generalization about apples' not being poisonous to human beings assumes that the universe won't change (either the nature of humans or the nature of apples) so that apples become poisonous to human beings. On this view, if induction can provide us with knowledge, it only provides us with knowledge of what is and has been, not of what will be. Thus, according to this version of skepticism, even if the fact that all observed whales have had lungs shows or confirms that all whales have had and have lungs (most skeptics probably would deny this), nevertheless it does not show that whales will continue to have lungs in the future.

Nonskeptics maintain that induction can provide knowledge (at least knowledge$_w$). They maintain that we are justified in inferring that all things that are F have the property of being G if all things that are F that have been observed have the property of being G. For example, nonskeptics maintain that you know that you have a brain inside your skull, even if no one has ever observed it, because no human being whose skull has been opened (or whose head has been x-rayed) has failed to have a brain. We know that every adult human being has a brain, a heart, and so on. So if you meet another human being tomorrow, you know that she has a brain and a heart even though you do not observe them.

But when we employ induction, inferring a generalization from a collection of individual observations, we must be careful. If you go through a house looking at the floors in every room and observe that each floor is covered with brown carpet, then you are very secure in inferring that every floor in the house is covered with brown carpet. No instances have escaped your observation. But often we go beyond what we are observing or have observed. There is no doubt that we risk error under those circumstances. That's why it is important to ensure a fair sample. If you observe that every student in your philosophy class is under 6 feet, you would not be justified in believing that every student in every philosophy class is under 6 feet.

When employing induction we also must employ all the relevant information or knowledge we possess. Suppose that I have been alive every day that I can remember. Then every day that I have observed has included me in it. Could I then infer that every day includes (or will include) me in it? That is, if I have observed that I have always been alive as far back as I can remember, may I infer that I will always be alive? No. Induction also tells me that every human being dies. Since I am a human being, some day I will die.

BRAIN TEASERS

1. There are about 6 billion human beings on Earth; more human beings are now alive than have ever existed. Thus, almost 6 billion human beings have not been observed to die. Do you know$_w$ that all human beings will die some day?

2. Don says that he knows$_w$ that all poor people in the United States are poor because they are lazy and don't work hard enough. How could he know$_w$ this?

3. John says that he knows lots of people who have had unprotected sex and not one of them has become HIV-positive or has contracted AIDS. Is he justified in believing on the basis of induction that if he has unprotected sex, he won't become HIV-positive or contract AIDS?

Observation and Causal Generalizations

Suppose that scientists wonder what causes AIDS. At one time people thought that standing in a draft or getting wet could cause a cold. But scientists have developed means for enhancing our ability to observe the world so that we do not have to rely on our unaided senses. They employ thermometers to precisely measure temperature, telescopes and microscopes to enhance their ability to see, x-ray and MRI machines to peer inside things, EEGs and EKGs to reveal various aspects of brain (EEG) and heart (EKG) functioning, Geiger counters to detect radiation, atomic accelerators to provide information about the nature of the atom, and so on.

By means of sense-enhancing instruments (as well as other kinds of instruments), scientists have discovered the existence of bacteria and viruses. Do either bacteria or viruses play a role in AIDS? How could scientists find out?

Scientists test causal hypotheses by appealing to observation (often sophisticated observation employing a variety of instruments). Because of prior experiences, scientists suspected that the breakdown of the human immune system in AIDS was caused by the activity of a virus. They hoped that they could identify the exact virus responsible for AIDS if their hypothesis was correct. How could a scientist test this hypothesis by appealing to observation? Testing a scientific hypothesis involves making predictions about what one will observe if the hypothesis is true. If one observes what one should observe if the hypothesis is true, then that tends to confirm the hypothesis—that is, provides reasons for believing the hypothesis. On the other hand, if one fails to observe what one should observe if the hypothesis is true, then that tends to disconfirm the hypothesis, or show that it is false.

If AIDS is caused by a particular virus, what should we observe? We should observe the presence of this virus in every AIDS patient. We should also observe that the virus is not present in people who do not have AIDS. (This requires instruments sensitive enough to detect the presence of viruses and to differentiate between different varieties of virus.) But this second requirement is not sufficient because it is possible that someone who does not have AIDS symptoms is nonetheless infected with whatever causes AIDS and will eventually develop it.

Scientists discovered a particular virus (actually several from the same family) in all AIDS patients they examined. (By induction they concluded that all AIDS patients are infected with this virus because all examined or observed AIDS patients were seen to be infected with it.) They hypothesized that this virus causes AIDS. To test the hypothesis, they examined people who did not have AIDS. If none of the non-AIDS people was infected with the virus, that would tend to confirm (but not prove conclusively) that this virus is the cause of AIDS. However, scientists found that some people who did not have AIDS were infected with this virus. Scientists had to make another prediction about what they would observe if their hypothesis was true. If this virus causes AIDS, then people infected with the virus should eventually develop AIDS. On the other hand, those people not infected with the virus should not develop AIDS. So scientists would have to observe people over a period of months and years. They found that almost everyone who was infected with the virus developed AIDS while no one who was not infected with the virus developed AIDS. That tended to confirm that this virus is the cause of AIDS.

Scientists do not accept a causal claim unless it has passed many tests based on observation. Before it has passed tests, a claim is merely a hypothesis. Testing a causal hypothesis requires the following steps:

TESTING CAUSAL HYPOTHESES

1. Specify what you will observe (under conditions C) if the hypothesis is true. (The predicted observations should be highly unlikely if the hypothesis is false.)
2. Make the relevant observations (under conditions C).
3. If you observe what you should observe if the hypothesis is true, then the hypothesis has been confirmed (but not conclusively proved).
4. If you do not observe what you should observe if the hypothesis is true, then the hypothesis has been disconfirmed (shown to be probably false).

Notice that the predicted observations should be highly unlikely if the hypothesis is false. For example, it would not do to reason in the following way:

1. You will observe the sun rising on Monday if this virus causes AIDS.
2. We observed the sun rising on Monday.

---

3. Therefore, the hypothesis that this virus causes AIDS has been confirmed.

The sun's rising on Monday is highly probable whether or not a particular virus causes AIDS. Therefore, it cannot be used to confirm the hypothesis that the virus causes AIDS.

One of the most famous confirmations of a scientific theory or hypothesis involves an experiment to confirm Einstein's theory of relativity. Prior to Einstein, scientists assumed that light always travels in straight lines and that the structure of space in which they travel is not affected by the presence or absence of physical objects. However, Einstein's theory of relativity claims that the structure of space is affected by the presence or absence of physical objects. Einstein claimed that space is distorted or curved by the mass of physical objects; the greater the mass of the object, the greater the distortion or curvature. The curvature would be noticeable only around very massive objects such as stars. (Scientists ask us to imagine that space is a rubber sheet and a star is a cannonball. Put the cannonball in the middle of the rubber sheet and it curves.)

According to Einstein, light would appear to bend as it passes a star because the space in which it is traveling curves around the star. Ordinarily the bending is not noticeable. However, Einstein predicted that it would be noticeable during a solar eclipse. He suggested the following experiment. During a solar eclipse, observe a star whose light traveling toward Earth will pass close by the sun and whose position relative to background stars is well known. Einstein predicted that the star would appear to have shifted its position relative to the background stars (see figure below). The explanation would be that the light rays traveling in straight lines appear to curve because space is curved near the sun.

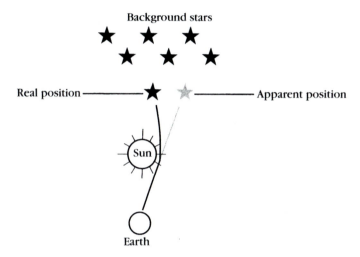

Einstein's prediction is a very risky one. If his theory is incorrect, then scientists probably would not observe what he predicted they would observe. However, if his theory is correct, scientists would almost certainly observe what he predicted. A team of astronomers set out to observe a solar eclipse to see whether Einstein's predictions were correct. Many scientists doubted his theory and doubted that the predicted observable phenomenon would occur. The scientific world was amazed when the astronomers reported that Einstein was right. Stars whose light passed very close to the sun appeared to have changed their position. That was strong confirmation that Einstein was right. Using his theory, he had predicted something that without the theory was very unlikely.

Smoking and Cancer

Jones, a two-pack-a-day cigarette smoker for forty years, has just died of lung cancer at the age of fifty-six. His children, who are also smokers, want to know whether his smoking caused his death because they've read so often that smoking causes lung cancer. Charles, his oldest son, insists that evidence proves that smoking doesn't cause lung cancer because he knows of many heavy smokers who lived into their eighties and even nineties. He has told his brothers and sisters that if smoking caused lung cancer, all smokers would have lung cancer. Since they don't, it's evident that smoking doesn't cause lung cancer and thus that their father's smoking didn't cause him to develop cancer. Tom, the youngest, disagrees. He thinks that smoking does cause lung cancer and that it's very likely that their father's heavy smoking did cause him to develop cancer. Who's right?

If smoking causes lung cancer, then shouldn't we expect to observe that (1) everyone who smokes develops lung cancer, and (2) no one who does not smoke develops lung cancer? If we don't observe either of these things, then wouldn't that disconfirm that smoking causes lung cancer? First, when scientists maintain that smoking causes lung cancer, they are not claiming that only smoking causes lung cancer. Therefore, we really should not expect to observe that no nonsmokers develop lung cancer. Furthermore, when they claim that smoking causes lung cancer, they are not maintaining that smoking will cause lung cancer under all conditions. Rather, they are maintaining that smoking causes cancer under the right conditions. Consider the claim that reducing the internal temperature of water to or below 32 degrees F will cause it to freeze. There is a caveat. It will cause it to freeze under the right conditions—for example, provided that the water is pure and is at a certain pressure. Similarly, scientists maintain that smoking cigarettes will cause lung cancer, but only under the right conditions. These conditions might involve the state of one's immune system, the composition of the tissue of one's lungs, and so on. Therefore, we should not expect to find that everyone who smokes develops lung cancer. However, there is a problem. If we should not expect to observe (1) that everyone who smokes develops lung cancer or (2) that everyone with lung cancer smoked, then what should we expect to observe in order to confirm the hypothesis that smoking causes lung cancer?

In a sense, we test this hypothesis by testing its denial—the hypothesis that smoking has nothing at all to do with developing lung cancer. If we can't directly test a hypothesis h, we may be able to test its rival, not h. If h is true, not h is false; if h is false, not h is true. If we can devise a test for not h—the hypothesis that smoking has nothing at all to do with developing lung cancer—and prove that it's false, we've shown that smoking does cause lung cancer.

If smoking doesn't cause lung cancer, what should we expect to find? If cigarettes have nothing to do with lung cancer, the percentage of smokers who develop the disease ought to be the same as the percentage of nonsmokers who develop it. This suggests a way of testing not h: Take a fair sample of smokers and a fair sample of nonsmokers and see how many of each has lung cancer. If we find that many more smokers than nonsmokers develop lung cancer, the hypothesis that smoking has nothing to do with lung cancer will have failed the test. And if the hypothesis fails the test, we've shown that smoking does have some connection with lung cancer. In fact, many more smokers than nonsmokers develop lung cancer, so there's reason to think that hypothesis not h is false.

We now have reason to think that h is true. Can we construct further tests of h? If smoking causes cancer, we should discover that the more cigarettes people smoke, the more likely it is that they'll develop lung cancer. That is, if we divide smokers according to the amount they smoke—for example, Group A, people who smoke half a pack a day; Group B, people who smoke a pack a day; Group C, people who smoke a pack and a half a day; and Group D, people who smoke two or more packs a day—we should find that the percentage of people who develop lung cancer is greatest among Group D and smallest among Group A. Performing this test, scientists discover that, indeed, the percentage of people with lung cancer is highest among heaviest smokers and lowest among lightest smokers. That finding further disproves the hypothesis that smoking has nothing to do with lung cancer and further confirms the hypothesis that smoking causes cancer. Can we devise further tests? Again the answer is yes. If smoking causes cancer, we ought to find that the longer people smoke, the greater is the incidence of lung cancer. That is, the percentage of people with lung cancer should be higher among people who have smoked for a long time than among people who have smoked for a shorter time. In fact, that's what we find.

Given these tests and others like them, scientists consider that they've proved beyond reasonable doubt that smoking causes lung cancer.

Scientists usually talk of probability and risk when they talk of cigarette smoking and cancer. For example, suppose that .01 percent of nonsmokers develop lung cancer but .1 percent of one-pack-a-day smokers develop it after twenty-five years. One-pack-a-day smokers thus have a .1 percent probability of developing lung cancer after twenty-five years, and their risk of developing it is ten times greater than that of nonsmokers. That smoking causes lung cancer doesn't mean that all smokers will eventually develop lung cancer; it means that smokers substantially increase the probability, or risk, of developing it.

Can we *know* that Jones's smoking caused his lung cancer? Probably not. According to skeptics, we can know that his smoking caused his cancer only if we know that nothing else caused it. But can we *know* that nothing else caused his cancer—for example, air pollution from a nearby coal-fired power station, automobile exhaust, radioactive gases, or hazardous chemicals at his place of work? The best we could do is say how probable it is that his smoking caused his lung cancer if we could eliminate some of the other possibilities. But it's not clear that we could eliminate all other possibilities. In this case, I don't think we could ever *know* that Jones's smoking caused his lung cancer.[2]

---

[2]Much of the information for this section came from Ronald Giere, *Understanding Scientific Reasoning*, 2d ed. (New York: Holt, Rinehart, and Winston, 1984).

The Virtue of Skepticism

Whether skepticism should be rejected remains an open question. But even if it should be rejected, skeptics do us a great service by reminding us of our fallibility. Many of us tend to be far less critical of ourselves and those we agree with than we should be. Skeptical challenges can keep us on our toes and encourage us to be far more careful about what we believe and about what we claim to know. Careful evaluation is more likely to lead us to truth than is uncritical acceptance of things, and truth, after all, should be our goal. Whether we can attain knowledge about the world may be an open question, but surely at least sometimes we can attain truth.

Bertrand Russell speaks eloquently of the value of philosophy and skepticism:

> The value of philosophy is, in fact, to be sought largely in its very uncertainty. The man who has no tincture of philosophy goes through life imprisoned in the prejudices derived from common sense, from the habitual beliefs of his age or his nation, and from convictions which have grown up in his mind without the co-operation or consent of his deliberate reason. To such a man the world tends to become definite, finite, obvious; common objects rouse no questions, and unfamiliar possibilities are contemptuously rejected. As soon as we begin to philosophize, on the contrary, we find . . . that even the most everyday things lead to problems to which only very incomplete answers can be given. Philosophy, though unable to tell us with certainty what is the true answer to the doubts which it raises, is able to suggest many possibilities which enlarge our thoughts and free them from the tyranny of custom.[3]

---

[3]Bertrand Russell, *The Problems of Philosophy* (New York: Oxford University Press, 1959), 156-157.

 RENÉ DESCARTES (1596–1650)

MEDITATIONS ON THE FIRST PHILOSOPHY

Meditation I

Of the things which may be brought within the sphere of the doubtful.

It is now some years since I detected how many were the false beliefs that I had from my earliest youth admitted as true, and how doubtful was everything I had since constructed on this basis; and from that time I was convinced that I must once for all seriously undertake to rid myself of all the opinions which I had formerly accepted, and commence to build anew from the foundation, if I wanted to establish any firm and permanent structure in the sciences.

From "Meditations on First Philosophy," *The Philosophical Works of Descartes,* Vol. 1 (Cambridge: Cambridge University Press, 1911). Reprinted with permission of Cambridge University Press.

Now for this object it is not necessary that I should show that all of these are false—I shall perhaps never arrive at this end. But inasmuch as reason already persuades me that I ought no less carefully to withhold my assent from matters which are not entirely certain and indubitable than from those which appear to me manifestly to be false, if I am able to find in each one some reason to doubt, this will suffice to justify my rejecting the whole. And for that end it will not be requisite that I should examine each in particular, which would be an endless undertaking; for owing to the fact that the destruction of the foundations of necessity brings with it the downfall of the rest of the edifice, I shall only in the first place attack those principles upon which all my former opinions rested.

All that up to the present time I have accepted as most true and certain I have learned either from the senses or through the senses; but it is sometimes proved to me that these senses are deceptive, and it is wiser not to trust entirely to any thing by which we have once been deceived.

But it may be that although the senses sometimes deceive us concerning things which are hardly perceptible, or very far away, there are yet many others to be met with as to which we cannot reasonably have any doubt, although we recognize them by their means. For example, there is the fact that I am here, seated by the fire, attired in a dressing gown, having this paper in my hands and other similar matters. And how could I deny that these hands and this body are mine, were it not perhaps that I compare myself to certain persons, devoid of sense, whose cerebella are so troubled and clouded by the violent vapours of black bile, that they constantly assure us that they think they are kings when they are really quite poor, or that they are clothed in purple when they are really without covering, or who imagine that they have an earthenware head or are nothing but pumpkins or are made of glass. But they are mad, and I should not be any the less insane were I to follow examples so extravagant.

At the same time I must remember that I am a man, and that consequently I am in the habit of sleeping, and in my dreams representing to myself the same things or sometimes even less probable things, than do those who are insane in their waking moments. How often has it happened to me that in the night I dreamt that I found myself in this particular place, that I was dressed and seated near the fire, whilst in reality I was lying undressed in bed! At this moment it does indeed seem to me that it is with eyes awake that I am looking at this paper; that this head which I move is not asleep, that it is deliberately and of set purpose that I extend my hand and perceive it; what happens in sleep does not appear so clear nor so distinct as does all this. But in thinking over this I remind myself that on many occasions I have in sleep been deceived by similar illusions, and in dwelling carefully on this reflection I see so manifestly that there are no certain indications by which we may clearly distinguish wakefulness from sleep that I am lost in astonishment. And my astonishment is such that it is almost capable of persuading me that I now dream.

Now let us assume that we are asleep and that all these particulars, e.g. that we open our eyes, shake our head, extend our hands, and so on, are but false delusions; and let us reflect that possibly neither our hands nor our whole body are such as they appear to us to be. At the same time we must at least confess that the things which are represented to us in sleep are like painted representations which can only have been formed as the counterparts of something real and true, and that in this way those general things at least, i.e. eyes, a head, hands, and a whole body, are not imaginary things, but things really existent. For, as a matter of fact, painters, even when they study with the greatest skill to represent sirens and satyrs by forms the most strange and extraordinary, cannot give them natures which are entirely new, but merely make a certain medley of the members of different animals; or if their imagination is extravagant enough to invent something so novel that nothing similar has ever before been seen, and that then their work represents a thing purely fictitious and absolutely false, it is certain all the same that the colours of which this is composed are necessarily real. And for the same reason, although these general things, to wit, [a body], eyes, a head, hands, and such like, may be imaginary, we are bound at the same time to confess that there are at least some other objects yet more simple and more universal, which are real and true; and of these just in the same way as with certain real colours, all these images of things which dwell in our thoughts, whether true and real or false and fantastic, are formed.

To such a class of things pertains corporeal nature in general, and its extension, the figure of extended things, their quantity or magnitude and number, as also the place in which they are, the time which measures their duration, and so on.

That is possibly why our reasoning is not unjust when we conclude from this that Physics, Astronomy, Medicine and all other sciences which have as their end the consideration of composite things, are very dubious and uncertain; but that Arithmetic, Geometry and other sciences of that kind which only treat of things that are very simple and very general, without taking great trouble to ascertain whether they are actually existent or not, contain some measure of certainty and an element of the indubitable. For whether I am awake or asleep, two and three together always form five, and the square can never have more than four sides, and it does not seem possible that truths so clear and apparent can be suspected of any falsity [or uncertainty].

Nevertheless I have long had fixed in my mind the belief that an all-powerful God existed by whom I have been created such as I am. But how do I know that He has not brought it to pass that there is no earth, no heaven, no extended body, no magnitude, no place, and that nevertheless [I possess the perceptions of all these things and that] they seem to me to exist just exactly as I now see them? And, besides, as I sometimes imagine that others deceive themselves in the things which they think they know best, how do I know that I am not deceived every time that I add two and three, or count the sides of a square, or judge of things yet simpler, if anything simpler can be imagined? But possibly God has

not desired that I should be thus deceived, for He is said to be supremely good. If, however, it is contrary to His goodness to have made me such that I constantly deceive myself, it would also appear to be contrary to His goodness to permit me to be sometimes deceived, and nevertheless I cannot doubt that He does permit this.

There may indeed be those who would prefer to deny the existence of a God so powerful, rather than believe that all other things are uncertain. But let us not oppose them for the present, and grant that all that is here said of a God is a fable; nevertheless in whatever way they suppose that I have arrived at the state of being that I have reached—whether they attribute it to fate or to accident, or make out that it is by a continual succession of antecedents, or by some other method—since to err and deceive oneself is a defect, it is clear that the greater will be the probability of my being so imperfect as to deceive myself ever, as is the Author to whom they assign my origin the less powerful. To these reasons I have certainly nothing to reply, but at the end I feel constrained to confess that there is nothing in all that I formerly believed to be true, of which I cannot in some measure doubt, and that not merely through want of thought or through levity, but for reasons which are very powerful and maturely considered; so that henceforth I ought not the less carefully to refrain from giving credence to these opinions than to that which is manifestly false, if I desire to arrive at any certainty [in the sciences].

But it is not sufficient to have made these remarks, we must also be careful to keep them in mind. For these ancient and commonly held opinions still revert frequently to my mind, long and familiar custom having given them the right to occupy my mind against my inclination and rendered them almost masters of my belief; nor will I ever lose the habit of deferring to them or of placing my confidence in them, so long as I consider them as they really are, i.e. opinions in some measure doubtful, as I have just shown, and at the same time highly probable, so that there is much more reason to believe in than to deny them. That is why I consider that I shall not be acting amiss, if, taking of set purpose a contrary belief, I allow myself to be deceived, and for a certain time pretend that all these opinions are entirely false and imaginary, until at last, having thus balanced my former prejudices with my latter [so that they cannot divert my opinions more to one side than to the other], my judgment will no longer be dominated by bad usage or turned away from the right knowledge of the truth. For I am assured that there can be neither peril nor error in this course, and that I cannot at present yield too much to distrust, since I am not considering the question of action, but only of knowledge.

I shall then suppose, not that God who is supremely good and the fountain of truth, but some evil genius not less powerful than deceitful, has employed his whole energies in deceiving me; I shall consider that the heavens, the earth, colours, figures, sound, and all other external things are nought but the illusions and dreams of which this genius has availed himself in order to lay traps for my credulity; I shall consider myself as having no hands, no eyes, no flesh, no blood, nor any senses, yet falsely believing myself to possess all these things; I shall remain obstinately attached to this idea, and if by this means it is not in my power to arrive at the knowledge of any truth, I may at least do what is in my power [i.e. suspend my judgment], and with firm purpose avoid giving credence to any false thing, or being imposed upon by this arch deceiver, however powerful and deceptive he may be. But this task is a laborious one, and insensibly a certain lassitude leads me into the course of my ordinary life. And just as a captive who in sleep enjoys an imaginary liberty, when he begins to suspect that his liberty is but a dream, fears to awaken, and conspires with these agreeable illusions that the deception may be prolonged, so insensibly of my own accord I fall back into my former opinions, and I dread awakening from this slumber, lest the laborious wakefulness which would follow the tranquillity of this repose should have to be spent not in daylight, but in the excessive darkness of the difficulties which have just been discussed.

Meditation II

The Meditation of yesterday filled my mind with so many doubts that it is no longer in my power to forget them. And yet I do not see in what manner I can resolve them; and, just as if I had all of a sudden fallen into very deep water, I am so disconcerted that I can neither make certain of setting my feet on the bottom, nor can I swim and so support myself on the surface. I shall nevertheless make an effort and follow anew the same path as that on which I yesterday entered, i.e. I shall proceed by setting aside all that in which the least doubt could be supposed to exist, just as if I had discovered that it was absolutely false; and I shall ever follow in this road until I have met with something which is certain, or at least, if I can do nothing else, until I have learned for certain that there is nothing in the world that is certain. Archimedes, in order that he might draw the terrestrial globe out of its place, and transport it elsewhere, demanded only that one point should be fixed and immoveable; in the same way I shall have the right to conceive high hopes if I am happy enough to discover one thing only which is certain and indubitable.

I suppose, then, that all the things that I see are false; I persuade myself that nothing has ever existed of all that my fallacious memory represents to me. I consider that I possess no senses; I imagine that body, figure, extension, movement and place are but the fictions of my mind. What, then, can be esteemed as true? Perhaps nothing at all, unless that there is nothing in the world that is certain.

But how can I know there is not something different from those things that I have just considered, of which one cannot have the slightest doubt? Is there not some God, or some other being by whatever name we call it, who puts these reflections into my mind? That is not necessary, for is it not possible that I am capable of producing them myself? I myself, am I not at least something? But I have already denied that I had senses and body. Yet I hesitate, for what follows from that? Am I so dependent on body and senses that I cannot exist without these? But I was persuaded that there was nothing in all the world, that there was no heaven, no earth, that there were no minds, nor any bodies: was I not then likewise persuaded that I did not exist? Not at all; of a surety I myself did exist since I persuaded myself of something [or merely because I thought of something]. But there is some deceiver or other, very powerful and very cunning, who ever employs his ingenuity in deceiving me. Then without doubt I exist also if he deceives me, and let him deceive me as much as he will, he can never cause me to be nothing so long as I think that I am something. So that after having reflected well and carefully examined all things, we must come to the definite conclusion that this proposition: I am, I exist, is necessarily true each time that I pronounce it, or that I mentally conceive it.

   DAVID HUME (1711–1776)

An Enquiry Concerning Human Understanding

Section IV: Sceptical Doubts Concerning the Operations of the Understanding

Part I

All the objects of human reason or enquiry may naturally be divided into two kinds, to wit, *Relations of Ideas,* and *Matters of Fact.* Of the first kind are the sciences of Geometry, Algebra, and Arithmetic; and in short, every affirmation, which is either intuitively or demonstratively certain. *That the square of the hypothenuse is equal to the square of the two sides,* is a proposition, which expresses a relation between these figures. *That three times five is equal to the half of thirty,* expresses a relation between these numbers. Propositions of this kind are discoverable by the mere operation of thought, without dependence on what is any where existent in the universe. Though there never were a circle or triangle in nature, the truths, demonstrated by Euclid, would for ever retain their certainty and evidence.

Matters of fact, which are the second objects of human reason, are not ascertained in the same manner; nor is our evidence of their truth, however great, of a like nature with the foregoing. The contrary of every matter of fact is still possible; because it can never imply a contradiction, and is conceived by the mind with the same facility and distinctness, as if ever so conformable to reality. *That the sun will not rise tomorrow* is no less intelligible a proposition, and implies no more contradiction, than the affirmation, *that it will rise.* We should in vain, therefore, attempt to demonstrate its falsehood. Were it demonstratively false, it would imply a contradiction, and could never be distinctly conceived by the mind.

It may, therefore, be a subject worthy of curiosity, to enquire what is the nature of that evidence, which assures us of any real existence and matter of fact, beyond the present testimony of our senses, or the records of our memory. . . .

All reasonings concerning matter of fact seem to be founded on the relation of *Cause and Effect.* By means of that relation alone we can go beyond the evidence of our memory and senses. If you were to ask a man, why he believes any matter of fact, which is absent;

From *An Enquiry Concerning Human Understanding,* ed. E. Steinberg (Indianapolis: Hackett, 1977). Footnotes are omitted.

for instance, that his friend is in the country, or in France; he would give you a reason; and this reason would be some other fact; as a letter received from him, or the knowledge of his former resolutions and promises. A man, finding a watch or any other machine in a desert island, would conclude, that there had once been men in that island. All our reasonings concerning fact are of the same nature. And here it is constantly supposed, that there is a connexion between the present fact and that which is inferred from it. Were there nothing to bind them together, the inference would be entirely precarious. The hearing of an articulate voice and rational discourse in the dark assures us of the presence of some person: Why? because these are the effects of the human make and fabric, and closely connected with it. . . .

If we would satisfy ourselves, therefore, concerning the nature of that evidence, which assures us of matters of fact, we must enquire how we arrive at the knowledge of cause and effect.

I shall venture to affirm, as a general proposition, which admits of no exception, that the knowledge of this relation is not, in any instance, attained by reasonings a priori; but arises entirely from experience, when we find, that any particular objects are constantly conjoined with each other. Let an object be presented to a man of ever so strong natural reason and abilities; if that object be entirely new to him, he will not be able, by the most accurate examination of its sensible qualities, to discover any of its causes and effects. Adam, though his rational faculties be supposed, at the very first, entirely perfect, could not have inferred from the fluidity, and transparency of water, that it would suffocate him, or from the light and warmth of fire, that it would consume him. No object ever discovers, by the qualities which appear to the senses, either the causes which produced it, or the effects which will arise from it; nor can our reason, unassisted by experience, ever draw any inference concerning real existence and matter of fact. . . . Present two smooth pieces of marble to a man . . . , he will never discover, that they

will adhere together, in such a manner as to require great force to separate them in a direct line. . . . Such events . . . are . . . known only by experience. . . .

Were any object presented to us, and were we required to pronounce concerning the effect, which will result from it, without consulting past observation; after what manner, I beseech you, must the mind proceed in this operation . . . ?

In vain, therefore, should we pretend to determine any single event, or infer any cause or effect, without the assistance of observation and experience. . . .

Part II

When it is asked, *What is the nature of all our reasonings concerning matter of fact?* the proper answer seems to be, that they are founded on the relation of cause and effect. When again it is asked, *What is the foundation of all our reasonings and conclusions concerning that relation?* it may be replied in one word, EXPERIENCE. But if we still carry on our sifting humour, and ask, *What is the foundation of all conclusions from experience?* this implies a new question, which may be of more difficult solution and explication. . . .

. . . We always presume . . . that effects, similar to those which we have experienced, will follow from them. If a body of like colour and consistence with that bread, which we have formerly eat, be presented to us, we make no scruple of repeating the experiment, and foresee, with certainty, like nourishment and support. Now this is a process of the mind or thought, of which I would willingly know the foundation. . . . As to past Experience, it can be allowed to give *direct* and *certain* information of those precise objects only, and that precise period of time, which fell under its cognizance: But why this experience should be extended to future times, and to other objects . . . , this is the main question on which I would insist. The bread, which I formerly eat, nourished me. . . . But does it follow, that other bread must also nourish me at another time . . . ?

The consequence seems nowise necessary. . . . I shall allow, if you please, that the one proposition may justly be inferred from the other: I know in fact, that it always is inferred. But if you insist, that the inference is made by a chain of reasoning, I desire you to produce that reasoning. The connexion between these propositions is not intuitive. There is required a medium, which may enable the mind to draw such an inference, if indeed it be drawn by reasoning and argument.

All reasonings may be divided into two kinds, namely demonstrative reasoning, or that concerning relations of ideas, and moral reasoning, or that concerning matter of fact and existence. That there are no demonstrative arguments in the case, seems evident; since it implies no contradiction, that the course of nature may change, and that an object, seemingly like those which we have experienced, may be attended with different or contrary effects. . . . Now whatever is intelligible, and can be distinctly conceived, implies no contradiction, and can never be proved false by any demonstrative argument or abstract reasoning *a priori*.

If we be, therefore, engaged by arguments to put trust in past experience, and make it the standard of our future judgment, these arguments must be probable only. . . . But . . . we have said, that all arguments concerning existence are founded on the relation of cause and effect; that our knowledge of that relation is derived entirely from experience; and that all our experimental conclusions proceed upon the supposition, that the future will be conformable to the past. To endeavour, therefore, the proof of this last supposition by probable arguments, or arguments regarding existence, must be evidently going in a circle, and taking that for granted, which is the very point in question.

In reality, all arguments from experience are founded on the similarity, which we discover among natural objects, and by which we are induced to expect effects similar to those, which we have found to follow from such objects. And though none but a fool or madman will ever pretend to dispute the authority of experience, or to reject that great guide of human life; it may surely be allowed a philosopher to have so much curiosity at least, as to examine the principle of human nature, which gives this mighty authority to experience, and makes us draw advantage from that similarity, which nature has placed among different objects. From causes, which appear *similar*, we expect similar effects. This is the sum of all our experimental conclusions.

Questions for Discussion and Review

1. Are there two different concepts of "knowing," a strong sense and a weak sense? Explain and defend your answer.

2. If you believe that you seem to see a red car in front of you, do you *know* that you seem to see a red car in front of you? Explain and defend your answer.

3. Do you *know* that there is a red car in front of you if you seem to see a red car in front of you? Explain and defend your answer.

4. At a murder trial, Roberto testifies that he saw the defendant, Cyril, murder the victim. Assuming that he is sincere, does Roberto know that Cyril committed the murder?

5. Assume that jurors in the case of #4 believe that Roberto is sincere in his testimony. Do they know that Cyril is the murderer? Would it

be reasonable to convict Cyril primarily on the basis of Roberto's testimony?

6. Let's call a property that simple observation reveals to us an observation property. The properties of being red and of being spherical are such observation properties. We can tell whether something is red or spherical just by looking at it. Other properties cannot be detected quite so easily. For example, to determine whether something has the property of weighing 150 pounds or being five feet tall, we cannot just look at it, we must use an instrument to measure the property—for example, a scale to measure its weight and a ruler to measure its height. How can observation reveal to us whether someone (a) is a bachelor, (b) has a Ph.D. in history, (c) is Ted's biological father, or (d) owns a yacht?

7. If you believe that Ron is Ted's biological father, what would it take for you to *know* that Ron is Ted's biological father? Explain and defend your answer.

8. A blood test to establish paternity is 99.9999% reliable. That is, if there is no genetic match between person X and person Y, then it is certain that person X is not the biological father of person Y. On the other hand, if there is a match, then the probability that X is Y's father is .999999. Tests show that Ron's blood genetically matches Ted's. Therefore, the probability that Ron is Ted's biological father is .999999. Do we now *know* that Ron is Ted's biological father? Explain and defend your answer. What, if anything, does this show about the concept of knowledge?

9. In the past, drinking warm milk just before bed has always enabled me to get to sleep. I did not drink warm milk before bedtime and I am having trouble getting to sleep now. Do I *know* on the basis of induction that if I drink warm milk now, it will enable me to get to sleep? Explain and defend your answer.

10. Every time I drive, I always make the sign of the cross before setting the car into motion. I have never had an accident. I believe that making the sign of the cross prevents me from having an accident. Do I *know* on the basis of induction that making the sign of the cross prevents me from having an accident? Explain and defend your answer.

11. I have eaten corn every day of my life since I can remember. It has always been nourishing rather than poisonous to me. Do I *know* on the basis of induction that corn will continue to be nourishing rather than poisonous to me? Explain and defend your answer.

12. Hume claims that inductive inferences about the future assume that the future will be like the past in relevant respects. For example, if

we infer that water will continue to freeze at 32 degrees F because it always has in the past, that assumes that the laws of nature will not change. Are we justified in believing that the laws of nature will not change? Do we know that the laws of nature will not change? Explain and defend your answers.

13. Consider the theory of evolution discussed in Chapter 2. Its core is the hypothesis that the living things around us today are descended from less complicated ancestors that may be extinct and that all living things are related by common lines of descent. Its primary competitor is the hypothesis that all living creatures (species) were created independently exactly as they are today rather than being the product of evolutionary development from less complicated organisms. Let's suppose that we're trying to decide which hypothesis is better. What should we find as we observe the world if all creatures alive today are descended from less complicated creatures of the past and are related by common lines of descent? What should we find as we observe the world if all creatures alive today (species) were created exactly as they are independently of one another? Given the available observational evidence, which theory is better confirmed?

14. Consider some of our philosophical questions: Does God exist? Are human beings a combination of physical body and nonphysical mind or soul? Is the thesis of Determinism true? Do human beings have free will? Such questions are not usually thought of as scientific questions. How do they differ from questions like "Does water expand when it freezes?" and "Is gold composed of atoms?" Can we devise observational tests for our philosophical questions the way we can for generalizations about the world? Why or why not?

15. How might you test the hypothesis that a high cholesterol level causes heart disease?

16. Many of us think that we *know* that different human races exist and that we can *know* what a person's race is simply by looking at him or her. Historically, humans have been divided into three major racial categories: European (caucasoid or White), African (negroid or Black), and Asian (mongoloid or Yellow). However, many scientists have become skeptical about the reality of race. For example, Alain Corcos, Professor Emeritus of Botany at Michigan State University, claims in his book, *The Myth of Human Races* published by Michigan State University Press, that the different human races are mere human constructs and that on the genetic and biological level there is only one race, the human race. Similarly, Alan Templeton, an evolutionary and population biologist at Washington University in St. Louis, "shows that while there is plenty of genetic variation in humans, most of it is individual variation." Templeton's research showed that "85 percent of genetic variation in the human DNA was due to

individual variation. A mere 15 percent could be traced to what could be interpreted as 'racial' differences. The 15 percent is well below the threshold that is used to recognize race in other species. . . ."[4]

Similarly, consider multiracial people. What race is someone with one Black and one White parent? What race is someone who has one parent who is Black and another who is biracial, half-Asian and half-White? What if someone has one great-grandparent who was Black, all the rest being White? (In that case, he or she was ⅛ Black and ⅞ White. In Louisiana, anyone who was more than ¹⁄₃₂ Black was classified as Black.)

Do we know that different races exist, or is there only one race, the human race? If race is something real, can we know what a person's race is simply by looking?

17. Suppose that someone claims that execution as punishment is a better deterrent to murder than is a sentence of life in prison without parole. How would you go about trying to confirm or disconfirm this claim?

Suggestions for Further Reading

Robert Audi. *Belief, Justification, and Knowledge.* Belmont, CA: Wadsworth, 1988. A rigorous introduction to the issues of Chapter 6 and the first part of Chapter 7 of this book. Suitable mainly for advanced students.

Roderick M. Chisholm. *Theory of Knowledge,* 3d ed. Englewood Cliffs, NJ: Prentice-Hall, 1989. A brief introduction to the issues of Chapter 6 and the first part of Chapter 7 by an eminent and influential contemporary philosopher. Suitable mainly for advanced students.

Roderick M. Chisholm and Robert Swartz, eds. *Empirical Knowledge: Readings from Contemporary Sources.* Englewood Cliffs, NJ: Prentice-Hall, 1973. A collection of essays primarily from twentieth-century philosophers; more suitable for advanced students.

Fred Dretske. "Conclusive Reasons." In *Essays on Knowledge and Justification,* ed. George Pappas and Marshall Swain. Ithaca, NY: Cornell University Press, 1978. An article sympathetic to the skeptics' claim that knowledge requires certainty.

---

[4]Tony Fitzpatrick, "Genetically speaking, race doesn't exist in humans." Washington University Office of Public Affairs, News and Information. http://news-info.wustl.edu/1998/Sept98-race.html.

Ronald Giere. *Understanding Scientific Reasoning,* 2d ed. New York: Holt, Rinehart & Winston, 1984. A rigorous but readable and highly recommended introduction to scientific reasoning.

David Hume. *An Enquiry Concerning Human Understanding.* First published in 1748, this is a lively, fascinating look at skepticism by one of the most important philosophers in the Western tradition.

Keith Lehrer. "Skepticism and Conceptual Change." In *Empirical Knowledge: Readings from Contemporary Sources,* ed. Roderick M. Chisholm and Robert Swartz. Englewood Cliffs, NJ: Prentice-Hall, 1973.

Keith Lehrer. "Why Not Skepticism?" In *Essays on Knowledge and Justification,* ed. George Pappas and Marshall Swain. Ithaca, NY: Cornell University Press, 1978. Both papers by Lehrer are sympathetic to the skeptics' claim that knowledge requires certainty.

George Pappas and Marshall Swain, eds. *Essays on Knowledge and Justification.* Ithaca, NY: Cornell University Press, 1978. A collection of essays suitable mainly for advanced students.

Karl R. Popper. *Conjectures and Refutations.* New York: Harper & Row, 1968. A collection of lively, forceful essays by an influential philosopher of science. Highly recommended.

W. V. Quine and J. S. Ullian. *The Web of Belief,* 2d ed. New York: Random House, 1978. A lively, readable introduction to the issues of this chapter.

Bertrand Russell. *The Problems of Philosophy.* New York: Oxford University Press, 1959. Russell's classic 1912 book is lively and provocative.

Brian Skyrms. *Choice and Chance: An Introduction to Inductive Logic,* 2d ed. Belmont, CA: Dickenson/Wadsworth, 1975. A rigorous introduction to some aspects of scientific reasoning.

Peter Unger. "A Defense of Skepticism." In *Essays on Knowledge and Justification,* ed. George Pappas and Marshall Swain. Ithaca, NY: Cornell University Press, 1978. A defense of Cartesian skepticism by a contemporary philosopher.

8 MORALITY

Objectives

Students are expected to:

- understand the Divine Command theory of morality.
- understand Moral Objectivism (MO).
- understand the three nonobjectivist moral theories: Moral Nihilism (MN), Moral Subjectivism (MS), and Moral Relativism (MR).
- understand Moral Egoism (ME).
- evaluate the different moral theories and reach conclusions about their plausibility.

Introduction

There was a time when almost everyone agreed that there's a clear and objective distinction between right and wrong, good and evil. They thought that some things are really wrong and other things are really right. While different individuals, different subcultures, and different societies had different moral beliefs, disagreeing about what's really right and wrong, they thought that their beliefs were really true and that those who disagreed with them were mistaken and had false moral beliefs. In some cases, at least, they thought that they knew what's right and wrong. For example, many people would have claimed to know that killing people for amusement and committing rape are wrong and that anyone who believes otherwise is mistaken.

Moral Objectivism

The view that some moral beliefs or statements are really objectively true and others really objectively false is called *Moral Objectivism (MO)* (sometimes called Moral Realism). (Its opposite is *Moral Nonobjectivism* or *Moral Antirealism*.) While many people today in all cultures are still moral objectivists who think that their moral beliefs are really objectively true, many others, especially in the highly industrialized societies of the West, such as the United States, reject Moral Objectivism. Sometimes it's because of moral disagreement. Prior to the Civil War in the United States, most people in the South believed that enslaving Blacks is right while most people in the North believed that it's wrong. (Southerners classified as Black and kept as slaves anyone that they believed had even one drop of "Black blood" going back five generations. If someone looked White but had even one great-great-grandparent who was Black, she was classified as Black.) Many Southerners said sincerely that they know that slavery is not wrong while many Northerners said that they know that slavery is wrong. Argument in most cases failed to persuade either side to change its views.

One way to look at this disagreement is to judge it from the perspective of our own moral beliefs. If you believe that slavery is wrong, then you might simply say that Northerners had true beliefs and were correct, while Southerners had false beliefs and were mistaken. If you think that you know that slavery is wrong, then you might further say that Northerners did know that slavery is wrong while Southerners didn't know that slavery isn't wrong.

But not all moral issues are as clear-cut as slavery for moral objectivists. A moral objectivist may be agnostic about a certain moral issue. Consider the question of whether it's wrong to eat meat. An objectivist may not believe that it is but also may not believe that it isn't. She may say, "I don't know." Then she can't judge this moral dispute by appealing to her own moral beliefs, because she doesn't have any moral beliefs on the subject. Then what?

An Objectivist in this situation would say something like the following. "I don't know whether it's morally wrong to eat meat. I haven't made up my mind. But there is an objectively true and an objectively false answer to the question, 'Is it morally wrong to eat meat?' Either it's morally wrong or it isn't. It can't be both morally right and wrong. It can't be neither morally right nor wrong. It must be one or the other. So if two people disagree about it, I don't know who's right and who's wrong, but I do know that one of them is right and the other wrong."

Thus, a moral objectivist might place each moral issue in one of the following three categories:

DEFINITELY WRONG   UNDECIDED   DEFINITELY RIGHT

A Moral Objectivist doesn't have to be a dogmatist or know-it-all.

A Moral Objectivist who believes that she knows that some things are right and others wrong can also concede that not all of her moral beliefs constitute moral knowledge. She can have a touch of skepticism and humility; she doesn't have to be a dogmatic fanatic. For example, she could say that while she knows that some things are wrong, such as racial discrimination, there are other things she believes to be wrong but doesn't know to be wrong, for example, premarital sex. This suggests, further, that a moral objectivist can have moral beliefs with different degrees of confidence. A moral objectivist may feel absolutely certain (maximum confidence) that her belief is correct or true, that racial discrimination is wrong but she may feel less confident that her belief that it's wrong to hunt is true.

Moral Nonobjectivism

But many people today reject MO and take a very different view, called *Moral Nonobjectivism*. They deny that anyone has moral knowledge. Further, they say that no one's moral beliefs, even their own, are more "privileged" than anyone else's. That is, they say that no moral belief or claim is any truer than another. If they have moral beliefs, they say that they shouldn't use their own moral beliefs to judge the moral beliefs of others. That's because their beliefs are not really true. There are no objective moral truths. Some moral nonobjectivists go further and say that no moral belief or claim is any more justified or reasonable than another. All are equally reasonable or equally unreasonable. While all moral non-objectivists agree on these basics, they do differ on other things. There are three nonobjectivist theories: *Moral Nihilism (MN)*, *Moral Subjectivism (MS)*, and *Moral Relativism (MR)*.

Moral and Nonmoral Beliefs

Before proceeding further, we should stop to reflect on our talk of moral beliefs, moral statements, and moral knowledge. Most people distinguish between moral and nonmoral beliefs. Moral beliefs are one kind of *evaluative* belief. Evaluative beliefs express evaluations, which are claims about what should or should not be the case. Examples of evaluative beliefs (and statements) include:

You shouldn't wear white running shoes with a tuxedo.

He's a good man.

This is a good car.

It's wrong to steal.

That's a bad argument.

This is a good paper.

He's a good writer.

Nonevaluative beliefs are beliefs that don't express evaluations. Some describe, others explain. Examples include:

This tuxedo is black.

He's six feet tall.

This car has rust spots and dents.

> Stealing is against the laws of this state.
>
> This argument has five premises.
>
> The water froze because the temperature dropped.

This distinction is enshrined in the social sciences as the distinction between facts and values. Evaluative beliefs and statements are on the "value" side while nonevaluative beliefs and statements are on the "fact" side of the divide. Generally, it's said that statements and beliefs on the evaluative side cannot be objectively true or false because they don't state facts, while statements on the nonevaluative side are either objectively true or objectively false because they do state facts. Many philosophers today doubt that this hard and fast distinction can be made. We'll return to this issue below.

Not all evaluative beliefs are moral beliefs. Which are? We can't distinguish solely on the basis of vocabulary. "He's a good man" and "It's wrong to steal" are moral beliefs; "This is a good car," "That's the wrong answer," and "It's wrong to wear jeans to a formal reception" are nonmoral beliefs. Let's use a rough and ready principle. An evaluative statement or belief is moral rather than nonmoral provided that it is intended to guide the behavior of people, and the behavior is likely to affect the well-being of other creatures or things. Thus, "It's wrong to steal" counts as moral because its use is to guide behavior and whether or not someone steals affects the well-being of other people. "It's wrong to wear white running shoes with a tuxedo" is not a moral claim because, although its use is also to guide behavior, whether someone wears white running shoes with a tuxedo ordinarily will not affect anyone's well-being.

Let's turn now to what is undoubtedly the most widely accepted objectivist moral theory, the Divine Command theory of morality.

The Divine Command Theory of Morality

Many people believe that there is one objectively true moral law by whose standards all moral beliefs should be judged: God's law. This is the Divine Command theory of morality. According to the Divine Command theory, God issues commands, either prohibitions, such as "Do not commit murder" and "Do not steal," or requirements, such as "Treat others with respect" and "Help others when the need is great and the cost or risk to you is small." According to this theory, it's morally wrong to violate God's commands or laws: it's wrong to do what God forbids and wrong to not do what God requires. A moral belief is true if it's consistent with God's law and false if it's not. If God forbids stealing, then "Stealing is morally wrong" is objectively true. If God doesn't forbid dancing, then "Dancing is morally wrong" is false.

There are two versions of the Divine Command theory. According to one, God's commands make things morally right and wrong: actions are morally right only because God commands us to do them and actions are morally wrong only because God forbids us to do them. On this view, if God did not forbid us to commit rape, then rape wouldn't be morally wrong. But on this view, God's commands (and morality itself) appear arbitrary. We can't say that God forbids rape because it's morally wrong, because it's not morally wrong unless God forbids it. And if God didn't exist, then nothing would be morally right or wrong. These consequences of the first version of the theory trouble many people.

According to the second version of the Divine Command theory, God's commands don't make things morally right or wrong. Rather, moral right and wrong are logically independent of God's will and commands. However, because of God's omniscience and infallibility, God knows moral right from wrong and Her commands reflect this moral knowledge. God forbids actions *because* they're morally wrong and requires actions *because* it's morally wrong to not do them. On this view, rape would be morally wrong even if God didn't forbid it. In fact, rape would be wrong even if God doesn't exist.

BRAIN TEASERS

Do you think that torture would be morally wrong even if God doesn't exist?

Both versions of the Divine Command theory solve problems. The theory provides a standard of moral right and wrong for action and a standard of moral truth for moral beliefs. And in many of its more popular incarnations, it provides an answer to a thorny question: "Why be moral?" That is, many people have pointed out that even if I believe that it's really wrong to do something, I may respond, "So what?" If it's in my self-interest to do it, I may consider the fact that it would be morally wrong to be irrelevant. I may not care about acting in morally acceptable ways.

Many people think that self-interest is the strongest motivator. If doing the right thing conflicts with what we believe to be in our self-interest, self-interest usually wins out. So how can morality get a grip on us? Many people who accept the Divine Command theory harness self-interest to morality. That is, they say that doing the morally right thing and not doing the morally wrong thing is always the best thing to do even from a purely self-interested point of view. Violating God's Law brings punishment that overwhelms any conceivable earthly gains and obeying God's Law brings rewards that overwhelm any conceivable earthly losses. God's punishments and rewards are eternal, so it's in our best self-interest to obey God and behave in morally acceptable ways.

BRAIN TEASERS

Do you think that God punishes people after death for violating Her commands and rewards people for obeying them?

But there are several problems with the Divine Command theory of morality, problems that have led some people to doubt that appeal to God's law can help resolve moral disagreement.

The Problem of God's Existence

The Divine Command theory is true only if God exists. But many people don't believe She exists, and even some believers have doubts. Anyone who doesn't believe in God will reject the Divine Command theory. And even if we accept it, we may have trouble appealing to it in moral argument when there's moral disagreement because we may be arguing with people who are agnostics or atheists. Therefore, many people, even theists who accept the Divine Command theory, look about for other secular or nonreligious bases for their moral beliefs and arguments.

Can We Know What God's Law Is?

Even if we believe in God, there are still problems for the Divine Command theory. Can we know what God's law is? If yes, how? And what about moral disagreement based on disagreement about God's Law? Most White Christian Southerners before the Civil War insisted that God doesn't forbid enslavement of Blacks. Most White Northerners insisted that She does. If people disagree about God's Law, how can we resolve it? We might turn to sacred scriptures, such as the Bible, but White Christian Southerners used Biblical passages to prove that God doesn't forbid enslaving Blacks while White Christian Northerners used other Biblical passages to prove that God does forbid it. How can we justify a claim to know God's law when there's so much disagreement, even among people of the same religion?

Perhaps God's law, the one true morality, is knowable by being *revealed* by God. But how can we tell if it's God really revealing the moral law to us, rather than our merely imagining that God is revealing it? And if such writings as the Bible or the Koran are presented as sacred scripture embodying God's voice, can we know it's really God's voice? If yes, how? How can we distinguish God's voice from the voices of the human authors of the texts? Sacred scriptures, even if they embody God's voice, often require interpretation. Can we know that our interpretation is the correct one? If so, how?

Because of such puzzles about the Divine Command theory, many people have rejected it. Some of those who reject it think that if the Divine Command theory is false, then there are neither objective moral truths nor moral knowledge. They embrace a nonobjectivist theory of morality.

Nonobjectivist Moral Theories

According to *nonobjectivist* moral theories, no moral belief is objectively true or false. Therefore, there is no moral knowledge. No acts are really morally right or wrong, so there are no moral rules that everyone should conform to. Furthermore, most people who accept Moral Nonobjectivism say that no moral claim or belief is objectively more reasonable or justified than another. We must keep in mind that these theories are extreme. They say that **no** moral claim or belief is objectively true and that **nothing** is "really" morally right or wrong. Let's test these theories by considering the following true story. It is grisly and horrible beyond belief.

In Romania in 1938, fourteen members of the Legion of the Archangel Michael, a rabidly anti-Semitic fascist group, were murdered by the police of King Carol because they publicly criticized the King for having a Jewish mistress. Later, King Carol was forced to abdicate and the Legion of the Archangel Michael got its revenge.

> On the night of January 22, 1941, the Legionnaires of the Archangel Michael . . . abducted 200 men, women, and children from their homes. The legionnaires packed the victims into trucks and drove them to the municipal slaughterhouse . . . in the southern part of Bucharest. . . . They made the victims, all Jews, strip naked in the freezing dark and get down on all fours on the conveyor ramp. Whining in terror, the Jews were driven through all the automated stages of slaughter. . . . The [limbless and headless] trunk of a five year old girl they hung upside down . . ., according to an eyewitness the next morning.[1]

Although the Legionnaires were probably Moral Objectivists who sincerely believed that what they did was not morally wrong, almost all other Moral Objectivsists would passionately insist that the Legionnaires committed a monstrously evil act. However, Moral Nonobjectivists would say that the Legionnaires' deed was neither really morally wrong nor morally right. They would say that my belief that the Legionnaires' deed was evil is not really objectively true, nor is the Legionnaires' belief that their deed wasn't evil really objectively false. There are no objectively true or false moral beliefs.

---

[1]Robert D. Kaplan, *Balkan Ghosts*. (New York: Vintage, 1996), xxii.

There are three different nonobjectivist moral theories: Moral Nihilism (MN), Moral Subjectivism (MS) and Moral Relativism (MR). Let's look at each in turn.

Moral Nihilism (MN)

Moral Nihilists deny that any moral beliefs or claims are objectively true or false. But unlike some other moral nonobjectivists, who say that some other kind of truth can be attributed to moral beliefs and claims, such as relative truth, they deny that moral beliefs can be even "relatively" true. Consequently, moral nihilists, unlike other moral nonobjectivists, have no moral beliefs; they don't believe that anything is right and they don't believe that anything is wrong. The word nihilism comes from the Latin *nihil*, meaning "nothing." Although moral nihilists don't have any moral beliefs of their own, they admit that other people do. It's just that the moral beliefs of other people are neither true nor false, reasonable nor unreasonable. If two individuals or societies disagree about a moral matter, neither is right and neither is wrong.

Thus, a Moral Nihilist will say that what the legionnaires did was neither really right nor really wrong. But further, a nihilist won't believe that it was morally wrong and won't believe that it wasn't morally wrong. He'll have no moral beliefs and make no moral judgment about the legionnaire's actions.

Many Moral Nihilists think that moral statements are neither true nor false because they're meaningless. From the nineteen thirties to the early nineteen sixties, a school of philosophy called Logical Positivism was very influential. In their view, a sentence used to make a statement is meaningful if and only if its truth or falsity can be conclusively proved by appeal to observation and perception. Since they believed that no moral claim can be conclusively proved by appeal to perception and observation, they concluded that moral sentences are meaningless. They can't be used to state facts, they can only express feelings or attitudes. Thus, on their view, "Rape is wrong" merely expresses a negative feeling or attitude toward rape. It doesn't attribute a moral property—wrongness—to acts of rape.

Logical Positivism fell out of favor in the 1960s. Now, few philosophers think that a sentence is meaningful if and only if its truth or falsity can be conclusively proved by appeal to perception and observation. In fact, few philosophers think that any statement's truth can be conclusively proved by appeal to perception and observation, given the arguments of GK skeptics who say we know nothing about the world. Most are content with something like justification or confirmation—nonconclusive reasons and arguments that make a conclusion probable rather than absolutely certain. And further, many philosophers think that many moral claims can be justified by arguments that appeal to perception and observation. (We'll return to this.)

Another factor that gives pause is that MN is contrary to the logical law according to which every statement is either true or false. According to this law, "Abe Lincoln was over six feet tall" is either true or false. It can't be both or neither. But according to MN, "Slaughtering Jews is morally wrong" is neither true nor false. If "Slaughtering Jews is morally wrong" were like "Slither recall alfalfa dents praise" in being meaningless, it would make sense to say that it's neither true nor false. But it's not meaningless.

Can we prove that MN is false? Perhaps not. But if we start out **not** believing in MN, then if we were right about justification in previous chapters, we're justified in continuing to not believe MN until we have very good reasons for adding it to our stock of beliefs. The burden of justification falls on those who say that MN is true. It is up to the moral nihilist to present us with powerful arguments showing that MN is true. It's difficult to see what arguments can be raised for MN. (We'll look at and evaluate some arguments in the next section that may apply to almost any version of Moral Nonobjectivism.)

Moreover, it seems likely that few people could be consistent nihilists. That would require them to make no moral judgments and have no moral beliefs. Thus, if someone brutally tortured to death someone a nihilist loved dearly, he couldn't claim or believe that it was morally wrong, nor could he say or believe that the murderer morally should not have done what he did. But most people do have moral beliefs that they judge and live by. It would be difficult for them to jettison their moral code and live without one.

Moral Subjectivism (MS)

According to *Moral Subjectivism* (MS), whatever an individual believes about a moral issue is true for that individual and there's no other kind of moral truth. No moral beliefs are objectively true or false, but they are subjectively true or false. It follows from this that no individual can have a false or mistaken moral belief. Unlike Moral Nihilists, Moral Subjectivists do have their own moral beliefs. But paradoxically, they say that their moral beliefs are no more true than the moral beliefs of those who disagree with them.

According to a moral subjectivist, if a legionnaire believes that what he did was not morally wrong, then he has a (subjectively) true belief. Similarly, if you believe that what he did is morally wrong, then you also have a (subjectively) true belief. You're both right, though not objectively right. Neither of you has an objectively true (or false) moral belief because there are none. Therefore, neither of you is mistaken. If we ask who's really right, a subjectivist says no one is really right. Most Moral Subjectivists also say that no moral belief is more justified or reasonable than another. According to MS, an individual's moral code is immune from rational criticism. Thus, the legionnaire's moral belief that it's not morally wrong to slaughter Jews is no less justified or reasonable than your belief that it is morally wrong to slaughter Jews.

But this poses a problem for a Moral Subjectivist, because he's committed to a view that threatens to make the idea of his having moral beliefs unintelligible. Suppose he says that he believes that what the legionnaires did is morally wrong. He says his belief is (subjectively) true. His commitments lead to this:

> I believe that slaughtering Jews is morally wrong, but my belief that it is morally wrong is no more true (or justified) than the belief that it is not morally wrong.

In that case, what could it mean to say that he "believes" that it's morally wrong?

Many people find Subjectivism implausible. It entails that principles condemning genocide, torture, rape, slavery, and child molestation as evil or morally wrong are simply not really true. Moral principles that say these actions are wrong are no better justified than principles that claim they're not wrong.

MS seems problematic for several reasons. It is unclear how Moral Subjectivists can be said to "believe" anything about moral matters. They are committed to views that most of us probably find deeply implausible—for example, the view that the belief that child rape is morally acceptable is no less true, correct, or reasonable than the belief that it is immoral. Finally, like MN, it is inconsistent with the law of excluded middle—that is, the claim that every statement is either true or false, that no statement is both true and false or neither true nor false. If we do not start out as moral subjectivists, it is up to the moral subjectivist to provide us with convincing arguments to show us that MS is true. What reasons are there for thinking that MS is true? (Some of these arguments might also be used to support MN.)

Who Am I to Say What's Right and Wrong?

Sometimes people ask the question, "Who am I to say what's morally right and wrong?" A question isn't really an argument, even a question for which we don't have an answer. But this is a particularly strange question. What kind of answer are we looking for? Here are some possible answers.

> I'm God.
>
> I'm the emperor of the world.
>
> I'm the Pope.
>
> I'm an ordinary human being.
>
> I'm nobody.

Suppose I'm not God, the emperor of the world, or the Pope. Does it follow that everyone's moral beliefs are (subjectively) true and that none are objectively true or false? Of course not.

Unhappily, people who ask this question seem to presuppose a certain answer: I'm nobody. And they take this to imply either that they have no right to have an opinion on a moral issue or that their view on the issue is no more true or justified than anyone else's. Now if I'm nobody—if I am not very intelligent or knowledgeable, if I haven't thought very deeply about a moral issue and looked carefully at the arguments for and against, then my opinion or belief may not be worth much. I may not be justified in believing what I believe or justified in having much confidence that what I believe is true. But it doesn't follow from "I'm nobody" that everyone's answer to the question is true and equally justified, unless you say "Everybody's nobody."

It strikes me as more than odd to ask, "Who am I to say that slaughtering Jews is morally wrong?" I don't have to be God or the Pope to see that it's wrong.

BRAIN TEASERS

Can we really "see" that slaughtering Jews is wrong?

Even with difficult moral issues, if I reach a conclusion based on informed and careful deliberation, why should I ask myself the question, "Who am I to say this is morally right or wrong?" Thus, if I have carefully thought about terrorism and come to believe that terrorism is morally wrong, what's the point of adding the question, "But who am I to say that terrorism is morally wrong?" If the answer to the question is, "I'm nobody," that seems to imply that one's moral beliefs can be objectively true or justified only if one is a special somebody, such as God or the Pope. But that's absurd.

Instead of asking, "Who am I to say what's morally right and wrong?" perhaps it would be more appropriate to ask, "What is it most reasonable to believe about this moral issue?"

People Disagree About Moral Issues

Perhaps the very fact of moral disagreement, and the difficulty of resolving it, is sufficient to show that MS is true. But does the mere fact that there's disagreement about the correct answer to a question show conclusively that there is no correct, better, or worse answer to the question?

People have disagreed about many things. Some people have thought that the world would be destroyed without human sacrifice; others have not. Some have believed that witches exist, others believe that they're figments of people's imagination. Does the mere fact that we disagree prove that there's no correct answer to a question? No. Witches can't both exist and not exist. Either they do or they don't. If people disagree about it, one must be right and the other wrong.

Moral disagreement isn't the only variety of disagreement. If the mere fact of disagreement doesn't prove that there's no correct answer to questions in history, medicine, and science, then it doesn't prove that there are no correct answers to moral questions. Moral disagreement doesn't prove that MS is true.

BRAIN TEASERS

> If one individual believes that Christopher Columbus was the first European to reach North America and another individual believes that he wasn't, can they both have true beliefs? Should we say that neither is wrong because they disagree?

One Can't Prove Who's Right in Moral Argument

One might claim that one can't prove who's right and who's wrong in moral argument; if one can't prove who's right, then no one's right. Perhaps the fact that we can't prove that our answer to a moral question is the correct one proves that there are no correct answers to moral questions.

Even if it's true that we can never prove that our answer to a moral question is correct, does it follow that there is no correct answer? We may never be able to prove whether there's life on other planets. Does it follow that there's no true answer to the question, Is there life on other planets? Does it follow that if one person believes there is and another person believes there isn't, they're both right? Of course not.

But is it true that no one can prove who's right when there's moral disagreement? It shouldn't be accepted as an assumption without more careful investigation. We need to examine moral "proof." What is a moral proof like? What are the standards of moral proof? Surely we need to answer these questions before accepting that there is no way to prove a moral claim. (In the next chapter we'll look more carefully at moral argument and moral proof.)

Moral Subjectivism Entails Tolerance and Open-Mindedness

Sometimes people embrace Moral Subjectivism because they think that it entails that we should be tolerant and open-minded on moral matters and they think these are good things. There are three problems with this. First, that fact that something entails another thing that we agree with or value doesn't show that the first thing is true. Even if MS entailed that we should be tolerant and open-minded about moral matters, it would not follow that MS is true. Second, tolerance and open-mindedness are not always good things. Would it be good to be tolerant of genocide, torture, and rape? Should we be open-minded about these things? Perhaps tolerance and open-mindedness are good things when it comes to some moral issues, but it is not obvious that they are good things with all moral issues. Finally, MS does not entail that we should be tolerant and open-minded about any moral issues. According to MS, if I believe that people should be intolerant of disagreement and should kill everyone who disagrees with us, I'm not mistaken. My belief is as true and justified as your belief that people who disagree should not kill each other.

Everyone Has a Right to Her Opinion

Sometimes people argue for MS by saying that everyone has a right to her own opinion. Unfortunately, even if this is true, it doesn't show that MS is true. When we say that everyone has a right to her own opinion, we seem to mean that it would be morally wrong to punish or persecute people for their beliefs and morally wrong to coerce people into changing their beliefs. But it doesn't follow from this that everyone's beliefs are equally true or justified. I might have a right to believe that there are witches and you a right to believe that there are no witches, but we can't both be right about this. One of us must have a false belief.

Even more troubling, the moral subjectivist can't say that the claim that everyone has a right to believe what they want is really true. If you believe everyone has this right and I believe they don't, we're both right. Can we use as a premise a claim that is neither objectively true nor objectively false?

Change in Belief

We sometimes change our minds about moral issues. If MS is true, why would we ever even consider changing our minds, since whatever we believe to be true is true? It's not as though I could decide to change my mind because I think that what I believed up to now is either false or unjustified. Whatever I believe and for whatever reason I believe it, MS guarantees that I'm right. I can't possibly make a moral mistake; changing my mind wouldn't make sense if I'm a moral subjectivist.

Moral Deliberation

Sometimes I haven't made up my mind on a moral issue. Then I have to deliberate before reaching a conclusion or before deciding what to believe (if we do decide such matters). But moral deliberation makes no sense if MS is true. It doesn't matter what I believe or why I believe it, I'm guaranteed to be right if MS is true. I could flip a coin about whether to believe that rape is morally wrong, and whether it's heads or tails, I'll be right.

The arguments in favor of MS are far from conclusive. And MS has consequences that most people find highly implausible.

Moral Relativism (MR)

According to *Moral Relativism* (MR), an individual's moral code is subordinate to his society's moral code. An individual's moral beliefs are true if and only if they're in conformity with the moral beliefs of his society. Whereas MS claims that there is no higher court of appeal in moral matters than an individual's own moral code, MR claims that there is a higher court of appeal: the moral code of the individual's society's.

Suppose that society A believes that slavery is morally acceptable while society B believes that it is immoral. Suppose further that individuals X and Y are members of society A while Z is a member of society B. Finally, suppose that X and Z believe that slavery is immoral while Y believes that slavery is morally acceptable. The situation would look like this:

SOCIETY A (SLAVERY IS ACCEPTABLE)	SOCIETY B (SLAVERY IS IMMORAL)
X believes slavery is immoral.	Z believes slavery is immoral.
Y believes slavery is acceptable.	

Whereas a moral subjectivist would say that individuals X, Y, and Z all have (subjectively) true moral beliefs, a moral relativist, would say that Y and Z have true moral beliefs, but X has a false moral belief. Individuals Y and Z have true moral beliefs because their beliefs are in conformity with the beliefs of their societies. Individual X has a false moral belief because her belief is contrary to what her society believes.

Suppose we ask which society has a true moral belief. The moral relativist would say that both societies have true (though not objectively true) moral beliefs, even though society A believes the exact opposite of what society B believes. According to MR, whatever a society believes about moral matters is true for that society and there is no other kind of moral truth. The correct standard of moral truth for individuals is their own society's moral code, which serves as a higher court of appeal on moral matters, and there is no higher appeal from that society's moral code. No society's moral code is more true, correct, or reasonable than another's.

Thus, if the society of the Legion of the Archangel Michael in Romania in 1941 believed that it's not morally wrong to slaughter Jews like pigs, while our society believes that it is morally wrong, neither society is mistaken, both are right. And both are equally justified.

Arguments Against Moral Relativism

Is a Society Always Right?   Is a society always right about moral issues, regardless of what its members believe and why they believe it? Many people find that view highly implausible. While a society may often or usually be right about moral issues, few people consider society omniscient or infallible. Societies make mistakes, even moral mistakes. And most people don't think that someone's moral judgments or principles are wrong simply because they disagree with the principles of their society. Many people think that a whole society could have false or unreasonable moral principles. For example, they think that the civil rights workers of the 1950s and 1960s who believed that people shouldn't be discriminated against solely because of the color of their skin were right, even if the moral code of their society held that such discrimination was acceptable. Many people are convinced that there's a difference between what a society *believes* to be right (or wrong) and what really *is* right (wrong).

Are the Majority's Moral Beliefs Always Right?   Most societies are not completely homogeneous. They are made up of many subgroups. And subgroups within societies often disagree. When we talk of a society's moral beliefs, we can only mean the beliefs of the *majority* in that society. In that case, MR reduces to the claim that whatever the *majority* in a society believes to be right is right for that society. Many people balk at this implication.

Change in Belief   If MR is true, then as moral beliefs change, moral truth changes. If the majority of people in the United States in the early 1800s believed that slavery is morally acceptable, then according to MR it was true (though not objectively true) that slavery was morally acceptable (not just believed to be morally acceptable). When a majority of people's views changed, then slavery changed from being morally right to being morally wrong. But how can changes in belief alter the truth of a moral claim?

Subcultures   A problem arises in identifying the society whose moral code serves as the standard of moral truth for an individual. Suppose a majority of people in the United States believe that birth control is wrong but a majority of people in California believe that it's not wrong. Is birth control wrong in California? Do the moral beliefs of a majority of people in the United States determine right and wrong in California, or do the moral beliefs of a majority of people in California determine right and wrong there? Which "society's" moral code is the proper standard?

You're an inhabitant of Earth, of North America, of the United States, of a certain state, and of a certain town in a state. Which society's moral code applies to you? You may be a member of a certain religion. Suppose you're a Muslim in a predominantly Christian society. Is the moral code of the majority of people in that society, who are Christians, the standard of right and wrong that applies to you, or is the moral code of the majority of Muslims in the world the proper standard of right and wrong for you? Which "society's" moral code is the standard of moral truth for a person? How do we decide? MR provides no answer.

Moral Deliberation Suppose that you haven't yet made up your mind on a particular moral issue. According to MR, how should you proceed? You should simply find out, perhaps by an opinion poll, what a majority of people in your society believes about it. Then you'll have the true answer. But surely that's preposterous.

MR has consequences that many people find deeply implausible, but are there strong arguments in favor of it that outweigh the objections? Before we can reach an enlightened decision, we need to look at the arguments for it. What reasons are there for thinking that MR is true?

Arguments for Moral Relativism

Societies Disagree One might argue that there are no moral beliefs that all societies agree on, no moral principles that all societies accept. Thus, some societies have accepted principles permitting infanticide, suttee, racial discrimination, and slavery, whereas others have rejected them. One might think that if there were correct moral principles binding on all people and all societies, there would be agreement among societies about such fundamental issues. Since there isn't agreement, in this view, one ought to conclude that there are no such correct moral principles.

This argument depends on two crucial assumptions. One is that there are no moral principles that all societies accept—that no matter what the principle, we'll find that some societies accept it and others reject it. The second assumption is that if there were correct moral principles binding on all people and all societies, there wouldn't be disagreement about them— all societies would accept them. Both assumptions are questionable.

Are there no moral principles that all societies agree on? It certainly seems that different societies accept different principles for certain issues: abortion, infanticide, euthanasia, suicide, slavery, premarital sex, number of spouses permitted at a time, and homosexuality come to mind. But are there no moral principles that all societies accept? To answer that question would require a lot of research. What, for example, of killing one's parents for amusement? What of killing and eating one's own children, even when food is plentiful? What of violating agreements freely entered into? Are these actions morally acceptable in some societies? Surely we'd need to carefully investigate a wide range of human societies to establish the claim that there are no moral principles that all societies accept. That claim, in fact, will not be at all easy to establish. Just showing some moral principles that not all societies accept hardly does much to establish the ambitious claim that there are no moral principles that all societies accept.

But if we can point to a society that rejects a basic moral principle that we accept—for example, a principle about killing—doesn't that lend some plausibility to the claim that there are no moral principles that all societies accept? If another society can reject a basic moral principle that we accept, then surely anything goes. For example, people might point to certain Polynesian societies that permitted killing one's parents at age sixty or so. Their morality permitted killing one's parents; our morality doesn't. Isn't that an example of a basic moral principle over which two societies differ? If two societies can disagree about whether it's acceptable to kill one's parents, surely there are no principles likely to be accepted by all societies.

However, before accepting this example at face value, we have to try to understand *why* the islanders' morality permitted killing one's parents. As it turns out, they believed that one spent eternity in the same condition in which one died. If one was blind, crippled, and deaf when one died, that's how one spent eternity. Children would thus express love and respect for their parents by killing them before old age could sap their vitality and bring on infirmity and disability that would make their lives in eternity a nightmare full of anguish. To these islanders, it would have been cruel and unloving to permit one's parents to live eternally with all the infirmities and disabilities that age brings.

The disagreement between their moral code, which required children to kill their parents, and our moral code, which forbids it, is not due to our accepting different fundamental principles. Both societies' moral codes require children to love and respect their parents, but because of other different beliefs about the world, those basic moral principles lead to different practical requirements. Thus, the difference between their morality and ours can be traced to their other beliefs about the world, rather than to their accepting different basic moral principles. I suspect that if we looked carefully enough, we'd discover there's more agreement among societies about basic moral principles than we're often led to believe by moral relativists.

But suppose that after careful examination we found that there really were no rules and principles that all societies accepted. Would that prove that MR is true? As we saw in the discussion of MS, the mere fact that people have different beliefs about the correct answer to a question doesn't prove that there is no correct answer to the question. People disagree about a whole host of issues, not just about moral matters. If the mere fact that people disagree doesn't prove that there are no correct or incorrect answers in other areas of inquiry, why should it be taken to prove that there are no correct or incorrect answers in moral matters? Further, this view assumes that if there were valid moral principles, all societies would accept them. But why should we think that? We don't expect to find universal agreement among societies about scientific theories. We recognize that even if a scientific theory is true, many societies in the past may not have accepted it and many societies in the present may not accept it. That usually doesn't tempt us to conclude that no scientific theories are true or false. Why should morality be treated differently?

We Can't Prove Which Society Is Right   According to MR, we can't prove that slavery, rape, murder, and torture are wrong. As with the same arguments for MS, we need to examine moral reasoning and the standards of "proof" in morality a bit more carefully before accepting this claim. We'll look more closely at moral proof in the next chapter, so we'll defer further consideration of this objection until then. But until we've looked at moral argument more carefully, we shouldn't be too quick to accept the claim that no one can prove a moral principle to be true.

MR is not beyond dispute. There are some powerful objections to it and the arguments supporting it are not as decisive as one might think. Whether MR is true remains an open question.

Moral Egoism

When all is said and done, many of us believe that there is a true morality, as opposed to false moralities. For many of us, the true morality is based on enlightened self-interest: the right thing to do is whatever is in one's own self-interest, and the wrong thing to do is whatever is contrary to one's own self-interest. That's *Moral Egoism* (ME).

According to ME, one never does wrong if one does what's in one's own self-interest; it's always morally acceptable to just look out for number one. According to a moral egoist, it's always all right for me to do what's in my self-interest, and it's always all right for you to do what's in your self-interest; you have no duties to me, and I have no duties to you.

There's something initially plausible about Moral Egoism. After all, aren't most people either exclusively self-interested or at least primarily self-interested? Don't we all seek our own happiness? And isn't self-interest—the quest for personal fulfillment, satisfaction, and happiness—the most powerful motive people have? Surely it's both rational and right to seek one's own happiness. What could be wrong about striving to be happy?

It seems indisputable that very often, doing what's in our own self-interest, doing what will make us happy, is not morally wrong. Going to a play or movie makes me happy, so it's in my self-interest to go. It's certainly not wrong for me to go to a play or movie. Going to the doctor, watching my diet, working to earn money by which to live, listening to music, and getting enough sleep are all in my self-interest, and it's surely not wrong for me to do those things. In fact, if I never or rarely did what's in my self-interest, I would soon die! Surely I ought to do things that are in my self-interest such as working, eating, sleeping, spending some time relaxing, and taking care of my health. Similarly, I surely ought to avoid doing things contrary to my self-interest, such as taking drugs, overeating and overdrinking, working too hard, smoking, and so on.

Usually, there's nothing wrong with doing what's in our self-interest, but is it *never* wrong to do what's in our self-interest? There seems to be no problem when we're talking about things like taking a bath or listening to music. It's in our self-interest to do things that bring us pleasure and happiness, but what if one gets pleasure from setting homeless people afire? What if one derives pleasure, happiness, and satisfaction from rape, assault, robbery, and murder? Is it morally acceptable to do *anything* that's in one's own self-interest? According to Moral Egoism, if it's in your self-interest to kill, rob, and assault people, then it's morally acceptable for you to kill, rob, and assault them.

According to moral egoists, we have no duties to others, whether negative duties not to do such things as murder, rape, enslave, and torture others, or positive duties to come to their aid, even if the need is very great and the potential cost or risk of helping is negligible. Let's test this out by considering a real case. In 1998, a college freshman named David Cash saw his friend pull a nine-year-old girl into a men's room late at night in a gambling casino in Nevada. Cash followed his friend in and saw him take the girl into a stall. Cash went to the other stall and peered over it to see what his friend was doing. He saw him ripping off the little girl's clothes while holding her mouth to prevent her from screaming. Cash told his friend to stop. When he didn't, Cash left the men's room and stood outside waiting for him. After about twenty minutes, his friend emerged from the bathroom and told Cash that he had raped and murdered the little girl. Cash's only response was to ask whether she had been sexually aroused.

Cash and his friend were apprehended. Because there's no law in Nevada (or in most other states) requiring people to come to the aid of others, even if they are being murdered, Cash wasn't prosecuted. He had broken no laws.

BRAIN TEASERS

> Should there be laws requiring us to come to the aid of others when the need is great and the cost or risk to ourselves is small?

When asked afterwards why he didn't do something to save the little girl's life, knowing that she was being assaulted, such as inform the security people at the casino, Cash said he didn't think he had any obligation to help.

BRAIN TEASERS

> If Cash didn't have a legal duty to help, did he have a moral duty to help? Is there a difference between legal and moral duties?

Many people consider Cash to be a Moral Egoist.

ME is plausible when one's self-interest doesn't conflict with the interests and well-being of others. But what of situations in which people's interests come into conflict? Is it quite so plausible when others may be harmed by people's actions or when others need help? Is it morally acceptable to do whatever is in one's own self-interest at such times, ignoring the needs and interests of other people? Is it morally acceptable to ignore someone's desperate need because it's not in one's self-interest to help? Is it morally acceptable to harm other people if it's in one's self-interest?

It must be difficult to be a consistent Moral Egoist. We surely must wonder whether Cash would have thought that no one had a duty to help him if he had been in the same situation as the little girl being raped and murdered. If he were being raped and murdered and someone could have helped him, he certainly would have wanted that help. But would he have believed that if someone able to help did not help, he would have been doing nothing morally wrong?

Are there any reasons to think that Moral Egoism is true? What arguments support it? ME is more often merely asserted than argued for.

Where does that leave us? We have yet to develop a fully plausible theory about morality. In the next chapter, we'll try to make some new beginnings by examining the structure of moral justification.

SAINT AUGUSTINE (354–430)

THE CONFESSIONS

[P]rior to my conversion] I . . . Did not know that true inward justice which judges not by custom but by the most righteous law of almighty God. By this law the moral customs of different religions and periods were adapted to their places and times, while the law itself remains unaltered everywhere and always. It is not one thing at one place or time, another thing at another. . . . Untrained minds . . . assess the customs of the entire race by the criterion of their own moral code. . . .

This is the style of those who are irate when they hear that something was allowed to the just in that age which was not granted to the just now, and that God gave one command to the former and another to the latter for reasons of a change in historical circumstances, though both ancient and modern people are bound to submit to the same justice. . . . An act allowed or commanded in one corner is forbidden and subject to punishment if done in an adjacent corner. Does that mean that justice is "liable to variation and change"? No. The times that it rules over are not identical.

From *Confessions*, trans. H. Chadwick (New York: Oxford University Press, 1991).

MOSES MAIMONIDES (1135–1204)

LAWS CONCERNING CHARACTER TRAITS
Chapter One

Every single human being has many character traits. [As for character traits in general,] one differs from another and they are exceedingly far apart from each other. One man is irascible, perpetually angry, and another man has a tranquil mind and does not become angry at all; if he does become angry, his anger is mild and only rarely aroused during a period of several years. One man has an exceedingly haughty heart, and another has an extremely lowly spirit. One is so full of desire that his soul is never satisfied by pursuing its desire; another has a body so exceedingly pure that he does not even desire the few things the body needs. One has a desire so great that his soul would not be satisfied with all the wealth in the world. As it is said: "He that loves silver shall not be satisfied with silver." Another is so constrained that he would be satisfied with some small thing not adequate for him, and he does not press to acquire whatever he needs.

One torments himself with hunger and is so tightfisted that he does not eat the worth of a small coin except when in great pain; another intentionally squanders all his wealth. All the rest of the character traits follow these patterns, which are [also] exemplified by the gay and the mournful, the miserly and the prodigal, the cruel and the merciful, the soft-hearted and the hard-hearted, and so on.

Between two character traits at opposite extremes, there is a character trait in the middle, equidistant from the extremes. Some character traits a man has from the beginning

From *Ethical Writings of Maimonides*, trans. R. L. Weiss, and C. E. Butterworth (New York: New York University Press, 1975).

of his creation, depending upon the nature of his body; some character traits a certain man's nature is disposed to receive in the future more quickly than other character traits; and some a man does not have from the beginning of his creation but learns from others, or he himself turns to them due to a thought that arose in his heart, or he hears that a certain character trait is good for him and that it is proper to acquire it and he trains himself in it until it is firmly established within him.

For any character trait, the two opposite extremes are not the good way, and it is not proper for a man to follow them nor to teach them to himself. If he finds his nature inclined toward one extreme or if he is disposed to receive one of them or if he has already learned one of them and has become accustomed to it, he shall make himself return to the good way and follow the way of good men, which is the right way.

The right way is the mean in every single one of a man's character traits. It is the character trait that is equally distant from the two extremes, not close to one or the other. Therefore the wise men of old commanded that a man continuously appraise his character traits and evaluate them and direct them in the middle way so that he becomes perfect.

How so? A man shall not be irascible and easily angered, nor like a corpse which feels nothing, but in between; he shall only become angry about a large matter that deserves anger so that something like it not be done again.

So too, he shall only desire the things which the body needs and without which it is impossible to live. As it is said: "A just man eats to satisfy his desire." Likewise, he shall only labor at his work to acquire what he needs for the present. As it is said: "Good is a little for the just man." He shall not be exceedingly tightfisted, nor squander all his wealth, but he shall give charity according to his means and lend a fitting amount to the needy. He shall not be gay and buffoonish nor sad and mournful, but rejoice all his days, calmly, with a cheerful demeanor. And thus shall he order the rest of his character traits. This way is the way of the wise men.

Every man whose character traits all lie in the mean is called a wise man. Whoever is exceedingly scrupulous with himself and moves a little toward one side or the other, away from the character trait in the mean, is called a pious man.

How so? Whoever moves away from a haughty heart to the opposite extreme so that he is exceedingly lowly in spirit is called a pious man; this is the measure of piety. If he moves only to the mean and is humble, he is called a wise man; this is the measure of wisdom. The same applies to all the rest of the character traits. The pious men of old used to direct their character traits from the middle way toward [one of] the two extremes; some character traits toward the last extreme, and some toward the first extreme. This is the meaning of "inside the line of the law."

We are commanded to walk in these middle ways, which are the good and right ways. As it is said: "And you shall walk in His ways." Thus they taught in explaining this commandment: Just as He is called gracious, you too be gracious; just as He is called merciful, you too be merciful; just as He is called holy, you too be holy.

In like manner, the prophets applied all these terms to God: slow to anger and abundant in loving-kindness, just and righteous, perfect, powerful, strong, and the like. They did so to proclaim that these ways are good and right, and a man is obliged to train himself to follow them and to imitate according to his strength.

How so? A man shall habituate himself in these character traits until they are firmly established in him. Time after time, he shall perform actions in accordance with the character traits that are in the mean. He shall repeat them continually until performing them is easy for him and they are not burdensome and these character traits are firmly established in his soul.

Since these terms applied to the Creator refer to the middle way that we are obliged to follow, this way is called the way of the Lord. That is what Abraham taught to his sons. As it is said: "For I have known him so that he will command his sons and his household after him to keep the way of the Lord, to do justice and righteousness." Whoever walks in this way brings good and blessing upon himself. As it is said: "In order that the Lord render unto Abraham that which He said concerning him."

Chapter Two

. . . In the case of some character traits, a man is forbidden to accustom himself to the mean. Rather, he shall move to the other [i.e., far] extreme. One such [character trait] is a haughty heart, for the good way is not that a man be merely humble, but that he have a lowly spirit, that his spirit be very submissive. Therefore it was said of Moses our master that he was "very humble," and not merely humble. And therefore the wise men commanded: "Have a very, very lowly spirit." . . . Likewise, anger is an extremely bad character trait, and it is proper for a man to move away from it to the other extreme and to teach himself not to become angry, even over something it is proper to be angry about. . . .

A man is forbidden to make a habit of using smooth and deceptive language. There shall not be one thing in his mouth and another in his heart, but what is within shall be like what is without. The matter in his heart shall be the same as what is in his mouth. It is forbidden to delude one's fellow creatures, even a Gentile. . . .

A man shall not be full of laughter and mockery, nor sad and mournful, but joyful. Thus the wise men said: "Laughter and levity bring about illicit sexual conduct." They commanded that a man not be unrestrained in laughter, nor sad and mournful, but that he receive every man with a cheerful demeanor. Likewise his desire shall not be so great that he rushes for wealth, nor shall he be lazy and refrain from working. But he shall live in contentment, have a modest occupation, and be occupied [mainly] with the Torah. No matter how small his portion, let him rejoice in it. He shall not be full of contention, envy, or desire, nor shall he seek honor. Thus the wise men said: "Envy, desire, and honor remove a man from the world." The general rule is that he

follow the mean for every single character trait, until all his character traits are ordered according to the mean. That is, in keeping with what Solomon says: "And all your ways will be upright."

Chapter Three

Perhaps a man will say: "Since desire, honor, and the like constitute a bad way and remove a man from the world, I shall completely separate myself from them and go to the other extreme." So he does not eat meat, nor drink wine, nor take a wife, nor live in a decent dwelling, nor wear decent clothing, but sackcloth, coarse wool, and so on, like the priests of Edom. This, too, is a bad way and it is forbidden to follow it. . . .

Chapter Four

Since preserving the body's health and strength is among the ways of the Lord—for to attain understanding and knowledge is impossible when one is sick—a man needs to keep away from things that destroy the body and to accustom himself to things that make him healthy and vigorous. They are as follows. A man should eat only when he is hungry and drink only when he is thirsty. . . . A man should not eat until his stomach is full. . . .

Day and night have altogether twenty-four hours. It suffices for a man to sleep one-third of them, i.e., eight hours, at the end of the night, so that there be eight hours from the beginning of his sleep until the sun rises. He should stand up from his bed before the sun rises. . . .

The business conduct of the disciples of wise men is truthful and faithful. His "no" is no and his "yes" yes. He is scrupulous with himself in his reckoning. He gives in and yields to others when he buys from them and is not exacting of them. He gives the sale-price on the spot. . . . [H]e stands by his word and does not change it. If others are obligated to him by law, he gives them time and is forgiving. He lends money and is gracious. He shall not take away business from his fellow man nor bring grief to any man in the world during his lifetime.

The general rule is that he be among the oppressed and not the oppressors, among the insulted and not those who insult. . . .

Chapter Six

Man is created in such a way that his character traits and actions are influenced by his neighbors and friends, and he follows the custom of the people in his city. Therefore a man needs to associate with the just and be with the wise continually in order to learn [from] their actions, and to keep away from the wicked, who walk in darkness, so that he avoids learning from their actions. That is what Solomon said: "He who walks with wise men will become wise, but he who associates with fools will become evil." . . .

It is a commandment for every man to love every single individual of Israel like his own body. As it is said: "And you shall love your neighbor as yourself." Therefore he needs to speak in praise of him and to have concern for his possessions, just as he has concern for his own possessions and wants to be honored himself. Whoever glorifies himself through the humiliation of his fellow man has no portion in the world-to-come.

There are two positive commandments to love the convert who comes under the wings of the *Shekhinah;* one, because he is in the class of neighbors, and the other, because he is a convert and the Torah said: "And you shall love the stranger." He [God] commanded the love of the convert, just as He commanded the love of his Name. . . .

 BUDDHA (557–477 B.C.)

THE TEACHINGS OF THE COMPASSIONATE BUDDHA

Universal Love and Good Will

From Suta-Wipata

May creatures all abound in weal and
peace; may all be blessed with peace
always; all creatures weak or strong,
all creatures great and small;
creatures unseen or seen, dwelling
afar or near, born or awaiting birth,—
may all be blessed with peace!

Let none cajole or flout his fellow
anywhere; let none wish others harm
in dudgeon or in hate.

Just as with her own life a mother
shields from hurt her own, her only

child,—let all-embracing thoughts for
all that lives be thine,

—an all-embracing love for all the
universe in all its heights and depths
and breadth, unstinted love,
unmarred by hate within, not rousing
enmity.

So, as you stand or walk, or sit, or lie,
reflect with all your might on this;—
'tis deemed a state divine.

The Brahmana

From Suta-Pitaka

Stop the stream valiantly, drive away the desires, O brahmana! When you have understood the destruction of all that was made, you will understand that which was not made.

From *The Teachings of the Compassionate Buddha*, ed. E.A. Burtt (New York: New American Library, 1955).

If the brahmana has reached the other shore in both insight, in restraint and contemplation, all bonds vanish from him who has obtained knowledge. . . .

I do not call a man a brahmana because of his origin or of his mother. He is indeed arrogant, and he is wealthy: but the poor who is free from all attachments, him I call indeed a brahmana.

Him I call indeed a brahmana who, after cutting all fetters, never trembles, is free from bonds and unshackled.

Him I call indeed a brahmana who, after cutting the strap and the thong, the rope with all that pertains to it, has destroyed all obstacles and is awakened.

Him I call indeed a brahmana who, though he has committed no offense, endures reproach, stripes, and bonds; who has endurance as his force and strength for his army.

Him I call indeed a brahmana who is free from anger, dutiful, virtuous, without appetites, who is subdued and has received his last body.

Him I call indeed a brahmana who does not cling to sensual pleasures, like water on a lotus leaf, like a mustard seed on the point of a needle.

Him I call indeed a brahmana who, even here, knows the end of his own suffering, has put down his burden and is unshackled.

Him I call indeed a brahmana whose knowledge is deep, who possesses wisdom, who knows the right way and the wrong, and has attained the highest end.

Him I call indeed a brahmana who keeps aloof both from laymen and from mendicants, who frequents no houses, and has but few desires.

Him I call indeed a brahmana who without hurting any creatures, whether feeble or strong, does not kill nor cause slaughter.

Him I call indeed a brahmana who is tolerant among the intolerant, mild among the violent, and free from greed among the greedy.

Him I call indeed a brahmana from whom anger and hatred, pride and hypocrisy, have dropped like a mustard seed from the point of a needle.

Him I call indeed a brahmana who utters true speech, instructive and free from harshness, so that he offends no one.

Him I call indeed a brahmana who takes nothing in the world that is not given him, be it long or short, small or large, good or bad.

Him I call indeed a brahmana who fosters no desires for this world or for the next, who has no desires and is unshackled.

Him I call indeed a brahmana who has no longings, and when he has understood the truth, does not express any doubt, and who has reached the deeps of the eternal.

Him I call indeed a brahmana who in this world has risen above bondage to both good and evil; who is free from grief, from sin, and from impurity.

Him I call indeed a brahmana who is bright like the moon, pure, serene, undisturbed, and in whom all unseemly gaiety is extinct.

Him I call indeed a brahmana who has traversed this miry road, the impassible world, difficult to pass, and its vanity; who has gone through and reached the other shore, is thoughtful, steadfast, free from doubts, free from attachment, and content.

Him I call indeed a brahmana who in this world, having abandoned all desires, travels about without a home, and in whom all concupiscence is extinct.

Him I call indeed a brahmana who, having abandoned all longings, travels about without a home, and in whom all covetousness is extinct.

Him I call indeed a brahmana who, after leaving all bondage to men, has risen above all bondage to the gods, and is free from all and every bondage.

Him I call indeed a brahmana who has left what gives pleasure and what gives pain, who is cold[1] and free from all germs of renewed life—the hero who has conquered all the worlds.

Him I call indeed a brahmana who knows the destruction and the return of beings everywhere, who is free from bondage, welfaring, and awakened.

_____

[1] I.e., free from passion.

Him I call indeed a brahmana whose path the gods do not know, nor spirits, nor men, whose passions are extinct, and who is an *arhat*.

Him I call indeed a brahmana who calls nothing his own, whether it be before, behind, or between; who is poor and free from the love of the world.

Him I call indeed a brahmana, the manly, the noble, the hero, the great sage, the conqueror, the sinless, the accomplished, the awakened.

Him I call indeed a brahmana who knows his former abodes, who sees heaven and hell, has reached the end of births, is perfect in knowledge, a sage, and whose accomplishments are all complete.

 HIS HOLINESS THE DALAI LAMA

THE VIRTUE OF COMPASSION

My message is the practice of compassion, love, and kindness.

Basically, universal responsibility is the feeling for other people's suffering just as we feel our own. It is the realization that even our own enemy is motivated by the quest for happiness. We must recognize that all beings want the same thing we want.

At the heart of Buddhist philosophy is the notion of compassion for others.

Love of one's neighbor, kindness, and compassion—these are, I believe, the essential and universal elements preached by all religions.

In spite of divergent philosophical views, we can establish harmony among all spiritual traditions on the basis of these common traits of love, kindness, and forgiveness.

[Of the ten virtues spoken of in Buddhism] three concern the body: one must not kill, steal, or engage in sexual misconduct. Four others are verbal: do not lie, defame others, speak offensive words, or engage in frivolous conversation. . . . Finally, the last three virtuous acts are of a mental nature: do not develop covetousness or malice and, finally, do not hold false or perverted views. . . .

 PLATO

REPUBLIC

Glaucon: They say that to do injustice is naturally good and to suffer injustice bad, but that the badness of suffering it so far exceeds the goodness of doing it that those who have done and suffered injustice and tasted both, but who lack the power to do it and avoid suffering it, decide that it is profitable to come to an agreement with each other neither to do injustice nor to suffer it. As a result, they begin

to make laws and covenants, and what the law commands they call lawful and just. This, they say, is the origin and essence of justice. It is intermediate between the best and the worst. The best is to do injustice without paying the penalty; the worst is to suffer it without being able to take revenge. Justice is a mean between these two extremes. People value it not as a good but because they are too weak to do

Plato: Complete Works, ed. John Cooper (Indianapolis: Hackett, 1997).

injustice with impunity. Someone who has the power to do this, however, and is a true man wouldn't make an agreement with anyone not to do injustice in order not to suffer it. For him that would be madness. This is the nature of justice, according to the argument, Socrates, and these are its natural origins.

We can see most clearly that those who practice justice do it unwillingly and because they lack the power to do injustice, if in our thoughts we grant to a just and an unjust person the freedom to do whatever they like. We can then follow both of them and see where their desires would lead. And we'll catch the just person red-handed travelling the same road as the unjust. The reason for this is the desire to outdo others and get more and more. This is what anyone's nature naturally pursues as good, but nature is forced by law into the perversion of treating fairness with respect.

The freedom I mentioned would be most easily realized if both people had the power they say the ancestor of Gyges of Lydia possessed. The story goes that he was a shepherd in the service of the ruler of Lydia. There was a violent thunderstorm, and an earthquake broke open the ground and created a chasm at the place where he was tending his sheep. Seeing this, he was filled with amazement and went down into it. And there, in addition to many other wonders of which we're told, he saw a hollow bronze horse. There were window-like openings in it, and, peeping in, he saw a corpse, which seemed to be of more than human size, wearing nothing but a gold ring on its finger. He took the ring and came out of the chasm. He wore the ring at the usual monthly meeting that reported to the king on the state of the flocks. And as he was sitting among the others, he happened to turn the setting of the ring towards himself to the inside of his hand. When he did this, he became invisible to those sitting near him, and they went on talking as if he had gone. He wondered at this, and, fingering the ring, he turned the setting outwards again and became visible. So he experimented with the ring to test whether it indeed had this power—and it did. If he turned the setting inward, he became invisible; if he turned it outward, he

became visible again. When he realized this, he at once arranged to become one of the messengers sent to report to the king. And when he arrived there, he seduced the king's wife, attacked the king with her help, killed him, and took over the kingdom.

Let's suppose, then, that there were two such rings, one worn by a just and the other by an unjust person. Now, no one, it seems, would be so incorruptible that he would stay on the path of justice or stay away from other people's property, when he could take whatever he wanted from the marketplace with impunity, go into people's houses and have sex with anyone he wished, kill or release from prison anyone he wished, and do all the other things that would make him like a god among humans. Rather his actions would be in no way different from those of an unjust person, and both would follow the same path. This, some would say, is a great proof that one is never just willingly but only when compelled to be. No one believes justice to be a good when it is kept private, since, wherever either person thinks he can do injustice with impunity, he does it. Indeed, every man believes that injustice is far more profitable to himself than justice. And any exponent of this argument will say he's right, for someone who didn't want to do injustice, given this sort of opportunity, and who didn't touch other people's property would be thought wretched and stupid by everyone aware of the situation, though, of course, they'd praise him in public, deceiving each other for fear of suffering injustice. . . .

As for the choice between the lives we're discussing, we'll be able to make a correct judgment about that only if we separate the most just and the most unjust. Otherwise we won't be able to do it. Here's the separation I have in mind. We'll subtract nothing from the injustice of an unjust person and nothing from the justice of a just one, but we'll take each to be complete in his own way of life. First, therefore, we must suppose that an unjust person will act as clever craftsmen do: . . . an unjust person's successful attempts at injustice must remain undetected, if he is to be fully unjust. Anyone who is caught should be thought inept, for the extreme of injustice is to be believed to be just without being just. And our completely unjust person must be given complete injustice; nothing may be subtracted from it. We must allow that, while doing the greatest injustice, he has nonetheless provided himself with the greatest reputation for justice. If he happens to make a slip, he must be able to put it right. If any of his unjust activities should be discovered, he must be able to speak persuasively or to use force. And if force is needed, he must have the help of courage and strength and of the substantial wealth and friends with which he has provided himself.

Having hypothesized such a person, let's now in our argument put beside him a just man, who is simple and noble and who, as Aeschylus says, doesn't want to be believed to be good but to be so. We must take away his reputation, for a reputation for justice would bring him honor and rewards, so that it wouldn't be clear whether he is just for the sake of justice itself or for the sake of those honors and rewards. We must strip him of everything except justice and make his situation the opposite of an unjust person's. Though he does no injustice, he must have the greatest reputation for it, so that his justice may be tested full-strength and not diluted by wrongdoing and what comes from it. Let him stay like that unchanged until he dies—just, but all his life believed to be unjust. In this way, both will reach the extremes, the one of justice and the other of injustice, and we'll be able to judge which of them is happier. . . .

[T]hose who praise injustice . . . say that a just person in such circumstances will be whipped, stretched on a rack, chained, blinded with fire, and, at the end, when he has suffered every kind of evil, he'll be impaled, and will realize then that one shouldn't want to be just but to be believed to be just. . . .

[The unjust man] rules his city because of his reputation for justice; he marries into any family he wishes; he gives his children in marriage to anyone he wishes; he has contracts and partnerships with anyone he wants; and besides benefiting himself in all these ways, he profits because he has no scruples about doing injustice. In any contest, public or private, he's the winner and outdoes his enemies. And by

outdoing them, he becomes wealthy, benefiting his friends and harming his enemies. He makes adequate sacrifices to the gods and sets up magnificent offerings to them. He takes better care of the gods, therefore, (and, indeed, of the human beings he's fond of) than a just person does. Hence it's likely that the gods, in turn, will take better care of him than of a just person. That's what they say, Socrates, that gods and humans provide a better life for unjust people than for just ones. . . .

Adeimantus: When fathers speak to their sons, they say that one must be just, as do all the others who have charge of anyone. But they don't praise justice itself, only the high reputations it leads to and the consequences of being thought to be just, such as the public offices, marriages, and other things Glaucon listed. But they elaborate even further on the consequences of reputation. By bringing in the esteem of the gods, they are able to talk about the abundant good things that they themselves and the noble Hesiod and Homer say that the gods give to the pious. . . .

Musaeus and his son make the gods give the just more headstrong goods than these.[1] In their stories, they lead the just to Hades, seat them on couches, provide them with a symposium of pious people, crown them with wreaths, and make them spend all their time drinking—as if they thought drunkenness was the finest wage of virtue. Others stretch even further the wages that virtue receives from the gods, for they say that someone who is pious and keeps his promises leaves his children's children and a whole race behind him. In these and other similar ways, they praise justice. They bury the impious and unjust in mud in Hades; force them to carry water in a sieve; bring them into bad repute while they're still alive, and all those penalties that Glaucon gave to the just person they give to the unjust. But they have nothing else to say. This, then, is the way people praise justice and find fault with injustice.

Besides this, Socrates, consider another form of argument about justice and injustice

---

[1] Musaeus was a legendary poet closely associated with the mystery religion of Orphism.

employed both by private individuals and by poets. All go on repeating with one voice that justice and moderation are fine things, but hard and onerous, while licentiousness and injustice are sweet and easy to acquire and are shameful only in opinion and law. They add that unjust deeds are for the most part more profitable than just ones, and, whether in public or private, they willingly honor vicious people who have wealth and other types of power and declare them to be happy. But they dishonor and disregard the weak and the poor, even though they agree that they are better than the others.

But the most wonderful of all these arguments concerns what they have to say about the gods and virtue. They say that the gods, too, assign misfortune and a bad life to many good people, and the opposite fate to their opposites. Begging priests and prophets frequent the doors of the rich and persuade them that they possess a god-given power founded on sacrifices and incantations. If the rich person or any of his ancestors has committed an injustice, they can fix it with pleasant rituals. Moreover, if he wishes to injure some enemy, then, at little expense, he'll be able to harm just and unjust alike, for by means of spells and enchantments they can persuade the gods to serve them. . . .

These initiations, as they call them, free people from punishment hereafter, while a terrible fate awaits those who have not performed the rituals.

When all such sayings about the attitudes of gods and humans to virtue and vice are so often repeated, Socrates, what effect do you suppose they have on the souls of young people? . . . And he'll answer: "The various sayings suggest that there is no advantage in my being just if I'm not also thought just, while the troubles and penalties of being just are apparent. But they tell me that an unjust person, who has secured for himself a reputation for justice, lives the life of a god. . . . I should create a façade of illusory virtue around me to deceive those who come near, but keep behind it the greedy and crafty fox. . . .

"But surely," someone will object, "it isn't easy for vice to remain always hidden." We'll reply that nothing great is easy. And, in any case, if we're to be happy, we must follow the path indicated in these accounts. . . .

Questions for Discussion and Review

1. Do you accept the Divine Command theory of morality? If not, why not? If yes, and you think you know God's Law, how do you know it?

2. Suppose that someone claims to have found a text actually written by Jesus. Would you believe it? What proof, if any, would you need?

3. Suppose that the text that the man in question 2 attributed to Jesus includes a command to enslave anyone who refuses to believe that he (Jesus) is divine. Would you believe it? If not, why not? What are the implications of your answer to the question of whether God's commands make things morally right and wrong?

4. Is nothing really morally right or wrong?

5. Suppose that Alpha believes that slaughtering innocent Jews is morally wrong while Omega believes that it's not morally wrong. What would a moral subjectivist say about this dispute? What would a moral objectivist say? With which, if either, would you agree?

6. Does everyone have a right to believe what he or she wants?

7. Does everyone have a right to act on his or her beliefs?

8. Society A believes that it's not morally wrong to enslave white people while society B believes it is morally wrong. What would a moral relativist say about this dispute? What would a moral objectivist say? With whom, if either, do you agree?

9. Society A believes that it's not morally wrong to slaughter innocent Christians. Abigail and Belinda are members of society A. Abigail believes it's morally wrong to slaughter innocent Christians while Belinda believes it isn't wrong. What would a Moral Relativist say about this dispute? What would a Moral Objectivist say about it? With whom, if either, do you agree?

10. Should people always conform to the moral code of their society? Why or why not?

11. Would a Moral Relativist be consistent if she said that people should always conform to the moral code of their society?

12. John is a financial consultant and money manager. He believes that it would be in his self-interest to steal the life savings of his clients and flee with his millions to another country where he could live out his life in luxury. As a moral egoist, he believes that it wouldn't be morally wrong because it's in his self-interest. Do you agree?

Suggestions for Further Reading

Fred Feldman. *Introductory Ethics.* Englewood Cliffs, NJ: Prentice-Hall, 1978. Chapters 6 and 11 provide a detailed, rigorous introduction to Egoism and Relativism.

Gilbert Harman. *The Nature of Morality.* New York: Oxford University Press, 1977. A well-written introduction to some of the issues of this chapter from a Relativist's perspective, suitable mainly for advanced students.

C. E. Harris, Jr. *Applying Moral Theories.* Belmont, CA: Wadsworth, 1986. Chapters 2 and 4 provide a readable, lively introduction to the issues of this chapter.

Louis J. Pojman, ed. *Ethical Theory.* Belmont, CA: Wadsworth, 1989. An excellent collection of articles on the topics of this chapter.

James Rachels. *The Elements of Moral Philosophy.* New York: Random House, 1986. Chapters 2–6 provide an excellent, readable introduction to the issues of this chapter.

Robert Van Wyk. *Introduction to Ethics.* New York: St. Martin's Press, 1990. Chapters 2 and 3 provide a well-written account of Egoism, Relativism, and the Divine Command theory.

MORAL JUSTIFICATION

Objectives

Readers are expected to:

- have formed an opinion on whether moral sentences can be true or false.
- understand the logical structure of moral arguments.
- understand the difference between nonmoral and moral reasons in moral arguments.
- understand how to critically evaluate moral arguments.
- understand the difference between absolute and non-absolute moral principles.
- understand what makes a moral principle universal and how the feature of universality can be used in moral arguments.
- understand the difference between basic and nonbasic moral principles.
- understand Intuitionism and self-evidence.
- understand social justifications of morality.
- understand reflective equilibrium as a process of moral justification.
- understand the various possible relationships between feelings and moral principles.
- understand Amoralism and various ways of answering the question, "Why be moral?"

Introduction

In August 1914, Germany invaded neutral Belgium as part of a plan to defeat France in a lightning stroke at the outbreak of World War I. The German high command believed that Belgium was the shortest and easiest route to the French armies. Although Germany had signed a treaty along with other major European powers to respect Belgian neutrality and to refrain from sending armies onto that country's soil, the German leaders decided that the treaty should be violated for strategic considerations.

When Belgian forces resisted the unprovoked German invasion, Germany turned to terror tactics directed at the civilian population to force the Belgian government to end all resistance to the German advance. On August 23, a German general, von Bülow, complained that the Belgian people were attacking his troops. So, "with my permission the General commanding these troops has burned the town to ashes and has had 110 persons shot."[1] Those shot were civilians. A few days later, a similar event occurred at another village. "On the second day at Tamines some 400 citizens were herded together under guard in front of the church in the main square and a firing squad began systematically shooting into the group. Those not dead when the firing ended were bayoneted."[2]

The Germans shot thousands of civilians in order to force the Belgian government to capitulate and sent thousands of able-bodied male civilians back to Germany to become virtual slave laborers. On August 23, another German general, von Hausen, saw that some civilians near the village of Dinant were trying to interfere with German efforts to build a bridge across a river. At his order, "His troops began rounding up 'several hundreds' of hostages, men, women, and children."[3] According to Barbara Tuchman:

> They were kept in the main square till evening, then lined up, women on one side, men opposite in two rows, one kneeling in front of the other. Two firing squads marched to the center of the square, faced either way and fired till no more of the targets stood upright. Six hundred and twelve bodies were identified and buried, including Felix Fivet, aged three weeks.[4]

Suppose that two individuals disagree about whether this action was morally wrong. Or suppose that two different societies disagree, Belgians claiming that the action was morally wrong and Germans claiming that it wasn't. Nonobjectivists would say that there's no objectively true or false answer to the question, "Was the German action morally wrong?" Objectivists would say that one of the individuals and societies must have a true moral belief and the other a false moral belief. But can we make sense of the idea of moral truths? And if Objectivists are right, how can we figure out what's true in moral matters? Can we know what's morally right and wrong?

We'll first look briefly at the idea of moral truth, then we'll examine moral justification. As we saw, justification is crucial for knowledge. It's also crucial for reasonable belief; as many philosophers emphasize, if we want to have true rather than false beliefs, the best strategy is to have justified rather than unjustified beliefs. This applies to moral matters as well as to other matters. If we want to discover the truth about moral issues (if

---

[1] Barbara Tuchman, *The Guns of August* (New York: Bantam Books, 1962), 351.
[2] Ibid., 351–352.
[3] Ibid., 353.
[4] Ibid., 353.

there are any moral truths to be discovered), then the most promising strategy is to weigh the reasons for and against the answers to our moral questions. Regarding the German massacre, we should look at the arguments for and against it and try to determine which side has the stronger case. The truth probably lies with the side with the stronger arguments. But that requires us to understand the nature of moral arguments.

Can Moral Statements Be (Objectively) True or False?

If no moral statement is objectively true or false, then there cannot be moral knowledge. Perhaps there cannot even be justified moral beliefs. Perhaps there cannot even be such things as moral beliefs at all. Ordinarily, when we talk of someone's believing something, we mean that she believes that a certain statement is true. And when we talk about someone's being justified, we mean that an individual who believes that p is true is justified in believing that it's true. Therefore, much may depend on the idea of moral truth. Are moral statements objectively true or false?

Why might we think that moral statements (and therefore moral beliefs) cannot be objectively true or false? Early in this century, many British and American philosophers embraced a view called Emotivism. According to Emotivism, only sentences used to describe or explain are true or false. Descriptions attribute properties and relations to things. "He's six feet tall," "he's older than John," and "He was running at 9:00 a.m." are examples of descriptions. Furthermore, they thought that only descriptions that can be conclusively proved to be true or false by appeal to perception and observation can be objectively true or false.

In their view, moral sentences are not used to describe or explain anything. For that reason alone they cannot be true or false. Instead, moral sentences express our emotions, attitudes, or feelings. According to their analysis of moral sentences, a sentence such as "Deliberately killing innocent civilians during wartime is immoral" is nothing but the expression of an emotion toward that action. The sentence should be analyzed as

Deliberately killing innocent civilians during war—Boo!

or as

Deliberately killing innocent civilians during war—(gesture of thumb down).

However, more recent moral philosophers have suggested that moral sentences may be used both to express attitudes and to describe things. Philosophers such as Ludwig Wittgenstein (1889–1951) and J. L. Austin (1910–1960) pointed out that we use language for a variety of purposes: to persuade, pray, frighten, threaten, warn, promise, describe, explain, apologize, express feelings (sympathy, outrage, fear), and so on. And we frequently use language for more than one purpose. Therefore, even if we use moral sentences to express attitudes or feelings, that may not be all we're using them for.

If we say "Antonio's a bachelor," we're describing Antonio. We're saying that he has the property of being a bachelor. Either he has that property or he doesn't, so "Antonio's a bachelor" is either true or false. Now if I say, "Antonio's a good man," I also seem to be describing him. I'm attributing to him the property of moral goodness (being a morally good man), just as in the other case I attributed to him the property of bachelorhood.

Of course, we have to understand the property of bachelorhood in order to understand the description of Antonio. We can say that bachelorhood is a complex property composed of other properties. Someone is a bachelor if he has the properties of being a male, being of a certain age (say, over 21), and being unmarried. (It's not clear whether one is a bachelor if one isn't currently married or instead is one only if one has never been married.) We can thus define the property of bachelorhood in terms of its constituent properties.

Can we define what it means to be a morally good man as we can define what it means to be a bachelor? If we can, then "He's a (morally) good man" can be used to describe just as "He's a bachelor" can. Similarly with actions. If we can define what "morally wrong" means, then "The German massacre was morally wrong" describes as much as "The German massacre occurred in 1914" describes. Descriptions convey information. Therefore, if moral sentences describe, they convey information. In the case of "He's a morally good man," if we know what "morally good" means when applied to a man (or human), or if we know the standards of moral goodness, the sentence "He's a (morally) good man" conveys information to us. "He's a (morally) good man" means that he satisfies the standards of moral goodness that apply to men or humans.

BRAIN TEASERS

What information, if any, does "he's a (morally) good man" convey?
What does "morally wrong" mean?

If moral sentences are used to describe things, as well as to express emotions and attitudes, then they are used to attribute moral properties to things. Just as "The sun is hot" attributes the property of being hot to the sun, "The massacre of innocent people by the Germans was morally wrong" attributes the property of moral wrongness to the massacre. Those who doubt that moral sentences can be true or false doubt that moral properties, such as moral wrongness and moral goodness, really exist.

The question of the reality and nature of properties is puzzling, whether we're talking about moral or nonmoral properties. Does the property of being a bachelor or being hot exist? Properties are not physical objects, so if they exist, they don't exist in the same way that loaves of bread and fish exist.

Let's sidestep questions about the reality of properties. Instead, let's focus on the similarities between moral sentences and certain nonmoral sentences. "Ray's a bachelor" describes Ray, attributing the property of bachelorhood to Ray. Similarly, "The German massacre was morally wrong" at least appears to attribute the property of moral wrongness to the massacre. We can't determine merely by looking at Ray whether he has the property of bachelorhood. Similarly, we may not be able to determine whether the massacre has the property of moral wrongness just by "looking" at it. Once we've defined what a bachelor is, we can employ perception and observation to confirm or disconfirm that Ray's a bachelor. (We can search marriage records, look for witnesses, and so on.) Similarly, if we can define moral wrongness, we may be able to confirm or disconfirm a claim such as "That was morally wrong" by using perception and observation. We may not be able to conclusively prove that Ray's a bachelor or prove that he's not a bachelor. (Suppose a woman claims to be married to him. Does that prove he's not a bachelor? No. Suppose we find a record of a marriage between Ray and the woman. Do we know that the marriage was valid? No.) Similarly, we may not be able to conclusively prove that the massacre was morally wrong.

We can define the term "bachelor." However, there may be some disagreement about its definition. We certainly wouldn't call a five-month-old unmarried male a bachelor. Most of us reserve the term for a male of a certain age, but the ages we have in mind probably differ. I may say that a male is a bachelor only if he's over 25 while you say he's a bachelor provided that he's over 18. Similarly, I may say he's a bachelor only if he's never been married while you say he's a bachelor provided that he's not currently married. I may say he's a bachelor if he's legally separated from his wife, living alone, and has filed for divorce, while you say he's not a bachelor until the divorce is actually granted.

Similarly, if we define moral wrongness, there may be disagreement. We may begin by defining moral wrongness as causing harm to a sentient creature, which many people would probably find initially plausible. But there are questions around the edges. Are all instances of causing harm to a sentient creature morally wrong? What if the legal system punishes someone for a crime he committed? What if a police officer shoots someone who is about to kill an innocent victim? Similarly, one may ask whether only harm caused to sentient creatures is morally wrong. We'll not follow up on these questions. Instead, we'll point out that similar questions can be raised regarding definitions of nonmoral terms. Take the old standby, baldness. How few hairs on one's head must one have in order to be bald?

We've raised questions that still remain open. But I hope I've said enough to make the idea of moral truth worth exploring. The next task is to look at moral justification.

Moral Justification

We looked at justification in a previous chapter. There we looked at four basic sources of justification (reason, sense perception, introspection, and memory), as well as at probability and explanation as justifiers. Here we'll begin by focusing on moral arguments.

When people disagree about a moral issue, they don't normally begin by throwing up their hands and saying that they'll just have to agree to disagree. Instead, they argue. I don't mean a shouting and shoving match. To argue is to present arguments to defend one's view and arguments to undermine the opposing views. For example, suppose that you and I disagree about affirmative action. You're in favor and I'm opposed. You'll probably present arguments that support affirmative action and I'll present arguments against affirmative action. Then you'll respond to my arguments with counterarguments and I'll do the same with yours. Our discussion or argument may lead to one of us changing his mind, but it may not. If we can't agree after arguing our respective cases, then either we'll stomp off in blind fury, assault each other, or amicably agree to disagree and go on to other subjects.

What do moral arguments look like? Let's begin with something pretty simple. Suppose that you and I agree that I was rude to a student and that it was deliberate. You say that it was morally wrong for me to be deliberately rude to her and I say it wasn't. We first have to decide on whom the burden of justification lays. Perhaps I should go first to present my arguments for the view that it wasn't wrong to be rude. Or perhaps you should go first to present your arguments for the view that it was wrong to be rude.

Let's think of moral argument as a little like a criminal trial. In a criminal trial, the burden of proof is on the prosecutor, not the defendant. The prosecutor goes first, presenting the evidence for guilt. Then the defense attorney responds. The defense attorney doesn't have to prove her client is innocent. (How could she?) All she has to do is prove that the prosecution's case has weaknesses. It's up to the prosecutor to prove that the defendant is guilty. If she can't prove it, then the defendant must be acquitted.

In moral disputes we might think of someone who says that doing (or not doing) an act is morally wrong as the prosecution. They are making the accusation, so it's up to them to prove their case. The other person in the dispute is in the position of the defense attorney. She just has to counter the prosecution's arguments. This suggests an important principle:

Moral claims require reasons. If someone claims that doing something or not doing something is morally wrong, they must have reasons. "It's morally wrong to do (or not do) that, but there are no reasons for thinking that it's morally wrong" doesn't make sense.

BRAIN TEASERS

Suppose I said it's morally wrong to cheat but there are no reasons for thinking that it's morally wrong. How would you respond?

Therefore, moral claims require reasons or arguments, and the burden of justification is on your shoulders to "prove" that it was wrong of me to be deliberately rude. Now you would probably say something like the following.

1. Being rude hurts people's feelings.
2. It's morally wrong to deliberately hurt people's feelings.

---

3. Therefore, it's morally wrong to be deliberately rude.

This moral argument has two premises. The first is a nonmoral claim. It simply states how the world is. The second premise is a moral principle. We might think of it as stating how the world should be. Moral principles can take many forms: "Don't be rude," "Being rude is morally wrong," "People shouldn't be rude," or "We have a moral duty not to be rude." Moral principles specify what morality prohibits and requires. This argument fits the pattern of the most common model of moral argument, according to which a moral argument has two kinds of premises: moral principles and nonmoral claims about the way the world is.

Evaluating Moral Arguments

Suppose that you and I continue to disagree about whether my deliberate rudeness to the student was morally wrong. You've given me an argument to support your view. If I accept your argument, I seem compelled to accept its conclusion. It certainly appears to be a valid argument: if its premises are true, then its conclusion must be true. So I must either accept it or not. If I don't accept it but do acknowledge that it's valid, I must reject one or more of its premises.

I may reject the nonmoral claim about the way the world is: rudeness hurts people's feelings. I may dispute that and reply that it doesn't hurt people's feelings. Then our dispute is a nonmoral one. It's about the way the world is rather than the way the world should be. And we each would try to marshall evidence to show that our view is the true or more reasonable one.

BRAIN TEASERS

> Which view is more reasonable—rudeness hurts people's feelings or rudeness doesn't hurt people's feelings?

So moral disagreement is sometimes based on disagreement about non-moral features of the world, about the way the world is.

On the other hand, I may reject the moral principle you appealed to: Deliberately hurting people's feelings is morally wrong. I may say it's not really morally wrong to deliberately hurt people's feelings. In that case, I may ask a question that's always appropriate in moral disputes: "Why?" That is, what reasons are there for thinking that? I'm then asking you to justify your claim that it's morally wrong to deliberately hurt people's feelings. I'm asking for another moral argument. It would probably take the same form. For example,

1. Hurting people's feelings causes them harm; for example, it lowers their self-esteem.
2. It's morally wrong to deliberately harm people.

---

3. Therefore, it's morally wrong to deliberately hurt people's feelings.

BRAIN TEASERS

> Construct an argument to show that it was morally wrong for the Germans to massacre innocent people in Belgium during World War I. Then construct an argument to show that it was morally right.

Evaluating Nonmoral Reasons (Premises)

Nonmoral claims can be true or false, reasonable or unreasonable, justified or unjustified. If the nonmoral claims supporting a moral judgment are false or unreasonable, the claims aren't good reasons and the moral argument is defective. For example, suppose I think it was wrong for you to have brushed your teeth early this morning and I argue as follows:

1. Brushing one's teeth early in the morning can cause an earthquake that will kill many people.
2. It's morally wrong to do something that can cause an earthquake.

---

3. Therefore, it was morally wrong of you to brush your teeth early this morning.

I hope you agree that this would be absurd. The nonmoral claim in the first premise is wholly unreasonable.

Take more realistic examples. Apologists for slavery argued as follows.

1. Blacks are inferior to Whites.
2. It's not morally wrong for a superior race to enslave an inferior race.

---

3. Therefore, it's not morally wrong for Whites to enslave Blacks.

Most people today (but, alas, not all) realize that the first premise, a nonmoral claim about the way the world is, is both false and unreasonable. For that reason alone, the argument is defective. The point is that moral arguments can be criticized for having nonmoral premises that are false, unreasonable, or doubtful.

Evaluating Moral Principles

Most people probably think that moral principles, too, can be true or false, reasonable or unreasonable. In that case, a moral principle can be a good reason only if it's true or reasonable. Consider the moral principle in premise (2) of the above argument: It's not morally wrong for a superior race to enslave an inferior race. Even if someone agrees that some races are superior, she may reject this moral principle as false or unreasonable. If the moral principle is false or unreasonable, the moral argument is defective.

But can moral principles be false or unreasonable? Suppose that Brad's best friend, Yasmin, is depressed and he argues as follows.

1. Yasmin is my best friend.
2. If one's best friend is depressed, one should try to persuade her to kill herself.

---

3. Therefore, I should try to persuade Yasmin to kill herself.

Surely the moral principle in premise (2) is unreasonable. It would be appropriate to ask Brad why he thinks that we should try to persuade depressed friends to commit suicide. If he has no answer, it's difficult to imagine conceding that the moral principle he appealed to is reasonable. But suppose he presents another argument:

1. Depression is incurable and causes much suffering.
2. We should not do nothing while our friends suffer; we should help them find relief.
3. The only relief from depression is death.

---

4. Therefore, we should try to persuade depressed friends to commit suicide to escape their suffering.

Now if all the premises of this argument were true, Brad might have a case. But they're not true. While depression does cause intense suffering, it is curable. There are many effective antidepressants that can relieve depression. Counseling and psychotherapy can help, as well. Death is not the only relief from depression. Given that the beliefs that underlie the moral principle that Brad applies are false and unreasonable, surely we can say that the moral principle itself is unreasonable, and even false.

BRAIN TEASERS

Which of the following moral principles are unreasonable? Why?

Rape is morally wrong.

Rape is not morally wrong.

It's morally wrong to gamble.

It's not morally wrong to gamble.

Prostitution is morally wrong.

Prostitution is not morally wrong.

Are Moral Principles Absolute?

Absolute principle: Permits no exceptions

Common sense moral principles are generally expressed as unqualified generalizations, such as "It's wrong to steal" or "Do not steal." That makes it appear that they are absolute. An absolute moral principle permits no exceptions. If "It's wrong to steal" is absolute, then there are no circumstances in which it wouldn't be wrong to steal.

But few unqualified moral principles are plausible candidates for absoluteness. Consider "It's wrong to kill." If that's an absolute or exceptionless moral principle, then no matter what living creature we kill and regardless of our reasons for killing it, it's morally wrong. For example, the following acts would be morally wrong: a doctor's giving you an antibiotic to kill bacteria that are causing you to be ill, a farmer's using pesticide to kill insects devouring his crops, and a gardener harvesting carrots to eat.

We make the moral principle a bit more plausible by qualifying it. Perhaps we don't mean that it's wrong to kill any living creature, such as a bee that's about to sting someone who has a life-threatening allergy to bee stings, but rather, we mean that it's wrong to kill *people*. So the unqualified "It's wrong to kill" becomes the qualified "It's wrong to kill people."

But most people still are uncomfortable with this principle because they think that there are circumstances in which it's not wrong to kill people. For example, most people seem to think that it's not wrong if, as a last resort, a police officer kills someone who is threatening serious harm to an innocent individual or a person kills someone in self-defense. If opinion polls are right, most people in the United States think it's not wrong to kill people as punishment for certain crimes. Thus, in order to make the principle more plausible, we may have to qualify it further. Perhaps we might express it as "It's wrong to kill people without a morally good or compelling reason." Of course, this leaves open the question of what constitutes a morally compelling reason, and there is likely to be substantial debate about that.

Another reason why it's not plausible to think of unqualified moral principles as absolute is that they can come into conflict. For example, a principle forbidding us to lie can come into conflict with a principle requiring us to save innocent lives. Suppose that a German citizen knows that a neighbor is hiding Jews from the Nazis and a Gestapo officer asks him whether he knows where there are any Jews. If he tells the truth, the Jews will be sent to a death camp and his neighbor imprisoned or worse. Lying will save lives. If we tell the truth, innocent people will be murdered. In this situation, we can't act on both principles. If they are both absolute, then whatever we do—lie or tell the truth—we do wrong. But surely common sense tells us that it's wrong to tell the truth and right to lie in this situation. In general, almost all plausible moral principles require qualification, such as "It's wrong unless there are morally good or compelling reasons to do it."

Are Moral Principles Universal?

According to many philosophers, moral principles are universal. That is, a moral principle is supposed to apply to everyone. "It's morally wrong to steal" applies to both me and you: it would be wrong for you to steal from me and for me to steal from you. If it's morally wrong to steal, it's morally wrong for everyone.

Universal principle: Applies to everyone

Universality can be a potent force in moral argument. It underlies the common question that people ask those they think have done something wrong: How would you like it if someone did to you what you just did? If it's not morally wrong for me to be rude to people, then it's not morally wrong for people to be rude to me. I can't consistently claim that it's not wrong for me to be rude, but it is wrong for others to be rude to me. If I think it would be wrong for you to be rude to me, consistency requires that I apply the same principles to myself that I expect others to live by.

Sometimes this strategy of stressing universality can persuade people in moral argument. If I would think it wrong for someone to murder me, it's difficult to see how I can justify the claim that it wouldn't be wrong for me to murder someone. It seems contradictory. It's morally wrong for you to murder me but not for me to murder you? That's the point of universality.

BRAIN TEASERS

Suppose that Byron thinks it's not morally wrong for him to beat up a smaller and weaker classmate in order to show his toughness. How might you appeal to universality to persuade him that it's morally wrong?

Apply universality to moral argument in the case of the German massacre at Dinant.

Is there a Foundation to Morality?

We can justify a moral principle by appealing to another deeper or more general moral principle as a premise. We then might be able to justify that deeper or more general moral principle by a yet deeper and more general moral principle. For example, we justified "It's wrong to be rude" by appealing to "It's wrong to hurt people's feelings." And we could justify "It's wrong to hurt people's feelings" by appeal to a more general moral principle, "It's wrong to harm people." How far can we go like this?

There seem to be three possibilities. We could go on forever; we could argue in a circle; we could come to basic moral principles that are a kind of foundation. We can't go on forever. That would require an infinite number of moral principles, each more general than the previous one. There aren't an infinite number of moral principles. We shouldn't argue in a circle, either, justifying principle A by appeal to principle B, principle B by appeal to principle C, principle C by appeal to principle D, and principle D by appeal to principle A. Such circular arguments are defective. So on this view there are (or we hope there are) basic moral principles.

Basic Moral Principles

A basic moral principle can justify a nonbasic moral principle, but it in turn is justified in a way that differs from how nonbasic principles are justified. If I justify "It's wrong to be rude" by appealing to the principle, "It's wrong to hurt people's feelings," then "It's wrong to be rude" isn't basic. Similarly, if I justify, "It's wrong to hurt people's feelings" by appeal to "It's wrong to harm people," then "It's wrong to hurt people's feelings" isn't basic. But suppose I have no more general moral principle to appeal to in order to justify "It's wrong to harm people"? Then "It's wrong to harm people" may be basic.

One possibility is that "It's wrong to harm people" is an arbitrary assumption and therefore isn't justified. In that case, its lack of justification infects everything built on it. Nothing it's used to justify is really justified because it has no justification to transmit to such principles as, "It's wrong to hurt people's feelings."

Another possibility is that basic principles are self-evident and necessarily justified. This is the view of Intuitionists.

Intuitionism and Basic Moral Principles

Many people are convinced that they know that it's wrong to harm people. At least, they know that it's wrong to harm people without a morally good reason, a more qualified principle. But how can we justify such a principle? Here we must distinguish between two aspects of justification. In one sense of justification, to say that I'm justified in believing something entails that it's not (epistemically[5]) wrong for me to believe it, that our reasons at least permit belief. But in a stronger sense, to say that I'm justified in believing something entails that it would be (epistemically) wrong for me not to believe it, that our reasons in a sense require belief. For example, suppose that you believe that Rhonda loves you. I might say that you're justified in believing that she loves you. I'm implying that your evidence permits you to believe it, that it's not (epistemically) wrong for you to believe it. I'm not implying that your evidence requires you to believe it.

But suppose you don't believe that Rhonda loves you and I claim that nevertheless, you're justified in believing that she does. On the one hand, I may be implying only that your evidence permits you to believe it, that it wouldn't be (epistemically) wrong to believe it. But I may mean something stronger. I may mean that it's (epistemically) wrong for you not to believe that she loves you, that it's unreasonable or irrational not to believe it, that you're not justified in not believing it.

When it comes to basic moral principles, many people want to establish that they're justified in the stronger sense, that we're not simply (epistemically) permitted to believe them, but that we're required to believe them. In moral disputes, we hope to reach agreement about basic moral principles. Suppose I'm justified in believing a basic moral principle. But suppose that you don't believe this principle. If I'm justified in believing it in the weaker sense, then it doesn't follow that you're justified in believing it. And even if you're justified in believing it in the sense that reason permits you to believe it, you might not believe it. Your reasons may permit you to believe it but it also permits you to not believe it. You would be justified if you believed it, but you'd also be justified if you don't believe it. What I would want to establish is the stronger claim that reason requires you to believe this basic moral principle, not just permits you.

---

[5]"Episteme" is the Greek word for knowledge. "Epistemically right/wrong" refers to rightness and wrongness from an epistemological rather than a moral point of view. It assumes that there is an ethics of belief, that it's wrong to believe under some conditions.

Intuitionists claim that there are basic moral principles and that they are self-evident. Different Intuitionists probably mean different things by "self-evident."

W. D. Ross (1877–1971), a well-known intuitionist, claims that it's self-evident that people have the following duties:

1. Duties to others you have because of previous acts of yours

    a. Duty of fidelity (duty to keep promises, keep your word, and the like)
    b. Duty of reparation (duty to compensate people for injuries and harm you cause)
    c. Duty of gratitude (duty to thank people for benefits they confer on you)

2. Duties to others not based on previous acts of yours

    a. Duty of beneficence (duty to help others in need)
    b. Duty of nonmaleficence (duty not to harm others without a compelling reason)
    c. Duty of justice (duty to be just to others)

3. Duty to oneself (duty to improve oneself physically, intellectually, and morally to reach one's fullest potential)."[6]

(We could express the same principles using "should" or the concept of moral wrongness. Thus, if we have a moral duty to keep promises, then it's morally wrong not to keep a promise and we should keep promises.)

Ross emphasizes that these basic principles are "prima facie." In part, that means that they're not absolute. There can be exceptions where it's not wrong to infringe or violate them. For example, in a particular situation, I may justifiably violate the principle requiring me to keep my promises in order to save a human life. That I have a prima facie duty to keep my promises seems to mean that keeping a promise is a consideration that always counts in favor of my doing rather than not doing something. Having a moral duty to do x always counts on the side of doing x, even if in concrete situations other reasons may weigh more strongly or heavily on the other side. In situations where prima facie duties conflict, I have to (and can only) reflect on which duty is more important in that situation.

Ross thought that moral right and wrong are undefinable but that "the rightness (prima facie) of certain types of act is self-evident . . . ; apprehended directly by minds which have reached a certain degree of maturity. . . ."[7] He goes on to say that, "the human mind . . . has . . . an a priori insight into certain broad principles of morality. . . ."[8] They are "self-evident . . . in the sense that when we have reached sufficient mental

---

[6] W. D. Ross, *The Right and the Good* (Indianapolis: Hackett, 1988), 21–22.
[7] Ibid., 12.
[8] Ibid., 14.

maturity and have given sufficient attention to the [principle] it is evident without the need of proof, or of evidence beyond itself."[9]

What Ross has in mind is less clear than we might like it to be. On the one hand, he may think that basic moral principles are necessarily true and therefore knowable a priori, just as "Bachelors are unmarried" and "Either it's raining or it's not" are. Some contemporary philosophers take that view, such as Judith Jarvis Thomson, who has said that the statement "Other things being equal, 'one ought not to cause others pain' is a necessary truth: it not merely is the case but could not have failed to be the case that an act's being an instance of 'causes a person pain' is favorably relevant to its being wrongful.[10] That is, Thomson would presumably say that it's necessarily true that the fact that you promised to do x is a reason for thinking that it would be wrong of you not to do x. That is, when weighing reasons for and against your doing x, necessarily, the fact that you promised to do x weighs in on the side of it's being wrong not to do it, not on the side of its being right not to do it. Similarly, it's necessarily true that the fact that doing y would cause harm is a reason for thinking that doing y would be wrong. Both these are akin to Ross's claim that we have a prima facie duty to keep our promises and not to harm others.

It's not clear whether "It's necessarily true that the fact that an act would cause harm is a reason for thinking it's wrong" means roughly the same as "It's necessarily true that causing harm to others is wrong." (You might want to read that sentence again.) If we say that the unqualified principle "Causing harm to others is wrong" is not absolute, then the two claims may be pretty much equivalent. They're both saying that necessarily, causing harm to others is a wrong-making characteristic. Perhaps a supporter of this view could maintain that that's just part of the meaning of "morally right" and "morally wrong," so that just as "Bachelors are unmarried" is true by definition, so, too, "Causing harm to others is a morally wrong-making characteristic" is true by definition.

Many philosophers deny that any moral claims are necessarily true, even the claim that causing harm to others is a wrong-making characteristic and that keeping a promise is a right-making characteristic. But the concept of necessary truth can be perplexing. There are obvious central cases of necessity, such as "Either it's raining or it's not" and "Raisins are dried grapes." But there are questions at the periphery. Most people say that "Nothing is red all over and blue all over" and "Things equal to the same things are equal to each other"

---

[9]Ibid., 29.

[10]Judith Jarvis Thomson, *The Realm of Rights* (Cambridge, MA: Harvard University Press, 1990), 15.

are necessarily true. Why? Some would even say that "Water freezes at 32 degrees Fahrenheit" is necessarily true because in every possible world in which water exists, it freezes at that temperature. If it freezes at some other temperature, then it's not water.[11] Given the puzzles at the periphery, it may not be easy to determine whether some basic moral principles are necessarily true.

Ross also talks of self-evidence in terms of "direct apprehension." To directly apprehend something is to "apprehend" it without any mediator. Common sense distinguishes between seeing an actor on a television or movie screen and seeing her "in person." Seeing her in person is like direct apprehension, while seeing her on a television or movie screen is like indirect apprehension. Of course, Ross doesn't mean this. But what does he mean? Perhaps he means that we can directly or immediately "see" that a particular action has the property of being prima facie morally right or wrong simply by reflecting on it carefully. We don't need to look at other things in order to "see" its moral rightness or wrongness. However, this view has difficulties. It suggests that we have a kind of sixth sense that enables us to "apprehend" the presence or absence of moral properties, especially if, as Ross seems to say, the moral properties of rightness and wrongness are undefinable.

But there's another thing that Ross may have in mind when he says that certain basic moral principles are self-evident. He may mean self-justifying in one or more of the following two senses.

SELF-EVIDENCE$_W$

A moral principle P is self-evident$_w$ means that necessarily, anyone who understands P, has reflected carefully on it, and believes it on the basis of that reflection, is justified in believing it.

But that gives us a weak sense of justification, being (epistemically) permitted to believe something. That's why we give it the w subscript. A stronger sense of self-evidence would be

SELF-EVIDENCE$_S$

A moral principle P is self-evident$_s$ means that necessarily, everyone who has reflected on and understands P is justified in believing it and is not justified in not believing it.

Thus, we might say that "It's morally wrong to harm people without a good moral reason" is at least self-evident$_w$ in that if you have reflected on it and believe it, then you're justified in believing it. We may find it difficult or impossible to imagine how you could not be justified.

---

[11]This is assuming that "water" is what Saul Kripky calls a "rigid designator."

BRAIN TEASERS

> If you understand and have reflected on "It's morally wrong to harm
> people without good moral reasons" and have come to believe it on
> the basis of that reflection, could you possibly be unjustified in believ-
> ing it? If yes, how or why?

What about self-evidence$_s$? Could we say that if you understand and
have reflected on the principle that it's morally wrong to harm people
without good moral reasons, but do not accept it, then you are not justified in refusing to accept it? That's an open question.

A Social Justification of Basic Moral Principles

Contemporary American philosopher Bernard Gert identifies ten moral
principles or rules that he seems to consider basic in a sense. They are:

1. Don't kill.
2. Don't cause pain.
3. Don't disable.
4. Don't deprive of freedom.
5. Don't deprive of pleasure.
6. Don't deceive.
7. Keep your promises.
8. Don't cheat.
9. Obey the law.
10. Do your duty.[12]

Gert says that the function of moral rules or principles is to minimize
evil.[13] By that he seems to mean that their purpose is to minimize the kind
of things that make social cooperation and interaction extremely difficult
or impossible. If members of a group systematically violated these rules
with respect to each other, the group would almost immediately dissolve.
The members couldn't possibly live together, let alone cooperate for
shared purposes.

According to Gert, "morality is a public system that applies to all
rational persons. A justified or rational morality is a public system that

---

[12]Bernard Gert, *Morality: A New Justification of the Moral Rules* (New York: Oxford
University Press, 1988), 157.
[13]Ibid., 6.

all impartial rational persons would advocate adopting to govern the behavior of all rational persons."[14] That is, morality is a public system, not a private one. We don't invent our own moralities, we learn them. For example, my moral code is by no means unique. It's pretty much the same as the moral code of most other people in my society. I probably agree with most others on far more issues than I disagree with them. I and others both live and judge by the considerable body of moral beliefs that we share. Our morality is a shared resource. I may disagree about some issues, but that may be because of disagreement about what the nonmoral facts are or because of disagreement about how a moral principle that we share should be applied, not because we disagree about basic moral principles.

Our moral code that we share is intended to govern everyone's behavior. It's universal. But in reflecting on moral principles, I must adopt a moral point of view, which is an impartial point of view. If I'm only going to accept principles that will benefit me or people I identify with, such as family members, then I'm not being impartial, I'm being biased. To count as a moral principle for me or our society, I (and others) must have reflected on it from an impartial point of view and have accepted it on the basis of that impartial reflection. Impartial reflection, for example, would not lead me to accept a moral principle that permits discrimination on the basis of race or sex.

BRAIN TEASERS

Should Gert add an eleventh basic rule: Don't discriminate on the basis of irrelevant characteristics?

We're justified in accepting a basic moral principle if after impartial reflection we're willing to publicly accept and defend it as a principle that will apply to everyone. And we count it as a justified moral principle because it is intended to minimize the evils that make social cooperation very difficult or impossible. On the other hand, we're not justified in accepting a basic moral principle if we're not willing to publicly accept and defend it as a principle that will apply to everyone.

Gert's view goes back to David Hume, who pointed out that there is no reason to adopt a moral code or take morality seriously unless it's useful. According to Hume, a moral code can be useful if its adoption by a group enables its members to get along together, if it helps establish conditions conducive to mutual cooperation. As Hume puts it, a moral code is useful if its adoption helps establish or maintain the conditions "by

---

[14]Ibid., 5.

which alone the social confederacy can be maintained, and every man reap the fruits of mutual protection and assistance."[15]

People live together rather than as isolated hermits because they will have better life prospects if they're part of a group that cooperates for mutual advantage. People are better able to survive and flourish as part of a group than as isolated hermits. Aristotle stresses that human beings are social animals; they depend on one another and live in groups as part of a community or society. Thus, the well-being of the individual depends on the health and well-being of the group. The health and well-being of the group depend on how the members treat one another. The function of a moral code is to help establish and maintain the health and well-being of the group to ensure that its members have a decent chance of surviving and flourishing.

If members of a group do not refrain from killing, robbing, and assaulting one another, the group will simply disintegrate. If members of the group don't help one another when the need is great and the cost of helping small, its members won't have a decent chance of surviving and flourishing, and it's likely that the group will disintegrate. Most people in a group must conform to certain fundamental principles most of the time if the group is to survive and if its members are to have a decent chance of surviving and flourishing. The core of any acceptable moral code must be those principles that will ensure the survival of the group or community and the survival and flourishing of its members. According to the view suggested here, a moral code has the function of helping establish and maintain the conditions required for social cohesion, the survival of the group, and the survival and flourishing of its members.

Members and Nonmembers

There is a problem with viewing morality as having the function of preserving the well-being of a group and its members. What of those who are not members of the group? Suppose that a group claims that Gert's ten moral rules apply only to its own members. Thus, suppose that group A claims that its members shouldn't kill each other, but that it's not morally wrong for them to kill nonmembers or "outsiders." It may not be an "evil" that threatens the group's survival. Thus, the moral code of Nazis probably forbade them from killing fellow "Aryans," but didn't forbid them to kill non-Aryans. Racists generally do not treat members of their own race the way they treat members of other races. Those inside the protective circle of the group are first-class citizens of the moral community;

---

[15]David Hume, *An Inquiry Concerning the Principles of Morals* (La Salle, IL: Open Court, 1960), 49.

those outside the circle of the group are often little more than prey to be ignored, exploited, or exterminated.

The following diagram illustrates how widely or narrowly one may define the group and thus the moral community:

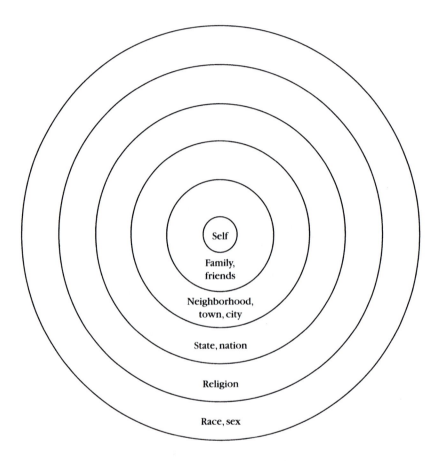

Self

Family, friends

Neighborhood, town, city

State, nation

Religion

Race, sex

Does morality permit limiting the application of the moral rules to members of one's narrowly defined group? Many people deny this. They believe that the circle must be widened to include all human beings. They think that it is arbitrary and therefore unreasonable to limit the protections of morality to some small group defined by race, religion, nationality, or gang affiliation. But further, one might argue that now, no group can survive for long if it treats nonmembers in ways inconsistent with the moral rules. It will create implacable enemies who eventually will find a way to destroy the group that's preying on them. On this view, morality has the function of enabling all people on this planet to live together in harmony and to live decent lives. According to this view, the group that counts is the group made up of all people—at the very least the entire human race.

There's another consideration that makes it dangerous for a group or society to discriminate against some of its members. Groups live in a world where they must interact with other groups. Sometimes those who are in a minority in one group are a majority in another group. Groups that discriminate may trigger intervention by other groups. Such intervention could take the form of economic sanctions or violence. For example, Serb atrocities against ethnic Albanians in the Serbian province of Kosovo led to NATO military action, even though Albanians certainly did not constitute a large percentage of the population of NATO countries.

Reflective Equilibrium

Contemporary American philosopher John Rawls points out that moral justification for individuals often takes the form of a search for what he calls a *reflective equilibrium*. The context seems to be one in which I'm asking myself whether I'm justified in either coming to believe or continuing to believe a moral claim. In some cases the answer may be that I'm justified in believing it in the sense that it's not (epistemically) wrong for me to believe it. In other cases the answer may be that I'm justified in believing it in the much stronger sense that it would be (epistemically) wrong for me to not believe it.

Reflective equilibrium appeals first to the fundamental rational requirement of logical consistency. We start out with a body of beliefs, including moral beliefs. Our moral beliefs include moral principles, such as "Stealing is wrong," and moral judgments about concrete individual cases, such as "It was wrong for John to steal Mary's book." Our goal as rational people is to have a set of beliefs, including our moral beliefs, that is coherent. Coherence entails logical consistency but may include more requirements than consistency. If our set of beliefs include some beliefs that contradict each other, then the set is incoherent.

Rawls points out that the search for a reflective equilibrium is a dynamic rather than static process. In moral justification, we start with the moral beliefs that we have the most confidence in.

> There are questions we feel sure must be answered in a certain way. For example, we are confident that religious intolerance and racial discrimination are unjust. We think that we have examined these things with care and have reached what we believe is an impartial judgment not likely to be distorted by an excessive attention to our own interests. These convictions are *provisional fixed points* which we presume any conception of justice must fit.[16]

---

[16]John Rawls, *A Theory of Justice* (Cambridge, MA: Harvard University Press, 1971), 19–20.

Rawls's discussion is limited to the political/moral concept of justice, but it applies generally to moral justification.

We must start somewhere in justification. We've seen that some philosophers believe that we start with basic moral principles. So far, we've talked as though a basic moral principle must always remain basic. That is, once accepted, it must always be accepted, perhaps because it's necessarily true. Rawls, too, may be taken to suggest that we start with basic moral principles. But Rawls calls them provisional starting points in justification. That is, they may be basic for us when we begin the process of justification, but they may not be basic for us at the end. We may justifiably change our minds about them and reject them, ceasing to believe them at all.

A feeling of certainty is not enough to establish a moral belief as basic, a provisional fixed point. It is important to emphasize the reflective in reflective equilibrium. It must be a principle that we have examined with care from an impartial point of view. And our confidence must be based on the results of that careful reflection. Only then can it legitimately function as a basic moral principle for us.

In justification we then consider individual concrete moral judgments and other moral principles in relation to what we (provisionally) take as basic. If another moral principle is consistent with our basic ones, then we are justified in accepting it. Suppose "Deception is wrong" is basic for me. Recognizing that misstating income on a tax return is a form of deception, I'm justified in believing that it's wrong to misstate one's income on a tax return. On the other hand, I'm not justified in believing that it's not wrong to misstate one's income on a tax return. Similarly for individual concrete moral judgments. I'm not justified in believing that it wouldn't be wrong for me to misstate my income on a tax return.

Sometimes coherence of my set of beliefs can be enhanced because a moral principle would explain a principle that's basic for me. That is, explain in the sense of justify. Suppose that "Deception is wrong" is basic for me. I might wonder why deception is wrong and reason that it's wrong because it harms people. Then I may be justified in believing the principle "It's wrong to harm people" because it explains my basic belief. The justification is even stronger if it explains several of my basic beliefs. Suppose that "Discrimination on the basis of religion is wrong" is basic for me. Why is it wrong? Among other things, it harms people. So "It's wrong to harm people" also explains my basic principle that discrimination on the basis of religion is wrong. Since it explains several of my basic beliefs, I'm justified in believing that it's wrong to harm people.

Reflection may lead me to refine a moral belief. I may realize that there are situations in which it's not wrong to harm people. Imprisoning is a form of harm, but I may have a firm conviction that imprisoning people for committing serious crimes is not wrong. Imprisonment for committing a crime is a good reason to harm someone. Similarly, I may reason that it's wrong to discriminate on the basis of religion, but it's not always wrong to discriminate. If I have one job to fill and there's more than one applicant, I must discriminate among the applicants. I could decide on the basis of any number of features that distinguish the applicants, for example, height, weight, race, sex, religion, hair color, hair length, eye color, experience, skills, test results, class, education, accent, and ethnic background. But I may feel very confident that some features are relevant and others aren't. For example, I may feel very confident that height, weight, and hair and eye color are irrelevant and that it wouldn't make sense to hire someone for a job on such a basis. I may also feel very confident that experience and education are relevant. I may then on reflection recognize that (ordinarily) race isn't relevant to hiring. Not hiring someone for a job she wants harms the person. But if the person chosen is reasonably considered to be more qualified for the job on purely job related features, then a person who is not hired was harmed with good reason. But if an applicant is rejected solely because of her race and race is not a bona fide job related qualification, then she is harmed without good reason. So I may revise my principle from "It's wrong to harm people" to "It's wrong to harm people without good reasons."

But sometimes, reflection can lead us to change our minds about a principle that's basic for us. Suppose I start out feeling very confident that racial discrimination is not wrong and I take it as basic. Presumably it would be based on my belief that some races are inferior to others. First, I may learn things that are inconsistent with my belief that some races are inferior. In that case, I would not be justified in believing that they are and I may recognize this and change my mind. In any case, if I'm no longer justified in believing that some races are inferior to others (even if I still unjustifiably believe it), I'm at the very least less justified in believing that discrimination on the basis of race is not wrong.

But I may have other moral beliefs also inconsistent with the belief that racial discrimination is not wrong. Perhaps I feel very confident that discrimination on the basis of religion is wrong. If I reflect on why it's wrong, I may see that the reasons why religious discrimination is wrong also show that racial discrimination is wrong. So reflection may lead me to change my mind about racial discrimination. Before reflection I took it to be basic for me; after reflection, I ceased believing it. That's why Rawls calls the moral principles that are basic for us provisional fixed points. They may be fixed for us now, but may not be fixed for us later.

According to Rawls, as a moral agent seeking reflective equilibrium, I continually work on making my set of beliefs, including beliefs about moral principles and judgments of individual cases, as coherent as possible. That often requires me to revise my beliefs, including principles I first took to be basic for me. If an alteration in my system of beliefs increases its coherence, then I'm justified in making that alteration.

BRAIN TEASERS

1. Employing reflective equilibrium, are you justified in believing that capital punishment for first-degree murder is not morally wrong?
2. Employing reflective equilibrium, are you justified in believing that it would be wrong for you to cheat?

Feelings and Moral Principles

Perhaps *feelings* have a greater role to play in the adoption of moral principles than we've so far allowed. Some people have said that moral beliefs are based solely on feelings. Perhaps we have certain feelings, either positive or negative, when we consider instances of certain actions, and we generalize on the basis of such feelings. For example, one might have strong negative feelings when reflecting on the case of Kitty Genovese, who was killed over a half hour period while her neighbors ignored her screams for help. On the basis of these negative feelings, such as revulsion, one may judge that it was wrong for her neighbors to ignore her screams. One might then generalize from the individual case, adopting the principle that in similar circumstances one would do wrong if one did the same thing that her neighbors did: not help when the need was great. Thus, moral beliefs would be based solely on our feelings. If someone didn't have feelings of revulsion for the act and of compassion and sympathy for the victim while reflecting on the Kitty Genovese case, then he would probably judge that it wasn't wrong for her neighbors to ignore her screams. And he might believe that in general, it's not wrong to ignore cries for help.

If moral beliefs are based solely on feelings, then they're purely subjective. But perhaps everyone is susceptible to the same feelings when reflecting on the same cases and principles. Hume stresses the importance of emotions and feelings in moral evaluation, but he claims that all human beings have characteristics of benevolence and sympathy; they have negative feelings when they consider instances of other people's being harmed and positive feelings when they consider other people's being benefited. As he puts it, "The view of human happiness or misery . . . excites in our breast a sympathetic movement of pleasure or uneasiness."[17] Hume seems to say that these feelings and susceptibilities are inherent in all humans. However, he also says, "If any man from a cold insensibility, or narrow selfishness of temper, is unaffected with the image of human happiness or misery, he must be equally indifferent to the

---

[17]David Hume, *An Inquiry,* 56.

images of vice and virtue."[18] That seems to suggest that some people can be without these feelings. But Hume maintains that everyone is capable of such feelings: "It . . . cannot be disputed, that there is some benevolence, however small, infused into our bosom; some spark of friendship for human kind; some particle of the dove kneaded into our frame, along with the elements of the wolf and the serpent."[19]

Whether these feelings are as universal as Hume implies is an open question. Surely our experience shows us that in some people, the particles of the wolf and serpent are much stronger than the particles of the dove, if there are any dove particles kneaded in. But what we've said above casts doubt on Hume's claim that moral beliefs are based solely on our feelings. It surely seems possible for someone to have no feelings prompted by reflection on the principle that it's wrong not to help others when the need is great and the cost or risk small, and yet to have the person believe the principle, perhaps because that's what she was taught. (This explains the origin of the belief; it doesn't necessarily justify the belief.) And in reflecting on the Kitty Genovese case, she could believe that it was wrong for Kitty's neighbors to do nothing, solely because she recognizes that a principle she accepts, when applied to this case, yields the conclusion that it was wrong.

However, there is probably at least something right about Hume's view of the role of feelings in moral belief. If someone has no feelings of sympathy or compassion for others, if they don't care about anyone else's pain or happiness, it's not likely that he will adopt moral principles forbidding harm or requiring help. The kind of viciousness exemplified in Kitty Genovese's attacker, who repeatedly stabbed her during three separate episodes over a half hour period, is probably due more to deficiencies in feeling and emotion than to deficiencies in reason. So we shouldn't ignore the role of feelings in moral belief and judgment.

But perhaps we can extend reflective equilibrium to include feelings as well as beliefs. In that case, a responsible moral agent tries to ensure that her feelings and emotions, as well as her beliefs, are coherent. In some cases, that may mean making moral judgments about emotions and feelings. If I believe that cold-blooded murder is morally wrong, but I have no negative feelings when reflecting on real instances of cold-blooded murder, I may judge that my feelings and emotions are inappropriate and that I should feel certain things, such as revulsion at the act and sympathy for the victim. Or suppose I feel revulsion when reflecting on a certain act, but I don't believe that such acts are morally wrong. My feelings may lead me to reconsider my belief. I may take my revulsion as a sign of wrongness and, after further reflection, comparing the belief with

---

[18]Ibid., 56.

[19]Ibid., 60.

other feelings and beliefs, come to revise it. For example, suppose I start out believing that it's not wrong for the strong to prey on the weak. However, I see a bully humiliate someone weaker than him and feel revulsion and outrage at the sight, as well as compassion and sympathy for the bully's victim. In that case, I might reconsider my belief that it's not wrong for the strong to prey on the weak. The feelings alone may lead me to change my mind and come to believe that it is wrong. Or it may lead to reflection. I may have a thought I hadn't had before. I may realize that I would think it wrong for someone stronger to prey on me. Again, that would (or should) lead me to change my mind.

Moral Belief and Action

Morality is not just a matter of belief; it's primarily a matter of action. But moral beliefs are relevant because for many if not most of us, our moral beliefs guide and influence our actions. If I believe that murder is morally wrong, my moral belief may motivate me to refrain from committing murder. If you believe that sex outside marriage is morally wrong, that may motivate you to refrain from sex until marriage.

Some people do wrong things because they don't believe that what they're doing is morally wrong. For example, someone may discriminate on the basis of race because he doesn't believe that it's morally wrong. However, some people do wrong things even when they believe it's morally wrong. For example, someone may believe that rape is wrong, yet rape anyway. How are we to explain situations where someone believes that an action is morally wrong but does it anyway?

Common sense tells us that in such cases, self-interest triumphs over our moral beliefs. In some cases, it's because of what Aristotle called weakness of will. Self-interest weighs in on the side of the wrong thing and it's too strong for us to resist. Our desire to do the wrong thing (e.g., rape) is stronger than our desire to do the right thing (not rape). We don't have enough willpower to resist the temptation of self-interest—the pleasure or satisfaction we'll get from the act—even though we believe that we should try to resist the temptation because the act is morally wrong.

BRAIN TEASERS

Can you think of any times when you have exhibited such weakness of will? What were the episodes like?

But sometimes people take a different view. They don't think that they should try to resist the temptations of self-interest. They think that they should ignore their moral beliefs. In a sense, they say to themselves, "The hell with morality. Who cares if something is wrong? I'm going to do it anyway."

This is different from weakness of will. When doing wrong is due to weakness of will, people generally feel guilty, remorseful, perhaps even angry with themselves. They may vow to try to do better at resisting temptation in the future. But if doing wrong is due to an attitude of "Who cares about morality? I don't," then one will not feel guilt or remorse. One won't vow to do better. Such a person is an Amoralist.

Why Be Moral? The Challenge of Amoralism

An Amoralist refuses to take moral beliefs as good reasons for action. He takes the attitude, "I don't care if it's morally wrong. There are no good reasons to be moral. Being moral is for suckers. I'll do what's in my self-interest." The Amoralist is different from the moral egoist. Moral egoists believe that it's not really wrong to do anything if it's in our self-interest. But Amoralists believe that many things in their self-interest are really morally wrong. And Amoralists, as I'm using the term, are different from moral nihilists. Moral nihilists have no moral beliefs. But Amoralists do. It's just that Amoralists refuse to act on their moral beliefs.

Some Amoralists take the position that the only good reasons for action are self-interested reasons. If something is in my self-interest, that's a good reason for doing it; if something is not in my self-interest, that's a good reason for not doing it. Now if something is morally wrong, Amoralists say that's not a good reason for not doing it. Similarly, if not doing something is wrong, that's not a good reason for doing it. So if rape is in my self-interest because it gives me pleasure, that's a good reason for doing it. However, if rape is morally wrong, that's not a good reason for not doing it.

Amoralists who take this view say that if moral requirements or prohibitions can be shown to be in their self-interests, then they are good reasons for action. If they can't, then they're not. So suppose we can show that raping, while in his immediate self-interest, is not in his long-run self-interest because of the high risk of being caught and punished. The Amoralist may conform his behavior to the moral principle that rape is wrong by not raping. But he doesn't refrain from raping because he believes it's wrong; he refrains from raping because he believes that it's not in his long-term self-interest.

Many philosophers have tried to justify a system of moral principles by trying to show that it's in a person's self-interest to live by them. They answer the Amoralist's question, "Why be moral?" by trying to show that it's in his self-interest to be moral. But there's one problem with this strategy. The arguments almost always show that it's in the Amoralist's self-interest to appear to others to be moral but not necessarily to actually be moral. If you appear to others to be honest, you'll benefit as much, perhaps even more, than if you actually are honest. If you're dishonest when you're not likely to be caught, you'll often benefit more than if you had been honest. Of course, one might try to persuade the Amoralist that it's always in his long-term self-interest to be moral because if he's not, God will punish him after death and God can't be fooled the way human beings can. But if the Amoralist doesn't believe this, it will have no effect.

One way to counter the Amoralist is to deny that self-interest is the only good reason for action. We may say that believing that something is morally wrong really is a good reason for not doing it. But we may have to rest content with a fairly modest conclusion. That is, if I'm not an Amoralist, then my moral beliefs are good reasons for action for me. If the Amoralist says they're not good reasons for anyone, I can deny that since I provide a counterexample; they are good reasons for me. If the Amoralist goes on to say that they may be good reasons for me but they shouldn't be, that it's unreasonable or unjustified to count moral beliefs as good reasons for action, I can simply deny that. I'm justified in the sense that reason at least permits me to count them as good reasons for action. There's no argument that the Amoralist can advance that could show that I'm not justified in counting moral beliefs as good reasons for action. I'm on firm ground.

However, I may have no grounds for saying that the Amoralist must take his moral beliefs as good reasons for his actions. Just as I'm justified in taking mine as good reasons, he may be justified in refusing to take his as good reasons. He may have no other reasons that would require him to accept his moral beliefs as good reasons for his actions. Thus, we may not be able to persuade the Amoralist to change his mind. But the Amoralist shouldn't be able to persuade us moralists to change our minds. We're justified in being and remaining moralists, just as he may be justified in remaining an Amoralist. The fact that we can't persuade him to agree with us does not show that we're not justified in being moralists.

BRAIN TEASERS

Are you a moralist or an Amoralist? Why?

How would you answer the question, "Why be moral?"

It's possible that Amoralists refuse to act on their moral beliefs because they lack feelings of compassion or sympathy and have no attitude of respect for others. We've seen that according to one influential model, actions are explained by appeal to the agent's beliefs and desires. Neither kind of reason alone can cause action. Thus, moral beliefs will lead to action only if the agent has the right desires. In this case, the right desire may be the desires to do the morally right thing and not do the morally wrong thing. If I believe that it would be wrong to steal but I don't desire to refrain from doing the wrong thing, then my belief won't affect my actions. Many agents may have the desire to do the right thing only because they have the right feelings, emotions, and attitudes, because they have sympathy, compassion, and respect for others.

  G. J. WARNOCK

THE OBJECT OF MORALITY

1. Some Options in Ethics

. . . Even a very sketchy acquaintance with history and anthropology may make one hesitate to assume that there is *any* way of behaving, considered, say, wrong at one time and place, which has not been considered unobjectionable, or even virtuous, at another. Deliberate killing, for instance, one might take to be an extreme case of, surely, undesirable conduct; but there have certainly been societies in which the deliberate, unprovoked killing of strangers was regarded as not merely unobjectionable, but positively meritorious.

However, it is plainly absurd, though it is sometimes done, to present this nearly limitless diversity as if it were a bald, brute, irreducible fact, insusceptible of explanation, as perhaps are, for instance, some differences of aesthetic taste. For it is really quite obvious that these differences of view, with their consequent differences of prevalent modes of behaviour, are at least in large part *consequences* of other differences—of, for instance, differences in belief about the natural consequences of actions, or, perhaps even more importantly, the supernatural consequences. A propensity to decapitate strangers is not really surprising in one who is convinced, however absurdly, that a regular supply of severed heads is a necessary condition of the survival and prosperity of his tribe;

and at a less exotic level, it is clear that at least some differences about, for instance, sexual morals are the result of divergent beliefs about the consequences, social or psychological, or various sorts of sexual behaviour—beliefs incidentally which, in many cases, are very far from being able to claim the dignity of knowledge. Then it is also plainly relevant that what, in human character and conduct, is *needed* for success, and even for survival, varies very widely in different social and physical conditions. Men living in, say, a prosperous commercial society in conditions of settled peace may not greatly esteem, because they will not encounter the need for, those traits and qualities of character that are most highly valued by, say, horse-breeding nomads, or jungle-dwellers, or sea-going brigands. So that consciousness, which indeed it is desirable to have, of the huge diversity of views that have been held as to good and bad, right and wrong, in human character and conduct, should be tempered by recognition that there is no reason to suppose that the *basis* of such views is correspondingly diversified. People who hold very different beliefs, particularly perhaps supernatural beliefs, and who live their lives in very different conditions and in the face of very different demands, would quite naturally arrive, on the very same basis of appraisal, at wholly different practical conclusions. . . .

From *The Object of Morality* (London: Methuen, 1971).

2. The Human Predicament

Moral concepts come into a certain kind, or perhaps one should say certain kinds, of evaluation. By this I do not mean to say that there is any one thing which we use them in doing, but only that "evaluation" is a good enough name for what, in one way or another, they have in general to do with. Moral discourse, in which moral concepts are employed, has to do, in one way or another, with issues about what is good or bad, right or wrong, to be commended or condemned. Obviously there is evaluation that is not moral. Good weather is not morally good; the wrong way to sew on a button is not morally wrong; commendation of your style as a golfer, or of you for your style as a golfer, would not be moral commendation. What morality has to do with is a *kind* of evaluation. The question, *what* kind, is, I suppose, just the question to which most of this book is intended to suggest an answer. Let us begin with a simpler question: evaluation of what? There is perhaps no very useful short answer to this question; but if we had to give one, the best answer, though it immediately calls for some qualification, seems to be: the actions of rational beings. Why "actions"? Well, it is clearly not *only* actions that are ever the topic of moral thought, or moral discussion or remark. Failures to act perhaps scarcely need separate mention. But also, people may be said to be morally good or bad; so may their characters or their motives, or their feelings; so may practices and institutions; perhaps even objects sometimes, like books or pictures. But it seems reasonable to say that, even in these other cases, some more or less direct reference to actions is always present, and is fundamental. A person is morally good or bad primarily at least because of what he does or omits to do. A morally bad character is a disposition to act morally badly, or wrongly. Motives typically, and feelings often, tend to issue in actions. A morally objectionable institution, like slavery perhaps or an oppressive system of law or government, is morally objectionable in that it permits, or even requires, things to be done that morally ought not to be done, or prevents things being

done that should be done. . . . So it seems that, when moral issues come up, there is always involved, more or less directly, some questions of the doings or non-doings of rational beings. Why "rational beings"? Why not simply say "people," or "human beings"? The distinction is perhaps not a very important one, in practice at any rate; but still, it does seem to be the case that what makes "people" eligible for consideration, and sometimes for judgement, as moral agents is that they are in a certain sense rational, and not that they constitute a particular biological species, that of humans. For one's doings to be a proper or possible object of moral evaluation whether by others or by oneself, it is a necessary condition that one should have at least some ability to perceive and consider alternative courses of action, to appreciate what is to be said for or against the alternatives, to make a choice or decision, and to act accordingly. . . .

To be rational in this sense, then, rather than simply to be human, is a necessary condition for one's doings or non-doings to be a proper object of moral evaluation. . . . It is perhaps . . . conceivable that the circumstances of life of some species of rational beings might have been such that no moral issues ever arose for them. If, for instance, though rational, they were all completely impassive, completely invulnerable, completely self-sufficient, not significantly affected in any way by anything that went on around them, and having to do with no sentient beings of any other sort, then it is perhaps hard to see how any of their doings could be judged morally better or worse than any alternatives. It would seem to make no difference of any morally assessable sort. However, it is surely of no great importance to decide this question; for we know well enough that human beings, who are in fact the only sort of rational beings we commonly encounter, are not like this, either by nature or with respect to their circumstances. So we may leave these rather fanciful speculations on one side, and move on to what we all actually know something about, that is, what may conveniently, if portentously, be called the "human predicament."

I had better make clear at once why I want to bring in, and indeed to start from, this perhaps archaic-looking topic. My idea is this. In general we evaluate things, it is to be supposed, for certain purposes; whenever, in any field, we rank or grade, commend or condemn, and so forth, we have—or should have, if there is to be any sense in what we are doing—some object in view, and quite possibly more than one. . . . Evaluation is surely never just pointless; at the very least, even if we may sometimes have no practical purpose in view, it will be because we have some *preference* as between one thing and another that we bother at all to evaluate items of that kind. Further, it seems to be that to understand some species of evaluation (as contrasted perhaps with mastering it as a mere drill) is essentially a matter of grasping what its object is, what it is done *for; and indeed if—only* if—one understands this, can one be in any position to assess the appropriateness, or even relevance, of the standards and criteria employed.

Consider, for instance, the "grading" of candidates in a school-leaving examination. Clearly, in considering how this is or should be done, it is essential to be clear as to what it is being done for. Is it the object, for instance, to determine and indicate how well candidates are judged to *have* done certain work at school? Or is it, differently, to indicate how well they are judged *likely* to do certain things in future, for instance in employment or at universities? Conceivably one might hold that these come to the same, on the ground that what a candidate has done is the only sound, or only assessable, indicator of what he may be expected to do; but if that is not so, clearly the two objects would make appropriate and relevant the employment of different criteria. Then again, it might be the object, or part of the object, to reward or reprove, encourage or stimulate, the examinees themselves; and this too would make "grading" a different sort of exercise.

Now it is not impossible to raise the question: what is *moral* evaluation for? What is its point? Why do we distinguish between, say, actions as morally right or wrong, between people or qualities of character as good or bad?

Why do we teach children to do this, by precept or example? Why do we think it worth doing? What are we trying to achieve, or bring about, by doing it? Well, it is by and large—with qualifications already noted—evaluation *of* the actions of rational beings. It does not seem plausible that in doing this we are simply, so to speak, disinterestedly awarding marks, for no particular reason or purpose, to ourselves or others. There is, it seems obvious here, some general practical end in view; and if so, it may seem manifest that the general object must be to bring it about, in some way or other, that rational beings act, in some respects or other, *better* than they would otherwise be liable to do. Put more pompously, the general object of moral evaluation must be to contribute in some respects, by way of the actions of rational beings, to the amelioration of the human predicament—that is, of the conditions in which *these* rational beings, humans, actually find themselves. . . . How are things liable to go wrong? And how exactly—or, perhaps, plausibly—can morality be understood as a contribution to their going better? . . .

It seems reasonable, and in the present context is highly relevant, to say, without necessarily going quite so far as Hobbes did, that the human predicament is inherently so, but not completely hopelessly so; that is, there are circumstances, not in the least likely to change significantly or to be changed by our own efforts, which cannot but tend to make things go badly, but also something at least can be done, many different things in fact, to make them go at least somewhat better than they would do, if no such things were done at all.

In the first place, a human being as a certain kind of animal has what may be called biological needs. The life-span of humans is in any case limited, but if a person is to survive at all he must have air and water, usually shelter, and appropriate food, and he must not be subjected to gross physical damage. Apart from this there are countless other things which, while not absolute needs for every member of the species, can reasonably be regarded as indispensable enough, and indispensable for enough humans, to be called needs also. Then, in addition to and overlapping with the things that people need, there are the things that they want. . . . Although there may be some things that almost every human being wants (but does not absolutely need), there is obviously also almost endless personal diversity in wants, attributable to differences of circumstances, information, and individual character and aims, or to pure vagaries of taste and fancy. . . . Now some human needs, wants, and interests are, special and exceptional circumstances apart, just naturally satisfied by the human environment and situation, and others frustrated. For instance, there is naturally available in the atmosphere of the planet, without any intervention of ours, enough air for everybody to breathe (not always clean air, but that is another matter); and there are doubtless some things that people want to do, or perhaps would like to do, or wish that they could do, which are simply physically impossible—either completely so, for everybody, or impossible in certain conditions, or for certain people. But, uncontroversially, over an enormous range of needs, wants, and interests, these are neither just naturally satisfied, nor naturally, ineluctably frustrated. In an enormous range of cases, something both needs to be done, and also at least in principle could be done. And of course this is where practical problems arise.

. . . At least as serious is the fact that the resources needed for doing things, again both in large matters and small, are practically always limited; not everything that is needed, or wanted, or would be advantageous can be done at the same time, or even could ever be done at all. This means, of course, that some "satisfactions" must be postponed to others, with consequent problems about priorities; and some, no doubt, cannot possibly be secured at all.

. . . In practice people cannot but be often in competition with other people; practically at any rate, even if not in Utopian theory, it is often the case that the full or even partial satisfaction of one, or some, is attainable only at the expense of others—that is, by bringing about a situation which in some degree frustrates or does not wholly satisfy them. Nor, it

seems, is this simply a practical difficulty of limited resources; for just as the wants, etc., of a single individual do not necessarily form a set such that satisfaction of all of them is possible even logically, the same may be true of the wants, etc., of pairs or of any larger groups of people. If, for instance, you want to exert absolute domination over me, and I over you, it is not logically possible that both these wants should be fully satisfied; and similarly if, say, you want exclusive possession of some particular thing that I possess, and want too.

. . . Human knowledge and intelligence set limits of one sort to what *can* be done; and limits of another sort are set by limited resources. Given these limitations, there is no practical possibility of everyone's having everything that he wants, or would be the better for having, or even perhaps everything that he needs. But further, there is not merely a practical difficulty here, however insuperable; for, whether for an individual or for a group (or, for that matter, for groups of groups), there is no reason to believe that total satisfaction is even a logical possibility. People may have, both as individuals and as members of groups, wants and even interests the joint satisfaction of which is not logically possible.

But of course that is not all that may reasonably depress us. Even if what we have vaguely called total satisfaction is not a practical or even a logical possibility, there is reason to think that there is a practical possibility of a good deal of satisfaction—practical, that is, from the point of view of available resources and known technical feasibility. We have been assured by a variety of prophets, in the H. G. Wells or (in some moods) Bertrand Russell manner, that, notwithstanding the perplexing diversity of people's interests and wants, and the doubtless lesser variety of their actual needs, there exist both the resources and the technical capacity to go at least a very considerable way towards the general satisfaction of the inhabitants of our planet, and not only in grossly material respects; and, discounting a little the blue-skies fervour characteristic of such prophets, there is no reason wholly to disbelieve what they say. But of course there are snags; and these have to do with certain further facts about human beings.

We have already mentioned, as limiting factors, limited resources, limited information, limited intelligence. What we need now to bring in might be called limited rationality, and limited sympathies. In the first place it may be said—certainly with extreme vagueness, but still with pretty evident truth—that human beings in general are not just naturally disposed always to do what it would be best that they should do, even if they see, or are perfectly in a position to see, what that is. Even if they are not positively neurotic or otherwise maladjusted, people are naturally somewhat prone to be moved by short-run rather than long-run considerations, and often by the pursuit of more blatant, intense, and obtrusive satisfactions rather than of those cooler ones that on balance would really be better. While mostly "rational" in the minimal sense mentioned above—that is, able in at least some degree to envisage practical alternatives, to deliberate, and to decide—they are not all just naturally, or indeed in any other way, rational in the more exacting sense of being regularly disposed to deliberate well and to act accordingly. And this is so, of course, even where a person has to consider no interests, wants, or needs but his own.

Next, limited sympathies. This may even be too mild a term for some of the things that I have in mind. One may say for a start, mildly, that most human beings have some natural tendency to be more concerned about the satisfaction of their own wants, etc., than those of others. A man who does not like being hungry, and who is naturally inclined to take such steps as he can to satisfy his hunger, may very well care less, even not at all, about the hunger of others, and may not care at all whether anything is done to satisfy them. Even if he does care to some extent about others, it is quite likely to be only about *some* others—family, friends, class, tribe, country, or "race." There is also, besides complete or comparative indifference, such a thing as active malevolence, perhaps even purely disinterested malevolence; a man will sometimes be not only unconcerned about, but actively malevolent towards, others whom he may see as somehow in competition with himself, and sometimes perhaps even towards some whose frustrations or sufferings are not even supposed to be for the advancement of any interest of his own. There are two obvious ways in which, consequently, things in the human predicament are liable to go badly. For people are not simply confronted, whether as individuals or groups, with the problems of getting along satisfactorily in material conditions that may, in varying degrees, be ungenial or hostile. They are also highly vulnerable to other people; and they often need the help of other people. But, given "limited sympathies," it cannot be assumed that needed help will naturally be forthcoming; and it cannot even be assumed that active malevolence will *not* be forthcoming. And perhaps above all, there may be the impossibility of trust. Whether, in pursuit of some end of my own, I need your help, or merely your non-interference, I may well be unable to trust you either to co-operate or to keep out of it, if I think that you are not only much less concerned about my ends and interests than your own, but possibly even actively hostile to my attainment of my ends. If so, then it may be impossible for either of us to do, either separately or together, things that would be advantageous to use both, and which perhaps we both clearly see would be advantageous to us both; and it may be necessary for us individually to do things, for instance in self-protection, the doing of which may be exceedingly laborious, wasteful, and disagreeable. It will be obvious that all this applies as fully to relations between groups as between individuals; and indeed that distrust and active hostility between groups has been, in the human predicament, as frequent and constant as between individuals, and vastly more damaging. . . .

. . . Then, finally, they are vulnerable to others, and dependent on others, and yet inevitably often in competition with others; and, human sympathies being limited, they may often neither get nor give help that is needed, may not manage to co-operate for common ends, and may be constantly liable to frustration or positive injury from directly hostile interference by other persons. Thus it comes about that—as Hobbes of course most memorably insisted—there is in what may be called the human predicament a certain "natural" tendency for things to go very badly; meaning thereby not, of course, in this connection, *morally* badly, but badly merely in the sense that, given the abovementioned wholly indisputable facts about people and the circumstances in which they exist, there is the very evident possibility of very great difficulty in securing, for all or possibly even any of them, much that they want, much that it would be in their interest to have, even much that they need. . . .

. . . It is only, after all, in comparatively unusual cases that the means of reasonable human existence are just ineluctably, physically unavailable (though it should not be forgotten that this may not always be the case); nor, one may well think (though possibly future generations will think differently), are many of the major ills of the human predicament more than partially attributable to sheer lack of knowledge and technical skills. One may well think that by far the most important matter is the poor use, or positive misuse, of resources and skills that for the most part are quite readily available; and it seems that this must be laid, in one way or another, at the door of limited rationality and limited sympathies. . . .

But now, if limited rationality and limited sympathies are crucial, which is one to regard as the more important of the two? Perhaps it is not very sensible to attempt a definite answer to this question, if only because in practice these two factors are extraordinarily difficult to disentangle from one another. One might be inclined, pursuing much of the same train of thought as in the last paragraph, to see limited sympathies as fundamental; for a man may be wholly rational, clear-headed, sane, and still, if he is not to act destructively towards others, it is essential that he should not simply see, but care, what becomes of them. Or again, if one society or group is not to oppress another, it is surely fundamental that it should not be either hostile or indifferent to that other's interests. Thus one may feel some sympathy with the common run of

uplifting—if unpractical—discourses about the fundamental necessity for improvement of a "change of heart." But one may also feel, rightly, for two reasons, that such discourses over-simplify. In the first place, much that is most damagingly done seems really attributable, not to the malevolence of men, but to sheer folly and confusion of mind; some wars, for example, though not indeed all wars, may well seem not so much wicked as nearly insane, owing far more to short-sightedness, thoughtlessness, and muddle than to actual ill-will. So one may sometimes feel that there is plenty of good-will about, plenty of humane intentions, if only men were saner in seeing how to bring them to bear. But secondly, is it not the case that much failure of human sympathy is itself the direct offspring of un-reason? Racial hostility, for instance, is not merely—though of course it is—a gross defect of human sympathy; it is also—in common no doubt with many other hatreds, hostilities, and fears—a gross deformation of rationality. If people were saner, their sympathies also would be less stunted and deformed; hearts would be in much better shape if heads were less tangled, and haunted, and befogged. Surely it has been a very common failing of moralists, professionally pre-occupied with the weakness of good-will in human affairs, enormously to under-rate the strength in that connection, not simply of ill-will, but of sheer un-reason. It is possible conceptually to distinguish one from the other, and in practice sometimes to recognize one in the other's absence. But so often they go together, each playing into the other's hand, and perhaps not realistically to be ranked in any order of precedence.

Precedence, though, in what respect? It may well be the case that, as things are, rationality may be in shorter world supply than human sympathy, so that what we need more of at the moment is rationality. Nevertheless, there still seems to be a good case for the contention that something like (not, I hasten to say, exactly like) Kant's "goodwill" is more fundamental still. If, for instance, I believe that you are both ready and able at any time to sacrifice me and my interests to the pursuit of your own, I shall not be reassured by any decrease in your muddle-headedness—unless, indeed, as might very well not be the case, in an unmuddled perspective the sacrifice of me would be seen to be irrational from your point of view. Rationality in fact seems, like intelligence and skill and resources, to be something that can be used to do harm (at least to some) as well as good; what is ultimately crucial is *how* it is to be used. Nothing in the end, then, seems to be more important, in the inherent liability to badness of the human predicament, than that limitation which I have called, vaguely enough, "limited sympathies."

Now, the general suggestion that (guardedly) I wish to put up for consideration is this: that the "general object" of morality, appreciation of which may enable us to *understand* the basis of moral evaluation, is to contribute to betterment—or non-deterioration—of the human predicament, primarily and essentially by seeking to countervail "limited sympathies" and their potentially most damaging effects. It is the proper business of morality, and the general object of moral evaluation, not of course to add to our available resources, nor—directly anyway—to our knowledge of how to make advantageous use of them, nor—again, not directly—to make us more rational in the judicious pursuit of our interests and ends; its proper business is to expand our sympathies, or, better, to reduce the liability to damage inherent in their natural tendency to be narrowly restricted. We may note at once that, if this is, as I think, in a sense the most important of the built-in tendencies of things to go wrong, the present suggestion fits well with the common idea that there is something peculiarly *important* about morality. But that is too vague to be much use. The only way, I suppose, to see whether there is anything much in this suggestion—to see whether it illuminates the nature of "the moral point of view"—is to see what follows from this general supposition, how it works out, and whether what it would imply is closely consonant enough with what we already think we know about moral judgement. It must be remembered, of course, that quite different ways of looking at the matter might quite well issue in just the same implications, so that argument of this pattern is certain not demonstrative. But we may give it a try, and see how persuasive we can make it look.

Questions for Discussion and Review

1. Is "It's morally wrong to harm people without good reasons" true? Is it self-evident?

2. Is it ever wrong to break a promise? Is it always wrong to break a promise? Why?

3. Is it ever wrong to lie? Is it always wrong to lie? Why?

4. Try constructing an argument to justify racial discrimination, then an argument against racial discrimination. Which argument is stronger? Why?

5. Is it morally wrong to discriminate against people on the basis of sexual orientation? Why/Why not?

6. Joan heard Kitty Genovese's screams for help and did nothing. She didn't even call the police. Did she do anything morally wrong?

7. If something is legal, does it follow that it's not morally wrong?

8. Imagine that you've been asked to create a moral code for a group of people who wish to live together and cooperate for mutual benefit. What would be some of the principles that you would include in this code?

9. White settlers in the Smokey Valley are preparing to attack Native Americans to drive them off the land. When challenged, the settlers claim that what they are doing is not morally wrong because the Native Americans are "nothing but savages." What would you say to them?

10. Brad says that because the thought of homosexual behavior revolts him, he knows it's morally wrong. How do you respond?

11. Suppose you believe that suicide assistance is morally wrong, but when you reflect on making a very sick person with no chance of recovery stay alive against her will, knowing that her condition will get even worse, you feel uneasy. How might you deal with this?

12. Are there any good reasons to be moral?

Suggestions for Further Reading

Steven M. Cahn and Joram G. Haber. *20th Century Ethical Theory.* Englewood Cliffs, NJ: Prentice-Hall, 1995. An excellent anthology of the most influential works in moral philosophy in this century.

R. M. Hare. *Freedom and Reason.* Oxford: Oxford University Press, 1963. An influential exposition of the role of universality in moral judgments, suitable mainly for advanced students.

David Hume. *An Enquiry Concerning the Principles of Morals.* Indianapolis: Hackett, 1977. A highly readable introduction to Hume's views on the nature of moral judgment and the roles of reason and emotion.

Walter Sinnott-Armstrong and Mark Timmons, eds. *Moral Knowledge? New Readings in Moral Epistemology.* New York: Oxford University Press, 1996. An excellent anthology of recent writing on moral truth, knowledge, and argument.

G. J. Warnock. *Contemporary Moral Philosophy.* New York: St. Martin's Press, 1967. A well-written introduction to influential twentieth-century views of moral judgments and moral reasoning.

TWO THEORIES OF RIGHT AND WRONG

10

Objectives

Readers are expected to:

- understand and be able to apply the Greatest Happiness version of Act Utilitarianism.
- understand and be able to apply Negative Act Utilitarianism.
- understand and be able to apply Rule Utilitarianism.
- understand and be able to apply the Universal Law formulation of Kant's Categorical Imperative.
- understand and be able to apply the Respect for Persons formulation of Kant's Categorical Imperative.

Introduction

What we might call common sense morality embodies two strands of moral thinking. One is that right and wrong are solely dependent on consequences. If the good consequences of an action outweigh the bad, it's the right thing to do; if the bad consequences outweigh the good, it's the wrong thing to do. On this view, we should do what has the best consequences. The other strand is golden rule reasoning. We could express it as a rule: "Treat others the way you want to be treated." Or we could express it as the principle: "It's wrong to treat people in ways that you wouldn't want to be treated." According to these strands of common sense morality, there's one basic moral principle, although they differ on what that principle is. Let's look first at the strand of common sense morality that says that right and wrong depend only on consequences.

Consequentialism

Consequentialism is the view that moral right and wrong depend only on consequences. For example, suppose there's a debate about capital punishment and someone says that it's morally right solely because its good consequences outweigh the bad—it saves innocent lives by reducing the murder rate and only leads to the death of people who have committed heinous crimes. The person is judging the moral issue as a consequentialist. Similarly, suppose someone says that gambling isn't really morally wrong because no one is harmed by it and the people who engage in it do so voluntarily because they want to. She's judging from a consequentialist position; She's saying that it's not wrong because the bad consequences don't outweigh the good consequences.

Moral Egoism is a consequentialist position. According to moral egoists, if the good consequences for me outweigh the bad consequences for me, it's the morally right thing to do. But many people say that's not really judging from a moral point of view, which is supposed to be impartial. I'm only considering the consequences to me. What if I benefit from robbing you? The consequences may be good for me, but they're bad for you. The most influential consequentialist position is Utilitarianism, which is opposed to Moral Egoism.

Utilitarianism

Would it be morally wrong for me to rob you if I'll benefit and you'll be harmed? Unlike Moral Egoism, Utilitarianism says that I must take into account not merely the consequences for me, but the consequences for everyone who will probably be affected by my action. Thus, suppose that the loss to you will be greater than the benefit to me. Because my action leads to more harm than good, it's the morally wrong thing to do. There would be more total good consequences if I don't rob you than there would be if I do rob you. On the other hand, if the benefit to me would be greater than the harm to you, it's the right thing to do. That could happen if, for example, I'm poor and need the money to buy food for my family and me so we won't starve, while you're rich and you'd use the money for gambling (and would probably lose it).

But I can't limit my thinking to you and me. I have to take into account everyone who will probably be affected by the action. Your family and friends might be affected by my robbing you. How? Your family may be called on to replace the money I've stolen. That's less money for them. They'll surely feel bad about your being robbed; they'll feel sorrow, sympathy, and compassion for you and anger toward the robber. They'll probably feel heightened insecurity and fear at a robbery happening to someone close to them because it means it could happen to them. So not only would you be harmed, but people who care about you would be harmed.

Others also might be affected, depending on what I'll use the money for. If I use it to buy drugs, the drug dealer will benefit. But in benefiting the drug dealer, I may be harming those who will be harmed by the drug dealer. If I use the money to buy an automatic weapon to employ in robbing banks, people I rob or kill will be harmed. On the other hand, if I use it to finance an operation for my dying mother to save her life, she is benefited, as are the medical personnel and institutions that get paid for their services. In applying Utilitarianism, I must sum up all the gains or benefits to everyone who will probably be affected, and sum up all the losses or harms to everyone who will probably be affected. If the benefits are greater than the harms, it's the right thing to do; if the harms are greater than the benefits, it's the wrong thing to do.

What Are Good Consequences and Bad Consequences?

Different Utilitarians have different conceptions of good consequences and bad consequences. Some insist that only pleasure is a good consequence and only pain is a bad consequence. Thus, they would say that the right thing to do is the action that will produce the most pleasure or the least pain. Others claim that only happiness counts as a good consequence and only unhappiness as a bad consequence. They say that the right thing to do is the action that, of the alternatives available, will produce the most happiness or least unhappiness. Still others use a wider concept, well-being. According to them, an increase in well-being is a good consequence and a decrease in well-being a bad consequence. They say that the right thing to do is the action that, of the available alternatives, will produce the greatest increase in well-being or the least decrease in well-being.

We'll use the wider concept of well-being: increased well-being is a benefit (+), and decreased well-being is a harm (−). But what counts as increased well-being and decreased well-being? I think we'll agree that death, pain, illness (physical and mental), disability, failure to satisfy one's needs and desires, and restricted freedom reduce well-being and their opposites increase well-being. Our commonsense notions of well-being will suffice.

Whose Well-Being Counts?

Utilitarians say that everyone's well-being counts, and counts equally. From an impartial point of view I cannot say that my well-being counts but yours doesn't, or that White people's well-being counts more than the well-being of people of color. We're all morally equal.

Act Utilitarianism (AU)

There are two different utilitarian theories: *Act Utilitarianism* (AU) and *Rule Utilitarianism* (RU). Let's look at AU first, starting with the most common form of AU that we can call the Greatest Happiness version.

John Stuart Mill and the Greatest Happiness Version of AU   John Stuart Mill (1806–1873), probably the most influential of the early British utilitarians, summed up the theory in this way. "The creed which accepts as the foundation of morals, Utility, or the Greatest Happiness Principle, holds that actions are right in proportion as they tend to promote happiness, wrong as they tend to promote the reverse of happiness."[1] According to Mill, "the conduct which, under any given circumstances, is objectively right, is that which will produce the greatest balance of good over evil in the universe."

Mill continues, "The happiness which forms the utilitarian standard of what is right in conduct is not the agent's own happiness, but that of all concerned. As between his own happiness and that of others, utilitarianism requires him to be as strictly impartial as a disinterested and benevolent spectator."[2]

Mill's theory has been called Act Utilitarianism (AU). Perhaps we should call it, though, the Greatest Happiness version of Act Utilitarianism. The core of it is the claim that the morally right thing to do is what will "produce the greatest balance of good over evil in the universe." But what does that mean?

Suppose that you did act A and doing A produced more total well-being than would have been produced if you hadn't done A. According to the Greatest Happiness version of AU, it seems that doing A was the right thing to do and not doing A would have been the wrong thing to do. However, we have to ask, "Did doing A produce the greatest balance of good over evil in the universe?" To answer that question, I can't simply look at the difference between doing and not doing A. I have to look at what other alternative actions I could have done. Suppose at that time I could have done acts B, C, and D, as well as A, and suppose that if I had done B instead of A, even more total well-being would have been produced. In that case, doing B was the right thing, not doing A.

We can sum up the Greatest Happiness version of AU in the following way.

GREATEST HAPPINESS VERSION OF AU

An action is morally right if and only if it would produce more total well-being than any alternative action.

We must do the following to apply the Greatest Happiness version of AU:

1.   Identify the alternative actions.

2.   Identify who is likely to be affected by each alternative.

---

[1]John Stuart Mill, "Utilitarianism," in *Essential Works of John Stuart Mill*, ed. Max Lerner (New York: Bantam Books, 1961), 194.

[2]Ibid., 204.

3. Determine for each alternative action and for each person affected, whether her well-being will be increased (+) or decreased (−).

4. Determine by how much each individual's well-being will increase or decrease.

5. Determine which alternative will probably have the greatest total well-being.

The action that will produce the greatest amount of total well-being is the morally right thing to do.

Suppose you could either go to a movie or visit your elderly aunt, who's alone and ill. Going to the movie would give you more satisfaction and happiness, but your aunt would be disappointed and sad if you didn't visit her. Suppose we've calculated the increases and decreases in well-being and have come up with the accompanying table. The first line represents your increase or decrease in well-being from (1) going to the movie or (2) visiting your aunt. The second line represents your aunt's increase or decrease in well-being. The third line represents the total change in well-being resulting from each action.

	GO TO MOVIE	VISIT AUNT
You	+10	−5
Aunt	−20	+25
TOTAL	−10	+20

According to the Greatest Happiness version of AU, the right thing to do is visit your aunt rather than go to the movie. That action would produce the greater amount of well-being.

Let's examine another example. Harold Heartless is an investment counselor. About a hundred people have entrusted their life's savings to him to invest for their retirement, a total of about $10 million. Heartless is considering taking his clients' money and leaving the country. If he can get away with it and live happily ever after, would it be the morally right thing to do?

Let's assume we've calculated the "utilities" that appear in the following table:

	STEAL THE MONEY	DON'T STEAL THE MONEY
Heartless	+2,000	0
Clients	−20,000	0
TOTAL	−18,000	0

There will be far greater total utility if Heartless doesn't steal the money. If he steals it, he'll gain 2,000 units of well-being, but each of his 100 clients will lose an average of 200 units for a total loss of 20,000 units. The bad consequences outweigh the good by 18,000 units. If he doesn't steal the money, neither Heartless nor his clients will suffer a reduction in well-being. According to AU, it would be morally wrong for Heartless to steal the money, even if he'd be better off if he stole it (assuming he wasn't caught and punished, and suffered no pain from a guilty conscience).

BRAIN TEASERS

Although it may be difficult to measure gains and losses in well-being with any precision, most of us can probably make educated guesses about comparative total gains and losses, about whether one act would result in more or less total well-being than another. Let's try some applications of AU. In each case, list everyone who would probably benefit and probably be harmed, and how much benefit or harm would probably be produced.

1. Consider a German general in 1914 trying to decide whether it would be wrong to kill civilians at Dinant. Let's suppose he believes that killing several thousand Belgian civilians will increase the probability of a German victory. According to AU, would it be right or wrong for him to order the killing of Belgian civilians?

2. Dawn and Dave aren't married, but they're having a sexual relationship. According to AU, is it right or wrong for them to have sex without being married?

3. The leader of a small Middle Eastern country unfriendly to the United States is working to secure nuclear weapons and sophisticated delivery systems. U.S. leaders believe that he intends to use these weapons either to blackmail his neighbors or to attack them. The Mideast is considered important to U.S. national interests. U.S. leaders believe that the threat to U.S. interests and the country's neighbors would significantly diminish if the leader could be gotten out of the way. The CIA believes that it could assassinate him. According to AU, would it be morally wrong to assassinate the leader?

Many people think that the Greatest Happiness version of AU has considerable plausibility as a fundamental moral principle. Although there can be disputes about the probable consequences of actions and the changes in well-being, the Greatest Happiness version of AU gives a framework for moral decision making and moral justification that seems reasonable to many people. Nonetheless, there are some serious problems with it.

The Greatest Happiness Principle Requires Too Much   The Greatest Happiness version of AU requires us to do what will produce maximum total well-being. If we could do any of four things and one, A, would produce more total well-being then the others, then doing anything other than A is morally wrong. Now suppose you listen to music for relaxation. What else could you be doing? You could be soliciting contributions for famine relief. Which would produce more total well-being? Probably soliciting contributions for famine relief. If you listen to music, you're the only one who will benefit; if you solicit contributions for famine relief, many people will probably benefit. Then, according to the Greatest Happiness principle, the right thing to do is to solicit contributions; it would be wrong to sit home and listen to music.

AU hardly lets us rest. No matter what you do to benefit yourself—for example, watch television—it's wrong because you could be doing something else that would produce more total well-being. You could be volunteering at a soup kitchen, visiting sick children in the hospital, or teaching illiterate adults to read. According to the Greatest Happiness version of AU, it would be wrong for you to watch television, read a book, listen to music, or play a video game because they'll produce less total well-being than other things you could be doing.

Critics of the Greatest Happiness version of AU think that it's unreasonable to accept a moral principle that puts such a burden of doing good on people. People have their own lives to live, their own needs and desires to satisfy. It would not be reasonable for human beings to adopt a moral code that always required them to sacrifice their own needs, desires, interests, plans, projects, and happiness for the well-being of others.

Negative AU   This criticism suggests a possible revision in AU. Perhaps rather than requiring an agent to produce the maximum possible total well-being, AU should require agents to minimize reductions in total well-being. This may be the view of Jeremy Bentham (1748–1832), who is generally considered the father of Utilitarianism and who preceded John Stuart Mill. According to Bentham, an action is morally right if "the tendency it has to augment the happiness of the community is greater than any it has to diminish it."[3] According to Bentham's version of AU, it seems that we can limit ourselves to looking at a single alternative action and comparing the consequences of doing it and not doing it. If doing A would increase total well-being while not doing A would reduce total well-being, then doing A is morally right and not doing A is morally wrong. On the other hand, if doing A would reduce total well-being while not doing A would not, then doing A is morally wrong.

Suppose, though, that I could do A, B, or C. Both A and B would increase total well-being while C would decrease it. However, doing B would produce more total well-being than doing A. According to

---

[3]Jeremy Bentham, "An Introduction to the Principles of Morals and Legislation," in *The Utilitarians* (New York: Doubleday, 1961), 18.

Bentham's version of AU, it would be morally wrong to do C, but both A and B would be morally right. Thus, I wouldn't be doing anything morally wrong by doing A rather than B. Bentham's version permits me to choose between A and B. According to the Greatest Happiness version of AU, though, the only morally right thing is B; it would be morally wrong to do A.

Bentham's version of AU can be called Negative AU:

NEGATIVE AU

An action is morally wrong if and only if doing it would reduce total well-being, provided that there are alternative actions that would not reduce total well-being.

Suppose that you could go to a movie, solicit contributions for famine relief, or rob a bank. Going to a movie would increase total well-being by 10 units; soliciting contributions for famine relief would increase total well-being by 20 units; robbing a bank would decrease total well-being by 500 units. It would be morally wrong to rob a bank; Negative AU forbids it. But it would not be morally wrong to go to a movie or to solicit contributions for famine relief; Negative Au permits both.

But perhaps the Negative AU requires too little. Suppose John is walking along the river and sees a young child in imminent danger of drowning. John can't swim, but he sees a rope on the shore that he could throw to the child, probably saving her. On the other hand, he could just walk away and let the child drown. How are we to think about this case? Here's one possibility.

	RESCUE	DON'T RESCUE
me	−10	0
child	+1000	0
child's family	+500	0
TOTAL	+1490	0

On this view, not rescuing leaves everything as it was. Even if the child drowns, my not rescuing her didn't cause her to drown, it merely did not change anything. So I could have done something that would have increased total well-being, but instead I didn't intervene and let things take their course. So I didn't reduce total well-being by not rescuing her. I did something wrong according to the Greatest Happiness principle, but not according to Negative AU. If you think I did wrong by not saving her, then if you're right, Negative AU may not require enough of me.

On the other hand, we might claim that inaction has consequences. If I had acted, I would have saved the child from drowning. So the child drowned because I did nothing. In that case, our reasoning might look like this.

	RESCUE	DON'T RESCUE
me	−10	0
child	+1000	−1000
child's family	+500	−500
TOTAL	+1490	−1600

In that case, I would have done wrong according to both versions of AU.

BRAIN TEASERS

> If I let the child drown when I could have saved her, does she drown because of my inaction? Is a loss of 1600 units of well-being a consequence of my inaction?

Act Utilitarianism Focuses Too Exclusively on the Future Shouldn't past actions count in moral evaluation? Suppose you borrowed $1,000 from a rich friend and promised to repay it in six months. When the six months has passed, you realize that contributing the $1,000 to a worthy charity would produce far more total well-being than would repaying it to your already rich friend:

	REPAY	CONTRIBUTE TO CHARITY
You	−100	−100
Friend	+20	−20
Needy People	0	+500
TOTAL	−80	+380

The $1,000 affects your well-being much more than it does your rich friend's well-being, because he's rich and you're not. It's pocket money for him. The $1,000 means a lot more to the poor than it does to you. It could feed a starving family or pay their rent for several months. If you contribute the money to charity, the total increase in well-being will be 380 units; if you pay your friend the money you owe him, there's a reduction of 80 units of well-being. What should you do?

It seems that according to both the Greatest Happiness version of AU and Negative AU, contributing the money to charity would be the right thing to do; it would be wrong to repay your friend. But would it be morally acceptable to give the money to charity rather than to repay the loan, even if contributing it to charity would produce more total well-being? Don't you have a duty to repay the loan because you borrowed the money and promised to repay it? Didn't your past action create an obligation that overrides considerations of total well-being? Many people think that the answer is yes and that AU's exclusive emphasis on future consequences ignores duties and obligations created by past actions. Do you think you should repay your friend or contribute the money to charity? Why? Is this a serious problem for AU?

Act Utilitarianism Can Lead to Injustice   According to AU, the only thing that's relevant to moral right and wrong is total well-being. The distribution of that well-being is irrelevant. But a long tradition going back at least to Aristotle claims that justice requires a certain kind of equality in the distribution of good and bad; too much inequality is unjust. AU under certain circumstances may violate those principles of justice.

Suppose that in a certain society, one percent of the population is green. They're slaves and are forced to do the worst jobs. Non-green people benefit enormously from having green people as slaves. Suppose that the total increase in well-being to the 99 percent of the people who are non-green is 10 million units while the total decrease in well-being to the green people who are enslaved is 9.5 million units. According to AU (both versions?), enslaving the green people is morally right; in fact, it would be morally wrong if they were allowed to be free. But our common sense views of justice surely rebel at this conclusion.

BRAIN TEASERS

Would it be morally wrong to permit green people to be free according to Negative AU?

Similarly, suppose you could do three things, A, B, or C. A would reduce well-being for each of 100 people by 5 units (–500 units); B would reduce well-being for each of 10 people by 50 units (–500 units); C would reduce well-being for 1 person by 500 units (–500 units). What would be the right thing to do here? According to both versions of AU, the three alternatives are equally right because all produce the same reduction in total well-being.

	A	B	C
Person 1	–5	–50	–500
Persons 2–10	–45 (5 ea.)	–450 (50 ea.)	0
Persons 11–100	–450 (5 ea.)	0	0
TOTAL	–500	–500	–500

But common sense morality says it would be worse to produce a reduction of 500 units of well-being in 1 person than to produce a reduction of 5 units of well-being in each of 100 persons. They think that insensitivity to the distribution of well-being is a weakness in AU.

BRAIN TEASERS

Jack murdered Wanda. The prosecutor is wondering whether she should ask for the death penalty or a sentence of life in prison with no possibility of parole if Jack is convicted. What kind of reasoning would an act utilitarian follow in trying to answer the prosecutor's question? What answer do you think an act utilitarian would give if she applied (a) the Greatest Happiness version of AU? (b) Negative AU?

The problems we've encountered with AU have led many people to reject it. Yet many people believe that appeal to total well-being is still important in moral reasoning and evaluation. Is there some alternative version of Utilitarianism that escapes the problems of AU?

Rule Utilitarianism (RU)

Act Utilitarianism requires us to apply the utilitarian standard directly to individual actions. *Rule Utilitarianism,* on the other hand, requires us to apply the utilitarian standard to rules or principles. RU tells us to follow rules that, if generally followed, would maximize total well-being for all.

Suppose I'm thinking of robbing you. I could follow a rule that says "Don't rob" (It's morally wrong to rob) or a rule that says "Rob" (It's not morally wrong to rob). RU says I should follow the correct rule, but which rule is correct? I have to determine whether there would be more total well-being for society if people followed the rule "Don't rob" or if they followed the rule "Rob." If there would be more total well-being if people followed the rule "Don't rob" than there would be if they followed the rule "Rob," then "Don't rob" is the correct rule. On the other hand, if there would be more total well-being if people followed the rule "Rob" than there would be if they followed the rule "Don't rob," then "Rob" is the correct rule.

Suppose I'm trying to decide whether to keep a promise I made you. If I apply AU, I have to determine the different consequences of keeping and of not keeping this particular promise. If I apply RU, I have to determine the consequences of the practices of (1) keeping promises and (2) not keeping promises. That is, I have to determine whether there would be more total well-being if people generally keep their promises or if instead there would be more total well-being if they generally do not keep their promises. If there would be more total well-being if people generally keep their promises, then the correct rule is to keep promises. However, if there would be more total well-being if people generally broke their promises, then the correct rule is to break promises. Now if according to RU the correct rule is to keep promises, then the morally right thing for me to do is to keep this particular promise. That way I'd be following the correct moral rule.

Suppose I have a rich, miserly old uncle who has a fortune of $10 million and I've learned that he intends to change his will next week to leave his money to the local chapter of the Ku Klux Klan instead of to me, his current sole beneficiary. He's very ill and, according to his doctors, has less than a month to live. If the Ku Klux Klan gets his money, it will use it to promote intolerance and hate. If I inherit his money, I'll contribute $9 million to an organization that works to foster harmony and world peace, and I'll keep only $1 million of it for myself. I could murder my uncle before he changes his will. He has at most a month to live, so the loss in well-being to him of a mere month of illness plagued life wouldn't be great. Suppose that if I kill him, total well-being will increase by 1,000 units; if I don't, total well-being will decrease by 100 units. According to both versions of AU, killing him is the morally right thing to do.

Rule Utilitarians think it would be wrong to murder my uncle even if murdering him would produce more total well-being. They think that killing my uncle violates a correct moral principle that forbids murder, a moral principle justified by appeal to considerations of utility. According to RU, the rule that would produce the most total well-being if generally followed is the correct rule. There would be greater total well-being if people generally follow a rule forbidding murder; therefore, a rule forbidding murder is a correct moral rule, and a rule permitting murder is not. It would be wrong for me to murder my uncle, because it would violate a correct moral rule. We might express the RU as follows:

RULE UTILITARIANISM STANDARD

1. An individual action is morally right if and only if it conforms to a correct moral rule.

2. A moral rule is correct if and only if there will be more total well-being if people follow it than there will be if they don't follow it.

Suppose an unpopular student, Jack, enters the snack bar. Jack is timid, and bullies find him a tempting target. Tom intends to pick on Jack in order to cultivate a "macho" image. Is it morally right for Tom to pick on Jack? To apply RU, we first have to identify the rules that Tom could follow. There are two:

Rule A: Pick on people to show your toughness.

Rule B: Don't pick on people to show your toughness.

Next, we have to determine whether there will be more total well-being if people generally follow A, or instead will be more total well-being if they follow B. Let's assume that it's obvious that there will be more total well-being if people generally follow B rather than A. Then, B is the correct rule and A is incorrect. If Tom picks on Jack, he will violate a correct moral rule; therefore, according to RU, it would be morally wrong for Tom to pick on Jack.

BRAIN TEASERS

1. Consider once more the German general trying to decide whether it would be right to kill the innocent civilians of Dinant. If he orders the execution, he will be following the rule "Deliberately kill innocent civilians in war if it will contribute to victory." Do you think it would be right for him to order the executions, according to RU? Why or why not?

2. Can the seven moral duties that W. D. Ross identified or the ten moral rules that Bernard Gert proposed (Chapter 9) be justified by appealing to RU?

Problems with All Versions of Utilitarianism

Applying either AU or RU requires that we compare changes in well-being among people. However, making such comparisons can be extremely difficult. In the example of enslaving green people, how do we precisely measure the loss in well-being of green people and the gain in well-being of nongreen people? Any numbers are arbitrary.

However, this objection may not be insurmountable. We may legitimately judge that one person's loss will be greater than another's gain, even if we can't precisely measure their gains and losses. We could insist that the total losses to the 1 percent of green people who are enslaved is greater than the total gains to the 99 percent who are not green. We can often make a reasonably accurate educated guess about what would increase or decrease well-being.

Utilitarianism also can't seem to accommodate the idea that some acts are what common sense calls above and beyond the call of duty. They're praiseworthy, but not morally required. At the extreme, they constitute heroism. For example, consider someone who rushes into a building to save someone. According to common sense morality, it wouldn't be morally wrong to not rush in, risking one's life. It's heroic and praiseworthy, but not a duty. But if there would be more total well-being if people followed a rule to risk their lives to save others, then according to RU it would be morally wrong not to. And if risking your life would produce more total well-being, then the Greatest Happiness version of AU says it would be wrong not to do it. It may even be that Negative AU says the same thing if your not acting is thought to cause the individual's death.

An adequate moral code should distinguish between what morality forbids or requires, on the one hand, and what's good but not required, on the other. It may be good to devote one's life to helping the poor, but not required. One may be permitted to do other things with one's life, even though devoting one's life to the poor is a good and praiseworthy thing. Morality must include more than requirements and prohibitions; it must include ideals to strive for, ideals "above and beyond the call of duty." If critics are right that Utilitarianism can't make room for such distinctions, then it isn't a completely adequate moral theory.

BRAIN TEASERS

The Greyair Chemical Company owns a chemical plant in a poor country that has weak environmental laws and lax enforcement of the environmental laws that exist. The plant produces chemicals that are exclusively for export to wealthy, highly industrialized countries. It employs about 250 people from the local population at wages that are considered high by the standards of this country, but low by the standards of rich countries. The company has been pouring untreated or barely treated toxic chemical waste into the air, soil, and water. The effect on the health of the nearby population, more than 500,000 people, is unknown, but local political activists claim that scientific studies suggest that the pollution directly or indirectly causes twenty five to thirty deaths each year as well as birth defects and a variety of illnesses. In order to significantly reduce the amount of toxic waste that the plant pours into the environment, engineers calculate that an initial investment of $10 million would have to be made and that subsequently the annual cost would be more than $1 million. The Greyair Chemical Company has refused to install the pollution control equipment because it claims that it would significantly reduce the profitability of the plant.

Furthermore, the company denies that the pollution that the plant generates poses a serious health hazard for the population around the plant. Finally, the company says that it is doing nothing wrong since it is in compliance with the laws of the country in which it is operating. From the perspective of (a) the Greatest Happiness version of AU, (b) Negative AU, and (c) RU, is the company doing anything wrong in not installing the pollution control equipment?

Kantian Moral Theory

Do not impose on others what you yourself do not desire.

—Confucius (551–479 B.C.E.), *Analects*

Always treat others as you would like them to treat you.

—Jesus, The Sermon on the Mount (Matthew 7:12)

The most influential moral theory competing with Utilitarianism derives from the work of Immanuel Kant (1724–1804). Kant and his followers reject the fundamental assumption of Utilitarianism that the consequences of an action, or of following a rule, determine moral right and wrong. Kant's views are an elaboration of golden rule reasoning in ethics. Kant begins his influential work on ethics, *Foundations of the Metaphysics of Morals,* with the observation "Nothing in the world . . . can possibly be conceived which could be called good without qualification except a GOOD WILL."[4] Kant points out that there are conceivable circumstances in which all other candidates for being good without qualification would not be good; if there are conceivable circumstances in which something would not be good, it's not good without qualification.

Consider pleasure, for example. One may think that pleasure is good without qualification, but what if someone derives pleasure from torturing people? In that circumstance, pleasure is not good; therefore, pleasure isn't good without qualification. Perhaps happiness is good without qualification. However, what if a mass murderer lives a happy life after her murders? In that case, happiness isn't good because it isn't deserved. Therefore, happiness isn't good without qualification. Or consider a character trait such as courage. Is courage good without qualification? Courage isn't good without qualification because it can be put to evil purposes. Courage in a Mafia hit man isn't good. Kant claims that only a good will is good without qualification.

According to Kant, each person has a will—a power or capacity to make decisions and perform actions. A person's will guides his or her actions and behavior. But what makes a will a good will? A will is good only when it wills actions that conform to moral laws because they conform to moral laws.

Suppose you return a wallet you found. Let's assume that returning the wallet conforms to a moral law requiring you to return things you've found. Does that show you have a good will? No. You may have returned it only because you feared getting caught, not because you

---

[4]Immanuel Kant, *Foundations of the Metaphysics of Morals,* 2d ed., trans. Lewis White Beck (New York: Macmillan, 1990), 9.

thought it was the right thing to do. Doing what conforms to moral law doesn't show a good will unless you've done it because you believe it is the right thing to do. Kant maintains that people do things for reasons and that to do things for a reason is to follow a policy, or maxim. What, then, are maxims?

Actions and Maxims

Kant claims that when an agent does something for a reason, the agent is following a *maxim*. A maxim is a policy, or blueprint, that specifies what one will do in certain circumstances and why. If you return a wallet you've found only because you fear being detected and punished, you're following a maxim. What maxim? Something like this: "I'll return something I've found when I believe I may be caught and punished if I don't." If you return a wallet you've found because you hope to get a reward for returning it, you're following a different maxim: "I'll return something I've found when I believe I'll get a reward for returning it." Notice that in each case you're doing the same action—returning the wallet—but the maxim of the action is different. Kant asserts that people are always following maxims when they act, although he probably didn't think that people always consciously formulate the maxims in their minds.

Does returning a wallet show that you have a good will? Not necessarily. It depends on the reason for returning it, on the maxim you're following. If the maxim you're following is "Return a wallet if you think you'll get caught," returning the wallet doesn't show you have a good will. However, if you return the wallet because you think it's the right thing to do, because you think the moral law requires returning it, then returning the wallet shows a good will.

According to Kant, the moral worth of an action is determined by the maxim the person is following. An action is morally valuable if and only if the maxim one is following is part of the moral law and one is following it because it's part of the moral law. A person with a good will does things out of respect for the moral law. But what is the moral law? What does morality require, forbid, and permit?

Kant's Categorical Imperative

According to Kant, there is one fundamental moral principle to which all rational creatures are obligated to conform. He calls it the *Categorical Imperative*, meaning an unconditional or absolute command.

First Formulation: Willing That a Maxim Become a Universal Law

Kant offers several formulations of the Categorical Imperative. His first version is as follows:

FIRST FORMULATION OF THE CATEGORICAL IMPERATIVE

Act only according to that maxim by which you can at the same time will that it should become a universal law.[5]

The Categorical Imperative is a test for maxims of action. Some maxims are morally acceptable, and one is permitted to follow them; other maxims are not morally acceptable, and one is not permitted to follow them. A maxim is morally acceptable only if one could will that the maxim become a universal law. But what does that mean?

Suppose you come to an intersection with a stop sign. Since you're in a hurry you don't stop; you drive right through the intersection without even looking. Is this action right or wrong? That depends on whether the maxim you were following is morally acceptable. Is it a maxim you could will to be a universal law? The relevant maxim here is the maxim that actually determined your action, the maxim you were actually following.[6] Let's say it was this: "I won't stop at stop signs when I'm in a hurry." Could you will that maxim to be a universal law?

If a maxim is a *universal law,* everyone follows it. If your maxim to drive through intersections without stopping when you're in a hurry were a universal law, everyone would drive through stop signs when they were in a hurry. In deciding whether it's wrong to drive through intersections without stopping, one must answer the question "Could I will that everyone drive through intersections without stopping when they're in a hurry?" If the answer is no, one should not follow the maxim.

You might be tempted to say that in at least one sense of "could," you could will anything. But Kant is interested in what you could will *without contradiction.* Kant's Categorical Imperative requires you to act only on maxims that you could will *without contradiction* to be universal laws. If willing a maxim to be a universal law would involve you in a contradiction, you're forbidden to act on that maxim.

There are at least two ways in which you could contradict yourself in willing that a certain maxim become a universal law. First, you could will to become a universal law a maxim that *couldn't* become a universal law. A maxim couldn't become a universal law if it would be impossible for everyone to follow it. Second, you could will to become a universal law a maxim that would conflict with needs, desires, or interests that you and all rational creatures have.

Let's look at the first kind of contradiction, in which it would be impossible for everyone to follow a certain maxim. One of Kant's examples is that of someone falsely promising to repay money he's borrowing in order to get the loan. He's acting on a maxim that we might express as

---

[5]Kant, *Metaphysics of Morals,* 38.

[6]Kant seems to have thought that one can always determine the maxim one is or was following. That may not be the case.

"I'll falsely promise to repay a loan when I need one and can't get it without promising to repay it." Could that maxim be willed to be a universal law? Could it be a universal law that everyone will falsely promise to repay a loan when they need the loan and can't get it without promising to repay it? Kant says no. He claims that if everyone followed the maxim, no promises would be believed anymore, and no loans would be made on the basis of a promise to repay. Then the entire institution of promising would die out, as would the convention of lending money on the basis of a promise to repay it. If the maxim became a universal law, in a brief time no one would be able to act on it anymore. Why? No one would take promises seriously, and no one would lend money on the basis of a promise to pay it. Once no one took promises seriously, there wouldn't be any sense in making promises, either; the practice of making and accepting promises would die out. Thus, the maxim couldn't become a universal law because it is self-defeating. If it became a universal law that everyone acted on, soon *no one could act on it.*

Thus, the first kind of contradiction involves willing that everyone do something x in circumstances c when, if everyone did x in circumstances c, eventually no one could do x. If you will that everyone falsely promise to repay money when they need it, eventually no one will be able to promise to repay money at all, whether falsely or not, because the convention of making loans on the basis of a promise to repay will die out. When the conventions of lending, borrowing, and promising to repay die out, no one can make false promises to repay borrowed money anymore, so no one can follow the maxim.

Perhaps we can make this point plainer in the following way. A maxim will always be expressed in the first person (using the pronoun "I") because it is a personal rule of action. The maxim I would be following may be expressed as:

> (M1) I will falsely promise to repay a loan when I need one and cannot get one without promising to repay it.

Is that a morally acceptable maxim to follow? The test is whether I can consistently will that it be a universal law—a rule followed by everyone, not just by me. We can transform (M1) from a personal maxim into a universal law by changing "I" to "everyone," yielding the universal law:

> (UL1) Everyone will falsely promise to repay a loan when they need one and cannot get one without promising to repay it.

Can I consistently will that my maxim (M1) become a universal law (UL1) without contradiction? No, I cannot because if everyone followed (UL1), soon no one could follow (UL1). (UL1) is self-destroying. The practice of lending money on the basis of a promise to repay would quickly die out if everyone followed (UL1). Since I cannot consistently will that my maxim (M1) become a universal law (UL1), it follows that (M1) is not a morally acceptable maxim to follow.

Let's return to the stop sign example now. Could you will without contradiction that the maxim not to stop at stop signs become a universal law? It would probably be at least possible for everyone to follow the maxim. Even if everyone ignored stop signs when they were in a hurry, stop signs might still have some value and might still be put up at intersections. As long as there were still stop signs, everyone could follow the maxim. So you wouldn't be contradicting yourself in the first sense, that of willing that everyone follow a maxim it would be impossible for everyone to follow.

But that's not the only way you might be contradicting yourself in willing that a maxim become a universal law. You couldn't will that a maxim become a universal law without contradiction if its becoming a universal law would conflict with desires, interests, and needs that you and all rational creatures have. Surely you desire to be happy, healthy, and alive. Surely you care about some other people and desire that they remain happy, healthy, and alive. What if it became a universal law that people would not stop at stop signs when in a hurry? Your chances of remaining happy, healthy, and alive would be significantly decreased, as would those of people you care about. In willing that the maxim become a universal law, you'd be willing that everyone follow a policy that would make it far less easy to satisfy your own needs and desires.

Again, to make this plainer, let's suppose the maxim you would be following is:

(M2) I will not stop at stop signs when I'm in a hurry.

(M2) is a morally acceptable maxim if and only if I can consistently will that it become a universal law. Again, we transform (M2) into a universal law by replacing "I" with "everyone," yielding:

(UL2) Everyone will not stop at stop signs when they are in a hurry.

Could you consistently will this universal law (UL2) without contradiction? No, because it would conflict with the desires that you and all rational creatures have to remain alive, healthy, and happy. If (UL2) became a universal law, there is a high probability that you or someone you care about would be injured or killed.

To summarize, there are two ways in which one could involve oneself in contradiction in willing that a maxim be made a universal law:

1. One could will that everyone follow a maxim that it would be impossible for everyone to follow.

2. One could will that everyone follow a maxim that, if followed by everyone, would significantly reduce the probability of one's satisfying the needs, desires, and interests that all rational creatures have.

Suppose you're producing and marketing a pesticide that you've just found to be a powerful carcinogen. A law has been passed in the United States prohibiting its manufacture and sale, but no such laws have been passed in Third World countries. You're thinking of moving your operation to South America. Your business could still be profitable, because few of your potential customers in the Third World will know that the pesticide is a powerful carcinogen and your prices will be competitive with similar pesticides that, although not as great a health hazard, are no more effective than yours. Should you produce and market in the Third World the pesticide you've discovered to be a carcinogen?

How could you apply the Categorical Imperative here? First, you have to specify an action and its determining maxim. The action under consideration is producing and marketing the carcinogenic pesticide without warning in a country where it's not illegal to do so. What maxim would determine your action? It's something like this: "I'll sell hazardous products to consumers without warning when it's not illegal to do so and I can make a profit." Let's call that maxim (M3). The question is whether you could will without contradiction that maxim (M3) become a universal law. The universal law would be:

> (UL3) Everyone will sell hazardous products to consumers when it's profitable and not illegal.

We need to ask two questions about (UL3) to determine whether you could will it without contradiction:

1.   Would it be impossible for everyone to act on (UL3)?
2.   If everyone followed (UL3), would it significantly reduce the chances of your satisfying the needs, desires, and interests that you, as a rational creature, have?

It doesn't seem as though it would be impossible for everyone to act on (UL3). It seems that it would be possible for everyone to sell hazardous products to consumers without warning when it's not illegal. There could still be sales of hazardous products. What of the second variety of contradiction? In willing that (M3) become a universal law, would you be willing something that significantly reduces the chances of satisfying your needs, desires, and interests? As a rational creature, you care about yourself and at least some other people; you want to remain alive and healthy and want the people you care about to remain alive and healthy. If (M3) were to become a universal law, wouldn't everyone's health be threatened, including your own and that of those you care about? You'd be willing that you and those you care about remain healthy, but also willing something that would make it more difficult for you and those you care about to remain healthy.

If you can't will (M3) to become a universal law without involving yourself in contradiction, it fails the test of the Categorical Imperative; therefore, acting on (M3) would be immoral, contrary to the moral law. You shouldn't produce and sell the carcinogenic pesticide in the Third World because you'd be acting on a maxim that you couldn't will to be a universal law.

BRAIN TEASERS

Suppose you're a soldier in wartime. A superior officer has given you an order that you believe is immoral: kill several prisoners you've captured, even though regulations clearly forbid it. You fear that if you refuse, he'll find a way of punishing you for disobeying his order; he'll give you the most dangerous duties and will try to find a way of getting you killed. You know that no one will back you up if you try to press charges against him and that no one will protect you from his vengeance. What would be the maxim of your action? Could you will without contradiction that the maxim become a universal law? Would it be morally acceptable, then, for you to obey the order and execute the prisoners of war? Why or why not?

Kant's Categorical Imperative seems to be a negative test. Applying it will tell us what actions are forbidden or prohibited, but will it tell us which actions, if any, are required? Actions that follow a maxim that you can't will to be a universal law are prohibited. Does the moral law only prohibit action? Does it require any action? Recall the tragic case of Kitty Genovese, who was murdered after her neighbors ignored her screams for help. Did her neighbors have a duty to call the police? If the Categorical Imperative is only a negative test for what is forbidden, how could it be applied to establish what people morally must do?

Kant claims that the Categorical Imperative test will show that people have a duty to help one another. He proposes the case of a man who has no desire to help others and follows the maxim "I won't help other people in need when I have no desire to help them." Kant writes:

> If such a way of thinking were a universal law of nature, certainly the human race could exist. . . . Now although it is possible that a universal law of nature according to that maxim could exist, it is nevertheless impossible to will that such a principle should hold everywhere as a law of nature. For a will which resolved this would conflict with itself, since instances often arise in which he would need the love and sympathy of others, and in which he would have robbed himself, by such a law of nature springing from his own will, of all hope of the aid he desires.[7]

Kant assumes that everyone will want the help of others; consequently, willing a universal law that people not help those in need would conflict with this desire. That would be a contradiction.

Suppose you have heard Genovese's blood curdling screams but don't want to get involved. Is it morally acceptable to return to bed

---

[7]Kant, *Metaphysics of Morals,* 39.

without calling the police? If *not* calling the police is morally unacceptable—that is, morally forbidden—you're morally obligated to call. But is *not* calling the police an action that can be judged by the standards of the Categorical Imperative?

Let's say you don't call the police because you don't want to get involved. The maxim of that action (or inaction) would be:

(M4) I won't help someone in great need when I don't want to get involved, even if the cost to me is small.

Could you will this maxim to be a universal law, followed by everyone? Such a universal law would be:

(UL4) Everyone will refrain from helping others in great need when they don't want to get involved, even if the cost to them would be small.

If everyone ignored the need of other people for help, everyone's health and happiness would be jeopardized. In willing that maxim to become a universal law, then, you'd be willing something that would conflict with what you, as a rational creature, want and need. In that case, the maxim to refrain from helping when the need is great and the cost small would fail the test of the Categorical Imperative; not helping would be wrong. Genovese's neighbors had a duty to help her by at least summoning the police, a duty they violated.

Second Formulation: Respect for People   Kant offers another version of the Categorical Imperative, which focuses on how persons or rational agents should be treated. Rather than stressing universal law, the second version stresses that rational agents, or people, aren't merely objects or machines, like typewriters, automobiles, or television sets. As we saw in Chapters 3 and 4, people have mental states and are capable of reasoning. They have beliefs, desires, interests, emotions, feelings, life plans, goals, sensations, and attitudes. Of the mental states that people can have, Kant focuses on reasoning and willing rather than sensing, but we can broaden our scope to include all features of people that set them off from mere objects. Kant contends that people are special because of their capacities and that we should not treat them the way we might treat objects.

The people with whom we're most familiar are normal, mature human beings. *Human being* is a biological category. As we know, there are other forms of biological life besides human beings: whales, elephants, horses, ducks, sharks, monkeys, snakes, bees, ants, and so on. *Person* is a metaphysical category, a kind of thing that has a developed capacity for a rich mental life. You're a human being; you're also a person. A fly is not a person; it doesn't have the capacity for a rich mental life or the wide variety of mental states required for being a person.

Human beings are people, and people are different from other things, living or nonliving, like television sets and flies. Therefore, Kant thinks, it would be inappropriate to treat people the same way we treat television sets and flies. Kicking my television set to vent my frustration is morally acceptable, but kicking you isn't. Why? You're not a mere object like a television set; you're a person. Kant's second formulation of the Categorical Imperative, then, insists that people shouldn't be treated as mere objects:

SECOND FORMULATIONS OF THE CATEGORICAL IMPERATIVE

Act so that you treat humanity, whether in your own person or in that of another, always as an end and never as a means only.[8]

According to this formulation, we're never to treat a person as merely a means to our own ends. We may merely use objects, but we may never merely use people. People, according to Kant, are to be treated with respect because they have inherent value or worth. They have dignity that demands respect. Treating a person with respect entails taking account of that person's desires, needs, goals, and interests.

Kant is not saying that it's always wrong to "use" people, to treat them as means to one's own ends. Rather, it's wrong to *merely* use them. If you hire someone to tutor you in calculus, you're using that person as a means to an end: passing calculus. Surely you're not doing anything wrong by using this person as a tutor. When you hire someone to tutor you, you're not merely using that person. Assuming that the transaction is fully voluntary, both parties benefit (you get tutored, the tutor earns income). The relationship is what we could call a two-way street. Each party in the relationship takes account of the needs, interests, and desires of the other.

There are various fairly obvious ways in which we might "merely" use a person. To kill someone for gain is to merely use that person. To enslave, rape, assault, rob, cheat, and lie, are all ways of merely using a person. In those cases, one totally ignores the interests, desires, needs, goals, and ends of the person being used. One also limits or eliminates the person's freedom to decide how to interact with others. Treating people as mere objects to be used without respect for their needs, interests, and desires is forbidden, according to Kant. When our treatment of people is shaped by our perception of their interests, desires, needs, and goals, we are treating them with *respect*. Kant's second formulation of the Categorical Imperative, then, can be considered a requirement to treat people with respect.

Let's return to your dilemma about producing and marketing the carcinogenic pesticide in the Third World. How would Kantian respect for people apply here? Kant might insist that you're merely using the people who might be affected by the pesticide to gain profits for your company and yourself. In selling them the dangerous pesticide without adequate warning about its health hazards, you're ignoring their needs, interests, desires, and goals. You're not treating them with the respect that their

---

[8]Ibid., 204.

dignity as people requires. You're then doing what is forbidden by the second formulation of the Categorical Imperative; you're treating those people merely as means to your own ends. Thus, what you contemplate doing is wrong.

It seems reasonable to suppose that we treat people with respect if we conform to the following general guidelines and that we fail to treat them with respect if we violate any of these guidelines:

1. Minimize the harm (physical and psychological) we cause other people.

2. Ensure that interactions with other people are genuinely voluntary. (Do not unjustifiably violate a person's freedom or autonomy.)

3. Help other people in need when the cost or risk to you is reasonable.

4. Do not exploit other people. (Make sure that your interactions with other people are mutually and roughly equally beneficial.)

BRAIN TEASERS

1. Suppose you're considering selling drugs to some of your friends who want to buy them. Would that action pass the test of always treating people as an end and never merely as a means? Why or why not? Would it pass the test of being able to will it to be a universal law without contradiction?

2. Suppose you've gotten in line to buy 100 tickets for the Super Bowl so that you can "scalp" them—that is, sell them to people for a higher price than you paid for them. Would that action pass the test of the second formulation of the Categorical Imperative? Why or why not? Would it pass the test of being able to will it to be a universal law without contradiction?

The Moral Community: Should All People Count Equally?   Ours is a world in which intolerance is common. People have a tendency to discriminate against others who are different from themselves. They have discriminated against others on the basis of race, nationality, religion, sex, sexual orientation, and social class. People often count as full members of the moral community only people like themselves. For example, many whites in the pre–Civil War South believed that other whites should be treated with respect, but not nonwhites. Nazis did not consider Jews full members of the moral community like themselves and so believed that exterminating them was morally acceptable. Many men have not considered women full members of the moral community. Some heterosexuals do not consider homosexuals full members of the moral community.

In the former Yugoslavia, ethnic divisions and hatred have led to some of the worst acts of savagery since the Nazi mass murder of Jews during World War II. After the collapse of the Soviet Union, Yugoslavia, an Eastern European satellite of the Soviet Union, broke apart into three states: Serbia, Croatia, and Bosnia. Serbs in Bosnia revolted and began a campaign of "ethnic cleansing"—a euphemism for torture, rape, and mass murder of Bosnian Muslims in the territory under Serbian control. The Serbs in Bosnia wanted to join with the Serbs in Serbia to create a "Big" Serbia. They wanted none but Serbs in their territory, so they murdered or drove out almost all non-Serbs. Similar events have occurred in Croatia, where Croatian Serbs revolted and murdered or drove out Croats. When Croatian troops defeated the Serb rebels, some Croats were guilty of atrocities against the Serbs in retaliation for Serb savagery. Tens of thousands of innocent people have been murdered, tortured, raped, and/or driven from their homes because of ethnic hatred.

What are the criteria of full membership in the moral community? Should religion, nationality, sex, race, sexual orientation, or political views be relevant? Kant would say no; only the rich mental life that makes someone a person is relevant for full membership in the moral community. The available evidence makes clear that those capacities do not systematically vary with religion, nationality, sex, race, sexual orientation, or political views. Thus for Kant, none of these differences between human beings would provide grounds for attributing different or unequal moral status. All fully developed, fully functioning human beings are people and thus are full members of the moral community, whether they are men or women; Christian, Jewish, Hindu, or atheist; white, brown, or red; Serb, Muslim, or Croat.[9]

---

[9]Ibid., 204.

 JOHN STUART MILL (1806–1873)

UTILITARIANISM

1. General Remarks

There are few circumstances among those which make up the present condition of human knowledge more unlike what might have been expected, or more significant of the backward state in which speculation on the most important subjects still lingers, than the little progress which has been made in the decision of the controversy respecting the criterion of right and wrong. From the dawn of philosophy the question concerning the

From *Essential Works of John Stuart Mill,* ed. Max Lerner (New York: Bantam Books, 1961).

summum bonum, or what is the same thing, concerning the foundation of morality has been accounted the main problem in speculative thought, has occupied the most gifted intellects, and divided them into sects and schools, carrying on a vigorous warfare against one another. And after more than two thousand years the same discussions continue, philosophers are still ranged under the same contending banners, and neither thinkers nor mankind at large seem nearer to being unanimous on the subject than when the youth Socrates listened to the old Protagoras, and asserted (if Plato's dialogue be grounded on a real conversation) the theory of utilitarianism against the popular morality of the so-called Sophist.

It is true that similar confusion and uncertainty, and in some cases similar discordance, exist respecting the first principles of all the sciences, not excepting that which is deemed the most certain of them, mathematics; without much impairing, generally, indeed without impairing at all, the trustworthiness of the conclusions of those sciences. An apparent anomaly, the explanation of which is that the detailed doctrines of a science are not usually deduced from, or depend for their evidence upon, what are called its first principles. Were it not so, there would be no science more precarious, or whose conclusions were more insufficiently made out, than algebra; which derives none of its certainty from what are commonly taught to learners as its elements, since these, as laid down by some of its most eminent teachers, are as full of fictions as English law, and of mysteries as theology.

The truths which are ultimately accepted as the first principles of a science, are really the last results of metaphysical analysis, practised on the elementary notions with which the science is conversant; and their relation to the science is not that of foundations to an edifice, but of roots to a tree, which may perform their office equally well though they be never dug down to and exposed to light. But though in science the particular truths precede the general theory, the contrary might be expected to be the case with a practical art, such as morals or legislation. All action is for the sake of some

end, and rules of action, it seems natural to suppose, must take their whole character and colour from the end to which they are subservient. When we engage in a pursuit, a clear and precise conception of what we are pursuing would seem to be the first thing we need, instead of the last we are to look forward to. A test of right and wrong must be the means, one would think, of ascertaining what is right or wrong, and not a consequence of having already ascertained it.

The difficulty is not avoided by having recourse to the popular theory of a natural faculty, a sense or instinct, informing us of right and wrong. For—besides that the existence of such a moral instinct is itself one of the matters in dispute—those believers in it who have any pretensions to philosophy, have been obliged to abandon the idea that it discerns what is right or wrong in the particular case in hand, as our other senses discern the sight or sound actually present. Our moral faculty, according to all those of its interpreters who are entitled to the name of thinkers, supplies us only with the general principles of moral judgments; it is a branch of our reason, not of our sensitive faculty; and must be looked to for the abstract doctrines of morality, not for perception of it in the concrete. The intuitive, no less than what may be termed the inductive, school of ethics, insists on the necessity of general laws. They both agree that the morality of an individual action is not a question of direct perception, but the application of a law to an individual case. They recognise also, to a great extent, the same moral laws; but differ as to their evidence, and the source from which they derive their authority.

According to the one opinion, the principles of morals are evidence *a priori,* requiring nothing to command assent except that the meaning of the terms be understood. According to the other doctrine, right and wrong, as well as truth and falsehood, are questions of observation and experience. But both hold equally that morality must be deduced from principles; and the intuitive school affirm as strongly as the inductive that there is a science of morals. Yet they seldom attempt to make out a list of the *a priori* principles which are to serve as the premises of the science; still more rarely do they make any effort to reduce those various precepts of morals as of *a priori* authority, or they lay down as the common groundwork of those maxims some generality which is much less obviously authoritative than the maxims themselves, and which has never succeeded in gaining popular acceptance. Yet to support their pretensions there ought either to be some one fundamental principle or law at the root of all morality, or, if there be several, there should be a determinate order of precedence among them; and the one principle, or the rule for deciding between the various principles when they conflict, ought to be self-evident.

To inquire how far the bad effects of this deficiency have been mitigated in practice, or to what extent the moral beliefs of mankind have been vitiated or made uncertain by the absence of any distinct recognition of an ultimate standard, would imply a complete survey and criticism of past and present ethical doctrine. It would, however, be easy to show that whatever steadiness or consistency these moral beliefs have attained has been mainly due to the tacit influence of a standard not recognized. Although the non-existence of an acknowledged first principle has made ethics not so much a guide as a consecration of men's actual sentiments, still, as men's sentiments, both of favour and aversion, are greatly influenced by what they suppose to be the effects of things upon their happiness, the principle of utility, or as Bentham latterly called it, the greatest happiness principle, has had a large share in forming the moral doctrines even of those who most scornfully reject its authority. Nor is there any school of thought which refuses to admit that the influence of actions on happiness is a most material and even predominant consideration in many of the details of morals, however unwilling to acknowledge it as the fundamental principle of morality, and the source of moral obligation. I might go much further, and say that to all those *a priori* moralists who deem it necessary to argue at all utilitarian arguments are indispensable. It is not my present purpose to criticize these thinkers; but I cannot

help referring, for illustration, to a systematic treatise by one of the most illustrious of them, *The Metaphysics of Ethics,* by Kant.

This remarkable man, whose system of thought will long remain one of the landmarks in the history of philosophical speculation, does, in the treatise in question, lay down a universal first principle as the origin and ground of moral obligation; it is this: So act that the rule on which thou actest would admit of being adopted as a law by all rational beings. But when he begins to deduce from this precept any of the actual duties of morality, he fails, almost grotesquely, to show that there would be any contradiction, any logical (not to say physical) impossibility, in the adoption by all rational beings of the most outrageously immoral rules of conduct. All he shows is that the *consequences* of their universal adoption would be such as no one would choose to incur.

On the present occasion, I shall, without further discussion of the other theories, attempt to contribute something towards the understanding and appreciation of the Utilitarian or Happiness theory, and towards such proof as it is susceptible of. It is evident that this cannot be proof in the ordinary and popular meaning of the term. Questions of ultimate ends are not amenable to direct proof. Whatever can be proved to be good must be so by being shown to be a means to something admitted to be good without proof. The medical art is proved to be good, by its conducing to health; but how is it possible to prove that health is good? The art of music is good, for the reason, among others, that it produces pleasure; but what proof is it possible to give that pleasure is good? If, then, it is asserted that there is a comprehensive formula, including all things which are in themselves good, and that whatever else is good is not so as an end but as a mean, the formula may be accepted or rejected, but is not a subject of what is commonly understood by proof. We are not, however, to infer that its acceptance or rejection must depend on blind impulse or arbitrary choice. There is a larger meaning of the word proof, in which this question is as amenable to it as any other of the disputed questions of philosophy. The subject is within the cognizance of the rational faculty; and neither does that faculty deal with it solely in the way of intuition. Considerations may be presented capable of determining the intellect either to give or withhold its assent to the doctrine; and this is equivalent to proof.

We shall examine presently of what nature are these considerations; in what manner they apply to the case, and what rational grounds, therefore, can be given for accepting of rejecting the utilitarian formula. But it is a preliminary condition of rational acceptance or rejection that the formula should be correctly understood. I believe that the very imperfect notion ordinarily formed of its meaning is the chief obstacle which impedes its reception; and that could it be cleared, even from only the grosser misconceptions, the question would be greatly simplified, and a large proportion of its difficulties removed. Before, therefore, I attempt to enter into the philosophical grounds which can be given for assenting to the utilitarian standard I shall offer some illustrations of the doctrine itself, with the view of showing more clearly what it is, distinguishing it from what it is not, and disposing of such of the practical objections to it as either originate in, or are closely connected with, mistaken interpretations of its meaning. Having thus prepared the ground, I shall afterwards endeavour to throw such light as I can upon the question, considered as one of philosophical theory.

II. What Utilitarianism Is

. . . The creed which accepts as the foundation of morals, Utility, or the Greatest Happiness Principle, holds that actions are right in proportion as they tend to promote happiness, wrong as they tend to produce the reverse of happiness. By happiness is intended pleasure and the absence of pain; by unhappiness, pain, and the privation of pleasure. To give a clear view of the moral standard set up by the theory much more request to be said; in particular, what things it includes in the ideas of pain and pleasure; and to what extent this is left an open

question. But these supplementary explanations do not affect the theory of life on which this theory or morality is grounded—namely, that pleasure and freedom from pain are the only things desirable as ends; and that all desirable things (which are as numerous in the utilitarian as in any other scheme) are desirable either for the pleasure inherent in themselves, or as means to the promotion of pleasure and the prevention of pain.

Now such a theory of life excites in many minds, and among them in some of the most estimable in feeling and purpose, inveterate dislike. To suppose that life has (as they express it) no higher end than pleasure—no better and nobler object of desire and pursuit—they designate as utterly mean and grovelling; as a doctrine worthy only of swine, to whom the followers of Epicurus were, at a very early period, contemptuously likened; and modern holders of the doctrine are occasionally made the subject of equally polite comparisons by its German, French, and English assailants.

When thus attacked, the Epicureans have always answered that it is not they, but their accusers, who represent human nature in a degrading light; since the accusation supposes human beings to be capable of no pleasures except those of which swine are capable. If this supposition were true, the charge could not be gainsaid, but would then be no longer an imputation; for if the sources of pleasure were precisely the same to human beings and to swine, the rule of life which is good enough for the one would be good enough for the other. The comparison of the Epicurean life to that of beasts is felt as degrading, precisely because a beast's pleasures do not satisfy a human being's conceptions of happiness. Human beings have faculties more elevated than the animal appetites; and, when once made conscious of them, do not regard anything as happiness which does not include their gratification. . . . But there is no known Epicurean theory of life which does not assign to the pleasures of the intellect, of the feelings and imagination, and of the moral sentiments, a much higher value as pleasures than to those of mere sensation.

It must be admitted, however, that utilitarian writers in general have placed the superiority of mental over bodily pleasures chiefly in the greater permanency, safety, uncostliness, etc., of the former—that is, in their circumstantial advantages rather than in their intrinsic nature. . . . It is quite compatible with the principle of utility to recognize the fact that some *kinds* of pleasure are more desirable and more valuable than others. It would be absurd that while, in estimating all other things, quality is considered as well as quantity, the estimation of pleasures should be supposed to depend on quantity alone.

If I am asked what I mean by difference of quality in pleasures, or what makes one pleasure more valuable than another, merely as a pleasure, except its being greater in amount, there is but one possible answer. Of two pleasures, if there be one to which all or almost all who have experience of both give a decided preference, irrespective of any feeling of moral obligation to prefer it, that is the more desirable pleasure. If one of the two is, by those who are competently acquainted with both, placed so far above the other that they prefer it, even though knowing it to be attended with a greater amount of discontent, and would not resign it for any quantity of the other pleasure of which their nature is capable, we are justified in ascribing to the preferred enjoyment a superiority in quality so far outweighing quantity as to render it, in comparison, of small account.

Now, it is an unquestionable fact that those who are equally acquainted with, and equally capable of appreciating and enjoying, both do give a most marked preference to the manner of existence which employs their higher faculties. Few human creatures would consent to be changed into any of the lower animals for a promise of the fullest allowance of a beast's pleasures; no intelligent human being would consent to be a fool, no instructed person would be an ignoramus, no person of feeling and conscience would be selfish and base, even though they should be persuaded that the fool, the dunce, or the rascal is better satisfied with his lot than they are with theirs. . . . A being of higher faculties requires more to make him happy, is capable probably of more

acute suffering, and certainly accessible to it at more points, than one of an inferior type; but in spite of these liabilities, he can never really wish to sink into what he feels to be a lower grade of existence.

We may give what explanation we please of this unwillingness; we may attribute it to pride. . . ; we may refer it to the love of liberty and personal independence . . . ; but its most appropriate appellation is a sense of dignity, which all human beings possess in one form or another, . . . and which is so essential a part of the happiness of those in whom it is strong that nothing which conflicts with it could be, otherwise than momentarily, an object of desire to them. . . . It is indisputable that the being whose capacities of enjoyment are low, has the greatest chance of having them fully satisfied; and a highly endowed being will always feel that any happiness which he can look for, as the world is constituted, is imperfect. But he can learn to bear its imperfections, if they are at all bearable; and they will not make him envy the being who is indeed unconscious of the imperfections, but only because he feels not at all the good which those imperfections qualify. It is better to be a human being dissatisfied than a pig satisfied; better to be Socrates dissatisfied than a fool satisfied. And if the fool, or the pig, are of a different opinion, it is because they only know their own side of the question. The other party to the comparison knows both sides. . . .

It may be . . . objected that many who begin with youthful enthusiasm for everything noble, as they advance in years sink into indolence and selfishness. But I do not believe that those who undergo this very common change voluntarily choose the lower description of pleasures in preference to the higher. I believe that before they devote themselves exclusively to the one, they have already become incapable of the other. Capacity for the nobler feelings is in most natures a very tender plant, easily killed not only by hostile influences but by mere want of sustenance; and in the majority of young persons it speedily dies away if the occupations to which their position in life has devoted them, and the society into which it has thrown them, are not favourable to keeping that higher capacity in exercise. . . .

. . . The utilitarian standard . . . is not the agent's own greatest happiness, but the greatest amount of happiness altogether; and, if it may possibly be doubted whether a noble character is always the happier for its nobleness, there can be no doubt that it makes other people happier, and that the world in general is immensely a gainer by it. . . .

According to the Greatest Happiness Principle . . . the ultimate end, with reference to and for the sake of which all other things are desirable (whether we are considering our own good or that of other people), is an existence exempt as far as possible from pain, and as rich as possible in enjoyments, both in point of quantity and quality. . . . This, being, according to the utilitarian opinion, the end of human action, is necessarily also the standard of morality, which may accordingly be defined, the rules and precepts for human conduct, by the observance of which an existence such as has been described might be, to the greatest extent possible, secured to all mankind; and not to them only, but, so far as the nature of things admits, to the whole sentient creation. . . .

When, however, it is . . . asserted to be impossible that human life should be happy, the assertion, if not something like a verbal quibble, is at least an exaggeration. If by happiness be meant a continuity of highly pleasurable excitement, it is evident enough that this is impossible. A state of exalted pleasure lasts only moments, or in some cases, and with some intermissions, hours or days, and is the occasional brilliant flash of enjoyment, not its permanent and steady flame. Of this the philosophers who have taught that happiness is the end of life were as fully aware as those who taunt them. The happiness which they meant was not a life of rapture, but moments of such, in an existence made up of few and transitory pains, many and various pleasures, with a decided predominance of the active over the passive, and having as the foundation of the whole not to expect more from life than it is capable of bestowing. A life thus composed, to those who have been fortunate

enough to obtain it, has always appeared worthy of the name of happiness. And such an existence is even now the lot of many, during some considerable portion of their lives. The present wretched education and wretched social arrangements are the only real hindrance to its being attainable by almost all.

The objectors perhaps may doubt whether human beings, if taught to consider happiness as the end of life, would be satisfied with such a moderate share of it. But great numbers of mankind have been satisfied with much less. The main constituents of a satisfied life appear to be two, either of which by itself is often found sufficient for the purpose: tranquillity and excitement. With much tranquillity, many find that they can be content with very little pleasure: with much excitement, many can reconcile themselves to a considerable quantity of pain.

There is assuredly no inherent impossibility in enabling even the mass of mankind to unite both; since the two are so far from being incompatible that they are in natural alliance the prolongation of either being a preparation for, and exciting a wish for, the other. It is only those in whom indolence amounts to a vice that do not desire excitement after an interval of repose; it is only those in whom the need of excitement is a disease that feel the tranquillity which follows excitement dull and insipid, instead of pleasurable in direct proportion to the excitement which preceded it. When people who are tolerably fortunate in their outward lot do not find in life sufficient enjoyment to make it valuable to them, the cause generally is caring for nobody but themselves. To those who have neither public nor private affections, the excitements of life are much curtailed, and in any case dwindle in value as the time approaches when all selfish interests must be terminated by death; while those who leave after them objects of personal affection, and especially those who have also cultivated a fellow-feeling with the collective interests of mankind, retain as lively an interest in life on the eve of death as in the vigour of youth and health.

Next to selfishness, the principal cause which makes life unsatisfactory is want of mental cultivation. A cultivated mind—I do not mean that of a philosopher, but any mind to which the fountains of knowledge have been opened, and which has been taught, in any tolerable degree, to exercise its faculties—finds sources of inexhaustible interest in all that surrounds it: in the objects of nature, the achievements of art, the imaginations of poetry, the incidents of history, the ways of mankind, past and present, and their prospects in the future. . . .

Now, there is absolutely no reason in the nature of things why an amount of mental culture sufficient to give an intelligent interest in these objects of contemplation should not be the inheritance of every one born in a civilized country. . . .

. . . No one whose opinion deserves a moment's consideration can doubt that most of the great positive evils of the world are in themselves removable, and will, if human affairs continue to improve, be in the end reduced within narrow limits. Poverty . . . may be completely extinguished by the wisdom of society, combined with the good sense and providence of individuals. Even that most intractable of enemies, disease, may be indefinitely reduced in dimensions by good physical and moral education, and proper control of noxious influences; while the progress of science holds out a promise for the future of still more direct conquests over this detestable foe. . . . As for vicissitudes of fortune and other disappointments connected with worldly circumstances, these are principally the effect either of gross imprudence, of ill-regulated desires, or of bad or imperfect social institutions. All the grand sources, in short, of human suffering are in a great degree, many of them almost entirely, conquerable by human care and effort. . . .

. . . Unquestionably it is possible to do without happiness; it is done involuntarily by nineteen-twentieth of mankind, even in those parts of our present world which are least deep in barbarism. . . .

I must again repeat . . . that the happiness which forms the utilitarian standard of what is right in conduct is not the agent's own happiness, but that of all concerned. As between his own happiness and that of others, utilitarianism requires him to be as strictly impartial as a disinterested and benevolent spectator. In the golden rule of Jesus of Nazareth we read the complete spirit of the ethics of utility. To do as you would be done by, and to love your neighbour as yourself, constitute the ideal perfection of utilitarian morality. As the means of making the nearest approach to this ideal, utility would enjoin first, that laws and social arrangements should place the happiness, or (as speaking practically it may be called) the interest, of every individual, as nearly as possible in harmony with the interest of the whole; and secondly, that education and opinion, which have so vast a power over human character, should so use that power as to establish in the mind of every individual an indissoluble association between his own happiness and the good of the whole; especially between his own happiness and the practice of such modes of conduct, negative and positive, as regard for the universal happiness prescribes; so that not only he may be unable to conceive the possibility of happiness to himself, consistently with conduct opposed to the general good, but also that a direct impulse to promote the general good may be in every individual one of the habitual motives of action, and the sentiments connected therewith may fill a large and prominent place in every human being's sentient existence. . . .

The objectors to utilitarianism cannot always be charged with representing it in a discreditable light. On the contrary, those among them who entertain anything like a just idea of its disinterested character, sometimes find fault with its standard as being too high for humanity. They say it is exacting too much to require that people shall always act from the inducement of promoting the general interests of society. But this is to mistake the very meaning of a standard of morals, and confound the rule of action with the motive of it. It is the business of ethics to tell us what are our duties, or by what test we may know them; but no system of ethics requires that the sole motive of all we do shall be a feeling of duty: on the contrary, ninety-nine hundredths of all our actions are done from other motives, and rightly so done, if the rule of duty does not condemn them. It is the more unjust to utilitarianism that this particular misapprehension should be made a ground of objection to it, inasmuch as utilitarian moralists have gone beyond almost all others in affirming that the motive has nothing to do with the morality of the action, though much with the worth of the agent. He who saves a fellow creature from drowning does what is morally right, whether his motive be duty, or the hope of being paid for his trouble. . . . But to speak only of actions done from the motive of duty, and in direct obedience to principle: it is a misapprehension of the utilitarian mode of thought to conceive it as implying that people should fix their minds upon so wide a generality as the world, or society at large. The great majority of good actions are intended not for the benefit of the world, but for that of individuals, of which the good of the world is made up; and the thoughts of the most virtuous man need not on these occasions travel beyond the particular persons concerned, except so far as is necessary to assure himself that in benefiting them he is not violating the rights, that is the legitimate and authorized expectations, of any one else. The multiplication of happiness is, according to the utilitarian ethics, the object of virtue; the occasions on which any person (except one in a thousand) has it in his power to do this on an extended scale . . . are but exceptional; and on these occasions alone is he called on to consider public utility; in every other case, private utility, the interest or happiness of some few persons, is all he has to attend to. . . .

We not uncommonly hear the doctrine of utility inveighed against as a *godless* doctrine. If it be necessary to say anything at all against so mere an assumption, we may say that the question depends upon what idea we have formed of the moral character of the Deity. If it be a true belief that God desires, above all things, the happiness of His creatures, and that this was His purpose in their creation, utility is not only not a godless doctrine, but more profoundly religious than any other. If it be meant that utilitarianism does not recognize the revealed will of God as the supreme law of morals, I answer that a utilitarian who believes

in the perfect goodness and wisdom of God necessarily believes that whatever God has thought fit to reveal on the subject of morals must fulfil the requirements of utility in a supreme degree. But others besides utilitarians have been of opinion that the Christian revelation was intended, and is fitted, to inform the hearts and minds of mankind with a spirit which should enable them to find for themselves what is right, and incline them to do it when found, rather than to tell them, except in a very general way, what it is; and that we need a doctrine of ethics, carefully followed out, to *interpret* to us the will of God. . . .

Again, defenders of utility often find themselves called upon to reply to such objection as this—that there is not time, previous to action, for calculating and weighing the effects of any line of conduct on the general happiness. This is exactly as if any one were to say that it is impossible to guide our conduct by Christianity, because there is not time, on every occasion on which anything has to be done, to read through the Old and New Testaments. The answer to the objection is that there has been ample time, namely the whole past duration of the human species. During all that time mankind have been learning by experience the tendencies of actions; on which experience all the prudence, as well as all the morality of life, are dependent. People talk as if the commencement of this course of experience had hitherto been put off, and as if, at the moment when some man feels tempted to meddle with the property or life of another, he had to begin considering for the first time whether murder and theft are injurious to human happiness. . . . It is truly a whimsical supposition that if mankind were agreed in considering utility to be the test of morality, they would remain without any agreement as to what *is* useful, and would take no measures for having their notions on the subject taught to the young, and enforced by law and opinion. There is no difficulty in proving any ethical standard whatever to work ill, if we suppose universal idiocy to be conjoined with it; but on any hypothesis short of that mankind must by this time have acquired positive beliefs as to the effects of some actions on their happiness; and the beliefs which have thus come down are the rules of morality for the multitude, and for the philosopher until he has succeeded in finding better.

That philosophers might easily do this, even how, on many subjects; that the received code of ethics is no means of divine right; and that mankind have still much to learn as to the effects of actions on the general happiness, I admit, or, rather, earnestly maintain. The corollaries from the principle of utility, like the precepts of every practical art, admit of indefinite improvement, and, in a progressive state of the human mind, their improvement is perpetually going on. But to consider the rules of morality as improvable, is one thing; to pass over the intermediate generalizations entirely, and endeavour to test each individual action directly by the first principle, is another. It is a strange notion that the acknowledgment of a first principle is inconsistent with the admission of secondary ones. . . . Rules of conduct cannot be so framed as to require no exceptions, and that hardly any kind of action can safely be laid down as either always obligatory or always condemnable. There is no ethical creed which does not temper the rigidity of its laws by giving a certain latitude, under the moral responsibility of the agent, for accommodation to peculiarities of circumstances. . . . There exists no moral system under which there do not arise unequivocal cases of conflicting obligation. These are the real difficulties, the knotty points both in the theory of ethics, and in the conscientious guidance of personal conduct.

. . . But it can hardly be pretended that any one will be the less qualified for dealing with them from possessing an ultimate standard to which conflicting rights and duties can be referred. If utility is the ultimate source of moral obligations, utility may be invoked to decide between them when their demands are incompatible. Though the application of the standard may be difficult, it is better than none at all: while in other systems, the moral laws all claiming independent authority, there is no common umpire entitled to interfere between them; their claims to precedence one over another rest on little better than sophistry, and unless determined, as they generally are, by the unacknowledged influence of considerations of utility, afford a free scope for the action of personal desires and partialities. We must remember that only in these cases of conflict between secondary principles is it requisite that first principles should be appealed to. There is no case of moral obligation in which some secondary principle is not involved; and, if only one, there can seldom be any real doubt which one it is, in the mind of any person by whom the principle itself is recognized.

 IMMANUEL KANT (1724–1804)

FOUNDATIONS OF THE METAPHYSICS OF MORALS

First Section: Transition from Common Sense Knowledge of Morals to the Philosophical

Nothing in the world—indeed nothing even beyond the world—can possibly be conceived which could be called good without qualification except a good will. Intelligence, wit, judgment, and other talents of the mind however they may be named, or courage, resoluteness, and perseverance as qualities of temperament, are doubtless in many respects good and desirable; but they can become extremely bad

From *Foundations of the Metaphysics of Morals,* 2nd ed. Trans. L. W. Beck (New York: Library of Liberal Arts, 1990). Copyright © 1990 Macmillan Publishing Co. Reprinted by permission of the publisher.

and harmful if the will, which is to make use of these gifts of nature and which in its special constitution is called character, is not good. It is the same with gifts of fortune. Power, riches, honor, even health, general well-being and the contentment with one's condition which is called happiness make for pride and even arrogance if there is not a good will to correct their influence on the mind and on its principle of action, so as to make it generally fitting to its entire end. It need hardly be mentioned that the sight of a being adorned with no feature of a pure and good will yet enjoying lasting good fortune can never give pleasure to an impartial rational observer. Thus the good will seems to constitute the indispensable condition even of worthiness to be happy.

Some qualities seem to be conducive to this good will and can facilitate its action, but in spite of that they have no intrinsic unconditional worth. They rather presuppose a good will. . . .

Moderation in emotions and passions, self-control, and calm deliberation not only are good in many respects but seem even to constitute part of the inner worth of the person. But however unconditionally they were esteemed by the ancients, they are far from being good without qualification, for without the principles of a good will they can become extremely bad, and the coolness of a villain makes him not only far more dangerous but also more directly abominable in our eyes than he would have seemed without it.

The good will is not good because of what it effects or accomplishes . . . ; it is good only because of its willing (i.e., it is good in itself). . . . Even if it should happen that, by a particularly unfortunate fate or by the niggardly provision of a stepmotherly nature, this will should be wholly lacking in power to accomplish its purpose, and if even the greatest effort should not avail it to achieve anything of its end, and if there remained only the good will—not as a mere wish, but as the summoning of all the means in our power—it would sparkle like a jewel all by itself, as something that had its full worth in itself. Usefulness or fruitlessness can neither diminish not augment this worth. . . .

We have, then, to develop the concept of a will which is to be esteemed as good in itself without regard to anything else. It dwells already in the natural and sound understanding and does not need so much to be taught as only to be brought to light. In the estimation of the total worth of our actions it always takes first place and is the condition of everything else. In order to show this, we shall take the concept of duty. It contains the concept of a good will. . . .

I here omit all actions which are recognized as opposed to duty, . . . for with these the question does not arise as to whether they may be done *from* duty, since they conflict with it. I also pass over actions which are really in accord with duty and to which one has no direct inclination, rather doing them because impelled to do so by another inclination. For it is easily decided whether an action in accord with duty is done from duty or for some selfish purpose. It is far more difficult to note this difference when the action is in accord with duty and, in addition, the subject has a direct inclination to do it. For example, it is in accord with duty that a dealer should not overcharge an inexperienced customer, and wherever there is much trade the prudent merchant does not do so, but has a fixed price for everyone so that a child may buy from him as cheaply as any other. Thus the customer is honestly served, but this is far from sufficient to warrant the belief that the merchant has behaved in this way from duty and principles of honesty. His own advantage required this behavior, but it cannot be assumed that over and above that he had a direct inclination to his customers and that, out of love, as it were, he gave none an advantage in price over another. The action was done neither from duty nor from direct inclination but only for a selfish purpose.

On the other hand, it is a duty to preserve one's life, and moreover everyone has a direct inclination to do so. But for that reason, the often anxious care which most men take of it has no intrinsic worth, and the maxim of doing so has no moral import. They preserve their lives according to duty, but not from duty. But if adversities and hopeless sorrow completely take away the relish for life; if an unfortunate man, strong in soul, is indignant rather than despondent or dejected over his fate and wishes for death, and yet preserves his life without loving it and from neither inclination nor fear but from duty—then his maxim has moral merit.

To be kind where one can is a duty, and there are, moreover, many persons so sympathetically constituted that without any motive of vanity or selfishness they find an inner satisfaction in spreading joy and rejoice in the contentment of others which they have made possible. But I say that, however dutiful and however amiable it may be, that kind of action has no true moral worth. It is on a level with actions done from other inclinations, such as the inclination to honor, which, if fortunately directed to what in fact accords with duty and is generally useful and thus honorable, deserve praise and encouragement, but no esteem. For the maxim lacks the moral import of an action done not from inclination but from duty. . . .

Thus the first proposition of morality is that to have genuine moral worth, an action must be done from duty. The second proposition is: An action done from duty does not have its moral worth in the purpose which is to be achieved through it but in the maxim whereby it is determined. Its moral value, therefore, does not depend upon the realization of the object of the action but merely on the principle of the volition by which the action is done irrespective of the objects of the faculty of desire. . . .

The third principle, as a consequence of the two preceding, I would express as follows: Duty is the necessity to do an action from respect for law. . . .

But what kind of law can that be, the conception of which must determine the will without reference to the expected result? Under this condition alone can the will be called absolutely good without qualification. Since I have robbed the will of all impulses which could come to it from obedience to any law, nothing remains to serve as a principle of the will except universal conformity to law as such. That is, I ought never to act in such a way that I could not also will that my maxim should be a universal law. Strict conformity to law as such (without assuming any particular law applicable to certain actions) serves as the principle of the will, and it must serve as such a principle if

duty is not to be a vain delusion and chimerical concept. The common sense of mankind (*gemeine Menschenvernunft*) in its practical judgments is in perfect agreement with this and has this principle constantly in view.

Let the question, for example, be: May I, when in distress, make a promise with the intention not to keep it? I easily distinguish the two meanings which the question can have, viz., whether it is prudent to make a false promise, or whether it conforms to duty. The former can undoubtedly be often the case. . . .

To be truthful from duty, however, is an entirely different thing from being truthful out of fear of untoward consequences, for in the former case the concept of the action itself contains a law for me, while in the latter I must first look about to see what results for me may be connected with it. . . . The shortest but most infallible way to find the answer to the question as to whether deceitful promise is consistent with duty is to ask myself: Would I be content that my maxim of extricating myself from difficulty by a false promise should hold as a universal law for myself as well as for others? And could I say to myself that everyone may make a false promise when he is in a difficulty from which he otherwise cannot escape? Immediately I see that I could will the lie but not a universal law to lie. For with such a law there would be no promises at all, inasmuch as it would be futile to make a pretense of my intention in regard to future actions to those who would not believe this pretense or—if they overhastily did so—would pay me back in my own coin. Thus my maxim would necessarily destroy itself as soon as it was made a universal law. I do not, therefore, need any penetrating acuteness to discern what I have to do in order that my volition may be morally good. Inexperienced in the course of the world, incapable of being prepared for all its contingencies, I only ask myself: Can I will that my maxim become a universal law? If not, it must be rejected, not because of any disadvantage accruing to myself or even to others, but because it cannot enter as a principle into a possible enactment of universal law, and reason extorts from me an immediate respect for such legislation. . . .

Second Section: Transition from Popular Moral Philosophy to the Metaphysics of Morals

. . . The conception of an objective principle, so far as it constrains a will, is a command (of reason), and the formula of this command is called an *imperative.*

All imperatives are expressed by an ought and thereby indicate the relation of an objective law of reason to a will which is not in its subjective constitution necessarily determined by this law. This relation is that of constraint. Imperatives say that it would be good to do or to refrain from doing something, but they say it to a will which does not always do something simply because the thing is presented to it as good to do. Practical good is what determines the will by means of the conception of reason and hence not by subjective causes but objectively, on grounds which are valid for every rational being as such. It is distinguished from the pleasant, as that which has an influence on the will only by means of a sensation from purely subjective causes, which hold for the senses only of this or that person and not as a principle of reason which holds for everyone.

A perfectly good will, therefore, would be equally subject to objective laws of the good, but it could not be conceived as constrained by them to accord with them, because it can be determined to act by its own subjective constitution only through the conception of the good. . . .

All imperatives command either *hypothetically* or *categorically*. The former present the practical necessity of a possible action as a means to achieving something else which one desires (or which one may possibly desire). The categorical imperative would be one which presented an action as of itself objectively necessary, without regard to any other end. . . .

. . . If the action is good only as a means to something else, the imperative is hypothetical; but if it is thought of as good in itself, and hence as necessary in a will which of itself conforms to reason as the principle of this will, the imperative is categorical. . . .

The hypothetical imperative . . . says only that the action is good to some purpose, possible or actual. . . . The categorical imperative, which declares the action to be of itself objectively necessary without making any reference to any end in view (i.e., without having any other purpose), holds as an apodictical practical principle. . . .

If I think of a hypothetical imperative as such, I do not know what it will contain until the condition is stated under which it is an imperative. But if I think of a categorical imperative, I know immediately what it will contain. For since the imperative contains, besides the law, only the necessity of the maxim of acting in accordance with the law, while the law contains no condition to which it is restricted, nothing remains except the universality of law as such to which the maxim of the action should conform; and this conformity alone is what is represented as necessary by the imperative.

There is, therefore, only one categorical imperative. It is: Act only according to that maxim by which you can at the same time will that it should become a universal law.

Now if all imperatives of duty can be derived from this one imperative as a principle, we can at least show what we understand by the concept of duty and what it means, even though it remain undecided whether that which is called duty is an empty concept or not. . . .

We shall now enumerate some duties, adopting the usual division of them into duties to ourselves and to others and into perfect and imperfect duties.[1]

1. A man who is reduced to despair by a series of evils feels a weariness with life but is

---

[1]It must be noted here that I reserve the division of duties for a future *Metaphysics of Morals* and that the division here stands as only an arbitrary one (chosen in order to arrange my examples). For the rest, by a perfect duty I here understand a duty which permits no exception in the interest of inclination; thus I have not merely outer but also inner perfect duties. This runs contrary to the usage adopted in the schools, but I am not disposed to defend it here because it is all one to my purpose whether this is conceded or not.

still in possession of his reason sufficiently to ask whether it would not be contrary to his duty to himself to take his own life. Now he asks whether the maxim of his action could become a universal law of nature. His maxim, however is: For love of myself, I make it my principle to shorten my life when by a longer duration it threatens more evil than satisfaction. But it is questionable whether this principle of self-love could become a universal law of nature. One immediately sees a contradiction in a system of nature whose law would be to destroy life by the feeling whose special office is to impel the improvement of life. In this case it would not exist as nature; hence that maxim cannot obtain as a law of nature, and thus it wholly contradicts the supreme principle of all duty.

2. Another man finds himself forced by need to borrow money. He well knows that he will not be able to repay it, but he also sees that nothing will be lent him if he does not firmly promise to repay it at a certain time. He desires to make such a promise, but he has enough conscience to ask himself whether it is not improper and opposed to duty to relieve his distress in such a way. Now, assuming he does decide to do so, the maxim of his action would be as follows: When I believe myself to be in need of money, I will borrow money and promise to repay it, although I know I shall never be able to do so. Now this principle of self-love or of his own benefit may very well be compatible with his whole future welfare, but the question is whether it is right. He changes the pretension of self-love into a universal law and then puts the question: How would it be if my maxim became a universal law? He immediately sees that it could never hold as a universal law of nature and be consistent with itself; rather it must necessarily contradict itself. For the universality of a law which says that anyone who believes himself to be in need could promise what he pleased with the intention of not fulfilling it would make the promise itself and the end to be accomplished by it impossible; no one would believe what was promised to him but would only laugh at any such assertion as vain pretense.

3. A third finds in himself a talent which could, by means of some cultivation, make

him in many respects a useful man. But he finds himself in comfortable circumstances and prefers indulgence in pleasure to troubling himself with broadening and improving his fortunate natural gifts. Now, however, let him ask whether his maxim of neglecting his gifts, besides agreeing with his propensity to idle amusement, agrees also with what is called duty. He sees that a system of nature could indeed exist in accordance with such a law, even though man (like the inhabitants of the South Sea Islands) should let his talents rust and resolve to devote his life merely to idleness, indulgence, and propagation—in a word, to pleasure. But he cannot possibly will that this should become a universal law of nature or that it should be implanted in us by a natural instinct. For, as a rational being, he necessarily wills that all his faculties should be developed, inasmuch as they are given him and serve him for all sorts of purposes.

4. A fourth man, for whom things are going well, sees that others (whom he could help) have to struggle with great hardships, and he asks, What concern of mine is it? Let each one be as happy as heaven wills, or as he can make himself; I will not take anything from him or even envy him; but to his welfare or to his assistance in time of need I have no desire to contribute. If such a way of thinking were a universal law of nature, certainly the human race could exist, and without doubt even better than in a state where everyone talks of sympathy and good will or even exerts himself occasionally to practice them while, on the other hand, he cheats when he can and betrays or otherwise violates the right of man. Now although it is possible that a universal law of nature according to that maxim could exist, it is nevertheless impossible to will that such a principle should hold everywhere as a law of nature. For a will which resolved this would conflict with itself, since instances can often arise in which he would need the love and sympathy of others, and in which he would have robbed himself, by such a law of nature springing from his own will, of all hope of the aid he desires.

The foregoing are a few of the many actual duties, or at least of duties we hold to be actual, whose derivation from the one stated principle is clear. We must be able to will that a maxim of our action become a universal law; this is the canon of the moral estimation of our action generally. Some actions are of such a nature that their maxim cannot even be *thought* as a universal law of nature without contradiction, far from it being possible that one could will that it should be such. In others this internal impossibility is not found, though it is still impossible to will that that maxim should be raised to the universality of a law of nature, because such a will would contradict itself. We easily see that a maxim of the first kind conflicts with stricter or narrower (imprescriptable) duty, that of the latter with broader (meritorious) duty. Thus all duties, so far as the kind of obligation (not the object of their action) is concerned, have been completely exhibited by these examples in their dependence upon the same principle.

When we observe ourselves in any transgression of a duty, we find we do not actually will that our maxim should become a universal law. That is impossible for us; rather, the contrary of this maxim should remain as a law generally, and we only take the liberty of making an exception to it for ourselves or for the sake of our inclination, and for this one occasion. Consequently, if we weighed everything from one and the same standpoint, namely, reason, we would come upon a contradiction in our own will, viz., that a certain principle is objectively necessary as a universal law and yet subjectively does not hold universally but rather admits exceptions. . . .

Now, I say, man and, in general, every rational being exists as an end in himself and not merely as a means to be arbitrarily used by this or that will. In all his actions, whether they are directed toward himself or toward other rational beings, he must always be regarded at the same time as an end. All objects of inclination have only conditional worth, for if the inclinations and needs founded on them did not exist, their object would be worthless. . . . Beings whose existence does not depend on our will but on nature, if they are not rational beings, have only relative worth as means, and are therefore called things; rational

beings, on the other hand, are designated persons because their nature indicates that they are ends in themselves (i.e., things which may not be used merely as means). Such a being is thus an object of respect, and as such restricts all [arbitrary] choice. . . .

. . . Man necessarily thinks of his own existence in this way, and thus far it is a subjective principle of human actions. Also every other rational being thinks of his existence on the same rational ground which holds also for myself; thus it is at the same time an objective principle from which, as a supreme practical ground, it must be possible to derive all laws of the will. The practical imperative, therefore, is the following: Act so that you treat humanity, whether in your own person or in that of another, always as an end and never as a means only. Let us now see whether this can be achieved. To return to our previous examples:

First, according to the concept of necessary duty to oneself, he who contemplates suicide will ask himself whether his action can be consistent with the idea of humanity as an end in itself. If in order to escape from burdensome circumstances he destroys himself, he uses a person merely as a means to maintain a tolerable condition up to the end of life. Man, however, is not a thing, and thus not something to be used merely as a means; he must always be regarded in all his actions as an end in himself. Therefore I cannot dispose of man in my own person so as to mutilate, corrupt, or kill him. (It belongs to ethics proper to define more accurately this basic principle so as to avoid all misunderstanding, e.g., as to amputating limbs in order to preserve myself, or to exposing my life to danger in order to save it; I must therefore omit them here.)

Second, as concerns necessary or obligatory duties to others, he who intends a deceitful promise to others sees immediately that he intends to use another man merely as a means, without the latter at the same time containing the end in himself. For he whom I want to use for my own purposes by means of such a promise cannot possibly assent to my mode of acting against him and thus share in the purpose of this action. This conflict with the principle of other men is even clearer if we cite examples of attacks on their freedom and property, for then it is clear that he who violates the rights of men intends to make use of the person of others merely as means, without considering that, as rational beings, they must always be esteemed at the same time as ends (i.e., only as beings who must be able to embody in themselves the purpose of the very same action.)[2]

---

[2]Let it not be thought that the banal "what you do not wish to be done to you. . . " could here serve as guide or principle, for it is only derived from the principle and is restricted by various limitations. It cannot be a universal law, because it contains the ground neither of duties to one's self nor of the benevolent duties to others (for many a man would gladly consent that others should not benefit him, provided only that he might be excused from showing benevolence to them). Nor does it contain the ground of obligatory duties to another, for the criminal would argue on this ground against the judge who sentences him. And so on.

Thirdly, with regard to contingent (meritorious) duty to oneself, it is not sufficient that the action not conflict with humanity in our person as an end in itself; it must also harmonize with it. In humanity there are capacities for greater perfection which belong to the purpose of nature with respect to humanity in our own person, and to neglect these might perhaps be consistent with the preservation of humanity as an end in itself, but not with the furtherance of that end.

Fourthly, with regard to meritorious duty to others, the natural purpose that all men have is their own happiness. Humanity might indeed exist if no one contributed to the happiness of others, provided he did not intentionally detract from it, but this harmony with humanity as an end in itself is only negative, not positive, if everyone does not also endeavor, as far as he can, to further the purposes of others. For the ends of any person, who is an end in himself, must as far as possible be also my ends, if that conception of an end in itself is to have its full effect on me.

Questions for Discussion and Review

For each of the following, apply the Greatest Happiness version of AU, Negative AU, RU, and the two formulations of Kant's Categorical Imperative to answer them.

1. A college basketball star has made a deal with gamblers to shave points for $12,000. Is his action morally wrong?

2. An athlete uses steroids to win a place on the college basketball team. Is her action morally wrong?

3. In 1965 the Crooked Path Construction Company bribed a city building inspector to overlook the fact that the company violated building code requirements by using substandard materials in constructing a six-story office building. The company paid the building inspector $20,000 and saved itself more than $750,000. In 1995 the building was torn down to make way for a new convention complex. The president of Crooked Path Construction, Larry Lyer, believes that his company did nothing morally wrong because its actions harmed no one. Did his company do anything morally wrong?

4. A student scrawls anti-Semitic, anti-Arab, anti-black, anti-Hispanic, and sexist remarks on lavatory walls. Is her action morally wrong?

5. To retaliate against an invasion of his country, a patriot blows up a civilian airliner of the invading nation. Is his action morally wrong?

6. An employee who has worked for a company for more than thirty years and is less than two years from retirement is fired by the vice president so that the company won't have to pay her a pension. Is his action morally wrong?

7. James and Gloria, both 24, are not married but they are having sex. Is this morally wrong?

8. Are homosexual acts immoral?

9. United States law forbids polygamy (having more than one spouse at a time) because many people believe that polygamy is immoral. Is polygamy immoral?

10. In *The Flame Trees of Thika,* her autobiographical account of growing up in East Africa in the early years of the twentieth century, Elspeth Huxley comments that the Kikuyu among whom she lived were indifferent to animal suffering. She writes:

   Perhaps the Kikuyu were not deliberately cruel to animals, but they were horribly callous. If they did not actively enjoy watching an animal suffer, they certainly did not mind, and it never occurred to any of them to put a beast out of pain. In their eyes, I suppose, pain was simply a thing that had to be suffered, whether you were a beast or a man; and for beasts, they did not seem to give them credit for any feelings.[10]

   Once the young Elspeth hoped to save a goat that was to be sacrificed in a religious ritual intended to save a young woman who was dying. (The sacrifice did not succeed; the young Kikuyu woman died anyway.) She writes:

   I was too late to save the goat. Its insides had been slit open, some of its organs lay on the ground and it had been partially flayed. . . . The point was that the goat was still alive. A man held its jaws to stop it bleating, but for a moment I saw its eyes, and the feeble twitchings of its raw and broken legs. I then turned and ran.[11]

   Is there anything wrong with the Kikuyu sacrificing the goat in this manner? Should human beings refrain from causing nonhuman animals to suffer or relieve animal suffering when they can?

11. John doesn't love Pamela, but he wants to seduce her and persuade her to have sex with him. He thinks he'll succeed if she believes he loves her; thus, to get what he wants, he tells her he loves her and can't live without her, writes her love poems, and sends her flowers. He believes that his attention makes her happy and that she would

---

[10]Elspeth Huxley. *The Flame Trees of Thika* (New York: Penguin Books, 1959), 129.
[11]Ibid., 135.

enjoy having sex with him. He knows she'll eventually find out that he doesn't really love her, but he thinks that she won't be made too unhappy and will quickly get over it when she finds out. Is John doing anything morally wrong?

12. Suppose you're the manager of a store. One of your employees has been consistently late to work in the morning because she has several small children. You've warned her several times to be on time, but she's still late once or twice a week. You've decided to fire her and replace her with someone who can get to work on time. Would it be morally wrong?

13. It's 1:00 a.m. Saturday and you're having a party. Your neighbor downstairs has complained about the loud music. One of your friends wants to turn the volume down, but another friend wants you to turn it up to punish your neighbor for complaining. Would it be morally wrong to turn the volume up?

Suggestions for Further Reading

Fred Feldman. *Introductory Ethics*. Englewood Cliffs, NJ: Prentice-Hall, 1978. Chapters 2–4, 5, 7–8. A rigorous, detailed introduction to Utilitarianism and Kant's views.

C. E. Harris, Jr. *Applying Moral Theories*. Belmont, CA: Wadsworth, 1986. Chapters 6–7. A readable introduction to Utilitarianism and Kant's views that emphasizes use of the theories to solve moral problems.

Immanuel Kant. *Foundations of the Metaphysics of Morals,* 2d ed. Trans. Lewis White Beck. New York: Macmillan, 1990. (Originally published in 1785.) A difficult yet fascinating exposition and defense of the test of the Categorical Imperative. Formidable, so appropriate only for very advanced students.

John Stuart Mill. *Utilitarianism*. Indianapolis: Hackett, 1977. (Originally published in 1861.) A readable, lively, enjoyable analysis of Utilitarianism by one of its most influential defenders.

Louis P. Pojman. *Ethics: Discovering Right and Wrong*. Belmont, CA: Wadsworth, 1990. Chaps. 5–6. A useful introduction to Utilitarianism and Kant.

Anthony Quinton. *Utilitarian Ethics*. New York: St. Martin's Press, 1973. A thoughtful, well-written analysis of the strengths and weaknesses of Utilitarianism and its development.

Robert N. Van Wyk. *Introduction to Ethics*. New York: St. Martin's Press, 1990. Chaps. 6–7. A readable, careful introduction to Utilitarianism and Kant.

11 JUSTICE AND RIGHTS

Objectives

Readers are expected to:

- understand and apply Aristotle's principle of Justice.
- understand the distinction between positive and negative rights.
- understand the distinction between legal and moral rights.
- understand how to justify moral rights claims.
- know the rights contained in the United Nations Universal Declaration of Human Rights.
- understand the Utilitarian approach to questions of Justice.
- understand and apply Rawls's theory of Justice.

Introduction

The world exhibits massive amounts of inequality. Lions are stronger than the antelope they prey on. Greyhounds are faster than dachshunds. Elephants are bigger than mice. Chimps are smarter than dogs. Dolphins can swim better than humans.

But these sorts of natural inequalities among species don't usually raise serious moral issues. Rather, it's inequalities within one species—Homo sapiens—that raise such issues. Some people are very rich while others are very poor. Some people have a lot of power; others have little or no power. Some people have more legal rights and privileges than others. Some people get more social respect than others.

For example, Blacks were once enslaved by Whites. They did not have the same legal rights and privileges as Whites. Similarly, at one time women did not have the same legal rights that men had; they couldn't vote. Often they couldn't enter certain professions, hold property in their own names, or earn a college degree. At one time in most societies, the legal right to participate in political decision-making belonged only to the rich. In the United States today, some people are homeless and hungry while others are billionaires who probably have trouble keeping track of how much they're worth from day to day. Physicians generally get a lot more respect than garbage collectors. The rich have more influence with elected politicians than do the nonrich. The rich live longer than the poor.

The natural inequalities among species are generally not alterable or under anyone's control. That's not true of the inequalities among humans. Much of the inequalities of income, wealth, power, rights, status, respect, and life prospects are under human control. Much of the inequality is caused by social institutions created and alterable by humans.

Many moral questions arise when reflecting on our political and social institutions. One set of questions involves the relationship between Justice and Equality. Are there forms or degrees of inequality that are morally wrong or unjust? Is it morally wrong for a society to permit some people to be very poor while others are very rich? Is it morally wrong to give different people different legal rights? Is it morally wrong for some people to have much more power than others?

The moral concept most often applied to social and political institutions is Justice. What does Justice require regarding equality and inequality? This raises a perplexing question. Are there any standards of Justice that we all can agree on?

Aristotle's Conception of Justice: Treating Equals Equally

According to Aristotle, justice requires treating people who are equal in relevant ways the same way and treating people who are unequal in relevant ways differently. As Aristotle puts it, "justice . . . is equality—not, however, for all, but only for equals. And inequality . . . is justice; neither is this for all, but only for unequals."[1] Aristotle summarizes his remarks about justice by saying that "what is just . . . should be equal for equals."[2]

I suspect that on reflection, most people would agree that Aristotle has identified the core of the concept of justice that we all share. Suppose I see one student cheat on an exam and I give everyone in the class a failing grade on it. Surely we'd all agree that that would be unjust. But why? Aristotle's explanation is that I'm treating people who are different in relevant respects in the same way. The fact that the one student cheated but the others didn't marks a relevant difference among them. Yet I'm treating them as if everyone cheated. I shouldn't treat noncheaters in the same way I treat cheaters.

Similarly, suppose that I give your paper a D and someone else's an A. You think both papers are pretty much the same in quality so you

---

[1]Aristotle, *Politics*, in *The Complete Works of Aristotle*, ed. Jonathan Barnes (Princeton, NJ: Princeton University Press, 1984), 11–14.

[2]Ibid., 20–21.

come to me for an explanation. I say that the papers are nearly identical in content and quality of writing, but that I just felt like giving one an A and the other a D. Surely if they're the same, then they deserve the same grade. I'm treating equal papers in relevant respects differently, and that's unjust. Aristotle's principle of Justice would explain our convictions that it would be wrong (unjust) for me to fail both cheaters and noncheaters, and wrong (unjust) to give different grades to very similar papers.

Justice requires treating people who are equal in relevant respects equally (in the same way), and people who are unequal in relevant respects unequally. Injustice occurs when people equal in relevant respects are treated differently and when people different in relevant respects are treated the same. What counts as a relevant difference depends on what's being distributed. What's relevant for a grade on a philosophy paper is not relevant for getting a part in a play. What's relevant for getting a part in a play is not relevant for being a starting player on a varsity basketball team.

We'll concentrate on the most important benefits that society produces and distributes: (1) civil and political rights and (2) economic resources (wealth and income). We want to know whether justice permits inequality in the distribution of these benefits. If it does, does justice place any limits on the degree of inequality permitted? Finally, if inequality in these basic benefits is permitted by the principles of justice, what constitutes a relevant difference justifying different shares?

Does Justice Permit Inequality in Civil and Political Rights?

Civil and political rights include such rights as the right to vote in elections and to hold public office, the right to voluntarily enter into contracts with other people, the right to own property, the right to a fair and impartial trial when accused of a crime, the right to a free choice of occupation, the right to freedom of movement, and the right to freedom of thought and expression. Does justice require that everyone in a society have equal civil and political rights?

Not all societies have granted equal civil and political rights. Consider a slave society. Obviously, slaves don't have the same civil and political rights as masters. Similarly, in some societies, women have been subordinate to men and have not had the same civil and political rights. For example, nineteenth-century American women didn't have the right to vote. Until late in the nineteenth century in most parts of Europe, poor people didn't have the same rights as people who weren't poor; they couldn't vote. Is it just to assign or distribute civil and political rights on the basis of sex, race, wealth, or hereditary class? Are these relevant differences for the distribution of civil and political rights?

Imagine that someone in the United States today advocates giving the right to vote only to men or only to the wealthy, or the right to a fair and impartial trial to everyone but Arabs and Asians, or the right to freedom of religion to everyone but non-Christians, or the right to freedom of movement to everyone but homosexuals. Won't most of us, on reflection, insist that sex, race, nationality, religion, wealth, and sexual orientation are irrelevant when it comes to assigning civil and political rights—that men and women, wealthy and poor, Arabs and non-Arabs, Asians and non-Asians, Christians and non-Christians, homosexuals and heterosexuals are all equal in all respects relevant to the assignment of civil and political rights? Isn't such discrimination unjust because it treats people who are equal in all relevant respects differently?

An influential tradition in Western thought proclaims that people are roughly equal in the features or characteristics relevant to the assignment of civil and political rights; therefore, justice requires equal civil and political rights for all people. Thomas Hobbes (1588–1679), for example, begins with the assumption that all people are relatively equal:

> Nature hath made men so equal, in the faculties of the body, and mind; as that though there be found one man sometimes manifestly stronger in body, or of quicker mind than another; yet when all is reckoned together, the difference between man, and man, is not so considerable, as that one man can thereupon claim to himself any benefit, to which another may not pretend, as well as he. For as to the strength of body, the weakest has strength enough to kill the strongest, either by secret machination, or by confederacy with others, that are in the same danger with himself.
>
> And as to the faculties of the mind, setting aside the arts which are grounded upon words, and especially . . . science; which very few have, and but in few things; as being not a native faculty, born with us . . . , I find yet a greater equality amongst men, than that of strength. For prudence, is but experience; which equal time equally bestows on all men, in those things they equally apply themselves unto. That which may perhaps make such equality incredible, is but a vain conceit of one's own wisdom, which almost all men think they have in a greater degree than the vulgar; that is, than all men but themselves, and a few others, whom by fame, or by concurring with themselves, they approve. For such is the nature of men, that howsoever they may acknowledge many others to be more witty, or more eloquent, or more learned; yet they will hardly believe there be many so wise as themselves; for they see their own wit at hand, and other men's at a distance.[3]

According to Hobbes, people are roughly equal in strength, intelligence, wit, and wisdom; only arrogance and ignorance lead us to think that people like ourselves are superior to people unlike ourselves. Similarly, Thomas Jefferson writes in the Declaration of Independence, "We hold these Truths to be self-evident, that all Men are created equal. . . ."

---

[3]Thomas Hobbes, *Leviathan* (New York: Collier Books, 1962), 98.

According to this tradition, people are roughly equal in the features relevant to the assignment of civil and political rights, despite the myriad ways in which they can be different and unequal. As we saw in the previous chapter, many moral theories, including Utilitarianism and Kantian theory, insist that all people's well-being must count equally from a moral perspective. According to this view, every person is a full member of the moral community simply because he or she is a person. From the perspective of this tradition, we could say that the only feature relevant for the distribution of civil and political rights is personhood. All people are equally people, and all people should have equal civil and political rights. For example, the contemporary philosopher William Frankena writes:

> All [people] are to be treated as equals, not because they are equal in any respect but simply because they are human [people]. They are human [people] because they have emotions and desires, and are able to think, and hence are capable of enjoying a good [happy] life in a sense in which other animals are not.[4]

Frankena goes on to endorse the "equal intrinsic value of individual human beings."[5] Bernard Williams, another contemporary philosopher, points out that the assumption "All human beings are equally human beings," or "All people are equally people," is a truism that may appear vacuous, especially as a basis for the claim that all people should have equal civil and political rights. Nonetheless, Williams says, such truisms are useful,

> serving as a reminder that those who belong anatomically to the species homo sapiens, and can speak a language, use tools, live in societies . . . , etc., are also alike in certain other respects more likely to be forgotten. These respects are notably the capacity to feel pain . . . , and the capacity to feel affection for others.[6]

Shakespeare eloquently expresses this idea in *The Merchant of Venice*. In the play, Shylock is the victim of the anti-Semitism of Christian Venice. In a powerful passage, he rages over the discrimination he has experienced and tells why he hates Antonio:

> He hath disgraced me, and hind'red me half a million, laughed at my losses, mocked at my gains, scorned my nation, thwarted my bargains, cooled my friends, heated mine enemies—and what's his reason? I am a Jew. Hath not a Jew eyes? Hath not a Jew hands, organs, dimensions, senses, affections, passions? fed with the same food, hurt with the same weapons, subject to the same diseases, healed by the same

---

[4]William Frankena, "The Concept of Social Justice," in *Social Justice*, ed. Richard B. Brandt (Englewood Cliffs, NJ: Prentice-Hall, 1962), 19.

[5]Ibid., 21.

[6]Bernard Williams, "The Idea of Equality," in *Justice and Equality*, ed. Hugo Bedau (Englewood Cliffs, NJ: Prentice-Hall, 1971), 118.

means, warmed and cooled by the same winter and summer as a Christian is? If you prick us, do we not bleed? If you tickle us, do we not laugh? If you poison us, do we not die?[7]

Frankena, Williams, and Shakespeare call on us to recognize all people as full members of the moral community, regardless of religion, race, nationality, sex, wealth, or sexual orientation. To discriminate against people on the basis of irrelevant characteristics—to assign unequal civil and political rights on the basis of irrelevant characteristics—is arbitrary, irrational, and unjust. All people deserve equal civil and political rights simply because they're people. A society that violates that principle is unjust.

Few people in the Western world today would suggest that poor people or women shouldn't have the right to vote. Few people would advocate preventing Blacks, Hispanics, or Asians from voting or running for public office. However, we should remember that long, difficult struggles were necessary before that consensus emerged in the twentieth century. And we should remember that even in the twentieth century, that consensus can be fragile. Germany in the 1920s and 1930s under Nazi rule attempted to exterminate Europe's Jews. Many Whites in the United States in the 1950s and 1960s resisted racial integration, sometimes with violence. South Africa has only recently dismantled its system of apartheid.

Justice and Relevant Differences

Not all discrimination is unjust. No college instructor gives all students the same grade; instructors discriminate, giving some students good grades and others bad grades. However, so long as the basis of discrimination is relevant, it's not unjust. If a paper receives a "D" rather than an "A" because it's disorganized and poorly written, that's not unjust. However, if it receives a "D" because it's written by a woman or because it's written by an athlete, that's unjust.

Similarly, colleges and universities discriminate, accepting some applicants and rejecting others. Employers discriminate, hiring some applicants but not others. You probably discriminate, selecting some people to be your friends but not others. Discrimination is only unjust if it's based on an irrelevant characteristic. What's relevant depends on what's at issue.

For example, consider a prestigious college or university that has fairly high admission standards. Suppose it generally accepts only applicants who have at least a "B+" average in high school or a combined score of 1200 on their Scholastic Aptitude Tests (SATs). Assuming the admission standards are designed to distinguish between those applicants likely to do well at the college and those likely not to do well,

---

[7]William Shakespeare, *The Merchant of Venice*, act 2, scene 1, lines 50–63.

discriminating against applicants on the basis of their high school grades and SAT scores is not unjust, because the differences on which the discrimination is based are relevant.

Similarly, consider a law firm hiring recent law school graduates. Suppose the firm generally only hires applicants from the top twenty or twenty-five law schools who have graduated in the top 10% of their classes. Is the law firm's procedure unjust? Why or why not? On the other hand, suppose the law firm generally hires only male applicants. Is that just?

Consider the right to serve on juries. Should all people have the right to serve on juries simply because they're people? No. A five-year-old human being is a person, but surely no five-year-old should serve on a jury. Serving on a jury is an important right, but juries have a function that requires a certain level of maturity in its members. Members of a jury must weigh evidence, evaluate the testimony of witnesses, and ultimately make judgments of extreme importance. A five-year-old hasn't the maturity, wisdom, experience, or knowledge to do what's required of a juror. Therefore, age is a relevant difference. Only after they've reached a certain age, the age of maturity (conventionally thought to be somewhere between eighteen and twenty-one), should people have the right to serve on juries.

For the same reason, one might contend that it would be just to deny the right to serve on juries to the mentally handicapped. Depending on the severity of the handicap, such a person may lack the judgment, wisdom, and maturity to do what's required of a juror. However, surely it would be unjust to deny to the physically handicapped the right to serve on juries. For example, being confined to a wheelchair would not interfere with one's ability to do what's required of a juror. Similarly, it would be unjust to deny the right to serve on juries to the poor, to Asians, to Hispanics, or to homosexuals.

BRAIN TEASERS

Would it be unjust to deny the right to serve on juries to people who are illiterate? Why or why not?

According to Aristotle's principle of justice, people equal in relevant respects are to be treated equally. Applying this principle is not easy, because what's relevant in one situation isn't relevant in another. A few decades ago, virtually no television commercials included Blacks. Almost all decision makers in business, advertising, and entertainment were white, and because of conscious or unconscious prejudice, they almost never chose Blacks for roles in their commercials. People were unable to get roles in television commercials not because they lacked talent and ability but because they were Black. Most people now agree that race should not have been a relevant factor; excluding Blacks on the basis of their race treated people who were equal in relevant respects unequally.

Once the injustice is recognized, what should be done? Suppose an advertising agency decides to reserve some of the roles in its commercials for Blacks, to ensure that they have opportunities heretofore denied them. Would that be unjust? In isolation, race is not relevant. To deny people roles because of their race is surely unjust; therefore, wouldn't it be unjust to reserve roles for members of a specific race? One might argue that reserving some roles for nonwhites doesn't violate the principle that people equal in relevant respects are to be treated equally. One might defend such a decision by claiming that in this situation, Whites and Blacks are not equal in all relevant respects; unlike Whites, that is, Blacks have been discriminated against in the past and excluded from television commercials because of their race. One might claim that the advertising agency is reserving roles for Blacks not merely because they're Black but because up to now they've been discriminated against and excluded on account of their race. To ensure that the patterns of unjust discrimination don't persist, positive steps must be taken to overcome the previously existing barriers to Blacks. Without positive steps, television commercials are likely to remain lily white.

BRAIN TEASERS

1. Would it be unjust to reserve some roles in television commercials for Blacks if they have been denied roles because of their race in the recent past?

2. Is it just to require men to register for Selective Service but not women? Would it be just to draft men into the armed forces but not women?

3. Two people apply to a prestigious, highly selective university. J has a "B+" average in high school, 1150 on her SATs, and good letters of recommendation from her teachers. She comes from an affluent suburb with excellent schools. She's White and upper middle class. K has a "B–" average, 1020 on her SATs, and good letters of recommendation from her teachers. She comes from an impoverished inner-city neighborhood and went to a substandard school. She's Hispanic and comes from a poor family. The prestigious university to which the two students have applied has a student body that's 82 percent White, 6 percent Black, 10 percent Asian, and 2 percent Hispanic. J is rejected by the university, but K is accepted, largely because she's Hispanic and the university is committed to increasing the percentage of Hispanics among its students. Is the university acting unjustly? Why or why not?

4. L and M apply to a prestigious, selective university. L has a "B+" average, 1150 on her SATs, and good letters of recommendation.

M has a "B" average, 1020 on her SATs, and good letters of recommendation. L is Jewish and M is Christian. The student population is 5 percent Jewish, and the administration doesn't want the percentage of Jewish students to rise any higher. M is accepted, but L is rejected, primarily because she's Jewish. Is the university acting unjustly? Why or why not? (Is there any relevant difference between the situation in item 3 and this situation?)

5. Would it be just to prevent homosexuals from teaching in public schools? Why or why not?

Are Inequalities of Wealth and Income Just?

Almost all societies have been divided between rich and poor. In some societies the rich live lives of incredible luxury, whereas the poor barely survive. Economic inequality has been almost a universal feature of human societies, but some societies have wider chasms between rich and poor than others.

In some societies, a small percentage of the people live like kings, whereas others are so poor that they're barely able to satisfy their basic needs for food, clothing, shelter, medical care, and basic education. Whereas the rich can satisfy their every whim, the poor suffer from chronic malnutrition, live in hovels, dress in rags, can't afford a doctor or medicine when they're ill, and have inferior educational opportunities.

Economic inequality among nations is huge. According to the 1998 United Nations Human Development Report, the richest 20% of the world's population consumes 86% of the world's goods and services while the poorest 20% struggles by with consuming a mere 1.3%. The report also maintained that in 1998 the world's richest three individuals had total income that equaled the total combined GDP of 48 of the world's poorest nations. Europeans spend $11 billion annually on ice cream, while it would take only an estimated $9 billion a year to ensure that everyone in the world has clean water and safe sewers. Americans and Europeans spend $17 billion per year on pet food; it would take an estimated $13 billion per year to ensure that everyone in the world has their basic needs for health and nutrition met.[8]

In 1997, the average annual income of the bottom 20% of U.S. households was $8,872 while for the top 20% it was $122,764. The bottom 20% received 3.6% of total income while the top 20% received 49.4%.[9] A recent study estimates that in 1999, the richest 1% will receive as much total after-tax income (12.9% of the total) as the poorest 38% combined. The average

---

[8]*The United Nations Human Development Report* (Oxford: Oxford University Press, 1998).

[9]U.S. Bureau of the Census, Official Statistics of the United States, 1998, Table B, xi.

annual before-tax income of the richest 1% in 1999 is projected to be $786,000 while its average annual after-tax income is projected to be $516,000. This same study estimates that between 1977 and 1999, the annual after-tax income of the richest 1% will have increased by 115%, that of the richest 20% will have increased by 43%, that of the middle 20% will have increased by 8%, and that of the poorest 20% will have actually declined by 9%. According to the study's authors, data compiled by Edward Wolff of New York University showed that in 1995, the richest 1% of households owned 39% of the nation's wealth while the richest 20% owned 84% of it. That means that the remaining 80% of households owns only 16% of the wealth in the United States.[10] The official median annual income for White households was $38,972, for Black households $25,050, and for Hispanic households $26,628.[11] About 3% of households had an annual income of less that $5,000 while about 9.5% had an annual income of $100,000 or more.[12] The median income for full time year round workers was : White males, $36,118; Black males, $26,897; Hispanic males, $21,799; White females, $26,470; Black females, $22,764; Hispanic females, $19,676.[13]

In 1997, 11.0% of Whites were below the official poverty level, with 16.1 percent of White children in poor families; 26.5 percent of Blacks were poor with 37.2 percent of Black children growing up in poor families; 27.1 percent of Hispanics were poor, with 36.8 percent of Hispanic children growing up poor.[14] Many experts claim that anyone who has an income that is less than 25 percent above the poverty level still suffers from significant deprivation. 15.2 percent of Whites and 21.0 percent of White children, 33.8 percent of Blacks and 45.4% of Black children, and 35.9 percent of Hispanics and 46.8 percent of Hispanic children were at this income level.

Census Bureau data show that there is much economic inequality in the United States, and the inequality is not distributed uniformly but rather is affected by an individual's sex, race, and ethnic background. There's no denying that on average, White males do best. Is such economic inequality just? If all people are full members of the moral community, does Aristotle's conception of justice imply that all people should share equally in a society's resources? The answer seems to be yes, if personhood is the only feature relevant for the distribution of a society's economic resources.

However, few Americans think that all people should have roughly equal shares of wealth and income simply because they're people. Most

---

[10]Isaac Shapiro and Robert Greenstein, "The Widening Income Gap," The Center for Budget and Policy Priorities. Released September 4, 1999.

[11]U.S. Bureau of the Census. Official Statistics of the United States, 1998, Table F, xvii.

[12]Ibid., *Income*, Table 2, p. 5.

[13]Ibid., *Income*, Table 7.

[14]Ibid., *Income*, Table 2, p. 2.

think that other characteristics besides personhood are relevant, for example, effort and contribution. Suppose Jones works ten hours a day, six days a week, with great intensity and efficiency, and Smith works six hours a day, four days a week, without much intensity or efficiency (Smith spends most of his time goofing off). Many people say that Smith and Jones should not be paid the same.

But on the other hand, suppose Thatcher is too ill or infirm to work. Whereas Jones works sixty hours a week with great intensity and efficiency, Thatcher doesn't work at all. Should Thatcher receive no share of society's economic resources because she doesn't work? Would it be just to let her starve to death or perish for lack of shelter or medical attention?

Many people think that features other than personhood are relevant to how society's economic resources should be distributed. Justice requires treating people who are equal in relevant respects equally and people who are unequal in relevant respects unequally. Many people think that effort, contribution, and need are relevant in addition to personhood. Consider the following principles of justice regarding the distribution of economic benefits:

1. People should have a *roughly equal* share of economic resources.

2. People should receive economic resources *proportional to their needs:* the greater their needs, the more economic resources they should receive.

3. People who cannot meet their basic needs by their own unaided efforts should have enough help *to ensure that their basic needs are met.*

4. People should receive economic resources *proportional to their contribution* to the society: the greater the contribution, the more economic rewards they deserve.

5. People should receive whatever economic rewards they can get in *a free market economy,* whether it's a lot or a little.

The first principle calls for rough equality. It's important to keep in mind that this doesn't mean absolute equality. In our society, the richest one percent of families have thousands of times the annual income of the poorest one percent of families. Some egalitarians (advocates of more equality) might be satisfied if the richest families had no more than fifty times the annual income of the poorest. Others might be satisfied only if the richest had no more than ten times the annual income of the poorest. One test of unjust inequality is proposed by Rosseau (1712–1778): "as for wealth, no citizen [should] be so very rich he can buy another, and none so poor that he is compelled to sell himself."[15] Rousseau means that there

---

[15]Jean Jacques Rousseau, "The Social Contract," in *The Social Contract and Other Later Political Writings,* ed. Victor Gourevitch (Cambridge: Cambridge University Press, 1997), 78.

should not be so much economic inequality that it gives some people great power over others. If the poor depend on the rich for their very lives, perhaps because the rich own all the economic resources so that they get to decide who shall work and who shall not, that's unjust according to Rousseau's egalitarian test.

The second principle takes need into account. Someone with one dependent needs less than someone with six dependents. Someone with serious medical problems needs more economic resources for medical treatment than someone who doesn't have medical problems. Someone with serious learning challenges needs more resources for education than someone who doesn't. According to the second principle, it is just that more economic resources go to those with greater needs.

The third principle focuses on basic needs, needs for adequate food, clothing, shelter, medical care, and education. According to this principle, it would be unjust to allow people's basic needs to go unmet if they can't meet them by their own unaided efforts, for example, the physically and mentally handicapped, the ill, the elderly, and children. Society should ensure that people's basic needs are met when they can't meet them themselves.

The fourth principle calls for rewards proportional to contribution to what we might call the common good. If teachers contribute more than advertising copywriters or if nurses contribute more than stockbrokers, they should receive greater economic rewards. If the CEO of a company makes a hundred times the contribution to the organization of a secretary, then she should have a hundred times the salary of a secretary.

The fifth principle puts no limits on economic inequality. If you have skills, abilities, or knowledge that are in high demand and low supply so that you can command an income of a million dollars a year, while someone else lacks these things and can only get part-time work at minimum wage with no benefits, there's nothing wrong with that. The same thing goes if I inherit a two hundred million dollar company that gives me an income of ten million dollars a year and control over substantial economic resources, while you inherit nothing. It ignores contribution and need.

The first three principles, if applied in a private enterprise economy, would require economic redistribution: taking from those who have a lot and giving it to those who have too little. For example, if someone has an income of one million dollars, $100,000 of it could be taken in taxes to be then used to provide for the basic needs of those who are helpless and without resources. But critics ask whether it would be just to take money from one person to give to another. The issue often is framed in terms of moral *rights*. Critics of redistribution claim that society or the government has no *right* to tax the rich in order to provide for the poor. They say that the rich have a right to all the income they receive. Supporters of redistribution, on the other hand, claim that society has a right to tax the rich to provide for the poor or to reduce economic inequality, that the rich don't have a right to keep all their income, and that the poor have a right to have their basic needs met.

Part of the concept of justice involves the concept of rights. It's unjust to violate people's rights. A crucial question must be answered if we are to be clear about how much economic inequality is just: What rights do people have?

Rights

To have a right is to have a legitimate or justified claim on some person or institution—a claim that should be recognized, accepted, and enforced. To say that you have a right to freedom of speech, for example, is to say that you have a legitimate claim on others not to be interfered with when you try to speak, and that this claim ought to be recognized, accepted, and enforced by society. Having a right generally entails that others have a duty toward the right-holder. For example, if you have a right to freedom of expression, it entails that others have a duty not to interfere with your efforts to express your thoughts and feelings; if you have a right to life, it entails that others have a duty not to kill you. We can at least partly define rights, then, in terms of duties.

Positive and Negative Rights

A right can entail either that others have a positive or a negative duty toward the right-holder. A *negative* duty is a duty *not* to do something; a *positive* duty is a duty to do something. If I have a duty not to kill you, that's a negative duty—a duty to not do something. If I have a duty to pay taxes, that's a positive duty—a duty to do something. *Negative rights* entail that others have negative duties toward the right-holder; *positive rights* entail that others have positive duties toward the right-holder. Thus, the right of freedom of speech is a negative right, because it entails that others have a duty *not* to interfere with your efforts to speak. On the other hand, the right to a fair trial before an impartial jury is a positive right, because it entails that others have a duty to supply an impartial jury and all the resources necessary for a fair trial.

Some people talk of rights as though all rights are entirely negative or entirely positive. But in fact, we might think of rights being located on a continuum. Some rights are located near the positive end, entailing primarily positive duties; other rights may be located closer to the negative end, entailing primarily negative duties. But many rights are located near the middle of the continuum because they entail both positive and negative duties. For example, the right to a fair trial entails the (positive) duty to provide judge, jury, and courtroom, as well as the (negative) duty to not undermine the integrity of a trial by bribing witnesses, threatening jurors, manufacturing false evidence, or suppressing evidence.

We can define a particular right by identifying the duties that others owe the right-holder. Consider the right to life. That's usually considered the most fundamental right. What do we mean if we say that you have a right to life? Obviously, it entails that others have a (negative) duty to you *not* to kill you (at least without a morally compelling reason). But it also may entail that others have a (positive) duty to you to preserve your life if it's threatened and they can save you at reasonable cost or risk to themselves.

BRAIN TEASERS

1. Suppose you and I are eating lunch out in the park and you begin choking on your food. I know you're choking, and I easily could save your life. If I don't help you, you'll choke to death. Would I violate your right to life if I let you die? Do I have a duty to save you?
2. If you have a right to freedom of religion, what duties do others owe you?

Absolute and Nonabsolute Rights

An *absolute right* is a right that may never legitimately be infringed or violated. To infringe an absolute right is always wrong. On the other hand, a *nonabsolute right* permits infringements in certain circumstances. It is not always wrong to infringe a nonabsolute right. For example, the unqualified right to life is absolute if it is never permissible to kill someone. It is not absolute if there are circumstances in which killing someone is not morally wrong.

BRAIN TEASERS

Are there situations in which it is not wrong to kill someone, even if he has a right to life?

If we express a right claim in an unqualified way, for example, claiming without qualification that people have a right of free speech, it's rarely plausible to consider the right absolute. For example, the right to free speech doesn't really give you the right to give a loud speech outside my window at 3:00 a.m. or to libel me. The police would be violating no duties they have toward you if they stopped you. If we qualify the right claim in various ways, however, we may more plausibly consider the qualified right claim absolute. For example, we might say that people have a right to speak freely when it doesn't pose a serious threat to the well-being of others.

Legal and Moral Rights

Legal rights are created by a system of laws. Laws, in turn, are created by those who have the authority to create them, such as the U.S. Congress or a state legislature. You have the legal right in the United States to smoke cigarettes, but not to smoke crack cocaine. Why? Because the legal rules of the United States permit the one but not the other. Legal rights are purely local. People in one society can have legal rights that people in another society don't have because their laws are different.

Sometimes people don't have legal rights that we think they should have, or do have legal rights that we think they shouldn't have. For example, American women didn't have the legal right to vote in the nineteenth century, but most of us think that they should have. On the other hand, Whites in many southern states had the legal right to own Blacks, but we now think that they shouldn't have. When we talk of what legal rights people should have, we often appeal to a different kind of right—a moral right. Thus, we might say that women had a moral right to vote that was violated because they didn't have the legal right to vote. Similarly, we might say that white slaveowners had a legal right to own Blacks, but not a moral right to own them.

But what are moral rights? Legal rights are the rights a legal code gives people. We might say that moral rights are the rights that an adequate or acceptable moral code gives people. Moral rights are those claims that are validated, or legitimated, by an adequate moral code, those claims for which there are good moral reasons. One has a moral right when there are good moral reasons that justify public acceptance, recognition, and enforcement of the claim. Are there any moral rights that people have simply because they're people?

Americans can look to the Bill of Rights in the Constitution to identify their most fundamental legal or Constitutional rights. Is there anything similar that applies universally? The United Nations Universal Declaration of Human Rights of 1948 constitutes the world's shared understanding of what moral rights people have. Almost all the world's governments and peoples accept it as the standard for moral rights.

The U.N. Universal Declaration of Human Rights

What follows is a selection of articles from that document:

> *Whereas* recognition of the inherent dignity and of the equal and inalienable rights of all members of the human family is the foundation of freedom, justice, and peace in the world,

Whereas disregard and contempt for human rights have resulted in barbarous acts which have outraged the conscience of mankind, and the advent of a world in which human beings shall enjoy freedom of speech and belief and freedom from fear and want has been proclaimed as the highest aspiration of the common people . . . ,

Now, therefore, the General Assembly Proclaims this Universal Declararion of Human Rights. . . .

ARTICLE 1

All human beings are born free and equal in dignity and rights. They are endowed with reason and conscience and should act towards one another in a spirit of brotherhood.

ARTICLE 3

Everyone has the right to life, liberty, and security of person.

ARTICLE 4

No one shall be held in slavery. . . .

ARTICLE 5

No one shall be subjected to torture or to cruel, inhuman, or degrading treatment. . . .

ARTICLE 11

1. Everyone charged with a penal offence has the right to be presumed innocent until proved guilty according to law in a public trial at which he has had all the guarantees necessary for his defence. . . .

ARTICLE 13

1. Everyone has the right to freedom of movement and residence within the borders of each state. . . .

ARTICLE 17

1. Everyone has the right to own property alone as well as in association with others.

2. No one shall be arbitrarily deprived of his property.

ARTICLE 18

Everyone has the right to freedom of thought, conscience, and religion. . . .

ARTICLE 19

Everyone has the right to freedom of opinion and expression. . . .

ARTICLE 23

1. Everyone has the right to work, to free choice of employment, to just and favourable conditions of work, and to protection against unemployment.

2. Everyone, without discrimination, has the right to equal pay for equal work.

3. Everyone who works has the right to just and favourable remuneration ensuring for himself and his family an existence worthy of human dignity. . . .

ARTICLE 25

1. Everyone has the right to a standard of living adequate for the health and well being of himself and of his family, including food, clothing, housing, and medical care. . . .

ARTICLE 26

1. Everyone has the right to education.[16]

We might classify the rights according to the following categories.

Right to Life: Article 3.

Right to Physical Security and Bodily Integrity: Articles 3 and 5.

Right to Equal Treatment: Articles 1, 2, 7, and 23.

Civil and Political Rights: Articles 7, 9, 11, and 21.

Liberty Rights: Articles 3, 4, 7, 13, 17, 18, 19, and 20.

Subsistence Rights: Articles 23, 25, and 26.

Justifying Rights Claims

Opponents of economic redistribution to reduce economic inequality or to help the poor meet their basic needs claim that people have moral rights that are violated by redistribution. But the U.N. Declaration doesn't include a right of unlimited acquisition or a right not to be taxed for social purposes. On the other hand, proponents of economic redistribution claim that people have moral rights that are violated if their basic needs go unmet in order to avoid taxing the rich. The U.N. Declaration states that all people have the right to "a standard of living adequate for . . . health and well-being. . . ." (Article 25) Whether we accept or reject the human or moral rights contained in the U.N. Declaration, the question is how we can justify a rights claim. If it's justified, it's reasonable to accept it and may be unreasonable to reject it. If it's not justified, it's not reasonable to accept it.

Generally, individual rights claims are justified by appealing to the most basic and important interests that people have because rights are supposed to protect them. Consider the right to life. Surely life is our most basic interest. If we're dead, we probably no longer have any interests that rights can protect.[17] The dead can't speak, think, or worship, so they have no need of rights to protect those activities. They don't need food,

---

[16]United Nations Universal Declaration of Human Rights.

[17]This may not be the case. For example, if you're dead, you may still have a right to have your reputation protected or a right not to have your body desecrated. Perhaps you still have at least some interests that deserve protection when you're dead.

shelter, clothing, or medical care, so they don't need rights to guarantee them. The right to life protects people by imposing on others certain duties toward the right-holder, both to refrain from killing her and to preserve her life when it's threatened. When others try to respect an individual's rights, it protects the right-holder.

The liberty rights listed in the U.N. Declaration do not include a right to do anything we want without interference from others. Instead, it specifies certain activities that we have a right to engage in without interference. The list does not include a right to sunbathe nude or wear hats in classrooms. Why not? What principles underlie the selection of activities that are to be protected by rights? The U.N. Declaration lists activities that are especially important to people's well-being: thinking, communicating our thoughts, worshipping, participating in political decision-making, working, marrying. It also lists activities that are forbidden because of how deeply they affect people's lives: slavery, torture, cruel and unusual punishment, and unjust discrimination.

Similarly, the positive rights included in the Declaration protect only our most basic interests. The rights to adequate food, shelter, clothing, medical care, employment, and education protect our lives, health, and autonomy. The list doesn't include rights to cosmetics or cosmetic surgery, a yacht, or a second vacation home.

The most basic interests we have are connected to our personhood. We have a right to those things that are necessary for our being able to function as persons. Imagine if you were homeless and society provided you with only a dog house for shelter, or starving and malnourished and society provided you with only a can of cat food. That would not be appropriate given your dignity as a human being. You shouldn't be treated as a dog or cat. Our most important interests include a level of well-being appropriate to our personhood, including our capacity for autonomy, the capacity to act freely. Rights protect these interests. That means we can justify a right claim by showing how it is necessary to protect people's most basic and important interests in well-being and autonomy. And that means we can justify rejecting a rights claim by showing that the interests it protects are not sufficiently important and basic to merit the protection afforded by rights.

In some cases, though, it may be argued that a society cannot respect all of these rights in the U.N. Declaration because of scarce resources. This is particularly true of positive rights to the things we need in order to survive with dignity as persons. If a society can only provide adequate food for 90% of its population, it simply cannot respect everyone's right to adequate food. In such a case, some people say that the 10% of people left without adequate food don't really have a right to adequate food because of their society's inability to provide it. However we think of such situations, we should keep several things in mind. First, in most societies today, there is no doubt that everyone's rights listed in the U.N. Declaration could be respected, including the positive rights to subsistence. Few societies face such scarcities of resources. The problem is generally one of distribution. In societies that are poor, some have so much that there's not enough left over to meet the basic needs of those at the bottom. Second, often scarcity of certain resources is due to human decisions. For example, if there's not enough food in a society, it's often because too much land is devoted to other purposes or because of inadequacies and inefficiencies in transportation. Sometimes it's because of policies pursued by other societies. A strong society may exploit a weak society, taking resources away that could be used to meet the needs of the people in the weak society. Finally, societies don't exist in a vacuum. National boundaries are artificial creations. Resources within one set of national boundaries may be inadequate, but there may be a surplus within other national boundaries. The U.N. Declaration is universal. Its rights and duties apply to everyone. If people are starving to death in a poor African country, their right to life imposes duties on everyone, including the rich nations. If Britain has a surplus of food, there are ways to ensure that it gets to the people who need it elsewhere. Britain could donate it. Other rich nations could donate money to enable the poor African nation to buy the food it needs. The moral relevance of national boundaries for human rights is an open question.

BRAIN TEASERS

If people are starving in Africa, does the United States have a duty to help alleviate the starvation? Do individual Americans who have more than enough resources to meet their basic needs have a duty to contribute to famine relief?

But we can give a more social and less individualistic justification for the rights in the U.N. Declaration, as well. If a society does not attribute these rights to everyone and does not protect everyone in their exercise of them, the society will probably be unstable. Vast resources may have to be devoted to repression instead of to projects that will better people's lives. There will be a constant threat of crime, riots, rebellion, and revolution.

BRAIN TEASERS

Would economic redistribution to ensure that the poor in the U.S. have a standard of living appropriate to their personhood violate anyone's human rights? Would failing to tax the comfortable in order to ensure the basic needs of the poor violate anyone's human rights?

Equal Opportunity

Many of us profess to value equal opportunity. Proponents of redistribution claim that it's necessary if there is to be genuine equal opportunity. They claim that someone brought up poor cannot compete on an equal footing with people who were not brought up poor. Similarly, someone disadvantaged by racism or sexism can't compete on equal terms with someone who escaped those disadvantages. The competition is unjust, as though some people are running a mile race with ten pound weights on their ankles, others are unimpeded, and still others begin the race a quarter mile ahead of the starting line.

Many people start off disadvantaged in the womb. If a mother is malnourished or unhealthy during pregnancy, or if she abuses drugs or alcohol, it can permanently affect the child in her womb, even to the point of interfering with normal brain development. Those who grow up suffering from poverty and discrimination often face intense family turmoil, neighborhood decay and pathology, and inadequate medical services and educational resources, as well as the assaults of hunger, fear, and insecurity. Because the comfortable in our society are so insulated from the poor, they generally have little idea of what the lives of the poor are really like. It's easy for them to turn away and blame the poor for their plight, thinking that if they'd only get a job, they'd be fine.

But most experts on poverty deny that the problems of the poor are their own fault. Many poor people work long and hard, such as farm workers who pick crops or garment workers, but their wages are so low that they remain impoverished. There isn't an unlimited number of good jobs that pay decent wages, offer benefits, and offer real opportunity for significant advancement. There are a lot of dead-end, low paying jobs, many offering only part-time employment. Given their disadvantages, it's difficult for the poor and discriminated against to wrest the good and best jobs from those who historically have had a near monopoly on them—middle- and upper-class White males. It's a cold hard truth that in our society, whiteness and maleness have provided privileges.

As for the poor who aren't working, many have worked in the past and will work in the future. Generally, they don't have the skills and education that are in high demand. Some suffer from physical or psychological illness; others are alcoholics or drug addicts; some have dependents that make it difficult for them to be employed outside the home. It is easy for us who are comfortable to blame the poor for their poverty, but we should remember the old Native American adage that says that we should walk a mile in another person's moccasins before judging him.

Many proponents of equal opportunity argue that people have to start out on equal terms if the race is to be fair. That means taking resources from someone who starts out very rich and giving some to those who start out very poor.

BRAIN TEASERS

1. If people have a right to own property, does that mean they have a right to do anything they want with it?

2. Sheila is young and poor. She needs an operation to correct a heart defect; if she doesn't have the operation, she will die within two or three years. Her mother doesn't have health insurance and doesn't have the money to pay doctors or a hospital. Does Sheila have a right to medical care that would be violated if she were denied the operation because she can't pay? Suppose her medical care depends on using some of the tax dollars collected from the nonpoor to pay for medical services for the poor? Would it violate any rights of the nonpoor? If yes, what specific rights?

3. Tom is a brilliant student who comes from a poor family. He can't afford to go to college. Are any of his rights violated if he's unable to attend college because he can't afford it? Are any rights of the nonpoor violated if they're taxed to pay for Tom's education?

4. Jim Thompson has just lost his job; his wife is disabled and unable to work. Because the family can no longer pay the rent, they've been evicted from their apartment, and Jim, his wife, and two children are now living in their station wagon. Their money is rapidly dwindling, and soon they will not be able to afford food. If society ignores the Thompson family's plight, would that be unjust? Are any of the Thompson family's rights being violated if society does nothing to help them? Are property rights of the nonpoor unjustifiably or illegitimately violated if they're taxed to help provide the Thompson family with food and shelter?

Utilitarian Justifications of Moral Rights

Another approach to the question of justice is based on Utilitarianism. A utilitarian would say that justice requires distributing economic resources in a way that maximizes total well-being. Principles of justice are ultimately founded on the Utilitarian principle, just as other moral principles are. Thus, suppose a society could be in either of two situations, A or B. Economic inequality is greater in situation A than in B. If there would be more total well-being in the society in situation A, the society is just if it's in situation A and unjust if it's in situation B. Conversely, if there would be more total well-being in the society in situation B, the society is just if it's in situation B and unjust if it's in situation A.

Suppose moving to a situation of more total well-being requires redistribution. Will redistribution violate anyone's rights? Most Utilitarians would say no. Just as justice is subordinate to the Utilitarian principle, so, too, are rights. What moral rights people have depends on total well-being; people have whatever set of rights maximizes total well-being. If acknowledging a certain right would not maximize total well-being, it's not a genuine right. In any conflict between an alleged right and total well-being, total well-being wins out. Thus, if someone claims to have a right that would be violated by redistributing economic resources to increase total well-being, increasing total well-being takes priority; either the claimed right is not a genuine right, or it is genuine but may legitimately be overridden to further the more fundamental value of increasing total well-being.

Do people have a right to a fair trial? If accepting the right produces more total well-being than denying the right, according to Utilitarianism, the right to a fair trial is a genuine right. Since almost all Utilitarians believe that accepting the right to a fair trial produces more total well-being than not accepting it, they agree that a right to a fair trial is a genuine right that all people have. Do people have a right to rape? If accepting it would produce more total well-being than not accepting it, it's a genuine right. However, it's fairly obvious that accepting a right to rape would produce less total well-being than not accepting it, so it's not a genuine right, according to Utilitarianism; no one has a right to rape people.

Utilitarians accept a right to own property, because property rights increase total well-being. However, total well-being would not be maximized by treating property rights as absolute. Therefore, property rights are genuine, but not absolute, rights; they may be overridden. If redistribution of economic resources would increase total well-being, redistribution is required even if some people's property rights would be infringed. It's legitimate to override property rights to increase total well-being. Utilitarians would probably also accept subsistence rights, such as those in Articles 23, 25, and 26 of the U.N. Declaration, because accepting such rights would probably produce more total well-being than not accepting them.

To determine whether a society is just, a Utilitarian would examine the distribution of economic resources to determine whether it produces maximum total well-being. Most Utilitarians think that, generally, a more equal distribution of a society's economic resources produces more total well-being than a less equal distribution. For example, suppose that total well-being would increase in our society if 10 percent of the income of the richest fifth of households was taken and given to the poorest fifth of households. The gain in well-being of the poor would probably be greater than the loss in well-being of the rich. Many utilitarians believe that almost all known societies have too much economic inequality; total well-being would be increased for most societies if inequality were reduced. Therefore, many utilitarians claim that justice requires redistribution of economic resources in most societies to increase total well-being and reduce economic inequality.

The Utilitarian principle of justice does not entail that everyone should receive exactly equal shares of income and wealth. Some inequalities will increase total well-being, and those that do are just. For example, if hard work and effort are rewarded with a greater share of income and wealth, more total well-being will probably result, because the reward will serve as an incentive to work and effort. If people received the same share of wealth and income, regardless of their contribution, work, or effort, they might not work very hard. In that case, everyone would suffer, because the economy would be far less productive; the supply of goods and services produced would probably decline, leading to a decline in everyone's standard of living.

According to Utilitarianism, an inequality is just only if it produces more total well-being than there would be without it. It's not that someone who works longer hours, with more intensity or more efficiency, deserves to receive a larger share of economic resources. Rather, the justification is solely in terms of the consequences of having the inequality versus not having the inequality. If an inequality doesn't produce more total well-being than there would be without it, it's unjust.

Application of the Utilitarian principle to principles of justice assumes that everyone's well-being in a society counts equally and that all the members of a society have equal worth. Society is a cooperative system designed to further the interests of all its members equally; everyone's interests are furthered when total well-being is maximized. However, as we've seen, many people object to Utilitarianism because it focuses exclusively on total well-being (see Chapter 10). As the contemporary philosopher John Rawls writes, many doubt that "the imposition of disadvantages on a few can be outweighed by a greater sum of advantages enjoyed by others."[18] Are everyone's interests furthered if total well-being is maximized? Many say no.

Rawls's Theory of Justice: Justification in the Original Position

Without doubt, the most influential theory of justice of the past thirty or forty years is that proposed by John Rawls in his monumental book *A Theory of Justice*. His theory of justice is in conscious opposition to Utilitarianism. He points out that societies are in a sense created or invented by human beings (or the ancestors of human beings) "to advance the good of those taking part in [them]."[19] A stable and healthy society is required for

---

[18]John Rawls, *A Theory of Justice* (Cambridge, MA: Harvard University Press, 1971), 33.
[19]Ibid., 4

the well-being of its members, and such stability and health require the members' willing cooperation. According to Rawls, justice provides the fundamental principles regulating members' relations with one another; members will be cooperative rather than disruptive only if they think that the rules of their association are fair and to their own advantage.

> The intuitive idea is that since everyone's well-being depends upon a scheme of cooperation without which no one could have a satis-factory life, the division of advantages should be such as to draw out the willing cooperation of everyone taking part in it, including the less well situated.[20]

Social rules should be to everyone's advantage, since society requires everyone's willing cooperation. The problem is to discover principles that would be to everyone's advantage that everyone could agree on, and that would lead to everyone's willingly cooperating with one another. How can we discover such principles?

Rawls provides an ingenious solution to the problem. According to him, if in a certain well-defined situation everyone would agree to a prin-ciple of justice regulating cooperative activities, that principle of justice would be justified and correct.

> The guiding idea is that the principles of justice for the basic structure of society are the objects of the original agreement. They are the prin-ciples that free and rational persons concerned to further their own interests would accept in an initial position of equality as defining the fundamental terms of their association.[21]

The correct or most reasonable principles of justice are those that people themselves would choose or agree to in a certain well-defined situation.

What is the well-defined situation that Rawls has in mind? He thinks that moral evaluation presupposes impartiality. In adopting principles of justice for a society, people should judge from an impartial perspective; they shouldn't think that what's just is simply what's advantageous to themselves. Justice requires a less self-interested perspective. The prob-lem is to find an impartial perspective from which to judge and select principles of justice. Thus, correct or reasonable principles of justice are those that rational, self-interested people would agree to if they were judging from an impartial perspective.

To guarantee impartiality, Rawls says, we are to choose principles of justice in an "original position" of rough equality behind a "veil of igno-rance." "Among the essential features of this situation is that no one knows his place in society, his class position or social status, nor does

---

[20]Ibid., 15.

[21]Ibid., 11.

anyone know his fortune in the distribution of natural assets and abilities, his intelligence, strength, and the like."[22] People in the original position don't know whether they're white, black, red, or brown; male or female; strong or weak; above or below average in intelligence; healthy or unhealthy; young or old; or born into a disadvantaged or advantaged position. Without this information, people cannot tailor the principles to their own advantage.

To rationally justify a principle of justice, according to Rawls, we must show that rational, self-interested people behind the veil of ignorance in the original position would select the principle to regulate the institutions that bind them. What principles would be accepted? According to Rawls, there are two:

> The first requires equality in the assignment of basic rights and duties, while the second holds that social and economic inequalities . . . are just only if they result in compensating benefits for everyone, and in particular for the least advantaged members of society.[23]

More specifically, the two principles are:

> [1.] Each person is to have an equal right to the most extensive basic liberty compatible with a similar liberty for others.[24]

> [2.] Social and economic inequalities are to be arranged so that they are both (a) to the greatest benefit of the least advantaged and (b) attached to offices and positions open to all under conditions of fair equality of opportunity.[25]

According to Rawls, people in the original position would want to protect their liberty, a basic good. They'd demand equal liberty; however, if everyone has no liberty, everyone has equal liberty. Not only would they demand equal liberty, they'd demand maximum liberty compatible with the liberties of everyone else. Without doubt, this would include the civil and political rights we examined previously. Rawls also thinks that rational, self-interested people in the original position would accept the second principle to regulate the distribution of the benefits and burdens of social cooperation. They would accept principles permitting inequality only if somehow they would benefit from the inequality.

We are to think of the choice of principles of justice as though we are in a constitutional convention charged with deciding on the principles that will regulate social cooperation. Being self-interested, we want to select principles that will benefit us, since we're expected to cooperate on the basis of the principles chosen in the convention. However, we don't know

---

[22]Ibid., 12.

[23]Ibid., 14–15.

[24]Ibid., 60.

[25]Ibid., 83.

who or what we'll be outside the constitution hall because of the veil of ignorance; therefore, our ability to tailor the principles to favor ourselves is limited. Most important, we can't even estimate the probability of finding ourselves at the top or at the bottom of the social heap. Rawls thinks that prudence demands that we prepare for the worst; we should ensure that the worst possible outcome is not intolerable. If we find ourselves at the bottom of the social heap when we leave the constitutional convention, we must be able to live with it.

The vote in the constitutional convention must be unanimous. I can't expect other delegates to accept a principle giving me more than others, and it would be foolish of me to accept a principle that gives others more than me; therefore, I and others would probably initially insist on an equal distribution of social resources as the best deal we can cut in the convention. However, if an inequality would ultimately benefit me by increasing my well-being, I'd be willing to accept it. Therefore, in the convention, I'd demand and agree to an equal distribution of economic resources unless an unequal distribution would be advantageous to me. Since I don't know my position in society, I best protect my interests by insisting that any inequality benefit the least advantaged. Thus, Rawls claims that rational, self-interested people like us, if we were in such a constitutional convention, would accept only the two principles he specifies. Thus, "all social values—liberty, and opportunity, income and wealth, and the bases of social respect—are to be distributed equally unless an unequal distribution . . . is to everyone's advantage." Therefore, "Injustice . . . is simply inequalities that are not to the benefit of all."[26]

Most contemporary societies, even the Unites States, violate Rawls's principles of justice. Few societies have degrees and kinds of economic inequality limited to those that benefit all, particularly the least advantaged. Economic inequality generally benefits only the strong and powerful, not the weak and vulnerable. Most societies have governments that have policies that support economic inequality rather than policies to reduce it to a level that would benefit everyone, especially the disadvantaged.

However, some of Rawls's critics doubt that rational, self-interested people in the original position behind the veil of ignorance would choose the two principles that he claims they would choose. Other critics think that the principles that rational, self-interested people in the original position would or wouldn't choose are irrelevant to what principles of justice are reasonable or correct. After all, none of us has ever been in the original position, in a constitutional convention charged with adopting principles of justice, so we haven't really agreed to such principles. Critics ask why the principles that people might or might not accept in a purely hypothetical situation are relevant in the real world.

---

[26]Ibid., 62.

Despite the criticisms, Rawls's *A Theory of Justice* provides a structure for thinking about the rational justification for principles of justice that continues to fascinate philosophers. If he is correct in thinking that moral evaluation in general and principles of justice in particular presuppose adopting an impartial perspective, the machinery of the original position and veil of ignorance may be a fruitful way of guaranteeing a form of impartiality that doesn't unduly sacrifice self-interest. In a sense, it can be thought of as an attempt to integrate the demands of morality and self-interest.

   THOMAS HOBBES (1588–1679)

LEVIATHAN

Chapter 13: Of the Natural Condition of Mankind as Concerning Their Felicity and Misery

Men by nature equal. Nature hath made men so equal, in the faculties of the body, and mind; as that though there be found one man sometimes manifestly stronger in body, or of quicker mind than another; yet when all is reckoned together, the difference between man, and man, is not so considerable, as that one man can thereupon claim to himself any benefit, to which another may not pretend, as well as he. For as to the strength of body, the weakest has strength enough to kill the strongest, either by secret machination, or by confederacy with others, that are in the same danger with himself.

And as to the faculties of the mind, setting aside the arts grounded upon words, and especially that skill of proceeding upon general, and infallible rules, called science; which very few have, and but in few things; as being not a native faculty, born with us; nor attained, as prudence, while we look after somewhat else, I find yet a greater equality amongst men, than that of strength. For prudence, is but experience; which equal time, equally bestows on all men, in those things they equally apply themselves unto. That which may perhaps make such equality incredible, is but a vain conceit of one's own wisdom, which almost all men think they have in a greater degree, than the vulgar; that is, than all men but themselves, and a few others, whom by fame, or for concurring with themselves, they approve. For such is the nature of men, that howsoever they may acknowledge many others to be more witty, or more eloquent, or more learned; yet they will hardly believe there be many so wise as themselves; for they see their own wit at hand, and other men's at a distance. But this proveth rather that men are in that point equal, than unequal. For there is not ordinarily a greater sign of the equal distribution of any thing, than that every man is contented with his share.

From equality proceeds diffidence. From this equality of ability, ariseth equality of hope in the attaining of our ends. And therefore if any two men desire the same thing, which nevertheless they cannot both enjoy, they become enemies; and in the way to their end, which is principally their own conservation, and sometimes their delectation only, endeavour to destroy, or subdue one another. And from hence it comes to pass, that where an invader hath no more to fear, than another

From *Leviathan*, ed. M. Ockeshott (New York: Crowell-Collier, 1962).

man's single power; if one plant, sow, build, or possess a convenient seat, others may probably be expected to come prepared with forces united, to dispossess, and deprive him, not only of the fruit of his labour, but also of his life, or liberty. And the invader again is in the like danger of another.

From diffidence war. And from this diffidence of one another, there is no way for any man to secure himself, so reasonable, as anticipation; that is, by force, or wiles, to master the persons of all men he can, so long, till he see no other power great enough to endanger him: and this is no more than his own conservation requireth, and is generally allowed. Also because there be some, that taking pleasure in contemplating their own power in the acts of conquest, which they pursue farther than their security requires; if others, that otherwise would be glad to be at ease within modest bounds, should not by invasion increase their power, they would not be able; long time, by standing only on their defence, to subsist. And by consequence, such augmentation of dominion over men being necessary to a man's conservation, it ought to be allowed him.

Again, men have no pleasure, but on the contrary a great deal of grief, in keeping company, where there is no power able to overawe them all. For every man looketh that his companion should value him, at the same rate he sets upon himself: and upon all signs of contempt, or undervaluing, naturally endeavours, as far as he dares, (which amongst them that have no common power to keep them in quiet, is far enough to make them destroy each other), to extort a greater value from his contemners, by damage; and from others, by the example.

So that in the nature of man, we find three principal causes of quarrel. First, competition; secondly, diffidence; thirdly, glory.

The first, maketh men invade for gain; the second, for safety; and the third, for reputation. The first use violence, to make themselves masters of other men's persons, wives, children, and cattle; the second, to defend them; the third, for trifles, as a word, a smile, a different opinion, and any other sign of undervalue, either direct in their persons, or by reflection in their kindred, their friends, their nation, their profession, or their name.

Out of civil states, there is always war of every one against every one. Hereby it is manifest, that during the time men live without a common power to keep them all in awe, they are in that condition which is called war; and such a war, as is of every man, against every man. For war consisteth not in battle only, or the act of fighting; but in a tract of time, wherein the will to contend by battle is sufficiently known: and therefore the notion of *time,* is to be considered in the nature of war; as it is in the nature of weather. For as the nature of foul weather, lieth not in a shower or two of rain; but in an inclination thereto of many days together: so the nature of war, consisteth not in actual fighting; but in the known disposition thereto, during all the time there is no assurance to the contrary. All other time is PEACE.

The incommodities of such a war. Whatsoever therefore is consequent to a time of war, where every man is enemy to every man; the same is consequent to the time, wherein men live without other security, than what their own strength, and their own invention shall furnish them withal. In such condition, there is no place for industry; because the fruit thereof is uncertain: and consequently no culture of the earth; no navigation, nor use of the commodities that may be imported by sea; no commodious building; no instruments of moving, and removing, such things as require much force; no knowledge of the face of the earth; no account of time; no arts; no letters; no society; and which is worst of all, continual fear, and danger of violent death; and the life of man, solitary, poor, nasty, brutish, and short.

It may seem strange to some man, that has not well weighed these things; that nature should thus dissociate, and render men apt to invade, and destroy one another: and he may therefore, not trusting to this inference, made from the passions, desire perhaps to have the same confirmed by experience. Let him therefore consider with himself, when taking a journey, he arms himself, and seeks to go well accompanied; when going to sleep, he locks his doors; when even in his house he locks his chests; and this when he knows there be laws, and public officers, armed, to revenge all injuries shall be done him; what opinion he has of his fellow-subjects, when he rides armed; of his fellow citizens, when he locks his doors; and of his children, and servants, when he locks his chests. Does he not there as much accuse mankind by his actions, as I do by my words? But neither of us accuse man's nature in it. The desires, and other passions of man, are in themselves no sin. No more are the actions, that proceed from those passions, till they know a law that forbids them: which till laws be made they cannot know: nor can any law be made, till they have agreed upon the person that shall make it.

It may peradventure be thought, there was never such a time, nor condition of war as this; and I believe it was never generally so, over all the world: but there are many places, where they live so now. For the savage people in many places of America, except the government of small families, the concord whereof dependeth on natural lust, have no government at all; and live at this day in that brutish manner, as I said before. Howsoever, it may be perceived what manner of life there would be, where there were no common power to fear, by the manner of life, which men that have formerly lived under a peaceful government, use to degenerate into, in a civil war.

But though there had never been any time, wherein particular men were in a condition of war one against another; yet in all times, kings, and persons of sovereign authority, because of their independency, are in continual jealousies, and in the state and posture of gladiators; having their weapons pointing, and their eyes fixed on one another; that is, their forts, garrisons, and guns upon the frontiers of their kingdoms; and continual spies upon their neighbours; which is a posture of war. But because they uphold thereby, the industry of their subjects; there does not follow from it, that misery, which accompanies the liberty of particular men.

In such a war nothing is unjust. To this war of every man, against every man, this also is consequent: that nothing can be unjust. The

notions of right and wrong, justice and injustice have there no place. Where there is no common power, there is no law: where no law, no injustice. Force, and fraud, are in war the two cardinal virtues. Justice, and injustice are none of the faculties neither of the body, nor mind. If they were, they might be in a man that were alone in the world, as well as his senses, and passions. They are qualities, that relate to men in society, not in solitude. It is consequent also to the same condition, that there be no propriety, no dominion, no *mine* and *thine* distinct; but only that to be every man's, that he can get: and for so long as he can keep it. And thus much for the ill condition, which man by mere nature is actually placed in; though with a possibility to come out of it, consisting partly in the passions, partly in his reason.

The passions that incline men to peace. The passions that incline men to peace, are fear of death; desire of such things as are necessary to commodious living; and a hope by their industry to obtain them. And reason suggesteth convenient articles of peace, upon which men may be drawn to agreement. These articles, are they, which otherwise are called the Laws of Nature: whereof I shall speak more particularly, in the two following chapters.

Chapter 14: Of the First and Second Natural Laws, and of Contracts

Right of nature what. THE RIGHT OF NATURE, which writers commonly call *jus naturale*, is the liberty each man hath, to use his own power, as he will himself, for the preservation of his own nature; that is to say, of his own life; and consequently, of doing any thing, which in his own judgment, and reason, he shall conceive to be the aptest means thereunto.

Liberty what. By LIBERTY, is understood, according to the proper signification of the word, the absence of external impediments: which impediments, may oft take away part of a man's power to do what he would; but cannot hinder him from using the power left him, according as his judgment, and reason shall dictate to him.

A law of nature what. Difference of right and law. A LAW OF NATURE, *lex naturalis,* is a precept or general rule, found out by reason, by which a man is forbidden to do that, which is destructive of his life, or taketh away the means of preserving the same; and to omit that, by which he thinketh it may be best preserved. For though they that speak of this subject, use to confound *jus,* and *lex, right* and *law:* yet they ought to be distinguished; because RIGHT, consisteth in liberty to do, or to forbear: whereas LAW, determineth, and bindeth to one of them: so that law, and right, differ as much, as obligation, and liberty; which in one and the same matter are inconsistent.

Naturally every man has right to every thing. The fundamental law of nature. And because the condition of man, as hath been declared in the precedent chapter, is a condition of war of every one against every one; in which case every one is governed by his own reason; and there is nothing he can make use of, that may not be a help unto him, in preserving his life against his enemies; it followeth, that in such a condition, every man has a right to every thing; even to one another's body. And therefore, as long as this natural right of every man to every thing endureth, there can be no security to any man, how strong or wise soever he be, of living out the time, which nature ordinarily alloweth men to live. And consequently it is a precept, or general rule of reason, *that every man, ought to endeavour peace, as far as he has hope of obtaining it; and when he cannot obtain it, that he may seek, and use, all helps, and advantages of war.* The first branch of which rule, containeth the first, and fundamental law of nature; which is, *to seek peace, and follow it.* The second, the sum of the right of nature; which is, *by all means we can, to defend ourselves.*

The second law of nature. From this fundamental law of nature, by which men are commanded to endeavour peace, is derived this second law; *that a man be willing, when others are so too, as far-forth, as for peace, and defence of himself he shall think it necessary,* *to lay down this right to all things; and be contented with so much liberty against other men, as he would allow other men against himself.* For as long as every man holdeth this right, of doing any thing he liketh; so long are all men in the condition of war. But if other men will not lay down their right, as well as he; then there is no reason for any one, to divest himself of his: for that were to expose himself to prey, which no man is bound to, rather than to dispose himself to peace. This is that law of the Gospel; *whatsoever you require that others should do to you, that do ye to them. . . .*

Renouncing a right, what it is. Transferring right what. Obligation. Duty. Injustice. Right is laid aside, either by simply renouncing it; or by transferring it to another. By simply RENOUNCING; when he cares not to whom the benefit thereof redoundeth. By TRANSFERRING; when he intendeth the benefit thereof to some certain person, or persons. And when a man hath in either manner abandoned, or granted away his right; then he is said to be OBLIGED, or BOUND, not to hinder those, to whom such right is granted, or abandoned, from the benefit of it: and that he *ought,* and it is his DUTY, not to make void that voluntary act of his own: and that such hindrance is INJUSTICE, and INJURY, as being *sine jure;* the right being before renounced, or transferred. . . . It is called injustice, and injury, voluntarily to undo that, which from the beginning he had voluntarily done. . . .

Not all rights are alienable. Whensoever a man transferreth his right, or renounceth it; it is either in consideration of some right reciprocally transferred to himself; or for some other good he hopeth for thereby. For it is a voluntary act: and of the voluntary acts of every man, the object is some *good to himself.* And therefore there be some rights, which no man can be understood by any words, or other signs, to have abandoned, or transferred. As first a man cannot lay down the right of resisting them, that assault him by force, to take away his life; because he cannot be understood to aim thereby, at any good to himself. . . . And lastly the motive, and end for which this renouncing, and transferring of right is introduced, is nothing else but the security of a man's person, in his life, and in the means of so preserving life, as not to be weary of it. And therefore if a man by words, or other signs, seem to despoil himself of the end, for which those signs were intended; he is not to be understood as if he meant it, or that it was his will; but that he was ignorant of how such words and actions were to be interpreted. . . .

Chapter 15: Of Other Laws of Nature

The third law of nature, justice. From that law of nature, by which we are obliged to transfer to another, such rights, as being retained, hinder the peace of mankind, there followeth a third; which is this, *that men perform their covenants made:* without which, convenants are in vain, and but empty words; and the right of all men to all things remaining, we are still in the condition of war.

Justice and injustice what. And in this law of nature, consisteth the fountain and original of JUSTICE. For where no covenant hath preceded, there hath no right been transferred, and every man has right to every thing; and consequently, no action can be unjust. But when a covenant is made, then to break it is *unjust:* and the definition of INJUSTICE, is no other than *the not performance of covenant.* And whatsoever is not unjust, is *just.*

Justice and propriety begin with the constitution of commonwealth. But because covenants of mutual trust, where there is a fear of not performance on either part, as hath been said in the former chapter, are invalid; though the original of justice be the making of covenants; yet injustice actually there can be none, till the cause of such fear be taken away; which while men are in the natural condition of war, cannot be done. Therefore before the names of just, and unjust can have place, there must be some coercive power, to compel men equally to the performance of their covenants, by the terror of some punishment, greater than the benefit they expect by the breach of their covenant; and to make good that propriety, which by mutual contract men acquire, in recompense of the universal right they abandon: and such power there is none before the erection of a commonwealth. And this is also to be gathered out of the ordinary definition of justice in the Schools: for they say, that *justice is the constant will of giving to every man his own.* And therefore where there is no *own,* that is no propriety, there is no injustice; and where there is no coercive power erected, that is, where there is no commonwealth, there is no propriety; all men having right to all things: therefore where there is no commonwealth, there nothing is unjust. So that the nature of justice, consisteth in keeping of valid covenants: but the validity of covenants begins not but with the constitution of a civil power, sufficient to compel men to keep them: and then it is also that propriety begins.

Justice not contrary to reason. The fool hath said in his heart, there is no such thing as justice; and sometimes also with his tongue; seriously alleging, that every man's conservation, and contentment, being committed to his own care, there could be no reason, why every man might not do what he thought conduced thereunto: and therefore also to make, or not make; keep, or not keep covenants, was not against reason, when it conduced to one's benefit. He does not therein deny, that there be covenants; and that they are sometimes broken, sometimes kept; and that such breach of them may be called injustice, and the observance of them justice: but he questioneth, whether injustice, taking away the fear of God, for the same fool hath said in his heart there is no God, may not sometimes stand with that reason, which dictateth to every man his own good; and particularly then, when it conduceth to such a benefit, as shall put a man in a condition, to neglect not only the dispraise, and revilings, but also the power of other men. The kingdom of God is gotten by violence: but what if it could be gotten by unjust violence? were it against reason so to get it, when it is impossible to receive hurt by it? and if it be not against reason, it is not against justice; or else justice is not to be approved for good. From such reasoning as this, successful wickedness hath obtained the name of virtue: and some that in all other things have disallowed the violation of faith; yet have allowed it, when it is for the getting of a kingdom. . . . This specious reasoning is nevertheless false.

For the question is not of promises mutual, where there is no security of performance on either side; as when there is no civil power erected over the parties promising; for such promises are no covenants: but either where one of the parties has performed already; or where there is power to make him perform; there is the question whether it be against reason, that is, against the benefit of the other to perform, or not. And I say it is not against reason. For the manifestation whereof, we are to consider; first, that when a man doth a thing, which notwithstanding any thing can be foreseen, and reckoned on, tendeth to his own destruction, howsoever some accident which he could not expect, arriving may turn it to his benefit; yet such events do not make it reasonably or wisely done. Secondly, that in a condition of war, wherein every man to every man, for want of a common power to keep them all in awe, is an enemy, there is no man who can hope by his own strength, or wit, to defend himself from destruction, without the help of confederates; where every one expects the same defence by the confederation, that any one else does: and therefore he which declares he thinks it reason to deceive those that help him, can in reason expect no other means of safety, than what can be had from his own single power. He therefore that breaketh his covenant, and consequently declareth that he thinks he may with reason do so, cannot be received into any society, that unite themselves for peace and defence, but by the error of them that receive him; nor when he is received, be retained in it, without seeing the danger of their error; which errors a man cannot reasonably reckon upon as the means of his security: and therefore if he be left, or cast out of society, he perisheth; and if he live in society, it is by the errors of other men, which he could not foresee, nor reckon upon; and consequently against the reason of his preservation; and so, as all men that contribute not to his destruction, forbear him only out of ignorance of what is good for themselves.

As for the instance of gaining the secure and perpetual felicity of heaven, by any way; it is frivolous: there being but one way imaginable; and that is not breaking, but keeping of covenant.

And for the other instance of attaining sovereignty by rebellion; it is manifest, that though the event follow, yet because it cannot reasonably be expected, but rather the contrary; and because by gaining it so, others are taught to gain the same in like manner, the attempt thereof is against reason. Justice therefore, that is to say, keeping of covenant, is a rule of reason, by which we are forbidden to do any thing destructive to our life; and consequently a law of nature.

There be some that proceed further; and will not have the law of nature, to be those rules which conduce to the preservation of man's life on earth; but to the attaining of an eternal felicity after death; to which they think the breach of covenant may conduce; and consequently be just and reasonable; such are they that think it a work of merit to kill, or depose, or rebel against, the sovereign power constituted over them by their own consent. But because there is no natural knowledge of man's estate after death; much less of the reward that is then to be given to breach of faith; but only a belief grounded upon other men's saying, that they know it supernaturally, or that they know those, that knew them, that knew others, that knew it supernaturally; breach of faith cannot be called a precept of reason, or nautre. . . .

The fourth law of nature, gratitude. . . . GRATITUDE . . . is the fourth law of nature; which may be conceived in this form, *that a man which receiveth benefit from another of mere grace, endeavour that he which giveth it, have no reasonable cause to repent him of his good will.* For no man giveth, but with intention of good to himself; because gift is voluntary; and of all voluntary acts, the object is to every man his own good; of which if men see they shall be frustrated, there will be no beginning of benevolence, or trust; nor consequently of mutual help; nor of reconciliation of one man to another; of war; which is contrary to the first and fundamental law of nature, which commandeth men to *seek peace.* The breach of this law, is called *ingratitude; and* hath the same relation to grace, that injustice hath to obligation by covenant.

The fifth mutual accommodation, or complaisance. A fifth law of nature is COMPLAISANCE; that is to say, *that every man strive to accommodate himself to the rest.* For the understanding whereof, we may consider, that there is in men's aptness to society, a diversity of nature, rising from their diversity of affections; not unlike to that we see in stones brought together for building of an edifice. For as that stone which by the asperity and irregularity of figure, takes more room from others, than itself fills; and for the hardness, cannot be easily made plain, and thereby hindereth the building, is by the builders cast away as unprofitable, and troublesome: so also, a man that by asperity of nature, will strive to retain those things which to himself are superfluous, and to others necessary; and for the stubbornness of his passions, cannot be corrected, is to be left, or cast out of society as cumbersome thereunto. For seeing every man, not only by right, but also by necessity of nature, is supposed to endeavour all he can, to obtain that which is necessary for his conservation; he that shall oppose himself against it, for things superfluous, is guilty of the war that thereupon is to follow; and therefore doth that, which is contrary to the fundamental law of nature, which commandeth *to seek peace.* The observers of this law, may be called SOCIABLE, the Latins call them *commodi;* the contrary, *stubborn, insociable, forward, intractable.*

The sixth, facility to pardon. A sixth law of nature, is this, *that upon caution of the future time, a man ought to pardon the offences past of them that repenting, desire it.* For PARDON, is nothing but granting of peace; which though granted to them that persevere in their hostility, be not peace, but fear; yet not granted to them that give caution of the future time, is sign of an aversion to peace; and therefore contrary to the law of nature.

The seventh, that in revenges, men respect only the future good. A seventh is, *that in revenges,* that is, retribution of evil for evil, *men look not at the greatness of the evil past, but the greatness of the good to follow.* Whereby we are forbidden to inflict punishment with any other design, than for correction of the offender, or direction of others. For this law is consequent to the next before it, that commandeth pardon, upon security of the future time. Besides, revenge without respect to the example, and profit to come, is a triumph, or glorying in the hurt of another, tending to no end; for the end is always somewhat to come; and glorying to no end, is vain-glory, and contrary to reason, and to hurt without reason, tendeth to the introduction of war; which is against the law of nature; and is commonly-styled by the name of *cruelty.*

The eighth, against contumely. And because all signs of hatred, or contempt, provoke to fight; insomuch as most men choose rather to hazard their life, than not to be revenged; we may in the eighth place, for a law of nature, set down this precept, that *no man by deed, word, countenance, or gesture, declare hatred, or contempt of another.* The breach of which law, is commonly called contumely.

The ninth, against pride. The question who is the better man, has no place in the condition of mere nature; where, as has been shewn before, all men are equal. The inequality that now is, has been introduced by the laws civil. I know that Aristotle in the first book of his *Politics,* for a foundation of his doctrine, maketh men by nature, some more worthy to command, meaning the wiser sort, such as he thought himself to be for his philosophy; others to serve, meaning those that had strong bodies, but were not philosophers as he; as if master and servant were not introduced by consent of men, but by difference of wit: which is not only against reason; but also against experience. For there are very few so foolish, that had not rather govern themselves, than be governed by others: nor when the wise in their own conceit, contend by force, with them who distrust their own wisdom, do they always, or often, or almost at any time, get the victory. If nature therefore had made men equal, that equality is to be acknowledged: or if nature have made men unequal; yet because men that think themselves equal, will not enter into conditions of peace, but upon equal terms, such equality must be admitted. And therefore for the ninth law of nature, I put this, *that every man acknowledge another for his equal by nature.* The breach of this precept is *pride.*

The tenth, against arrogance. On this law, dependeth another, *that at the entrance into conditions of peace, no man require to reserve to himself any right, which he is not content should be reserved to every one of the rest.* As it is necessary for all men that seek peace, to lay down certain rights of nature; that is to say, not to have liberty to do all they list: so is it necessary for man's life, to retain some; as right to govern their own bodies; enjoy air, water, motion, ways to go from place to place; and all things else, without which a man cannot live, or not live well. If in this case, at the making of peace, men require for themselves, that which they would not have to be granted to others, they do contrary to the precedent law, that commandeth the acknowledgment of natural equality, and therefore also against the law of nature. The observers of this law, are those we call *modest,* and the breakers *arrogant* men. . . .

The eleventh, equity. Also if *a man be trusted to judge between man and man,* it is a precept of the law of nature, *that he deal equally between them.* For without that, the controversies of men cannot be determined but by war. He therefore that is partial in judgment, doth what in him lies, to deter men from the use of judges, and arbitrators; and consequently, against the fundamental law of nature, is the cause of war.

The observance of this law, from the equal distribution to each man, of that which in reason belongeth to him, is called EQUITY, and, as I have said before, distributive justice: the violation, *acception of persons.* . . .

The twelfth, equal use of things common. And from this followeth another law, *that such things as cannot be divided, be enjoyed in common, if it can be; and if the equality of the thing permit, without stint; otherwise proportionably to the number of them that have right.* For otherwise the distribution is unequal, and contrary to equity.

The thirteenth, of lot. But some things there be, that can neither be divided, nor enjoyed in common. Then, the law of nature, which prescribeth equity, requireth, *that the entire right; or else, making the use alternate, the first possession, be determined by lot.* For equal distribution, is of the law of nature; and other means of equal distribution cannot be imagined.

The fourteenth, of primogeniture, and first seizing. Of *lots* there be two sorts, *arbitrary,* and *natural.* Arbitrary, is that which is agreed on by the competitors: natural, is either *primogeniture . . .* or *first seizure.*

And therefore those things which cannot be enjoyed in common, nor divided, ought to be adjudged to the first possessor; and in some cases in the first born, as acquired by lot.

The fifteenth, of mediators. It is also a law of nature, *that all men that mediate peace, be allowed safe conduct.* For the law that commandeth peace, as the end, commandeth intercession, as the *means;* and to intercession the means is safe conduct.

The sixteenth, of submission to arbitrement. And because, though men be never so willing to observe these laws, there may nevertheless arise questions concerning a man's action; first, whether it were done, or not done; secondly, if done, whether against the law, or not against the law; the former whereof, is called a question of *fact;* the latter a question of *right,* therefore unless the parties to the question, covenant mutually to stand to the sentence of another, they are as far from peace as ever. This other to whose sentence they submit is called an ARBITRATOR. And therefore it is of the law of nature, *that they that are at controversy, submit their right to the judgment of an arbitrator.*

The seventeenth, no man is his own judge. And seeing every man is presumed to do all things in order to his own benefit, no man is a fit arbitrator in his own cause; and if he were never so fit; yet equity allowing to each party equal benefit, if one be admitted to be judge, the other is to be admitted also; and so the controversy, that is, the cause of war, remains, against the law of nature.

The eighteenth, no man to be judge, that has in him a natural cause of partiality. For the same reason no man in any cause ought to be received for arbitrator, to whom greater profit, or honour, or pleasure apparently ariseth out of the victory of one party, than of the other: for he hath taken, though an unavoidable bribe, yet a bribe; and no man can be obliged to trust him. And thus also the controversy, and the condition of war remaineth, contrary to the law of nature.

The nineteenth, of witnesses. And in a controversy of *fact*, the judge being to give no more credit to one, than to the other, if there be no other arguments, must give credit to a third; or to a third and fourth; or more: for else the question is undecided, and left to force, contrary to the law of nature.

These are the laws of nature, dictating peace, for a means of the conservation of men in multitudes; and which only concern the doctrine of civil society. There be other things tending to the destruction of particular men; as drunkenness, and all other parts of intemperance; which may therefore also be reckoned amongst those things which the law of nature hath forbidden; but are not necessary to be mentioned, nor are pertinent enough to this place.

A rule, by which the laws of nature may easily be examined. And though this may seem too subtle a deduction of the laws of nature, to be taken notice of by all men; whereof the most part are too busy in getting food, and the rest too negligent to understand; yet to leave all men inexcusable, they have been contracted into one easy sum, intelligible even to the meanest capacity; and that is, *Do not that to another, which thou wouldest not have done to thyself; which sheweth him, that he had no more to do in learning the laws of nature, but, when weighing the actions of other men with his own, they seem too heavy, to put them into the other part of the balance, and his own into their place, that his own passions, and self-love, may add nothing to the weight; and then there is none of these laws of nature that will not appear unto him very reasonable.*

The laws of nature oblige in conscience always, but in effect then only when there is security. The laws of nature oblige *in foro interno;* that is to say, they bind to a desire they should take place: but *in foro externo;* this is, to the putting them in act, not always. For he that should be modest, and tractable, and per-

form all he promises, in such time, and place, where no man else should do so, should but make himself a prey to others, and procure his own certain ruin, contrary to the ground of all laws of nature, which tend to nature's preservation. And again, he that having sufficient security, that others shall observe the same laws towards him, observes them not himself, seeketh not peace, but war; and consequently the destruction of his nature by violence.

And whatsoever laws bind *in foro interno,* may be broken, not only by a fact contrary to the law, but also by a fact according to it, in case a man think it contrary. For though his action in this case, be according to the law; yet his purpose was against the law; which, where the obligation is *in foro interno,* is a breach.

The laws of nature are eternal. The laws of nature are immutable and eternal; for injustice, ingratitude, arrogance, pride, iniquity, acception of persons, and the rest, can never be made lawful. For it can never be that war shall preserve life, and peace destroy it.

And yet easy. The same laws, because they oblige only to a desire, and endeavour, I mean an unfeigned and constant endeavour, are easy to be observed. For in that they require nothing but endeavor, he that endeavoureth their performance, fulfilleth them; and he that fulfilleth the law, is just.

The science of these laws, is the true moral philosophy. And the science of them, is the true and only moral philosophy. For moral philosophy is nothing else but the science of what is *good,* and *evil,* in the conversation, and society of mankind. *Good,* and *evil,* are names that signify our appetites, and aversions; which in different tempers, customs, and doctrines of men, are different: and divers men, differ not only in their judgment, on the senses of what is pleasant, and unpleasant to the taste, smell, hearing, touch, and sight; but also of what is conformable, or disagreeable to reason, in the actions of common life. Nay, the same man, in divers times, differs from himself; and one time praiseth, that is, calleth good, what another time he dispraiseth, and calleth evil: from whence arise disputes, controversies, and at last war. And therefore so long as a man is in the condition of mere nature, which is a condition of war, as private appetite is the measure of good, and evil: and consequently all men agree on this, that peace is good, and therefore also the way, or means of peace, which, as I have shewed before, are *justice, gratitude, modesty, equity, mercy,* and the rest of the laws of nature, are good; that is to say; *moral virtues,* and their contrary *vices,* evil. Now the science of virtue and vice, is moral philosophy; and therefore the true doctrine of the laws of nature, is the true moral philosophy. But the writers of moral philosophy, though they acknowledge the same virtues and vices; yet not seeing wherein consisted their goodness; nor that they come to be praised, as the means of peaceable, sociable, and comfortable living, place them in a mediocrity of passions; as if not the cause, but the degree of daring, made fortitude; or not the cause, but the quantity of a gift, made liberality.

These dictates of reason, men used to call by the names of laws, but improperly: for they are but conclusions, or theorems concerning what conduceth to the conservation and defence of themselves; whereas law, properly, is the word of him, that by right hath command over others. But yet if we consider the same theorems, as delivered in the word of God, that by right commandeth all things; then are they properly called laws.

 KARL MARX (1818–1883) AND FRIEDRICH ENGELS (1820–1895)

MANIFESTO OF THE COMMUNIST PARTY

A spectre is haunting Europe—the spectre of Communism. All the powers of old Europe have entered into a holy alliance to exorcise this spectre. . . .

Where is the party in opposition that has not been decried as Communistic by its opponents in power? Where the Opposition that has not hurled back the branding reproach of Communism . . . ?

Two things result from this fact.

I.   Communism is already acknowledged by all European Powers to be itself a Power.

II. It is high time that Communists should openly, in the face of the whole world, publish their views, their aims, their tendencies, and meet this nursery tale of the Spectre of Communism with a Manifesto of the party itself.

To this end, Communists of various nationalities have assembled in London, and sketched the following Manifesto, to be published in the English, French, German, Italian, Flemish and Danish languages.

I. Bourgeois and Proletarians

The history of all hitherto existing society is the history of class struggles.

Freeman and slave, patrician and plebeian, lord and serf, guild-master and journeyman, in a word, oppressor and oppressed, stood in constant opposition to one another, carried on an uninterrupted, now hidden, now open fight, a fight that each time ended, either in a revolutionary re-constitution of society at large, or in the common ruin of the contending classes.

In the earlier epochs of history, we find almost everywhere a complicated arrangement of society into various orders, a manifold gradation of social rank. In ancient Rome we have patricians, knights, plebeians, slaves;

From *The Marx-Engels Reader,* 2d ed., ed. Robert Tucker (New York: W. W. Norton, 1978). Copyright © 1978, 1972 by W. W. Norton & Co. Reprinted by permission of the publisher. Footnotes are omitted.

in the Middle Ages, feudal lords, vassals, guild-masters, journeymen, apprentices, serfs; in almost all of these classes, again, subordinate gradations.

The modern bourgeois society that has sprouted from the ruins of feudal society has not done away with class antagonisms. It has but established new classes, new conditions of oppression, new forms of struggle in place of the old ones.

Our epoch, the epoch of the bourgeoisie, possesses, however, this distinctive feature: it has simplified the class antagonisms: Society as a whole is more and more splitting up into two great hostile camps, into two great classes directly facing each other: Bourgeoisie and Proletariat. . . .

The feudal system of industry, under which industrial production was monopolised by closed guilds, now no longer sufficed for the growing wants of the new markets. The manufacturing system took its place. The guild-masters were pushed on one side by the manufacturing middle class; division of labour between the different corporate guilds vanished in the face of division of labour in each single workshop.

Meantime the markets kept ever growing, the demand ever rising. Even manufacture no longer sufficed. Thereupon, steam and machinery revolutionised industrial production. The place of manufacture was taken by the giant, Modern Industry, the place of the industrial middle class, by industrial millionaires, the leaders of whole industrial armies, the modern bourgeois.

Modern industry has established the world-market, for which the discovery of America paved the way. This market has given an immense development to commerce, to navigation, to communication by land. This development has, in its turn, reacted on the extension of industry; and in proportion as industry, commerce, navigation, railways extended, in the same proportion the bourgeoisie developed, increased its capital, and pushed into the background every class handed down from the Middle Ages. . . .

Each step in the development of the bourgeoisie was accompanied by a corresponding political advance of that class. An oppressed class under the sway of the feudal nobility, an armed and self-governing association in the mediaeval commune; here independent urban republic (as in Italy and Germany), there taxable "third estate" of the monarchy (as in France), afterwards, in the period of manufacture proper, serving either the semi-feudal or the absolute monarchy as a counterpoise against the nobility and, in fact, corner-stone of the great monarchies in general, the bourgeoisie has at last, since the establishment of Modern Industry and of the world-market, conquered for itself, in the modern representative State, exclusive political sway. The executive of the modern State is but a committee for managing the common affairs of the whole bourgeoisie.

The bourgeoisie, historically, has played a most revolutionary part.

The bourgeoisie, wherever it has got the upper hand, has put an end to all feudal, patriarchal, idyllic relations. It has pitilessly torn asunder the motley feudal ties that bound man to his "natural superiors," and has left remaining no other nexus between man and man than naked self-interest, than callous "cash payment." It has drowned the most heavenly ecstasies of religious fervour, of chivalrous enthusiasm, of philistine sentimentalism, in the icy water of egotistical calculation. It has resolved personal worth into exchange value, and in place of the numberless indefeasible chartered freedoms, has set up that single, unconscionable freedom—Free Trade. In one word, for exploitation, veiled by religious and political illusions, it has substituted naked, shameless, direct, brutal exploitation.

The bourgeoisie has stripped of its halo every occupation hitherto honoured and looked up to with reverent awe. It has converted the physician, the lawyer, the priest, the poet, the man of science, into its paid wage labourers.

The bourgeoisie has torn away from the family its sentimental veil, and has reduced the family relation to a mere money relation.

The bourgeoisie . . . has accomplished wonders far surpassing Egyptian pyramids, Roman aqueducts, and Gothic cathedrals; it has conducted expeditions that put in the shade all former Exoduses of nations and crusades.

The bourgeoisie cannot exist without constantly revolutionising the instruments of production, and thereby the relations of production, and with them the whole relations of society. Conservation of the old modes of production in unaltered form, was, on the contrary, the first condition of existence for all earlier industrial classes. Constant revolutionising of production, uninterrupted disturbance of all social conditions, everlasting uncertainty and agitation distinguish the bourgeois epoch from all earlier ones. All fixed, fast-frozen relations, with their train of ancient and venerable prejudices and opinions, are swept away, all new-formed ones become antiquated before they can ossify. All that is solid melts into air, all that is holy is profaned, and man is at last compelled to face with sober senses, his real conditions of life, and his relations with his kind.

The need of a constantly expanding market for its products chases the bourgeoisie over the whole surface of the globe. It must nestle everywhere, settle everywhere, establish connexions everywhere.

The bourgeoisie has through its exploitation of the world-market given a cosmopolitan character to production and consumption in every country. To the great chagrin of Reactionists, it has drawn from under the feet of industry the national ground on which it stood. All old-established national industries have been destroyed or are daily being destroyed. They are dislodged by new industries, whose introduction becomes a life and death question for all civilised nations, by industries that no longer work up indigenous raw material, but raw material drawn from the remotest zones; industries whose products are consumed, not only at home, but in every quarter of the globe. In place of the old wants, satisfied by the productions of the country, we find new wants, requiring for their satisfaction the products of distant lands and climes. In place of the old local and national seclusion and self-sufficiency, we have intercourse in every direction, universal interdependence of nations. And as in material, so also in intellectual production. The intellectual creations of individual nations become common property. National one-sidedness and narrow-mindedness become more and more impossible, and from the numerous national and local literatures, there arises a world literature.

The bourgeoisie, by the rapid improvement of all instruments of production, by the immensely facilitated means of communication, draws all, even the most barbarian, nations into civilisation. The cheap prices of its commodities are the heavy artillery with which it batters down all Chinese walls, with which it forces the barbarians' intensely obstinate hatred of foreigners to capitulate. It compels all nations, on pain of extinction, to adopt the bourgeois mode of production; it compels them to introduce what it calls civilisation into their midst, i.e., to become bourgeois themselves. In one word, it creates a world after its own image.

The bourgeoisie has subjected the country to the rule of the towns. It has created enormous cities, has greatly increased the urban population as compared with the rural, and has thus rescued a considerable part of the population from the idiocy of rural life. Just as it has made the country dependent on the towns, so it has made barbarian and semibarbarian countries dependent on the civilised ones, nations of peasants on nations of bourgeois, the East on the West.

The bourgeoisie . . . has agglomerated population, centralised means of production, and has concentrated property in a few hands. The necessary consequence of this was political centralisation. Independent, or but loosely connected provinces, with separate interests, laws, governments and systems of taxation, became lumped together into one nation, with one government, one code of laws, one national class-interest, one frontier and one customs-tariff.

The bourgeoisie, during its rule of scarce one hundred years, has created more massive and more colossal productive forces than have all preceding generations together. Subjection of Nature's forces to man, machinery, application of chemistry to industry and agriculture, steam-navigation, railways, electric telegraphs, clearing of whole continents for cultivation, canalisation of rivers, whole populations conjured out of the ground—what earlier century had even a presentiment that such productive forces slumbered in the lap of social labour?

We see then: the means of production and of exchange, on whose foundation the bourgeoisie built itself up, were generated in feudal society. At a certain stage in the development of these means of production and of exchange, the conditions under which feudal society produced and exchanged, the feudal organisation of agriculture and manufacturing industry, in one word, the feudal relations of property became no longer compatible with the already developed productive forces; they became so many fetters. They had to be burst asunder; they were burst asunder.

Into their place stepped free competition, accompanied by a social and political constitution adapted to it, and by the economical and political sway of the bourgeois class.

A similar movement is going on before our own eyes. Modern bourgeois society with its relations of production, of exchange and of property, a society that has conjured up such gigantic means of production and of exchange, is like the sorcerer, who is no longer able to control the powers of the nether world whom he has called up by his spells. For many a decade past the history of industry and commerce is but the history of the revolt of modern productive forces against modern conditions of production, against property relations that are the conditions for the existence of the bourgeoisie and of its rule. It is enough to mention the commercial crises that by their periodical return put on its trial, each time more threateningly, the existence of the entire bourgeois society. In these crises a great part not only of the existing products, but also of the previously created productive forces, are periodically destroyed. In these crises there breaks out an epidemic that, in all earlier epochs, would have seemed an absurdity—the epidemic of over-production. . . . And how does the bourgeoisie get over these crises? On the one hand by enforced destruction of a mass of productive

forces; on the other, by the conquest of new markets, and by the more thorough exploitation of the old ones. That is to say, by paving the way for more extensive and more destructive crises, and by diminishing the means whereby crises are prevented. . . .

But not only has the bourgeoisie forged the weapons that bring death to itself; it has also called into existence the men who are to wield those weapons—the modern working class— the proletarians.

In proportion as the bourgeoisie, i.e., capital, is developed, in the same proportion is the proletariat, the modern working class, developed—a class of labourers, who live only so long as they find work, and who find work only so long as their labour increases capital. These labourers, who must sell themselves piecemeal, are a commodity, like every other article of commerce, and are consequently exposed to all the vicissitudes of competition, to all the fluctuations of the market.

Owing to the extensive use of machinery and to division of labour, the work of the proletarians has lost all individual character, and consequently, all charm for the workman. He becomes an appendage of the machine, and it is only the most simple, most monotonous, and most easily acquired knack, that is required of him. Hence, the cost of production of a workman is restricted, almost entirely, to the means of subsistence that he requires for his maintenance, and for the propagation of his race. But the price of a commodity, and therefore also of labour, is equal to its cost of production. In proportion, therefore, as the repulsiveness of the work increases, the wage decreases. Nay more, in proportion as the use of machinery and division of labour increases, in the same proportion the burden of toil also increases, whether by prolongation of the working hours, by increase of the work exacted in a given time or by increased speed of the machinery, etc.

Modern industry has converted the little workshop of the patriarchal master into the great factory of the industrial capitalist. Masses of labourers, crowded into the factory, are organised like soldiers. As privates of the industrial army they are placed under the command of a perfect hierarchy of officers and sergeants. Not only are they slaves of the bourgeois class, and of the bourgeois State; they are daily and hourly enslaved by the machine, by the overlooker, and, above all, by the individual bourgeois manufacturer himself. The more openly this despotism proclaims gain to be its end and aim, the more petty, the more hateful and the more embittering it is.

The less the skill and exertion of strength implied in manual labour, in other words, the more modern industry becomes developed, the more is the labour of men superseded by that of women. Differences of age and sex have no longer any distinctive social validity for the working class. All are instruments of labour, more or less expensive to use, according to their age and sex.

No sooner is the exploitation of the labourer by the manufacturer, so far, at an end, that he receives his wages in cash, than he is set upon by the other portions of the bourgeoisie, the landlord, the shopkeeper, the pawnbroker, etc.

The lower strata of the middle class—the small tradespeople, shopkeepers, and retired tradesmen generally, the handicraftsman and peasants—all these sink gradually into the proletariat, partly because their diminutive capital does not suffice for the scale on which Modern Industry is carried on, and is swamped in the competition with the large capitalists, partly because their specialised skill is rendered worthless by new methods of production. Thus the proletariat is recruited from all classes of the population.

The proletariat goes through various stages of development. With its birth begins its struggle with the bourgeoisie. At first the contest is carried on by individual labourers, then by the workpeople of a factory, then by the operatives of one trade, in one locality, against the individual bourgeois who directly exploits them. They direct their attacks not against the bourgeois conditions of production, but against the instruments of production themselves; they destroy imported wares that compete with their labour, they smash to pieces machinery, they set factories ablaze, they seek

to restore by force the vanished status of the workman of the Middle Ages. . . .

But with the development of industry the proletariat not only increases in number; it becomes concentrated in greater masses, its strength grows, and it feels that strength more. The various interests and conditions of life within the ranks of the proletariat are more and more equalised, in proportion as machinery obliterates all distinctions of labour, and nearly everywhere reduces wages to the same low level. The growing competition among the bourgeois, and the resulting commercial crises, make the wages of the workers ever more fluctuating. The unceasing improvement of machinery, ever more rapidly developing, makes their livelihood more and more precarious; the collisions between individual workmen and individual bourgeois take more and more the character of collisions between two classes. Thereupon the workers begin to form combinations (Trades Unions) against the bourgeois; they club together in order to keep up the rate of wages; they found permanent associations in order to make provision beforehand for these occasional revolts. Here and there the contest breaks out into riots.

Now and then the workers are victorious, but only for a time. The real fruit of their battles lies, not in the immediate result, but in the ever-expanding union of the workers. This union is helped on by the improved means of communication that are created by modern industry and that place the workers of different localities in contact with one another. It was just this contact that was needed to centralise the numerous local struggles, all of the same character, into one national struggle between classes. . . .

This organisation of the proletarians into a class, and consequently into a political party, is continually being upset again by the competition between the workers themselves. But it ever rises up again, stronger, firmer, mightier. It compels legislative recognition of particular interests of the workers, by taking advantage of the divisions among the bourgeoisie itself. Thus the ten-hours' bill in England was carried. . . .

Finally in times when the class struggle nears the decisive hour, the process of dissolution going on within the ruling class, in fact within the whole range of society, assumes such a violent, glaring character, that a small section of the ruling class cuts itself adrift, and joins the revolutionary class, the class that holds the future in its hands. . . .

Of all the classes that stand face to face with the bourgeoisie today, the proletariat alone is a really revolutionary class. The other classes decay and finally disappear in the face of Modern Industry; the proletariat is its special and essential product.

The lower middle class, the small manufacturer, the shopkeeper, the artisan, the peasant, all these fight against the bourgeoisie, to save from extinction their existence as factions of the middle class. They are therefore not revolutionary, but conservative. Nay more, they are reactionary, for they try to roll back the wheel of history. . . .

. . . The proletarian is without property; . . . modern industrial labour, modern subjection to capital, the same in England as in France, in America as in Germany, has stripped him of every trace of national character. Law, morality, religion, are to him so many bourgeois prejudices, behind which lurk in ambush just as many bourgeois interests. . . .

All previous historical movements were movements of minorities, or in the interests of minorities. The proletarian movement is the self-conscious, independent movement of the immense majority, in the interests of the immense majority. The proletariat, the lowest stratum of our present society, cannot stir, cannot raise itself up, without the whole superincumbent strata of official society being sprung into the air.

Though not in substance, yet in form, the struggle of the proletariat with the bourgeoisie is at first a national struggle. The proletariat of each country must, of course, first of all settle matters with its own bourgeoisie.

In depicting the most general phases of the development of the proletariat, we traced the more or less veiled civil war, raging within existing society, up to the point where that war breaks out into open revolution, and where the violent overthrow of the bourgeoisie lays the foundation for the sway of the proletariat.

Hitherto, every form of society has been based, as we have already seen, on the antagonism of oppressing and oppressed classes. But in order to oppress a class, certain conditions must be assured to it under which it can, at least, continue its slavish existence. . . . The modern labourer, . . . instead of rising with the progress of industry, sinks deeper and deeper below the conditions of existence of his own class. He becomes a pauper, and pauperism develops more rapidly than population and wealth. And here it becomes evident, that the bourgeoisie is unfit any longer to be the ruling class in society, and to impose its conditions of existence upon society as an over-riding law. It is unfit to rule because it is incompetent to assure an existence to its slave within his slavery, because it cannot help letting him sink into such a state, that it has to feed him, instead of being fed by him. Society can no longer live under this bourgeoisie, in other words, its existence is no longer compatible with society.

The essential condition for the existence, and for the sway of the bourgeois class, is the formation and augmentation of capital; the condition for capital is wage-labour. Wage-labour rests exclusively on competition between the labourers. The advance of industry, whose involuntary promoter is the bourgeoisie, replaces the isolation of the labourers, due to competition, by their revolutionary combination, due to association. The development of Modern Industry, therefore, cuts from under its feet the very foundation on which the bourgeoisie produces and appropriates products. What the bourgeosie, therefore, produces, above all, is its own grave-diggers. Its fall and the victory of the proletariat are equally inevitable.

II. Proletarians and Communists

. . . The immediate aim of the Communists is the same as that of all the other proletarian parties: formation of the proletariat into a class, overthrow of the bourgeois supremacy, conquest of political power by the proletariat. . . .

. . . The abolition of existing property relations is not at all a distinctive feature of Communism. All property relations in the past have continually been subject to historical change consequent upon the change in historical conditions.

The French Revolution, for example, abolished feudal property in favour of bourgeois property. The distinguishing feature of Communism is not the abolition of property generally, but the abolition of bourgeois property. But modern bourgeois private property is the final and most complete expression of the system of producing and appropriating products, that is based on class antagonisms, on the exploitation of the many by the few.

In this sense, the theory of the Communists may be summed up in the single sentence: Abolition of private property.

We Communists have been reproached with the desire of abolishing the right of personally acquiring property as the fruit of a man's own labour, which property is alleged to be the groundwork of all personal freedom, activity and independence.

Hard-won, self-acquired, self-earned property! Do you mean the property of the petty artisan and of the small peasant, a form of property that preceded the bourgeois form? There is no need to abolish that; the development of industry has to a great extent already destroyed it, and is still destroying it daily.

Or do you mean modern bourgeois private property?

But does wage-labour create any property for the labourer? Not a bit. It creates capital, i.e., that kind of property which exploits wage labour, and which cannot increase except upon condition of begetting a new supply of wage-labour for fresh exploitation. Property, in its present form, is based on the antagonism of capital and wage-labour. Let us examine both sides of this antagonism.

. . . Capital is a collective product, and only by the united action of many members, nay, in the last resort, only by the united action of all members of society, can it be set in motion.

Capital is, therefore, not a personal, it is a social power.

When, therefore, capital is converted into common property, into the property of all members of society, personal property is not thereby transformed into social property. It is only the social character of the property that is changed. It loses its class-character.

Let us now take wage-labour.

The average price of wage-labour is the minimum wage, i.e., that quantum of the means of subsistence, which is absolutely requisite to keep the labourer in bare existence as a labourer. What, therefore, the wage-labourer appropriates by means of his labour, merely suffices to prolong and reproduce a bare existence. We by no means intend to abolish this personal appropriation of the products of labour, an appropriation that is made for the maintenance and reproduction of human life, and that leaves no surplus wherewith to command the labour of others. All that we want to do away with, is the miserable character of this appropriation, under which the labourer lives merely to increase capital, and is allowed to live only in so far as the interest of the ruling class requires it.

In bourgeois society, living labour is but a means to increase accumulated labour. In Communist society, accumulated labour is but a means to widen, to enrich, to promote the existence of the labourer.

. . . In bourgeois society capital is independent and has individuality, while the living person is dependent and has no individuality.

And the abolition of this state of things is called by the bourgeois, abolition of individuality and freedom! And rightly so. The abolition of bourgeois individuality, bourgeois independence, and bourgeois freedom is undoubtedly aimed at.

By freedom is meant, under the present bourgeois conditions of production, free trade, free selling and buying. . . .

You are horrified at our intending to do away with private property. But in your existing society, private property is already done away with for nine-tenths of the population; its existence for the few is solely due to its non-existence in the hands of those nine-tenths.

You reproach us, therefore, with intending to do away with a form of property, the necessary condition for whose existence is the non-existence of any property for the immense majority of society.

In one word, you reproach us with intending to do away with your property. Precisely so; that is just what we intend. . . .

Communism deprives no man of the power to appropriate the products of society; all that it does is to deprive him of the power to subjugate the labour of others by means of such appropriation.

It has been objected that upon the abolition of private property all work will cease, and universal laziness will overtake us.

According to this, bourgeois society ought long ago to have gone to the dogs through sheer idleness; for those of its members who work, acquire nothing, and those who acquire anything, do not work. . . .

But don't wrangle with us so long as you apply, to our intended abolition of bourgeois property, the standard of your bourgeois notions of freedom, culture, law, &c. Your very ideas are but the outgrowth of the conditions of your bourgeois production and bourgeois property, just as your jurisprudence is but the will of your class made into a law for all, a will, whose essential character and direction are determined by the economical conditions of existence of your class.

The selfish misconception that induces you to transform into eternal laws of nature and of reason, the social forms springing from your present mode of production and form of property—historical relations that rise and disappear in the progress of production—this misconception you share with every ruling class that has preceded you. . . .

Abolition of the family! Even the most radical flare up at this infamous proposal of the Communists.

On what foundation is the present family, the bourgeois family, based? On capital, on private gain. In its completely developed form this family exists only among the bourgeoisie. But this state of things finds its complement in the practical absence of the family among the proletarians, and in public prostitution.

The bourgeois family will vanish as a matter of course when its complement vanishes, and both will vanish with the vanishing of capital.

Do you charge us with wanting to stop the exploitation of children by their parents? To this crime we plead guilty.

But, you will say, we destroy the most hallowed of relations, when we replace home education by social.

And your education! Is not that also social, and determined by the social conditions under which you educate, by the intervention, direct or indirect, of society, by means of schools, &c.? The Communists have not invented the intervention of society in education; they do but seek to alter the character of that intervention, and to rescue education from the influence of the ruling class.

The bourgeois clap-trap about the family and education, about the hallowed co-relation of parent and child, becomes all the more disgusting, the more, by the action of Modern Industry, all family ties among the proletarians are torn asunder, and their children transformed into simple articles of commerce and instruments of labour.

But you Communists would introduce community of women, screams the whole bourgeoisie in chorus.

The bourgeois sees in his wife a mere instrument of production. He hears that the instruments of production are to be exploited in common, and, naturally, can come to no other conclusion than that the lot of being common to all will likewise fall to the women.

He has not even a suspicion that the real point aimed at is to do away with the status of women as mere instruments of production.

For the rest, nothing is more ridiculous than the virtuous indignation of our bourgeois at the community of women which, they pretend, is to be openly and officially established by the Communists. The Communists have no need to introduce community of women; it has existed almost from time immemorial.

Our bourgeois, not content with having the wives and daughters of their proletarians at their disposal, not to speak of common prostitutes, take the greatest pleasure in seducing each other's wives.

Bourgeois marriage is in reality a system of wives in common and thus, at the most, what the Communists might possibly be reproached with, is that they desire to introduce, in substitution for a hypocritically concealed, an openly legalised community of women. For the rest, it is self-evident that the abolition of the present system of production must bring with it the abolition of the community of women springing from that system, i.e., of prostitution both public and private.

The Communists are further reproached with desiring to abolish countries and nationality.

The working men have no country. We cannot take from them what they have not got. . . .

National differences and antagonisms between peoples are daily more and more vanishing, owing to the development of the bourgeoisie, to freedom of commerce, to the world-market, to uniformity in the mode of production and in the conditions of life corresponding thereto. . . .

In proportion as the exploitation of one individual by another is put an end to, the exploitation of one nation by another will also be put an end to. In proportion as the antagonism between classes within the nation vanishes, the hostility of one nation to another will come to an end. . . .

Does it require deep intuition to comprehend that man's ideas, views and conceptions, in one word, man's consciousness, changes with every change in the conditions of his material existence, in his social relations and in his social life?

What else does the history of ideas prove, than that intellectual production changes its character in proportion as material production is changed? The ruling ideas of each age have ever been the ideas of its ruling class.

When people speak of ideas that revolutionise society, they do but express the fact, that within the old society, the elements of a new one have been created, and that the dissolution of the old ideas keeps even pace with the dissolution of the old conditions of existence.

When the ancient world was in its last throes, the ancient religions were overcome by Christianity. When Christian ideas succumbed in the 18th century to rationalist ideas, feudal society fought its death battle with the then revolutionary bourgeoisie. The ideas of religious liberty and freedom of conscience merely gave expression to the sway of free competition within the domain of knowledge.

"Undoubtedly," it will be said, "religious, moral, philosophical and juridical ideas have been modified in the course of historical development. But religion, morality, philosophy, political science, and law, constantly survived this change."

"There are, besides, eternal truths, such as Freedom, Justice, etc., that are common to all states of society. But Communism abolishes eternal truths, it abolishes all religion, and all morality, instead of constituting them on a new basis; it therefore acts in contradiction to all past historical experience."

What does this accusation reduce itself to? The history of all past society has consisted in the development of class antagonisms, antagonisms that assumed different forms at different epochs.

But whatever form they may have taken, one fact is common to all past ages, viz., the exploitation of one part of society by the other. No wonder, then, that the social consciousness of past ages, despite all the multiplicity and variety it displays, moves within certain common forms, or general ideas, which cannot completely vanish except with the total disappearance of class antagonisms.

The Communist revolution is the most radical rupture with traditional property relations; no wonder that its development involves the most radical rupture with traditional ideas.

But let us have done with the bourgeois objections to Communism.

We have seen above, that the first step in the revolution by the working class, is to raise the proletariat to the position of ruling class, to win the battle of democracy.

The proletariat will use its political supremacy to wrest, by degrees, all capital from the bourgeoisie, to centralise all instruments of production in the hands of the State, i.e., of the proletariat organised as the ruling class; and to increase the total of productive forces as rapidly as possible.

Of course, in the beginning, this cannot be effected except by means of despotic inroads on the rights of property, and on the conditions of bourgeois production; by means of measures, therefore, which appear economically insufficient and untenable, but which, in the course of the movement, outstrip themselves, necessitate further inroads upon the old social order, and are unavoidable as a means of entirely revolutionising the mode of production.

These measures will of course be different in different countries.

Nevertheless in the most advanced countries, the following will be pretty generally applicable.

1. Abolition of property in land and application of all rents of land to public purposes.

2. A heavy progressive or graduated income tax.

3. Abolition of all right of inheritance.

4. Confiscation of the property of all emigrants and rebels.

5. Centralisation of credit in the hands of the State, by means of a national bank with State capital and an exclusive monopoly.

6. Centralisation of the means of communication and transport in the hands of the State.

7. Extension of factories and instruments of production owned by the State; the bringing into cultivation of waste-lands,

and the improvement of the soil generally in accordance with a common plan.

8. Equal liability of all to labour. Establishment of industrial armies, especially for agriculture.

9. Combination of agriculture with manufacturing industries; gradual abolition of the distinction between town and country, by a more equable distribution of the population over the country.

10. Free education for all children in public schools. Abolition of children's factory labour in its present form. Combination of education with industrial production, &c., &c.

When, in the course of development, class distinctions have disappeared, and all production has been concentrated in the hands of a vast association of the whole nation, the public power will lose its political character. Political power, properly so called, is merely the organised power of one class for oppressing another. If the proletariat during its contest with the bourgeoisie is compelled, by the force of circumstances, to organise itself as a class, if, by means of revolution, it makes itself the ruling class, and, as such, sweeps away by force the old conditions of production, then it will, along with these conditions, have swept away the conditions for the existence of class antagonisms and of classes generally, and will thereby have abolished its own supremacy as a class.

In place of the old bourgeois society, with its classes and class antagonisms, we shall have an association, in which the free development of each is the condition for the free development of all.

 SUSAN MOLLER OKIN

JUSTICE, GENDER, AND THE FAMILY

Introduction: Justice and Gender

We as a society pride ourselves on our democratic values. We don't believe that people should be constrained by innate differences from being able to achieve desired positions of influence or to improve their well-being; equality of opportunity is our professed aim. The Preamble to our Constitution stresses the importance of justice, as well as the general welfare and the blessings of liberty. The Pledge of Allegiance asserts that our republic preserves "liberty and justice for all." Yet substantial inequalities between the sexes still exist in our society. In economic terms, full-time working women (after some very recent improvement) earn on average 71 percent of the earnings of full-time working men. One-half of poor and three-fifths of chronically poor households with dependent children are maintained by a single female parent. The poverty rate for elderly women is nearly twice that for elderly men. On the political front, two out of a hundred U.S. senators are women, one out of nine justices seems to be considered sufficient female representation on the Supreme Court, and the number of men chosen in each congressional election far exceeds the number of women elected in the entire history of the country. Underlying and intertwined with all these inequalities is the unequal distribution of the unpaid labor of the family.

An equal share between the sexes of family responsibilities, especially child care, is "the great revolution that has not happened." Women, including mothers of young children, are, of course, working outside the household far more than their mothers did. And the small proportion of women who reach high-level positions in politics, business, and the professions command a vastly disproportionate amount of space in the media, compared with the millions of women who work at low-paying, dead-end jobs, the millions who do part-time work with its lack of benefits, and the millions of others who stay home performing for no pay what is frequently not even acknowledged as work. Certainly, the fact that women are doing more paid work does not imply that they are more equal. It is often said that we are living in a postfeminist era. This claim, due in part to the distorted emphasis on women who have "made it," is false, no matter which of its meanings is intended. It is certainly not true that feminism has been vanquished, and equally untrue that it is no longer needed because its aims have been fulfilled. Until there is justice within the family, women will not be able to gain equality in politics, at work, or in any other sphere.

. . . The typical current practices of family life, structured to a large extent by gender, are not just. Both the expectation and the experience of the division of labor by sex make women vulnerable. . . . A cycle of power relations and decisions pervades both family and workplace, each reinforcing the inequalities between the sexes that already exist within the other. Not only women, but children of both sexes, too, are often made vulnerable by gender-structured marriage. One-quarter of children in the United States now live in families with only one parent in almost 90 percent of cases, the mother. Contrary to common perceptions—in which the situation of never-married mothers looms largest—65 percent of single-parent families are a result of marital separation or divorce. Recent research in a number of states has shown that, in the average case, the standard of living of divorced women and the children who live with them plummets after divorce, whereas the economic situation of divorced men tends to be better than when they were married.

A central source of injustice for women these days is that the law, most noticeably in the event of divorce, treats more or less as equals those whom custom, workplace discrimination, and the still conventional division of labor within the family have made very unequal. Central to this socially created inequality are two commonly made but inconsistent presumptions: that women are primarily responsible for the rearing of children; and that serious and committed members of the work force (regardless of class) do not have primary responsibility, or even shared responsibility, for the rearing of children. The old assumption of the workplace, still implicit, is that workers have wives at home. It is built not only into the structure and expectations of the workplace but into other crucial social institutions, such as schools, which make no attempt to take account, in their scheduled hours or vacations, of the fact that parents are likely to hold jobs.

Now, of course, many wage workers do not have wives at home. Often, they *are* wives and mothers, or single, separated, or divorced mothers of small children. But neither the family nor the workplace has taken much account of this fact. Employed wives still do by far the greatest proportion of unpaid family work, such as child care and housework. Women are far more likely to take time out of the workplace or to work part-time because of family responsibilities than are their husbands or male partners. And they are much more likely to move because of their husbands' employment needs or opportunities than their own. All these tendencies, which are due to a number of factors, including the sex segregation and discrimination of the workplace itself, tend to be cyclical in their effects: wives advance more slowly than their husbands at work and thus gain less seniority, and the discrepancy between their wages increases over time. Then, because both the power structure of the family and what is regarded as consensual "rational" family decision making reflect

the fact that the husband usually earns more, it will become even less likely as time goes on that the unpaid work of the family will be shared between the spouses. Thus the cycle of inequality is perpetuated. Often hidden from view within a marriage, it is in the increasingly likely event of marital breakdown that the socially constructed inequality of married women is at its most visible.

This is what I mean when I say that gender-structured marriage *makes* women vulnerable. These are not matters of natural necessity, as some people would believe. Surely nothing in our natures dictates that men should not be equal participants in the rearing of their children. Nothing in the nature of work makes it impossible to adjust it to the fact that people are parents as well as workers. That these things have not happened is part of the historically, socially constructed differentiation between the sexes that feminists have come to call *gender*. We live in a society that has over the years regarded the innate characteristic of sex as one of the clearest legitimizers of different rights and restrictions, both formal and informal. . . .

The family is a crucial determinant of our opportunities in life, of what we "become." It has frequently been acknowledged by those concerned with real equality of opportunity that the family presents a problem. But though they have discerned a serious problem, these theorists have underestimated it because they have only seen half of it. They have seen that the disparity among families in terms of the physical and emotional environment, motivation, and material advantages they can give their children has a tremendous effect upon children's opportunities in life. We are not born as isolated, equal individuals in our society, but into family situations: some in the social middle, some poor and homeless, and some superaffluent; some to a single or soon-to-be-separated parent, some to parents whose marriage is fraught with conflict, some to parents who will stay together in love and happiness. Any claims that equal opportunity exists are therefore completely unfounded. Decades of neglect of the poor, especially of poor black and

Hispanic households, accentuated by the policies of the Reagan years, have brought us farther from the principles of equal opportunity. To come close to them would require, for example, a high and uniform standard of public education and the provision of equal social services—including health care, employment training, job opportunities, drug rehabilitation, and decent housing—for all who need them. In addition to redistributive taxation, only massive reallocations of resources from the military to social services could make these things possible.

But even if all these disparities were somehow eliminated, we would still not attain equal opportunity for all. This is because what has not been recognized as an equal opportunity problem, except in feminist literature and circles, is the disparity *within* the family, the fact that its gender structure is itself a major obstacle to equality of opportunity. This is very important in itself, since one of the factors with most influence on our opportunities in life is the social significance attributed to our sex. The opportunities of girls and women are centrally affected by the structure and practices of family life, particularly by the fact that women are almost invariably primary parents. What nonfeminists who see in the family an obstacle to equal opportunity have *not* seen is that the extent to which a family is gender-structured can make the sex we belong to a relatively insignificant aspect of our identity and our life prospects or an all-pervading one. This is because so much of the social construction of gender takes place in the family, and particularly in the institution of female parenting.

Moreover, especially in recent years, with the increased rates of single motherhood, separation, and divorce, the inequalities between the sexes have *compounded* the first part of the problem. The disparity among families has grown largely because of the impoverishment of many women and children after separation or divorce. The division of labor in the typical family leaves most women far less capable than men of supporting themselves, and this disparity is accentuated by the fact that children of separated or divorced parents usually live with their mothers. The inadequacy—and frequent nonpayment—of child support has become recognized as a major social problem. Thus the inequalities of gender are now directly harming many children of both sexes as well as women themselves. Enhancing equal opportunity for women, important as it is in itself, is also a crucial way of improving the opportunities of many of the most disadvantaged children.

As there is a connection among the parts of this problem, so is there a connection among some of the solutions: much of what needs to be done to end the inequalities of gender, and to work in the direction of ending gender itself, will also help to equalize opportunity from one family to another. Subsidized, high-quality day care is obviously one such thing; another is the adaptation of the workplace to the needs of parents. . . .

Vulnerability by Marriage

. . . I argue that marriage and the family, as currently practiced in our society, are unjust institutions. They constitute the pivot of a societal system of gender that renders women vulnerable to dependency, exploitation, and abuse. When we look seriously at the distribution between husbands and wives of such critical social goods as work (paid and unpaid), power, prestige, self-esteem, opportunities for self-development, and both physical and economic security, we find socially constructed inequalities between them, right down the list. . . .

. . . Few people would disagree with the statement that marriage involves, in some respects, especially emotionally, *mutual* vulnerability and dependence. It is, clearly, also a relationship in which some aspects of unequal vulnerability are not determined along sex lines. For example, spouses may vary in the extent of their love for and emotional dependence on each other; it is certainly not the case that wives always love their husbands more than they are loved by them, or vice versa. Nevertheless, as we shall see, in crucial respects gender-structured marriage *involves women in a cycle of socially caused and distinctly asymmetric vulnerability.* The division of labor within marriage (except in rare cases) makes wives far more likely than husbands to be exploited both within the marital relationship and in the world of work outside the home. To a great extent and in numerous ways, contemporary women in our society are *made* vulnerable by marriage itself. They are first set up for vulnerability during their developing years by their personal (and socially reinforced) expectations that they will be the primary caretakers of children, and that in fulfilling this role they will need to try to attract and to keep the economic support of a man, to whose work life they will be expected to give priority. They are rendered vulnerable by the actual division of labor within almost all current marriages. They are disadvantaged at work by the fact that the world of wage work, including the professions, is still largely structured around the assumption that "workers" have wives at home. They are rendered far more vulnerable if they become the primary caretakers of children, and their vulnerability peaks if their marriages dissolve and they become single parents.

. . . Women are made vulnerable, both economically and socially, by the interconnected traditions of female responsibility for rearing children and female subordination and dependence, of which both the history and the contemporary practices of marriage form a significant part. . . .

The traditional idea of sex-differentiated marital responsibility, with its provider-husband and domestic-wife roles, continues to be a strong influence on what men and women think and how they behave. Husbands, at least, tend to feel this way even when their wives *do* work outside the home; and when there is disagreement about whether the wife should work, it is more often the case that she wants to but that he does not want to "let" her. Thirty-four percent of the husbands and 25 percent of the wives surveyed by Blumstein and Schwartz did not think that couples should share the responsibility for earning a living. These percentages rise sharply when children are involved: 64 percent of husbands and 60 percent of wives did not think that the wife should

be employed if a couple has small children. Given the emphasis our society places on economic success, belief in the male provider role strongly reinforces the domination of men within marriage. Although, as we shall see, many wives actually work longer hours (counting paid and unpaid work) than their husbands, the fact that a husband's work is predominantly paid gives him not only status and prestige, both within and outside the marriage, but also a greater sense of entitlement. As a consequence, wives experiencing divorce, especially if they have been housewives and mothers throughout marriage, are likely to devalue their own contributions to the marriage and to discount their right to share its assets. "Many divorcing women still see the money their husbands have earned as 'his money.'" In ongoing marriages too, it is not uncommon for husbands to use the fact that they are the primary breadwinners to enforce their views or wishes.

It is no wonder, then, that most women are, even before marriage, in an economic position that sets them up to become more vulnerable during marriage, and most vulnerable of all if their marriage ends and—unprepared as they are—they find themselves in the position of having to provide for themselves and their children.

Vulnerability Within Marriage

Marriage continues the cycle of inequality set in motion by the anticipation of marriage and the related sex segregation of the workplace. Partly because of society's assumptions about gender, but also because women, on entering marriage, tend already to be disadvantaged members of the work force, married women are likely to start out with less leverage in the relationship than their husbands. As I shall show, answers to questions such as whose work life and work needs take priority, and how the unpaid work of the family will be allocated—if they are not simply assumed to be decided along the lines of sex difference, but are live issues in the marriage—are likely to be strongly influenced by the differences in earning power between husbands and wives.

In many marriages, partly because of discrimination at work and the wage gap between the sexes, wives (despite initial personal ambitions and even when they are full-time wage workers) come to perceive themselves as benefiting from giving priority to their husbands' careers. Hence they have little incentive to question the traditional division of labor in the household. This in turn limits their own commitment to wage work and their incentive and leverage to challenge the gender structure of the workplace. Experiencing frustration and lack of control at work, those who thus turn toward domesticity, while often resenting the lack of respect our society gives to full-time mothers, may see the benefits of domestic life as greater than the costs.

Thus, the inequalities between the sexes in the workplace and at home reinforce and exacerbate each other. . . . *A cycle of power relations and decisions pervades both family and workplace, and the inequalities of each reinforce those that already exist in the other.* Only with the recognition of this truth will we be able to begin to confront the changes that need to occur if women are to have a real opportunity to be equal participants in either sphere. . . .

. . . Those who seek to explain women's comparative disadvantage in the labor market by their preference for domestic commitments do not consider whether at least some of the causality may run in the opposite direction. But there is considerable evidence that women's "choices" to become domestically oriented, and even whether to have children, may result at least in part from their frequently blocked situations at work. Kathleen Gerson's study shows that, though they usually did not notice the connection, many of the women in her sample decided to leave wage work and turn to childbearing and domesticity coincidentally with becoming frustrated with the dead-end nature of their jobs. Conversely, she found that some women who had initially thought of themselves as domestically oriented, and who had in many cases chosen traditionally female occupations, reversed these orientations when unusual and unexpected opportunities for work advancement opened up to them.

Even if these problems with the human capital approach did not exist, we would still be faced with the fact that the theory can explain, at most, half of the wage differential between the sexes. In the case of the differential between white men and black women, 70 percent of it is unexplained. At *any* given level of skill, experience, and education, men earn considerably more than women. The basic problem with the human capital approach is that, like much of the neoclassical economic theory, it pays too little attention to the multiple constraints placed on people's choices. It pays too little attention to differentials of power between the sexes both in the workplace and in the family. It thus ignores the fact that women's commitment and attachment to the workplace are strongly influenced by a number of factors that are largely beyond their control. As we have seen, a woman's typically less advantaged position in the work force and lower pay may lead her to choices about full-time motherhood and domesticity that she would have been less likely to make had her work life been less dead-ended. They also give her less power in relation to her husband should she want to resist the traditional division of labor in her household and to insist on a more equal sharing of child care and other domestic responsibilities. Those who stress the extent to which both husbands and wives cling to the "male provider/female nurturer" roles as unobjectionable because efficient and economically rational for the family unit need to take a step back and consider the extent to which the continued sex segregation of the work force serves to perpetuate the traditional division of labor within the household, even in the face of women's rising employment.

Housework and the Cycle of Vulnerability

It is no secret that in almost all families women do far more housework and child care than men do. But the distribution of paid and unpaid work within the family has rarely—outside of feminist circles—been considered a significant issue by theorists of justice. Why should it be? If two friends divide a task so that each takes primary responsibility for a different aspect of it, we would be loath to cry "injustice" unless one were obviously coercing the other. But at least three factors make the division of labor within the household a very different situation, and a clear question of justice. First, the uneven distribution of labor within the family is strongly correlated with an innate characteristic, which appears to make it the kind of issue with which theorists of justice have been most concerned. The virtually automatic allocation to one person of more of the paid labor and to the other of more of the unpaid labor would be regarded as decidedly odd in any relationship other than that of a married or cohabiting heterosexual couple. . . . The distribution of labor within the family by sex has deep ramifications for its respective members' material, psychological, physical, and intellectual well-being. One cannot even begin to address the issue of why so many women and children live in poverty in our society, or why women are inadequately represented in the higher echelons of our political and economic institutions, without confronting the division of labor between the sexes within the family. Thus it is not only itself an issue of justice but it is also at the very root of other significant concerns of justice, including equality of opportunity for children of both sexes, but especially for girls, and political justice in the broadest sense.

The justice issues surrounding housework are not simply issues about who does *more* work. However, on average, wives living with their husbands *do* now work slightly more total hours than their husbands do. In addition, this averaging obscures a great variety of distributions of both quantity and type of work within marriages. For the purposes of this discussion, it will be helpful to separate couples into two major categories: those in which the wife is "predominantly houseworking" (either a full-time housewife or employed part-time) and those in which the wife is "predominantly wage-working" (employed full-time or virtually full-time). Within each category, I shall look at issues such as the distribution of work (paid and unpaid), income, power, opportunity to choose one's occupation, self-respect and esteem, and availability

of exit. As we shall see, wives in each category experience a somewhat different pattern of injustice and vulnerability. But, except in the case of some of the small number of elite couples who make considerable use of paid help, the typical divisions of labor in the family cannot be regarded as just.

Predominantly Houseworking Wives
When a woman is a full-time housewife—as are about two-fifths of married women in the United States who live with their husbands—she does less total work, on average, than her employed husband: 49.3 hours per week, compared with his 63.2. This is also true of couples in which the wife works part-time (defined as fewer than thirty hours per week, including commuting time), though the average difference per week is reduced to eight hours in this case. This is, of course, partly because housework is less burdensome than it was before the days of labor-saving devices and declining fertility. Not surprisingly, however, during the early years of child rearing, a nonemployed wife (or part-time employed wife) is likely to work about the same total number of hours as her employed husband. But the *quantity* of work performed is only one of a number of important variables that must be considered in order for us to assess the justice or injustice of the division of labor in the family, particularly in relation to the issue of the cycle of women's vulnerability.

In terms of the quality of work, there are considerable disadvantages to the role of housewife. One is that much of the work is boring and/or unpleasant. Surveys indicate that most people of both sexes do not like to clean, shop for food, or do laundry, which constitute a high proportion of housework. Cooking rates higher, and child care even higher, with both sexes, than other domestic work. In reality, this separation of tasks is strictly hypothetical, at least for mothers, who are usually cleaning, shopping, doing laundry, and cooking at the same time as taking care of children. Many wage workers, too, do largely tedious and repetitive work. But the housewife-mother's work has additional disadvantages. One is that her hours of work are highly unscheduled; unlike virtually any other worker except the holder of a high political office, she can be called on at any time of the day or night, seven days a week. Another is that she cannot, nearly as easily as most other workers, change jobs. Her family comes to depend on *her* to do all the things she does. Finding substitutes is difficult and expensive, even if the housewife is not discouraged or forbidden by her husband to seek paid work. The skills and experience she has gained are not valued by prospective employers. Also, once a woman has taken on the role of housewife, she finds it extremely difficult, for reasons that will be explored, to shift part of this burden back onto her husband. Being a housewife thus both impairs a woman's ability to support herself and constrains her future choices in life.

Many of the disadvantages of being a housewife spring directly or indirectly from the fact that all her work is unpaid work, whereas more than four-fifths of her husband's work is paid work. This may at first seem a matter of little importance. If wives, so long as they stay married, usually share their husbands' standards of living for the most part, why should it matter who earns the income? It matters a great deal, for many reasons. In the highly money-oriented society we live in, the housewife's work is devalued. In fact, in spite of the fact that a major part of it consists of the nurturance and socialization of the next generation of citizens, it is frequently not even acknowledged as work or as productive, either at the personal or at the policy level. This both affects the predominantly houseworking wife's power and influence within the family and means that her social status depends largely upon her husband's, a situation that she may not consider objectionable so long as the marriage lasts, but that is likely to be very painful for her if it does not.

Also, although married couples usually share material well-being, a housewife's or even a part-time working wife's lack of access to much money of her own can create difficulties that range from the mildly irritating through the humiliating to the devastating,

especially if she does not enjoy a good relationship with her husband. Money is the subject of most conflict for married couples, although the issue of housework may be overtaking it. Bergmann reports that in an informal survey, she discovered that about 20 percent of the housewife-mothers of her students were in the position of continually having to appeal to their husbands for money. The psychological effects on an adult of economic dependence can be great. As Virginia Woolf pointed out fifty years ago, any man who has difficulty estimating them should simply imagine himself depending on his wife's income. The dark side of economic dependence is also indicated by the fact that, in the serious predivorce situation of having to fight for their future economic well-being, many wives even of well-to-do men do not have access to enough cash to pay for the uncovering and documentation of their husband's assets.

At its (not so uncommon) worst, the economic dependence of wives can seriously affect their day-to-day physical security. As Linda Gordon has recently concluded: "The basis of wife-beating is male dominance—not superior physical strength or violent temperament . . . but social, economic, political, and psychological power. . . . Wife-beating is the chronic battering of a person of inferior power who for that reason cannot effectively resist." Both wife abuse and child abuse are clearly exacerbated by the economic dependence of women on their husbands or cohabiting male partners. Many women, especially full-time housewives with dependent children, have no way of adequately supporting themselves, and are often in practice unable to leave a situation in which they and/or their children are being seriously abused. In addition to increasing the likelihood of the more obvious forms of abuse—physical and sexual assault—the fear of being abandoned, with its economic and other dire consequences, can lead a housewife to tolerate infidelity, to submit to sexual acts she does not enjoy, or experience psychological abuse including virtual desertion. The fact that a predominantly houseworking wife has no money of her own or a small paycheck is not necessarily insignificant, but it can be very significant, especially at crucial junctures in the marriage.

Finally, as I shall discuss, the earnings differential between husband and housewife can become devastating in its significance for her and for any dependent children in the event of divorce (which in most states can now occur without her consent). This fact, which significantly affects the relative potential of wives and husbands for exit from the marriage, is likely to influence the distribution of power, and in turn paid and unpaid work, *during* the marriage as well.

Predominantly Wage-Working Wives and Housework Despite the increasing labor force participation of married women, including mothers, "working wives still bear almost all the responsibility for housework." They do less of it than housewives, but "they still do the vast bulk of what needs to be done," and the difference is largely to be accounted for not by the increased participation of men, but by lowered standards, the participation of children, purchased services such as restaurant or frozen meals, and, in elite groups, paid household help. Thus, while the distribution of paid labor between the sexes is shifting quite considerably onto women, that of unpaid labor is not shifting much at all, and "the couple that shares household tasks equally remains rare." The differences in total time spent in all "family work" (housework and child care plus yard work, repairs, and so on) vary considerably from one study to another, but it seems that fully employed husbands do, *at most,* approximately half as much as their fully employed wives, and some studies show a much greater discrepancy.

Bergmann reports that "husbands of wives with full-time jobs averaged about two minutes more housework per day than did husbands in housewife-maintaining families, hardly enough additional time to prepare a soft-boiled egg." Even unemployed husbands do much less housework than wives who work a forty-hour week. Working-class husbands are particularly vocal about not being equal partners in the home, and do little housework. In general, however, a husband's income and job prestige are *inversely* related

to his involvement in household chores, unless his wife is employed in a similarly high-paid prestigious job. Many husbands who profess belief in sharing household tasks equally actually do far less than their wives, when time spent and chores done are assessed. In many cases, egalitarian attitudes make little or no difference to who actually does the work, and often "the idea of shared responsibility turn[s] out to be a myth."

Some scholars are disinclined to perceive these facts as indicating unequal power or exploitation. They prefer to view them as merely embodying adherence to traditional patterns, or to justify them as efficient in terms of the total welfare of the family (the husband's time being too valuable to spend doing housework). There are clear indications, however, that the major reason that husbands and other heterosexual men living with wage-working women are not doing more housework is that *they do not want to, and are able, to a very large extent, to enforce their wills.* How do we know that the unequal allocation of housework is not equally women's choice? First, because most people do not like doing many of the major household chores. Second, because almost half of wage-working wives who do more than 60 percent of the housework say that they would prefer their husbands to do more of it. Third, because husbands with higher salaries and more prestigious jobs than their wives (the vast majority of two-job couples) are in a powerful position to resist their wives' appeal to them to do more at home, and it is husbands with the highest prestige who do the least housework of all. Even when there is little conflict, and husbands and wives seem to agree that the woman should do more of the housework, they are often influenced by the prevailing idea that whoever earns less or has the less prestigious job should do more unpaid labor at home. But since the maldistribution of wages and jobs between the sexes in our society is largely out of women's control, even *seemingly nonconflictual* decisions made on this basis cannot really be considered fully voluntary on the part of wives. . . .

Vulnerability by Separation or Divorce

. . . Many studies have shown that whereas the average economic status of men improves after divorce, that of women and children deteriorates seriously. Nationwide, the per-capita income of divorced women, which was only 62 percent that of divorced men in 1960, decreased to 56 percent by 1980. The most illuminating explanation of this is Lenore Weitzman's recent pathbreaking study, *The Divorce Revolution*. Based on a study of 2,500 randomly selected California court dockets between 1968 and 1977 and lengthy interviews with many lawyers, judges, legal experts, and 228 divorced men and women, the book both documents and explains the differential social and economic impact of current divorce law on men, women, and children. Weitzman presents the striking finding that in the first year after divorce, the average standard of living of divorced men, adjusted for household size, increases by 42 percent while that of divorced women falls by 73 percent. . . .

The basic reason for this is that the courts are now treating divorcing men and women more or less as equals. Divorcing men and women are not, of course, equal, both because the two sexes are not treated equally in society and, as we have seen, because typical, gender-structured marriage makes women socially and economically vulnerable. The treatment of unequals as if they were equal has long been recognized as an obvious instance of injustice. In this case, the injustice is particularly egregious because the inequality is to such a large extent the result of the marital relationship itself. Nonetheless, that divorce as it is currently practiced in the United States involves such injustice took years to be revealed. There are various discrete parts of this unjust treatment of unequals as if they were equals, and we must briefly examine each of them.

The first way in which women are unequally situated after divorce is that they almost always continue to take day-to-day responsibility for the children. . . . In approximately 90 percent of cases, children live with mothers rather than fathers after divorce. This is usually the outcome preferred by both parents. Relatively few fathers seek or are awarded sole custody, and in cases of joint custody, which are increasing in frequency, children still tend to live mainly with their mothers. Thus women's postdivorce households tend to be larger than those of men, with correspondingly larger economic needs, and their work lives are much more limited by the needs of their children. . . .

As we have seen, most married couples give priority to the husband's work life, and wives, when they work for wages, earn on average only a small fraction of the family income, and perform the great bulk of the family's unpaid labor. The most valuable economic asset of a typical marriage is not any tangible piece of property, such as a house (since, if there is one, it is usually heavily mortgaged). In fact, "the average divorcing couple has less than $20,000 in net worth." By far the most important property acquired in the average marriage is its career assets, or human capital, the vast majority of which is likely to be invested in the husband. As Weitzman reports, it takes the average divorced man only about *ten months* to earn as much as the couple's entire net worth. The importance of this marital asset is hard to overestimate, yet it has only recently begun to be treated in some states as marital property for the purposes of divorce settlements. Even if "marital property" as traditionally understood is divided evenly, there can be no equity so long as this crucial piece is left in the hands of the husband alone. Except for the wealthy few who have significant material assets, "support awards that divide income, especially future income, are the most valuable entitlements awarded at divorce." Largely because of the division of labor within marriage, to the extent that divorced women have to fall back on their own earnings, they are much worse off than they were when married, and than their ex-husbands are after divorce. In many cases, full-time work at or around the minimum wage, which may be the best a woman without much job training or experience can earn, is insufficient to pull the household out of poverty. . . .

Questions for Discussion and Review

1. Suppose there's an island with 1,000 families on it and no way for anyone to leave. The island has 1 million acres of prime agricultural land, all of which is owned by 10 families. The other 990 families are landless; they must work for one of the 10 landed families if they are to survive, for there are no other resources for meeting their basic needs. No one remembers how the 10 families acquired all the land, because they've owned it as long as anyone can remember. The current members of the 10 families inherited it from their predecessors, who inherited it from their predecessors, and so on going back at least five or six generations.

    The members of the 10 families live in great luxury. They can afford anything their hearts' desire. Another 90 families live comfortably as favored clients of the 10 families and include skilled workers whose services are in continual demand by the 10 families. In contrast, the members of the other 900 families barely survive. They work steadily only during the planting and harvesting seasons, about three months a year. The rest of the time, they pick up odd jobs as the need arises. They live in hovels rented from the owners. The landless cannot earn enough from laboring for the owners to save money to become owners themselves; in fact, most of the landless are perpetually in debt to the landowners.

    Landowners farm only 10 percent of the land, which means that the landless are chronically hungry and that food prices are high. The remaining 90 percent of the land is kept as private game preserves and parks for the wealthy. The landless are not permitted to enter the land to gather wood to heat their hovels or cook their meals, to hunt or fish to feed themselves, or to enjoy the scenery. Landless people found trespassing on the owner's land are punished severely.

    The majority of the people live in grinding poverty, uneducated and illiterate. Their average life expectancy is half that of the owners and the favored client families. However, there's more than enough land, if it were more equally distributed, for everyone to live a reasonably long, healthy, and prosperous life. Would it be unjust to redistribute land on the island, to take some from the owners and give it to the landless?

2. Reflecting on the U.N. Declaration, which rights do you think that you have? Which rights do you think that you don't have?

3. Jones is opposed to any form of social insurance or welfare that takes tax money from him to provide for the needs of others. He says that he works hard for his money and that the government doesn't have a right to force him to support other people. He claims

that he has a right to spend his money as he wants to. He thinks that all welfare programs should be abolished; if people can't or won't support themselves, that's tough—he's not responsible for them. He insists that it's unjust to tax him to support others. Do you agree or disagree with him? Why?

4. Are economic inequalities just only if they maximize total well-being? Why or why not? Are economic inequalities just only if they're to everyone's advantage? Why or why not?

5. With a flat income tax, everyone is taxed at the same rate; with a graduated income tax, people with higher incomes are taxed at a higher rate. For example, a flat tax might levy a 20% tax on all taxable income. On the other hand, a graduated tax might levy taxes on taxable income according to the following rate schedule: (1) under \$30,000—15%, (2) \$30,001 to \$75,000—25%, (3) over \$75,000—35%. Thus, under the 20% flat tax, someone with an income of \$25,000 would pay \$5,000 while someone earning \$250,000 would pay \$50,000. With the graduated tax, someone earning \$25,000 would pay \$3,750 while the person earning \$250,000 would pay \$76,950 (\$4,500 + \$11,200 + \$61,250).

    Some people argue that the rich should pay a larger percentage of their income in taxes than the nonrich because it's less of a burden to them. If the person earning \$25,000 is taxed at 20%, just like the person earning \$250,000, she only has \$20,000 left to live on while the rich person has \$200,000 to live on. Others say equals should be treated equally and the rich and poor are equals. Which tax schedule is more just?

6. Johann suggests the imposition of a high inheritance tax. He complains that being able to inherit a fortune from one's parents or grandparents gives one an unfair advantage over people who don't have rich relatives. He also says that people who inherit fortunes have done nothing to earn or deserve them. He says that he wants to "level the playing field" for people. He suggests a 75 percent tax on all inheritances over \$250,000. Sal disagrees. He claims that such a high tax violates people's property rights. If a rich person wants to bequeathe his fortune to his children or nieces and nephews, he should be able to do anything he wants with his property. With whom do you agree? Why?

7. Sara advocates government-subsidized childcare, which would make it easier for women, especially poor and working-class women, to get and keep jobs. Dirk says that it would be unjust to take money in taxes from some people in order to subsidize childcare for other people's children. With whom do you agree? Why?

8. Phil is homeless. He is an alcoholic who has not been able to hold down a job for ten years. At night in winter he often sleeps in bus

or subway stations. He says that there are not enough shelters for the homeless in the city and the ones that exist are often unsafe because of low funding and minimal security. Merchants and others complain that the homeless are smelly and dirty, that they urinate and defecate in public places such as parks, and that they frighten people who fear that they are dangerous. The mayor wants to solve the homeless problem by closing the few shelters that exist in the city. If there are no shelters for the homeless, then either the homeless, such as Phil, will get jobs or they will move somewhere else. Pam says that what the mayor wants to do is unjust. What do you think? Why?

9.   If you were in Rawls's original position behind the veil of ignorance, would you agree to tax income for social programs such as homeless shelters, child care, and medical care? Why or why not?

Suggestions for Further Reading

John Arthur and William Shaw, eds. *Justice and Economic Distribution,* 2d ed. Englewood Cliffs, NJ: Prentice-Hall, 1991. An anthology of some of the most important recent articles about economic justice.

Hugo A. Bedau, ed. *Justice and Equality.* Englewood Cliffs, NJ: Prentice-Hall, 1971. An excellent anthology that includes some classic essays on justice and equality.

Richard Brandt, ed. *Social Justice.* Englewood Cliffs, NJ: Prentice-Hall, 1962. An anthology of papers from the early 1960s, notable primarily for Gregory Vlastos's contribution, "Justice and Equality."

Joel Feinberg. *Social Philosophy.* Englewood Cliffs, NJ: Prentice-Hall, 1973. Chapters 4, 6, and 7 provide an excellent introduction to the issues of justice and rights.

Kenneth Kipnis and Diana Meyers, eds. *Economic Justice.* Totowa, NJ: Rowman & Allanheld, 1985. An excellent anthology of recent papers on economic justice.

Walter Laquer and Barry Rubin, eds. *The Human Rights Reader,* rev. ed. New York: Meridian, 1989. A fine collection of articles, book excerpts, and international documents on human rights. Especially noteworthy for the fine selection of United Nations Declarations and Covenants.

David Lyons, ed. *Rights.* Belmont, CA: Wadsworth. 1979. An excellent anthology of articles on rights.

Robert Nozick. *Anarchy, State, and Utopia.* New York: Basic Books, 1974. See especially Part 2. The now-classic statement and defense of Nozick's laissez-faire view of economic justice. The central arguments are widely anthologized and more accessible than the complete text.

John Rawls. *A Theory of Justice.* Cambridge, MA: Harvard University Press, 1971. The most influential work of political philosophy of the second half of the twentieth century. A gigantic book best approached by beginners in the small doses provided in some of the anthologies mentioned here.

Henry Shue. *Basic Rights: Subsistence, Affluence, and U.S. Foreign Policy.* Princeton, NJ: Princeton University Press, 1980. Part 1 offers an excellent, readable defense of the view that people have subsistence rights.

James Sterba, ed. *Justice: Alternative Political Perspectives,* 2d ed. Belmont, CA: Wadsworth, 1992. An excellent anthology of articles and book excerpts on economic justice.

Objectives

Readers are expected to:

- understand the concepts of freedom and liberty.
- understand the concept of autonomy.
- understand how liberties can be justified by appeal to autonomy and well-being.
- understand how to justify limitations on liberty.
- understand how to apply Mill's Harm principle.
- understand how to apply the Offense principle.
- understand how to apply Hard and Soft Paternalism.
- understand how to apply Legal Moralism.
- decide which liberty limiting principles to accept.
- understand the differences among democratic and non-democratic systems.
- understand economic democracy.

Introduction

Should people be free to use drugs such as marijuana, cocaine, and heroin? Should people be free to watch movies, look at art, listen to music, or read books that most people find pornographic? Should people be free to criticize government leaders or public policy? Should people be free to have abortions?

Freedom, or liberty, is a fundamental value for many people. The Bill of Rights, the first ten amendments to the U.S. Constitution, makes certain freedoms a matter of constitutional right. For example, the First Amendment makes freedom of religion, freedom of speech, freedom of the press, and freedom of assembly a matter of right:

> Congress shall make no law respecting establishment of religion, or
> prohibiting the free exercise thereof; or abridging the freedom of
> speech, or of the press; or the right of the people peaceably to assem-
> ble, and to petition the government for a redress of grievances.

The French Declaration of the Rights of Man and Citizen (1789) similarly proclaims moral rights to certain fundamental freedoms:

1. Men are born and remain free and equal in rights. . . .

2. The aim of every political association is the preservation of the natural and inalienable rights of man; these are liberty, property, security, and resistance to oppression. . . .

4. Liberty consists of the power to do whatever is not injurious to others; thus the enjoyment of the natural rights of every man has for its limits only those that assure other members of society the enjoyment of those same rights.

5. The law has the right to forbid only actions which are injurious to society. . . .

10. No one is to be disquieted because of his opinions, even religious, provided their manifestation does not disturb the public order established by law.

11. Free communication of ideas and opinions is one of the most precious of the rights of man. Consequently, every citizen may speak, write, and print freely. . . .[1]

Similarly the U.N. Universal Declaration of Human Rights declares that a variety of freedoms are moral rights:

ARTICLE 4

No one shall be held in slavery or servitude. . . .

ARTICLE 13

1. Everyone has the right to freedom of movement and residence within the borders of each state. . . .

ARTICLE 18

Everyone has the right to freedom of thought, conscience and religion. . . .

ARTICLE 19

Everyone has the right to freedom of opinion and expression. . . .

ARTICLE 20

1. Everyone has the right to freedom of peaceful assembly and association. . . .

Many of us today take these freedoms for granted, but such freedoms have not always been considered a matter of right. For example, the idea that people have a right to freedom of religion is only a few centuries old. Prior to the eighteenth century, most rulers thought they had a right to

---

[1]"The French Declaration of the Rights of Man and Citizen," in *The Human Rights Reader,* rev. ed., ed. Walter Laequeur and Barry Rubin (New York: New American Library, 1989), 118–119.

decide the religion of their subjects; the idea that their subjects had a right to freedom of religion would have struck them as ridiculous. During the Counter-Reformation, when Catholicism and Protestantism struggled for people's allegiance, wars were fought to force people to change their religious beliefs, and Inquisitions were instituted to stamp out "heresy" and ensure religious orthodoxy.

For example, from 1618 to 1648, war raged in Europe as Catholics tried to forcibly convert Protestants, and Protestants tried to resist or do some converting of their own. Richard Smoke writes:

> The climax of this trend was the Thirty Years' War (1618–1648). Armies from all over the Continent came to fight over whether central Europe would be Catholic or Protestant. Neither side could defeat the other, and in the end, the dividing lines were drawn not too far from where they had been at the outset. But the scale and duration of the destruction was like nothing Europeans had ever seen. As the fortunes of war ebbed and flowed over the years, cities would be taken and retaken many times. Each time there would be a slaughter of civilians and unrestrained looting and rape. . . . Millions who escaped the sword died from starvation or were so weakened by hunger that they fell victim to plagues. The population of central Europe fell drastically. . . . In some districts one could ride for days seeing nothing but gutted towns, burned-out farms, and rotting corpses.[2]

Because freedom of religion was not recognized as a right, millions of people died.

Several centuries ago, almost everyone would have denied that people have a moral right to freedom of speech, freedom of thought, freedom of conscience, or other freedoms we take for granted. Most people thought that governments had a right to decide what people said or thought. Even today, many governments don't act as though their subjects or citizens have rights to such freedoms. In many countries, publicly (or even privately) criticizing one's government can get one killed. Recall the demonstrations in Beijing in 1989, when soldiers of the People's Republic of China massacred hundreds of students protesting government policies. A few years ago, in many South and Central American countries, publicly criticizing the government or the military could bring swift and violent death from so-called death squads.

Liberty

People are free to do something if nothing prevents them from doing it. They're free to not do something if nothing compels them to do it. Thus,

---

[2]Richard Smoke, *National Security and the Nuclear Dilemma*, 2d ed. (New York: Random House, 1987), 6–7.

you're not free to fly like a bird because gravity and your physical structure prevent it. You're not free to not grow older while you're alive because nature makes you age.

When it's human actions that prevent or compel, we speak of liberty. If you're tied to a chair, you're not at liberty to get up. If a mugger is pointing a gun at you and ordering you to hand over your wallet, you're not at liberty to keep your wallet.[3]

Here we are concerned with one particular form of human action—law. Laws forbid some actions and require others. If the law forbids you to steal, then you're not at liberty to steal. If you steal and are caught, you'll be punished. If the laws require you to pay taxes, then you're not at liberty to not pay taxes. If you don't pay taxes and are caught, you'll be punished.

Almost everyone recognizes that people should not be at liberty to do anything they want. For example, people should not be at liberty to commit rape. Laws limiting people's liberty by forbidding rape surely are legitimate. Similarly, almost everyone thinks that people should not be at liberty to not pay their taxes. Laws limiting people's liberty by requiring them to pay taxes seem legitimate to most people. However, most people also think that there are liberties that people should have, for example, liberty of thought, speech, and religion. People have liberty of religion if, first, no laws prevent or require certain religious beliefs and actions, and second, if laws forbid others from interfering with people's religious life. (We'll discuss below whether specific liberties should be absolute.)

What principles should guide us in deciding what liberties people should have (have a moral right to) and what liberties they shouldn't have (don't have a moral right to)?

BRAIN TEASERS

Which of the following liberties should people have? Liberty to:

attend religious services of their choice

not attend any religious services

drive while intoxicated

download sexually explicit pictures of adults from the Internet

download sexually explicit pictures of children from the Internet

not wear clothes in public

not wear clothes in one's own house

use heroin in one's own home

---

[3]The mugger has narrowed your alternatives to only two, both of which are undesirable: give him your wallet or die.

Why Should People Have Any Liberty?

The Bill of Rights, the French Declaration of the Rights of Man and Citizen, and the U.N. Declaration of Universal Human Rights specify a number of basic liberties that people should have. But why should people have any liberty? As with other moral rights, a right to certain liberties is justified as necessary to protect people's autonomy and well-being.

Many people consider our capacity for autonomy to be one of our most valuable characteristics. Most other species act on instinct. Their behavior is based on relatively simple stimulus–response patterns that are hard wired into their systems. Birds don't build nests and spiders don't weave webs on the basis of conscious reflection, planning, and decision. They act as they are programmed to act, with little, if any, room for deviation from their programming. Birds don't decide to not feed their young—rather than abandon them—because they love them. They feed them because they are programmed and as they are programmed to do.

It seems to many people that human behavior is not like this. Of course, some, perhaps much, of our behavior is programmed. But some of it isn't. We seem to have the ability to deliberate and make choices. An architect designing a building, unlike a bird building a nest or a spider weaving a web, can use her imagination to select from many alternative designs and even may invent entirely new features to include in a building. She makes her choices deliberately, after reflection. Humans can decide how to act after reflecting on the alternatives available. You decided to go to college, but you could have done something else. You decided on a major but you could have chosen (and still can choose) a different major. You can decide whether to marry, where to live, and what occupation to pursue. If you have the capacity for autonomy, then you're not pre-programmed to follow just one path in life.

Autonomous people have the ability to act in accordance with their own beliefs, desires, preferences, plans, feelings, moral code, and so on. An autonomous person also has some control over these mental states. An autonomous person thinks for herself. She isn't a blind conformist in behavior or thought. She can and does critically evaluate the worldview of her family or society. For example, taught to be a racist, she can, after reflection, change her mind and believe that we're all equal and should be treated as equals, regardless of so-called racial differences. She can resist the message that people's success and worth are measured by the amount of wealth they've accumulated and the power they have over others. Autonomous people are independent thinkers.

A long tradition going back to Plato and Aristotle asserts that autonomous people also are not "enslaved" by their irrational and non-rational parts—their feelings, emotions, and passions. They're also not enslaved by addictions. Thus, a person is not behaving autonomously unless her reason is in control of her behavior. For example, someone in the grip of uncontrollable rage is not behaving autonomously if he throws a brick through his television screen because his favorite sports team lost. Similarly, a drug addict is not behaving autonomously when he injects heroin into his veins. (Perhaps we can rationally decide after deliberation to sometimes relinquish the control of reason and temporarily give ourselves up to passion, as in sex. Then we may still be behaving autonomously when nonrational parts are in control.)

If you have the capability for autonomous behavior but don't have some room (liberty) to exercise it, then that capability is forever left dormant. It's as though you don't have it. Rights to certain liberties, then, protect your capability for autonomous behavior by enabling you to exercise it. That's one reason for thinking that you have rights to some liberties. But liberty also protects our well-being. We have needs and desires to satisfy, life plans to follow, and happiness to pursue (and perhaps even catch), but because we aren't carbon copies of one another, we need to pursue our own paths in life in order to meet our particular needs, satisfy our particular desires, and attain some measure of happiness. Certain fundamental freedoms are necessary for us to find our own individual paths to happiness, satisfaction, and well-being. We might say that people cannot flourish if they have no liberty at all. We can justify a particular liberty, then, by showing that it is necessary for people's autonomy and basic well-being.

Justifying Limiting People's Liberty If people have a right to liberty, are there any legitimate limitations? Should people be at liberty to do anything they want? No. For one thing, we justify giving people liberty in part by claiming that it protects their capacity for autonomous behavior. But we've already seen that if we're merely doing what we want to do, we're not necessarily behaving autonomously. I'm not behaving autonomously if, in the grip of crowd hysteria, I help lynch someone, even if at the time I want to lynch him. When the hysteria dissolves, I may feel profoundly ashamed and guilty, and may wish that my reason or my "better self" had been more in control of my behavior. Thus, we don't really protect people's autonomy if we simply let them do whatever they want, and the appeal to autonomy can't justify giving people the liberty to do whatever they want. To put it vaguely, the appeal to autonomy justifies only giving people the liberty to do what rational, autonomous people would want to do.

Then, too, liberty is justified by appeal to individual well-being. People need some liberty in order to protect their important interests, meet their needs, satisfy their desires, and achieve happiness. The liberty to do anything we want is not necessary to achieve these goals; therefore, appeal to these goals can't justify giving people the liberty to do anything they want.

Finally, social life would be impossible without limits on liberty; human life would be, in the words of Thomas Hobbes (1588–1679), "solitary, poor, nasty, brutish, and short."[4]

Without laws, a truly human life would be impossible. Unfortunately, people often want to do things that would harm other individuals or harm society. Some people want to murder, rape, assault, steal, intimidate, oppress, and exploit others. Some want to drive while intoxicated, others want to build unsafe structures or pollute the environment to maximize their profits. We would not be able to form societies and cooperate to make human life better if people were at liberty to do whatever they want. Human life would not rise much above that of bears in the woods.

Liberty must be limited. There is no way to justify unlimited liberty. We must reject the claim that we should be at liberty to do anything we want. But people should have some liberty or liberties. How do we decide what liberties people should have and what liberties they shouldn't have? One influential answer to this question was given by the British philosopher John Stuart Mill (1806–1873).

Mill and the Harm Principle

John Stuart Mill proposes that

> the sole end for which mankind are warranted, individually or collectively, in interfering with the liberty of action of any of their number is self-protection. That the only purpose for which power can be rightfully exercised over any member of a civilized community, against his will, is to prevent harm to others.[5]

As Mill says, "All that makes existence valuable to anyone depends on the enforcement of restraints upon the actions of other people."[6] Thus, "The only part of the conduct of anyone for which he is amenable to society is that which concerns others."[7]

Mill claims that people should be at liberty to do or not do what they want, so long as they aren't harming other individuals or society collectively. The harm principle sets out an important limitation on people's liberty. It asserts that we don't have a right to act in ways that harm others. Laws forbidding acts that cause such harm are legitimate, and cannot be criticized as unjust limitations on people's liberty.

---

[4]Thomas Hobbes, *Leviathan*, ed. and trans. Edwin Curley (Indianapolis, IN: Hackett, 1994), 76.

[5]John Stuart Mill, *On Liberty* (Indianapolis, IN: Hacket, 1978), 9.

[6]Ibid., 5.

[7]Ibid., 9.

Mill asserts that certain fundamental freedoms must be protected, both for the good of society as a whole and for the good of the individual. These fundamental freedoms include (1) liberty of thought and discussion and (2) liberty to live according to one's own beliefs, values, desires, and preferences—that is, liberty "of framing the plan of our life to suit our own character." According to Mill, "The only freedom which deserves the name is that of pursuing our own good in our own way, so long as we do not attempt to deprive others of theirs or impede their efforts to obtain it."[8]

Liberty of Thought and Expression

Mill distinguishes between thought and action. Liberty of thought should be absolute. We should not punish someone for his thoughts or attempt to brainwash people into believing or disbelieving certain things. If someone has racist beliefs, we probably have a right to employ reason—to argue with him in order to persuade him rationally to change his mind. But we don't have a right to imprison him for his beliefs or to try to use force to change his beliefs. In part, this is because it's difficult to get people to change their beliefs, and almost impossible to know whether we've really succeeded. People can say they've changed their minds when they haven't. It virtually invites dishonesty. But it's also because thoughts don't cause harm to others the way that actions do.

Actions include words and deeds. Racist thoughts can lead to racist speech and racist acts, such as discrimination or even murder. Mill says that if acts harm others, we're justified in forbidding them by law. That might include the expression of our thoughts.

BRAIN TEASERS

Would we be justified in forbidding the expression of racist beliefs on the grounds that racist speech harms people?

Disciples of Mill point out that merely asserting that an act, including what we might call a speech act, is harmful is not sufficient grounds for forbidding it. First, we must have good reasons for thinking it highly probable that harm will be a consequence of the action. The mere possibility of harm is not grounds enough. And the probable harm to others must be great enough to outweigh the costs of forbidding the acts, both to society and to the people whose acts are forbidden.

---

[8]Ibid., 12.

Mill says that preventing harm to others is the only justification for limiting people's liberty. That would surely justify laws against libel. If someone falsely accuses you of child abuse, that harms you, even if you're not indicted or tried for it, let alone convicted and punished. You have an important interest in your reputation, which would be harmed if someone maliciously made false accusations against you. But what if someone makes a speech outside your bedroom window at 3:00 A.M.? Does that harm you? If they do it once, an hour of lost sleep may not be so harmful, but if they do it frequently, the lost sleep could cause serious harm.

BRAIN TEASERS

During a peaceful student demonstration, should one be at liberty to shout out that the demonstrators should burn down the administration building and hang the president?

Mill claims that it is always objectionable to stifle thought and the expression of thought except in very circumscribed circumstances. It may be acceptable to protect the immature from dangerous ideas, but not people who are mature. Why?

First, Mill points out that sometimes the thoughts being stifled are true. If they're stifled, people "are deprived of the opportunity of exchanging error for truth."[9] Even if the thoughts are not the whole truth, they may be part of the truth. Often the conventional wisdom is only partly true and needs supplementation by other parts of the truth. To suppress an opinion, Mill claims, is to assume one's own infallibility.

Second, free discussion is the best way for people to differentiate truth from falsity. "The beliefs which we have most warrant for have no safeguard to rest on but a standing invitation to the whole world to prove them unfounded."[10] How else are people to know what's true and what's false other than by free discussion? We can be confident we've arrived at truth only if all opinions have been carefully and critically examined.

Third, the mental development of people will be cramped without full and fearless opportunity to discuss every idea and thought. People will not be able to think for themselves if others think for them. If one is fed a steady diet of predigested and packaged thoughts from others, one's brain soon turns to mush.

Finally, if there's no opportunity for free discussion of all ideas, however dangerous, the beliefs that people have will degenerate into dead dogmas. Rather than being a living presence in one's mind, beliefs that

---

[9]Ibid., 16.

[10]Ibid., 20.

are not the product of free discussion and reflection degenerate into meaningless verbal formulas stored in some cobweb-covered corner of one's mind. On this fourth point, Mill uses the example of Christianity. According to him, Christians profess to be committed to the ethical doctrines taught by Jesus in the New Testament; however, they are not living beliefs but rather dead dogmas for the mass of Christians:

> All Christians believe that the blessed are the poor and humble, and those who are ill-used by the world; that it is easier for a camel to pass through the eye of a needle than for a rich man to enter the kingdom of heaven; that they should judge not, lest they be judged; that they should swear not at all; that they should love their neighbor as themselves; that if one take their cloak, they should give him their coat also; that they should take no thought for the morrow; that if they would be perfect they should sell all that they have and give it to the poor. They are not insincere when they say that they believe these things. They do believe them, as people believe what they have always heard lauded and never discussed. But in the sense of that living belief which regulates conduct, they believe these doctrines just up to the point to which it is usual to act upon them.[11]

BRAIN TEASERS

1. Do beliefs become dead dogmas if there isn't free discussion? Is Christianity a dead dogma for most Christians?

2. Suppose a scientist says publicly that cigarette smoking is beneficial. Would it be wrong to attempt to suppress these ideas as false and dangerous and forbid them to be publicly expressed?

The Power of Public Opinion

Mill recognizes that government and law are not the only threats to freedom; public opinion can be tyrannical. For example, people expressing unpopular views can be shouted down by people who disagree or punished or intimidated by employers. One duty of government may be to protect people's liberty from being limited by private tyranny. For example, laws may be enacted and enforced prohibiting employers from punishing employees for expressing their ideas. To protect people's freedom, it's not enough for government to leave them alone and refrain from enacting laws that limit liberty. Often government must enact and enforce laws to restrain those who would limit or interfere with others' liberty.

---

[11]Ibid., 39–40.

BRAIN TEASERS

1. A professor of mathematics believes that women are intellectually inferior to men, and he has publicly expressed his views orally and in writing. He's acknowledged to be an excellent math teacher and a talented scholar who has published widely in his field. However, female students have petitioned the president of the college to fire him because of his views. Would the president be justified in firing him?

2. The female students in the first Brain Teaser are picketing the math professor's classes and office, protesting his views and his remaining on the faculty. The administration believes that the picketing is disruptive and has ordered the students to stop or face disciplinary action. The students claim that the administration's order violates their right to free speech. Is the administration justified in ordering the students to stop their demonstrating? Would the administration be justified in punishing the students if they refused to stop?

Liberty of Action

Most societies are more tolerant of talk than they are of action. A crucial question is whether people should be free to act on their opinions. Mill admits "no one pretends that action should be as free as opinions." As he says, "Acts, of whatever kind, which without justifiable cause do harm to others may be, and in the more important cases absolutely require to be, controlled by the unfavorable sentiments, and, where needful, by the active interference of mankind."[12]

Suppose you and your roommate are applying for the same scholarship and only one of you can get it. If you get it, your roommate doesn't. If your roommate doesn't get it, he's been harmed. Would that justify society's interfering to prevent you from applying for or receiving the scholarship? Surely not. Society may not limit liberty to prevent all harms to others; it only may limit *unjustified* harms.

Mill's harm principle justifies denying people the liberty to drive at night with their lights off, to speed, or to drive while intoxicated. These are actions that have a high probability of causing unjustifiable harm to others. But almost all of us agree that harming another is justified if it's required for self-protection or the protection of others. A police officer may shoot a suspect if the individual is shooting at the officer or if he's about to murder an innocent person. The point is that we must use our judgment in deciding whether harm is justified or unjustified.

---

[12]Ibid., 53.

BRAIN TEASERS

1. In order to conserve energy and reduce pollution, would it be legitimate to limit people's liberty to use snowmobiles and motorboats?

2. In order to reduce urban pollution and congestion, would it be legitimate to limit people's liberty to drive wherever they want by blocking off many streets to traffic or even banning private autos within city limits?

3. If human population rises to the point that Earth cannot support that many people, would it be legitimate to limit people's liberty to have as many children as they want?

Paternalism

Mill claims that the only justification for limiting people's liberty is to prevent harm to others. This means that it's never legitimate to limit liberty merely to protect people from themselves. Mill opposes those who think that society has a right or duty to protect mature, competent people from themselves. Minors shouldn't be at liberty to drive, drink alcoholic beverages, buy cigarettes, make contracts, not go to school, work any hours they please, or marry. The mentally disabled should be protected from the harm they might cause themselves. But some people believe that society has a duty also to protect competent adults from themselves.

Consider motorcycle helmet and seat belt laws. These laws restrict people's liberty to ride a motorcycle without a helmet and to drive an automobile without wearing a seat belt. If these laws are justified only on the grounds that they protect people from their own folly, then they are paternalistic. (Most proponents of such laws insist that they protect other people from higher costs of medical care and medical insurance caused by the greater injuries to people who aren't wearing helmets or seat belts.) Mill says that paternalism is not a legitimate ground for limiting people's liberty. Therefore, he would oppose seat belt laws if their only justification is to protect the wearer's health.

BRAIN TEASERS

1. Are laws forbidding the use of marijuana, heroin, and cocaine justified purely paternalistically? Should there be such laws?

2. If the government is justified in forbidding the smoking of marijuana and the use of heroin, would it be justified in forbidding smoking cigarettes?

3. Paula loves both Gary and Tom and they love her. She wants to marry both of them and they both want to marry her. All three agree that they want to live together as husbands and wife. Should Paula be free to marry both Gary and Tom?

Four Liberty Limiting Principles

Mill says that only harm justifies limiting people's liberty. The contemporary American philosopher Joel Feinberg identifies four different liberty-limiting principles that we could accept, one of which is Mill's Harm principle.

The Harm principle: Laws limiting people's liberty in order to prevent serious, unjustified harm to others are legitimate.

The Offense principle: Laws limiting people's liberty in order to prevent serious, unjustified offense to others are legitimate.

Paternalism:

Soft Paternalism: Laws temporarily limiting people's liberty in order to ascertain whether someone who is engaged in very risky activities or intending to harm herself is competent, are legitimate.

Hard Paternalism: Laws limiting people's liberty in order to permanently prevent them from harming themselves, even if they are competent, are legitimate.

Legal Moralism: Laws limiting people's liberty in order to prevent them from doing what most people believe to be immoral are legitimate, even if the behavior does not pose a significant threat of serious harm or offense.

Feinberg accepts the Harm principle, a restricted version of the Offense principle, and Soft Paternalism. He rejects Hard Paternalism and Legal Moralism.[13]

With regard to the Offense principle, the case for limiting people's liberty depends on the seriousness of the offense, how deeply the behavior affects people. I might be offended if someone gives me the finger, but the seriousness of the offense is surely not sufficient to justify laws against giving people the finger. On the other hand, if I'm Black and someone uses an offensive racial epithet, the offense may go much deeper. In fact, I might feel threatened and intimidated by it.

---

[13]Joel Feinberg, *The Moral Limits of the Criminal Law* Oxford, Oxford University Press. Vol. I, *Harm to Others* (1984); Vol. II, *Offense to Others* (1985); Vol. III, *Harm to Self* (1986); Vol. IV, *Harmless Wrongdoing* (1988).

Another consideration is how easily the offense is avoided. If a couple are having sex in their bedroom with the curtains open and I'd have to climb a tree to see them, I can refrain from climbing the tree and looking in their window if I'm offended. On the other hand, if they're having sex on the sidewalk in front of my house, it's much more difficult for me to avoid perceiving it. Similarly, if pictures that would offend me are in a museum, I can avoid the offense by not entering the museum. Not so if they're posted on a billboard on a street I frequently walk down. I can close my eyes, but I might get hit by a car if I do.

Feinberg also says that to justify limiting people's liberty, a lot of people must be seriously offended by the activity. A few oversensitive people shouldn't dictate what should be permitted.

As for Paternalism, Feinberg accepts Soft Paternalism, which justifies us in preventing the incompetent from harming themselves, such as children, the mentally ill, and the mentally disabled. And it justifies us in temporarily stopping someone from engaging in risky activity or harming herself in order to ascertain whether she's competent. But Soft Paternalism does not justify us in permanently protecting competent people from themselves. For example, if a competent person suffering from a terminal illness wants to commit suicide, Soft Paternalism does not justify us in preventing her from killing herself. However, Hard Paternalism may.

With Legal Moralism, conduct considered immoral by the majority of people or the powerful, such as oral or anal sex, or sex between consenting competent adults of the same sex, may be forbidden even if no one is harmed and even if no one is offended because the acts occur in private.

BRAIN TEASERS

Which of the liberty limiting principles do you accept? Which do you reject?

Is Democracy the Best Form of Government?

Governments have great power over us. They make decisions that can determine how we live, even whether we live or die. Governments can contribute greatly to human well-being or they can make life miserable for a lot of people. The government of the United States aims to protect our lives and property, enforce contracts, provide medical care, fund medical and scientific research, protect the environment, foster economic growth, prevent unjust discrimination, provide transportation (by building and maintaining railroads, highways, and airports), protect us from foreign invaders, support education, and protect corporate interests worldwide. It has passed laws that govern health and safety in the work-place, provide for unemployment benefits and income if one cannot work because of injuries sustained on the job, protect some industries from unfair competition from other countries, and set minimum wages. The governments of some other countries allow the rich to exploit and oppress the poor. They severely limit liberty of expression and sometimes murder dissidents. They may launch unjust wars. They may persecute or fail to protect despised minorities.

In classical political theory (the political theory of the ancient Greeks and Romans), three basic forms of government were defined according to how many people shared in the rule of the state: one person, a few people, or many people. According to Aristotle's scheme of classification, rule by one person was called *monarchy* if the ruler governed in order to further and protect the public or common interest and *tyranny* if he ruled primarily in his own behalf. Rule by a few people was called *aristocracy* if the few ruled or governed in the common interest and *oligarchy* if they governed for the benefit of the wealthy. Finally, rule by the many was called *constitutional* government if the many governed in the common interest and *democracy* if the many governed primarily or exclusively in order to further the interests of the poor. For our purposes we will ignore these qualifications and define *democracy* as rule by the many as opposed to either rule by one person or rule by a few people.

Democracy

In a democracy, then, the many rule rather than the few. In a *direct* democracy, the many decide directly on legislation. The most familiar example of direct democracy in the United States is the New England town meeting, in which local government decisions are made by a vote of the entire citizen body (that cares to participate). In an *indirect* or *representative* democracy, citizens select representatives (such as members of Parliament, or members of the House of Representatives and Senate) who in turn determine government decisions by their votes (in Parliament or Congress). Democracy, whether direct or representative, is a matter of degree.

Democracy is rule by the many rather than by the few, but how many is "many"? If only 5 to 10 percent of adults have the right to participate in political decision making even in the most modest way, by voting, for example, the government is clearly aristocratic. But if 20 percent of adults have the right to participate in political decision making, is that rule by the few or by the many? What if 51 percent of adults have the right to participate? There is no hard and fast dividing line between aristocracy and democracy. It makes sense to speak of degrees of democracy. One government is more democratic than another if a greater percentage of people have the right to participate in political decision making. The maximally democratic society gives 100 percent of adults the right to participate in political decision making. (Perhaps the degree of democracy is also determined by the nature of the participation. If people merely vote for leaders and have little input into their decisions, it's less democratic than if they have great influence over the decisions.)

Democracy is sometimes referred to as rule by the majority. Therefore, the degree of democracy may also be a function of the extent to which government decisions are determined by the will of the majority. Decision making is less democratic if it gives a minority of voters a veto over decisions of the majority.

There are also some institutional features of democracy (at least of representative democracy). Rawls summarizes the features of a fully democratic government as follows:

> First of all, the authority to determine basic social policies resides in a representative body selected for limited terms by and ultimately accountable to the electorate. . . . All sane adults, with certain generally recognized exceptions, have the right to take part in political affairs, and the precept one elector one vote is honored as far as possible. Elections are fair and free, and regularly held. . . . The principle of participation also holds that all citizens are to have an equal access, at least in the formal sense, to public office. Each is eligible to join political parties, to run for elective positions, and to hold places of authority. Finally, decision making uses the procedure of so-called bare majority rule . . . for all significant political decisions.[14]

Justifying Democracy

Until recently, most of the articulate classes considered democracy to be a bad form of government because they believed that most people are not competent or qualified to participate in political decision making. They believed that the intelligence, knowledge, and virtue required for governing well is limited to a small group of superior people—the natural aristocrats. Therefore, they generally favored either monarchy or aristocracy rather than democracy, often sarcastically referring to democracy as "mobocracy."

In the twentieth century, contempt for ordinary people has become less acceptable. The pretensions of those who claim to be superior and who claim a right to govern because of their superiority have been challenged in many parts of the world. Egalitarian claims that people are much more equal than opponents of democracy say have been widely accepted among those once considered common and inferior. Democracy has not triumphed, but the world seems to be moving in the direction of democratization. The pressure for greater democracy may be nearly irresistible.

---

[14]John Rawls, *A Theory of Justice* (Cambridge, MA: Harvard University Press, 1971), 222–224.

Many people insist that everyone has a right to a democratic form of government. The U.N. Universal Declaration of Human Rights proclaims in Article 21 that "everyone has the right to take part in the Government of his country, directly or through freely chosen representatives." From the perspective of Rawls's theory of justice, one might claim that rational, self-interested people in the original position behind the veil of ignorance would insist on a fully democratic government. In the Original Position behind the Veil of Ignorance, we don't know whether we're political insiders or outsiders. If some people are denied the right to participate in political decision making, their well-being could be jeopardized because government could ignore their interests. Democracy would ensure at least that everyone has input, voice, and influence.

History seems to show that while even democratic governments are imperfect, for example, some having permitted slavery and unequal rights for women, the record of democracies in protecting people's well-being, autonomy, and rights is superior to that of nondemocratic governments.

What's Wrong with Democracy?

Sometimes, opposition to democracy is based purely on self-interest. If a privileged minority has seized the reins of government and has directed it primarily to benefit itself, it will be loath to give the reins back to the majority if it thinks it will lose its privileges and benefits. Others oppose democracy because they believe that people are not equal in respects relevant to the right to participate in government decision making. Opponents of democracy may claim that the majority of people lack the capacities for democracy. They say that most people are too ignorant, stupid, and foolish to govern wisely and well.

Some people complain that democracy takes too much time to solve problems and isn't efficient. In a democracy, they say, too much time is wasted talking because the majority must reach agreement before anything can be done. Sometimes the majority can't agree, other times major compromises among competing interests are necessary, so the best policies aren't followed. We may feel tempted to turn our problems over to a few experts who can act quickly and decisively. Perhaps they could do something about environmental threats, poverty, crime, drugs, and education.

None of this should tempt us from democracy. The alternatives to democracy are far more dangerous to the well-being and autonomy of the vast mass of people. We can't depend on the altruism of others to protect our interests. Democracy gives everyone the opportunity to protect their own interests by participating fully in political decision making. The politically powerless are almost always victimized by the politically powerful.

Then, too, people denied a right to participate in governing are not being treated as full members of the moral community. Treating them as inferiors who are not qualified to participate is not treating them with respect.

The Subversion of Democracy

Sometimes, political elites praise democracy and claim that their government is democratic when in fact there are many things that undermine it and make it operate more like an aristocratic than a democratic government. Governing elites can rig elections to ensure that their candidates win. But there are more subtle ways to undermine democracy. In a representative democracy, if elections are privately financed, the rich and powerful can be pretty much in the driver's seat because they will be the primary source of campaign contributions. Candidates for party nominations must please those who have the money to finance their campaigns. However popular a candidate, if she can't raise the money to compete, she has virtually no chance of being nominated. Individuals who pass the first considerable hurdle and are nominated must please those who have the money to finance their general election campaigns. Once elected, an office holder must think about reelection and where the money will come from. Obviously, the wealthy have far more power and influence than the nonwealthy.

Similarly, the wealthy can influence public opinion through ownership and control of the major media (television and radio stations, newspapers, magazines, and movies). They may be able to persuade a majority to favor or oppose various government policies. Again, democracy is undermined.

Voting has reached an all time low in the United States. Even during presidential elections, fewer than half of the people eligible to vote bother to vote in national elections. In off years, less than a third of those eligible actually vote. The low interest in politics leads to willful ignorance and misinformation about issues. Many people don't know who their own state senator and representative are. They know more about sports statistics than about economic statistics. They don't know how much the United States spends each year on foreign aid and how much it spends on the military. They don't know how many children are living in poverty and how many people lack health insurance. They don't know what the government is doing in its war on drugs and they don't know who's winning and why. Citizen apathy cannot only undermine democracy; it can destroy it.

BRAIN TEASERS

What could we do to make the United States more democratic?

Economic Democracy

So far we have talked only of democracy in the political sphere. However, what of democracy in the economic sphere? Most people in the United States and elsewhere are more immediately affected by the decisions of their employers than by the decisions of their governments. Consider the importance of such things as where you work, your job responsibilities, working conditions, salary, and benefits. Most working people have very little control or influence over these things. They are part of organizations that are structured hierarchically, like the military, with minimal democracy in decision making. Robert A. Dahl observes:

> Work is central to the lives of most people. For most people, it occupies more time than any other activity. Work affects—often decisively—their income, consumption, savings, status, friendships, leisure, health, security, family life, old age, self-esteem, sense of fulfillment and well-being, personal freedom, self-determination, self-development, and innumerable other crucial interests and values. Of all the relations of authority, control, and power in which people are routinely involved, none are as salient, persistent, and important in the daily lives of most persons as those they are subject to at work. What governments have such immense consequences for daily life as the government of the workplace?[15]

Dahl notes that

> typically in all [democratic] societies these [economic] organizations . . . stand out starkly because of their nondemocratic governments. . . . By and large, . . . the belief that [business] firms are best governed by nondemocratic means goes pretty much unchallenged in democratic countries.[16]

Workers don't elect their bosses and supervisors, although bosses and supervisors often have more power over an individual's life and life prospects than do senators or presidents. Workers have virtually no input into business decisions, practices, and policies that have profound effects on their lives. The hierarchical structure of work for all but the highest echelons of the work force influences the development of character in the direction of obedience and conformity.

Dahl advocates democratization of the workplace that parallels democratization of the political sphere. Such "economic democracy" would give workers far more influence than they now have over the decisions, practices, and policies of the firms where they work. Instead of all

---

[15]Robert A. Dahl, *Democracy and Its Critics* (New Haven, CT: Yale University Press, 1989), 327.

[16]Ibid., 327.

decisions being made at the highest levels with orders running downward through the organization, perhaps they would be made in conjunction with workers' councils in a kind of direct democracy. Or perhaps the workplace could be organized as a representative democracy with workers (along with stockholders?) electing managers and supervisors, including top management.

Dahl points out that the reasons that have been given for rejecting economic democracy are the same as those that have been given for rejecting democracy in the political sphere. Some people claim that workers have no right to participate meaningfully in the governance of firms, only the owners do. Dahl responds, first, that owners buy shares in a company in order to share in its profits, not to share in the management of the firm. Furthermore, he claims, the principle that underlies democracy in the political sphere—that those affected by policies and decisions have a *right* to participate in making those decisions—applies in the economic sphere just as much as in the political sphere.

Others claim that workers are simply not qualified, or not as qualified as managers and stockholders, to participate in business decision making. In response, Dahl points out that workers usually know far more about the place in which they work than do stockholders, who often know nothing more about a firm than the price of its stock. Managers govern firms and although in theory they are accountable to stockholders, in reality they are virtually autonomous. It is almost impossible for stockholders to organize to throw out poor managers, let alone oversee managerial decisions. Dahl concedes that direct democracy may not work in a company because workers lack expertise that managers are supposed to have, but he suggests that workers are in a better position than most stockholders to vote periodically on who should manage a company. Therefore, he suggests that managers should be periodically elected by workers (or at least with substantial worker input).

Finally, some critics of economic democracy claim that nondemocratic business organizations are far more efficient than democratic business organizations would be. Dahl claims that there is no reason to believe this assertion, even if "efficient" is narrowly defined as "profitable."[17]

---

[17]Ibid., 329–331.

BENJAMIN CONSTANT (1767–1830)

THE KIND OF LIBERTY OFFERED TO MEN AT THE END OF THE LAST CENTURY

The liberty which was offered to men at the end of the last century was borrowed from the ancient republics. . . .

That liberty consisted in active participation in collective power rather than in the peaceful enjoyment of individual independence. And to ensure that participation, it was even necessary for the citizens to sacrifice a large part of this enjoyment. . . .

In the republics of antiquity, the exiguous scale of the territory meant that each citizen had, politically speaking, a great personal importance. The exercise of the rights of citizenship represented the occupation and, so to speak, the amusement of all. The whole people contributed to the making of the laws, pronounced judgements, decided on war and peace. The share of the individual in national sovereignty was by no means, as it is now, an abstract supposition. The will of each individual had a real influence; the exercise of that will was a vivid and repeated pleasure. It followed from this that the ancients were prepared for the conservation of their political importance, and of their share in the administration of the state, to renounce their private independence.

This renunciation was indeed necessary; since to enable a people to enjoy the widest possible political rights, that is that each citizen may have his share in sovereignty, it is necessary to have institutions which maintain equality, prevent the increase of fortunes, proscribe distinctions, and are set in opposition to the influence of wealth, talents even virtue. Clearly all these institutions limit liberty and endanger individual security.

Thus what we now call civil liberty was unknown to the majority of the ancient peoples. All the Greek republics, with the exception of Athens,[4] subjected individuals to an almost unlimited social jurisdiction. The same subjection of the individual characterized the great centuries of Rome; the citizen had in a way made himself the slave of the nation of which he formed part. He submitted himself entirely to the decisions of the sovereign, of the legislator; he acknowledged the latter's right to watch over his actions and to constrain his will. But the reason was that he was himself, in his turn, that legislator and that sovereign; and he felt with pride all that his suffrage was worth in a nation small enough for each citizen to be a power; and this consciousness of his own worth was for him an ample reward.

It is quite a different matter in modern states. Because their territory is much larger than that of the ancient republics, the mass of their inhabitants, whatever form of government they adopt, have no active part in it. They are called at most to exercise sovereignty through representation, that is to say in a fictitious manner.

The advantage that liberty, as the ancients conceived it, brought people, was actually to belong to the ranks of the rulers; this was a real advantage, a pleasure at the same time flattering and solid. The advantage that liberty brings people amongst the moderns is that of being represented, and of contributing to that representation by one's choice. It is undoubtedly an advantage because it is a safeguard; but the immediate pleasure is less vivid; it does not include any of the enjoyments of power; it is a pleasure of reflection, while that of the ancients was one of action. It is clear that the former is less attractive; one could not exact from men as many sacrifices to win and maintain it.

From *Political Writings*, ed. B. Fontana (Cambridge: Cambridge University Press, 1988). Reprinted with the permission of Cambridge University Press. Footnotes omitted.

At the same time, these sacrifices would be much more painful: the progress of civilization, the commercial tendency of the age, the communication among the peoples, have infinitely multiplied and varied the means of individual happiness. To be happy, men need only to be left in perfect independence in all that concerns their occupations, their undertakings, their sphere of activity, their fantasies.

The ancients found greater satisfaction in their public existence, and fewer in their private life; consequently, when they sacrificed individual to political liberty, they sacrificed less to gain more. Almost all the pleasures of the moderns lie in their private life. The immense majority, always excluded from power, necessarily take only a very passing interest in their public existence. . . .

 JEAN JACQUES ROUSSEAU

THE SOCIAL CONTRACT

[4] As soon as this multitude is thus united in one body, one cannot injure one of the members without attacking the body, and still less can one injure the body without the members being affected. Thus duty and interest alike obligate the contracting parties to help one another, and the same men must strive to combine in this two-fold relation all the advantages attendant on it.

[5] Now the Sovereign, since it is formed entirely of the individuals who make it up, has not and cannot have any interests contrary to theirs; consequently the Sovereign power has no need of a guarantor toward the subjects, because it is impossible for the body to want to harm all of its members, and we shall see later that it cannot harm any one of them in particular. The Sovereign, by the mere fact that it is, is always everything it ought to be. . . .

[7] Indeed each individual may, as a man, have a particular will contrary to or different from the general will he has as a Citizen. His particular interest may speak to him quite differently from the common interest; his absolute and naturally independent existence may lead him to look upon what he owes to the common cause as a gratuitous contribution, the loss of which will harm others less than its payment burdens him and, by considering the moral person that constitutes the State as a being of reason because it is not a man, he would enjoy the rights of a citizen without being willing to fulfill the duties of a subject; an injustice, the progress of which would cause the ruin of the body politic. . . .

[8] Hence for the social compact not to be an empty formula, it tacitly includes the following engagement which alone can give force to the rest, that whoever refuses to obey the general will shall be constrained to do so by the entire body: which means nothing other than that he shall be forced to be free; for this is the condition which, by giving each Citizen to the Fatherland, guarantees him against all personal dependence; the condition which is the device and makes for the operation of the political machine, and alone renders legitimate civil engagements which would otherwise be absurd, tyrannical, and liable to the most enormous abuses. . . .

[1] This transition from the state of nature to the civil state produces a most remarkable change in man by substituting justice for instinct in his conduct, and endowing his actions with the morality they previously lacked. Only then, when the voice of duty succeeds physical impulsion and right succeeds appetite, does man, who until then had

In *The Social Contract and Later Writings*, ed. and trans. V. Gourevitch (Cambridge: Cambridge University Press, 1997).

looked only to himself, see himself forced to act on other principles, and to consult his reason before listening to his inclinations. Although in this state he deprives himself of several advantages he has from nature, he gains such great advantages in return, his faculties are exercised and developed, his ideas enlarged, his sentiments ennobled, his entire soul is elevated to such an extent, that if the abuses of this new condition did not often degrade him to beneath the condition he has left, he should ceaselessly bless the happy moment which wrested him from it forever, and out of a stupid and bounded animal made an intelligent being and a man.

[2] Let us reduce this entire balance to terms easy to compare. What man loses by the social contract in his natural freedom and an unlimited right to everything that tempts him and he can reach; what he gains is civil freedom and property in everything he possesses. In order not to be mistaken about these compensations, one has . . . to distinguish clearly between natural freedom which has no other bounds than the individual's forces, and civil freedom which is limited by the general will, and between possession which is merely the effect of force or the right of the first occupant, and property which can only be founded on a positive title.

[3] To the preceding one might add to the credit of the civil state moral freedom, which alone makes man truly the master of himself; for the impulsion of mere appetite is slavery, and obedience to the law one has prescribed to oneself is freedom. But I have already said too much on this topic, and the philosophical meaning of the word *freedom* is not my subject here.

Questions for Discussion and Review

1. Should people be free to engage in homosexual acts, or should (or may) society forbid homosexual acts between consenting adults? Defend your answer.

2. Letticia claims that adultery is immoral because the seventh of the Ten Commandments is "You shall not commit adultery" (Exodus 20:14). She also claims that divorce is immoral because several passages in the New Testament (such as Matthew 19:3–8 and Mark 10:2–12) condemn divorce. She says that people should not be free to do immoral things. Therefore, people should not be free to commit adultery or to divorce; there should be laws forbidding adultery and divorce. Do you agree with her? Why or why not?

3. Should people be free to have more than one spouse at a time? Defend your answer.

4. Should people be free to buy and sell sex, or should society forbid prostitution? Defend your answer.

5. Should students be free to cheat on examinations? Defend your answer.

6. Should people be free to use such drugs as heroin and cocaine? Defend your answer.

7. May society forbid the sale of cigarettes to people under age 18? Why or why not?

8. Acirema is at war. Justin, at a public meeting, criticizes the war as unjust. Some local toughs beat him up and intimidate other critics of the war into silence. The police do nothing to protect Justin and the other critics of the war. Justin claims that the government has violated his right to freedom of speech because it did not protect him from the violence of those who sought to silence him. He claims that his right to freedom of speech imposes on the government not merely the negative duty to refrain from preventing him from speaking but also the positive duty to protect him from the threats of private citizens who might try to silence him. Do you agree with him? Why or why not?

9. Should people be free to burn the American flag (provided that it is their flag) in order to protest government policy or draw attention to political causes, even though many people are offended by flag burning, or instead may society pass laws prohibiting flag burning and other forms of "desecration" of the flag? Defend your answer.

10. Since we now know that smoking cigarettes is very hazardous to people's health and causes hundreds of thousands of deaths each year, should people be free to smoke cigarettes, or would the government be justified in prohibiting cigarette smoking? Why or why not?

11. Should people be free to be cruel to animals, for example, free to torture puppies? Why or why not?

12. Should people be free to buy stolen goods? Why or why not?

13. Should people be free to yell "Fire!" in a crowded theater? Defend your answer.

14. Should music groups be free to record and sell songs with sexually explicit lyrics or with lyrics that advocate violence against women or against the police? Defend your answer.

15. Should homosexuals be free to serve in the military? Why or why not?

16. The editor of the student newspaper at Jefferson High School has written an article that advocates contraception and safe sex to prevent pregnancy and sexually transmitted diseases. In the article, various means of contraception and disease prevention are described in great detail to educate the readers. The school principal forbids publication of the article on the grounds that it would encourage sexual activity among high school students, many of whom are under age 16. The principal believes that premarital sex and teenage sex are immoral and undesirable and that the article would be dangerous and harmful. Is the principal justified in limiting the editor's freedom to publish her views in the student newspaper? Has the freedom of the readers of the newspaper been limited? If so, is that justified? Why or why not?

17. Many European countries and some states in the United States have laws requiring people to come to the aid of others in an emergency when the threat to the victim is great and the risk to the potential rescuer is small (sometimes called Good Samaritan laws after the story of the Good Samaritan that Jesus tells in Luke 10:25–37). Violation of the law—failure to act as the Good Samaritan acted—may result in fines or imprisonment. Suppose that the state of Euphoria has such a Good Samaritan law. Adolf sees a child drowning. He could save her by throwing a rope to her, or he could at least summon help. He says that he should be free to do nothing, free to just walk away. He says that laws requiring him to do something to save the child unjustifiably interfere with his freedom. He says that he should not be punished if he lets her drown. Do you agree with him? Why or why not?

18. Should people be free to commit suicide, especially if they are terminally ill? Why or why not?

19. Dr. Slocum has been Dave's physician for twenty years. Recently Dave, who is 74, was diagnosed with a variety of very serious illnesses. He almost certainly has less than a year to live, but his death will be slow. He will soon lose his physical and mental vigor; during his last months he will be physically helpless and his mental faculties will be impaired. Dave wants to die quickly and painlessly—"with dignity," as he puts it—rather than slowly waste away physically and mentally. After discussing it with his family, he has decided to commit suicide. His family supports his decision. In order to spare his family the pain of a grisly death, he does not want to shoot or hang himself. Therefore, he confers with Dr. Slocum and asks him to prescribe medications that will quickly and painlessly kill him. Dr. Slocum believes that people should be free to commit suicide and that doctors should be free to help their patients die swiftly and painlessly in order to minimize their and their family's suffering. Should there be laws absolutely prohibiting physician-assisted suicide? Defend your answer.

20. The leader of the New Nazi party has applied for a permit to hold a public rally. City leaders know that the Nazis will express ideas that most people find abhorrent: that Hitler was a hero and that Jews, Blacks, Hispanics, and other "undesirables" should be repressed and persecuted to make the country safe for the "superior" white race. They also fear violence, because opponents of Nazi ideas will probably disrupt the meeting. Therefore, the city denies the application for a permit and forbids the Nazis to hold a public rally. The Nazis complain that their right to free speech has been violated by the city. Would the city be justified in denying the Nazis a permit?

21. Bigotburg is a town that is 100 percent white. Recently it passed a
    law forbidding anyone who is not white from living in the town.
    The law prohibits residents from selling their property to nonwhites.
    Any sale to a nonwhite will automatically be voided. Eighty percent
    of the town's residents voted in favor of this law, so they claim that
    the decision was arrived at by democratic means. They say that the
    majority should decide the town's laws and they should be free to
    preserve their town's "unique character." They claim that federal
    laws that prohibit them from passing and enforcing such local laws
    violate their right to freely decide who may live in their town. On
    the other hand, nonwhites claim that Bigotburg's new law violates
    their freedom to live where they want to live. They say that the fed-
    eral government should protect their freedom not to be discrimi-
    nated against on the basis of race rather than protect the residents
    of Bigotburg's freedom to discriminate on the basis of race. Critics
    of Bigotburg think that the federal government should invalidate
    Bigotburg's new law. With whom do you agree? Why?

22. How does democracy differ from other forms of government or
    political organization?

23. Explain the difference between direct and indirect (representative)
    democracy. Are both forms of democracy equally practical or feasi-
    ble on (a) the federal level, (b) the state level, and (c) the
    city/town level? Why or why not? Which form of democracy is
    preferable? Why?

24. What is the least democratic organization with which you have been
    personally acquainted? What is the most democratic organization
    with which you have been personally acquainted? Do you think that
    the least democratic organization should have been more demo-
    cratic? Do you think that the most democratic organization should
    have been less democratic? More democratic? Explain and defend
    your answers.

25. If you belong to a particular religion, do you think that your reli-
    gion is organized democratically or nondemocratically? How should
    it be organized? Why?

26. Do you think that government in the United States (at the federal,
    state, or local level) is (a) not democratic enough, (b) democratic
    enough, or (c) too democratic? Explain and defend your answers.

27. Is your philosophy class run democratically? Explain and defend
    your answer. If it is not run democratically, what would have to be
    changed to make it a democracy? Should your philosophy class be
    run democratically? Should it be run "more" democratically? Explain
    and defend your answers.

28. Have any of the places where you have worked been run demo-
    cratically? Explain. Should they have been run democratically (or

more democratically)? How could the organization have been run democratically (or more democratically)? Explain and defend your answers.

29. When you were growing up, was your family organization (a) too democratic, (b) sufficiently democratic, or (c) not democratic enough? Explain and defend your answers.

30. Is democracy better than all alternative forms of government? Defend your answer.

31. There are three candidates in a presidential election. A receives 30 percent of the votes, B receives 34 percent of the votes, and C receives 36 percent of the votes. None of them has a majority (50 percent plus 1) of votes. Should C win under democratic rules? If not, what should be done to ensure that the election is run democratically? Why?

32. The United States has many allies in the world that are not democracies. Should the United States support and ally itself with nondemocratic governments? Should the United States try to assist nondemocratic governments to evolve into democracies? Why or why not?

33. Suppose scientists develop a supercomputer and a computer program designed to identify the 100 "best" people in the United States: the 100 wisest, most knowledgeable, most intelligent, most virtuous, most compassionate, most honest, most competent people in the country. The scientists recommend replacing elections for public officials with selection by computer every ten years of a Council of 100 with absolute power to cure society's ills: threats of war, environmental degradation, poverty, crime, drugs, and so on. The scientists aren't going to force their scheme on people. Instead, they present it to the people for a vote. They want a democratic election to determine whether democracy will be replaced by a technologically more sophisticated system. The scientists point out that rarely do the best people get elected to public office. They also point out the imperfections of U.S. democracy: the way wealth buys power and influence, the way democracy seems paralyzed, unable to act decisively. They argue that the well-being of everyone would be increased by their scheme. Would you vote for or against their proposal? Why? If the majority votes in favor of it, will the minority opposed to it have legitimate grounds for complaint if their right to vote is taken away from them, along with everyone else's right to vote? Would any of their rights be violated by such a scheme?

34. Suppose the majority of people in a country vote democratically to limit their liberty by abolishing freedom of speech, thought, religion, and conscience. Would that be objectionable? Why or why not? Could such a thing happen?

Suggestions for Further Reading

Aristotle. *Politics.* A classic examination of the nature and role of the state and of types of government. In an often fascinating excursion, Aristotle rambles through a landscape of issues and problems, making some acute observations.

John Arthur, ed. *Democracy: Theory and Practice.* Belmont, CA: Wadsworth, 1992. An excellent anthology of classical and contemporary writers on democracy.

S. I. Benn and R. S. Peters. *The Principles of Political Thought.* New York: Free Press, 1959. Chapter 10 gives a solid introduction to the nature and problems of political freedom; Chapter 15 provides an equally good introduction to the nature and justification of democracy.

Cicero. "On the Commonwealth." In *Classical Political Theories.* Robert Brown, ed. New York: Macmillan, 1990. A classic statement of the virtues of a "mixed" form of government, which includes aspects of monarchy, aristocracy, and democracy.

Carl Cohen. *Democracy.* New York: Free Press, 1971. An authoritative, detailed introduction to the nature and requirements of democracy, this book offers a defense of democracy by a respected theorist of democracy.

Robert A. Dahl. *Democracy and Its Critics.* New Haven, CT: Yale University Press, 1989. A detailed examination and defense of democracy by an eminent political theorist.

Joel Feinberg. *Social Philosophy.* Englewood Cliffs, NJ: Prentice-Hall, 1973. Chapters 1–3 provide a stimulating introduction to liberty and its problems by one of the foremost contemporary political and legal philosophers.

John Stuart Mill. *On Liberty.* Indianapolis: Hackett, 1978. An influential defense of liberty and an exploration of the legitimate grounds for limiting liberty.

Plato. *The Republic.* An enjoyable dialogue wherein Socrates, after an initial discussion of justice, proceeds to construct his vision of the ideal state. It includes an early version of the distinction between monarchy, aristocracy, and democracy by a brilliant theorist hostile to democracy.

A REACHING PHILOSOPHY

R eading philosophy isn't like reading a novel or like reading a history or science textbook. It requires greater skill, attention, and concentration. Here are a few brief tips on how to approach a work in philosophy.

1. Identify the question the author is trying to answer or the problem the author is trying to resolve. (*What's the point?*)

2. Identify the author's answer to the question or solution to the problem. (*What's the author arguing for or against?*)

3. Identify the reasons and arguments presented for the author's views. (*Why does the author think this answer or solution is correct or better than alternative answers and solutions?*)

4. Identify any opposing views that the author mentions but disagrees with. (*What are some alternative answers to the question or solutions to the problem?*)

5. Identify the reasons and arguments the author presents *against* opposing views. (*Why does the author think those views are wrong?*)

6. Decide whether you agree with the author's views and reasoning.

   a. Does the author's answer to the question or solution to the problem seem correct to you?
   b. Do you find the author's reasoning or arguments persuasive?
   c. Does the author bring up opposing views? Do you agree that they're mistaken? Why or why not?
   d. Does the author have good reasons for thinking that the opposing views are wrong?
   e. Can you think of any alternative answers or solutions that the author hasn't mentioned or thought of?

When reading a work of philosophy, always try to keep these questions in mind and try to answer them as you read along. Keep a pad and pen beside you at all times. Underline parts of the text that seem important to you. *Don't hesitate to reread sentences, paragraphs, or pages that you don't understand the first time you read them!* Most important, jot down notes as you read. Write a summary of the argument as you read and write down any questions, doubts, or challenges that occur to you. Always read actively and critically, trying to ensure that you understand the argument and trying to decide whether you agree with what you're reading.

WRITING A PHILOSOPHY PAPER

The Basic Format

1. Think of your paper as an attempt to answer a specific question or resolve a specific problem. When choosing a topic, try putting it in the form of a question, as in the following examples:

   Is theism more reasonable than either atheism or agnosticism?

   Is the Design argument a good argument for God's existence?

   Is Dualism more reasonable than Physicalism?

   Is Hard Determinism more reasonable than either Soft Determinism or Indeterminism?

   Do we *know* anything about the world?

   Is Moral Egoism correct?

   Is Utilitarianism an adequate moral theory?

   Do people have subsistence rights?

2. *Defend your answer.* The core of your paper should be a defense of the answer you give to the question. The most important goal is to define a position and to defend it with reasons, information, and arguments.

3. Identify what you take to be the strongest potential objection(s) to your view. Respond to the objection(s), explaining why you think they're not strong enough to show that your view is mistaken.

Tips on Good Writing

1. Your goal should be to *communicate* your ideas clearly and concisely. Keep in mind that you want your reader to understand you and your position.

2. There is no substitute for a *well-organized* paper.

    a. You should have a clear thesis that controls the development of your paper.

    b. Every paragraph should be directly related to your thesis and should contribute to the development of your ideas.

    c. Every paragraph should be clearly and logically related to the preceding and succeeding paragraphs (like links in a chain). Use transitions where necessary to ensure that your reader is following you and knows where you are in your argument and how you got there.

    d. Every paragraph should have one and only one topic, which is fully developed. (Beware of a lot of anemic paragraphs of only two or three sentences each; they are probably not fully developed.)

    e. Every sentence in each paragraph should be clearly and logically linked to the topic of that paragraph (like links in a chain).

3. *Define* important concepts or words when they're crucial to the argument you are developing.

4. *Revise! Revise! Revise!* Don't hand in to your instructor what should be a first draft of a paper. Write a first draft, then set it aside for at least a day or two. Go back and read it critically. *Rethink* your paper. Concentrate on the quality of your arguments and the clarity and organization of the material; don't just revise for spelling and grammar. Don't be afraid to eliminate whole sections of your first draft if they are merely digressions, to shift paragraphs and sections around, to reorganize your paper, or to add new material. Ask a friend to *read it critically* to see if he understands it, then quiz him on it to see if he really does understand what you've written. Revise again if you haven't made yourself clear.

5. *Use an outline or map of your paper for revising!* Few students feel comfortable starting out with an outline. I suggest turning to an outline or map only after you've produced your first draft of the paper. Make an outline or map *of the paper you've written*. This will give you the skeleton or frame of the paper without the meat and flesh and will enable you to see more clearly whether the organization is adequate. Now work on the outline or map to improve the structure if you think it needs improving. Here are two schematic examples of what an adequate structure or organization might look like.

SAMPLE OUTLINE

1. Introduction. This should include a clear statement of purpose—
    what you're going to argue for or against

2. Reasons/arguments supporting your position

3. Strongest challenge(s)/argument(s) against your position

4. Reasons/arguments in response to challenge(s)—why they don't
    show that you're mistaken

5. Conclusion

SAMPLE MAP

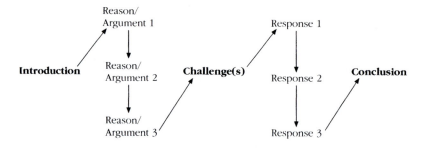

Revise the organization of your paper now following the organization of the revised outline or map.

Glossary/Index